Introduction to Media Production

Introduction to Media Production

The Path to Digital Media Production

Fourth Edition

Robert B. Musburger

Gorham Kindem

AMSTERDAM • BOSTON • HEIDELBERG • LONDON
NEW YORK • OXFORD • PARIS • SAN DIEGO
SAN FRANCISCO • SINGAPORE • SYDNEY • TOKYO

Focal Press is an imprint of Elsevier

Focal Press is an imprint of Elsevier
30 Corporate Drive, Suite 400, Burlington, MA 01803, USA
Linacre House, Jordan Hill, Oxford OX2 8DP, UK

∞ Recognizing the importance of preserving what has been written, Elsevier prints its books on acid-free
paper whenever possible.

Library of Congress Cataloging-in-Publication Data
Musburger, Robert B.
   Introduction to media production : the path to digital media production by Robert B. Musburger and
Gorham Kindem.
        p. cm.
   Previous editions entered under Gorham Kindem.
   Includes bibliographical references and index.
   ISBN 978-0-240-81082-9 (pbk. : alk. paper) 1. Motion pictures–Production and direction.
   2. Television–Production and direction. 3. Analog electronic systems. 4. Digital electronics.
   I. Kindem, Gorham Anders. II. Title.
   PN1995.9.P7K538 2009
   791.4302'32–dc22

                                                                                          2008043914

British Library Cataloguing-in-Publication Data
A catalogue record for this book is available from the British Library.

ISBN: 978-0-240-81082-9

For information on all Focal Press publications
visit our website at www.elsevierdirect.com

09 10 11 12 13 5 4 3 2 1

Printed in the United States of America

To Nancy and Pat
In return for their patience, understanding, and support.

CONTENTS

PREFACE TO THE FOURTH EDITION

This fourth edition of *Introduction to Media Production* approaches the process of teaching media production from a slightly different perspective from previous editions. Given the wide range and diversity of means by which a production will finally reach different audiences today, a consideration of potential audiences overrides nearly all other considerations in the planning and production of a program, whether it is an audio, video, or graphics production. Although the chapters in this book are arranged in a logical progression, each chapter can be taught as a stand-alone unit, or in any order that fits the curriculum of the school or of the individual faculty member teaching the course. A detailed index and a comprehensive glossary with 128 new digital entries provides definitions to new terms and concepts regardless of the order of presentation to the reader. Each chapter discusses developments in digital media technologies as they affect various topics. All chapters have been streamlined and bulleted for added readability and improved access to key concepts. Some chapters have been combined to recognize important changes in the rapidly evolving digital media production world. In addition to the original 168 images plus 12 color plates, 105 new photographs and illustrations have been added where they best facilitate understanding and illustrate important recent developments. Finally, although all media must start and end as an analog signal, digital technology in preproduction, production, postproduction, and distribution dominate analog technology. The structure and content of the fourth edition of *Introduction to Media Production* reflect those important changes. The authors are grateful to the external reviewers for their valuable suggestions and to Elinor Actipis, Michele Cronin, Lianne Hong, and the staff of Focal Press for their encouragement and strong support for this edition.

INTRODUCTION FOR IMP IV

The goal of this book is to help young media producers understand the entire process of media creativity, beginning with concepts and audience considerations and continuing through the preproduction, production, and postproduction processes, including distribution and exhibition. A final chapter considers how to plan and guide your future in the field of media production.

The authors feel you need to learn why decisions are made given the many choices involved in producing a media project, which is as important as knowing how to push buttons and turn knobs. Understanding how a piece of equipment works helps to explain what that equipment can and will accomplish for the operator and director. Unrealistic expectations based on ignorance leads to frustration and poor production qualities.

The chapters in this book are written so that you may read them in any order, although the authors feel that, based on their own experience, the chapter order in the text makes the best sense from a professional media producer's point of view.

Topics, professional terminology, and the language of media production are introduced and explained as the text moves from chapter to chapter. If you do not understand a term, you will find it defined and explained in the glossary at the end of the book.

CHAPTER 1: PRODUCING: EXPLOITING NEW OPPORTUNITIES AND MARKETS IN THE DIGITAL ARENA

This chapter is placed first in the book to underline the importance of knowing how the end result of a production will finally meet its intended audience. The radical changes in media production equipment, techniques, and methods of operation have been matched equally with radical changes in the distribution and exhibition of media productions. The quality of a production can now range from such extremes as a high-definition, widescreen, multichannel audio program to a small, low-quality picture on a cell phone. The production could be distributed by a major multinational distribution company placing the project on network television or in motion picture theaters around the world, or a few friends may view it on a personal web site.

CHAPTER 2: THE PRODUCTION PROCESS: ANALOG AND DIGITAL TECHNOLOGIES

Chapter 2 breaks the production process down into three primary stages—preproduction, production, and postproduction—and explains the relationship between the three. Much of the chapter covers the use of digital technology and equipment in the three stages. Finally, the chapter explains the relationships and duties of each member of the production team: audio, video, film, and multimedia.

CHAPTER 3: PRODUCING AND PRODUCTION MANAGEMENT

Chapter 3 describes the different types, duties, and responsibilities of producers and their chief assistants, production managers. The many critical duties and responsibilities of the producers and their teams are more often hidden from public view. These duties include supervising script preparation, writing proposals, and managing a budget.

CHAPTER 4: SCRIPTWRITING

Chapter 4 describes the many genres and methods of writing scripts. Details on writing dramatic, commercial, educational, news, situation comedy, and animation scripts for digital production are illustrated with various rhetorical, expository, and dramatic theories of writing.

CHAPTER 5: DIRECTING: AESTHETIC PRINCIPLES AND PRODUCTION COORDINATION

Chapter 5 describes the functions and skills required of directors of video, audio, film, and animation productions. Scene construction, the use of sound, and the differences between single-camera and multiple-camera productions in the digital age are clearly explained.

CHAPTER 6: AUDIO/SOUND

Chapter 6 covers all aspects of audio and sound production, concentrating on digital techniques. The discussion covers microphones and their uses, the control and monitoring of sound, and mixing for digital productions, along with an explanation of the theories of sound perspective and benefits of using sound in visual productions.

CHAPTER 7: LIGHTING AND DESIGN

Chapter 7 describes and organizes the techniques of lighting and design for digital production. The common areas of lighting and designing sets, costumes, and handling of props for digital production are covered in this chapter. New lighting instruments and techniques specific to digital productions are also explored.

CHAPTER 8: THE CAMERA

Chapter 8 discusses all types of digital cameras, as well as film cameras in common use today. Camera operation techniques, lens operation, and a breakdown of various specific types of digital cameras and their differences emphasize the wide range of digital cameras and their technical variations.

CHAPTER 9: RECORDING

Chapter 9 describes each of the many digital, analog, and film recording methods. Descriptions of audio and video digital formats, their compatibility, and their level of use are provided in great detail. Specific techniques required for digital recording of both audio and video constitute a portion of this chapter.

CHAPTER 10: EDITING

Chapter 10 describes each of the steps of editing digital audio, video, and digital film. Both the physical processes and the theoretical processes of dealing with digital editing as opposed to older analog editing methods are covered. Theories of editing a story, whether it is a commercial, news, or dramatic production, are described.

CHAPTER 11: GRAPHICS, ANIMATION, AND SPECIAL EFFECTS

Chapter 11 describes the digital techniques used in creating all visuals, including the methods used both on camera and off camera. The chapter explores the use of animation, special effects, and time-proven art techniques. The use of color and color theory along with framing and composition make up a major portion of this chapter.

CHAPTER 12: THE FUTURE AND YOUR CAREER

Chapter 12 describes the future of the media production business, as well as it can be determined at this point in time. The chapter then describes, point-by-point, the method of preparing for a career by earning an internship, preparing the paperwork for a résumé and cover letter, and designing and creating a portfolio. The chapter also offers tips for preparing for and handling an interview and negotiating pay and benefits for that first and succeeding jobs.

Producing: Exploiting New Opportunities and Markets in the Digital Arena

- What new markets and opportunities has the digital area fostered?
- Why are distribution and exhibition so important to the production process?
- What effect does the audience have on the production process?
- What are the chief means of exhibiting media productions?
- How does the economics of a production and distribution affect the content?
- What systems will be used to distribute and exhibit media in the future?

Introduction

The new world of advanced digital media production abruptly appeared in the studios, editing suites, radio and TV operations, independent production operations, and film studios with a suddenness that caught most people in the media production business by surprise. At first, digital equipment and technology appeared at a steady pace, bringing smaller equipment, lower costs in both equipment and production methods, and surprising higher quality. Then the Internet, originally considered as a supersized mail system, became a practical means of distributing all forms of media—audio, video, graphics—at a low cost and within reach of anyone with a computer and an Internet connection. Because of the two factors of low cost and accessibility, most concepts of media production distribution, and exhibition had to be reconsidered and restructured for producers to remain competitive, gain funding for productions, and reach targeted audiences.

This chapter considers the relationship of the audience to distribution of productions, the changing technologies of distribution and exhibition, the economics of distribution, and the future of exhibition.

THE AUDIENCE
Audience Analysis

An accurate estimate of the size, demographic makeup, and needs of a prospective audience is essential for the development of workable funded projects and marketable media ideas. What media should a producer use to reach a specific audience? How large is the potential audience? What size budget is justified? What needs and expectations does a particular audience have? What television, film, or graphics format should be used? These questions can only be answered when the prospective audience is clearly defined. Even in noncommercial productions, the overall budget must be justified to some degree on the basis of the potential size and demographics of the audience:

Audience Analysis
- Choice of medium
- Size of audience
- Budget justification
- Audience expectations
- Choice of medium format

Audiences differ in size and demographics. The age and gender of the members of an audience are often just as important as the overall number of people who will see the production. Television advertisers, for example, often design television commercials to reach specific demographic groups. Even documentary filmmakers, such as Michael Moore who produced the documentaries *Sicko* and *Bowling for Columbine*, often pretest films on audiences to see how effective they are in generating and maintaining interest and waging arguments. The process of assessing audience preferences for and interest in specific projects has become more scientific in recent years, but it inevitably requires an experienced and knowledgeable producer to interpret and implement research findings:

Audience Demographics
- Age
- Gender
- Income
- Education
- Religion
- Culture
- Language

Detailed audience information can facilitate later stages of the production process by giving the audience input into production decisions. The nature and preferences of the audience can be used to determine a project's format, subject matter, and structure, as well as its budget. For example, the reality series *Survival* (2007) was targeted specifically for working-class families interested in outdoor-adventure dramas. Everything from the actual locations to specific character types was selected on the basis of audience pretesting. While the artistic merit of using audience-survey research to make production decisions may be questionable, since it can produce a hodgepodge of styles and content rather than a unified work, its success has to some degree validated the technique in the commercial marketplace. It has also proved vital for noncommercial productions, where audience response is a primary measure of program effectiveness. Research can also be used during postproduction to assess the impact and effectiveness of a project. While audience research is no substitute for professional experience, it can give scientific, statistical validity to production decisions that might otherwise be based solely on less reliable hunches and guesses.

Estimating the size and demographics—for example, the age, gender, and other characteristics, of the potential audience for a prospective media project—can be quite complicated. Sometimes a project's potential audience can be estimated from the prior success of similar productions. For example, producers can consult the A.C. Nielsen and Arbitron ratings for television audiences drawn to previous programming of the same type. Television ratings provide audience information in the form of program ratings, shares, and demographic breakdowns for national and regional television markets. *Ratings* or rankings refer to the percentage of all television households—that is, of all households with a television set regardless of whether that set is on or off at a particular time—that are tuned to a specific program. If there are 80 million television households and 20 million of them are tuned to a specific program, then that program has a rating of 25, which represents 25 percent of the total television population.

Shares indicate the percentage of television households with the set turned on at a specific time that are actually watching a specific program. Thus, if 20 million households are watching something on television at a particular time and 10 million of those 20 million households are watching the same program, then that program has an audience share of 50, which represents 50 percent of the viewing audience (Figure 1.1).

Methods of determining audience value on the Internet is made easier by the system of counting the number of times a web site has been opened, or "hit," in a search. The hits provide an exact count of the number of times an audience has opened a site, but it does not tell how often they stayed to read or comprehend what was shown on the site. The method measuring hits is more accurate than ratings, but it is still not an absolute measurement of audience reaction—pleasure or displeasure. A new measuring system, the Total Audience Measurement Index (TAMI) is in development to include an audience's participation in all media simultaneously—broadcasting, cable, satellite, Internet, and mobile use—as a total research value.

Commercial producers and distributors often rely on market research to estimate audience size and the preferences of audiences that might be drawn to a particular project. The title of the project, a list of the key talent, the nature of the subject matter, or a synopsis of the story line, for example, might be given to a test audience, and their responses are recorded and evaluated. Research has shown that by far the best predictor of feature film success is advertising penetration—that is, the number of people who have heard about a project—usually through advertising in a variety of media. Other significant predictors of success appear to be the financial success of the director's prior work, the current popularity of specific performers or stars, and the interest generated by basic story lines pretested in written form.

Audience research has been used for a variety of purposes in commercial production. Sometimes before production, researchers statistically compare the level of audience interest (the "want-to-see" index) generated by a synopsis, title, or credits of a production to the amount of audience satisfaction resulting from viewing the completed project. A marketing and advertising strategy is often chosen on the basis of this research. A film that generates a great deal of audience interest before production, but little audience

THE LANGUAGE OF RATINGS

TERM	ABBREVIATION	DEFINITION
Universe estimate	UE	Total persons or homes in a given population: TV households in the United States
Ratings %	Ratings	Percentage of all households viewing a TV program at one time
Share of audience	Share	Percentage of TV sets in use tuned to a program
Coverage	Coverage	Percentage of TV households that could receive a program
Gross average audience	GAA Rating	Sum of the percentage of households tuned to the program, including repeat telecasts
Gross ratings points	GRPs	Sum of all ratings for all programs in a schedule
Households using TV	HUT%	$\frac{\text{Number of HH with TVs turned on}}{\text{Total HH universe estimate}}$
Persons using TV	PUT%	$\frac{\text{Number of Persons viewing TV}}{\text{Total persons universe}}$
Viewers per viewing HH	VPH	$\frac{\text{Persons projection}}{\text{Household projection}}$
Reach	Reach or CUME	Number of different homes exposed at least once to a program or commercial
Cost per thousand	CPM	$\frac{\text{Media cost}}{\text{Impressions}} \times 1,000$
GRPs	GRP	Rating x frequency
Impressions	Impressions	GRPs x UE

FIGURE 1.1 The terminology used by programmers and salespeople in broadcast media is a language of its own. The terms are both descriptive and analytical at the same time, but they are meant for professionals in the field to be used for accurate and concise communication.

satisfaction after viewing a prerelease screening of the completed film, might be marketed somewhat differently from a film that generates little interest initially but is well received in its completed form. The former might be marketed with an advertising blitz and released to many theaters before "word of mouth" destroys it at the box office, while the latter might be marketed more slowly to allow word of mouth to build gradually.

Some television programs and commercials will be dropped and others aired solely on the basis of audience pretesting. Story lines, character portrayals, and editing are sometimes changed after audience testing. Advertising agencies often test several versions of a commercial on sample audiences before selecting the version to be aired. A local news program may be continuously subjected to audience survey research in an attempt to discover ways to increase its ratings or share. A sponsor or executive administrator may desire concrete evidence of communication effectiveness and positive viewer reaction after a noncommercial production has been completed.

Audience research has to be recognized as an important element in the production process. While it is no substitute for professional experience and artistic ability, research nonetheless can provide some insurance against undertaking expensive projects that have no likelihood of reaching target audiences or generating profits.

Noncommercial audience research often focuses on assessments of audience needs and program effectiveness. A project that is not designed to make money often justifies production costs on the basis of corporate, government, or cultural needs as well as audience preferences and size. Sponsors need to have some assurance that the program will effectively reach the target audience and convey its message. Audience pretesting can help to determine the best format for conveying information and reaching the audience. Successful children's programs are often based on audience research that assures program effectiveness. For example, the fast-paced, humorous instructional style of *Sesame Street*, which mirrors television commercials and comedy programs, was based on exhaustive audience research. Whether it is used during preproduction or postproduction, audience research can strengthen a program and widen its appeal.

THE TECHNOLOGY OF DISTRIBUTION

Media production requires both analog and digital technologies. The advent of digital technologies stimulated a number of important changes in media production, including the convergence of technologies as well as corporate integration. The digital revolution describes a process that started several decades ago. Technicians developed uses for the technology based on "1" and "0" instead of an analog system of recording and processing audio and video signals. Rather than a revolution, it has been an evolution, as digital equipment and techniques have replaced analog equipment and processes where practical and efficient. Digital equipment may be manufactured smaller, requiring less power, and producing higher-quality signals for recording and processing. As a result, reasonably priced equipment, within the reach of consumers, now produces video and audio productions that exceed the quality of those created by professional equipment of less than two decades ago. But it must be remembered every electronic signal begins as an analog signal and ends as an analog signal, since the human eye and ear cannot directly translate a digital signal (Figure 1.2).

MEDIA SIGNAL PATH FROM ORIGINATION TO DESTINATION

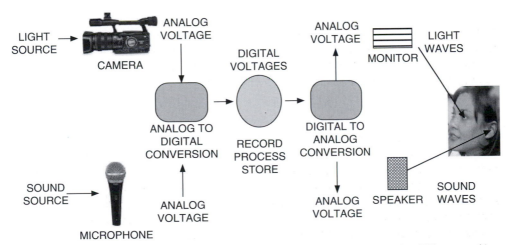

FIGURE 1.2 All sounds and light rays are analog signals as variations in frequency from below 60 Hz as sound to a range above 1 MHz for light. Any frequency may be converted to a digital signal duplicating the original analog signal, but for humans to be able to see and hear an audio or video signal it must be converted back to an analog signal.

The signals that create light and sound are analog signals. The types of equipment that make up optics in lenses and cameras, physical graphics, sets, and the human form all exist as analog forms. The signals a camera and microphone must convert from light and vibrations to an electronic signal must be an analog signal first and then may be converted to a digital signal. At the opposite end of the media process, a human cannot see an image or hear sound as a digital signal but must wait for the digital signal to be converted back to analog to be shown on a monitor and fed through a speaker or headset.

Communication production systems now move from the analog original to a digital signal, not a digital rendering of a video or audio signal, but straight to a pure digital signal without compression or recording on any media such as tape or disc. The analog of the light and sound need not be converted to a video, audio, film, or graphic signal but may remain as a digital stream until converted back to analog for viewing and or listening. All acquisition, storage, manipulation, and distribution will be in the form of a simple digital signal. Digital systems obviously will continue to improve from 8-16-32-64-128 bits as storage and bandwidth factors improve and expand. The number of bits indicates the level of conversion to a digital signal. The higher the bit rate, the better the quality of the digital signal, although the higher bit rate also requires greater bandwidth for storage and for transmission during distribution.

Tape will slowly disappear as the primary means of recording, distribution, and storage of media systems before discs and film disappear as a useful and permanent medium. Some forms of tape recording for high-end cameras will continue to be used to record digital, but not visual or aural signals that are then fed directly to postproduction operations. The lifetime of discs also may be dated as solid-state recording media such as P2 and other flash-type drives increase their capacity and costs decrease.

NEW PRODUCTION CONSIDERATIONS

Today production personnel may take advantage of the digital evolution to change the production technologies now available as well as the increased range of the methods of distribution of media productions. Production and distribution methods now must be considered together or the value of the production may never be realized.

Digitized signals of any media production now may reach an audience in almost infinite different paths of distribution. The traditional mass communication systems of radio-TV-film, cable, and satellite now are joined by digital signals distributed via a vast number of new systems by means of the Internet and Web variations now joined by mobile systems of podcasts, cell telephones, and other handheld computers (Figure 1.3).

Instead of media distribution via terrestrial radio and television broadcasts, cable, and motion pictures, the ubiquity of wireless digital signals distributed via WiFi, WiMax, and other "open" distribution systems has necessitated changes in media production theory, methods, technology, distribution, and profit sources. Digital production methods and operations are covered in Chapter 2.

There are four areas of consideration that must be contemplated to make key decisions between the birth of the original production concept and the first rollout of equipment:

- Which distribution method will be used?
- Which production format will be used?
- Which electronic media will be used?
- Which genre will tell the story best?

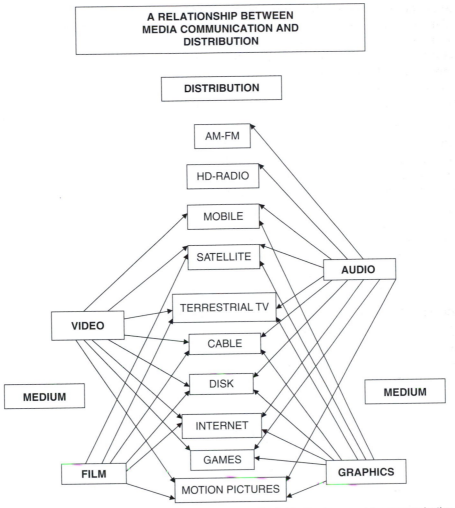

FIGURE 1.3 The relationship between the many possible media distribution forms and the communication media production formats indicate an interlocking relationship that is neither linear nor hierarchical.

THE BIG TEN OF DISTRIBUTION
AM-FM Terrestrial Radio

Terrestrial radio programming consists of music, news, public affairs, documentaries, and dramas, programming aimed at the largest possible audience. Except for public radio there is very little niche or specialized programming on standard radio channels. Terrestrial radio includes high-definition (HD) digital radio along with traditional analog radio, now often simulcast together.

HD-Radio (IBOC)

In-band on-channel (IBOC) and HD radio are trademark brands of digital radio broadcasting that allows for multichannels, both digital and analog programming to be broadcast on the same primary channel. The primary audience target of digital radio is the car driver, who is enticed with specialized high-quality, static-free programming.

Mobile

Mobile equipment consists of a rapidly expanding range of miniature digital-based equipment designed to provide the same services fixed position equipment provides in sending and receiving telephone messages, Internet information, photographs, video, audio, and streaming programs. Mobile systems also use wireless public systems to deliver a wide variety of mass communication programming.

Satellite

Separate radio and television systems use satellites to feed signals from central head-ends to a wide area of receiving antennas aimed at the satellite. Both systems, like digital radio and cable television, require a monthly subscription fee. Satellite radio offers programs that might not be available on terrestrial radio, as producers seek to reach audiences dissatisfied with standard broadcast radio. Satellite television competes directly with cable, offering the same program channels, but it may provide local stations to specific areas (Figure 1.4).

Terrestrial Television

By the spring of 2009, all terrestrial television in the United States will be broadcasting a digital signal on new or reassigned channels. Broadcast television, like broadcast radio, aims to please the largest audience to serve advertisers who pay for free television. Digital channels will allow broadcast television to carry more than one line of programming simultaneously on the assigned channel, opening the possibility of new and more varied programming opportunities. After that date, all digital broadcast signals may be viewed only on specific digital receivers, cable, and cable satellite systems with converter boxes, or a converter box between an antenna and the receiver to allow a standard analog receiver to view the new digital signals.

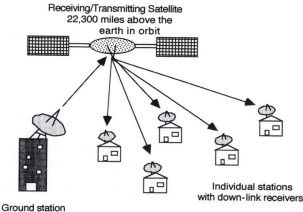

SATELLITE OPERATION

Receiving/Transmitting Satellite
22,300 miles above the
earth in orbit

Individual stations
with down-link receivers

Ground station
with up-link
transmitter

FIGURE 1.4 A basic satellite system consists of three parts: a ground station that gathers programming and transmits the signals to an orbiting satellite, which then retransmits the signals back to individual stations equipped with down-link receivers.

Cable/Telcos

Cable and telephone companies provides direct, wired video, telephone, and Internet connections to their subscribers. Cable stations originally merely carried broadcast channels but expanded to creating many of their own channels. Telephone companies originally served only to provide person-to-person telephone connections but expanded into the digital world by also offering Internet services and television channels. Both telephone and cable companies now compete head-to-head in all three of their areas of service—telephone, television, and Internet services—and they compete with satellite for programming services (Figure 1.5).

Disk/Disc

Magnetic media are referred to as "disks," whereas optical media are "discs." The disk/disc industry has offered varying degrees of different media services. For the foreseeable future, hard drives with multidisks will serve as valuable storage media. DVDs, and blue-laser discs (Blu-ray and holographic versatile discs), and CDs of all types provide relatively inexpensive and accessible media for recording and playing back video and audio signals. Music, motion pictures, television programs, and audio collections provide the majority of the programming for prerecorded and self-recorded discs.

Many of the purposes and uses of disc/disks have been replaced by solid-state items called flash drives among other titles. These small blocks of chips may be attached to computers or other digital equipment with a USB or other digital connector. The capacity is continually increasing, but 2 to 4 gigabytes of inexpensive miniature drives provide easily accessible and transportable means of storing and moving digital signals from one source to another. Larger desktop drives holding terabytes or more of storage provide backup drives and alternate storage locations for editing and other postproduction work.

The Internet

The Internet has become so pervasive, so all-encompassing, it is difficult to accurately analyze its individual value as a distribution system, or systems. The Internet now and in the future will hold a major position in distribution of all forms of media content, whether professionally created or from the cameras, microphones, computers, and minds of amateurs. How media will be placed on the Internet, who will control media on the Internet, and how Internet distribution systems will function may determine the future of media financing, production, and distribution.

CABLE SYSTEM OPERATION

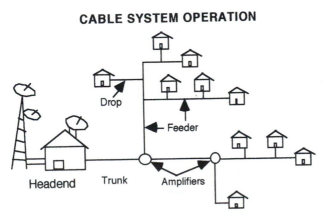

FIGURE 1.5 A cable system collects broadcast signals from off the air and downlinks programs fed by satellite at the headend. At the headend the signals are modulated onto a series of frequencies that are refed down a single cable. From the headend, the signal is fed to trunk lines that feed a fairly large area. Feeder lines take the signal from the trunk line to feed a smaller area, and then the drop is the final line that runs to the individual subscriber.

Games

The growth of the gaming industry reveals an interesting comment on the power of a media form that originated outside of the mainstream of society and gradually became important both for financial reasons and as a cultural symbol. As simple toys attached to a computer, videogames were primarily ignored, then derided as overly simple, too violent, and intentionally sexist. Whether the simplicity (which quickly disappeared with complex multilevel and multiplayer games), the sexism, or the violence made games as successful as they have become is less important. Games are here to stay. Because of their pervasive distribution, the amount of money spent to create them, the number of people employed in the industry, and the amount earned by the game companies, games must be considered a legitimate distribution system.

Motion Pictures

The distribution system with the longest history continues to maintain its position of importance in producing, distributing, and exhibiting motion pictures. The history of film has proven again the truth that new media seldom ever totally replace existing media. First radio, television, then high-definition media were touted to spell the doom and eventual demise of motion pictures. Producers keep creating motion pictures, and the manufacturers of film keep improving the quality and means of shooting motion pictures in ways that have yet to be matched by any other media format. In this discussion, "film" is the acetate-based, emulsion-coated flexible substance that filmmakers expose to light and then edit. The complete production that is distributed and shown in theaters, on television, and on the Internet is a "motion picture." The medium is "film," and the industry that distributes the final product is called the "motion picture" industry.

Video and digital visual productions often are labeled by the print media as "film" when such systems should be labeled "motion pictures", not "film".

> Note: There is intentionally no mention of tape, either video or audio, as a means of distribution. By the time this book is published, most formats of tape will have been replaced by other recording, distribution, and archival systems. Disc(k)s may be part of that process, but it will not be many years before the use and need for discs as a recording, distribution, and archiving system also will cease. Motion pictures may follow down that same path, but it will be many years before we see the end of film as a reliable, safe, and permanent media production system.

SOLID-STATE STORAGE

The arrival of digital technologies in media production systems brought about a problem not considered or needed in analog systems, a means of storing the vast amount of data created and that by its very nature needed to be stored indefinitely. Digital magnetic tape systems borrowed from analog tape worked for some time, but they immediately became insufficient for storing large amounts of data if that data needed to be accessed immediately and nonlinearly. The physical size of tape also became a problem. Disk and disc drives were developed specifically for digital storage and duplication. Both work well; hard disks provide all of the criteria needed for large amounts of storage and are easily accessible, but the cost is higher per gigabyte than optical discs, which are easily duplicated but not easily modified. Flash memory systems arrived later, bringing a new method of storing digital data. Flash cards and flash drives used in games, cameras, telephones, and portable media players as well as stand-alone storage devices have become popular and seemingly ubiquitous. In 2007, hard drives were used for 56% of total digital storage, optical drives 22%, magnetic tape 18%, and flash media approximately 2%. It is estimated that by 2010, hard drive use will decrease to 55%, optical drives will increase to 29%, tape will decrease to 13%, and flash memory will increase to approximately 3% of total storage. Over the years, tape will probably disappear as a storage media, supplemented by variations of discs and disks and a form of flash memory.

THE ECONOMICS OF DISTRIBUTION

In most media-related business operations, production is analogous to manufacturing, distribution to wholesaling, and exhibition to retailing. A distributor acts as a middleman or intermediary between the people who produce something and those who consume it. Exhibiting film, video, audio, Internet programming, and multimedia productions is similar to running a retail store from which individual consumers buy things. In media production, distribution and exhibition are aspects of postproduction, but producers must consider them during preproduction as well (Figure 1.6).

As digital technology advances, it becomes obvious that sending and receiving audio, video, motion pictures, and other digital signals via the Internet will take its place as a major means of distribution and exhibition. Streaming will become more practical as digital memory and compression techniques provide high-quality programming, and the capability of homes to receive that same quality programs at a reasonable rate increases. The ability of home viewers/listeners to receive a digital signal faster than a 59 K modem allows is the key to the success of streaming. Fiber-optic lines to the home, increased use of the digital subscriber line (DSL) in the home, or wireless Internet systems will allow streaming to become universal. Streaming of video and audio information on the Internet or World Wide Web (WWW) usually takes the form of either Web broadcasting, also known as video or audio on demand, or live webcasting.

MEDIA PRODUCTION BUSINESS COMPARED
TO RETAIL BUSINESS

MOTION PICTURES TELEVISION GAMES	BUSINESS
PRODUCER	MANUFACTURER
DISTRIBUTOR/NETWORK	WHOLESALE
EXHIBITOR STATION STORES	RETAIL SALES

FIGURE 1.6 In media production businesses, the producer is the equivalent of the manufacturer in a retail business. The distributor is the equivalent of a wholesaler, and the owner of the theater, TV station, or store that sells DVDs where the films are screened or exhibited is the equivalent of a retailer.

Video/audio on demand streaming occurs whenever a computer operator/receiver decides to download prerecorded audio or video information, while live webcasting occurs at a specific time determined by the sender rather than the receiver.

Distribution and exhibition marketing strategies and technologies will also be affected by the phenomenon known as convergence. Convergence refers to the coming together of previously separate technologies, such as computers and television sets. For example, as more and more computer manufacturers, such as Apple, become involved in audio/video and multimedia technologies, and more and more audio/video product manufacturers, such as Sony, become involved in computer technologies, previously separate entities are coming together. Early examples of convergence include WEB-TV where Web searches can be conducted using a conventional TV set, and liquid crystal display (LCD) TV sets which can also function as computer screens. As convergence progresses, media producers will need to become increasingly cognizant of new and emerging means and methods of distributing and exhibiting audio, video, and multimedia productions.

The selection of a specific production format or technology and the preparation of a budget must mesh with the anticipated distribution and exhibition technology and outlets. The initial planning for a feature film or television series, for example, may have to consider a wide variety of distribution and exhibition channels and markets, from major theatrical distribution, to network broadcasting, cable, DVDs, the Internet, and nontheatrical or educational distribution to college campuses, including unwanted and illegal piracy of copyrighted material via miniature video cameras in movie theaters and subsequent Internet streaming. Even a corporate or institutional in-house production is designed with specific types of exhibition in mind. The final product may be sent out as DVD, Blu-ray, CD, or flash card copy, or it may be presented "live" via satellite or over the Internet on video monitors or large screens at various corporate locations.

In Chapter 3, Producing and Production Management, we indicate that specific programs must be targeted for specific audiences. In this chapter, we will see how a television or film producer attempts to reach that target audience by selecting the best distribution and exhibition channel(s). Specific projects are tailored for specific forms of presentation in the media, such as cable television or theatrical film, as well as for specific target audiences. A consideration of the technology and economics of distribution and exhibition follows logically from the concern for the audience begun in our study of preproduction. Selecting the best channels requires an understanding of media technology and economics.

It is imperative that producers have a basic understanding of the potential markets for a film, television program, or multimedia production. Projects that are initiated without any consideration for, or knowledge of, the economics of distribution and exhibition will rarely if ever reach their target audience. There are many distribution and exhibition channels, including broadcasting, cable, satellite, theatrical and nontheatrical channels, home video, audio, multimedia, the Internet, and corporate and in-house channels. Each distribution/exhibition channel has different needs, requirements, and economic structures.

Broadcasting, Cable, and Satellite

Commercial broadcasting network television programming in the United States is produced for and by four primary networks—ABC, CBS, NBC, and Fox—and smaller networks such as CW, a combined Warner Bros. television network; U/PN, or United Paramount network; and the Spanish-language network, Univision. The four primary networks themselves originate news, sports, and most daytime programming. Most prime-time evening entertainment programming is produced by a limited number of independent producers and production companies.

Network television programming executives rarely take chances on unproven talent. They depend to a great extent on prior success as a guarantee of future success. Executive producers, such as Aaron Spelling, Michael Crichton, and Steven Bochco, have had repeated commercial success and are in a much better negotiating position with the networks than neophyte producers. Although the networks sometime take a chance on unproven talent, there is usually some compensating factor, such as a pre-sold property that was popular in another media or a major star who is willing to play a lead role. To be seriously considered, a producer must put together an extremely attractive package that guarantees some measure of success in terms of attracting a sizable audience.

The economics of commercial broadcast, cable, and satellite television revolves around the selling of audiences to advertisers. Entertainment programming is an indirect product. It provides revenues to the network or the station only when it attracts a large audience with the right demographic characteristics. The broadcast network, local station, cable channel, local cable operator, or satellite channel sells commercial time to advertisers on the basis of the size of the audience it is able to attract. Some advertisers believe that the most desirable audience in terms of demographics is women from 18 to 34 years of age, since they do the bulk of the buying of commercial products at retail stores. But males from 18 to 35 years of age with disposable income became a target of the advertisers, as well as Hispanic and other minority demographic groups. The newest target demographic group consists of males and females over 50 years old, known as "boomers," many retired with disposable income. This new targeted group may bring about a major shift in both programming and commercial production. Of course, all demographic groups are also sought for specific products and services, and programming is rarely aimed at just one demographic group.

A successful program is one that obtains a relatively high rating and audience share. The rating suggests the percentage of all 80 million-plus television households that are tuned to a specific program. Ratings translate into profit-and-loss figures, since advertisers are charged for commercial airtime on a cost-per-1,000 viewer basis. A *share* refers to the percentage of television households actually watching TV at a specific time, called households using television (HUT), that are tuned to a specific program. All the shares would add up to 100 percent (Figure 1.7).

Ratings and shares of television programs are determined by organizations such as A.C. Nielsen and Arbitron, which collect data about what viewers watch by means of diaries kept by viewers or meters attached to home sets. Generally a network program that garners around a 30 percent share is doing quite well. Good ratings can vary from above 10 percent in daytime to over 20 percent in prime time. Shows that consistently fail to achieve these ratings or shares are likely to be canceled in midseason or by the next season.

There are, of course, many factors that can affect a show's ratings. Scheduling is a crucial factor. Some time slots and days of the week are simply better than others in terms of ratings. Audience flow is another important factor. The popularity of the shows that

COMPARATIVE TV RATINGS FOR
SYNDICATED PROGRAMS BY GENRE

TALK

Oprah	5.0
Dr. Phil	3.2
Regis/Kelly	2.6
Ellen DeGeneres	2.2
Rachel Raye	1.7
Maury	1.5
Tyra	1.1
Springer	0.9

COURT

Judge Judy	4.3
Judge Joe Brown	2.4
People's Court	2.3
Judge Mathis	1.8
Judge Alex	1.6
Judge Karen	1.1
Family Court	0.6

MAGAZINE

Entertainment Tonight	4.3
Inside Edition	2.9
TMZ	2.1
Access Hollywood	2.0
Insider	1.9

GAME

Wheel of Fortune	6.6
Jeopardy	5.5
Millionaire	2.6
Deal/No Deal	1.6
Family Feud	1.5

FIGURE 1.7 In any one week the number of people or homes watching any one syndicated program varies from less than 0.1% to 20%. Syndicated programs are produced by independent producers and purchased by individual stations for airing at various times during the day so there is little cumulative viewership of any single program, but ratings may be compared between programs, not time of day. (Courtesy of *TV Newsday*)

precede and follow a specific program directly affects its share and ratings, because audiences often stay tuned to the same channel for a long period of time.

From the independent producer's standpoint, the survival of a show for at least five seasons is crucial to financial success. The amount of money that independent producers are given by the network to produce pilots and series episodes rarely covers the complete cost of production. This strategy is known as *deficit financing*. The producer usually signs a contract at the proposal or initial pilot script stage, granting a network exclusive rights to the series for at least five years. The contract specifies the year-by-year increase in network payments for each of the years that a series survives. After five years a sufficient number of episodes have usually been produced for the series to go into syndication.

Syndicated programming, often called *stripping*, is marketed to local stations for morning, early-afternoon, or early-evening broadcast, five days of the week. Independent producers make money from syndication, but they rarely make any revenues from network showings of series. Networks no longer are forbidden by law to directly syndicate their old shows, which now allows the networks a share of syndication revenues. Producers take substantial risks in terms of program development, which only pays off if the program goes into syndication. The probability of a show lasting long enough to go into syndication is actually quite low, but the success of a single show can pay for many disasters. Now that networks may purchase their own programs, independent producers must compete with their potential client's own programming.

Syndicated programming generally bypasses the major commercial networks. Syndicated programs are broadcast by network-affiliated local television stations during times of the day when there is no network programming, such as late afternoon and early evening. Independent local television stations show syndicated programming during any time slot, including prime time: 8 p.m. to 11 p.m. eastern standard time. Affiliates may also broadcast syndicated programming during prime time. In the past, networks paid their affiliated stations a fee for broadcasting network programming, although affiliates in sparsely populated areas may actually receive no fee other than the free use of the programs as a means to attract or draw viewers for the local commercials that are run during local station breaks between shows. Today networks expect affiliates to pay for programming provided by the networks. An affiliate can, of course, reject the network programming and substitute syndicated or its own local programming. Some major network affiliates have switched networks or combined affiliation with one growing network such as CW, and one major network such as NBC. Of course, an affiliated local station that continually rejects its network's programming or also affiliates with a growing network risks losing its primary network affiliate status. However, because of limited television channel space, local affiliates are usually in a strong bargaining position with the networks.

Affiliates and independents have sometimes banded together to partially finance their own entertainment programming. Although entertainment programming usually comes to a local station through a network or through an independent syndicator, local news, sports, and public service and information programming is usually produced by the station itself. Local news is one of the most competitive and profitable areas of local TV programming. It is important in terms of both the audience it draws to the local news program itself and the audience drawn to the syndicated programming that surrounds the news. During these non-network time slots, local stations sell commercial time to advertisers, who pay relatively high cost-per-thousand prices for commercial time, especially in the top 50 local television markets.

Obviously, the economic conditions of commercial broadcast television make it difficult for a small, unproven independent film or television producer to sell a single entertainment or informational program to commercial television stations. Television stations are interested in buying or showing a continuous supply of programming, such as a series or even a miniseries, rather than isolated or individual programs. Local stations will often show independently produced documentaries of local or regional interest during slow or weak time slots, such as Sunday morning or Saturday afternoon, but they will rarely pay much, if anything, for this type of programming. An independent producer would do better to find a corporate or individual sponsor for a single program and then guarantee that sponsor a credit line and a certain amount of exposure during slow or off-hours of commercial broadcasting than to try marketing a speculative program to television stations after it has been produced.

Similar kinds of marketing problems plague an independent producer who hopes to market a single program to cable television. Cable operators are often more interested in filling time slots on a regular basis than in buying isolated programs. Nonetheless, there is greater marketing potential for small, independently produced programming through cable television than through commercial broadcasting. The larger number of cable television channels ensures wider access and a greater ability to *narrowcast*, or to target a small, relatively specialized audience. The economic structure of cable television is quite different from that of commercial broadcasting. The cable operator sells specific channels or packages of channels to individual consumers or subscribers, and the program producer or supplier often receives a percentage of the subscription fee or commercial advertising revenues. Some channels are allocated to locally produced programs and provide community access. They are usually available free of charge to anyone who wants to show something of community interest.

Producers can advertise their own programs by publicizing a specific program topic and show time and date in print media. Unlike commercial broadcasters, a cable operator will often accept smaller-format, lower-quality video recordings, such as material on mini-DV digital videotape or other formats not of broadcast quality. Network broadcasters usually demand digital formats or 16 mm or 35 mm films of high quality that meet or exceed National Association of Broadcasters (NAB) standards. Some cable television programs—such as those produced by Turner Broadcasting (superstation WTBS Atlanta and Cable News Network, CNN, a cable program service), as well as the sports channel ESPN—depend to a significant extent on commercial advertising for their revenues and must meet broadcast standards. Other program channels, such as various movie channels, distribute and sometimes produce expensive entertainment programs and are almost totally dependent on percentages of subscription charges for their revenue.

It is possible to initiate the production and marketing of some cable programs for far less money than is required for commercial broadcasting. Many cable producers are nonunion and thus can save substantial production costs by paying lower salaries to their personnel. Cable distributors and suppliers have to sell their programming to local cable operators, invest in satellite transmission services, and assume the cost of program advertising. In return, they demand a portion of subscription receipts. It is possible to produce isolated programs on an independent basis for specific cable channels, such as WTBS, or to produce cable programming speculatively for Arts and Entertainment (A&E) or other cable distributors with a greater hope of finding a potential buyer than is the case with commercial broadcasting.

Public television is a noncommercial broadcasting distribution and exhibition channel. In the United States, it is partially supported by the Corporation for Public Broadcasting (CPB), which was set up by an act of Congress in 1967 that also authorized funds for its operation. The CPB created the current network of public broadcasting stations. There are basically four types of public broadcasting stations: those owned and operated by colleges and universities, such as stations at the universities of Houston, Wisconsin, and North Carolina; those owned and operated by school systems, such as that in Cincinnati (only 7 percent); those owned and operated by municipal (state) authorities, such as those in Georgia, New Jersey, and Iowa; and those developed and operated by nonprofit corporations, such as stations in Boston, New York, and Chicago.

Public broadcasting is often threatened by inadequate financial support. Federal budget allocations to the CPB are in constant jeopardy. The pursuit of large audiences through popular programming often attracts major corporate sponsors; however, such sponsorship is sometimes criticized on the basis that it gives these corporations power over noncommercial as well as commercial broadcasting. Some critics charge that on-the-air credits are tantamount to advertising and should not be permitted in noncommercial broadcasting. Public television stations frequently raise money through funding drives. The money they collect is used to fund local productions, to purchase national Public Broadcasting Service (PBS) programming (which they have a hand in selecting), and to defray operating costs. PBS is responsive to member stations that are involved in determining which programs will be nationally distributed. This relationship is quite different from that between commercial networks and affiliates, although the extent to which public stations should be controlled by the national network as opposed to local management is an often hotly debated issue.

Public television programming comes from a variety of sources. Some of the programming is at least partially funded by the Corporation for Public Broadcasting and corporate sponsors at the national level and is then distributed through PBS to its member stations. PBS member stations produce much of the programming that is distributed through PBS to other stations. The largest producers of this type of national PBS programming are PBS member stations in Boston, Pittsburgh, Columbia, South Carolina, New York, Washington, Chicago, and Los Angeles. However, member stations usually produce a series of programs on a specific topic rather than single, isolated programs.

Some programming comes from foreign producers, most notably the British Broadcasting Corporation (BBC). Individual stations themselves often produce a certain amount of local or regional public-interest programming, much of which never receives national distribution. At the local or state level, it is sometimes possible for an independent producer to air an individual program on a PBS station or state system. Such programs are often independently funded by other sources, although partial funding can come from a PBS station in return for broadcast rights, usually specifying a specific number of airings over a two- or three-year period. The quality standards of PBS are similar to those of commercial broadcast television.

The subject matter and format of PBS programming can be quite different from that of commercial broadcast programming, although PBS stations have become increasingly concerned about attracting large audiences which help to generate public financial support. The length of a half-hour PBS program is currently about 26 minutes, compared to about 22 minutes for most programs intended for commercial television stations and cable channels.

Commercial spots are short (often 15- or 30-second) television messages that attempt to sell commercial products and services to consumers. The production of network television commercials and national spot sales is largely controlled by major advertising agencies, such as J. Walter Thompson, Leo Burnett, N. W. Ayer, and McCann-Erickson, who contract with production specialists on a bidding basis. The advertising agency usually develops the basic story line for a commercial in consultation with the client whose product, name, or services are being promoted. The advertising agency also develops a storyboard of hand-drawn images to visualize the spot. The director's job is to capture this idea on 35 mm film, HDTV, or other digital formats. Some creative innovation and play with the basic script idea is allowed with a talented director, but the work of production companies is primarily that of technical and aesthetic execution, rather than of developing creative, original ideas.

The production budget for a network commercial is often extremely high, given the relatively short duration of the final product. It is not unusual for a company to spend from half a million to 1 million dollars for a single 30-second network-level spot.

The production company must be technically perfect in its execution of the commercial. Sometimes as much as 90,000 feet of 35 mm film is shot to produce just 45 feet of the final product for a beverage commercial, for example. Major advertisers often contract with a separate individual or company for different aspects of production and postproduction on a commercial, rather than allowing any single production company to have complete control. Many of the most talented creative producers of network-level commercials work on a freelance basis or have their own production companies.

A local television station or a small production company often produces local commercials. Television stations often sell local commercial time to businesses in their area and then offer to produce the commercial themselves. Small independent production companies sometimes produce the entire commercial for a client, from script to screen. The budgets for locally produced television commercials are low compared with network-level commercials. Some are produced on mini-DV or 16 mm film for a few thousand dollars. Only rarely is 35 mm film used for the production of local commercials. In the largest local television markets, the production of commercials is handled by major advertising agencies. National spot sales place network-quality spots that are not part of the network schedule on smaller market TV stations. The costs of commercial production represent but a small fraction of the total advertising budget for the promotion of a product, name, or service. Television time costs are usually much higher than production costs, and many other media besides television, such as magazines, newspapers, and radio, may be involved in a particular advertising campaign.

Public service announcements, or *PSAs*, are the least expensive type of commercial. They are usually shown free of charge in the public interest to help promote public service agencies and nonprofit organizations. While PSAs must meet broadcast standards in terms of technical quality, they are often produced in the most economical format possible, such as 16 mm film, mini-DV or other low-cost digital format. PSAs offer an excellent opportunity for neophyte producers to become involved in a serious production, allowing them an opportunity to perfect their technical competence and to experiment with new techniques.

Theatrical and Nontheatrical

Power in the feature film industry is concentrated primarily in distribution. Major distributors, such as Disney, Paramount, Warner Bros., MGM, United Artists, Columbia, Universal, and Twentieth Century-Fox, receive the bulk of the distribution receipts from feature films. They negotiate with exhibition chains, such as National General, and independent theaters for a split of exhibition receipts. One of the most common splits for a major film is a 90/10 split, which gives 90 percent of the admission receipts to the distributor and 10 percent to the exhibitor, above and beyond the latter's fixed operating costs for a specified period of time, such as several weeks. The distributor's percentage decreases gradually over time as the exhibitor's percentage increases. Exhibitors compete with each other for specific films by bidding a specific split and exhibition duration. About 50 percent of the major U.S. distributors' total theatrical receipts come from foreign distribution. Distributors also negotiate with television networks, cable television movie channels, and consumer videotape retailers (Figure 1.8). Income from the sale of DVDs and ancillary items now exceeds that of ticket sales in theaters for most feature films and has done so since the mid-1990s.

**RANKING U.S. MOTION PICTURES
BY DOMESTIC BOX OFFICE INCOME**

RANK	TITLE	RELEASE	RECEIPTS
1	*Titanic*	1997	$600,779,824
2	*Dark Knight*	2008	522,341,786
3	*Star Wars*	1997	460,935,665
4	*Shrek 2*	2004	436,471,036
5	*ET. The Extraterrestrial*	1982	434,949,459
6	*Star Wars I: The Phantom Menace*	1999	431,065,444
7	*Pirates of the Caribbean: Dead Man's Chest*	2006	423,032,628
8	*Spiderman*	2002	403,706,375
9	*Star Wars III: Revenge of the Sith*	2005	380,262,555
10	*The Lord of The Rings: The Return of the King*	2003	377,019,252
11	*Spider-Man 2*	2004	373,377.893
12	*The Passion of Christ*	2004	370,270,943
13	*Jurassic Park*	1993	356,784,000
14	*Lord of the Rings: The Two Towers*	2002	340,478,898
15	*Finding Nemo*	2003	339,714,978
16	*Spider-Man 3*	2007	336,530,303
17	*Forrest Gump*	1994	329,694,499
18	*The Lion King*	1994	328,423,001
19	*Shrek the Third*	2007	320,706,665
20	*Transformers*	2007	318,759,914

ACTUAL DOMESTIC BOX OFFICE DOLLARS
(not adjusted to 2008 dollars)

FIGURE 1.8 The calculation of actual dollars earned by motion pictures is a complex and often mistrusted process. One of the most telling figures is actual box office receipts, but that may not be a fair judgment of a film's popularity because some films are shown in many theaters, others in relatively few. Also the calculation should be adjusted to today's dollars, which would make many films of many years ago appear to have earned much more than their actual income at the time when they were exhibited. (Courtesy of *Imdb.com.*)

An average Hollywood-produced feature film today costs more than $80 million to produce. The distributor spends about 30 percent more than these production costs for advertising, release prints, and other distribution costs. It is virtually impossible to acquire financial backing for even an average budgeted feature film without a major distributor's endorsement. That endorsement usually requires the involvement of previously proven talent, such as well-known stars and directors, in a dramatic production. The distributor then either puts up the money for a production or provides some sort of guarantee to banks, which then finance the cost of production with a loan. Only rarely do major distributors later pick up independently produced feature films that do not have an initial major distributor endorsement. But major motion pictures are being produced in right-to-work states, especially in the South, to lower production costs by avoiding unions and obtaining considerable state and local cooperation.

Low-budget feature films are largely distributed by independent distributors, who do not have as much bargaining power with the largest theater chains and independent theaters as do the majors. Of course, a producer can always distribute his or her own film either by negotiating directly with theaters for a split, which is rarely done, or by renting a theater, doing some local advertising, and then receiving any and all gate receipts, a technique known as *four-walling*.

Producers negotiate with distributors for a percentage of the distribution receipts. A producer can demand a certain percentage of either the gross receipts or the net receipts (after the distributor has subtracted certain fixed costs) or sell the film outright to the distributor. Obviously a producer who is able to negotiate a percentage of the gross receipts is in a strong bargaining position. The producer must consider a number of factors before deciding on a specific plan, such as the true earning potential of the film, the length of time before real receipts will be received, during which interest on loans must be paid, the reliability of distributor accounting, and the hidden costs of production and distribution (Figure 1.9).

An increasingly important area of negotiations is *ancillary rights* and *commercial tie-ins*, such as toys and T-shirts. Receipts from markets in addition to commercial theaters, such as network and cable television, must be considered. Musical records, books, posters, dolls, toys, clothing, and games that are offshoots of a

**RANKING WORLDWIDE MOTION PICTURES
BY BOX OFFICE INCOME IN U.S. DOLLARS**

RANK	TITLE	RELEASE	RECEIPTS
1	*Titanic*	1997	$1,835,300,000
2	*Lord of the Rings: Return of the King*	2003	1,129,252,000
3	*Pirates of the Caribbean: Dead Man's Chest*	2006	1,060,332,628
4	*Dark Knight*	2008	971,446,786
5	*Harry Potter and the Sorcerer's Stone*	2001	969,600,000
6	*Pirates of the Caribbean: At World's End*	2007	958,404,152
7	*Harry Potter: The Order of the Phoenix*	2007	937,000,866
8	*Star Wars I: The Phantom Menace*	1999	922,379,000
9	*Lord of the Rings: The Two Towers*	2002	921,600,000
10	*Jurassic Park*	1993	919,700,000
11	*Harry Potter: The Goblet of Fire*	2005	892,194,397
12	*Spider-Man 3*	2007	885,430,303
13	*Shrek 2*	2004	880,871,036
14	*Harry Potter: Chamber of Secrets*	2000	866,300,000
15	*Finding Nemo*	2003	865,007,000
16	*Lord of the Rings: Fellowship of the Ring*	2001	860,700,000
17	*Star Wars III: Revenge of the Sith*	2005	848,462,555
18	*Independence Day*	1996	811,200,000
19	*Spiderman*	2002	806,700,000
20	*Star Wars*	1997	797,900,000
21	*Shrek the Third*	2007	791,900,000
22	*Harry Potter: The Prisoner of Azkabar*	2004	789,458,727
23	*Spider-Man 2*	2004	783,577,893
24	*The Lion King*	1994	783,400,000
25	*Indiana Jones and the Kingdom of the Crystal Skull*	2008	760,969,461

WORLDWIDE BOX OFFICE DOLLARS
(not adjusted to 2008 dollars)

FIGURE 1.9 Much of the income from feature films comes from both the sales of tapes and discs and from international distribution. The total income worldwide may be triple the receipts earned within the United States. The calculation of actual value is made even more difficult with the constantly shifting value of the American dollar against international currency. (Courtesy of *lmdb.com*.)

successful film can make huge profits. Sometimes an especially popular movie star will demand either a large initial payment of several million dollars or a percentage of the gross distribution receipts. The involvement of major stars directly affects not only the production budget but also the producer's negotiations with the distributor and the banks.

The producer and financial backers of a feature film understand that film production is an extremely risky business. Few feature films earn a substantial profit, and most of those that do either are produced on an extremely tight budget for somewhat smaller domestic and foreign markets or are extremely high-budget films heavily promoted by major distributors. In both of these cases, the successful commercial producer understands the target audience and designs a film and budget that are realistic in terms of audience expectations, preferences, and size.

The term *nontheatrical* refers to films and videos that are shown in places other than commercial film theaters. Nontheatrical films, DVDs, and videos are shown by colleges and universities, other educational institutions, civic groups, and other organizations. They are not always exhibited for profit but often as a cultural or informational service. Although nontheatrical exhibition is usually a nonprofit undertaking, nontheatrical distribution is largely a commercial business. Feature films, for example, are rented to various groups, institutions, and individuals in 16 mm film and various video formats for public showing. Renting these works for public showing is often far more expensive than purchasing a home videotape or disc copy, but videotapes and discs, which can be rented or purchased in retail stores, are strictly intended for individual, home use. Higher royalties are demanded for public showings of these films and videos when they are rented from commercial, nontheatrical distributors.

Nontheatrical distribution is not limited to feature films. Individual film and video artists, documentary producers, and producers of other short informational and educational materials often have their work distributed by a nontheatrical distributor. Nontheatrical distributors who make a profit pass on a certain percentage of their gross receipts to producers. Some independent producers and artists cooperatively organize their own distribution systems. The New York Filmmaker's Cooperative, for example, passes on a greater share of distribution receipts to individual artists and keeps only a small percentage of the receipts from rentals or sales for its own operating costs.

Many commercial nontheatrical distributors, such as Pyramid Films, distribute successful short films. Many of the short subjects they distribute have previously won major awards, such as Academy Awards or major festival awards. One of the best means for beginning producers and directors to find good distributors for short works is to win awards at major festivals and contests. A nontheatrical distributor will often offer winners of major awards the opportunity to use the distributor's promotional and advertising services for a major percentage of the distribution receipts or offer an outright payment for exclusive distribution rights. These short films are then distributed individually to nonprofit institutions; as packages of shorts to cable television services, such as HBO (Home Box Office); and to colleges and universities. Nontheatrical distributors actively seek projects that have specialized audiences or limited markets, since they do not always have to distribute these works through mass media channels such as commercial broadcasting or commercial film theaters.

Home Video, Audio, and Multimedia

An expanding market for film and video productions includes home videotapes and DVDs, Blu-ray discs (BDs), audio CDs, and various forms of multimedia, including CD-ROMs. There are other digital discs besides Blu-ray including HD-DVD and V-DVD, but in this text, Blu-ray will refer to all consumer blue laser discs. These products are rented and sold to individual consumers. Feature films, popular music with accompanying video images, and informational and educational materials can be marketed in this manner. The individual consumer buys a DVD or Blu-ray disc and plays it on his or her own deck or computer and monitor. Most entertainment films and videos currently being sold as commercial products were initially produced for distribution to commercial theaters, network television, or cable television. As more consumers possess their own players, more programming will be designed for initial sale to consumers, just like records, books, and computer games in retail stores. The rental/sale of home DVDs has been a rapidly expanding market for entertainment programming for some time. In fact, 1985 was the first year that videotape plus DVD sales of Hollywood products equaled domestic feature film distribution receipts from theaters. DVD sales and rentals have replaced tape sales and rentals as of the end of 2007.

Emerging new audio recording and duplication technologies have had an impact on audio production and distribution. Recordable CD-ROM technology, CD-R, can be used for temporary or permanent information storage and retrieval, including "burning" or making copies of audio CDs. Storage of audio recordings on computer hard drives has been facilitated by the MP3 digital compression format, which provides nearly CD-quality sound reproduction with significantly reduced storage size. MP3 files may then be downloaded to portable audio players like the iPod. This format has also led to legal complications for some Internet companies, such as Napster, which facilitated the sharing of audio recordings on individual computers across the World Wide Web, angering some musical artists and recording companies by potentially reducing the size of their markets and royalties on copyrighted materials. Illegal operations such as Napster have been shut down and now have been replaced by share programs that charge a minimum for each shared musical recording. Apple, Microsoft, and AOL as well as other Internet companies have joined this expanding field.

The rental and sale of DVD and Blu-ray discs is an area that can be easily exploited by smaller producers because many DVD/Blu-ray rentals and sales outlets are operated as small businesses (although many regional and local markets are dominated by major chains, such as Blockbuster) and distribution is not as tightly controlled as is the theatrical outlet for feature films. Advertising expenses can be substantial, however, and these must be born by the producer who wants to sell DVD/Blu-ray to rental outlets and individual consumers. Most Hollywood films have already had a great deal of publicity and have generated much public interest before their availability as DVD and Blu-ray discs.

Programming designed specifically for the home DVD/Blu-ray market differs in many important respects from programming designed primarily for theatrical distribution. The production of programming for small-screen exhibition raises a number of aesthetic problems. Composition within the frame in a small-screen format must keep key information in the essential area of a TV receiver. Important details cannot be presented on the fringes of the screen, as in a wide-screen feature film production designed primarily for theatrical release. Close-ups are used much more frequently for small-screen productions, and wide vistas and panoramic shots are kept to a minimum. The pacing of entertainment programming intended for television and disc distribution is often faster and more action-packed to hold the audience's attention. Framing and aspect ratio problems become more acute when portable video players and cell telephones with square or odd format shapes defy traditional composition planning.

At present, using DVDs for mastering is still fairly expensive initially, although the cost of mass duplication is relatively low. Initial recordings and editing are not done on DVD but directly on the CPU of a computer before transferring to a DVD duplication facility. Film recordings are produced, edited, and then duplicated on DVD, creating a master pressing or copy from which individual DVD copies are made. Because the cost of this master runs high, it is only economical to use this technology when a large number of copies are needed. But the ease, low cost, and simplicity of burning a DVD-R on a typical home computer has made creating DVDs as attractive as burning individual CDs (Figure 1-10). The high information capacity, relative permanence, and durability of DVDs make them an ideal information storage and retrieval medium. The low cost of producing numerous copies once the master disc is made makes the disc an excellent means of distributing promotional materials to salespeople or consumers in retail stores throughout the country. When a large number of DVDs are made from the same master, the actual duplicating cost can be as low as $1 to $2 per disc.

In terms of direct sales to consumers, the main advantage offered by the sale of a product (rather than the sale of a seat in a theater or time on commercial television) and the relatively low cost of making multiple video copies is that DVD or Blu-ray discs can be made for and marketed to specialized demographic groups. Distribution channels are not constrained by limited channels of access, as they are in the case of network television and commercial film theaters, where a product must be marketed to a mass, heterogeneous audience. Individual copies can be manufactured and sold to smaller groups of consumers, just as popular rock, country, soul, and classical music can be marketed by the recording industry to smaller groups of people. Individual discs can sell for anywhere from about $5 to $50, depending on the size of the market and the cost of production. As the consumer market

FIGURE 1-10 The ability to create quality media productions in a home setting has developed an entirely new distribution network. Now, an individual may record, process, and distribute his or her own work from a relatively inexpensive set of media equipment without relying on any outside organizations.

expands, independent producers will undoubtedly proliferate, and disc production may become as decentralized as production in the audio recording industry or music business has become.

Consumer marketing of multimedia products is made somewhat complex by virtue of the diversity of standards in terms of hardware, such as Mac versus PC platforms (a problem that plagued the consumer videocassette rental business early on, when both Beta and VHS were fairly common), and the diversity of distribution channels, such as computer retail store sales versus catalog sales (more Mac-based software and DVDs are marketed via the latter than the former channel, for example). Many CDs and DVDs, of course, can be used on both platforms. Publishers finance and market multimedia products, while distributors manage the flow of the product of the publisher to the customer.

Publishers coordinate printing, duplication, and packaging, as well as marketing. Marketing usually involves promotion and advertising, as well as sales. Focus groups may provide responses concerning what potential consumers want and what prices they are willing to pay. Products may then be test-marketed in specific locations before they are mass-marketed across the country. Different pathways to the consumer constitute the distribution channels, such as retail chain stores and catalog sales. Although the distribution of multimedia products is not as concentrated in the hands of a few major companies as is the case with feature films and network television broadcasting, nonetheless major multimedia publishers are emerging who have distinct advantages in terms of access to capital and distribution channels as well as other means necessary to successfully mass-market DVD and Blu-ray discs and other multimedia technologies to consumers.

Hollywood's involvement in multimedia, for example, has been stimulated by the fact that the videogame business currently generates about the same revenues as the box-office portion of the film industry at more than $5 billion per year, and the videogame business is expected to more than double in the next few years. A number of DVD/Blu-ray discs and interactive videogames have been produced that carry the same titles as Hollywood motion pictures, giving viewers an opportunity to further their involvement with their favorite plots and characters using multimedia. Interactive multimedia divisions of major studios attempt to establish connections between computer games and movies, although important differences still exist between these media. For example, successful interactive multimedia products usually focus on the user, rather than a Hollywood actor, as the star.

The probability of succeeding in either medium with a particular product remains relatively low, since only about 6 DVD titles out of every 200 are financially successful. Success and name recognition in one medium can carry over to another. Mass market DVD production costs average about $500,000 compared with about $80 million for a Hollywood feature film, and Hollywood distributors spend as much as 30 percent of their total budgets on advertising and distribution, which can translate into significant name recognition for a multimedia product. However, some hit videogames have appeared that are based on Hollywood films. Some multimedia firms have joined forces with television and music companies to produce arty, experimental stories that draw name recognition from rock groups and successful television programs. A number of other multimedia publishers have focused on developing DVD and Blu-ray discs or videogames as an independent art form, relying on imaginative graphics, animation, and sounds to stimulate the user's involvement and interaction with unique multimedia worlds and characters.

Corporate and In-House

The overwhelming majority of production in the United States is done by corporations and institutions in-house. This is one of the largest and fastest growing areas of possible employment in production. According to Department of Labor statistics, roughly 193,000 people in this country make their living in broadcast television, while 235,000 people make their living in nonbroadcast television, most of which consists of corporate and institutional production done in-house. At the turn of the century, for example, the largest growth in sales of video equipment came from the industrial/business/institutional market, not the broadcast market.

In-house production by corporations, government agencies, and educational institutions constitutes a special type of distribution and exhibition channel. Much corporate video production is designed to train and motivate employees, to communicate with employees scattered all over the country or around the world, or to communicate with customers and clients. Different kinds of information can be represented in a more entertaining fashion than might be the case with a brochure or other publication. Sales representatives can be trained in the latest techniques and strategies for selling products. Corporate productions often demonstrate these techniques through dramatizations. Some corporations use digital facilities to record executive speeches and sales meetings, so that corporate information can be widely disseminated.

Specific products are often advertised and demonstrated in automobile showrooms or department stores using DVDs produced in-house. Hospitals and educational institutions often produce programs that are helpful to patients and students. Health care information is often disseminated via closed-circuit television or by a mobile DVD unit that can be moved from room to room. Special diets, medications, and surgical procedures that a patient is about to undergo can be clarified and explained better and more efficiently on videotape than in person.

One of the fastest growing areas of in-house production is the production of instructional DVDs and computer interactive programs and videodiscs for corporate or institutional training. Discs can help students learn an incredible range of tasks at their own individual rate, using a student-controlled player; an interactive video unit, which consists of a computer and a videodisc player controlled by the computer; or an interactive computer with a CD-ROM. The viewer's response can be recorded on a touch pad that controls the operation of the computer and the rate at which new information or questions are presented.

An in-house production unit has varying degrees and types of accountability. The production unit may be directly accountable to management in a corporation in terms of its production budgets and production management. Government agencies and educational units are usually accountable to government or academic administrators. Since the programming that is produced is usually aimed at an internal audience or a specialized audience outside the institution, the means of assessing program success is sometimes quite informal, although major corporations often do sophisticated research into program effectiveness. Policy is sometimes controlled by a few individuals. There is usually a specific message to tell, and communication usually takes place in a one-way direction down the hierarchy, although programming ideas sometimes originate from employee, patient, or student suggestions.

Most in-house production units produce DVDs that can be played at a time and place that is convenient for the recipient of the information. The in-house producer often has all of the facilities needed to produce a completed product and to internally distribute and exhibit it. Medical schools, telephone companies, and public utilities, as well as government agencies, may have completely outfitted video production units with state-of-the-art equipment, such as digital formats, recording and editing equipment, as well as high-quality video cameras, lighting, and sound equipment. Small companies and agencies may only have a single mini-DV camcorder, a digital tape deck with a monitor, and no sophisticated production or editing facilities.

Individual project production costs are often kept low by having producers, directors, and technical support people on staff who can serve a variety of functions. Personnel who work in corporate or institutional production often have to be more flexible and have a broader range of skills than those who work in a particular broadcast television position. The staff for an in-house production unit is generally small. New personnel may be expected to work with slides, audiotape, and film on occasion, as well as digital formats. Production costs are usually kept to a minimum as well by using the most economical medium to communicate a specific message. If motion is not essential, a slide and tape show may be a more economical and effective means of presenting the material. Technical information and statistics might be communicated more effectively and inexpensively by writing and illustrating a brochure or a pamphlet. Regardless of the specific medium that is eventually selected, basic writing and production skills are essential qualifications for anyone pursuing a career in the rapidly expanding area of corporate and institutional in-house production.

INTERNET DISTRIBUTION

Of all new media, the Internet as it emerged has had a greater effect on all previous media than any of the other media on their predecessors; radio on music and motion pictures, television on radio and motion pictures, and cable on television. The Internet has moved into communication and distribution areas that it was never designed for nor intended to be used. As a simple widespread research communication tool, the Internet has entered or begun to compete in virtually every type of information distribution system.

Radio DJs use web sites for contests, chatting, and blogging with listeners while on the air. The radio stations stream their live broadcast programming and add features and repeated programs for which they do not have available airtime. Web radio services allow listeners to personalize their listening preferences by connecting them to genre-preferred sites of their own choosing. Internet-based radio stations operate out of basements, garages, and bedrooms, without Federal Communications Commission (FCC) licenses. But faced with new music-licensing fees high enough to keep the small operations from earning their operating costs, much less earn a profit, Internet radio stations will need to reconsider their business models to continue to exist.

Internet radio offers the listener an alternate source for their listening pleasure, whether it is for music, opinion, news, or genre and specific opinions not available from commercial or public radio.

Internet Protocol Television (IPTV), the logical coalition between TV and the Internet, originally faced consumer resistance as the advantages of viewing television programs on a computer were outweighed by the inconvenience of watching television on the small computer screen under minimal broadband reproduction of signals using limited, inconsistent scanning systems. IPTV is a system used to send packets of segments of a video signal through the Internet. The normal video signal through the Internet appears as a small picture in-frame, probably not at 60 frames per second, so the picture jumps and lags as the digital signal arrives slowly. IPTV solves the problem by breaking the signal into digital packets and sending them at various times (in nanoseconds) through various Internet connections so that the signal arrives and is assembled in a complete form at the receiver. The system requires special sending and receiving equipment, usually a set-up box on the television monitor for home use. The advantages of IPTV are more for the telephone companies or cable companies pressing for the technology. Once in place, whichever company has made the connection to a home then has the means of providing all three communication services to that home on one wire, at one price: telephone, television, and a high-speed computer connection. Home media centers that include computer CPUs connected to a large, high-definition screen served by a high-speed broadband network and server will open consumers to adapt their television viewing to IPTV. The low bandwidth and slow delivery systems continue to be solved and improved with upgraded compression systems and fiber-optic connections to the home (FTTH). Cable and telephone companies race to meet the demand first.

Internet news has contributed to the decline in newspaper readers, broadcast newscast viewers, and even cable news channel viewers. Internet news consists of five basic types of newscasts; newspaper web sites; broadcast news web sites; cable news channel web sites; and newscasts from a variety of specialized news Web organizations, blogs, and commercial news aggregators; and news services like AP, Reuters, and Al Jazeera. Online news readership exceeded the readership of all print media by the end of 2007. TV news web sites attract fewer viewers than print web sites, but the numbers continue to grow to make up for the late start in entering the Web news business. Aggregators on the Internet with a particular bias show the strongest increase in traffic as fans find their preferred voice. Although bloggers receive major publicity and attention, they attract fewer visits than a typical midsized city newspaper site.

A political-economic question yet to be resolved surrounding the Internet is the concept known as "Net Neutrality." At the present time, broadband Internet service providers (ISP) follow a tradition (but not codified as of 2008) that prohibits favoring or impeding the use of their communication lines. The content companies, telecommunication companies, and most individual users would like to see the prohibition policy made final with legislation on a national basis. The ISPs would like to avoid any legislation that impedes their greater freedom to decide who they serve and what they charge for their services. The question puts two large, rich, and powerful groups of communication corporations against each other with the small individual users watching from the sidelines.

Distribution of network television programs available on the Internet is a rapidly growing market, which also contributed to labor actions, specifically among screenwriters in late 2007 and 2008. Many young viewers watch broadcast television with less frequency than they access the World Wide Web. They often view episodes or sections of episodes of television series via the Internet. Networks originally made these programs freely available ostensibly to attract young viewers and develop new markets. Writers and other craft groups, on the other hand, have demanded participation in the revenue streams generated by these new markets they feel erode traditional sources of income such as residuals from syndication and other markets. Advertising and other revenue streams are growing slowly on the Internet, which offers potential for producers in terms of new media markets as well as employment opportunities for media students.

Internet distribution, like all new media before it, will change all preceding media— especially news gathering and reporting. Whether the unrestricted, unedited, or unauthorized nature of the Internet will bring about a more accurate and reliable source of information or destroy the centuries-old tradition of professional, responsible journalism may or may not become apparent until sometime in the future.

THE FUTURE OF DISTRIBUTION AND EXHIBITION

The digital evolution transformed a linear pattern of distribution of media programs from production-distribution-exhibition to a multiarmed pattern that has yet to completely stabilize. The high cost of advertising is beginning to bring about the simultaneous multiple release of motion pictures and other media products in different formats. The traditional sequential revenue stream and markets were theatrical film, broadcast and cable television, foreign markets, DVD and Blu-ray discs, and the Internet. Producers from now on must consider more than a single linear path for their work; from their first concept they must consider multiple paths to move the project from the camera, microphone, or computer to the targeted audience. It will not matter if the original production medium format is audio, video, film, graphics, the Internet, or any new digital format, the delivery will be via disc, satellite or terrestrial signals, film, solid-state memory, or the Web. The actual signal may be distributed by cable, fiber optics, radio frequencies, or magnetic pulses.

The audience may view or hear the program in a video monitor, a film or digital image projected on a screen, a computer desktop or laptop monitor, a cell telephone, an automobile dashboard, a handheld PDA, a miniature computer, or any number of mobile devices. All aspects of distribution and exhibition of the digital evolution have yet to be fully explored. The race between improved and expanded production technology and systems to maximize the potential of exhibited digital technology is an ongoing process. Video systems moved from 2K to 4K to 4-4-4 and full digital signals to match ultrahigh definition TV (UHD-TV). Film projection systems and film emulsions continue to surpass the resolution and contrast range of even those video systems and will continue to improve.

Increased bandwidth, memory, and transmission systems open new levels of quality, storage, and speed of handling signals for delivery on new high-speed networks. The technical figures published in this text will be surpassed by the time you read this chapter. The rapid changes in media technology, production techniques, distribution networks, and exhibition methods will not slow down—for better or for worse, the hectic uncontrolled changes will provide whatever is necessary for the field to continue to mature and evolve.

Summary

The digital changes in media production have opened new avenues for the use of production in the home, business, and in entertainment areas not used before. The media producers or workers must have a clear understanding of where their intended production will be distributed before they actually begin production to take advantage of the many options open to them. That understanding must include knowledge of the intended audience and the methods of analyzing who the audience is and why that audience may watch a particular production.

The wide variety of means of distributing media productions include all of the traditional means but add many new means of showing works including the Internet, games, and mobile outlets that did not exist 10 years ago. Broadcasting refers to the transmission of television and radio signals through the airwaves. Cable television distributes video transmissions, often received via satellite dish, to individual homes by way of coaxial cables. HDTV offers the prospect of providing high-quality television images, which can be used by large-screen electronic projection systems in commercial theaters and in private homes. Theatrical film/electronic exhibition requires some form of large-screen projection. Nontheatrical screenings usually involve smaller groups of viewers and significantly less, if any, admission fees than theatrical screenings, reducing the need and demand for high-quality, large-screen projection. A number of media products are designed or marketed for the home, such as DVD/Blu-ray discs, CD-ROMs, photo CDs, and audio CDs. Corporate and in-house media technologies are diverse. A closed-circuit television system interconnects various recording, transmitting, and receiving devices within a single building or building complex. Teleconferencing refers to "live" or instantaneous group interaction that takes place via simultaneous transmission of video, voice, or data from several locations.

Producers also need to be familiar with the economics of broadcasting, cable, satellite, theatrical, nontheatrical, home videocassette, videodisc, and multimedia, and corporate and in-house distribution and exhibition. Commercial broadcasters sell audiences to advertisers. Syndicated programming consists of reruns of old network series, movies, and other non-network programming. Public television is partially supported by the Corporation for Public Broadcasting and contributions from corporations, foundations, endowments, and individuals. PBS programming is produced largely by member stations, although some programming is purchased from foreign producers, such as the BBC. Member stations produce their own regional programming as well as programming of national interest that is distributed through PBS. Cable television offers a somewhat better potential market for independent, small-scale productions. However, most cable operators are interested in filling time with continuing series, rather than with isolated individual programs. Commercials are brief messages used on commercial television to sell products, names, and services to consumers. At the national and major local market levels, they are usually produced on 35 mm film by production specialists for advertising agencies. At the local level, they are produced by local stations themselves and by small independent producers. Public service announcements (PSAs) are noncommercial messages broadcast free of charge.

Economic power in the theatrical feature film industry resides in the major distributors, such as Paramount, Warner Bros., MGM, United Artists, Columbia, Sony, Universal, and Twentieth Century-Fox. An average feature film distributed by the majors costs more than $80 million. Videocassettes, DVDs, videodiscs, and multimedia products are often marketed to individual customers via video sales/rental stores for home use. They are also used for corporate communications. Consumer marketing of multimedia products is made somewhat complex by virtue of the diversity of standards in terms of hardware. Interactive multimedia divisions of major studios attempt to establish connections between computer games and movies, although important differences still exist between these media. In-house production refers to the production of programming by an organization for itself. In-house production units exist in industry, government, and education, and collectively they represent the largest producer of video programming in the United States. A production unit usually maintains a sufficient staff and supply of equipment to produce a videotape or film completely in-house, using the most economical and efficient medium to communicate with employees, patients, students, and other groups.

EXERCISES

1. Make a list of all the potential distribution and exhibition outlets for a specific production project. Then prioritize this list by arranging the potential distribution/exhibition outlets in a hierarchy from most to least important in terms of the funding sources or your own expectations and potential returns on production investments. Determine the ideal production, editing, and distribution medium (film, video, multimedia, etc.) and format(s) (16mm, DVD, CD, etc.) for the most important outlet(s).

2. Calculate the cost of producing a film, video, or multimedia product using this (or these) format(s). Determine if the potential financial investments and returns from the outlets justify these expenses. If not, determine which media and format(s) will work most effectively within the desired distribution/exhibition channels without exceeding potential investments and returns.

3. Ask a program director of a television station to let you see an outdated ratings book from your market. Read it carefully and determine where you would place your commercials for maximum effect. Do the same for a local radio station. If this is not possible, find old issues of trade magazines like *Broadcasting* or *Entertainment Weekly* and use the summaries of ratings published in those periodicals.

4. Check to see if one of the larger corporations in your market maintains an in-house production unit. Ask for a tour and find out what the corporation produces, where it is exhibited, and how the corporation budgets its operation.

5. Plan on producing a short, one- to two-minute documentary. Write a distribution plan for at least five different means of distribution. Compare costs, audiences, and methods of distribution.

Additional Readings

Albarran, Alan. 2006. Management of Electronic Media, third ed. Wadsworth, Belmont, CA.
Albarran, Alan. ed. 2006. Handbook of Media Management and Economics, Earlbaum, Mahwah, NJ.
Albarran, Alan, Pitts, Gregory G. 2001. The Radio Broadcasting Industry, Allyn & Bacon, Boston.
Alberstat, Philip. 1999. Independent Producer's Guide to Film and TV Contracts, Focal Press, Boston.
Alexander, Alison, et al. 2003. Media Economics, third ed. Erlbaum, Mahwah, NJ.
Bielby, William T., Bielby, Denise D. 2003. Controlling prime-time: Organizational concentration and network television programming strategies. *Journal of Broadcasting & Electronic Media*, 47(4), 573–596.

Brooker, Will, Jermyn, Deborah. eds. 2002. The Audience Studies Reader, Routledge, New York.

Caldwell, John T. 2000. Electronic Media and Technoculture, Rutgers University Press, Piscataway, NJ.

Christensen, Lars Thoger, et al. 2008. Corporate Communications Convention, Complexity and Critique, Sage, Thousand Oaks, CA.

Croteau, David, Hoynes, William. 2001. The Business of Media: Corporate Media and the Public Interest, Pine Forge Press, Thousand Oaks, CA.

Dimmick, John W. 2003. Media Competition and Coexistence, Erlbaum, Mahwah, NJ.

DiZazzo, Ray. 2003. Corporate Media Production, second ed. Focal Press, Boston.

Eastman, Susan Tyler, Ferguson, Douglas. 2002. Broadcast/Cable Programming: Strategies and Practices, sixth ed. Wadsworth, Belmont, CA.

Eastman, Susan Tyler, Ferguson, Douglas. 2009. Media Programming: Strategies and Practices, eighth ed. Wadsworth, Belmont, CA.

Einstein, Mara. 2003. Media Diversity: Economics, Ownership, and the FCC, Erlbaum, Mahwah, NJ.

Groebel, Jo, Noam, Eli M, Feldmann, Valeria. 2006. Mobile Media: Content and Services for Wireless Communications, Erlbaum, Mahwah, NJ.

Hall, Phil. 2006. Independent Film Distribution, Michael Wiese Books, Studio City, CA.

Kindem, Gorham. ed. 1982. The American Movie Industry: The Business of Motion Pictures, Southern Illinois University Press, Carbondale, IL.

Kindem, Gorham. ed. 2000. The International Movie Industry, Southern Illinois University Press, Carbondale, IL.

Lutzker, Arnold. 2002. Content Rights for Creative Professionals, second ed. Focal Press, Boston, MA.

Lee, Jr., John J. 2000. The Producer's Business Handbook, Focal Press, Boston.

Marich, Robert. 2006. Marketing to Moviegoers: A Handbook of Strategies Used by Major Studios, Focal Press, Boston.

Middleton, Kent, Lee, William E. 2008. Law of Public Communication, seventh ed. Allyn & Bacon, Boston.

Miller, Philip. 2003. Media Law for Producers, fourth ed. Focal Press, Boston.

Parks, Stacy. 2007. The Insider's Guide to Independent Film Distribution, Focal Press, Boston.

Wasko, Janet. 2003. How Hollywood Works, Sage, Thousand Oaks, CA.

The Production Process: Analog and Digital Technologies

- What are the three stages of production?

- What are the differences between digital and analog production techniques?

- Why is production terminology different?

- Who makes up the production team?

- What is production aesthetics?

- How has the history of production developed?

Introduction

Media production requires both analog and digital technologies. The advent of digital technologies stimulated a number of important changes in media production, including the convergence of technologies as well as corporate integration. This chapter explores significant developments encouraged by digital media at the same time that it confirms the continuing value of some analog technologies and provides an overview of the media production process.

The digital revolution describes a process that started several decades ago. Technicians developed uses for the technology based on a two-value or binary system of "1" and "0" ("on" and "off") instead of a multiple continuous-value analog system of recording and processing audio and video signals. Rather than a revolution, it has been an evolution, as digital equipment and techniques have replaced analog equipment and processes where practical and efficient. Digital equipment may be manufactured smaller, requiring less power and producing higher-quality signals for recording and processing. As a result, reasonably priced equipment, within the reach of consumers, now produces video and audio productions that exceed the quality of those created by professional equipment of two decades ago. But every electronic signal begins as an analog signal and ends as an analog signal, as the human eye and ear cannot directly translate a digital signal (Figure 2.1). Nonetheless, digital technologies have

FIGURE 2.1 (A–D) Digital equipment and technologies have entered all phases of audio, video, film, and graphics production. Although digital production techniques are basically the same as analog techniques, there have been marked increases in efficiency, flexibility, lossless duplicability, and, in some cases, reproductive quality. (Courtesy KCTS 9, Seattle, ElectroVoice, Audio-technica, Canon, Vinten, Ross, and Sony Corporations.)

increased the efficiency, flexibility, duplicability, and, in some cases, the reproductive quality of media work in all three stages of production: preproduction, production, and postproduction.

STAGES OF PRODUCTION

The production process can be organized into three consecutive stages: preproduction, production, and postproduction. Everything from the inception of the project idea to setting up for actual recording is part of the preproduction stage. This includes the writing of a proposal, treatment, and script, and the breakdown of the script in terms of production scheduling and budgeting. The second major phase of production is the production stage. Everything involved in the setup and recording of visual images and sounds, from performer, camera, and microphone placement and movement to lighting and set design, makes up part of the production stage. Postproduction consists of the editing of the recorded images and sounds, and all of the procedures needed to complete a project in preparation for distribution on various media.

Preproduction

Preproduction consists of the preparation of project proposals, premises, synopses, treatments, scripts, script breakdowns, production schedules, budgets, and storyboards. A *proposal* is a market summary used to promote or sell a project. A *premise* is a concise statement or assertion that sums up the story or subject matter. For example, the basic premise of Joan Didion's film *The Panic in Needle Park* (1971) is "Romeo and Juliet on drugs in New York's Central Park."

A *synopsis* is a short paragraph that describes the basic story line. *Treatments* are longer plot or subject-matter summaries in short-story form, which often accompany oral pitches of a premise or concept, and *scripts* are virtually complete production guides on paper, specifying what will be seen and heard in the finished product. One can *break down* a script by listing all equipment and personnel needs for each scene so that a production can be scheduled and budgeted. A *budget* describes how funds will be spent in each production category. A *storyboard* provides a graphic visualization of important shots that the camera will eventually record.

Production

Production begins with setup and rehearsal. The film, video, or multimedia director stages and plots the action by rehearsing scenes in preparation for actual recording. Charting the movement of talent on the set is known as *performer blocking*, while charting the movements of the cameras is called *camera blocking*. Every camera placement and movement of the talent must be carefully worked out before recording. If the action cannot be controlled, as in the live transmission of a sporting event or the production of a documentary, the director must be able to anticipate exactly where the action is likely to go and place the camera or cameras accordingly. During actual production, the entire project is essentially in the hands of the director. In multiple-camera studio or location production, for example, the director often selects the shots by commanding the technical director (TD) to press certain buttons on a device called a *switcher*, which makes instantaneous changes from one camera to another. In single-camera production, the director remains on the set and communicates directly with the talent and crew. The script supervisor or continuity person watches the actual recording session with a sharp eye to ensure that every segment in the script has been recorded. Perfect continuity between shots, in such details as a consistent left-to-right or right-to-left direction and identical flow of performer movements (matched action) from one shot to the next, must be maintained so that these shots can be properly combined during editing.

In an audio production or recording session, the producer maintains the same authority and responsibilities as a video or film director: rehearsing the musicians, instructing the engineer, and supervising the actual recording session. In a digital *multimedia* production or an interactive session, whether for a computer game, CD-ROM, blue-laser disc, or DVD recording, the producer's authority and responsibilities are the same except that the producer may be gathering and working totally with digital material instead of people. In multimedia and interactive production sessions, the producer may very well perform all aspects of the production—from writing the entire process including preproduction through postproduction to creating the graphics, entering code in order to create the program in a digital form, and performing final editing functions.

Postproduction

Postproduction begins after the visual images and sounds have been recorded (although in live television, production, and postproduction stages occur simultaneously). Possible edit points can be determined during the preview stage, when the recorded images and sounds are initially viewed. Pictures and accompanying sounds are examined and reexamined to find exact edit points before various shots are combined. Separate soundtracks can be added later to the edited images, or the sounds can be edited at the same time as the pictures. The postproduction stage ties together the audio and visual elements of production and smoothes out all the rough edges. The visual and audio elements must be properly balanced and controlled. Sophisticated digital devices help editors and technical specialists mold sounds and images into their final form.

In audio postproduction, the emphasis is placed on choosing the best of the many sound takes and combining the various tracks onto one or, in the case of stereo, two finished tracks, or, as in the case of audio for high-definition television (HDTV) for theaters and home theaters, as many as six or more tracks. In motion picture production, the sound editor may use as many as 64 or more tracks to complete the production. Games and other interactive and animated productions also require multichannel audio tracks. Signal processing, including equalization, adding effects, and balancing tracks against each other, is often performed during the sound mix, that is, during the final process of combining various soundtracks. Such processing operations may be performed either in an analog or in a digital format. The tendency is to manipulate audio in a digital format to avoid any degeneration or degradation of the signal.

The three stages of production are separate only in a chronological sense. Proficiency in one stage of the production process necessarily requires some knowledge of all other stages. A director or writer cannot visualize the possibilities for recording a particular scene without having some awareness of how images can be combined during editing. In short, although the overall organization of this text into three stages (preproduction, production, and postproduction) follows a logical progression, mastery of any one stage demands some familiarity with other stages as well.

DIGITAL VERSUS ANALOG TECHNOLOGY

Although all three stages of media production have been affected by the advent of digital technologies, analog technologies continue to play important roles in each stage as well. For many years, equipment used in media production was exclusively analog, and many analog technologies, including motion picture film, are still used widely today. In fact, the size and quality of images recorded by some film technologies have never been surpassed. The potential screen size and image detail, or resolution, of projected large-format film images, such as IMAX and even standard 35 mm film, are still superior to video projection systems, including digital HDTV projection systems, and it is likely to remain so for some time. The look of film, the softness of the film image, the intense saturation of colors, and film's superior reflectance contrast range (from bright white to dark black) over electronic media (300+:1 versus 100:1) translate into a sophisticated and subtle visual medium. As Nicholas Negroponte, MIT Media Lab founder and author of *Being Digital*, said about 10 years ago, "The subtlety and nuance of film is so far out of reach right now. Film is still by far the highest, best-resolution medium we have" (*American Cinematographer*, May 1995, p. 79). But advances in digital equipment and technology have made the visible differences to the audience less discernible between the two media. The increased efficiency in production, creative options, and greater choices in distribution methods make digital techniques in feature film and commercial productions much more attractive to producers.

New media technologies rarely eliminate older technologies, although they often make the use of older technologies more specialized. The use of film has become more and more specialized with every advance in electronic imaging technology. For example, advances in videotape recording and editing made it less advantageous for television news operations to use news film during the 1970s, but many prime-time dramatic programs used film and continue to do so. Today, digital editing systems offer a number of advantages over conventional film editing, and digital technologies have virtually replaced analog audiotape and videotape recording and editing technologies in most situations as well.

Digital systems encode audio and video information as a series of ones and zeros, or "on" and "off" signals. A full range of sounds (from loud to soft and from high pitch to low) and images (from bright to dark and from high color saturation to low) can be digitally encoded as a series of zeros and ones. Analog audio and video information, on the other hand, contains a vast range of incremental electrical or photochemical values that are analogous to the sound and image spectrum.

Digital recordings are more permanent and are much less likely to experience a loss in quality when they are copied from one generation to the next than are analog recordings, because only one value is used for encoding "on" or "off," one or zero. Digital encoding also offers increased flexibility and efficiency in terms of manipulating and shaping recorded sounds and visual images during postproduction editing and special effects, because it is easier to manipulate a two-value or binary system (one or zero; on or off) than a vast range of incremental values (Figure 2.2).

Despite the many advantages of digital signals in the production process, there are some disadvantages. The conversion of an analog signal to a digital signal by the nature of sampling—that is, trying to rapidly and sequentially encode incremental values as a series of ones and zeros—drops a portion of the original analog signal in order to convert the constantly changing analog signal to the stair-step digital signal. In audio, these omissions are small enough that they are seldom missed. In video, the missing portions are small details not easily missed by the human eye. A greater problem with digital signals is the need to compress signals to save bandwidth, or transmission and storage space. Compression also removes portions of each digital signal that is not missed in the reconstruction of the signal in recompression.

Digital technologies have increased the speed, efficiency, duplicability, and flexibility of film and TV production. It is important to recognize some of the contributions that digital technologies have made to each stage of media production, including preproduction writing, producing, and storyboarding; production recording and lighting; and postproduction editing and special effects. Overall, digital technologies have significantly increased production efficiency in each of these areas, and they have begun to alter conventional notions of reality and history through a proliferation of imaginative and realistic special effects.

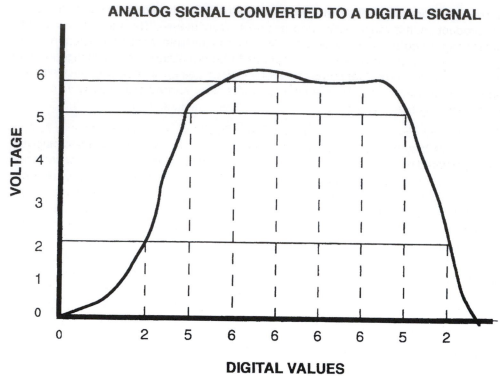

FIGURE 2.2 Digital signals are determined by periodically sampling the values of comparable analog signals: the greater the number of samples per second, the higher the quality of the digital signal.

Digital Technologies Used in Preproduction

Film and TV preproduction stages consistently use digital computers. Scriptwriting and word-processing computer software programs help writers efficiently format and revise scripts. Producers and production managers use scheduling and budgeting software programs to quickly break down scripts and preplan their productions. Breakdown sheets list all equipment and personnel needs for each scene in a film or TV script. The cost of each of these items can quickly be totaled to produce an overall budget, whereas the duration and sequence of recording each scene can be used to create an overall production schedule. Computers quickly and efficiently make changes in a script, a budget, or a schedule.

Computer graphics software facilitates the creation of storyboards, which can provide visual guidelines for camera shots, editing, and overall storytelling. A storyboard consists of a series of graphic images that indicate the camera framing and composition for each shot in a film or TV program. Previsualization (pre-viz) has extended the use of preproduction storyboards by creating digital storyboards that may be full-motion, full-color scenes created in a graphics computer. These carefully planned computer scenes help the director share his vision of what he wants a scene to look like and how it is to be blocked and shot with the key members of the creative staff: the director of photography, scenic designers, and the actors. The pre-viz storyboard artist becomes the writer, director, camera operator, lighting director, and art director by converting what is written in the script to a digital visual form. This computer program may then be easily manipulated as each member of the creative staff works with the director to make suggestions and modifications to reach an understanding of the common goal of the production. It is much easier and less expensive to make the changes in the computer program before sets are built and time-consuming rehearsals have begun. Other graphics programs allow sets and costumes to be visualized and coordinated before they are actually made. Lighting plots can be revised quickly when computer programs offer the potential to visualize the lighting effects on simulated characters and settings before actually hanging the lights.

Computerized casting networks and performer databases help talent agencies to promote actors they represent and casting directors to find them. Location scouting has been facilitated by computer databases, and the World Wide Web's ability to provide pictures of possible locations via computer networks offers the potential to both cut down on travel expenses and shorten preproduction schedules. The ability to capture and send images and sounds as well as text around the world via digital computer networks, such as the Internet and the World Wide Web, offers tremendous potential regarding the international flow of information. The Internet and its developing potential for video streaming also offers a new means of marketing motion pictures, and as Negroponte has suggested, "the Net will perhaps be the primary form of world commerce. . . . And the cinematography community will enjoy an extraordinary new marketplace" (*American Cinematographer*, May 1995, p. 80). Web sites such as NetFlix and 2.0 sites such as YouTube have already demonstrated the importance and viability of the Internet.

Digital Technologies Used in Production

New digital recording devices for video cameras offer a number of advantages for news recording. For example, a computer hard disk, digital disk, or solid-state RAM chip or a digital videotape recorder can be built into a portable video camera to record news stories for television. Dockable (camera-attachable) hard disks, flash drives, digital disks, or RAM chips, memory drives, such as P2, or digital videotape recorders allow up to two hours or more of professional-quality video to be recorded. Digital images and sounds can be edited immediately on a digital nonlinear editing system, greatly speeding up the production of news stories. Just as analog videotape recording and editing offered significant advantages over news film in the 1970s, digital recording and editing devices offer potential advantages over conventional analog videotape recording and editing news stories today.

Computerized digital lighting boards facilitate production by allowing a cinematographer or lighting director to preprogram a lighting setup and hang several lighting setups simultaneously using different computer files on the same lighting board program. Special lighting effects, such as projecting images and graphics on the walls of sets to add atmosphere or create laser light shows, can also be preprogrammed into a computerized lighting board and software program. Virtual sets created in a computer program inserted behind performers bypass the time-consuming and expensive process of set construction, assembling, and lighting. For example, the lighting director for a popular American film, *Batman Forever* (1995), made extensive use of digital lighting techniques and equipment during production in order to control more complicated lighting setups and changes than would be possible using conventional analog technology. This film returned to the original 1939 comic-book source of the mythical crime fighter, the Caped Crusader, to create a more active and action-oriented hero than the 1989 version of *Batman*, as well as active comic-book villains. In one scene at a circus, where the villain, Two-Face (played by Tommy Lee Jones) staged a deadly threat to Batman (played by Val Kilmer), more than 225

Xenon lamps were controlled by a computerized lighting board so that they could do color changes and chases. In another "pan-Asian" sequence within Gotham City, the lighting director used computer-controlled lighting to project saturated colors and Chinese motifs onto the sides of the buildings on Figueroa Street in downtown Los Angeles, where filming was done. The lighting director's extensive experience with rock and roll concerts and theatrical shows greatly facilitated his use of computerized lighting equipment in the film.

Sound recording has been greatly facilitated by digital audiotape (DAT) direct to MiniDisk, CD-R, solid-state memory (flash drives), and audio-DVD recording processes and equipment.

Flash Drives

USB flash drives are flash memory data storage devices integrated with a universal serial bus (USB) connector. Originally known as thumb drive or jump drive, the more common names of USB drive, memory drive, memory data storage drive, or compact flash drive. The units are small enough to be attached to a key chain or carried in a pocket and sturdy enough to stand a fair amount of physical abuse because there are no moving parts within the case. Instead a series of microchips on a circuit board process, store, and distribute the data presented in a form recognized by virtually all operating systems, whether PC, Mac, or Linux based. The connector is a standard USB male connector. Some 2.0 drives require more power than the standard model, but they all derive their operating power directly from the computer they are plugged into.

Flash drives and memory cards are superior to portable hard drives because they have no moving parts and operate with most equipment without special drivers. They are quite handy in terms of passing files back and forth between computers without wires or complex connectors, sometime called "Sneaker Drive" referring to walking in sneakers between computers. They are easily rewritable without destroying other data on the drive or card. Unless they have special circuits, most are not copy protected, however, and can be easily overwritten if they are not carefully handled.

Other solid-state storage devices include magnetic cards like Mini and MicroSD cards, smart media, and multimedia cards (MMC). Each of these must be matched to a specific circuit like those in cameras and recorders.

Digitally recorded sounds can be filtered more effectively and efficiently on location than analog recordings, for example, to remove unwanted background sounds. Digital sound recordings also minimize hiss as well as generational loss in sound quality when they are copied and dubbed for editing purposes, and they blend well with digitally recorded sound effects, music, and automatic dialogue replacement (ADR) recorded in a sound studio during postproduction. Multimedia audio stays in the digital domain throughout the production process.

Digital Technologies Used in Postproduction

Some of the most significant contributions of digital technology to film and TV production have come in the postproduction area. Digital videotape recorders and direct-to-digital servers facilitate the creation of special effects during final or online editing by allowing images to be layered on top of one another in successive recordings without loss of quality.

Digital editing systems make editing and revising a film or video as simple and quick as operating a computer word processor. In addition to increasing postproduction efficiency, digital editing systems allow an editor to visualize a final edited program. Special effects such as conforming and answer printing or digital video editing may be previewed before the final stages of video or film postproduction. Remarkably versatile and sophisticated three-way color correction and audio mixing and sweetening features and programs are becoming standard in basic digital video editing software systems.

Both film and TV postproduction use digital editing systems throughout the processes. Most digital editing systems employ computer hardware that is capable of processing and storing vast amounts of visual and audio information. A digital editing system may include a central processing unit (CPU) that has a processing speed of more than 2 gigahertz (GHz), eight *or more* gigabytes (GB) of random access memory (RAM), a keyboard, a mouse, one or two computer monitors, a digital recorder, an amplifier and loudspeakers, and one or more hard disk drives designed for large memory storage (in excess of 1 terabyte or 1,000 gigabytes).

Digital editing software offers several advantages over conventional means of editing film, audiotape, and videotape, including increased flexibility, as well as potential time and cost savings. A common cliché is that digital editing is the equivalent of word processing and desktop publishing for audio, film, and video postproduction. The analogy holds for many aspects of editing that are shared by word processing and various digital editing software programs. For example, most word processing software programs allow a writer to cut, copy, paste, and delete words, paragraphs, and pages of text. Digital editing affords an editor similar flexibility in terms of instantaneously changing the order and duration of sounds and images. For example, clips of video or audio information can be cut, trimmed, copied, pasted, inserted, and deleted along a timeline (Figure 2.3).

A *clip* is usually the smallest unit of digital video (or audio) information that can be stored and manipulated during editing. It can range in duration from just one frame to an entire movie, but it often consists of a single shot, that is, a continuous camera recording or take. Digitized clips are usually imported (or copied) into a particular editing project file where they are edited along a timeline with other images and sounds. Images and sounds from each clip are often displayed as a series of representative still frames along the timeline. Clips can be copied and inserted at various points along the timeline, and they can also be deleted from the timeline and the remaining images and sounds attached to one another.

Every edit made using a digital software program is usually a virtual edit. No digitized material is discarded when clips are trimmed, cut, or deleted along an editing timeline, because each clip is usually stored separately outside the timeline window. Every clip stored on a disk drive is instantaneously accessible in its entirety and can be grabbed in the project or clip window and reinserted at any point along the timeline. Many alternative versions of a scene or sequence can thus be quickly edited and examined without prematurely eliminating material that may be needed later. Transitions from one shot to another can be previewed, as can the superimposition of titles and various digital video effects without ever actually cutting, discarding, eliminating, or deleting any originally digitized video or audio.

The ability to manipulate clips of video and sound along a timeline not only adds flexibility to the editing process; it can also make editing more efficient and cost-effective. Clips can be rapidly trimmed, cut, inserted, and deleted. Digital editing is extremely

FIGURE 2.3 (A–D) Digital equipment may be used to record, control, or edit audio, video, or lighting signals. (Courtesy of KCTS 9, Seattle, Yamaha, Fairfield, ETC, and Ross Corporations.)

fast compared with physically cutting and splicing a conventional feature film, and the time it takes to find and insert videotape images and sounds from a source onto a master videotape can be dramatically reduced by using instantaneously accessible digital clips along a timeline. The amount of time scheduled for postproduction editing can be significantly diminished, facilitating the editing of projects that require a short turnaround time, such as topical news magazine segments and minidocumentaries. Increased editing efficiency can also translate into cost savings that affect the overall budget of longer-term projects when an editor's time and salary can be reduced. Clearly, digital editing offers a number of advantages in terms of flexibility and efficiency over conventional videotape and film editing.

Digital editing systems can be used at many different production levels. Some low-end digital editing systems are designed for use on home computers, and the range of graphics and special effects that are available on relatively inexpensive consumer programs to edit home videos is truly remarkable. Inexpensive digital editing systems also provide an excellent means of teaching video and sound editing, graphics, and special effects to students at a variety of educational levels. High-end professional systems can be used to efficiently edit feature films, relying on Kodak film KeyKode numbers and SMPTE timecode numbers (discussed in Chapter 6, Audio/Sound) as references for film conforming and online editing. Large corporations whose video production units use high-end digital editing systems sometimes finish their programs in digital form, avoiding the added time and cost of online videotape editing. A large number of audio tracks can usually be edited initially using digital editing software, and additional editing, mixing, and sound "sweetening" can be done later using a compatible digital audio workstation (DAW).

Special effects techniques have been greatly expanded and enhanced by digital technologies, and the Academy of Motion Picture Arts and Sciences recently granted full-branch status (similar to the acting and cinematography branches of the academy) to visual effects supervisors and artists. Digital effects are often combined with miniatures (smaller copies of objects) and models (full-size mockups) to produce startlingly realistic special effects in Hollywood feature films, such as J. K. Rowling's *Harry Potter* series. (Miniatures and models are discussed more fully in Chapter 11, Graphics, Animation, and Special Effects.) Computer graphics hardware and software have played an important role in the creation of special effects.

Many of the special effects used in the Hollywood film *Apollo 13* (1995), for example, were achieved by compositing (combining digital images) miniatures and models using computer graphics and digital video effects. *Apollo 13* focuses on the nearly tragic story of the Apollo 13 astronauts: an accident occurred on-board their spacecraft in April of 1970 that forced their moon landing to be aborted and nearly left them stranded in space. These events took place at the height of the space race and the Cold War competition between the United States and the Soviet Union.

The ability to manipulate and control individual pixels (single dots of colored light on a dimensional graphic image) has led to a proliferation of effects that challenge conventional conceptions of history and reality. For example, the NASA space program astronaut who advised the producers of *Apollo 13* regarding the authenticity of various space-launch procedures and restagings asked the producers where they had obtained actual documentary footage of the launch of the Apollo 13 spacecraft, when in fact the images were digital special effects created on a computer.

The Hollywood film *Forrest Gump* (1994) placed the fictitious main character inside the frame of an actual documentary recording of former President Lyndon B. Johnson, while President Johnson's lips were animated and he appeared to speak to Forrest Gump. These examples illustrate the power of digital special effects to potentially rewrite history and to create artificial worlds that sometimes seem more real than authentic documentary recordings. Film history has itself been revised and manipulated through the digital colorization of old black-and-white feature films. Colorizing old (and sometimes new) Hollywood films has clearly distorted the original artist's intentions and has altered film history. In the hands of media moguls, such as Ted Turner, who acquired the MGM library for use on Turner Network television, it has also significantly added to the television markets and viewing audiences for older films. Digital film and TV technologies have had a significant impact on conventional notions of history and reality, and they have challenged traditional legal, ethical, and aesthetic conceptions as well.

Digital technologies that offer potential connections to film and video are CD-ROM, DVDs, Blu-ray, high-definition versatile multilayer disc (HD-VMD), holographic video disc (HVD), computer games, and other interactive software. Many Hollywood film companies work with CD-ROM producers to create interactive computer games in conjunction with the release of feature films to theaters. The same settings or locations used in a feature film can be recorded in virtual 360-degree space using several film cameras. These images can then be mapped three dimensionally via various computer programs so that a DVD player can move throughout the space, interacting with characters and situations from the film. DVDs that incorporate film and video material also offer tremendous potential in education, including interactive film and TV production training, such as learning how to operate specific pieces of equipment. Films and television programs released on DVDs include many extra features and supplementary materials, which expand the information on how and why a production was completed. Digital technologies have clearly increased the speed, efficiency, and flexibility of media production in all three stages of film and TV production: preproduction, production, and postproduction. Although they have not yet eliminated superior analog technologies, such as film recording and theater screenings, digital devices have made the use of traditional analog technologies more specialized. In addition, digital technologies have begun to alter conventional notions of history and reality through the use of sophisticated computer graphics and special effects. Finally, as we move through the twenty-first century, new digital technologies, such as various forms of digital discs, hard drives, the Internet, and the World Wide Web (WWW), will undoubtedly provide new markets for films and videos and new educational opportunities for film and TV students and scholars.

The advent of digital technology has blurred many traditional distinctions in media production, such as offline versus online editing, film versus video production, and (active) artists versus (passive) viewers. Originally, videotape editing occurred in two stages, often referred to as offline and online editing. During offline editing, the sequential order of visual images and sounds were arranged and rearranged using small-format dubs or copies of the original videotape recordings. During online editing, the final decisions resulting from offline editing were performed again using the original, high-quality videotape or digital recordings and more sophisticated equipment. Today a high-quality digital editing system can perform both functions; that is, it can be used for both (preliminary) offline editing and for (final) online editing, making the passage from one stage to the next less distinct. In addition, the flexibility afforded by digital editing systems is similar to the flexibility of traditional film-cutting techniques but much more efficient. For example, a digital editing system allows an editor to reduce the overall length or duration of a program by deleting or removing images and sounds along a timeline and simply bringing the remaining images and sounds together so that they directly precede and follow one another. This technique is similar to the removal of frames of film or a shot and accompanying sound from the middle of a film. The potential to change the overall program duration at will is often referred to as a nonlinear approach to editing because the order of shots and sounds can be reordered at any time. Digital systems can be used to edit productions that were originally recorded on either film or videotape using a nonlinear approach. In so doing, digital editing equipment has brought film and video editing closer together.

Digital HDTV cameras capture electronic images that have an aspect ratio (width-to-height ratio) and resolution (clarity and amount of detail in the image) that more closely approximates some wide-screen theatrical film formats than it does traditional television or video images. Professional as well as consumer HDTV cameras are designed to operate in either 16:9 or 4:3 (consumer and prosumer HDV cameras, for example, can often record in non-HDTV formats, such as DVSP or DVCAM) aspect ratios and in a variety of scan formats (see Chapter 9, Recording). Finally, computers and interactive multimedia software allow traditionally passive media viewers and listeners to analyze and manipulate audio, video, and film productions and to actively recreate their own versions of existing media texts, as well as to learn new skills interactively, play computer games, and control where they find and use media productions. Traditional distinctions between (active) artists versus (passive) viewers or listeners, film versus video production, and offline versus online editing are becoming less meaningful as digital technologies erase differences between traditional forms of media production.

PRODUCTION TERMINOLOGY

Acquiring basic media production terminology is crucial to understanding the entire production process. The use of production technology and techniques requires a rather specialized vocabulary. As key words are introduced in this text, they are usually defined. When chapters are read out of sequence, the reader can refer to the glossary and index at the end of the book to find a specific definition or the initial mention of a term. We almost intuitively understand the meaning of such words as television, video, audio, and film, but it is important to be as precise as possible when using these and other terms in a production context. *Television* refers to the electronic transmission and reception of visual images of moving and stationary objects, usually with accompanying sound. The term *television* has traditionally referred to images and sounds that are broadcast through the airwaves. Electronic television signals can be broadcast by impressing them on a carrier wave of electromagnetic energy, which radiates in all directions from a television tower and is picked up by home receivers. Electrical energy travels in waves, much like ocean waves that crash on the sand at the beach. A carrier wave is usually rated in thousands of watts of power channeled through a television transmitter (Figure 2.4).

BROADCAST ELECTROMAGNETIC SPECTRUM

VERY LOW & LOW FREQUENCIES LONG WAVE 3 kHz–300 kHz	MEDIUM FREQUENCIES MEDIUM WAVE 300 kHz–3 mHz	HIGH FREQUENCIES SHORT WAVE 3 mHz–30 mHz
Audio—10/20 Hz Military & Experimental Broadcast	AM Broadcasting	Marine, Air, Land mobile Amateur (Ham) radio International Shortwave
VERY HIGH FREQUENCIES 30 mHz–300 mHz	ULTRA HIGH FREQUENCIES 300 mHz–3 GHz	SUPER & EXTREME HIGH FREQUENCIES 3 GHz–300 GHz
Television Channels 2–13 FM Broadcast	Television Channels 14–69 L-Band satellites Land Mobile	Microwave C, Ku, & Ka Band satellites Radar

FIGURE 2.4 Broadcast carrier frequencies share space on the international electromagnetic spectrum with a variety of other signals and broadcast users.

Electromagnetic energy ranges from sound to long radio waves to very short radio waves and on to light and gamma rays. The radio waves can travel through the atmosphere, the sea, and the earth, and they can be picked up by receivers. Television signals can also be sent through closed-circuit or cable television systems, that is, along electrical wires rather than through the airwaves. Before the 1930s, experimental television was primarily closed circuit, but the commercial exploitation of this technology as a mass medium and as a means of distributing television to large numbers of private homes, known as *cable television*, did not occur until much later. Since the 1960s, it has been possible to transmit television signals via satellites across continents and around the world. *Satellites* are communications relay stations that orbit the globe. Line-of-sight microwave (i.e., high-frequency) transmissions of television signals are frequently used for live, nondelayed, real-time news reports in the field and for sending signals to outlying areas where broadcast signals are not well received. Satellite program distribution systems now compete with cable program distribution systems. Telephone companies through the installation of fiber-optic cables directly to the home also are capable of distributing programming to the home in competition with both cable, satellite, and off-the-air broadcasting. All except broadcasting and satellites are capable of also offering Internet service.

The terms *television* and *video* are sometimes used interchangeably, but it is generally agreed that television is a means of distributing and exhibiting video signals, usually over the air. *Video*, on the other hand, is a production term. Also, the term *video* is used narrowly to refer to the visual portion of the television signal, as distinguished from the audio or sound. The more general definition of *video* as a production term refers to all forms of electronic production of moving images and sounds. This is the preferred use in this text. The term *video* can refer to a three- to five-minute popular song with accompanying visuals on a videotape, DVD, or Blu-ray disc, and it is actually a shortened form of the term *music video*. A *video* can also refer to a videotape copy of a feature film available at a video rental store. *Videotape* refers to magnetic tape, which is used to record both the video and the audio portions of the television signal. Videotape, digital servers, and other digital media allow television signals to be transmitted on a time-delayed basis, rather than live, and when used with various electronic editing devices, they allow recorded images and sounds to be changed and rearranged after they have been recorded. A videotape and a DVD or Blu-ray disc also allows feature films to be played at home on a *VCR* (video cassette recorder) or a DVD/Blu-ray disc player, respectively. Videotape (VTR) traditionally has meant the tape is mounted and played from an open reel. A VCR is a tape that has been encased in a closed cassette from which the tape is withdrawn as it is played. DVDs are disks containing video and audio recorded using a laser beam to embed the digital information in the surface of the disk. New forms of DVDs continue to be developed offering longer recording time, higher-quality signals, and increased interactive features, Blu-ray, HD-VMD, and HVD all are marketed with the expectation of replacing the original DVD.

Film has a variety of meanings in production. Defined narrowly, it simply refers to the light-sensitive material that runs through a motion picture camera and records visual images. When film is properly exposed to light, developed chemically, and run through a motion picture projector, moving objects recorded on the film appear to move across a movie screen. In a more general sense, the term *film* can be used interchangeably with such words as *motion picture(s), movie(s),* and *cinema*. The first two words in the singular refer to specific products or works of art that have been recorded on film, whereas in the plural they can also refer to the whole process of recording, distributing, and viewing visual images produced by photochemical and mechanical, that is, nonelectronic, means.

Audiotape refers to magnetic tape that is used to record sounds. *Digital audiotape* (DAT) is used to record audio signals in digital form on high-density magnetic tape in a DAT recorder. *Compact discs* (CDs) are digital audio recordings that are "read" by a laser in a CD player for high-quality audio reproduction.

Making clear-cut distinctions between video and film is becoming increasingly difficult, especially in the context of new digital technologies. For example, when a feature film, a television series, a music video, or a commercial advertisement is initially recorded on film but edited in digital form and distributed on digital tape, broadcast on television, satellite transmitted, or sold or rented as a DVD or Blu-ray disc, is this a video, a film, or a new type of digital hybrid? Using a single video camera to record a program in segments, rather than using multiple video cameras to transmit it live or to record it live on tape, has frequently been called *film-style video production* because the techniques used in single-camera video production are often closer to traditional film practice than to those of multiple-camera studio or remote video production. On the other hand, the techniques of multiple-camera film production used to record stunts in feature films are often closer to traditional multiple-camera studio television practice than to traditional single-camera film practice. As mentioned earlier, digital editing techniques often combine traditional film and videotape editing techniques at the same time that they mimic computer word processing. All of these developments make it difficult to make firm distinctions between film, video, and digital media today. Too often the term *film* is inaccurately applied to video and digital media productions when the term *motion pictures* would be more appropriate. The term *digital motion pictures* refers to distributing films to a theater via digital means rather than physically shipping the film to each theater.

Multimedia refers to the creation of works that combine video, audio, graphics, and written text. Combining these media involves digitizing all of the various elements so that they can be computer controlled and stored in a variety of forms, such as on hard disk drives, memory flash dives, and DVDs. *Interactive media* refers to various forms of viewer/reader/listener manipulation of and interaction with computer-controlled multimedia forms. Multimedia and interactive media have both been widely used in training and education, as well as computer games, but they are also developing into important new art forms and means of personal expression, especially as distributed on the Internet and the World Wide Web. These terms are often used in combination, with *interactive multimedia,* referring to works that are interactive and involve the use of multimedia.

New forms of media are constantly being developed and existing media forms are constantly changing. Thus, although it is important to be as precise as possible in the use of media terms, it is equally important to realize that the meanings of these terms can change over time, reflecting changes in the technology on which these media are based and the ways in which that technology is used.

SINGLE-CAMERA VERSUS MULTIPLE-CAMERA PRODUCTION, AND STUDIO VERSUS LOCATION PRODUCTION

A producer or director of a live-action production must make two basic decisions before production begins. First, she must decide whether one or more than one camera should be used to record or transmit images. Using one camera is called *single-camera production*, whereas using more than one camera is referred to as *multiple-camera production*. Second, a decision must be made about whether the images should be recorded inside or outside the studio. Recording inside the studio is known as *studio production*, whereas recording outside the studio is called *location production* in film and *remote production* (involving cable/microwave links to the studio) or *field production* in video.

Multiple-camera production techniques are used to record continuous action quickly and efficiently without interruption. Such techniques are the basis for television news programs, entertainment programs involving a studio audience, as well as much corporate, educational, and religious programming. Remote coverage of sporting events almost always requires multiple cameras. Multiple film cameras are frequently used to record dangerous stunts simultaneously from a variety of angles for feature films. Multiple film cameras also are used to film some television situation comedies.

In single-camera production, each separate shot is set up and recorded individually. The main artistic advantage of single-camera production is that few compromises have to be made in lighting or microphone placement to accommodate the viewing requirements of several different cameras. Logistically, only one camera needs to be set up or carried into the field at a time. Single-camera production of dramatic fiction usually begins with the recording of a master shot, which covers as much of the action in a scene as possible from a single camera position. Then the same actions are repeated and recorded again with the camera placed closer to the action. The resulting material is combined during postproduction editing. Single-camera production techniques are used to record feature films, documentaries, and television commercials, as well as in news recording. Except for live coverage of sports events, single-camera production is the norm for location and remote production situations.

In some production situations, it is simply impossible to record events inside a studio, even though studio production facilities and techniques are usually more efficient and economical. Lighting and sound recording are more easily controlled in a studio than at a remote location. Most production studios are designed to provide ideal recording conditions by insulating the recording space from outside sounds, reducing the echo of interior sounds, and allowing easy overhead or floor positioning of lights and access to power supplies. Location production can give a film or television production a greater sense of realism or an illusion of reality.

Exterior locations often create a sense of authenticity and actuality. But location settings rarely provide ideal lighting and acoustical environments. Extraneous sounds can easily disrupt a production. Confined settings often create sound echo and make it difficult to position lights and to control the shadows they create. Inclement weather conditions outdoors can delay the completion of a project. Because location production sometimes increases production risks and costs, a producer must have strong justification for recording outside the studio. Of course, the construction of sets inside a studio can also be extremely expensive, in addition to creating an inappropriate atmosphere, and location production in this case is easily justified on the basis of both costs and aesthetics.

Planning for Positive Production Experiences

Everyone wants to have positive production experiences. Although no secret formula for success exists, a thorough understanding of production principles and a positive attitude toward the overall production process is certainly helpful. Exuding confidence in a project enlists the support of others. This requires knowing what is needed and how to get it. Making good creative choices demands careful advance planning of every logistical and conceptual aspect of production.

Many production techniques can be mastered through practice exercises, such as those recommended at the end of each chapter in this book, and through actual production experience. Truly benefiting from these experiences requires taking risks and learning from one's mistakes. Learning to work within present levels of ability, avoiding unnecessary or repeated errors through careful planning, and the development of strong conceptualization skills are also essential.

Avoiding Negative Production Experiences

The first law of production is Murphy's law: *Anything that can go wrong, will go wrong.*

Every production person has vivid memories of his or her first encounter with Murphy's law, such as an essential piece of equipment that the camera crew forgot to take on location or one that failed to work properly. The second law of production is an antidote to Murphy's law: Proper prior planning prevents poor productions.

Many production problems are preventable. Ignoring conceptual and aesthetic considerations, failing to learn how to operate a camera properly, forgetting to bring necessary equipment, and having no backup or replacement equipment are preventable mistakes. No one is beyond the point of needing to think carefully about what he or she is doing or learning how to use new equipment. Everyone should use detailed equipment checklists, specifying every necessary piece of equipment, which are checked and rechecked before going into the field. Every production needs to have some backup equipment and contingency plan to turn to when things start to go other than planned.

Some production problems are not preventable. No one can precisely predict the weather or when a camera will stop working. But everyone must have an alternative or contingency plan if such a problem occurs. Equipment should be properly maintained, but not everyone can or should try to repair equipment in the field. Certainly, the option to record another day, if major problems should occur, must be available. Good quality productions are rarely made in a panic atmosphere, and careful planning is the best anecdote to panic, Murphy's law, and negative production experiences (Figure 2.5).

Quality productions are shaped and reshaped many times on paper before they are recorded and edited. Preproduction planning is extremely important. It is always cheaper and easier to modify a project before actual recording takes place than to do so after production is under way. The organization of this text reflects the importance of preproduction planning and the development of conceptualization skills. The first section is devoted entirely to preproduction planning. Some degree of advance planning and conceptualization is implicit in later stages of production and postproduction as well.

THE PRODUCTION TEAM IN AUDIO, VIDEO, FILM, AND MULTIMEDIA PRODUCTION

The production team can be organized hierarchically or cooperatively. In a hierarchical situation, the commands flow downward from the producer to the director, and from her to the rest of the creative staff or production crew. In a cooperatively organized production, every member of the production team has equal authority and control, and decisions are made collectively. Most production situations combine aspects of both the

STAGES OF MEDIA PRODUCTION		
PREPRODUCTION	**PRODUCTION**	**POST PRODUCTION**
PRODUCER	*DIRECTOR*	*EDITOR*
Research	Visualization	Offline
Writing	Interpretation	Online
Law/Ethics	Selection	Titles
Budgets	Visual/Sound	Visual Effects
Scheduling	Integration	Narration
Production	Graphics	Sound Effects
Management	Lighting	Sweetening
	Casting	Integration
	Blocking	Distribution
	Rehearsing	
	Recording/Airing	

FIGURE 2.5 Each of the three stages of media production fulfills critical facets of the production process. Each of the three stages relies on the professional completion of the other two stages. No one stage is more important than any other.

hierarchical and the cooperative models, although the former approach is clearly dominant in the commercial world. Combining approaches, the producer or director makes most of the important decisions, but the help, support, guidance, and input of all the creative staff and some of the technical crew is actively sought and obtained (Figure 2.6).

Production is rarely a purely democratic process, but it is almost always a collective process that requires the support and cooperation of large numbers of people.

The members of any media production team usually can be divided into two distinct groups: the creative staff and the technical crew. This basic division is often used for budgeting purposes. Dividing the team and costs into above-the-line creative aspects and below-the-line technical aspects allows for a quick financial comparison between investments in the creative and technical sides of a production. The costs of paying the producer, director, scriptwriter, and performers are considered above the line, whereas those for equipment and the crew are below the line. The two should be roughly equivalent in terms of the allocation of financial support to ensure that neither the creative nor the technical side of the production is being overemphasized (Figure 2.6).

Creative Staff in Media Production

The creative staff in audio, video, multimedia, and film production includes the producer, director, assistant director, scriptwriter, designers, and the talent or performers.

Producer

There are many different types of television and film producers: executive producers, independent producers, staff producers, line producers, and producer hyphenates (e.g., producer-writer-directors). The exact responsibilities of the producer vary greatly between different commercial and noncommercial production categories and levels. In general, the producer is responsible for turning creative ideas into practical or marketable concepts. The producer secures financial backing for a television or

COMPARISONS BETWEEN MEDIA PRODUCTION TEAMS				
PERSONNEL CLASSIFICATIONS	MOTION PICTURES	AUDIO	VIDEO	GRAPHICS
ABOVE THE LINE				
EXECUTIVE	Executive Producer Producer Production Manager	Producer	Executive Producer Producer Production Manager	Developer Publisher Producer
CREATIVE	Director Writer Art Director	Arranger Director	Director Writer Art Director	Designer Writer Video Director
PERFORMANCE	Actor Narrator	Musician Announcer	Actor Announcer	Voice Talent
BELOW THE LINE				
TECHNICAL	Stage Manager Lab Technician Sound Engineer	Operator	Technical Director Technician Audio Director Lighting Director	Computer Technician
PRODUCTION	Director/Photography Camera Operator Recordist Editor Mixer Grip-Gaffer	Mixer Board Assistant	Camera Operator CG/Graphics Operator Audio Operator Assistant Director Editor Stage Manager Stage Crew	Art Director Graphics Artist Animator Programmer

FIGURE 2.6 Parallels exist between the organization of production teams, depending on the media used, but each medium has unique personnel categories for each level depending on whether the classification is above the line or below the line.

film production and manages the entire production process, including budgeting and scheduling, although production managers often handle many of these tasks at major studios. Some producers become directly involved in day-to-day production decisions, whereas others function as executive managers who largely delegate production responsibilities to others. The producer ensures that the financial support for a production is maintained and usually represents the views of his or her clients, investors, or superiors, as well as those of prospective audiences, throughout the production process. The producer in radio or in an audio recording session also may hire the musicians, arrange for facilities and studio time, and in some cases actually operate the audio board or other recording medium (Figure 2.7).

Director

The director creatively translates the written word or script into specific sounds and images. He or she visualizes the script by giving abstract concepts concrete form. The director establishes a point of view on the action that helps to determine the selection of shots, camera placements and movements, and the staging of the action. The director is responsible for the dramatic structure, pace, and directional flow of the sounds and visual images. He or she must maintain viewer interest. The director works with the talent and crew, staging and plotting action, refining the master

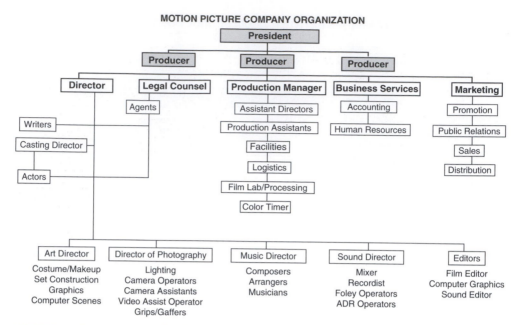

MOTION PICTURE COMPANY ORGANIZATION

FIGURE 2.7 The organization of motion picture companies varies with the number of films in production at any one time. Some company services are shared between productions, and others are unique to each individual production.

shooting script, supervising setups and rehearsals, as well as giving commands and suggestions throughout the recording and editing.

The director's role changes with different types of production situations. In live, multiple-camera video, the director usually is separated from the talent and crew during actual production, remaining inside a control room. In the control room, the director supervises the operation of the *switcher*, a live-television editing device that controls which picture and sound sources are being recorded or transmitted. The director also gives commands to the camera operators from the control room. A stage manager or floor manager (FM) acts as the live television director's representative in the studio, cueing the talent and relaying a director's commands. In single-camera production, the director remains in the studio or on the set or location and works closely with the talent and the director of photography (DP) (Figure 2.8).

Assistant/Associate Director

The assistant or associate director helps the television or film director concentrate on his or her major function, controlling the creative aspects of production. In feature film production, the assistant director (AD) helps break down the script into its component parts before the actual production for scheduling and budgeting purposes. The AD then reports to the production manager, who supervises the use of studio facilities and personnel. During actual production, the AD becomes involved in the day-to-day paperwork and record keeping, sometimes actually taking charge of a shooting unit, but always making sure that the talent and the crew are confident, well-informed, and generally happy. In studio video production the associate director (AD) keeps track of the time, alerts the crew members and performers of upcoming events, and sometimes relays the director's commands to the camera operators, video switcher, and other crew members.

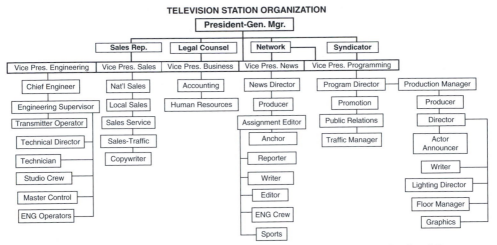

FIGURE 2.8 The organization of a television station varies considerably depending on the size of the market and whether the station is a network affiliate, network owned and operated, or a totally independent operation.

Scriptwriter

The scriptwriter is a key member of the production team, particularly during preproduction. A scriptwriter outlines and, in large part, determines the overall structural form of a production project. He or she writes a preliminary summary of a production project, called a *treatment*. A treatment lays the groundwork for the script and is written in the third person, present tense, much like a short story. The script provides a scene-by-scene description of settings, actions, and dialogue or narration, and functions as a blueprint that guides the actual production.

The Production Crew in Media Production

The production crew in media production includes the director of photography, camera operator, lighting director, art director or scenic designer, editors, and perhaps a number of specialized engineers and technicians, depending on the size and sophistication of the production. Figures 2.7 and 2.8 illustrate a more complete breakdown of the organization of a motion picture company and a television station.

Director of Photography

The overall control of film lighting and cinematography, or the creative use of a movie camera, is usually given to one individual, the director of photography (DP). A DP supervises the camera crew, who are sometimes called *cameramen* (referred to as *camera operators* in this text), assistant camera operators, grips, and the electrical crew, who are sometimes called *engineers* or *gaffers* and who actually control the lighting setup. The DP works closely with the director to create the proper lighting mood and camera coverage for each shot.

The DP is considered an artist who paints with light. He or she is intimately familiar with composition, as well as all technical aspects of camera control and is frequently called on to solve many of the technical and aesthetic problems that arise during film recording. The DP rarely, if ever, actually operates the camera.

Lighting Director

In video production, the camera operation and lighting functions are usually kept separate. The lighting director is responsible for arranging and adjusting the lights in the studio or on location according to the director's wishes or specifications. The lighting director supervises the lighting crew, who hangs and adjusts the various lighting instruments.

Camera Operator

The camera operator controls the operation of the film or video camera. Many adjustments of the video camera must be made instantaneously in response to movements of the subject or commands from the director, such as changing the positioning of the camera or the focus and field of view of the image. The director's commands come to the camera operator in the studio via an intercom system connected to the camera operator's headset. The camera operator must smoothly, quietly, and efficiently control the movement of the support to which the camera is attached in the studio and avoid any problems with the cable, which connects the camera to the switcher or videotape recorder. A film camera operator works much more independently than a video camera operator, following the directions that the DP and the director give before the camera rolls. While shooting, it is the operator's responsibility to maintain framing and follow the action. In 2D animation, the camera operator shoots each cel or sets of cels following the director's instructions.

Art Director or Scenic Designer

The art director (film or graphics) or scenic designer (video) supervises the overall production design. He or she determines the color and shape of sets, props, and backgrounds. Art directors frequently work closely with costume designers and carpenters to ensure that costumes and sets properly harmonize or contrast with each other. In feature film, the art director delegates the supervision of set construction and carpentry to the set designer, and in video the scenic designer often supervises both the abstract design of a set on paper and its actual construction.

Technical Director

The technical director (TD) operates the switcher, a multiple-video-camera editing device, in the control room. At the director's command, the TD presses the buttons that change the television picture from one camera or playback device to another. In some television studios, the technical director supervises the entire technical crew, including relaying the director's commands to the camera operators, while also operating the switcher.

Editor

In video postproduction, the editor operates an editing system that electronically connects the individually recorded segments into a sequential order. A film editor physically cuts together various pieces of film into a single visual track and an accompanying soundtrack. The sound editor is a specialist who constructs and organizes all the various sound elements so that they can be properly blended or mixed together into a final soundtrack. In film, the sound segments can be physically spliced together, but in video they are edited electronically. Film and film audio can also be transferred to digital formats for digital editing.

Audio Engineer or Mixer

In video production the individual responsible for all aspects of initial audio recording is called the *audio engineer*. In film production, this person is referred to as the *mixer* or *audio (or sound) recordist*. In studio video production, the audio engineer sits behind a large audio console in the control room, where he or she controls the sound from the microphones and playback units. The audio engineer also supervises the placement of microphones in the studio. The film mixer or audio recordist, like the audio engineer in video, adjusts and controls the various audio recording devices, but unlike the audio engineer, he or she remains on the set rather than in the control room. The film mixer usually operates an audiotape recorder that runs synchronously with the film camera. The mixer tries to record a consistent, balanced audio signal throughout all the different single-camera setups so that a smooth, even soundtrack can be created during subsequent editing and mixing.

Video Engineer or Laboratory Color Timer

The quality of video and film images depends on technical specialists who can control image, color, brightness, and contrast levels. In video production, a video engineer usually controls the setting and adjustment (shading) of camera recording and transmission levels. The engineer is responsible for ensuring that all cameras are functioning properly and that multiple cameras all have comparable image qualities. A video engineer can also make color corrections to individual shots during postproduction. The color timer at a film laboratory performs a similar role, but does so after the film has been edited and before copies are made. In video postproduction and in film that has been transferred to video, the color in each shot can be adjusted using special digital equipment. Color can also be adjusted within individual frames using computer-controlled colorizing equipment, which digitizes images and allows a colorist to control individual pixels in the frame. Many digital editing programs contain a wide range of image-control devices, allowing precise adjustments of the color, brightness, and contrast of scenes, sequences, shots, and individual frames during postproduction. Including three-way color correction controls that allow an editor to separately adjust shadow areas, midtones, and highlights for color hue and saturation, ensures proper color balance.

The Production Team in the Recording Industry

The employees involved with the actual production of audio programs in the recording industry may be as few as one: the producer/operator working with the musician or performer. Or the team may be as complex a group as arrangers, producers, engineers, operators, as well as the musicians or performers (Figure 2.9).

Producer and Operator

The producer and operator function the same as in a video production, except that they are concerned only with the sound of the program. The operator will spend much time and effort adjusting equalization, levels, and effects of each input channel several times on a single microphone. Overall equalization, levels, and effects must then be set relative to all inputs for the best balanced sound.

Arranger

Arrangers work with the musicians to assemble the best possible musical composition. Often the musicians will arrange their own music or arrive at a recording session with the composition ready to record.

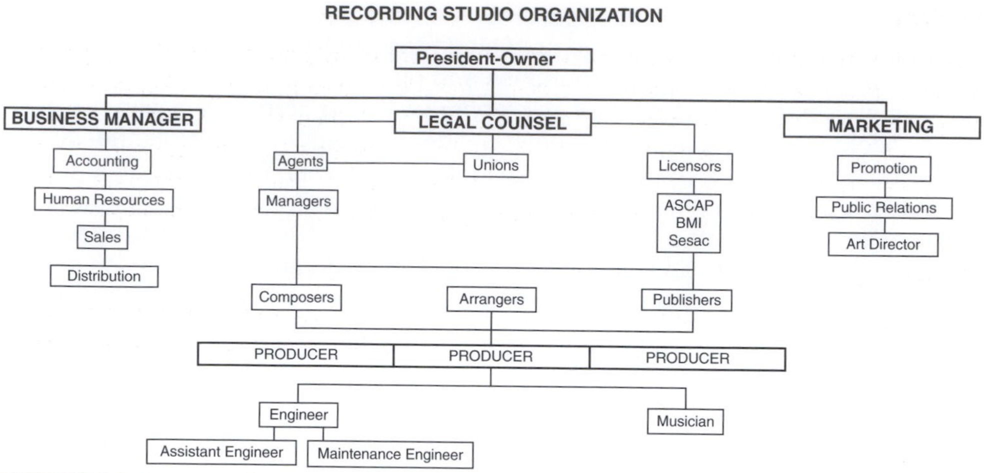

RECORDING STUDIO ORGANIZATION

FIGURE 2.9 The organization of a recording studio varies depending on the size of the studio, the type of recordings that are made in that facility, and the number of artists using the facility on a regular basis.

The Production Team on an Interactive Multimedia Production

The interactive multimedia creative staff and production team includes the developer, publisher, producer, designer, writer, video director, graphic artist/animator, and programmer.

Developer

The developer is the individual or corporation that creates an interactive multimedia product. The developer oversees program content and programming and delivers the product to the publisher. Developers are analogous to the production side of the film and video business. Production companies are developers.

Publisher

The publisher provides financial backing and ensures that the product will be successfully distributed. Publishers are analogous with the distribution side of the film and video business.

Producer

The producer manages and oversees a project, interacts with the marketing people and executives in the publishing company, and coordinates the production team. The producer is sometimes referred to as a project director, project leader, project manager, or a director.

Designer

The designer is basically a writer who visualizes the overall interactive multimedia experience and then creates the design document that specifies its structure, that is, a product's necessary and unique attributes. In an interactive computer game, for example, the design document may include the basic elements of the story, locations, and problems to be solved by the person playing the game. Animation, music, and sound effects are included in the design document, which is then handed over to a producer, who coordinates the creation of the design elements into a product.

Writer

The writer may consult with the designer who initially envisioned a particular product but is usually hired by the producer to help create and develop design elements and to shape them into their final form. The writer may flesh out the characters, dialogue (which may appear as text in one platform but may be spoken in another), music, sound effects, and possible scenarios envisioned by the designer, or she may invent entirely new material. Interactive multimedia writers are generally very skilled at nonlinear storytelling.

Video Director

If a video recording is needed to add live-action material to an interactive multimedia experience, a video director is brought in to handle staging the action, actors, and crew.

Art Director

The art director is responsible for converting the written script into a visual production. Usually the art director draws or supervises the production of the storyboards, especially in animation and games, that guide the production from conception to completion. The art director develops the basic concept of color, style, and character design before assigning the work to individual artists.

Graphic Artist/Animator

The graphic artist or animator draws and animates characters, backgrounds, and computer environments, which make up the visual elements of an interactive multimedia product.

Programmer

The programmer is the person who develops computer programs that integrate the various aspects of a multimedia product and facilitate interaction with it on various computer platforms, such as on a Macintosh computer. The programmer is responsible for writing each line of computer code that controls each line of dialogue and movement of a character. Several computer programmers may be involved in the creation of interactive multimedia, which will be used on different platforms or computer environments, such as Windows, Mac, and NT. Programmers are sometimes referred to as engineers (Figure 2.10).

VISUALIZATION: IMAGES, SOUNDS, AND THE CREATIVE PROCESS

Visualization can be defined as the creative process of translating abstract ideas, thoughts, and feelings into concrete sounds and images. This demands strong conceptualization skills and a thorough understanding of media production methods and techniques. Scriptwriters and directors must have something significant to say and the technical means to say it. Quality production work requires an ability to organize one's creative thoughts and to select and control many devices that record, edit, and transmit visual images and sounds. Scriptwriters and directors must acquire a basic understanding of the overall production process before they can fully develop their visualization skills. A knowledge of production principles and practices stimulates the search for innovative ways to translate abstract ideas into concrete sounds and images. It also sets limits on a writer's creative imagination. A scriptwriter must be practical and realistic about production costs and logistics. An imaginative script may be too difficult or expensive to produce. A scriptwriter

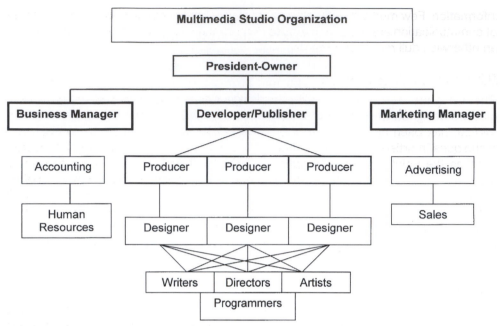

FIGURE 2.10 The organization of a multimedia operation varies widely depending on the type, number, and budgets of the projects the individual studio specializes in within its specialized field.

must also have some knowledge of camera placement, graphics design, composition, timing, and editing, even though his or her work is basically completed during the preproduction stage.

To visualize means to utilize the full potential of audio, video, film, and multimedia for creative expression, film, video, audio, and multimedia communicators must be constantly open to new ideas, technologies, and techniques, because these media are constantly changing. But they cannot ignore traditional communicative practices and ways of structuring messages. Other media and older forms of communication provide a wealth of information about the communication process.

In a sense, the attempt to use visual images and sounds to communicate with others is as old as the human species. Early human beings, for example, drew pictures of animals on the walls of caves. Cave drawings may have been created out of a desire to record a successful hunt for posterity, to magically influence the outcome of future hunts by controlling symbolic images, or to express the feelings and thoughts of an artist toward an animal or hunt. These three purposes of communication can be summarized as conveying information, rhetorical persuasion, and artistic expression. To some extent, these explanations are also applicable to contemporary uses of video, film, audio, and multimedia.

Conveying Information

Communicating with pictures and sounds may have a single purpose, to convey information. What is communicated, the specific content or meaning of the message, consists of informative signs and symbols, images and sounds, which are transmitted from one person to another. We tend to think of certain types of films, television, and multimedia programs, such as documentaries, educational films, videotapes, audio recordings, news programs, and interactive programs, as primarily intended to convey information. Few media messages are exclusively informational, however. Other types of communication are needed to arouse and maintain audience interest and to enliven an otherwise dull recitation of facts.

Rhetorical Persuasion

Rhetoric is the art of waging a successful argument. Persuasive devices and strategies are designed to shape opinions, change attitudes, or modify behavior. The term *rhetoric* has been applied to the use of stylistic as well as persuasive devices and techniques in artistic works such as novels. An artist can select a rhetorical device, such as the point of view of a specific character, to tell or stage a story, so that the reader or audience becomes more emotionally involved. Rhetorical devices often stimulate emotions. They can make a logical argument more persuasive and a work of fiction more engaging and emotionally effective. In television, radio, film, and multimedia we tend to think of editorials, commercials, political documentaries, and propaganda as rhetorical forms of communication. Many fictional dramas can also be thought of as rhetorical in structure and intent.

Artistic Expression

Artistic works often communicate an artist's feelings and thoughts toward a person, object, event, or idea. Sometimes artistic expressions are extremely personal, and it is difficult for general audiences to understand them. At other times, the artist's thoughts and feelings are widely shared within or even between cultures. An artistically expressive film, graphic, television, audio, or multimedia program can convey a culture's ethos and ideology, its shared values and common experiences, in unequaled and innovative ways. Works of art can communicate an artist's unique insight into his or her own self, culture, and medium of expression. Artists often experiment with new expressive techniques and devices, presenting ordinary experiences in new and provocative ways. They can challenge a viewer's preconceptions and stimulate a serious and profound reexamination of personal or cultural goals and values. They can also reinforce traditional conceptions and cultural values.

PRODUCTION AESTHETICS

Media production requires more than a mastery of technology and techniques. It is also an artistic process that demands creative thinking and the ability to make sound aesthetic judgments. How should you approach a specific topic? What techniques should you use? Important aesthetic choices have to be made. To make these decisions, you must be aware of many different possibilities and approaches. Every production choice implicitly or explicitly involves aesthetics. Some production techniques go unnoticed and enhance an illusion of reality, for example, whereas others are devices that call attention to themselves and the production process. The aesthetic alternatives from which you must choose at each stage of the production process can be divided into three basic categories: realism, modernism, and postmodernism.

Realism

A realist approach to production creates and sustains an illusion of reality. Realist techniques rarely call attention to themselves. Spaces seem to be contiguous to one another within a specific scene, and time seems to flow continuously and without interruption, similar to our experience of the everyday world.

FIGURE 2.11 A realist production strives to create an illusion of reality through spatial and temporal continuities that mirror real-life experiences, as Tom Hanks and his platoon are depicted in the Dreamworks production of *Saving Private Ryan*. (Courtesy of Dreamworks Pictures.)

Many Hollywood films, for example, sustain an illusion of reality and make us forget that we are watching a movie. This illusion of reality in Hollywood films is based, however, on stylistic conventions that audiences readily accept as real. Conventional editing techniques, such as matching a character's action over a cut from one shot to the next shot in traditional Hollywood films, help to sustain an illusion of reality, and are often referred to as realist conventions of classical Hollywood cinema (Figure 2.11).

As William Earl has suggested in his cogent description of modernism as a revolt against realism in films, realist films, which include many classical Hollywood films, define reality as familiar, recognizable, and comprehensible. Realist art feels most at home living among familiar things in their familiar places, or among persons with recognizable characters acting or suffering in comprehensible ways (Earl, "Revolt Against Realism in the Films," *Journal of Aesthetics and Art Criticism*, 27(2), Winter 1968).

Modernism

A modernist approach to production, which is reflected by many avant-garde works of video and film, often calls attention to forms and techniques themselves. Modernist works fail to create a realistic world that is familiar, recognizable, and comprehensible. A modernist media artist instead feels free to explore the possibilities and limitations of the audio, video, or film medium itself without sustaining an illusion of reality (Figure 2.12).

As viewers of modernist works, we often see familiar objects and events portrayed in a new light through the use of innovative techniques. Modernist art often appears less objective than realist art. Modernist works sometimes probe the subjectivity or inner psychological world of the individual artist/creator. In addition to self-expression, modernist productions often reflect feelings of ambiguity, as opposed

FIGURE 2.12 A modernist production goes beyond realism to create an artist's symbolic or imaginative world, as is depicted in Tim Burton's production of *Big Fish,* in which Ewan McGregor tries to come to an understanding of his past life and relationship with his father. (Courtesy of Columbia Pictures.)

to objective certainty. Time is not always continuous, and space is not always contiguous. Modernist art tends to be more elitist and private, as opposed to popular and public. The surrealist, dreamlike images in paintings by Salvador Dali and early avant-garde films such as Salvador Dali's and Luis Bunuel's *Un Chien Andalou* or *Andalusian Dog* (1929) illustrate these aspects of modernism, as do some experimental dramatic films, such as the beginning of Swedish film director Ingmar Bergman's film *Persona* (1966). Many other European art films and some contemporary music videos are distinctly modernist in approach as well.

Postmodernism

The emergence of digital technologies coincides with the rise of postmodernist films, videos, and audio art. Postmodernism literally means "after" or "beyond" modernism. Whereas modernist art emphasizes the individual artist's self-expression and the purity of artistic form, postmodernist art is anything but pure. It often features a collage or grab bag of past styles and techniques, rather than a pure or simple form. What emerges from this menagerie of styles and grab bag of techniques is not an individual artist's self-expression but rather a hodgepodge of different expressive forms from different periods and artists.

The absence of a single artist as a controlling presence (controlling what a piece of art means or how it should be viewed) encourages the viewer or listener to interact with the artwork, to play with it, and reshape it into another form. The artist doesn't control the meaning of a postmodernist text; the viewer or listener does. Postmodernist works often question human subjectivity itself. Sometimes they seem to suggest that the world is made of simulations rather than real experiences. Human characters can become indistinguishable from cyborgs in postmodernist films, just as individual artists become less distinguished by their unique styles and somewhat indistinguishable from audiences who create their own texts through viewer/listener free play.

Postmodernist films and television programs often combine popular culture with classical and elite art, mixing a variety of traditionally distinct genres or modes, such as documentary and dramatic fiction, and encouraging viewer and listener interaction with (if not the actual recreation of) art works. Postmodernist art borrows images and sounds from previous popular and classical works of art with which most viewers and listeners are often already familiar. Rather than inventing entirely new and perplexing original forms (modernism) or trying to establish explicit connections to the real world (realism), postmodernist art plays with previously developed images and sounds and recreates a self-contained, playfully simulated world of unoriginal forms, genres, and modes of expression. Interactive multimedia works, such as Peter Gabriel's CD-ROM music videos, allow viewers and listeners to adjust the volume and remix separate music tracks, creating their own versions of his music. A modernist piece of music would never allow the viewer/listener to freely play in this way with the work of art, because the artwork is presumed to have been perfected and completed by the artist (Figure 2.13).

FIGURE 2.13 A postmodernist production far exceeds realism and modernism by suggesting that the audience must contribute to the production by mixing genres, such as science fiction and hard-boiled detective, as well as other styles. A postmodernist production may question, for example, what it means to be a human by making cyborg simulations indistinguishable from "real" people, such as the character depicted by Harrison Ford in the Ladd Company's production of the *Blade Runner*. (Courtesy of the Ladd Company.)

Postmodernism may be more difficult to define than realism or modernism because it is a more recent development, and it is still evolving. Nonetheless, some of the main characteristics associated with postmodernism are already apparent. These include the production of open-ended works that encourage viewer participation and play, rather than a concern for the human subjectivity of either the individual artist or the main character in a fictional drama or a social actor in a documentary or docudrama. Postmodernist art frequently offers a pastiche or collage of simulated images and sounds drawn from a variety of different modes and genres (both fiction and nonfiction, for example), a feeling of nostalgia for the past, a plundering of old images and sounds from previous works, simulations rather than "real experiences," and a mixture of classical and contemporary forms as well as popular and elite culture.

Combining Aesthetic Approaches

Obviously the three aesthetic movements and choices that have just been described (realism, modernism, and postmodernism) are neither definitive nor exhaustive. Many projects combine aesthetic approaches in various ways. Modernist sequences can be incorporated into realist movies, such as dream sequences in classical Hollywood cinema. Some Hollywood movies, such as *The Lord of the Rings* series (2001–2004), *The Triplets of Belleville* (2003), and *Last Samurai* (2003), seem to combine realism with postmodernism. The choice of one aesthetic approach is neither absolute nor irreconcilable with other approaches. But although different approaches can be combined, the decision to combine them should be a matter of conscious choice.

Because aesthetic decisions are basic to different stages of the production process, many of the chapters in this text begin with a discussion of realist, modernist, and postmodernist approaches. This is followed by a discussion of production practices that are relevant to the use of digital and analog technologies. Combined with actual hands-on production experience, this text provides the basic information needed to make valid production decisions with the confidence that many possible alternatives have been explored and the best possible approach and techniques have been selected.

A SHORT HISTORY OF AUDIO, FILM, AND VIDEO PRODUCTION TECHNOLOGY

The basic technology for the eventual development of radio, audio recording, motion pictures, and television was available as early as the beginning of the nineteenth century. The predecessors for motion pictures may be considered to be still photography; for audio systems, the telegraph and telephone; and for television, the electrical discharge of light-sensitive materials. Each of these was discovered or invented before 1840 (Figure 2.14).

From 1839 to the end of the nineteenth century, experiments and practical models of both selenium-based electrical systems and rotating disc-based systems were developed to convert and transmit visual images. By 1870, Thomas Edison had produced a primitive mechanical cylindrical audio-recording device called the phonograph. During the last half of the nineteenth century, a variety of toylike machines, such as the Thaumatrope, Phenakistoscope, Zoetrope, and lantern shows with delightful titles such as Phantasmagoria and Magasin Pittoresqueó were used to display projected pictures that appeared to move.

A   B

FIGURE 2.14 Early media production equipment by today's standards was primitive and ineffective. But production techniques that were developed to produce shows on that early equipment still provide the basis for today's digital media production. (A) An early twentieth-century film camera compared with (B) a modern 35 mm camera. (Courtesy of Arri USA, Inc.)

Before the introduction of film, a perceptual mechanism of the illusion on which motion pictures depend was based on and is called "an instance of the phi phenomenon" by the early twentieth-century perceptual psychologists Wertheimer and Termus. Gestalt psychologists were fascinated by perceptual tricks and illusions because they provided a convenient means of studying the way our brains process sensory information. The phi phenomenon produces apparent motion out of stationary lights or objects. It occurs when two lights, separated by a short distance, are flashed or strobed very rapidly. Above a certain threshold of flashes per second, the human eye is deluded into thinking that one light is moving, rather than those two stationary lights flashing. This same phenomenon may help to explain the perception of apparent motion from rapidly flashed still photographs. Some researchers believe the mind fills in the gaps between frames and produces apparent, not real, motion.

A period of invention at the end of the nineteenth century brought about the telephone, the electric telescope that was designed to convert moving images into an electrical signal, and early carbon, crystal, and ceramic microphones. Before the turn of the century, the disc record player and recorder were improved in France as well as the beginnings of motion pictures. In this country, Edison and W. K. L. Dickson developed a workable motion picture camera and projector, and George Eastman invented the flexible film base that made motion pictures possible. The century ended with the first "wireless" broadcasts, film projected on a screen for an audience, and a working model of a wire recorder.

Television experiments continued into the early twentieth century, alternating between rotating disc and electrical scan systems. Motion picture sound systems early in the century utilized sound recorded on discs with primitive methods designed to maintain synchronization between picture and sound. Many of the frustrations of workers in all three industries—motion pictures, radio, as well as television—were partially solved by Lee De Forest's invention of the triode-amplifying vacuum tube. This invention provided the means to send voices over the air for the first time and for the motion picture industry to use sound-reinforcing systems for theater.

Before 1900, the all-electronic television system now in use was described by a variety of experimenters, but it took 17 years before a practical model became operational. Today's television technology is based on light coming through a camera lens and striking a light-sensitive surface on the surface of one or more charged couple device (CCD) chips in the camera. Fluctuations in current on the surface of the chip are read by the circuitry of the camera as direct variations in the light striking the surfaces. These fluctuations in electrical current are then fed to a television screen, which reverses the process. Bright light striking specific points on the camera pickup chip correspond to bright light emitted by the phosphors of the television receiver's monitor. A television screen is scanned completely 30 times every second; thus, the images move at a speed of 30 frames per second, rather than the 24 frames per second of sound film. Some believe television, like film, depends on the phi phenomenon to produce apparent motion, but it also relies on persistence of vision to fuse the continuous scanning of the picture tube into complete frames of picture. *Persistence of vision* refers to the temporary lag in the eye's retention of an image, which some researchers believe may fuse one image with those that immediately precede or follow. This phenomenon does not explain apparent motion, because the fusion of images in the same position within the frame would result in a confused blur, rather than the coherent motion of objects.

The first two-color, two-negative Technicolor film process was developed in 1917. It was followed three years later by the first AM radio stations in the United States receiving licenses and some experimental television stations being licensed to use the spinning disc system. By the early 1920s, the Hollywood motion picture industry had become pervasive enough to dominate foreign screens and to be threatened with domestic censorship. The first sound-on-film system was developed by De Forest in 1930, the same year that Vladimir Zworykin invented the iconoscope television camera tube, which opened the way for an all-electronic television system. The all-electronic system was first demonstrated in 1927 by Philo Farnsworth in the United States and in 1925 by John Logie Baird in Britain. Within that same decade, the recording industry moved from acoustical recording to electronic methods, and AT&T started the first radio network. Twentieth Century Fox first used the Movietone sound-on-film system for newsreels. Warner Bros. used the Vitaphone disc system for its first sound features.

During the 1930s, modern dynamic and ribbon microphones were invented, and both British and American inventors continued to experiment with audio wire recorders. By 1932, Technicolor introduced their three-color, three-negative film process, and FM radio continued to be developed. German scientists perfected an audio-tape recording system based on paper coated with iron oxide, and Eastman Kodak introduced 16 mm film as an amateur format. The format quickly became popular with professional military, educational, and industrial filmmakers, as well as documentary producers.

Immediately preceding the entry of the United States into World War II, RCA promoted its all-electronic television system with the Federal Communications Commission (FCC), who later approved that system over the CBS rotating disc system in 1953.

Although World War II interrupted the rapidly expanding field of electronics, many developments in communication technology came from the war effort. The higher frequencies, miniaturization of equipment and circuits, and advances in radar that were used in television, and eventually computers, all were perfected. Following the war, magnetic tape became a standard for recording audio, television stations and receivers increased in number rapidly, and motion picture studios experimented with theater TV and close relationships with television stations and networks. The Paramount 1948 decree by the U.S. Supreme Court motivated the film industry to divorce the motion picture production and distribution from theater exhibition, bringing an end to the major studio era and stimulating greater independent production. The transistor was invented, CBS developed the 33⅓ long-playing (LP) records, and RCA followed with the 45 rpm.

Television saved the record business by forcing radio stations to turn to all-music formats, and the motion picture industry felt compelled to turn to widescreen, 3D, and all-color films to compete with the small-screen, black-and-white television systems of the 1950s. Eventually, greater interaction occurred between film and television as film studios produced television series and feature films that were shown on television. By the middle of the decade, the FCC approved the National Television Standards Committee (NTSC) color-TV standard, and stereo recordings on tape were marketed, leading to the development of multitrack recording techniques. Within the next two years, all three industries moved forward: television with the invention of the quadraplex videotape recorder, motion pictures with the Panavision camera and lens systems, and audio with the perfection of stereo discs.

The beginning of the rapid acceleration of technical developments occurred in 1959, when the integrated circuit was invented, leading to the development of computer chips. For the next 20 years, computers moved from room-sized operations that could perform limited calculations (by today's standards) to pocket-sized computers and a variety of other applications priced for small companies and individuals. Within the next 10 years, professional helical videotape recorders and electronic editing of videotape were developed; satellites were launched to permit transmission of audio, visual, and digital information instantaneously worldwide; the FCC approved a stereo standard for FM; quadraphonic and digital sound systems were developed; and cable moved from the country to the cities. During the period of these great advances in the electronic communication fields, motion pictures also utilized the same inventions to improve sound recording, lighting and editing systems, and theater exhibition systems. The expansion of cable television brought television to many rural areas that were out of reach of the TV stations of the time.

During the 1970s, miniaturization produced smaller cameras, recorders, and receivers, leading to new production techniques in both radio and television. Videotape formats began to proliferate, with systems both for the home (Betamax and VHS) and for the professional (U-matic and 1-inch). Cable became a major player in distributing both films and video productions as pay channels took to the satellites. HBO provided movies, ESPN provided sports, and CNN provided 24-hour news.

Technical advances continued through the 1980s, with two events setting the stage for massive changes in all communication fields: In 1981, HDTV was first demonstrated, and in 1982, a consent decree between the Department of Justice and American Telephone and Telegraph (AT&T) separated the long-distance and equipment-supply portions of the corporation from the individual local telephone systems. Less earth-shattering but still important developments were the authorization of lower-power TV (LPTV) stations, direct broadcast satellite (DBS) systems, the invention and rapid spread of compact discs (CDs), and the agreement on a Musical Instrument Digital Interface (MIDI) standard. The FCC approved a stereo TV standard, and RCA introduced the charge coupled device (CCD) camera, which used computer chips in place of camera tubes. By the middle of the 1980s, digital systems were used in new videotape formats, motion picture editing and synchronizing systems, and digital audio decks and editing systems (Figure 2.15).

Fox, Universal-Paramount (UPN), and Warner Bros. (WB) television networks began operations as the other three networks—American Broadcast Company (ABC), Columbia Broadcasting System (CBS), and National Broadcasting Corporation (NBC) — changed ownership. Later UPN and WB merged to form CW, which stands for CBS plus Warners. Experiments with teletext and videotext found limited use, and a once-failed system, videodisc, returned and began making inroads in the home market. Professional videotape formats shrunk in size as half-inch BetaCam and Recam were followed by BetaSP and MII, which became the standards of the production and broadcast studios before digital cameras and recording formats were developed.

In the 1990s, computer workstations and digital audiotape (DAT) integrated audio production into a complete digital world, and nonlinear digital editing systems for video programs became the standard. The motion picture industry turned to digitized video for postproduction and special effects, as the two visual industries began to share many more technologies. Black-and-white movies were colorized, and graphics were created through the expanded use of digital systems. Interactive multimedia production of CDs incorporated audio, video, text, and graphics into interactive computer programs. The computer slowly encompassed virtually the entire field of communications in rapid sequences of developing technologies.

At the beginning of the twenty-first century, each of the production areas—audio, video, and motion pictures—has continued to merge, overlap, and grow closer together through the use of digital technology and equipment. A fourth area of

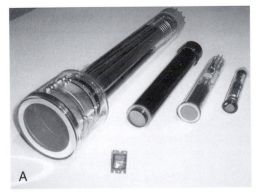

A

B

FIGURE 2.15 (A) Television camera tubes passed through a series of modifications and shapes and sizes from the 1930s until chips replaced tubes. From left to right: an Image Orthicon (IO) tube, the first practical camera tube used until the mid-1960s. The original color cameras required four IOs, one each for red, green, and blue colors and a fourth for luminance. Later cameras used the green tube for luminance. Next to the IO are a series of vidicon, saticon, and newvicon tubes, each smaller and offering higher resolution, requiring lower power, and allowing a smaller camera. (B) The Image Orthicon tube's two-inch, light-sensitive surface compared to the one-half-inch or smaller, light-sensitive surface of a camera chip.

production, multimedia, emerged during the last decade of the twentieth century and has become a dominant force in media production of the twenty-first century. By FCC ruling, broadcasters are required to replace analog NTSC broadcasting with digital TV in one of the 18 different formats by February 2009. By the end of the first quarter of 2004, over 99 percent of all television homes had access to digital television broadcasts over the air, but fewer than 16 percent actually owned and used full digital HDTV receivers and monitors. More than 1000 TV stations were broadcasting some programs in digital format. Whether the TV signal may be viewed and heard in its full digital format depends on special HD on the television receiving equipment in each individual home. This transition from analog to digital by a portion of the audience at a time is comparable to the conversion from monochrome to full-color television in the 1950s except the new signal is not compatible with NTSC, and there will no longer be any analog broadcasts or reception. The availability of digital TV and HDTV equipment and consumer interest has increased during the first decade of the century. Distribution of home video on digital video disk, or digital virtual disk (DVD), quickly surpassed that of VHS videocassettes. The high quality of audio and video information contained on DVDs, as opposed to VHS cassettes, including Dolby Digital five- and six-track audio for home theater sound and component video for various wide-screen and HDTV formats, stimulated the proliferation of DVDs. The vast number of VHS decks in homes has kept VHS as a relatively popular home video recording system, but the ability to record (burn) directly onto DVD or CD-ROM disks on many personal computers makes the end of VHS a certainty. Newer forms of DVD, including Blu-ray discs, have been developed and probably will continue to be invented in order to pack high-quality and more information on each side of the disk. By late 2003, high-quality, easy-to-operate digital recording and editing equipment and software became a reality on most home computers. Radio stations, graphics, animation, and postproduction techniques now all relied heavily on digital technology.

The problem of copyright violations through the use of MP3 equipment for downloading and distributing music reached a legal stalemate in 2003. As music producers lowered their prices and the Recording Industry Association of America (RIAA) filed hundreds of civil lawsuits, the number of illegal downloaded records began to fade. Apple computers and others began paid download systems that provided a practical and affordable alternative to illegal downloading of music. Comparable systems are in development for video programs, but the battle over copyright infringement will continue.

The wars fought in the first five years of the century saw the development of miniaturized cameras, direct-to-satellite video and audio feeds from cell phones, and other digital technologies that were used by both the military and news-gathering organizations. Handheld or camera-mounted satellite transmission equipment allowed live footage to be fed to the world from the battlefield. Cell phones allow reporters to feed live sound and low-level video from the field without the need to any base operation. Cell phones also serve as video receivers via the web, and more and more short-form, small-screen video programming is being produced for cell phones and personal digital assistants (PDAs). Miniature and night-vision cameras provide footage not attainable before the conflicts in the Middle East. Satellite maps show accurate locations and relationships of battles, cities, and areas of conflict as background for stories. New high-definition cameras mounted on guns show targets and the results of firing of weapons. High-frequency radio signals allow for smaller and more portable communication equipment. Each of the many newer digital systems developed for the military will eventually reach both the consumer and professional communication operations by the time this conflict ends or shortly thereafter.

Summary

Production is divided into three stages: preproduction, production, and postproduction. Preproduction designates all forms of planning that take place before actual recording, including producing, production management, and writing. Production begins with the director's preparations to record sounds and images. It includes all aspects of sound and image recording. Postproduction refers to the last stage of production, when the editing of recorded images and sounds begins and the completed project is distributed and exhibited.

Digital technology has revolutionized media production and is replacing analog technology in a number of media production areas, but analog technologies, such as film, continue to play important roles in each stage of production. Digital technology has opened up a wide range of fascinating production and postproduction techniques, such as special effects that have begun to alter conventional notions of history and reality. Digital technology significantly reduces, if not eliminates, the degradation of sounds and images when copies are made. It has also blurred traditional distinctions and has brought media technologies closer together.

Careful advance planning during the preproduction stages is the best way of avoiding negative production experiences. A producer initiates a project by drafting a proposal, obtaining financial support, and attempting to circumvent the operation of Murphy's law: Anything that can go wrong, will go wrong. Production can take place either in a studio or on location, again depending on the nature of the events to be recorded.

The production team is usually organized somewhat hierarchically, in the sense that a producer or director is in charge, and everyone is accountable to a staff head, who specializes in a particular area. But to work together effectively, a production team should also be cooperatively organized, so those individual specialists function collectively as a team.

Visualization is the creative process of image and sound construction. Video, film, and multimedia record moving images and sounds. These recordings can be edited. Writers and directors must be skilled at visualization. They must understand the relation between abstract words in a script and the concrete sounds and images that are recorded and edited.

There are three basic aesthetic approaches to media production: realism, modernism, and postmodernism. A realist approach relies on techniques that enhance an illusion of reality, a modernist approach emphasizes the artist's active shaping and manipulation of his or her material, and a postmodernist approach offers a pastiche of simulated images and sounds, questioning human subjectivity and the centrality of the individual artist. The choice of an aesthetic approach guides the selection of specific production techniques.

The histories of film, television, and audio technology are interrelated and overlap. Film is a nineteenth-century technology based on photochemical means. Television and video technology, developed commercially somewhat later, reproduces images by electronic means. Audio technology developed simultaneously with film and television because both visual media eventually required sound to match their pictures. All three media underwent substantial changes during the twentieth century. During the twenty-first century, all media production technology used in video, film, and audio productions will continue to converge within the realm of digital formats. Computers will continue to play a greater role in all aspects of media production from preproduction, to production, on through postproduction stages. Solid-state digital equipment will replace all equipment requiring moving parts.

EXERCISES

1. Find examples of realistic, modernistic, and postmodernistic films. Compare how each tells its story, and describe why each fits in the category you have chosen.

2. Find examples of television/cable programs that fit the three aesthetic categories. Compare how each tells its story, and describe why each fits in the category you have chosen.

3. Using both the Internet and your library, find references to the early development of technologies that led to modern-day motion picture, television, and audio production techniques. Arrange your findings in chronological order.

4. Watch an evening of network programming on one network. Make a list of the programs, and determine by watching whether each program was originally produced on film or video (or totally digitally) and whether the production used a single camera or multiple cameras.

5. Call a local television station and ask to visit the station for a tour. While there, ask if an organizational chart of the station is available or if someone would explain while you take notes how the station is organized by departments and what each department is responsible for.

6. Follow the same steps as requested in Exercise 5 but for a recording studio, a film studio, or a graphics studio.

Additional Readings

Badal, Sharon. 2008. Swimming Upstream: A Lifesaving Guide to Short Film Distribution, Focal Press, Boston.

Benedetti, Robert. 2002. From Concept to Screen: An Overview of Film and TV Production, Allyn & Bacon, Boston.

Block, Bruce. 2008. The Visual Story: Creating the Visual Structure of Film, TV and Digital Media, second ed. Focal Press, Boston.

Bordwell, David, Thompson, Kristin. 2006. Film Art, eighth ed. McGraw-Hill, New York.

Braudy, Leo, Cohen, Marshall. 2004. Film Theory and Criticism, sixth ed. Oxford University Press, New York.

Cook, David A. 2004. A History of Narrative Film, fourth ed. W.W. Norton & Company, New York.

Earl, William. 1968. Revolt against realism in films. Journal of Aesthetics and Criticism, 27(2), Winter.

Ellis, Jack C, McLane, Betsy A. 2005. A New History of Documentary Film, Continuum, New York, NY.

Everett, Anna, Caldwell, John T. 2003. New Media: Theories and Practices of Digitextuality, Routledge, New York.

Grant, August, Meadows, Jennifer. 2008. Communication Technology Update and Fundamentals, eleventh ed. Focal Press, Boston.

Gross, Lynne, et al. 2005. Programming for TV, Radio & The Internet: Strategy, Development & Evaluation, Focal Press, Boston.

Harrington, Richard, Weiser, Mark. 2008. Producing Video Podcasts: A Guide for Media Professionals, Focal Press, Boston.

Hofstetter, Fred. 2005. Internet Literacy, McGraw-Hill, New York.

Hutchison, Tom. 2008. Web Music Marketing and Promotion, Focal Press, Boston.

Levison, Louise. 2007. Filmmakers and Financing: Business Plans for Independents, fifth ed. Focal Press, Boston.

Orlik, Peter B. 2001. Electronic Media Criticism: Applied Perspectives, second ed. Erlbaum, Mahwah, NJ.

Perebinossoff, Phillipe. 2008. Real-World Media Ethics: Inside the Broadcast and Entertainment Industries, Focal Press, Boston.

Rayburn, Dan. 2007. Streaming and Digital Media: Understanding the Business and Technology, Focal Press, Boston.

Roberts-Breslin, Jan. 2007. Making Media: Foundations of Sound and Image Production, second ed. Focal Press, Boston.

Sterling, Christopher H, Kittross, John Michael. 2002. Stay Tuned: A History of American Broadcasting, third ed. Erlbaum, Mahwah, NJ.

Udelson, Joseph H. 1982. The Great Television Race: A History of the American Television Industry, 1925–1941, University of Alabama Press, Tuscaloosa, AL.

Wasko, Janet, MacDonald, Paul. 2008. Contemporary Hollywood Film Industry, Wiley & Sons, Hoboken, NJ.

CHAPTER 3

Producing and Production Management

- Who is a producer, and what does this person do?

- What is preproduction paperwork, and why is it needed?

- What are the laws, restrictions, and ethics of production?

- What is production management?

Introduction

A producer is often the only key member of the production team who guides a project through all phases of production, from preproduction planning through postproduction editing and distribution. A producer initiates a project by drafting a proposal, obtaining financial support, assembling the necessary personnel, and then managing and overseeing the entire production process. She also ensures that the completed project reaches its target audience and satisfies people who have financially supported it. A producer provides the necessary continuity between one stage of production and the next, and tries to ensure consistency in the final product. Although the producer plays an important part in all three production stages, this chapter focuses on the producer's role during preproduction and production.

PRODUCING
Role of the Producer

A producer is a risk taker, someone who seizes an idea, runs with it, and convinces others to participate in a project. Producers are creative administrators who act as links between the corporate executives, managers, financial concerns, investors, or distributors who finance video and film productions and the artists who create them. Such productions can require large sums of money, which come in the form of bank loans, outright grants, risk capital, and governmental or corporate "in-house" budget allocations. These productions also require a great deal of logistical planning and administration. Creative artists rarely have the time or the desire to deal with many of these administrative tasks, such as financing, budgeting, scheduling, and overall production management. Producers try to create high-quality products as efficiently as possible.

They know how to turn unappealing or extravagant ideas into workable material and marketable concepts. They understand the diverse needs of creative people, corporate executives, investors, product buyers, and audiences. Producers tread a fine line between the creative talent's need for artistic expression and the necessity of providing concrete returns on production investments.

Good producers must be effective decision makers and people managers. A producer's ability to understand and work with many different individuals is constantly tested throughout the entire production process. Ultimately, the production buck stops with the producer, who assumes responsibility for the successful completion of the project. If the production runs over schedule or over budget—that is, beyond the initial guidelines in terms of production time or money—it is the producer who must step in and decide what to do. Should production be terminated, a key individual replaced, or additional time and funds allocated to complete the project? These decisions can be extremely difficult. If a problem develops with a particularly unruly and disruptive actor or staff member, the producer or the director must try to resolve the dispute amicably or take disciplinary action.

Producers often specialize in particular types of programs. Specialists who work with television commercials, dramas, sports news, or interactive multimedia, for example, rarely work outside of their program type because success in one type of production does not guarantee success in another. Producers in charge of sound recordings, multimedia, videogames, and animation carry responsibilities differently than producers of television and film productions because of the nature of the differences in the media and the differences in the methods of finishing these types of productions.

Producers are further typed into at least four different categories according to the nature and extent of their responsibilities: staff producers, independent producers, executive producers, and producer hyphenates.

Staff producers are employed on a continuing basis by a production company or organization. Producers are often assigned to specific projects in a small video or film production company. Local television station staff producers often work in several areas simultaneously, sometimes floating from news to sports to public affairs. At the network television level, staff producers are assigned to specific divisions, such as news or sports, and they work exclusively within these domains. Staff producers in film often specialize in the production of feature films, educational films, commercials, documentaries, sports films, or industrial films. Unit production managers at major Hollywood studios are staff producers who are intimately involved with and extremely knowledgeable about almost every aspect of production. They are directly involved in production decisions on a daily basis. Staff producers of interactive multimedia productions and computer games coordinate a team of artists, designers, programmers, and writers for a developer or publisher.

Independent producers put together and sell production ideas to studios, film distributors, network and cable television executives, syndicators, and publishers. Independent producers are responsible for the bulk of all theatrically released entertainment films and prime-time television programming. They put together marketable story, staff, and talent packages. An independent producer is not employed on a continuing basis by a film studio or a television network or station. He or she works on a specific project on a freelance basis.

Executive producers are often less involved in day-to-day production decisions than other types of producers. They may delegate many production tasks to others and focus on project development and evaluation instead. In television, production executive producers are sometimes legendary figures, such as Norman Lear, Grant Tinker, Michael Crichton, Steven Botchco, or David E. Kelly, who have supervised several productions simultaneously and are constantly developing and promoting new program concepts and ideas. In feature film production, executive producers vary from people whose participation ensures sufficient funding to peripheral nonparticipants whose involvement in any aspect of production is minimal. Co-producers of feature films are rarely if ever involved in production in a major way or on a daily basis.

Finally, producer "hyphenates" combine the role of producer with those of writer or director. Writer-producer-directors immerse themselves in preplanning and the day-to-day production process, almost totally controlling the quality of the final product and preserving the integrity of their original idea. But, at the same time, they must also fulfill the responsibilities of director or writer. Often producers are intimately involved in the writing of those productions they produce.

Production Strategies

Producers often rely on production strategies to help ensure that a project is successful in obtaining necessary funding, fulfilling its purposes, and reaching an audience. The development of a production strategy involves at least four steps:

1. Turning a provocative idea into a funded and marketable media package
2. Defining the goals and objectives of the project
3. Researching the topic
4. Assessing the potential audience

Market Research

Where do media production ideas come from? Creative minds? Obviously creativity is a necessary asset in production, but it is not sufficient in itself to guarantee success. Producers must also be sensitive to the needs, preferences, and desires of potential funding sources, investors, executives, managers, buyers, distribution channels, and audiences. Project ideas can arise from a variety of sources, including personal experiences, such as a chance encounter with an impressive human being, an unusually committed or effective organization, or a compelling social problem. An idea might be generated by a current event in a newspaper; a presold property, such as a successful book or play that suddenly becomes available; a desire to make a statement or to explore a specific issue for the public good; a need expressed by a corporate executive, government administrator, or a consumer or labor group; or a previously successful television program, film, or computer game. Exactly where an idea comes from is not as important (unless it involves copyrighted material whose media rights have already been secured and are unavailable) as what is done with that idea to make it appeal to potential funding sources, distribution channels, and audiences. Successful producers are people who not only develop or recognize good ideas but also know how to package, promote, and execute their ideas and to communicate them to others.

To transform good ideas into funded, marketable, and doable material, producers put together marketable packages featuring components of known or presumed value to reduce the uncertainty that sponsors and investors feel about whether or not a proposed project will be successful. Many people believe that the prior success of a similar venture or previous productions by members of the creative staff enhances the chances of success for a new project. According to this view, a producer, writer, director, or star performer who has recently had successful films or television programs is likely to be successful again. Obtaining production financing for proven talent is always easier than doing so for unproven talent. The prior success or notoriety of the subject of a documentary or of a novel or play on which a dramatic film or television program is based is also presumed to provide some guarantee of success.

Noncommercial projects initiated by people who have been previously successful are also more likely to receive funding than those undertaken by neophytes, but inexperienced producers can overcome this problem by involving at least a few experienced creative staff members in their project. Previous success in production can be defined in terms of awards, published reviews, specialized showings, and satisfied clients, as well as in terms of profits. In any case, an attractive media idea and package plays on prior success to appease sponsors and partially reduce financial risks inherent in production support and investments.

Unfortunately, producers rarely have the luxury of waiting for prior success of a similar project or property to be amply demonstrated before they initiate a project. Screen rights to novels and plays are often secured before publication or staging. A hot topic may have lost its popularity before a project is actually completed because of the long lead time between project initiation and completion. Successful producers anticipate trends almost before they happen, but they are also able to package these new concepts and ideas in traditional ways that help a sponsor or investor to see how appealing or marketable a new concept can be.

Production Goals and Objectives

Defining the goals and objectives for a project begins with the formation of a project idea, which must be refined as it is transformed into workable material. The importance of defining the goals and objectives of a project cannot be overestimated (Figure 3.1).

For example, when major film producers and directors David O. Selznick, who had previously produced *Gone with the Wind* (1939), and Alfred Hitchcock, who subsequently directed *Psycho* (1960), vehemently disagreed about how literal the adaptation process—that is, how true to the novel a film should be—the initial result *Rebecca* (1940) was a major success which won the Academy Award for Best Picture. But subsequently they produced a complete disaster—*The Paradine Case* (1948). Bitter disagreements over goals, objectives, and methods of producing and directing films led to major headaches and problems for everyone involved in the production process during all of their "collaborations," and despite their early success, they parted ways soon after experiencing failure, and Selznick in fact closed down his production studio.

Members of the production team need to be aware of a program's overall objectives and to share common goals to prevent unnecessary conflicts from arising during the production process. Obtaining financial support for a project is much easier when the goals and objectives of the project are clearly specified. Any potential sponsor or funding

```
┌─────────────────────────────────────────┐
│        PRODUCTION GOALS & OBJECTIVES      │
└─────────────────────────────────────────┘
```

PRODUCTION GOALS (General Assertions and Statements of Purpose)

GOAL #1	
GOAL #2	
GOAL #3	

PRODUCTION OBJECTIVES (Specific, Concrete Anticipated Results)

OBJECTIVE #1	
OBJECTIVE #2	
OBJECTIVE ##	

FIGURE 3.1 Precisely conceived and researched production goals and objectives keep a production on track and moving toward a complete and finished production.

source wants to know what you are trying to accomplish. If your goals and objectives remain vague and unspecified, your project is unlikely to generate much support.

Although the goal or objective of a project may be primarily a commercial one, it is rarely exclusively to make money. Project goals may be quite specific, such as winning a particular award, or they may be more general, such as reaching a new level of artistic expression. They may involve a political agenda, such as changing people's minds about an important issue or problem, or motivating concrete actions, including voting for a particular candidate or buying a specific product. The goal might be primarily educational, such as teaching students to use a new computer program through the production of an interactive CD. On the other hand, the goal might be to produce a challenging computer game, an emotional piece of music on an audio CD, or a compelling or exciting animation using computers or traditional techniques. It might be to increase public appreciation of work undertaken by a fascinating person or a highly committed organization. It might also be to increase public awareness about compelling social problems, such as hunger, disease, and violent conflict at home or abroad, or to serve the needs of children or a minority group for nonviolent entertainment and educational programming.

Whatever the goals and objectives of a project may be, it is important to write them down so that they can be clarified, carefully considered, and discussed before developing a script or recording and editing a project. Enumerating the goals and objectives of a project will help to galvanize support and to ensure that everyone on the production team is using the same playbook. It will help to reduce future conflicts and to increase the appeal of a project to potential funding sources.

Researching a topic is another important step in the development of a production strategy. Topic research allows a producer to gather accurate information about a specific film or television topic. Careful research ensures that productions do not misinform. The quality of the research directly affects the integrity of the entire project. A hastily produced, poorly researched production can generate a great deal of antipathy from its audience. Sometimes pressure groups are aroused and legal actions, such as libel suits, are taken against the producer or production company. Careful research can make the difference between promoting misinformation versus carefully examining the key issues and stimulating a reasonable debate. Exciting action and intense, well-acted performances contribute a great deal to the impact and success of any dramatic production, but thorough topic research gives a project significance, depth, and lasting value and promotes the long-term interests of the producer.

Topic research requires imagination and determination. New sources of information are only uncovered with extreme diligence and persistence. Research can involve the collection and inspection of at least four different types of data or material records: written, visual, oral, and digital. Data banks of information are produced daily as vast quantities of information of all types are collected and released in digital form, either on disc, CD-ROM, or through the Internet or various web sites. Producers or their researchers can save many hours traditionally spent in libraries by using digitized sources. Books, magazines, newspapers, diaries, and private correspondence are written materials that often need to be uncovered, read, and analyzed. Good producers read extensively about their subject in preparation for production. Unlike scholars, producers may perform their research with a broad brush and with little attention to footnotes and minute details in order to get an overall understanding of their topic. This will facilitate the presentation of information in an accessible and logical manner.

Visual records may include photographs, and drawings of relevant settings, props, and costumes may also need to be examined. Actual locations may need to be visited as well. Historical visual and audio records and stock footage may need to be examined. Performing research in archives often requires considerable time and effort. Location scouts may use the World Wide Web and electronic mail (e-mail) to provide a rapid method of corresponding with location sources and interviewing subjects without waiting for mail service or a telephone response. Stock footage of historical events is expensive, because rights to duplicate this material must be obtained.

It is often important to examine or conduct oral interviews with people who are knowledgeable about specific topics. Interviews might be conducted with actual participants in events or recognized experts in a field. Interview questions should be written down and carefully planned, but the interviewer should not read them but rather remember them as a guide so that a more lively and spontaneous interview can be recorded. In some cases, experts who are interviewed during preproduction may be retained as consultants throughout the production phase. Sometimes consultants are supplied by specific organizations, such as the American Medical Association, which do not want to be slighted by improper or inaccurate information. In any case, extensive topic research often helps a producer make intelligent production decisions, while impressing potential sponsors and funding sources with her or his knowledge of the subject, adding program depth, and avoiding a variety of ethical pitfalls and problems.

Proposal Writing

One of a producer's first responsibilities is to create a proposal. A proposal is a written document designed to help raise money and obtain other kinds of support for a project. It may be submitted to a group of investors, a private foundation, or a government agency such as the National Endowment for the Arts, or a regional, state, or local arts council. An effective proposal generates enthusiastic support. It should be written in clear and engaging language that any nonspecialist can understand, but it should also be sufficiently thorough to meet the expectations of media and subject area specialists.

Good proposals usually contain the following elements: a provocative opening statement of purpose; a rationale of the need for such a project; its structure, organization, and approach; a preliminary budget and schedule; specific information concerning the anticipated audiences and the means of reaching them; and short, paragraph-length summaries of the careers of the producer, director, and other key creative personnel. Proposals are sometimes accompanied by videotape "show reels" containing clips from previously successful works by members of the creative staff (Figure 3.2).

The opening statement of purpose for any proposal is extremely important. It should provide a concise summary of the goals and objectives of your project. It should also generate interest and enthusiastic support. Try to imagine that you have just read about 100 proposals, and, although some of them are stimulating, you are becoming quite bored with the whole process. Suddenly something hits you like a breath of fresh air. One proposal stands out above the others. The writer is particularly clever, insightful, or committed. The proposal generates a contagious feeling of excitement. This is what you must try to accomplish in your opening statement of purpose. What is it that has stimulated your own interest? Now encapsulate this feeling and communicate it to someone else by putting it into powerful prose that relies on active rather than passive verbs in every sentence.

The opening statement usually includes a tentative title for the project. It also identifies the subject matter and convinces the reader of its importance and impact, often by providing a taste and flavor of the story that will unfold, including at least a hint of the conflicting forces and elements of dramatic structure that stimulate and propel it. Try to specify what you want your project to accomplish and who you hope will be moved by it.

What important need justifies the expenditure of the money and resources required to undertake and complete your project? Will it serve the public good? How? Will it be commercially successful? Why? Does it help to solve a social problem or promote greater understanding among and between different groups of people? Does it have a particular appeal to young or old people?

Proposal writers often provide some essential background information so that nonspecialists can begin to understand why this need is so compelling. Background statements provide the reader with sufficient grounding in a subject area to be able to understand and accept a basic premise and to make informed judgments concerning the importance, feasibility, and effectiveness of your project. They should be concise, providing basic and essential information. Writers use computers to access data and information sources during proposal writing to gather accurate and comprehensive information. Two of the resources are Lexis and Nexis. Lexis is a legal database,

SAMPLE PROPOSAL FORMAT

TITLE: Safety Training   PAGE: 1
WRITER: T. Bartlett   LENGTH: 10 mins
CLIENT: Mountain Industries   DATE: 10-10-08

Rivers and Streams Productions, Inc. will produce a ten minute, color videotape to be used as a training medium for new and present employees of Mountain Industries. The tape will target specific safety procedures necessary to be followed in the unique operation of logging in the mountains of Montana. The tape will emphasize personal safety actions and procedures required by the Occupational Safety and Health Administration.

The shooting schedule will last for ten days, weather and other acts of nature not withstanding. Postproduction will last for four weeks following the completion of principal videography. Taping will start within two weeks of final script approval. Research and preparing of the treatment will last three weeks following the acceptance of the proposal. The final script will be prepared within three weeks of acceptance of the proposed treatment.

The budget will be approximately $35,000.00, depending on specific technical requirements of the script. Because the script calls for a series of dangerous actions requiring stunt actors and technicians, some allowances for costs and shooting overruns may be required.

The format will be semi-documentary/instructional with the tape narrated and techniques explained by an actor representing a skilled and knowledgeable logger. Both incorrect and correct operational procedures will be illustrated. Employees, equipment, and facilities of Mountain Industries logging operation will be required for the production of this tape.

FIGURE 3.2 A proposal is a sales tool that needs to be written clearly and to describe completely the intended project, including all critical or unusual aspects of the production involvement in this project.

containing court cases and other legal information in the United States. Nexis is a news-retrieval system, listing most major newspaper, magazine, and newsletter contents. Both systems are designed for searching under a variety of methods to quickly reach the specific information that the research requires.

The approach, organization, and structure of a proposal indicate how you plan to tell your story and from whose point of view. For example, you might classify your project as a serious drama about an imminent separation and divorce, told from a child's view, or as a documentary portrait of an artist exploring an upbeat former stage designer's views on his pending blindness as he creates wall hangings and fabric designs that are enriched by his newly stimulated tactile senses. A documentary may consist of vérité sequences, "talking-head" interviews, and traditional voice-over narration. Or it may present dramatic reenactments of what "witnesses" convinced themselves happened at a violent crime scene, such as those presented in Errol Morris's *Thin Blue Line*. Each of these descriptions of a project characterizes its approach and structure.

The anticipated audience may be quite narrow or very broad, but it should be described in specific terms. The primary audience for a documentary might be a specific ethnic group, such as African-American communities in northern urban areas. A dramatic Appalachian folktale might be aimed at young Anglo-American teenage girls. In the latter case, the means of reaching that audience, or the specific distribution channel, might be motion picture theaters, prime-time public television, or afternoon commercial television. The former project might be designed for prime-time commercial or public television broadcast, as well as for rental to schools and universities through a nontheatrical distributor.

A proposal should also contain short biographies of the primary creative staff, written in paragraph form. These should highlight previous productions that are most closely related in content and approach to the project being proposed. Citing earlier works that have received major awards or national distribution will encourage potential funding sources to believe that prior success will ensure continued success. If you have a limited track record yourself, you should enlist the participation and support of creative staff members who have extensive experience and impressive track records, if at all possible. Letters of endorsement and support from highly regarded individuals, especially from people with whom the funding source is already familiar, should also be included with a proposal whenever possible. You should also try to make personal contact with the funding source, which, one hopes, will lead to an oral presentation of your project proposal. Writers use computers to prepare all written preproduction materials, such as proposals, treatments, and scripts. A computer allows the writer flexibility to make changes, deletions, and additions quickly and efficiently. Working in the digital domain allows information to be distributed to all involved personnel in either digital or hard-copy form (Figure 3.3).

Project Presentations

A producer who has interest in a potential funding source usually tries to make a personal, face-to-face, oral presentation to the investor, sponsor, or executive who is considering funding the project. Sometimes the presentation will be made over lunch or dinner. At other times it will be a more formal presentation in an office. At the very least, it will consist of a telephone conversation. Regardless of the setting, it is essential that the producer capitalize on any interest generated by a written proposal during

PROPOSAL REQUIREMENTS

- Concise statement – indicate what you hope to say

- Background and need (Purpose and Objectives)

- Your approach, structure, and style

- Preliminary budget

- Shooting schedule

- Equipment list

- Summary of credits, experiences

TREATMENT REQUIREMENTS

- Written in third person, present tense

- Describe all action sequences

- Describe main characters

- Indicate conflicts and resolutions

- List stylistic features

- Limit dialog

FIGURE 3.3 A proposal and a treatment together are key tools that a producer uses to sell a production in order to gain financing. They must be concise and accurate if the nontechnical client is to understand them.

the presentation. A producer who lacks enthusiasm in presenting his or her project to a prospective sponsor or investor is destined to fail. Sometimes the acceptance of a dramatic project hinges on the availability of a well-known creative staff member or star performer. If a producer has some well-known talent under contract before the face-to-face presentation, that presentation is more likely to solidify funding support. The presentation also offers a producer the opportunity to present additional, less fully developed future project ideas to a funding source, to gauge his or her interest, and to make adjustments later based on some of the funding source's reactions and recommendations. You should always go to a "pitch" or presentation with another idea in your back pocket, just in case you are given the opportunity to present it.

Legal Rights and Concerns

Producers are often involved in legal matters, many of which require the involvement of a qualified entertainment lawyer. Music and written materials are usually protected by copyright. Any use of copyrighted materials is usually secured on the basis of a royalty fee that is paid to the owner of this property. Legal releases free the producer from threat of lawsuits from people who appear in a film or television program and must be secured before that work is publicly exhibited. Private citizens can sue for libel, slander, invasion of privacy, or defamation of character if they believe they have been unfairly portrayed. The law is somewhat different for public figures, but they are still protected to some extent, and, as noted earlier, producers must exercise great care in the treatment of human subjects to avoid lengthy and expensive legal actions. The large number of legal services that are often required for commercial production has resulted in legal specialists, known as entertainment lawyers, who cater to the specific needs of the industry.

Producers are generally responsible for obtaining permissions and releases. Permissions to use personal property and copyrighted works, such as specific locations and music, require negotiations with the property owners. For example, a student who wishes to use a piece of popular music in a film or video needs to obtain permission from both the owner of the musical recording or CD, such as Sony music, *and* the publisher of the music, such as the American Society of Composers, Authors, and Publishers (ASCAP), Broadcast Music Incorporated (BMI), and the Society of European Stage Authors and Composers (SESAC). Personal releases signed by people appearing in the film or video inhibit subsequent legal suits brought by them against the producer, especially when they are dissatisfied with the final product or outcome.

Some producers maintain their own music libraries, so that they do not have to commission expensive original music for every production need. These music libraries are collections of musical recordings that are available from organizations such as ASCAP, BMI, and SESAC. These music recordings on CDs or digital formats require royalty payments in the form of needle-drop fees, which simply means that every time a cut from the CD or recording is used, a specific fee must be paid, regardless of how long the recording runs. Production music libraries are available on CD, audio DVD, digital and analog tape, and via web site downloads. Regardless of the medium, including downloading from the Internet, the needle-drop fee still applies.

Unions, Guilds, and Nonunion Working Conditions

Talent and technicians in many states are protected by union or guild contracts that have been worked out with major producers and production companies. Union or guild-negotiated contracts specify salary scales, working conditions and policies, and many other factors, such as residual payments. The unions or guilds with which a producer may work, or at least honor in terms of salary and working conditions represent the highest level of professionals in the entertainment industry.

Media Guilds and Unions
- AFTRA—American Federation of Radio and TV Artists
- SAG—Screen Actors Guild
- WGA—Writers Guild of America
- DGA—Directors Guild of America
- AFM—American Federation of Musicians
- IATSE—International Alliance of Theatrical and Stage Employees
- NABET—National Association of Broadcast Employees and Technicians
- IBEW—International Brotherhood of Electrical Workers

Some states, of course, have right-to-work laws, which prohibit the formation of completely closed shops; that is, they prevent unions from requiring all workers to join their union, pay dues, and abide by union-negotiated contracts. Texas and Florida are examples of such states.

Production in most metropolitan areas is heavily unionized, especially at the highest levels of production, such as network and broadcast station television, feature films, and 35 mm film commercials. In these areas, salary levels must meet or exceed certain specified minimum levels. A union member who fails to abide by these conditions and works for less pay is vulnerable to disciplinary fines or expulsion from the union, and the producer or production company may have to renegotiate a union contract, because its violation of the agreement makes the document null and void. In right-to-work states, union contracts of this type do not always exist, and salaries and working conditions are often negotiated on an individual basis.

Nonunion productions are often difficult to distribute or air at the highest, most lucrative levels. It is well known, for example, that the major Hollywood feature film distributors cannot purchase or distribute more than one nonunion-produced film per year without jeopardizing their union contracts. Most producers of feature films and network television programs must face the added costs of union salary scales during production or accept the added difficulties of finding an effective means of national distribution. Although the highest levels of television and film production are heavily unionized, except in right-to-work states, a great deal of commercial and noncommercial production is accomplished without union talent and crews throughout the country. Much public, cable, local, corporate, government, educational, and religious television and film production takes place in nonunion or partially unionized work environments. It is often easier to obtain initial production experience and employment in these nonunionized production settings.

The "illusion of reality" inherent in nonfiction programming and films, it has been argued, gives television and film producers the power to shape as well as reflect public opinion. Some nonfiction programming, such as network news broadcasts, functions as a primary source of public information about current events. Because nonfiction media producers can influence public opinion, they have an ethical responsibility not to intentionally mislead the public. The fact that many nonfiction film and television producers are concerned with making a profit as well as performing a useful social function often means that individuals will be tempted to compromise their ethical responsibilities. Although it is true that nonfiction works must have entertainment or dramatic value to attract audiences and prove cost-effective, there is a point at which a shortsighted pursuit of profit forces abandonment of long-term social goals and values. Self-serving creators of nonfiction programming have the potential to do harm to individuals and our democratic institutions. The Federal Communications Commission (FCC) attempts to ensure that broadcasters operate in "the public interest, convenience, and necessity."

Private citizens are protected from media abuse by the possibility of bringing libel, slander, or invasion of privacy suits. Documentary filmmakers, for example, must obtain written permission (releases) from private citizens before they can publicly exhibit television or film recordings of them. Public figures are less well protected than private citizens, and even private citizens who are involved in bona fide, public news events may legally be filmed or recorded without their permission. Generally speaking, in a court of law public figures need to prove a producer's "intent" to do them harm, but private citizens only need to demonstrate a harmful "effect."

Beyond the legal and public policy limitations and implications of their work, writers and producers of films and television programs have an ethical responsibility to use the "illusion of reality" inherent in nonfiction and fiction formats wisely and to treat their human and nonhuman subjects fairly. From a production standpoint, documentary and news people must be concerned about the potentially negative effects a publicly exhibited work may have on the people who are photographed or recorded. What is done to a human being when his or her picture is shown to thousands or millions of viewers, especially when that person is a private citizen rather than a public figure?

Lance Loud, the gay son who appeared along with the rest of his family before a national public television audience when *An American Family* (1973) was broadcast on PBS, made a public exhibition of coming out of the closet. In 2001, PBS broadcast a follow-up after Lance had died of AIDS, titled *Lance Loud! A Death in an American Family*, which explored some of the benefits and burdens of being publicly exposed, as well as the ethical implications of the earlier documentary. Ross McElwee's probing and insightful but also highly personal explorations of Southern culture, such as *Sherman's March* (1986) (his most recent Southern adventure is titled *Bright Leaves* [2003]), sometimes exposed Southern women to possible humiliation or embarrassment as he pursued romantic relationships with them on camera. However, some of McElwee's documentary subjects have been performers who were actively seeking exposure and public recognition. In the latter cases, who was using whom? Are we talking about exploitation or the pursuit of mutual self-interest?

Other questions to consider include: How are releases to use the images of private citizens obtained? Are people coerced into signing a release, or do they freely choose to be publicly exhibited? Does the unannounced appearance of a news or documentary camera crew at a private citizen's home or office constitute a form of coercion? Does the subject's initial permission allow the producer or editor to use the recordings in any manner that he or she sees fit, or does a writer, editor, director, or producer have some responsibility to show the completed work to the subject before it is publicly shown so that a follow-up permission can be obtained? These are ethical questions that should concern documentary and newswriters, directors, and producers, who must weigh the public's right-to-know against the citizen's right-to-privacy. These questions frequently arise in many different types of nonfiction programming, not only documentaries and news stories, but also commercials and educational programming.

PRODUCTION MANAGEMENT

Producers are usually responsible for production management. Production management includes the supervision, acquisition, use, and scheduling of the production staff, equipment, and facilities. The producer, or another member of the staff under the producer's direction, such as a production manager for a major film studio (often called a unit production manager or unit manager), breaks a script down according to its component locations and settings. An experienced individual who is intimately familiar with essential production equipment needs, budget limitations, personnel contracts, and salary scales easily specifies the personnel and facilities needed for each scene.

Script Breakdown

A script breakdown helps a producer estimate and follow realistic schedules and budgets by providing a complete record of all equipment, personnel, and facilities needed for every scene or sequence. It also makes it possible to shoot the production efficiently out of continuity, that is, ignoring the chronology of sequences in the script and shooting all the scenes that take place in one setting at the same time, regardless of where they will appear in the finished product. This procedure is obviously more efficient than returning to the same settings or locations several times in the course of production. After the script has been broken down according to its settings and locations, breakdown sheets are filled out. Each sheet lists the cast members, staff, sets, props, costumes, and equipment needed at one setting or location. An overall shooting schedule and equipment and personnel list can be made and total costs estimated from all the breakdown sheets put together. All of the production management forms are now available as computer programs, allowing for such forms to be manipulated as easily as any word processing program. Shooting schedules, script breakdowns, production reports, and budgets all may be processed in a digital format (Figure 3.4).

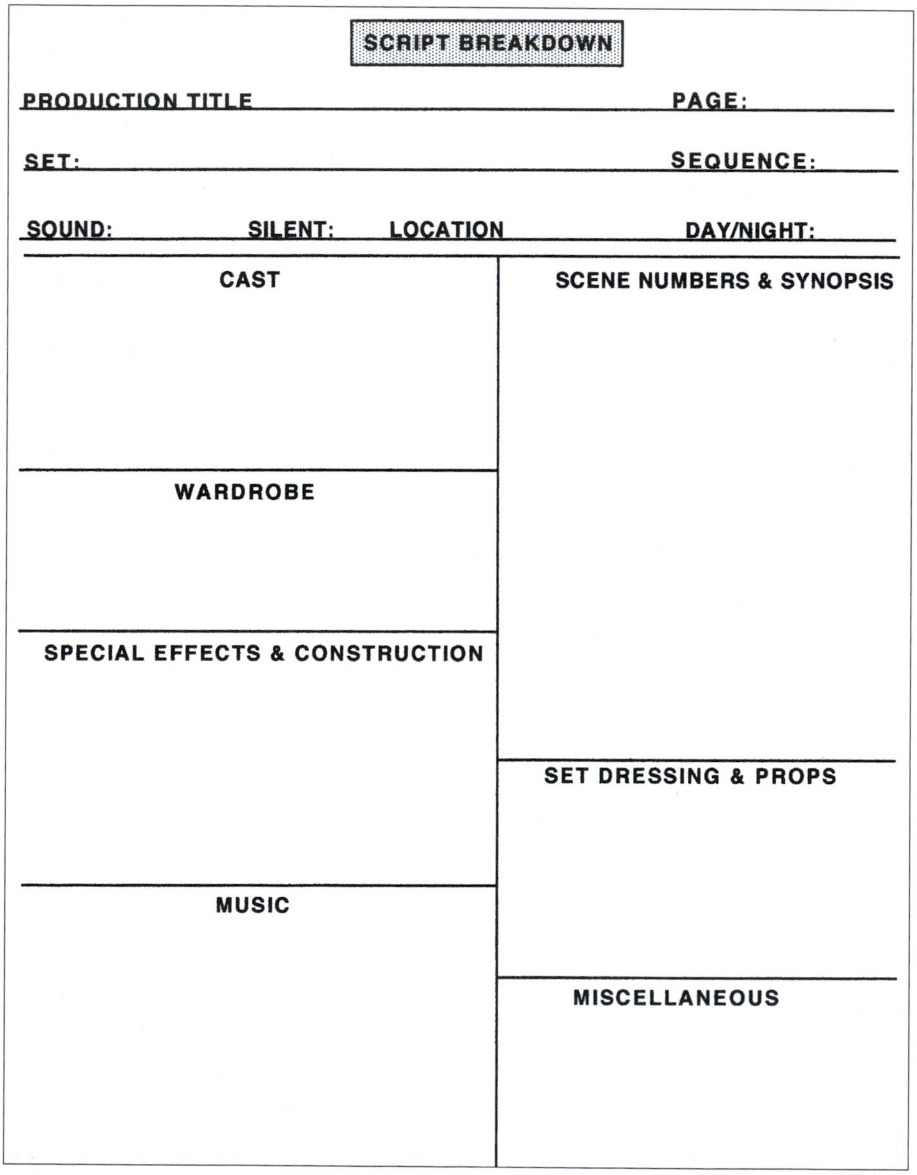

SCRIPT BREAKDOWN

PRODUCTION TITLE _____ PAGE: _____

SET: _____ SEQUENCE: _____

SOUND: _____ SILENT: ____ LOCATION ____ DAY/NIGHT: _____

CAST	SCENE NUMBERS & SYNOPSIS
WARDROBE	
SPECIAL EFFECTS & CONSTRUCTION	
	SET DRESSING & PROPS
MUSIC	
	MISCELLANEOUS

FIGURE 3.4 The script breakdown form needs to indicate everything that will be used on a production during a specific shooting period, usually a day or a single location.

Shooting Schedule

A shooting schedule indicates the total number of days of recording that will actually be required to complete the project. Shooting schedule information is often assembled using a computer program that segments a schedule into units of one day's shooting at a specific location or studio. An individual segment indicates all major personnel and equipment needs for one day at one place. The segments can be moved around if the production schedule must be altered. Because shooting is scheduled primarily on the basis of scenes and locations, the segments for all the days of shooting of the same scene or location usually appear sequentially on a schedule board.

The expense or lack of availability of key production personnel at a certain period can complicate scheduling, sometimes forcing a producer to return to a location or studio more than once during actual production. Once the shooting schedule is finalized, the production schedule for a feature film at a major studio, for example, can be fitted into a master production schedule governing a production company's overall use of facilities and personnel for several simultaneous or overlapping projects. Scheduling computer software can generate as many hard copies as needed and allow instantaneous changes to be made in production scheduling (Figure 3.5).

Production Budget

Production budgets are usually divided into above-the-line and below-the-line costs. *Above-the-line* costs include the salaries of the creative staff members, such as the producer, the director, the designer (in interactive multimedia production), and

SHOOTING SCHEDULE

DATE:_____

DIRECTOR: PROD. NO.:   PROD. TITLE:

Date	No. of Days	Name of Set & Scene Numbers	Cast	Location

FIGURE 3.5 The shooting schedule form lists the key requirements for an entire production broken down by shooting days or portions of days if more than one location is scheduled in any one day.

the scriptwriter, and the fees paid to performers or talent, such as actors or narrators. *Below-the-line* costs cover technical facilities, equipment, and personnel, such as production engineers and crew. When below-the-line costs are approximately equal to above-the-line costs, the production values, or overall level of sophistication of the equipment and crew, are usually appropriate for the investment in creative talent.

Running time, the total duration (as well as the complexity) of a completed project, is an important determinant of overall budget. Although it is generally true that longer running times require larger budgets, the case of high-budget, network-level television commercials suggests that there are some exceptions to this rule. Running times for specific types of programs are often standardized. A public television program might run for about 26 or 52 minutes, whereas the same program would be only about 23 or 46 minutes long if it were to be commercially broadcast, to allow time for the commercials. Theatrical films, those that are shown in commercial theaters, are rarely more than three hours in duration, because it is difficult for a theater owner to show films longer than this more than twice a day—once in the afternoon and once in the evening. Film length can directly affect box office revenues.

Shooting ratios represent the ratio of footage shots during production to footage actually used in the final edited version. Such ratios vary considerably from format to format. Shooting ratios for a cinema vérité, a documentary approach in which a single camera is used to record unstaged events, can range anywhere from 20:1 to more than 100:1 of recorded material shot to material used. An efficiently produced, sponsored film or videotape, on the other hand, may be produced at a 4:1 or 5:1 shooting ratio of footage shot to footage used. An average feature film or television action drama requires a shooting ratio of 15:1 or more. Television commercials can easily run up shooting ratios as high as 50:1 or more. In some categories, such as certain soft drink commercials, as much as 50,000 feet of 35 mm film may be originally exposed in order to produce just 45 feet (30 seconds) of the final product.

Shooting Ratios Footage Shot: Footage Used	
Sponsored film/video	4:1–5:1
Feature or drama	15:1–20:1
Documentary	20:1–100:1
Commercials	50:1–1,000:1

Producers must determine the exact cost of almost every production item, from equipment rental or purchase to union salary scales, talent residuals, and copyright royalty fees. Television and film equipment can be rented from businesses that specialize in these services, or it can be purchased by a studio or individual and amortized, that is, depreciated in value for tax purposes on a yearly basis over the period of time that it is actually used. *Residuals* are payments that performers and talent receive for repeat uses of productions in which they appear that continue to earn money (Figure 3.6).

Every final budget should include a contingency fund that represents from 10 percent to 30 percent of the estimated budget. The contingency fund permits some latitude for error, which can arise in a number of areas, for unpredictable circumstances such

```
                              PRODUCTION  BUDGET
                              DATE:
         TITLE:               DIRECTOR:
         PRODUCER:            PHONE:
         CLIENT:              MEDIUM:              FORMAT:
         ADDRESS:             PHONE:
         CONTACT:             PHONE:
         ALTERNATE:


    1. SCRIPT (Rights, research, writing, duplication)          _____

    2. STAGING (Sets, costumes, location fees, props)           _____

    3. EQUIPMENT (Rental, lease, use fees)                      _____

    4. SPECIAL EQUIPMENT (Mounts, aerials, submarine)           _____

    5. RAWSTOCK                                                 _____

    6. DUPING (Time code copies, off-line copies)               _____

    7. AUDIO (Effects, fees, rights, sweetening, looping, etc.) _____

    8. MUSIC (Fees, rights, performance)                        _____

    9. GRAPHICS (Titles, animation, art)                        _____

   10. EDITING                                                  _____

   11. PERSONNEL:     Staff        _____
                      Crew         _____
                      Talent       _____                   _____

   12. TRAVEL (Transportation, lodging, per diem)               _____

   13. DISTRIBUTION (Dubs, promotion)                           _____

   14. POSTAGE/INSURANCE                                        _____

   15. OTHER                                                    _____


                                    SUB-TOTAL                   _____
         OVERHEAD      _____ 0

         CONTINGENCY   _____ 0
                                    GRAND TOTAL                 _____
```

FIGURE 3.6 The production budget form must indicate all costs, regardless of how small, and if unknown, a professional estimate must be made. This is the summary page; each of the categories indicated necessitates one or more pages to include every category of funds required for the production.

as inclement weather that delays production and for talent or labor difficulties. A budget that does not include a contingency fund is unlikely to attract any but the most naive sponsors or investors.

There are many ways to organize and structure production personnel and the production process, but most approaches can be placed somewhere along a continuum from a strict hierarchy to a loose cooperative. A hierarchical model is basically a pyramid structure. Authority flows downward from the producer to the director and other members of the production team. In short, everyone has an immediate supervisor who is responsible for making production decisions. These decisions flow downward from the top. A cooperative model divides production tasks and responsibilities equally among each of the various areas of specialization. A different individual or group is responsible for each aspect of production, and all decisions are made cooperatively and collectively within and between different divisions.

Few actual production situations are exclusively hierarchical or cooperative in approach. Television and film production is necessarily a cooperative, collective process to some extent. In large-scale productions, specialization forces producers and directors to delegate responsibility to experts, whose cooperation and creative innovation is essential to the completion of a quality product. But media production is rarely a purely democratic art. Most productions are organized somewhat hierarchically around the funding source or the producer, who represents that source. Responsibility for daily decisions is frequently delegated to the director, and by the director to specialists in each area, such as the stage manager, the art director, and the lighting director. The producer and the director must coordinate and supervise the overall production. They must create an effective communication network that ensures that information flows freely from the bottom up as well as from the top down.

One means of ensuring adequate communication among the various staff and crew members is to schedule regular production meetings before, during, and after actual production. Coordinating the overall production minimizes the risk that continuity will be lost, that costumes will clash with sets, that lighting will be inappropriate to the mood of a particular scene, or that staff members will simply misunderstand the overall purpose and design of the production. Involving people in production decision making encourages their support and cooperation. A production meeting may also require some exercise of authority on the part of the producer or director to ensure production efficiency and consistency. In general, the more time allocated to production meetings (provided that these are not simply drink fests or "bull sessions"), the less time and money the production team will later need to spend on costly reshooting.

Producers must constantly evaluate the efficacy of procedures being used in production. Short-term evaluations focus on gathering daily information. The producer fills out daily production reports, based on information received from each production area. Accurate records are kept for financial purposes, and some secretarial or clerical skills are essential. The forms to be filled out concerning a feature film production, for example, are almost endless. There are daily call sheets, weekly budget summaries, revised shooting schedules, lab reports, and work orders. The producer must supervise a staff of assistants and secretaries who are able to organize and maintain production records and quickly respond to daily production needs. Long-term evaluations focus on applications to future projects.

The producer often works in concert with the director in casting the major talent for a specific production. Many variables must be considered before casting decisions are made. Individual agents sometimes suggest selections from the available talent pool, but actors are finally selected and tested at auditions, in which they read segments of the script in the presence of the director, the producer, and sometimes the casting director. The actor's appearance, voice quality, talent, and salary have to be carefully considered. Sometimes an inexperienced actor or "real" person from the actual locale will offer a more authentic portrayal than a professional actor.

Producers often consider the box-office appeal (theatrical film popularity) or television quotient (or TVQ, an index of popularity that is based on the star's fame and popularity and that is used by television networks) of specific star performers as a means of justifying the added expense of acquiring proven talent. Directors are often more concerned about aesthetic values, such as whether or not a particular actor or individual is perfectly right or natural for the role, than is the producer, who also worries about salaries and box-office appeal. The producer is often the funding source's sole representative during production and must therefore consider many financial, as well as aesthetic, factors.

Staff producers in small corporate, government, educational, and local cable television production units function much the same way as other producers. Their budgets may be smaller, and the people they work with are fewer in number, but the same basic skills are required. To illustrate the fact that all producers perform essentially the same role, let us consider a student production made in an academic setting. A student who is producing an assigned project for a grade must obtain funding for the project, either by earning the money, negotiating with parents, or finding a sponsor who can use the finished product. The student producer must procure the necessary equipment, supplies, and personnel to make the best possible film or video project with limited resources. Scheduling the production and acquiring talent within an academic environment is often extremely difficult because students have different class schedules and responsibilities.

Once the actual shooting is scheduled, the weather may not cooperate and the shoot may have to be rescheduled. Perhaps special costumes or props are needed, and the student must undertake delicate negotiations with the drama department or the head of buildings and grounds on campus. If the work is to be publicly screened or used on a local cable channel, the producer must be sure to pay all copyright fees for prerecorded music or commission original music from a friend in the music department. Release forms should be obtained from people who appear in a work that will be publicly exhibited. Finally, when the project is finished, the student must evaluate feedback from a number of people, including an instructor's unexpectedly high or low grade. The producer, then, has to be an effective supervisor of people, an administrator, a salesperson, a sensitive but objective critic, and, above all, a good fundraiser and money manager. These diverse skills, which combine business acumen and organizational ability with creativity and sensitivity to people, are not plentiful in the profession, nor are they easily acquired. Good producers should be recognized for their unique value to both the artistic and the business sides of the production process.

Summary

Producers plan, organize, and supervise the production process from the initial idea to its eventual distribution and exhibition. Producers adopt conscious production strategies to turn creative ideas into marketable concepts. A production strategy involves at least four steps: generating funded and workable ideas, defining the goals and objectives of the project, researching the topic, and assessing the potential audience. Producers must also estimate the production budget and make a proposal to a potential source of funding during a face-to-face presentation of the project's ideas and goals.

Effective producers possess a variety of supervisory skills—from the ability to manage people and resolve disputes, to strong organizational skills—which facilitate the flow and recording of information as well as budgetary decisions. Production team interaction can be structured hierarchically or cooperatively. Together with the director, the producer becomes involved in casting decisions. The producer is frequently the sponsor's or investor's sole representative during actual production.

Production management involves breaking down the script into its component parts so that the project can be shot cost-effectively out of continuity and coordinating the use of facilities, personnel, and equipment. Script breakdown sheets aid in the preparation of a budget and the scheduling of production facilities and personnel.

EXERCISES

1. Rent four movies. Watch each until the end credits have finished. List the number of producers and their titles, including associate and assistant producers for each production. Also list the first assistant director(s), because they are responsible to the producers.

2. Watch four major television programs, and list the producers, associates, and assistant producers on each production. Compare the number with your list of movie producers from Exercise 1.

3. Write a concept of a production that you would like to produce. Create a budget. Decide where you can get funding, and attempt to do so. If unsuccessful, decide what was wrong with your approach to gain funding.

4. Find a complete script of a movie (some are available on the web). Break down the script based on how you would organize the shooting of the script.

5. For Exercise 4, decide what would be the most efficient order in which to shoot the scenes and to most efficiently use your cast and crew.

6. Hold a casting call among your friends and fellow students. Cast the script from Exercise 4 as objectively as possible. Keep in mind that the perfect cast might not exist, and create the best choices you can.

Additional Readings

Albarran, Alan B, Areese, Angel. 2003. Time and Media Markets, Erlbaum, Mahwah, NJ.

Alberstat, Philip. 1999. Independent Producer's Guide to Film and TV Contracts, Focal Press, Boston.

Alberstat, Philip. 2001. Law and the Media, fourth ed. Focal Press, Boston.

Block, Peter, Houseley, William, Southwell, Ron. 2001. Managing in the Media, Focal Press, Boston.

Cartwright, Steve R, Cartwright, G Phillip. 1999. Designing and Producing Media-Based Training, Focal Press, Boston.

Chater, Kathy. 2001. Research for Media Production, second ed. Focal Press, Boston.

Cleve, Bastian. 2006. Film Production Management, third ed. Focal Press, Boston.

Creech, Kenneth. 2007. Electronic Media Law and Regulation, fifth ed. Focal Press, Boston.

Crowell, Thomas A. 2007. The Pocket Lawyer for Filmmakers: A Legal Toolkit for Independent Producers, Focal Press, Boston.

DiZazzo, Ray. 2003. Corporate Media Production, second ed. Focal Press, Boston.

Gates, Richard. 1999. Production Management for Film and Video, third ed. Focal Press, Boston.

Gripsrud, Jostein. 2002. Understanding Media Culture, Oxford University Press, New York.

Jacobs, Bob. 1999. The Independent Video Producer, Focal Press, Boston.

Kindem, Gorham. 1982. The American Movie Industry, Southern Illinois University Press, Carbondale, IL.

Kindem, Gorham. 2000. The International Movie Industry, Southern Illinois University Press, Carbondale, IL.

Koster, Robert. 2004. Budget Book for Film & Television, second ed. Focal Press, Boston.

Lee, Jr, John J. 2005. The Producer's Business Handbook, second ed. Focal Press, Boston.

Lutzker, John B. 2002. Contents Rights for Creative Professionals, fourth ed. Focal Press, Boston.

Miller, Philip. 2002. Media Law for Producers, Focal Press, Boston.

Pryluck, Calvin. Ultimately we are all outsiders: The ethics of documentary filming. *Journal of Film and Video*, 28(1), 21–29.

Radford, Marie L, Barnes, Susan B, Barr, Linda R. 2002. Web Research: Selecting, Evaluating, and Citing, Allyn & Bacon, Boston.

Rosenthal, Alan. 2002. Writing, Directing, and Producing Documentary Films, third ed. Southern Illinois University Press, Carbondale, IL.

Stone, Chris, Goggin, David. 2000. Audio Recording for Profit: The Sound of Money, Focal Press, Boston.

Tomaric, Jason. 2008. Power Filmmaking Kit: The Make Your Professional Movie on a Next-to-Nothing Budget, Focal Press, Boston.

Van Tassel, Joan. 2006. Digital Rights Management: Protecting and Monetizing Content, Focal Press, Boston.

Warnick, Barbara. 2002. Critical Literacy in a Digital Era, Earlbaum, Mahwah, NJ.

Weise, Michael. 2001. Film and Video Budgets, Focal Press, Boston.

Scriptwriting 4

- Why is it necessary to think visually?

- What are the preparations for scriptwriting?

- What are the script formats?

- How do fiction and nonfiction scripts differ?

- What are dramatic and narrative script structures?

- What are rhetorical and expository script structures?

Introduction

Scriptingwriting is narrative art that requires great storytelling capabilities, familiarity with specific screenwriting formats, and an understanding of visualization, that is, how written words are transformed into concrete sounds and images.

Scriptwriting can be divided into two basic categories: fiction and nonfiction. Many feature films, television series, miniseries, serials, made-for-TV movies, interactive games, and animated productions originated from works of fiction, and most documentaries, news programs, commercials, corporate videos, and interactive educational or training productions are works of nonfiction. Fiction scripts generally present dramatic stories imaginatively invented by the scriptwriter. Nonfiction scripts often convey information or rhetorical arguments concerning various topics regarding issues and actual historical events.

The line separating fiction from nonfiction is not always clear and distinct, however. Some projects fall into a gray area between the two. For example, historical dramas and docudramas are often based on actual events, and some documentaries involve staged or dramatized reenactments. Dramatic and narrative structures associated with fiction are sometimes relevant to the presentation of historical or contemporary events in works of nonfiction, and rhetorical structures associated with nonfiction are sometimes relevant to the presentation of characters and themes in fiction.

Every scriptwriter should be familiar with the basic elements of both fiction and non-fiction writing. Many principles of dramatic structure that are used in fiction are also applicable to the development of audience interest in a documentary or news story. Principles of rhetorical persuasion and expository structures used in documentaries and commercials can be helpful in terms of presenting a social issue or problem in a dramatic production, such as a children's afternoon special program or a made-for-TV movie.

This chapter provides an introduction to visual thinking and a sequential overview of the scriptwriting process. It also examines some of the ways in which fiction and non-fiction scripts can be effectively organized. The focus is on elements of dramatic, narrative, rhetorical, and expository structure, which are of practical value to scriptwriters working in a variety of areas and formats.

VISUAL THINKING

A script that guides the production of a film, video, audio, or interactive multimedia program can be compared with an architectural drawing or blueprint. A script orients the director and other key members of the creative staff to the overall story or topic. It provides a preliminary sketch or outline for a project that is to be constructed and gives it concrete form. Just as an architect must be knowledgeable about building construction methods and materials, a scriptwriter must understand the entire production process. Scriptwriting cannot be completely divorced from the other preproduction, production, and postproduction activities discussed in this book.

A scriptwriter should only write what he or she is confident can actually be staged and recorded. Abstract concepts and ideas have a more limited place in scriptwriting than they do in forms of writing that are not intended to be performed or pictorially rendered. Thinking visually demands that a scriptwriter think in practical terms of actual settings, concrete actions, and specific dialogue that will actually be performed or observed and recorded. A good feature film scriptwriter or screenwriter, for example, often begins a script visually with an image that will give the audience a strong sense of place, atmosphere, mood, and even the theme of the picture.

Television, film, audio, and interactive multimedia are visual and acoustic media. A fiction scriptwriter establishes settings, describes actions, and defines characters through concrete sounds and visual images. Settings are established economically as specific buildings, locations, and props. Characters are defined by their actions and reactions, as well as by what they say to other characters. The emotional texture of settings, actions, and characters is developed through the actual performance and recording of concrete sounds and visual images. A sound or image does not speak in terms of "people" or "screams" in general, but of this specific person and this specific scream.

Unlike a playwright, a scriptwriter does not need to rely exclusively or even primarily on dialogue or just a few settings to tell a story. Dialogue can be substantial, or it can be practically nonexistent. A scriptwriter can use a variety of settings to reflect different moods, atmospheres, and aspects of a character, or just one setting to provoke a feeling of confinement. Actions can occur outdoors or indoors, in quick succession at different times and at a variety of geographic locations, or slowly at one time and place. A stage play is usually restricted to just a few settings, which must be set up quickly between different scenes or acts. Time is usually continuous within each scene. Time and place in a film, television program, audio recording, or interactive game can be continuous or discontinuous. A media production can depict many existing settings around the world, reconstruct them in a studio, or create a purely imaginative acoustic or animated environment. Actions occurring in a character's past can be intercut with those in the present or future.

Economy of expression is one of the hallmarks of good scriptwriting. Every setting, prop, or character in a fictional story, for example, can only be briefly described. Its presence in the script indicates that it is an essential and integral part of the story or topic, rather than a peripheral detail. Unlike a novelist or short story writer, a scriptwriter rarely writes long passages describing the setting or a character's state of mind and feelings.

One of the skills that scriptwriters must develop is visual thinking. A script facilitates the recording of specific moving images and sounds, and it is based on a firm understanding of the production process. By reading the production and postproduction sections of this book, especially those chapters that focus on the aesthetics of generating, recording, and editing sounds and images, a beginning scriptwriter can acquire some understanding of the creative potential of moving images and sounds, or visual thinking. Quality scriptwriting demands a firm grasp of production aesthetics and the entire production process.

PREPARATION FOR SCRIPTWRITING

The scriptwriting process has several distinct stages, beginning with the research phase. Before a script is written, considerable research must be carried out. Research provides insurance against presenting implausible stories or conveying factually incorrect information. It also provides a source of inspiration and creative ideas.

A premise, synopsis, and several story outlines may be drafted after the research phase before a treatment is prepared. A treatment is a plot description in short-story form and is used primarily as part of a proposal submitted to a potential funding source. It is often submitted to a funding source or producer as an accompaniment to an oral presentation or pitch. It provides a guide for the writing of a complete script.

The next stage in the scriptwriting process is the writing of the script itself. A script may go through several drafts and involve the participation of several writers before it is completed and production can begin. The final stage is the preparation of a shooting script, which indicates all camera placements, transition devices, and various types of effects. These are usually added by the director (or the designer in multimedia production).

Stages of Scriptwriting
- Research
- Premise, synopsis
- Story outline
- Treatment
- Proposal
- Rough draft
- Final draft
- Scene script
- Shooting script

Research

The first stage of scriptwriting is the research phase. Every aspect of the topic should be carefully and thoroughly researched before the script is written. Whether the project is to be primarily entertaining, informative, or persuasive, its overall quality directly depends on the quality of research that has gone into the development of the script. The more carefully documented the information contained in a script is, the more realistic, authentic, accurate, and responsible the finished product will seem to be.

Many documentary writers feel research is like an iceberg; seven-eighths of it is below the surface and can't be seen.

Careful research is both a form of insurance and a source of inspiration. Carefully documenting sources of information can protect a producer from legal prosecution. News and documentary writers, for example, have an obligation to research their stories carefully. It is often necessary to find hard evidence from reliable sources to support a basic statement or argument. Thorough investigation of a subject frequently leads to the revelation of information that stimulates the creative process and challenges and excites the viewer.

Research is a creative process of uncovering new sources of information. A project researcher or scriptwriter begins by acquiring a general background in the area on which the project will focus. She collects as many books and articles as possible that deal with the general topic area and reads those that seem to be most helpful and pertinent to the specific issues at hand. Searching the web, computer files, and systems such as Lexis and Nexis, as well as other databases, is one of the fastest and most accurate methods of acquiring the basic information needed when researching a project. Armed with this general knowledge, the researcher progresses by focusing more narrowly on specific problems and concerns. General understanding of the topic stimulates the creation of insightful questions that can be raised during interviews with an expert or a participant in the events. The more knowledgeable a writer or researcher becomes, the more information she will elicit from additional sources of information. Like a good detective, a writer learns that one piece of evidence leads to the discovery of another.

Production research is usually either novelistic or journalistic in approach. A fiction writer or novelist conducts research to find details that stimulate reader interest and authenticate events and settings. A fictional film, television program, or computer game is often researched in this manner. Strict authenticity is sometimes sacrificed for dramatic interest and action. Journalistic research, on the other hand, aims at uncovering sources of documentary evidence that can be used to support the presentation of information and editorial arguments (Figure 4.1).

Premise, Synopsis, and Outline

Every good treatment is preceded by the writing of a simple idea or concept, called a *premise*. A premise is basically a "what if" statement, which describes the basic story idea. For example, "what if" Romeo and Juliet sang and danced, and were caught between rival gangs and ethnic groups in New York City? This is the basic premise of *West Side Story* (1961). "What if" Romeo and Juliet were involved with drugs in Central Park? A feature film titled *The Panic in Needle Park* (1971) operates on the basis of this simple premise. A good treatment is always based on a simple but

FIGURE 4.1 The beginning of any media production is the research stage. Information must be gathered, facts checked, and information documented before the script is written.

interesting concept. The premise can be used later as a strong opening "pitch" of a script or screenplay to a producer by providing a concise label for the project.

The next preparatory step before writing a treatment is to compose a synopsis, which consists of one or more paragraphs that describe the basic *story line*: "Tony and Maria fall in love, but because they are associated with rival gangs, the Sharks and the Jets, many obstacles are placed in the path of their love. After Tony accidentally kills Maria's brother in a fight, the couple's relationship is filled with suffering and frustration."

On the basis of this synopsis of *West Side Story*, an *outline* can be written, developing the major plot lines and characters in the story. This outline also defines all major actions and character reactions. Usually several outlines are written and revised before the treatment is created.

Treatments

A treatment is an important step in the development of a script. Usually written in the third person, present tense, it provides a narrative summary of the basic story lines. A treatment visualizes the story as it will unfold on the screen and gives a play-by-play of all major actions and scenes in reduced form. A writer composes a treatment so that he or she can receive an approval or commission to write a fictional script or undertake a documentary project. When a producer initiates a project, the treatment sometimes accompanies a proposal, which is submitted to a funding source. Scriptwriters (and their agents) often initiate a film or television project by writing a treatment.

The major portion of the treatment is devoted to a highly visual, but concise, narrative presentation of characters and events. Some examples of dialogue spoken by characters are usually included, and the treatment adopts a short-story format. A good treatment adopts a lively prose style that dramatizes the basic premise and effectively communicates the tone and flavor of a piece. Camera directions and shot descriptions are used sparingly, if at all. Highly visual nouns or adjectives and action verbs are used to convey resonant images. A treatment is not a legal document fashioned with dry regularity and precision. It must excite and interest a producer or funding source and serve as a thorough and helpful guide for the writing of a script or screenplay. A treatment provides some protection against future writing problems by forcing the writer to resolve many difficulties before the actual scriptwriting phase.

How long should a treatment be? A treatment for a feature-length film screenplay, which will run about two hours, usually has about 20 to 70 double-spaced, typewritten pages. The finished screenplay will be 100 to 140 pages, because each page of a screenplay usually translates into about one minute of actual screen time. A treatment for a work of short fiction should probably be from 5 to 10 pages in length. It is always preferable to err on the side of brevity, because verbose, overwritten treatments are not likely to be read with interest and enthusiasm.

Nonfiction treatments, such as a documentary treatment that is included in a proposal submitted to a potential funding source, are concise narrative descriptions of what the viewer will see and hear written in the present tense. Like dramatic fiction treatments, the purpose is to evoke interest, excitement, and, if possible, the same emotional response from the reader that you hope your production will elicit from the viewer or listener. A separate paragraph is usually devoted to each sequence that will appear in the completed project (Figure 4.2).

SCRIPTWRITING FORMATS

After the preliminary stages of scriptwriting have been completed, a writer or group of writers begin to write a full script. The script conforms to one of the following formats: split-page, full-page, or a semiscripted format, such as a script outline. Scriptwriters rely on a basic set of terms as well as these common formats to effectively communicate with other members of the creative staff, such as the director. A discussion of three standard scriptwriting formats—full-page, split-page, and semiscripted—is presented next.

Full-Page Master Scene Script Format

A full-page master scene script format is frequently used in dramatic fiction programs, including single-camera film and video productions, such as live-action dramas and feature films, and multiple-camera live-on-tape productions, such as television situation comedies. In a full-page master scene script format, a single column, which is devoted to both visuals and audio, fills the entire page. The script is organized into scenes, which are numbered in consecutive order. The location and time of day of each scene are specified. Actions and camera movements are described in full paragraphs. Scriptwriting computer programs are available for all computer operating systems. These programs format the script in a professional layout, relieving the scriptwriter of the tedium of worrying about margins and spacing while attempting to create a workable script (Figure 4.3).

Because a full-page master scene script is organized by scenes, it can easily be reorganized so that all the scenes requiring a single set or location can be shot consecutively. As we noted in the previous chapter, producers and production managers try to organize production so that all the scenes at a specific location can be shot at one

SAMPLE TREATMENT FORMAT

TITLE: Safety Training   PAGE: 1
WRITER: T. Bartlett   LENGTH: 10 mins
CLIENT: Mountain Industries   DATE: 10-10-08

   The ten-minute training tape will open with a montage of incorrect logging operations followed in each case by the possible disastrous and life-threatening results of such actions. Examples of such scenes are:

   A logger without a safety belt steps back and falls from a tree stand.

   A chainsaw jams and flips back into the logger.

   A tractor tips over on the driver because it exceeded its tilt limit.

   A logging truck driven too fast forces an on-coming car from the road.

   A log falls from a truck being loaded and strikes a logger who was standing too close to the truck.

   A logger refuels his saw improperly, causing a fire.

   A truck or tractor becomes a runaway when left improperly locked down.

   A logger dumped into the river and crushed by logs.

   A log avalanche occurs because of careless blocking of a log stack.

   This series of accidents will be enhanced with sound effects and dramatic music as well as the actual sound of each accident.

   Following this montage, the narrator will walk into the scene and describe in general the dangers and reasons for following OSHA safety requirements for those working in dangerous occupations such as the

(continued)

FIGURE 4.2 The treatment of a production is, along with the proposal, another sales tool. Potential funding sources need to be able to accurately visualize in their minds, while reading the treatment, exactly what the producer has in mind. If the treatment is not clear and complete, funding is highly unlikely.

MASTER SCENE SCRIPT FORMAT

(Margins and tabs set as indicated below, assuming 80 space wide paper)

| 5 | 10 | 20 | 25 | 55 | 60 | 70 | 75 |

FADE IN:

1. INT./EXT.   DAY/NIGHT   1.
    BRIEF SCENE OR SHOT DESCRIPTION, CAM. ANGLE.

    In upper and lower case, a more detailed description of the scene giving
    setting, props, and CHARACTERS position if needed with margins set at
    10/70.

                              CHARACTER
                        (Mode of delivery, upper and
                        lower case, margins at 25/55)

                    The dialog is typed in upper and lower case
                    centered within 20/60 margins.

    Any other descriptions of shot framing, movement of CAMERA or
    CHARACTER is at margins set at 10/70.

                                                              (TRANSITION)

2.   INT   WS   UNIVERSITY CLASSROOM   DAY   2.

    Classroom is full of students, some wide awake, gossiping, others sleeping
    or nodding off as they wait for the professor to arrive.

                                JANE
                    (Quietly so only Jack can hear her.)
                    Are you sure there isn't going to be an exam
                        during tomorrow's class?

                                JACK
                    (With a bravado, all-knowing tone)
                    Of course not, have I ever lied to you?

    The professor enters the room, downstage right, walks to the lecturn and the
    room becomes quiet.

                            PROFESSOR
                        (Emphatically as a reminder)
                    If I am forced to repeat myself again, I WILL
                    be forced to give you your first examination in
                    tomorrow's class.

(DISSOLVE TO)

3.   EXT   WS   CAMPUS   DAY   3.

    The clouds suddenly darken the sky as rain, thunder and lightning start
    and the lights go out plunging the room into darkness.

        (A scene script describes the entire scene in very general terms, a shooting script
                contains much more detailed descriptions and shot instructions)

FIGURE 4.3 A master scene script gives the screenwriter the opportunity to notify the director of the writer's intent without limiting the director to specific shots. But the script must include enough information so that the director understands what the writer had in mind and wants the actors to say and do.

time, because it is usually more efficient and cost-effective than recording the scenes in chronological order as they appear in the script.

Every scene presented in a master scene script usually begins with a "scene heading," indicating an indoor/interior (INT.) or outdoor/exterior (EXT.) setting, the name of the specific location, and the time of day. There may be a number of different setups, dialogue sequences, and descriptions of actions and characters until the location, time of day, and interior or exterior setting change:

EXT: XANADU—NIGHT—EXTREME LONG SHOT—FENCE AND MANSION

The full-page master scene script describes few, if any, camera movements and shots. It is much more common for the director to select and indicate specific shots during the preparation of the final shooting script immediately before production. A director's shot descriptions often specify camera-to-subject distance, angle of view, and camera movement when they are incorporated into the stage directions following the scene heading. Rather than providing shot descriptions, a scriptwriter can artfully visualize the scene in prose following the header without specifying camera-to-subject distances, angles, and so forth. In any case, camera shots, angles, movements, transition devices, times of day, interior and exterior settings, specific character names, and sound effects are generally typed in uppercase letters, whereas actions, events, and specific stage directions, including sets, props, characters, and actions, as well as dialogue, are usually typed in lowercase letters. Dialogue to be spoken by a specific character normally follows the stage directions and has the character's name listed in the middle of the page immediately above his or her lines of dialogue, which are slightly indented from the paragraph descriptions of actions and camera movements. The end of a scene is usually indicated by a "scene close," such as CUT TO: or DISSOLVE TO:, which indicates the transition to the next scene.

The information highlighted in UPPERCASE LETTERS throughout a master scene script is emphasized for the convenience of the producer or production manager, who will break down the script into its component parts for scheduling and budgeting. Each scene is numbered for easy reference, and each revision of a master scene script is dated, to ensure that all performers, creative staff, and crew members are using identical copies of the script during production.

Split-Page Script Format

In a split-page script (also called a dual-column script), the visual information appears in one column on a sheet of paper and the audio information in the other column. The split-page script format is often used for commercials and other forms of nonfiction production, such as documentaries. The dialogue and narration are written out fully on the audio side of the page. Visual images are indicated on the opposite side of the page. The latter are sometimes described sparingly in live multicamera productions, such as awards ceremonies and performances, leaving wide margins, so that the director or assistant director can make copious notes about specific cameras and shots in these blank areas. Visual cues and segment durations are written in full uppercase letters in the visual column, and any information in the script that should not be read on-air is set in upper case letters (Figure 4.4).

DUAL COLUMN SCRIPT FORMAT

TITLE: PAGE:
WRITER: LENGTH:
CLIENT: DATE:

VIDEO	AUDIO
1. SINGLE SPACE VIDEO INSTRUCTIONS	1. ANNCR: Audio copy is lined up directly across the page from its matching video.
2. TRIPLE SPACE BETWEEN EACH SHOT	2. Double space between each line of audio copy.
3. EACH SHOT MUST BE NUMBERED ON THE SCRIPT	3. The audio column's number must match that of its video.
4. EVERYTHING THE VIEWER IS TO SEE; ALL VISUALS, VIDEO TAPES, CG, CAMERA SHOTS, ARE INCLUDED IN THE LEFT-HAND COLUMN.	4. Everything the viewer is to hear; all sounds, music, voices, sound effects, narration and all audio cues are included in the right-hand column.
5. EVERYTHING ON THE VIDEO SIDE IS TYPED IN CAPITAL LETTERS.	5. Everything spoken by the talent is typed in upper and lower case letters. All instructions in the audio column are typed in capital letters.
6. THE TALENT'S NAME STARTS EACH NEW LINE, BUT DOES NOT HAVE TO BE REPEATED IF THE SAME PERSON OR SOUND SOURCE CONTINUES.	6. SAM: Note--the name is in caps, what Sam says is in upper and lower case.
7. AVOID SPLITTING SHOTS AT BOTTOM OF THE PAGE.	7. Avoid splitting words or thoughts at the end of the line.

FIGURE 4.4 A split-page format defines clearly how each shot is to be framed, the action within that shot, and the accompanying audio.

The obvious advantage of the split-page format is that visual and audio elements can be directly compared and coordinated. An empty column suggests that one aspect is being focused on to the exclusion of the other. A rough equality in terms of space devoted to these two tracks or creative elements ensures that both will be fully utilized in the completed project.

Semiscripted Formats

Many types of nonfiction television programs and films do not need to be fully scripted in advance of production. A talk show, game show, or even a documentary film or videotape may only be partially or semiscripted. A semiscripted format may consist of a simple rundown sheet, which is a basic outline of the show from beginning to end, indicating what material or performer is needed at specific times. It is organized on the basis of the running time of each segment and of the entire program. Different electronic sources of material, such as remote feeds and videotape playbacks, are also specified (Figure 4.5).

A script outline is another semiscripted format. Portions of a script outline may be fully scripted, such as the opening or closing segments of a news, talk, or game show that remain the same from show to show. Other elements are simply outlined in rough

| Client: | WEMPLE'S DUTCH MILL | DATE: | 7-7-08 |
| JOB: | #WDM-94-7-3 | MEDIA: | TV |

SCENE 1:

SCENE:	Kitchen, middle class	MOM: A little more mustard?
TALENT:	Mom and Male kid	
ACTION:	Mom busily fixing lunch	KID: That's great, you make the best cheeseburgers in the whole world

SCENE 2:

SCENE:	Backyard	KID: But I'd rather be eating at Wemple's
TALENT:	Male kid	
ACTION:	Kid runs out of back door	

SCENE 3:

SCENE:	Mom in kitchen	
TALENT:	Mom	MOM: Never mind burgers, I'd rather be eating at Wemple's
ACTION:	Mom puts away lunch, hurries out front door	

SCENE 4:

| KEY LOGO & TAG | VO: Everybody'd rather be eating at Wemple's |

FIGURE 4.5 A semiscript provides the director with a rough outline of the production, allowing much greater freedom for deciding on shots. The form also is used for productions that cannot be scripted: sporting events, game shows, and special events.

form, either because they must be ad-libbed during recording or because the exact information to be read may not, in fact, be available until just before air or recording time, such as with quiz and game shows. Documentary, sports, and talk show directors often use a script outline because it is difficult to precisely script live or uncontrolled events. The questions to be asked during an interview show can be written down in advance, but the answers cannot, unless the interview is staged. A director or camera operator must be able to respond instantly to unpredictable events as they happen. The actual selection of shots to be used may be delayed to later stages of production, such as postproduction editing. Only the general type of shot or action may be specified in a script outline.

FICTION SCRIPTWRITING

Drama and narrative are fictional art forms that have a basis in everyday life. A drama is basically a series of actions performed by actors, such as a stage play. A narrative is a chain of events that is told or narrated, such as a novel or short story. Although most dramas and narratives draw on everyday life and experience, effective works of fiction are often shaped and refined by carefully organizing and structuring these actions and events and removing the dull moments of life so that viewer, listener, or reader interest can be intensified. The organization of dramatic actions and narrative events is often referred to as the elements of dramatic and narrative structure. Fiction scriptwriting has the potential to combine certain elements of dramatic and narrative structure, and a successful work of fiction, be it a film, video, audio, or multimedia production, is usually one that makes effective use of these basic structural elements.

Dramatic Structure

Dramatic films and television programs can be plotted into a framework that consists of a basic three-act structure and a series of rising and falling actions, which culminate in a climax and resolution. Act One of a drama usually sets up the main plot by establishing the central characters, their goals and conflicts, as well as the basic time, place, and situation of the story. Act Two and Act Three each begin with a turning point, such as a major shift in the main plot, which moves the drama in a different direction from the previous act, generating audience interest and maintaining story momentum. Secondary as well as primary characters and themes are usually more fully developed through both main plot and subplot actions in Act Two. Conflicts and problems eventually reach a climax and are resolved as the main plot and subplot are brought together near the end of Act Three.

Rising actions include build sections, where conflicts build into a series of crises, and a final climax. Falling and horizontal actions include temporary resolutions or pauses in the action following crises, which allow the audience to catch its breath before proceeding to the next crisis or climax. Then the final resolution of the conflicting elements that led to the climax are revealed, bringing the drama to a close.

These classic forms of dramatic structure ensure that actions build in a logical and exciting way on the basis of major conflicts that must be resolved. A drama may have limited or extensive expositions of characters, situations, and settings and few or many complications, reversals, and crises; but it almost always relies on internal or external conflicts, which build toward a climax and resolution, if it is to sustain interest, arouse excitement, and evoke a sense of fulfillment. *Crime dramas*, such as *Medium, CSI*, and *CSI Miami*, or *CSI NY*, and medical dramas, such as *ER*, illustrate classic dramatic structure.

Act One

Act One usually begins with powerful images that convey the essential focus, pace, and style of the film or television program. We not only sense the time and place of the story, but we are often introduced to a major theme as well. Generally without writing any dialogue, the scriptwriter is able to convey the basic ideas, thoughts, and feelings that the unfolding story will eventually develop in great detail through character actions, dialogue, or interior monologue.

The main plot action is usually initiated and propelled by a precipitating event or catalyst in Act One. The precipitating event may consist of an action, such as a murder; a piece of dialogue, such as one character informing another that he or she has found the secret to eternal life; or a situation, such as the appearance of a young unmarried woman who is obviously pregnant. The precipitating event helps to establish the basic spin or direction of the main plot.

Learning more about the characters in Act One might require some back story, such as flashbacks into a character's past or some discussion of a particular character's life by other characters. The plot unfolds in Act One as a series of dramatic beats or actions that reveal who characters are by what they do and say. A dramatic scene—that is, a series of actions or events occurring at one time and place—may consist of several *beats* or dramatic moments.

Act Two

Act Two usually begins with the first turning point. A turning point substantially changes or reverses the direction of the plot. For example, one character may believe that another character is her best friend, but new information reverses her opinion and suggests that her supposed friend is really someone to be feared and avoided. During Act Two the subplot is more fully developed than in Act One. For example, the main plot of the story may focus on a woman whose career objective is to succeed as an executive in a major corporation, whereas the subplot may focus on her romantic involvement with the chief executive at a rival company. In Hollywood films, subplots often focus on romantic love and develop important themes, and main plots often focus on characters' pursuit of material goals, actions, and concrete objectives.

During Act Two, secondary as well as primary characters are more fully developed, along with resulting conflicts between characters. Subsequent events, such as the eventual death of a particular character, are often foreshadowed, although the payoff may not occur until Act Three. Complications develop, which sometimes act as barriers to a character's successful accomplishment of his or her goals. For example, a long-distance runner who is very religious may discover that a major competition is scheduled to take place on an important religious holiday, and his participation in that event violates his own ethical and religious standards.

Act Three

The second turning point usually initiates Act Three and speeds up the action. Act Three provides a sense of urgency and propels the story toward its conclusion. Actions build toward a climax, where the conflicts originating in Act One are resolved and the main plot and the subplot come together.

Rising Action: Crises and Climax

Dramatic action that has progressed through several complications inevitably builds to a crisis. A drama may have several crises, in which the conflict that has stimulated the action intensifies to the point that something or someone is threatened. We all encounter crises in our lives, but drama removes most of the dull moments between these crises, so that characters' actions and emotions and viewers' interest and involvement are intensified. The major character or characters may have to make an important decision. Perhaps it is a life-and-death situation. Should a risky surgical procedure be performed? Can a murderer be identified and sacrificed? Should a character choose between a lover or a spouse? The dramatic action usually builds through several important crises that finally culminate in a major crisis or climax.

A climax is the most decisive point of confrontation in a drama. It simply demands some form of resolution. One side must win or a compromise must be reached. The climax brings the major conflicting forces together so that they may be openly confronted and resolved. The climax is usually the highest, most intense emotional peak of the drama.

Falling Action: Resolution

Overcoming the basic conflict or fulfilling the goals and motivations that have stimulated the dramatic action is known as a resolution. The defeat of the antagonist, the death of the hero, the marriage of the loving couple, or the attainment of the major goal may each represent the culmination of the action. A resolution is considered a falling action compared with the rising action of a crisis or climax. The resolution section of the drama considers the implications of the climactic actions and gives the audience time to contemplate what has just transpired before new actions are initiated or the drama ends. Emotionally, the audience may need sufficient time to recuperate from the emotional experience of the climax. A drama that ended immediately after the climax might leave some of the audience's expectations unfulfilled.

The resolution of a drama can be ambiguous or unambiguous. An ending can appear to resolve all major conflicts or allow the hero to achieve his or her major goals. In a mystery story, the discovery of a secret can answer all questions. But an ending can also be ambiguous. Conflicts can persist and goals remain unachieved. Some dramatic forms have virtually no resolution at all. Soap operas rarely, if ever, reach any resolution. They consist of a series of crises. Any apparent solution, such as a marriage, is usually the source of another conflict. The absence of any resolution establishes a new convention that is unique to the open-ended, serial dramatic form. A closed dramatic form uses resolution to enforce a sense of finality or closure at the end. The drama is essentially self-contained, although the dramatic action may continue in the form of a sequel.

Text and Subtext

A good writer not only plays with the surface text of the dialogue while telling a story but often develops a subtext through character actions and reactions. The subtext defines what the characters are really feeling—that is, the feelings that underlie their dialogue. For example, a man and a woman may be discussing something rather innocuous, such as the weather. Their dialogue defines the text. "Don't you think that it's getting warmer?" "Yes, but my hands are freezing." "There's still a touch of winter in the air, but the ice is melting." The text indicates that the characters are aware that spring is coming and the weather outside is getting warmer. But by staging the action so that the characters gradually get closer together and begin holding hands and touching one another, the subtext (and double entendre of the dialogue), of course, is that they are gradually warming up to each other romantically. This example may be rather trite or cliché, but it illustrates the basic principle involved in creating subtext, which in the hands of a talented screenwriter gives drama depth and distinction.

Narrative Structure

In addition to having dramatic structure, the structure of action, scripts also have narrative structure, the structure of time and point of view. A story can follow an uninterrupted chronological structure from beginning to end, or it can have flashbacks and flash-forwards, which disrupt the continuous flow of time. A great deal of screen time can be devoted to some events and very little to others. For example, a character in a soap opera can go upstairs in one scene and come down in the next, having aged several years (and sometimes having been replaced by another actor). On the other hand, it may take several episodes or even several weeks of episodes to develop all the intrigues occurring at a party that supposedly lasted for only two hours on one day. The difference between the actual screen time and the supposed story or historical time devoted to specific events is sometimes referred to as *narrative duration*, and the difference between the actual order of presentation and the supposed historical chronology of specific events in the story is sometimes referred to as *narrative order*. Scriptwriters can manipulate narrative order and duration to effectively relate one event to another, such as providing character back story by using a flashback to break the chronological order of the narrative and to relate a character's history to his or her present actions.

A fictional work can also be narrated by someone. A story can be told from a specific point of view. An omniscient or effaced (hidden) narrator tells the story but does not appear as a character within it, whereas a dramatized narrator is a specific character who also tells the story. In media production, the director can use the camera to enhance the point of view of a specific character whom the scriptwriter is using to tell the story by placing the camera in that character's approximate physical position on the set. We, the audience, then see and understand what that character sees and understands from his or her point of view throughout the story. An effaced or omniscient narrator acts as a substitute for the scriptwriter. He or she is an unseen person who presents the story when no character takes responsibility for it. An effaced narrator selects what we will see and understand by adopting a more "objective" point of view, and a director can use the camera more "objectively" by not placing it in the approximate spatial position of any specific character.

Narrative point of view is an extremely important structural component. How something is presented is just as important as what is presented. If we experience a series of events through the eyes of a character as opposed to omnisciently through an effaced narrator, our experience of these events is quite different. Adopting the point of view of a particular character makes a difference in terms of how actions, events, and their meanings are perceived. Imagine, for example, the presentation of the Battle of the Little Big Horn through the eyes of a Sioux warrior versus those of a U.S. cavalryman. Arthur Penn's film *Little Big Man* (1970) presents a shifting point of view on General Custer through the ambiguous cultural identity and affiliation of its main character/narrator. The adoption of a specific point of view colors and even distorts events in a particular way, and such a perspective must be carefully and thoughtfully selected.

A well-known short film called *An Occurrence at Owl Creek Bridge* (1964), based on the short story of the same name by Ambrose Bierce, illustrates most major aspects of narrative structure. It tells the story of a southerner during the Civil War who is about to be hanged from a bridge by Union soldiers. The story is generally presented from the victim's point of view. The victim dreams about his wife as he is about to be hanged, and the images intercut pleasant memories of the past with the present horror of imminent death as he watches the Union soldiers prepare for his execution. We are shown his memories of his wife as the victim narrates historical time. Cutting back to his present predicament, the camera often assumes his physical position within the setting at the bridge. Just when he seems about to die, the rope snaps and he falls into the river. Writer-director Robert Enrico expands historical time underwater. It takes the victim more than three minutes of film time to free himself underwater from the ropes that bind him and swim to the surface. Enrico then condenses the time it takes him to swim away down the river, eluding the gunfire of the soldiers along the shore. But when he gets home and is about to embrace his wife, the scene cuts directly to his hanging at the bridge again. In retrospect, the escape scenes can be interpreted by the audience as a wish fulfillment of the victim's hope of escaping death, which is shattered by the reality of his death. The events of the escape have only occurred in the victim's mind. They have been narrated by the victim and exist as a dream outside of the normal "present" time of the dramatic scenes of the hanging.

Characterization and Theme

There are almost as many ways to initiate the writing of an original piece of fiction as there are works of fiction. Some writers begin with specific characters. Once they have these characters firmly in mind, they begin to imagine specific, exciting situations within which these people find themselves. Conflicts arise from interactions among characters who have different goals and values. Certain themes begin to emerge as the characters initiate or become involved in specific actions. This "organic" approach to fiction writing tries to ensure that actions and themes flow "naturally" out of "real" characters (Figure 4.6).

Another approach to writing fiction begins with a basic theme, idea, or message. In some ways it is more difficult to begin with the theme and then find three-dimensional characters who can initiate actions to reinforce the theme. There is a real danger that the theme will become overbearing. The opposite danger faced by the "character-first" approach is that the actions undertaken by certain characters will not be thematically significant or interesting.

A third way to initiate a fictional script is to begin with the plot or story structure and then work in both directions—that is, toward characters who can carry out those actions and the themes that those actions reflect or represent. In using this method, there is a danger that characters will simply become pawns to carry out actions and that themes will be tacked on from the outside.

Where a scriptwriter begins is probably less important than paying attention to the development of all three fictional aspects: plot, characters, and themes. Plot (that is, the telling or presentation of specific actions and events) has already been discussed in terms of dramatic and narrative structure, but characterization and theme need further consideration.

Developing strong, believable, and interesting characters is just as important as creating an exciting series of actions and events. Complex characters give a story depth

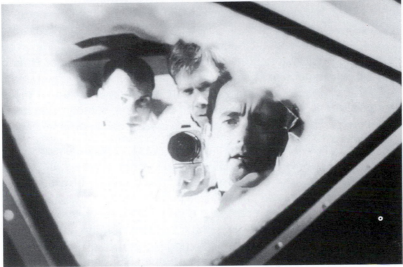

FIGURE 4.6 A dramatic production should draw the audience into the story through a combination of quality acting, directing, and production values. Universal Pictures' production of *Apollo 13* provided the audience with such an experience. (Courtesy of Universal Pictures.)

and three-dimensionality. A character's values and beliefs lead to conflicts with other characters who hold opposing values. If these values are significant and strongly held, the entire fictional experience is enhanced.

Character can be revealed through two primary vehicles: actions and words. What characters do and say reveals in large part who they are. But actions and behavior are usually more important than dialogue. Characters should show us what they believe through their actions. The important thing for the writer to remember is that communication takes place through concrete sounds and images. A character is largely created through external appearances, actions, and speech. But the external surface of a character must reflect a complex internal value system and a set of abstract thoughts, beliefs, and feelings. An external surface that is not based on a solid psychological foundation lacks depth, understanding, and true artistic potential.

Characters can be roughly divided into three categories: central characters, principal characters, and secondary or incidental characters. The central character or characters figure prominently in a story. They are the primary sources of audience satisfaction, interest, and identification. The decisions they make and the actions they initiate propel the drama. Their values, beliefs, feelings, and goals determine, to a great extent, how meaningful and significant the entire drama will become. The principal characters are usually friends or foils to the central character(s). They can offer support to the actions and thoughts of the central character, or they can present significant obstacles to the attainment of his or her goals. In a longer drama, there is usually enough time to give most or all of the principal characters sufficient depth so that their interactions with the central character become important and convincing.

Secondary and incidental characters may help create a situation that provokes a conflict, but they are contributors to (rather than initiators of) major actions. There is rarely time to fully develop all the minor characters in a drama into complex individuals. They have certain traits and mannerisms that distinguish them in a crowd and add spice to the drama, but these can easily deteriorate into stereotypes or clichés. Stereotyping secondary or incidental characters often runs the risk of stereotyping certain occupational or ethnic groups and minorities. Some reliance on character types (as opposed to stereotypes) ensures immediate audience recognition of the most important aspect of a character and contributes to the drama as a whole. What minor characters say about any major character helps to develop the latter's characterization. A good deal of information about the central character can be communicated to the audience through the words of secondary and incidental characters, sometimes reinforcing and sometimes contradicting the central character's own speech and actions.

A *theme* is basically a significant statement that a work of fiction asserts or an important issue that it raises. Themes generally emanate from the values, beliefs, and goals of the central characters, but a general theme may be much broader and universal than the attitudes of any single character. The film *Citizen Kane* (1941) has several broad themes, for example. The portrayal of Kane's life focuses on such issues as the absence of love in his life and his pursuit of fame, fortune, and power. Images, symbols, and motifs, such as "Rosebud," suggest, perhaps, that the absence of a happy childhood or family or parental love and guidance can lead to an inability to love and a meaningless pursuit of money and power. This film also develops other themes concerning democracy, politics, and the press, including, perhaps, a criticism of American society and capitalism in general. Of course, not all films are so heavily thematic, but the greatness of this film is that it does not sacrifice characterization and dramatic structure in order to make meaningful statements. Important themes coexist with strong characters and a complex plot. The themes are not the sole interest of the story (Figure 4.7).

Adaptation

An adaptation is a relatively faithful translation of a play, short story, a novel, or even a comic strip into a film or television program. The scriptwriter is usually very familiar with the original literary work and makes every attempt to translate it into a different medium with the central characters and themes virtually intact. A television or film script that is less faithful to the original is frequently said to be based on that source, whereas a work that uses the original written piece as a springboard for essentially new ideas is said to be freely adapted or simply suggested by the original (Figure 4.8).

FIGURE 4.7 The acclaim of *Citizen Kane* is based in part on its strong characters, complex plot, and important themes. (Courtesy of RKO Pictures.)

FIGURE 4.8 The *Spiderman* films produced by Columbia TriStar were adapted from the original Spiderman cartoon strip and an animated television series. (Courtesy of Columbia TriStar Pictures.)

The adaptation process usually begins with a consideration of the author's intent. What is the basic theme and point of view from which the story is told? Which characters are particularly memorable or attractive, disturbing or sympathetic? The plot must be analyzed in detail, using some of the basic elements of dramatic and narrative structure discussed earlier as a guide to good storytelling technique in media production. Does the story have a basic three-act structure? Does it build logically and dramatically toward a climax and resolution? Does the story have a plot and a subplot, and do the two coalesce at the denouement, that is, at the point of their final solution and clarification? Are there dead spots that can be eliminated or conflicts that need to be intensified? How many different scenes and settings are required? Is the story told from an omniscient or a specific character's point of view? Is there substantial dialogue and action, or will a character's interior monologue need to be dramatized and shown rather than simply told? Does the story follow a chronological structure, or does it involve flashbacks or flash-forwards in time?

After completing a careful analysis of the basic plot, subplot, characters, and themes, the scriptwriter who is adapting a work from one medium to another will write a treatment and then a screenplay that usually provides a number of changes from the original work. These changes may include the following: creating or eliminating subplots; eliminating, combining, adding, or altering (usually secondary or minor) characters; cutting, shortening, or expanding and enhancing specific scenes; and adding, subtracting, or altering settings. The scriptwriter makes these changes to improve a story's dramatic and narrative structure; to enhance the characterization and theme of the original novel, play, or short story; and to increase the efficiency and often decrease the cost of actual production.

A full and complete adaptation of a lengthy novel, for example, could substantially exceed the normal time restrictions of most media productions. A scriptwriter must then decide which elements are crucial to the story, which will be the most dramatic, what scenes or portions of the plot can be eliminated entirely, and how others can be shortened. Sometimes characters can be combined, so that the ideas and values they espouse are not lost but simply condensed. Dialogue or action scenes may have to be added, however, to dramatize information that was presented in the novel as pure description or characters' inner thoughts. The story should be shown not just told. Literary dialogue must work well as spoken dialogue, and dialogue should not become so lengthy and informative that it substitutes for action. An adaptation scriptwriter must understand the production problems and costs involved in composing a faithful adaptation of an original piece of writing. He or she must also understand the needs and expectation of the audience so that an effective, exciting, and interesting presentation of characters, actions, and themes will be created on the screen (Figure 4.9).

Before the adaptation process commences, the rights to a published or copyrighted work must be secured, of course. An original novel, short story, play, history, or biography may be protected by copyright for up to 75 years, and any television or film producer who attempts to adapt it, however freely, without paying for the right to do so can be held liable for damages to the value of that property.

Short Fiction Forms and Formats

Some short fiction forms, such as television situation comedies, may require different treatment, including the use of alternative dramatic and narrative structures and story construction, from that of longer forms, such as feature films. For example, half-hour episodes in a television situation comedy series present the same set of characters in a slightly different situation each week. The relatively short duration of an individual episode encourages a different organization and approach.

A sitcom episode is usually organized into two acts with three scenes per act and a tag or epilogue after the last commercial to keep the audience tuned in and to reinforce any message or theme. The opening of an episode must grab the attention of

FIGURE 4.9 The *Harry Potter* films produced by Warner Bros. were adapted by a series of books written by J. K. Rowling. (Courtesy of Warner Bros.)

the audience to prevent viewers from switching channels. A major conflict or problem must be presented in the first five minutes (Act One, Scene One), before the first commercial break. The dramatic device that grabs the audience is called a *hook*. It often takes the form of a problem or conflict that excites the viewer and foreshadows events that occur later in the story. A specific object or idea introduced early in a drama, which becomes an important factor during the final resolution, is called a *plant*. Planting and foreshadowing are effective devices in terms of hooking the audience. The conflict builds through a series of complications or misunderstandings until the end of Act One, where a new complication is introduced. In Act Two, things begin to get sorted out, and the main conflict is resolved in Act Two, Scene Three. With the opening credits, closing tag, and commercials between scenes, a series episode writer only has about 20 minutes to quickly develop the basic conflict or situation, add a few complications, and then neatly resolve it. The structure of a situation comedy follows this basic formula, regardless of the exact setting and characters. There is a constant need for imagination and creativity within this tight, somewhat restrictive format.

Other types of short fiction are not as formulaic as situation comedy, but they nonetheless demand tight dramatic structure. There simply isn't enough time to develop many minor characters or a complicated subplot. A short drama usually has a short exposition section. New characters and situations must be developed quickly and efficiently. A few lines of dialogue can establish who new characters are and their basic motivations. The plot must develop several complications to promote interest and variation, but it must also build toward a climax. Loose ends are quickly tied up and resolved.

Interactive Stories and Games

Interactive scripts differ from traditional dramatic and narrative scripts in a number of ways. Traditional noninteractive scripts tend to be linear in terms of narrative structure. There may be flashbacks and flash-forwards in time, but dramatic narratives follow a relatively fixed linear progression. Interactive stories and game scripts, on the other hand, are distinctly nonlinear. Players can select characters and a variety of story paths to pursue during a game.

Scriptwriters and programmers use one of two types of logic systems for interactive story construction: branching and artificial intelligence. *Branching* refers to a structure that is similar to the structure of a tree or a series of highways that intersect. Choosing a specific action sends the player character along a path that consists of a series of branches off the initial road or tree trunk. Branches may intersect, bringing the character back toward the center, or they may send the character farther and farther away from the center. A scriptwriter specifies various branches by placing single words in brackets, such as [ATTACK] or [RETREAT], which indicate actions the player or player character (PC) has chosen. Actors and computer characters (CCs) then respond to the player character's actions with various forms of text-based or spoken dialogue, and in so doing the story proceeds along various paths or branches.

Artificial intelligence (AI) refers to the ability to insert variables into a text so that a wide variety of text-based dialogue can be created and displayed very efficiently. Using standard terms, such as computer character (CC) and player character (PC), the scriptwriter uses a % mark to indicate a variable set of dialogue that can be accessed elsewhere. A # mark is used to locate the name of a set of dialogue and instructions, and a series of "if/then" statements indicates actions and dialogue that will be inserted as the PC makes various choices and the CC responds.

One method of organizing scenes for interactive stories is a flowchart, which is also discussed in more detail later in this chapter in reference to interactive educational scriptwriting under "Interactive Learning and Training." Flowcharts allow writers and programmers to visualize various branches and variables that can be followed throughout a game. Computer programs are available that allow a standard full-page master scene script to be married to a flowchart program.

An interactive script consists of a series of instructions to programmers concerning player characters, computer characters, text-based and spoken dialogue, actions, and responses, which follow a branching or artificial intelligence logic system for story construction. An interactive story or game may be designed for one or more platforms, including CD-ROM, Sega, Genesis, or online. Dialogue is usually written as text or spoken dialogue to be recorded using actors. In either case, it is usually very brief. Writers need to be conscious of the limitations of various platforms, such as CD-ROM, in terms of storage space for both graphics and text.

Every line of dialogue needs to have a specific purpose in terms of moving the story forward, and this restriction makes it somewhat more difficult to build character through dialogue in interactive than in motion picture and television scripts. There should be enough variety that a player is not bored by endless repetitions of the same line of dialogue. If the dialogue will appear on the screen in written form, remember that the screen is generally restricted to 80 characters of 12-point type per line or less. Scripts are often written in ASCII unformatted style so that they can be directly input into the computer. Full caps are used to emphasize the most important information, such as if/then statements, character names, and actions the player character may choose. Notation and style are generally based on a standard computer programming language known as C++.

NONFICTION SCRIPTWRITING

Many different types of nonfiction programs and films are used as informative or persuasive media devices. Documentaries, news stories, instructional programs, and commercials are examples of nonfiction films and television programming. These types of products seem to share some common characteristics. There is usually an emphasis on actuality or the presentation of real people, things, situations, actions, and problems. They are often structured or organized to transmit information or to motivate people to change their attitudes or behavior. They make frequent use of expository and rhetorical structures to convey information and to make persuasive appeals to an audience.

Nonfiction shares certain characteristics with dramatic fiction. All scriptwriters attempt to stimulate viewer interest through the portrayal of dramatic conflicts. The theorist Kenneth Burke has argued that all media presentations (both fictional and nonfictional) are essentially dramatic social devices. Reuven Frank, as executive producer of the NBC Evening News in the 1960s, sent the following memorandum to his news staff:

> Every news story should, without any sacrifice of probity or responsibility, display the attributes of fiction, of drama. It should have structure and conflict, problem and denouement, rising action and falling action, a beginning, a middle, and an end. These are not only the essentials of drama; they are the essentials of narrative.

In short, elements of dramatic and narrative structure are important to nonfiction scriptwriters, and the material presented earlier in this chapter concerning fiction scriptwriting is relevant to nonfiction scriptwriting as well. In addition, nonfiction scriptwriters utilize rhetorical and expository structure to present argument and convey information.

Rhetorical and Expository Structure

Nonfiction scriptwriters know how to wage effective arguments and to present information in a logical manner that facilitates understanding. Arguments are fashioned on the basis of rhetorical strategies. An argument can take the form of inartistic or artistic proof. Inartistic proofs are dependent on factual material available to the writer, editor, or speaker, such as interviews with various participants, witnesses, and observers. There are three main types of artistic proof: ethical, emotional, and demonstrative. An ethical proof relies quite heavily on the moral integrity and credibility of the speaker. An emotional proof relies on the appeal to audience emotions and feelings. A demonstrative proof relies on a series of expositions (showing, not just telling), which have recourse to actual events or opposite/alternative points of view. A specific script might rely on all of these different forms of proof and argument.

We can also distinguish rhetorical strategies and approaches on the basis of whether the argument focuses on its source, its subject, or the viewer. The credibility of the source of an argument in part determines its effectiveness. For example, a highly trusted or reliable person, such as a news anchor or a narrator with a commanding voice, carries a certain persuasive power. Utilizing widely shared beliefs about a subject can also be highly persuasive, such as the idea that all politicians are corrupt or that many large corporations are insensitive to environmental issues. Other arguments focusing on the subject include leaving out various alternative solutions to a problem and implying that the solution presented is the only one possible. This form of argument conceals its basic premise. Emotional arguments, such as waving the flag or castigating someone as a communist, on the other hand, focus more on viewers (and the assumption that certain emotional responses are widely shared) than on the subject or the source of the argument.

A nonfiction scriptwriter relies on expository structures that help to organize information in a logical manner. Widely used expository structures include effects-to-causes, problem/solution, enumeration, classification into logical categories, and theme/countertheme. Many network television documentaries, for example, begin with scenes that dramatize the effects of a particular social problem. These highly charged, emotional scenes act as a hook to grab the audience's attention. A dispassionate narrator then begins to explore some of the causes that have produced these effects. In a classic documentary, such as *The River* (1936) or *Harvest of Shame* (1960), the film or television program ends with proposed solutions to the problem. Specific goals are cited, and specific courses of action are recommended to viewers concerning flood control (the Tennessee Valley Authority) and migrant worker welfare (federal legislation), respectively. Each documentary is structured as an argument for the elimination of a pressing social problem, and the information is logically presented through a problem/solution and effects-to-causes organization (Figure 4.10).

Visual and audio information can also be edited to compare and contrast different opinions and points of view. This can take the form of a theme/countertheme structure, where one idea or point of view clashes repeatedly with another, much like a theme and countertheme in a piece of music. For example, the documentary film *Hearts and Minds* (1975) uses a theme/countertheme structure to alternate between anti-Vietnam War and pro-Vietnam War interviews and statements. *Enumeration* refers to a listing of various possibilities or realities, whereas logical categories might consist

FIGURE 4.10 A documentary, such as *The River* (1936), not only needs to tell a coherent story, but it must make a specific point or argument for or against a social issue.

of different aspects or approaches to a subject. For example, an educational documentary about a Latin American country might examine political, social, economic, cultural, and artistic aspects of that country.

A nonfiction scriptwriter uses dramatic as well as expository structure. Events in a documentary, for example, can be considered to be rising and falling actions. The overall structure of a documentary can obtain emotional power by building toward a climax where a central problem or conflict is resolved. The pace of a nonfiction work is extremely important in terms of maintaining audience interest. The pace should vary to provide an effective emotional (as well as a logical) flow of events. Pacing is difficult to control during the writing stage, because it depends on so many factors that are evident only when the actual sound and image recordings are available. Although the writer must exhibit some concern for pacing during the scriptwriting phase, it is really the documentary director and editor who finally determine the pace of specific elements and of the documentary film or videotape as a whole. Pacing is affected by the editing together of long- and short-duration camera shots as well as the speed of actions within shots, dialogue, and narration.

The opening of a nonfiction film or video should define what the piece is about and where it is going. It should serve as a hook to grab the viewer's attention, pique his or her curiosity, and generate a sense of expectation. Presenting a problem or conflict in dramatic, human terms is one of the best ways of gaining immediate audience attention. Presenting a particularly exciting segment of scenes or vignettes, which will be shown in their entirety somewhat later, acts as a teaser that can stimulate interest. Short segments from longer interviews can be edited together to dramatize a conflict or to present alternative points of view at the start. The writer's job is to find a way in which the documentary's main idea, theme, point of view, or conflict can be concisely dramatized in human terms that the intended audience will immediately understand. Later, near the conclusion of the piece, a sense of completion and fulfillment can be achieved by providing a definitive ending that leaves few questions raised in the opening sequence unanswered.

Voice and Point of View

Many nonfiction and documentary scripts establish a particular point of view. A point of view is an important angle or perspective from which an issue or problem can be productively approached. Television documentaries and news magazines such as *60 Minutes*, for example, sometimes adopt the point of view of a person in an underdog role, such as an individual consumer, as opposed to a large anonymous corporation or bureaucracy. Establishing a specific point of view helps to dramatize and humanize the problem. The audience frequently identifies with the individual, underdog, or injured party, and this can be used to increase the audience's emotional involvement in the problem.

Nonfiction scriptwriters and directors often assert their own voices and opinions. The assertion of a voice can be direct and explicit, such as when a narrator states an opinion, belief, or argument. It can also be indirect and implicit in the expository structure and order in which information is presented. For example, the film *Hearts and Minds* (1975) shows a Vietnamese woman crying over a family member's grave immediately after General William Westmoreland states that Vietnamese people don't value life as dearly as Americans do. Here the expository structure and order of presentation undercuts General Westmoreland and asserts the filmmaker's editorial opinion.

Direct or indirect assertions of a voice are associated with a variety of nonfiction and documentary approaches. Classic rhetorical and expository documentaries, such as *The River* (1937) and *Harvest of Shame* (1960), for example, rely on direct address through an authoritative narrator or reporter/anchor person. Observational approaches to nonfiction film and video, such as the so-called cinema vérité approach, on the other hand, generally suppress the voice of the filmmaker, avoid using a narrator, and require little, if any, scriptwriting. Events are recorded as they happen in long, continuous camera and sound takes. Nonetheless, the order of presentation of these events, which is determined during editing and postproduction, can rely on indirect means of asserting the filmmaker's opinion, such as the order of presentation cited earlier with respect to *Hearts and Minds*. An interactive approach encourages the subjects of a documentary to assert their own voices, often highlighting their interaction with the filmmaker. In this case, the subjects directly assert their own voices, whereas the filmmaker relies on both direct and indirect means of asserting his or her voice. Finally, a self-reflexive approach makes a filmmaker's implicit assertions explicit by self-consciously analyzing his or her own role in the filmmaking process. A self-reflexive approach turns the filmmaker's voice into the subject of the nonfiction film or video.

Narration and Interviews

A nonfiction scriptwriter needs to tell an interesting story in a gripping and imaginative way, using facts, anecdotes, and opinions collected during research. Sometimes narration facilitates telling a story. At other times it gets in the way. If a nonfiction story effectively unfolds through compelling sounds and images, leave it alone. There is no need to retell the story with narration. Narration should clarify images and provide important additional information rather than redundantly describing what sound and images themselves convey. Narration can also emphasize and explain important points and details.

Narration needs to be written so that it can be spoken by a narrator rather than read silently as text by the viewer. It should be colloquial and down to earth. It should also be personalized whenever possible. Narration written in the first person, which will be spoken by a participant in the events that the sounds and images depict, for example, usually works much more effectively than narration written in the third person, which will be spoken by someone who has no connection to the events.

A nonfiction scriptwriter should use simple sentences and action verbs. Words should be particular rather than general, concrete and specific rather than abstract and indefinite. Narration should be factual and informative, directing the viewer's attention to specific details or enhancing the mood and atmosphere by using adjectives that create a more vivid and memorable experience. Using long lists of data, recitations of statistics, and difficult specialized terminology rarely provide narration that is sufficiently informal, subtle, and effective (Figure 4.11).

Interviews often add emotion and personalize events. They should be carefully planned by writing down questions on a piece of paper after carefully and thoroughly researching the subject, but the interviewer should memorize these questions and never simply read them during the interview. An interviewer needs to maintain eye contact with the interviewee and use questions to facilitate rather than disrupt a personal or emotional response to questions. Interview questions should not be able to be answered by a simple yes or no from the interviewee. They should be specific

FIGURE 4.11 The writer or producer must gather information before the script is written. Interviewing the sources of information provides basic and accurate information on which to base the script.

and directive rather than rambling or excessively general. They should encourage the interviewee to divulge information through personal anecdotes as well as through the expression of attitudes, feelings, and opinions that generate enthusiasm or emotional power. An interviewer should come prepared with a bevy of specific questions whose order of presentation will be determined in large part by the interviewee's responses.

Short Nonfiction Forms and Formats

Many scriptwriting principles used with longer nonfiction forms, such as documentaries, are also applicable to shorter forms, such as news stories, talk shows, instructional programs, and commercials, but each of these shorter forms of nonfiction writing has its own principles and practices as well.

News Stories

A television newswriter, for example, writes *copy* or narration to be spoken by on-camera or off-camera news anchors and reporters. Most reporters write their own stories. Only in larger markets do news anchors generally read copy written by a newswriting specialist. Network and most local station newscasters are generally involved in writing their own copy. Whether one is working as a news anchor, reporter, producer, or director, some knowledge of basic newswriting is essential.

Unlike print journalism, television newswriting does not begin with a who, what, when, where, and why approach. There isn't time to answer all of these questions immediately. Television *story leads* quickly identify the situation. Key information is usually delayed until the second sentence delivered by the newscaster. The first sentence orients the viewer to the general issue to be discussed. "Another accusation of voter fraud surfaced today" leads into a story about a close senatorial election. "Candidate Sherlock Holmes accused the committee to reelect Senator Moriarty of foul play in Baskerville County" then provides the specific information. News copy generally plays

FIGURE 4.12 Many television news stories are produced and shot in the field. A crew of a reporter, a producer, and a camera operator make up the basic electronic news-gathering (ENG) crew. In some markets a crew as small as one person or as large as five persons may make up the ENG crew.

a subservient role to accompanying sounds and pictures. Like good documentary narration, good newswriting doesn't try to compete with visual information but rather sets a context for its interpretation (Figure 4.12).

Newswriting does not have to describe what happened, when news clips are available. The writer simply sets a context for the viewing experience, establishes links or transitions between different stories, and provides a limited summary or conclusion. When commentary accompanies images and sounds, it should identify key participants. Because the camera cannot jump from one participant to another as quickly as they can be verbally identified, a descriptive phrase about each person allows sufficient time for close-ups to be edited together. The alternative to this practice is to use a less dramatic long shot, which includes all participants at once and allows them to be quickly identified as a group or, in any case, by no more than three individual identifications.

Newswriting should be simple and conversational, so that a newscaster can clearly and concisely communicate the essential information as though he or she is talking to a friend. Remember that a newscaster is an invited guest in private homes. A writer must use discretion when discussing difficult issues. Shocking or disturbingly violent visuals should be clearly identified in advance, giving children and sensitive adults an opportunity to avoid them.

Newswriters, like print reporters, must be careful to attribute information to specific sources and to protect themselves from charges of falsehood. All too often, careless TV news reporters present suppositions as facts. False broadcast news reports can have an immediate and profound effect on viewers.

The first component of a field-recorded news story to be written and recorded is usually the reporter's on-camera commentary. This commentary introduces the subject, provides bridges between various segments, and offers a summary at the end. It is used as voice-over narration to order dramatic visual images and sounds that illustrate what the reporter is talking about.

A newswriter must be concerned with pace. Numerous stories are presented during a half-hour newscast (actually 23 minutes plus commercials). Each must be cut down to minimal length in a way that retains excitement, interest, and essential information. Although a newscaster often seems calm and in control, the delivery and pace of the entire newscast must be both rapid and smooth. A television newswriter emphasizes active rather than passive verbs to increase pace and viewer interest. The sources of information must be given at the beginning of a sentence rather than at the end of a sentence for better oral communication. The order of words should result in an unambiguous interpretation of events. The purpose of a television newscast is to describe events rather than to interpret them or editorialize about them.

Each story is written as a separate computer file so that the producer can assemble the show as she or he sees fit. When the producer determines the best order of the stories, the computer files can be arranged in that order. Stories must be accurately timed. A good average reading speed is about 150 words of copy per minute. The combination of written copy and edited visuals and sounds must be precisely timed so that the total program fits into the allotted time slot. The completed script indicates if and when commercials will be inserted, and it functions as a timing and source guide to live production for the entire staff and crew. A copy of the script goes to the producer, the director, and all on-set newscasters, often called talent. The copy to be read should include phonetic spellings, so that pronunciation is understood. The script is automatically formatted in news script format and is also sent to the teleprompters on the cameras for the anchors to read. It is possible and often necessary to make last-minute changes to the script while the newscast is on the air, moments before the story being changed is seen by the anchors on the prompter.

The material a newswriter edits, rewrites, condenses, or originates comes from a variety of sources. Broadcast news often relies on wire services, such as the Associated Press. Some stories are simply downloaded from computer files provided by wire services. However, using these stories verbatim fails to establish a unique news style. Although wire services usually offer different story renditions for print and broadcast news clients, it can be quite risky to present unedited copy written by print-oriented wire-service journalists. Relying on wire-service copy also fails to provide viewers with news of local or regional interest. Assigning print journalists who have no experience with broadcast journalism to write broadcast copy can also be disastrous. Network news and the most comprehensive local news usually originate from experienced reporters in the field who are investigating specific events, issues, and topics, and who receive tips from interested participants. Local stations also keep a close eye on the print media and competing newscasts to catch up on stories they might otherwise miss. Follow-ups on major stories from preceding days are another important news source.

The news producer must determine the significance of each story and the viewer interest it is likely to arouse so that the lead story, or most important beginning segment, can be selected and the other stories coherently ordered. Which stories will actually be aired depends on a number of factors, including program length, the availability of accompanying still images or videotape, the number of major events that have occurred that day, and the producer's own preferences and priorities. A large number of stories will be written each day; some of those will actually be aired and others either presented later, if they have accompanying visuals of continuing interest, or abandoned entirely. The selected stories are usually presented in blocks that reflect geographical or topical relationships. Innate interest and importance to the audience are equally valid considerations. Many producers try to end a news program with a humorous or human-interest story.

Many factors, including the quality of the news writing, affect the selection and placement of news stories for a particular broadcast. Ordering stories in a newscast can be somewhat subjective and quite complex. The trend in commercial television broadcasting is toward many short items, rather than a few long reports on selected topics, and significant use of actual footage and flashy graphics. Although a fast-paced structure and format for a news broadcast raises many questions about the quality of in-depth understanding available to the American public on any single topic through commercial television, this approach is obviously economically advantageous to commercial broadcasters because it attracts many viewers.

Talk Show

News and entertainment functions are combined on many talk shows. Late-night talk shows are weighted toward entertainment and depend quite heavily on writers for their humorous opening monologues by the talk show host. The importance of writers for this television format was reflected by the fact that late-night talk shows were some of the first programs to be shut down during the 2007–2008 writer's strike. There are basically two types of interviews conducted on talk shows: celebrity interviews and authority interviews. Celebrity interviews are frequently seen on afternoon and evening entertainment programs. Comedy or singing performances often accompany such interviews. Celebrity interviews generally try to explore the human side of guests and coax them into revealing more about themselves than they may have initially intended. The interview can be purely a performance to entertain the audience or an occasion for self-disclosure, depending on the interviewer's success in gaining the confidence of the celebrity. Celebrity interviews almost always have a commercial purpose. The guest is often promoting a recent book, film, or television program when they appear on the *Tonight Show* or on the *Late Show with David Letterman*. Sometimes he or she simply wants to become better known to the general public. Authority interviews focus for the most part on issues, information, ideas, and attitudes rather than personalities. The interviewer's purpose is often to play devil's advocate and force the guest to clarify and substantiate a position and possibly to reveal some important detail that has been omitted in previous reports and interviews. It is not the authority's personality that is of primary interest, but his or her knowledge of and opinion on some significant topic. The authority interview comes perilously close to the celebrity interview, however, when the primary objective is simply to find a political skeleton in the guest's closet.

Writers and researchers must carefully prepare the interviewer for his or her interaction with the guest. A good interviewer is at least as well informed as the audience and has anticipated what questions audience members would ask if they could. Interviewers often write the questions they plan to ask on note cards. They then go over these cards, paring them down to a reasonable number of questions that they are confident will appeal to their audience. A good interviewer is less concerned with impressing the audience with brilliant questions than with functioning as an effective representative of the audience during the interview. Background information on the guest and topic must be thoroughly researched. But the interviewer must also be a glib respondent to unpredictable events, a careful and sensitive listener, at times a cajoler, and at other times a provocateur or a catalyst.

Although a tremendous amount of writing may be compiled before the interview, only a small fraction of it will actually be used during the interview. The interview must appear to be unrehearsed and spontaneous. Questions cannot be read from a sheet of paper. They must be presented as though they are spontaneous. A written script provides a general outline of guests to be interviewed and topics to be discussed. Introductions and background material can be written out and displayed at the appropriate time on a teleprompter, which projects copy on a see-through mirror in front of the camera lens. Cue cards are also created for the interviewer's use. A script also indicates when commercials will appear and the precise timing of the segments of a show.

Talk-show writers and interviewers, like good documentarians and newswriters, are concerned about ethical issues, such as the potential conflict between the public's right to know and the citizen's right to privacy. When a sensitive topic or personal problem is to be discussed, the interviewer must satisfy the audience's curiosity without embarrassing the guest or placing him or her in an awkward position. A good interviewer knows how to phrase questions in a tactful manner so that the guest is not offended, although the audience's curiosity and expectations are fully satisfied. Indirect methods of questioning can be quite effective, and they raise fewer ethical dilemmas about pressuring a private citizen into revealing more personal details than he or she really cares to have the public know.

Barbara Walters, in discussing her celebrity-interviewing techniques, has said that she often uses indirect methods of questioning. For example, she felt that it would be in bad taste to ask Mamie Eisenhower, the former president's widow, any direct question about her supposed problem with alcohol. Instead, she simply asked Mrs. Eisenhower if there was ever a time that she felt concerned about her public impressions in the White House. Mrs. Eisenhower revealed that she had an inner ear problem that sometimes caused her to lose her balance and that the press had misinterpreted this as a sign of alcoholism.

Commercials and Public Service Announcements

Commercials are brief messages that advertise products, company names, and services. Unlike many other types of nonfiction, commercials aim directly at modifying audience behavior and attitudes. The chief test of a commercial's success is not whether people watch and enjoy it. The true test is whether people buy a specific product or are positively predisposed toward a particular company. Commercials are primarily persuasive; they are informative only to the extent that audiences become aware of the existence of new products and services or corporate goodwill.

Commercials vary considerably in terms of their production values and formats. Network commercials and national spot commercials (network-level commercials aired on local stations in major markets) are generally written and controlled by major advertising companies, such as Leo Burnett, J. Walter Thompson, and McCann-Erickson. These companies oversee all aspects of the creation of a commercial from writing, through storyboarding, to actual production by an independent production company. They are often shot on 35 mm film, and budgets can run as high as several hundred thousand dollars. On the local level, commercials are usually made on videotape by a television station or by a small production studio. The people who produce local commercials often write them as well. Many regional and local commercial producers use digital production effects and transitions as well as computer graphics, whether the commercial was originally shot on film or videotape.

The first step in writing a commercial is to establish the main goal. In most cases the goal is to sell a specific product or service, but some commercials sell corporate goodwill. Public utilities do not always compete directly with other companies supplying the same type of power or service. They nonetheless need to maintain a positive public image, if only to obtain periodic rate increases. Targeting a goal for products, services, or corporate goodwill is helpful in terms of selecting a specific selling strategy.

Commercial scriptwriters rely quite heavily on advertising research to determine the best way to sell a product or service. Audience testing and positioning often dictate the look and selling approach of a television commercial. Positioning refers to the most effective means of reaching prospective buyers for a product or service. Audience testing and positioning determine the overall approach that a writer should take, how a commercial will look, and how it will communicate to a selected target audience. Market research reveals the best selling strategy.

Writers of commercials try to define three things before they begin writing the script: the intended audience, the major selling points of the product, and the best strategy or format with which to sell the product. The audience can be defined generally or specifically in demographic terms of sex, age, race, socioeconomic status, and so on. Airtime for the presentation of the commercial can be selected on the basis of this well-defined target audience. The writer must be familiar with the types of expressions and selling techniques that will appeal to the intended audience. Advertising agencies conduct research before actual writing begins, trying to ascertain why a particular group of people likes or uses a product and why others do not. A commercial is usually designed to broaden the appeal of the product without alienating the current users or consumers. Writing a commercial requires a firm understanding of the specific product or service that is being sold. Listing the major selling points of the product will help the writer to select those elements that appeal primarily to the main target audience and to determine the best selling format, whether it is a hard sell or a soft sell, a serious or a humorous tone, a testimonial, or a dramatization.

Both hard-sell and soft-sell commercials are used to promote specific products. They are usually based on a careful study of the nature of the product and its appeal. Consumer testing reveals that a hard sell works well with automobiles and soap products, for example. An aggressive pitch does not turn off potential customers. Many soap-product commercials present "real-life" dramatizations that end in a hard sell from a typical consumer who is satisfied with the product. Other products rely on a soft sell or less direct appeal. They create a particular image that entices consumers to seek beauty aids or brand-name clothing in order to have a more satisfying social life. A commercial can create an attractive image that is associated with the product and that the customer aspires to emulate. This approach often reinforces social stereotypes, such as traditional or emerging trends in male and female roles. Commercials generally reinforce the status quo because advertisers are afraid of offending potential customers. Testimonials, which are celebrity endorsements of a product or service, often rely on hard-sell techniques. Dramatizations, except in the soap products, usually offer a more direct approach. The viewer is left to his or her own conclusions about why someone is so attractive, successful, or satisfied.

Generally, humorous treatments work well in some cases but not others. Humorous treatments of products or services related to death, personal hygiene, or profound social problems are generally in poor taste and can be offensive to audiences and thus counterproductive. Humor can be used effectively to deflate the sophisticated image of a specialized foreign product, such as Grey Poupon mustard, or to associate a product with fun and good times, as McDonald's commercials have done. Humor can create amusement and attention, but if poorly handled it can also distract attention from the product or company name. Appropriate use of humor generally requires talented performers. A variety of means can be used to help the audience remember the product or company name, such as simple name repetition or a song with a catchy phrase or slogan, called a *jingle*. Many commercials begin with the creation of a song to which the visual elements will be edited. The lyrics and music are frequently performed by top-name musicians and performers, and they often set the tone and pace for the entire commercial. The emphasis in jingles is on repeatable phrases that will help the consumer remember the product or company name.

Commercials are often extensively tested on audiences and potential consumers before any purchase of expensive airtime. The objective of most scientific tests is to determine the effect of the commercial on product recall or name retention. It is assumed that if viewers can recall the product or company name, they are likely to buy the product. Other tests examine actual or simulated purchasing behavior, such as the opportunity to select a soft drink from among several competing products after viewing commercials. Sometimes several versions of a commercial may be tested, only the most effective of which will actually be used.

Written or spoken advertising copy must be clear, succinct, concrete, and active. Clarity is of utmost importance. If the message is to be understood, it must be expressed in terms that the average viewer can easily comprehend. Time for commercials is both limited and expensive, so the message must be short and direct. There is no time for wasted words that distract attention from the central point. It is usually best to use concrete nouns and adjectives, as well as active verbs. Passive verbs are too tentative and rarely help sell products. Writers of commercials try to use words that will be popular with the anticipated audience and consumer. Key words or *buzzwords*, such as "natural" or "no artificial ingredients," can increase the appeal of a product for potential buyers, despite the fact that chemists often consider such words to be imprecisely applied to soft drinks and food, as few edible substances are actually artificial.

A *storyboard* is a preproduction tool consisting of a series of drawings and accompanying written information. In some ways a storyboard is similar to a comic strip. The storyboard tells the commercial story or message in still pictures. Narration or dialogue, camera movements, sound effects, and music are usually specified under or next to each frame. An advertising agency usually creates a storyboard to show clients and producers what a commercial will look like. The storyboard suggests how images and sounds will be ordered, the placement of the camera, and the design of the set. Today, computer storyboard programs or programs that combine both word processing and a storyboard segment provide a flexible and efficient method of creating and editing scoreboards. As commercial production moves toward HDTV, storyboards for HDTV are drawn 16 units wide by 9 units high to match the 16:9 ratio of the widescreen format.

Directors sometimes use storyboards along with the script as a guide to the actual recording of the finished commercial on film or videotape, and their use is highly recommended for any type of production for which step-by-step planning is possible. Many feature film directors compose their shots on storyboards before actual production. A television storyboard consists of four elements: hand-drawn sketches, camera positions and movements, dialogue or narration, and sound effects or music. Each hand-drawn sketch is composed within a frame that has the same proportions as a television screen (4 units wide by 3 units high, a ratio of 4:3). A frame is drawn for each shot. Camera positions and movements, lines of dialogue or narration, and sound effects (SFX) and music are specified under or next to each frame.

A public service announcement, or PSA, is produced much like a commercial. PSAs are usually aired free of charge by commercial broadcasting stations, and most noncommercial stations offer no other form of announcements. PSAs often promote nonprofit organizations. They can attempt to raise public awareness of specific social problems and social service agencies and are usually persuasive in the sense that they have clear behavioral objectives, such as appeals for help or money. In the case of a social need or charity event, the emphasis is usually on developing audience empathy for people in need rather than on appealing to the audience's materialistic needs and drives.

The writing of a PSA is virtually identical to that of a commercial. The same steps and procedures can be followed, including researching the particular organization or cause, specifying the goal, matching the selling or promotional strategy to the intended audience, and creating a storyboard. PSAs offer an opportunity for students and beginning production people to obtain valuable experience in writing and production, because they are usually produced on very low budgets and incur few, if any, expensive airtime costs.

Instructional Films and Videos

Instructional films and videos often serve one of the following purposes: to supplement lectures in the classroom; to inform the public and government employees about new government policies; or to inform employees or the public about corporate practices, policies, and points of view. These three purposes reflect the institutional needs of producers in educational, government, and corporate environments, respectively. Instructional programs are designed as either supplementary or primary materials. They may accompany an educational, government, or corporate speech, or they may have to stand on their own without the help of a person who can set a context for viewing or answering questions.

The most important factor in planning instructional programs is to understand the needs, expectations, and level of knowledge of the audience. Groups with different demographics (age, socioeconomic status, and educational level) often require entirely different instructional strategies. A 4-year-old child requires a different approach than a 10-year-old. Although the overall objective of any instructional program is to impart knowledge, effective communication depends on the writer's awareness of the audience's sophistication, age, and educational level. A writer must use terms with which the audience is already familiar or define new terms in words that the audience already understands.

Instructional information must be clear and well organized. Each step or concept must follow logically from preceding steps and concepts. Suppose, for example, that a program is designed to instruct beginning photography students about basic concepts of developing film. It is logical to begin with a description and graphic demonstration of a piece of film, showing the various light-sensitive layers and substances. The camera can be described next, along with the process of exposing the film to light. Finally, the stages of developing and printing the film, using different chemicals and pieces of equipment, can each be described sequentially. A short review of the fundamental steps then summarizes the overall process.

An instructional program must be more than clear and logical, however. It must graphically demonstrate concepts and ideas. Otherwise, what is the point of making a videotape or film? Cross-sections of a piece of film and the working parts of a camera can be drawn. Actual scenes might be shot in a photographic darkroom under red lights, which give the impression of a darkroom setting but provide sufficient light for recording purposes. A photographer can actually demonstrate the various stages of developing and printing photographic images, so that students are brought out of the classroom into an actual work environment. Educational films and videotapes present materials that cannot be easily demonstrated through a lecture or the use of other less-expensive media, such as slides, audiotapes, or graphic projections. Moving images should move. There is no justification for using film or videotape recording for something that can be done just as well and much less expensively with still pictures. Noted communications researcher Carl I. Howland's experiment comparing slides and lectures with movies as teaching devices demonstrated that slides and lectures were better, not just less expensive. Of course, motion is an important component of many educational subjects. The narration that accompanies this graphic material must be concise, clear, and easily comprehended. A sense of drama, like a sense of humor, can add interest and excitement, but it can also be overdone. The main objective is to show rather than tell. The narration should be authoritative, but not condescending. It must impart accurate information, link various parts of the demonstration, and establish a context within which the accompanying images can be clearly and completely understood.

Interactive Learning and Training

Writing for interactive multimedia educational applications is an important aspect of authoring. *Authoring* includes everything from designing a flowchart for the interactive learning or training process to writing actual text that will appear on a computer monitor when the application is run. Authoring begins with the development of an interactive training concept. An author clarifies the training concept and specifies the intended audience, the purpose of the application, and the basic subject matter by writing a treatment document, which provides a narrative description of the proposed project. The treatment may also indicate the anticipated platforms (Mac, PC, and so on), operating systems (Mac OS 10, Windows Vista, XP, and so on), style (command or object), and interface (text based or graphical). Like a treatment for an interactive game, the latter information defines the authoring environment, that is, the computer hardware and software that will be used to design the application as well as the intended avenues of its distribution. This aspect of authoring is also similar to a producer's development of a proposal and treatment for a (noninteractive) film or video. The author defines the objectives for a project and the means by which those objectives will be accomplished (Figure 4.13).

The scriptwriting phase of interactive educational multimedia production, similar in many respects to authoring or writing computer games and other forms of interactive entertainment, is sometimes referred to as the *design stage*. The purpose of the design stage is to provide an architectural blueprint for the overall project that will

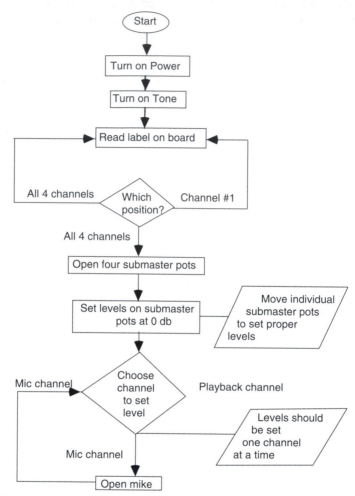

SETTING LOUDNESS LEVEL ON AUDIO CONTROL BOARD

FIGURE 4.13 An interactive program diagram shows the various paths or choices that the person using the program has to follow. Arrows indicate directions that the paths may take in moving forward, retracing, or starting a new path.

guide the selection and arrangement of content. Creating a design can take the form of flowcharting as well as actual scriptwriting. A flowchart indicates the possible avenues that a student can pursue to acquire information or to be trained in the use of various hardware or software. A fixed flowchart on paper can become complex and somewhat confusing when there are many interactive choices and options that result in numerous intersecting lines. Using computer software for authoring, which includes screen icons that move the flowchart to different levels by means of double-clicking a mouse pointer on an icon, can increase the clarity and flexibility of a flowchart.

The script for an interactive learning or training application indicates all the content that will appear in the completed project, including graphics, animation, video, and audio, as well as written text. The flowchart provides an overview of the program architecture and interactive training options, whereas script material added to the flowchart indicates in some detail all of the content that will appear at various points along the flowchart. Descriptions of visual images and sounds are generally kept to a minimum. Various icon symbols are often used to indicate repeated (as opposed to unique) sounds, graphic images, animation sequences, and live-action video that will appear at different points along the flowchart. Text may appear as spoken narration or written text that accompanies visual images and sounds. For example, CD-ROMs and DVD/Blu-ray discs of music videos or feature films can include written text that provides additional information about its production. An interactive CD-ROM or DVD/Blu-ray disc can also allow a student to manipulate various components, such as remixing the sound or altering special effects in the image. In this case, a viewer/listener becomes an active participant in the creative process and learns how to control sounds and images through hands-on experience. Educational multimedia products can also provide written text in the form of specific questions and correct or incorrect answers to these questions, which test a student's knowledge, providing immediate feedback. Several incorrect responses might indicate to a student that he or she needs to repeat one section before going on to the next.

Interactive multimedia provides obvious educational advantages over published manuals and textbooks that an author or scriptwriter should utilize whenever possible. Because some students are primarily auditory learners and others learn better through visual or tactile stimulation, authors should make some attempt to vary the form of media presentation. Sometimes media redundancy—that is, conveying similar information using audio, visual, and hands-on interaction—can be extremely effective for all types of learners. Authors should also allow for different learning rates or speeds of information acquisition. Flowcharts should provide enough options to facilitate the learning process for students who learn relatively quickly or slowly.

Summary

Scriptwriting can be divided into two basic categories: fiction and nonfiction. Every scriptwriter should be familiar with the basic elements of both fiction and nonfiction writing. Principles of dramatic and narrative structure used in fiction may also be applicable to nonfiction, and principles of rhetorical persuasion and expository structures used in nonfiction can be helpful in a dramatic production. Elements of dramatic, narrative, rhetorical, and expository structure are of practical value to scriptwriters working in a variety of areas and formats.

Scriptwriting demands visual thinking. Scriptwriters know how to use the full creative potential of moving images and sounds. Preparation for scriptwriting includes performing research and writing a treatment. Research is a creative process of uncovering new sources of information. A synopsis of the story or subject matter is called a treatment. A treatment provides a summary of the project in short-story form. It provides an outline of the script that can serve as a guide for future writing.

There are three basic script formats: full-page master scene, split-page, and semi-scripted.

Dramatic films and television programs can be plotted into a framework that consists of a basic three-act structure and a series of rising and falling actions, which culminate in a climax and resolution. Dramatic structure includes rising actions and falling actions, text, and subtext.

Fictional stories are usually told or narrated by someone. Narrative structure has two basic elements: time and point of view.

Dramatic narratives develop characters and themes. Characters' values reveal themselves through actions and words. The writer's job is to externalize these values through speech, mannerisms, and actions.

Nonfiction scripts often convey information about actual events. Nonfiction scriptwriters work in a variety of formats, including documentary, news and talk shows, commercials, and educational programs, such as interactive multimedia applications. They make frequent use of expository and rhetorical structures to convey information and to make persuasive appeals to an audience.

Arguments are fashioned on the basis of rhetorical strategies. Rhetorical strategies and approaches can also be distinguished on the basis of whether the argument focuses on its source, its subject, or the viewer.

A nonfiction scriptwriter relies on expository structures that help to organize information in a logical manner. Widely used expository structures include effects-to-causes, problem/solution, enumeration, classification into logical categories, and theme/countertheme.

Narration needs to be written so that it can be effectively spoken.

Short nonfiction formats include news stories, talk shows, and commercials. A newswriter's job is to organize a story and to describe events in a straightforward, clear, and succinct way. There are basically two types of talk show interviews: celebrity interviews and authority interviews. Commercials are brief messages that are broadcast as persuasive appeals.

Instructional films and videos must be clear and well organized. Writers must rely on terms and concepts that will be easily comprehended by the appropriate educational level or demographic group to which the instructional material is directed.

The script for an interactive learning or training application indicates all the content that will appear in the completed project, including graphics, animation, video, and audio, as well as written text. A flowchart provides an overview of the program's architecture and interactive training options. Interactive multimedia can be tailored to meet the needs of students who are primarily auditory, visual, or tactile learners.

EXERCISES

1. Write a synopsis of a short, five-minute script of a simple drama.

2. Write the script from Exercise 1 in a single column full-master script format. Second, reorganize the script in a two-column format. Finally, organize the material into a semiscripted format.

3. Outline the script into three acts.

4. Choose a favorite fairytale or short story, and write a script adaptation.

5. Choose a controversial topic of the day, research the topic, and then write an eight-minute script in the model used by the CBS-TV program *60 Minutes*.

6. Using a product you use, write three 30-second commercials. Each one should use a different selling strategy.

Additional Readings

Bernard, Sheila Curran. 2007. Documentary Storytelling, Making Stronger and More Dramatic Nonfiction Films, Focal Press, Boston.

Cook, Martie. 2007. Write to TV: Out of Your Head and onto the Screen, Focal Press, Boston.

Cooper, Pat, Dancyger, Ken. 2005. Writing the Short Film, third ed. Focal Press, Boston.

Dancyger, Ken, Rush, Jeff. 2007. Alternative Scriptwriting: Successfully Breaking the Rules, Focal Press, Boston.

De Abreu, Carlos, Smith, Howard Jay. 1995. Opening the Doors to Hollywood: How to Sell Your Idea/Story, Custos Morum, Beverly Hills, CA.

DiZazzo, Ray. 2000. Corporate Media Production, Focal Press, Boston.

Em, Michele. 1994. The ever-changing story: Writing for the interactive market. Journal of the Writers Guild of America West, June, 16–21.

Emm, Adele. 2001. Researching for Television and Radio, Routledge, New York.

Field, Syd. 1984. Screenplay: The Foundations of Screenwriting, DTP.

Garrand, Timothy. 2006. Writing for Multimedia and the Web, third ed. Focal Press, Boston.

Johnson, Claudia H. 2000. Crafting Short Screenplays That Connect, Focal Press, Boston.

Luther, Arch C. 1992. Designing Interactive Multimedia, Bantam Books, New York.

MacDermott, Felim, McGrath, Declan. 2003. Screenwriting: Screencraft Series, Focal Press, Boston.

Marx, Christy. 2007. Writing for Animation, Comics, and Games, Focal Press, Boston.

Miller, Carolyn Handler. 2008. Digital Storytelling: A Creator's Guide to Interactive Entertainment, Focal Press, Boston.

Musburger, Robert B. 2007. An Introduction to Writing for Electronic Media: Scriptwriting Essentials Across the Genres, Focal Press, Boston.

Rabiger, Michael. 2006. Developing Story Ideas, second ed. Focal Press, Boston.

Rosenthal, Alan. 2003. Writing, Directing, and Producing Documentary Films, third ed. Southern Illinois University Press, Carbondale, IL.

Rosenthal, Alan. 1995. Writing Docudrama, Focal Press, Boston.

Thompson, Kristin. 1999. Storytelling in the New Hollywood: Understanding Classical Narrative Technique, Harvard University Press, Cambridge.

Van Nostran, William J. 2000. The Media Writer's Guide: Writing for Business and Educational Programming, Focal Press, Boston.

Directing: Aesthetic Principles and Production Coordination

- What are directing aesthetics approaches?

- How do shots vary?

- What does composition mean to a director?

- How are shots combined into sequences and scenes?

- How do single- and multiple-camera directing differ?

Introduction

Video and film directors are artists who can take a completed script and imaginatively transform it into exciting sounds and images. Directors creatively organize many facets of production to produce works of art. They know how and when to use different types of camera shots and have mastered the use of composition, image qualities, transition devices, and relations of time and space. Directors know when and how to use different types of sound and how to control sound and image interaction. They understand how to work with people, especially actors and various creative staff and crew members. Above all, they know how to tell good stories. By using all of their creative powers, directors are able to produce films and video programs that have lasting value.

A director may concentrate on a sound production—including radio drama, commercial, or documentary—as director of a soundtrack for a visual production or as a director of a music recording. In those cases, the responsibilities are similar to those of a visual director. Of course, the energy of the director is aimed at melding the voice, music, and sound effects all into a coherent whole matching the meaning of the script. Directing a sound production involves fewer people, less equipment, and, even with digital operations, far less complex operations than a visual production. In some cases, the term "producer" is substituted for "director" in sound productions, as many of the responsibilities of both directing and producing are combined under one person.

As with sound, multimedia, interactive, and animation productions, directors often accept multilevel responsibilities in addition to their primary functions as director. The multichannel nature of these productions requires a different mental set requiring concentration on more than the one aspect of simultaneous action and movement. Multiple directors in such productions often fulfill the multichannel responsibilities, as is often the case in feature length animated films and complex games.

Directors prepare a shooting script by indicating specific types of images and sounds to be recorded within each scene. Armed with a final shooting script, a director is ready to organize production. To record the different scenes and sequences described in the script, the director must organize the activities of many different people who are involved in production. The role of the director is quite different in multiple-camera versus single-camera productions. The director must be able to communicate precisely and quickly with cast and crew. Each person must be able to understand and follow a specific communication system and language as it is directed at him or her. This chapter covers each of these facets of the director's responsibility in the production process. The director usually selects and organizes images and sounds according to one of the three basic aesthetic approaches introduced in Chapter 2, The Production Process: Analog and Digital Technologies.

AESTHETIC APPROACHES

A convenient way to organize *aesthetics*, or approaches to the creative process, is to use three very general categories: realism, modernism, and postmodernism. Most artistic approaches reflect one or more of these three aesthetic tendencies, which differ in their emphases on function, form, and content. *Function* refers to why something is expressed: its goal or purpose. *Form* can be thought of as how something is expressed in a work of art. *Content* refers to what is expressed. Function, form, and content are closely connected aspects of any creative work.

Aesthetics
- Function—Why
- Form—How
- Content—What
- Realism—Content over form
- Modernism—Form over function
- Postmodernism—Audience's involvement over artist's form and content

Realism

Realism stresses content more than form. In realist works, artists use forms and techniques that do not call attention to themselves, or a so-called transparent style. Realist artists depict a world of common experience as naturally as possible. Smooth, continuous camera movements and actions, continuity of time and place, and the use of actual locations and real people (i.e., nonactors) help to sustain a sense of reality. Realist art relies on conventions that some artists and viewers believe will preserve an illusion of reality. Although realist techniques and conventions change, as in the shift from black-and-white to color images for added realism in photography, film, and television during the 1950s and 1960s, the mimetic tradition of art and literature imitating reality and the intent to preserve an illusion of reality in Western art has persisted over time. A realist artist is a selector and organizer of common experience, rather than a self-conscious manipulator of abstract forms, principles, and ideas.

Many prime-time network television dramas, such as *CSI* and *Law and Order*, and nonfiction programs, such as *60 Minutes*, *48 Hours*, and *20/20*, select and organize common experience as naturally as possible. Continuity of space and time is evident even in the titles of some of these programs, such as *48 Hours*. Forms and techniques rarely call attention to themselves. Instead a transparent but dramatic style helps to depict worlds of common experience and sustain an illusion of reality.

Modernism

Modernism stresses the idea that form is more important than function. Creators of avant-garde works of video and film art explore their medium beyond the usual restrictions and limitations of a realist approach without considering the illusion of reality. A modernist director's works show less objectivity, tend to explore feelings of ambiguity, and may lack continuity in space and time. Many music video productions and some science fiction programs may be classified as modernist.

Some European feature film directors, such as Ingmar Bergman in Sweden and Luis Bunuel in Spain and France, have used modernist aesthetics to guide their approaches to filmmaking. Bergman's film *Persona* (1966), for example, offers a collage of images that reflect the psychological states of mind of an actress who refuses to speak and a nurse who is trying to take care of her both inside and outside a Swedish mental hospital. Their personalities and faces seem to merge during the course of the film. The editing of this film and the world that Bergman depicts often conform more closely to internal mental states than they do to an external illusion of physical reality. Space and time are often discontinuous. Luis Bunuel's early surrealist avant-garde film *Un Chien Andalou* (*An Andalusian Dog*, 1929), which he co-directed with the surrealist painter Salvador Dali, and his later narrative feature films, such as *The Discreet Charm of the Bourgeoisie* (1973) and *Tristana* (1970) or *Viridiana* (1961), often defy logic and rational thought as well as continuity in space and time. The surrealist world that Bunuel depicts allows the irrational thoughts and unconscious feelings and desires of his characters to be freely exposed at the same time that it makes a satirical comment on social conventions and institutional religious practices. Ingmar Bergman and Luis Bunuel are strongly personal, modern artists who sometimes stress style more than content and explore feelings of ambiguity and interior states of mind in their films rather than present an external illusion of reality.

Postmodernism

Postmodernism stresses viewer participation within open-ended works with vaguely defined characteristics. A scattered blending or pastiche of new and old images, genres, and production techniques may intentionally confuse the audience, yet at the same time attempt to emotionally and sometimes interactively involve viewers or listeners in the creation of texts rather than treat them as passive consumers of entertainment. Film and video directing and production in the postmodernist mode continue to evolve, and their precise definitions remain somewhat elusive.

An example of a postmodernist work is Peter Gabriel's CD-ROM titled *Explora 1 Peter Gabriel's Secret World* (1993), which was developed and directed by Peter Gabriel, Steve Nelson, Michael Coulson, Nichola Bruce, and Mic Large. This interactive CD-ROM contains Peter Gabriel's music and music videos as well as minidocumentaries about the artist and the production of his works, including information about performing artists with whom Gabriel has collaborated as well as other visual artists. Viewers and listeners control the sequence and duration in which the entertainment and information contained on this CD-ROM are presented in the "INTERACT" mode, whereas the "WATCH" mode takes them on a guided journey through the disk. Viewers and listeners have to correctly put together an image of Peter Gabriel to gain entry and to select different worlds to explore and different areas with which to interact. In one section, viewers and listeners can even add or subtract different musicians and control the sound levels of the audio mix for a selection from Peter Gabriel's music during an interactive recording session. The ways in which this CD-ROM combines animation, live action, and documentary recordings, information, and entertainment and the "INTERACT" and "WATCH" modes of presentation clearly offer a postmodernist approach to directing that directly involves the viewer and listener in the creative process.

Realism, modernism, and postmodernism are not mutually exclusive, nor do they exhaust all aesthetic possibilities, but they offer a convenient means of organizing the field of aesthetics from the standpoint of production. The relation of expressive forms and techniques to program content and purposes often reflects these three general tendencies. They are applicable to all the aspects of production that will be covered in the following sections, including visualization, lighting, and set design, as well as postproduction editing.

VISUALIZATION

The director decides what types of pictures should be used to tell the story specified in a script by considering the choices available. The visualization process includes an analysis of the types of shots possible, composing those shots, and deciding how to combine the shots visually and with the proper sounds into a comprehensive whole. The visualization process follows in interactive, animation, and multimedia productions as in linear film or TV production.

A director's ability to select and control visual images begins with an understanding of specific types of shots. The camera can be close to or far away from the subject. It can remain stationary or move during a shot. The shots commonly used in video and film production can be described in terms of camera-to-subject distance, camera angle, camera (or lens) movement, and shot duration.

Types of Shots

Long Shot (LS)

The long shot orients the audience to subjects, objects, and settings by viewing them from a distance; this term is sometimes used synonymously with the terms *establishing shot, wide shot*, or *full shot*. An establishing shot (ES) generally locates the camera at a sufficient distance to establish the setting. Place and time are clearly depicted. A full shot (FS) provides a full frame (head-to-toe) view of a human subject or subjects (Figure 5.1). Extreme long shots in production for micro displays such as cell phones and iPods are not as effective because the small detail will be lost on the small-low resolution screen.

Medium Shot (MS)

A medium shot provides approximately a three-quarter (knee-to-head) view of the subject. The extremes in terms of camera-to-subject distance within this type of shot are sometimes referred to as a *medium long shot* (MLS) and a *medium close-up* (MCU) (Figure 5.2). The terms *two-shot* and *three-shot* define medium shots in which two or three subjects, respectively, appear in the same frame.

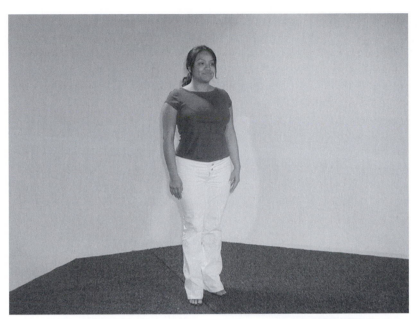

FIGURE 5.1 A long shot (LS) may refer to the framing of a human figure from head to foot, or the longest shot in the sequence.

FIGURE 5.2 A medium shot (MS) may refer to the framing of a human from the head to just below the knees, or a shot framing two persons, sometimes called a two-shot.

Close Shot (CS) or Close-Up (CU)

The terms *close shot* and *close-up* are often used synonymously. A close-up refers to the isolation of elements in the shot and normally indicates the head and shoulders of a person. When someone is making an important or revealing statement or facial gesture, a close-up will draw the audience's attention to that event. Close-ups focus and direct attention and create dramatic emphasis. When they are overused, how-ever, their dramatic impact is severely reduced. A very close camera position is some-times called an *extreme close-up* (ECU). See Figures 5.1, 5.2, and 5.3 for illustrations of long, medium, and close-up shots, respectively. There are times when the standard nomenclature of framing is not appropriate. If the widest shot in a program is from a

FIGURE 5.3 A close-up (CU) may refer to the framing of a person from the top of the head to just below the neckline, or if framing an object, filling the frame with the object.

FIGURE 5.4 A point-of-view (POV) refers to framing as if the observer were viewing from inside the camera or if the camera lens represented what a character would be viewing from his or her position in the set.

FIGURE 5.5 An over-the-shoulder (OS) refers to a two-shot from behind one of the subjects who is facing the other subject. Generally the framing is a medium shot.

blimp and the tightest shot is of one football player, then the blimp shot would be the LS and the player shot would be a CU. Conversely, if the entire commercial is shot in close-ups, the tightest shot would be an ECU, and the widest shot would be an LS, even if it were only a shot of a hand holding a product.

Camera Angle

The camera angle is frequently used to establish a specific viewpoint, such as to involve the audience in sharing a particular character's perspective on the action. The goal may be to enhance identification with that person's psychological or philosophical point of view (Figures 5.6, 5.7, 5.8).

Point-of-View Shot (POV Shot)

A point-of-view shot places the camera in the approximate spatial positioning of a specific character. It is often preceded by a shot of a character looking in a particular direction, which establishes the character's spatial point of view within the setting, followed by a shot of that same character's reaction to what he or she has seen. The latter shot is sometimes called a reaction shot. A closely related shot is the *over-the-shoulder shot* (OS). The camera is positioned so that the shoulder of one subject appears in the foreground and the face or body of another is in the background. Another variation on the point-of-view shot is the *subjective shot*, which shows us what the person is looking at or thinking about. Like point-of-view shots, subjective shots offer a nonobjective viewpoint on actions and events and can enhance audience identification with more subjective points of view (Figures 5.4 and 5.5).

Reverse-Angle Shot

A reverse-angle shot places the camera in exactly the opposite direction of the previous shot. The camera is moved in a 180-degree arc from the shot immediately preceding it.

FIGURE 5.6 A low-angle shot is the view from a camera positioned well below the eye level of the subject looking up at the subject.

FIGURE 5.7 A high-angle shot is the view from a camera positioned well above the eye level of the subject looking down on the subject.

Stationary versus Mobile Camera Shots

An objectively recorded scene in a drama establishes a point of view that conforms to the audience's main focus of interest in the unfolding events. This objective placement of cameras can still be quite varied. A director can use a continuously moving camera gliding through the scene to follow the key action. This approach establishes

FIGURE 5.8 Among many other means of mounting either film or video cameras is the gyroscope mount, which can be mounted on an airplane, helicopter, or any moving vehicle. The stabilizing system provides a solid, smooth picture, and the operator inside the vehicle can pan, tilt, and zoom the camera as the shot requires.

a point of view that is quite different from recording a scene from several stationary camera positions. Both approaches can be objective in the sense that neither attempts to present a specific person's point of view, although a moving camera creates a greater feeling of participation and involvement as the audience moves through the setting with the camera.

A moving camera adds new information to the frame and often alters spatial perspective. A moving camera shot can maintain viewer interest for a longer period of time than a stationary camera shot. But a moving camera shot can also create difficulties. It is often difficult to cut from a moving camera shot to a stationary camera shot. The camera should be held still for a moment at the beginning and end of a moving camera shot so that it can easily be intercut with other shots. One moving camera shot can follow another so long as the direction and speed of movement remain the same. Both moving the camera and cutting from one stationary camera shot to another can give us a spatial impression of the setting from a variety of perspectives, but the former generates feelings of smoothness and relaxation, and the latter creates an impression of roughness and tension, which can be used effectively to stimulate a feeling of disorientation, as in the film *Natural Born Killers* (1994). Many types of mobile camera shots can be recorded with the camera remaining in a relatively fixed position. Depending on the type of digital camera and compression used in the camera, artifacts may be created by rapid movement of the camera.

Pan Shot

A camera can be panned by simply pivoting it from side to side on a fixed tripod or panning device. This shot is often used to follow action without having to move the camera from its fixed floor position. A pan is always a horizontal movement.

Tilt Shot

A camera tilt is accomplished by moving the camera up and down on a swivel or tilting device. This shot is also used to follow action, such as a person standing up or sitting down. It can also be used to follow and accentuate the apparent height of a building, object, or person. A tilt is always a vertical movement.

Pedestal Shot

A camera can be physically moved up and down on a pedestal dolly. A hydraulic lift moves the camera vertically up and down within the shot, such as when a performer gets up from a chair or sits down. A pedestal shot allows the camera to remain consistently at the same height as the performer, unlike a tilt shot, where the camera height usually remains unchanged. Pedestal shots are rare, but a pedestal is often used to adjust the height of the camera between shots (Figure 5.9).

Zoom Shot

A zoom can be effected by changing the focal length of a variable focal-length lens in midshot. A zoom shot differs from a dolly shot in that a dolly shot alters spatial perspective by actually changing the spatial positioning of objects within the frame. During a zoom shot, the apparent distance between objects appears to change because objects are enlarged or contracted in size at different rates. During a *zoom-in*, objects appear to get closer together, and during a *zoom-out*, they seem to get farther apart. Other types of mobile camera shots require camera supports that can be physically moved about the studio.

FIGURE 5.9 A studio pedestal is designed to allow the heavy weight of a studio camera, lens, and prompter to be moved about the studio with relative ease. The direction of the wheels under the skirt of the pedestal can be changed to allow the camera to be guided in any direction. The vertical pedestal column is counterweighted or controlled by compressed air to allow the operator to raise or lower the camera easily and smoothly. The pan head is mounted on the top of the pedestal column. (Courtesy of KCTS 9, Seattle.)

Dolly Shot

A dolly shot is a shot in which the camera moves toward or away from the subject while secured to a movable platform on wheels. It is often needed to follow long or complicated movements of performers or to bring us gradually closer to or farther away from a person or object.

Trucking Shot

In a trucking shot, the camera is moved laterally (from side to side) on a wheeled dolly. The camera may truck with a moving subject to keep it in frame. If the dolly moves in a semicircular direction, the shot is sometimes referred to as an *arc* or *camera arc*.

Tracking Shot

A tracking shot uses tracks laid over rough surfaces to provide a means of making smooth camera moves in otherwise impossible locations.

Crane or Boom Shot

The camera can be secured to a crane or boom so that it can be raised and lowered or moved from side to side on a pivoting arm. This type of shot can create a dramatic effect when it places the subject in the context of a large interior space or a broad exterior vista.

COMPOSITION

Composition is a term used by painters, graphic artists, and still photographers to define the way in which images can be effectively structured within a frame. Frame dimensions or the aspect ratio of the specific media format affect the composition. Two basic principles of composition that will be discussed in Chapter 11 are symmetry and closure. Composition is complicated by the fact that video and film images move in time. Therefore, composition is constantly changing.

Aspect Ratio

A frame limits the outer borders of the image to specific dimensions. The ratio of these dimensions—that is, the ratio of a frame's width to its height—is called the aspect ratio of the frame. Composition is obviously slightly different for different aspect ratios. If you were to put identical paintings in frames with different dimensions and aspect ratios, for example, the paintings would look very different: the relations between the shapes and objects or the composition within the frames would not be the same. American analog video, standard digital video (SD), Super-8mm, 16mm, and standard 35mm film all have the same aspect ratio: 4:3 or 1.33:1. But feature films in Super-16mm, 35mm, and 65mm, which are made for wide-screen projection in theaters, have aspect ratios that vary from 1.85:1 to 2.35:1.

High-definition TV (HDTV) is set at 16 × 9, or 1.78:1, which closely approximates the 1.85:1 academy aperture feature film format or aspect ratio. Wide-screen images can enhance an illusion of reality by involving more of our peripheral or edge vision, but they also alter the aesthetics of object placement and composition within the frame. Consider the different impressions created by a wide gulf between two characters on a wide-screen frame and the greater proximity of two characters in a video frame. It is difficult to copy or transfer visuals from one aspect ratio to another intact, as in copying magazine photographs with a video camera or showing a wide-screen film on television (Figure 5.10).

ASPECT RATIO – ESSENTIAL AREA

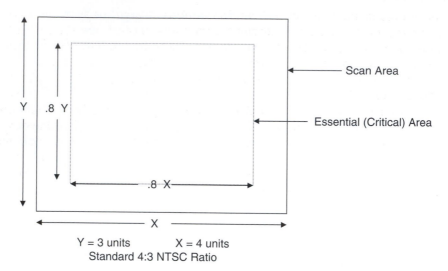

Y = 3 units   X = 4 units
Standard 4:3 NTSC Ratio

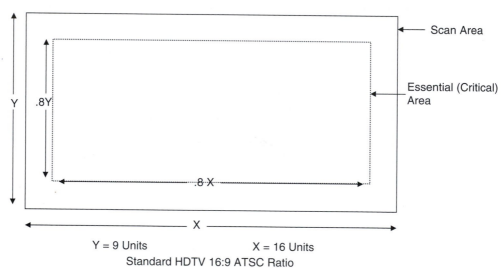

Y = 9 Units   X = 16 Units
Standard HDTV 16:9 ATSC Ratio

FIGURE 5.10 The aspect ratio is the ratio of the width (X-axis) of a frame to the height (Y-axis). The NTSC television and traditional film ratio is 4 units × 3 units. The HDTV aspect ratio is 16 units × 9 units, and wide-screen films range from 16 × 9 to 2 × 1. The critical or essential area is considered to be the portion within the frame outlined by a 10 percent border of the full scanned area. This is true of both 4 × 3 and 16 × 9 aspect ratios.

Essential Area

An important factor in terms of frame dimensions is the concept of essential area. The full video or film camera frame is rarely, if ever, viewed in its entirety. Part of the border or edge of the full frame is cut off during transmission and conversion in the home receiver. *Essential* or *critical area* refers to the portion of the full frame that will actually be viewed. All key information, actions, and movements must be safely kept within this essential area (Figure 5.10).

Rule of Thirds

One well-practiced theory of composition involves dividing the frame into thirds, both horizontally and vertically. If you mentally draw two vertical and two horizontal lines that divide the frame into thirds, objects can then be arranged along the lines. Important objects may be placed at the points where these lines intersect for added interest or emphasis. Following the rule of thirds allows a picture to be quickly comprehended in an aesthetically pleasing way. Placing subjects in this manner is more interesting than simply bisecting the frame. Other slightly more complicated forms of visual composition can also be used with success, but they are not always comprehended so quickly and easily. The framing composition changes radically with a 16:9 aspect ratio when the rule of thirds is applied. The vertical area remains the same, but much more space needs to be filled in the horizontal areas. Those areas increase the possibilities of using many more multiple images in a single frame than in a 4:3 ratio (Figure 5.11).

FRAMING RULE OF THIRDS

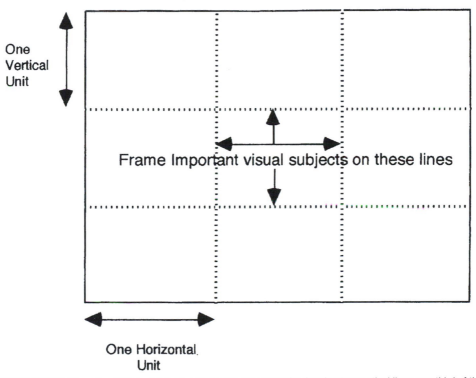

FIGURE 5.11 The rule of thirds divides the frame into nine areas by drawing two vertical lines one-third of the way in from each side and two horizontal lines one-third of the way from the bottom and the top of the frame.

Symmetry

Symmetry is an important aesthetic principle of composition in any two-dimensional, framed visual medium. A director can create a symmetrical or balanced spatial pattern by using objects in the frame. A symmetrical frame appears stable and solid, but it is eventually uninteresting and boring as well. An asymmetrically or unbalanced frame is more volatile and interesting but can also be extremely distracting. When properly used, both symmetrically and asymmetrically organized frames can be pleasing and effective.

The key is to know when it is appropriate to use one form of composition rather than the other. Framing the head of one person talking directly into the camera in an asymmetrical pattern can be distracting. The audience's attention is supposed to focus on the spokesperson, but it is distracted by the lack of balance in the frame. An asymmetrical image of one or more people in the frame can suggest that someone or something is missing. The entrance of another person or character then balances the frame (Figures 5.12 and 5.13).

An asymmetrical frame can suggest that something is wrong or that the world is out of balance. The concept of symmetry must be integrated with the rule of thirds and other concepts, such as lookspace, walkspace, and headroom. *Lookspace* refers to the additional space remaining in the frame in the direction of a performer's look or glance at something or someone outside the frame. *Walkspace* is the additional space in the frame remaining in front of a moving performer. When following the rule of thirds, the performer's face (in the case of a look or glance) or the performer's body (in the case of a walk or run) is placed on one of the trisecting vertical lines, leaving two thirds of the remaining space in the direction of the glance or movement. This asymmetrical composition is much better than having the performer in the exact center of the frame (Figure 5.15). *Headroom* refers to the space remaining in the frame above the subject's head, which is most pleasing visually when there is a slight gap between the top of the head and the top of the frame.

SYMMETRICAL FRAMING

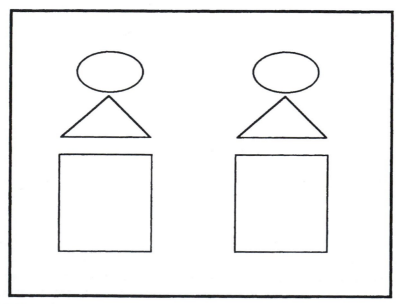

FIGURE 5.12 Symmetrical balance in composing the objects within a frame shows exactly the same items on each side of a line drawn down the middle of the frame.

ASYMMETRICAL FRAMING

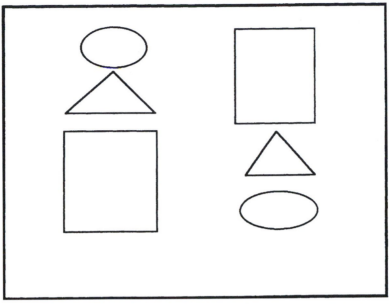

FIGURE 5.13 Asymmetrical framing can vary from an equal weight of objects on each side of the frame to totally unbalanced weight, as well as asymmetrical groupings of objects.

Closure

The concept of lookspace is related to another aspect of visual composition called *closure*. On-screen space—that is, space within the frame—often suggests continuity with off-screen space. An open frame suggests that on-screen space and objects continue into off-screen space. A completely closed frame, on the other hand, gives the illusion of being self-contained and complete in itself.

The way in which an image is framed and objects are arranged can create a sense of closure or a sense of openness. Symmetrically framing a performer's head in the center of the frame creates a sense of closure. The composition does not allude to parts of the body that are missing off-screen. Framing body parts between normal joints of an arm, leg, or waist, on the other hand, suggests continuity in off-screen space. Something appears to be missing, although our memories readily fill in the missing parts (Figure 5.14).

Depth and Perspective

Screen composition can enhance an illusion of depth and three-dimensionality. Lighting can add depth to the image by helping to separate foreground objects from their backgrounds. Placing the camera at an angle so that two sides of an object are visible at the same time creates three-dimensionality. Including foreground objects in a frame can enhance the illusion of depth by setting a yardstick by which the distance, size, and scale of the background can be determined. A person, tree branch, or object of known scale in the foreground can set a context for depth. Diagonal or parallel lines, such as those of a railroad track, can guide the eye to important objects in the frame and create a greater illusion of depth. Placing objects or people at several different planes of action within the frame, or creating frames within frames, such as a person standing inside a doorway, increases the perception of depth within the frame.

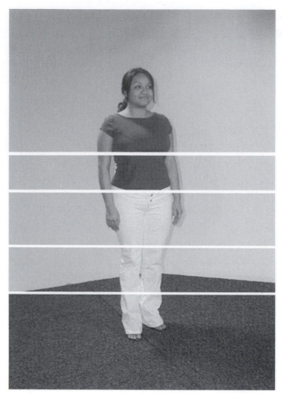

FIGURE 5.14 Logical cutoff points to keep in mind when framing subjects *should not* fall at the joints of the body. To allow for closure and the assumption that the body continues beyond the cutoff point, camera operators must frame the subject *between* the joints, that is, between the ankle and knee, or between the waist and breast.

Of course, a certain degree of care must be exercised when using multiple planes of action so that two planes do not unintentionally connect to create one confused plane, as when a plant in the background appears to be growing out of a person's head. *Image perspective* refers to the apparent depth of the image and the spatial positioning of objects in different planes. The type of lens that is used can affect perspective. Telephoto or long focal-length lenses often seem to reduce apparent

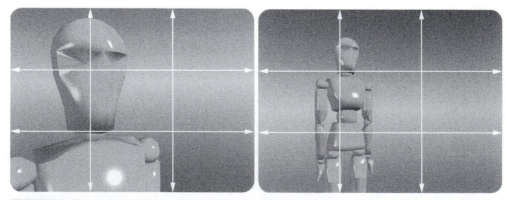

FIGURE 5.15 Any object, either moving in the frame or facing in an obvious direction, needs room to "move" and "look" within the frame. A common framing practice is to place such subjects on either of the lines splitting the frame into nine sections.

depth, whereas wide-angle or short focal-length lenses seem to expand space and apparent depth. Lenses help an image look deep or shallow. A moving camera, as in a dolly shot, can also affect the apparent depth and perspective by changing the relationship between objects in the frame. Cutting from one camera angle to another can help create an illusion of three-dimensionality out of two-dimensional video and film images.

Frame Movement

A moving frame changes visual composition. In video and film, composition is constantly in flux because of camera or subject movement. In this respect, film and video are quite unlike photography and painting, which present motionless images. One type of composition can quickly change to its opposite. A symmetrical frame can quickly become asymmetrical, or an open frame can appear closed. The illusion of depth can be enhanced by the movement of a camera or of objects within the frame. Objects that move toward or away from the camera naturally create a greater sense of depth than those that move laterally with respect to the camera. Diagonal lines of movement, such as diagonal lines within a static frame, add dynamism and force to the composition. A canted frame is created by tilting the camera to the left or right. This adds a sense of dynamic strength to an image, such as an exciting shot within a car chase, but a canted frame used in less intense action sequences often looks out-of-place.

Image Qualities

A director must be conscious of subtle differences in image tonality, especially when editing or combining images. *Image tonality* refers to the overall appearance of the image in terms of contrast (gradations of brightness from white to black) and color. Lighting and recording materials can affect image contrast. Combining two shots that have very different contrast levels can be disconcerting to the viewer, but it can also arouse attention. A high-contrast scene—that is, one that has a limited range of gray tones with mostly dark black and bright whites—will look quite different from a low-contrast scene, which has a wide range of intermediate tones. Matching image tonalities in terms of contrast and color can help effect smooth transitions from shot to shot and scene to scene. Combining mismatched tones can have a shock or attention-getting value. Excessive contrast is a common problem in video production, especially field production, where outdoor lighting is difficult to control. High contrast is sometimes more of a problem in video than in film, because of the narrower range of contrasting shades or tonalities that video can record, but it is an important consideration in both media.

Scale and Shape

Scale refers to the apparent size of objects within the frame. Camera-to-subject distance, camera angle, and the type of lens used can affect the apparent size of objects. Lower camera positions and angles sometimes increase the apparent size of an object in the frame. The apparent size of an object can increase or decrease its importance.

Directors can create a balanced and symmetrical frame by arranging objects of equivalent size or similar shape in different parts of the same frame. Graphic similarities, such as similarities in the shape or color of objects, can create smooth transitions between shots. Graphic differences can be used to create an asymmetrical frame or to emphasize transitions from one shot to another.

Speed of Motion

Images can have different speeds of motion. *Speed of motion* refers to the speed at which objects appear to move within the frame. This speed can be changed by altering the film recording speed or the video playback speed to produce fast motion or slow motion. Editing many short-duration shots together can enhance the speed of motion, whereas using fewer shots of longer duration can help slow down actions and the speed of motion. The pace of editing is called *editing tempo*. Camera placement, lenses, and the actual motion of the photographed objects also affect the apparent motion of objects. A long focal-length lens often slows down apparent motion by squashing space, whereas a wide-angle lens can speed up motion by expanding the apparent distance traveled in a given period of time.

COMBINING SHOTS

One of the director's key jobs, which is shared by the editor during postproduction, is to determine the precise duration of each shot. An exposition section may call for a number of long takes that slow down the action and allow the audience to contemplate character, situation, and setting. A dramatic climax, on the other hand, may call for many different short-duration shots, which help intensify the action. The famous three-minute shower-scene murder in Alfred Hitchcock's *Psycho* (1960), for example, is made up of more than 100 separate pieces of film cut together to intensify the action. Modernist film aestheticians, such as Sergei Eisenstein, have sometimes advocated the use of many short-duration shots, whereas realist aestheticians, such as André Bazin, have often recommended the use of longer-duration shots.

A good director is usually a good editor; that is, directors know how and when to combine specific images. Editing begins with an understanding of composition, image qualities, and different types of shots. Shots can be combined using a variety of transition devices, including straight cuts, fades, dissolves, wipes, and digital transitions.

Straight Cut or Take

A *straight cut* or *take* is a direct, instantaneous change from one camera shot to another, say from a long shot of a scene to a close-up of a performer's face. Time is assumed to be continuous over a straight cut, except in the case of *jump cuts*, where actions are discontinuous and do not match from one shot to the next, suggesting a gap in time. If a cut is made from a shot of a person talking to someone on one side of a room to a second shot showing the same person talking to someone else on the opposite side, the result is a jump cut. Jump cuts are widely used in commercials, in which stories are condensed to 30 seconds by using rapid editing tempos, and in documentary and news interviews, where this procedure is sometimes considered more honest than using cutaways to mask deletions. It is becoming more and more common to use jump cuts to compress time in fiction as well.

Fade

The picture of a video program or film can fade in from blackness to image or fade out from image to blackness. A fade-out followed by a fade-in usually indicates a significant passage of time. A fade, like a curtain on the stage, can be used to mark the beginning and the end of a performance and to separate acts or scenes (Figure 5.16).

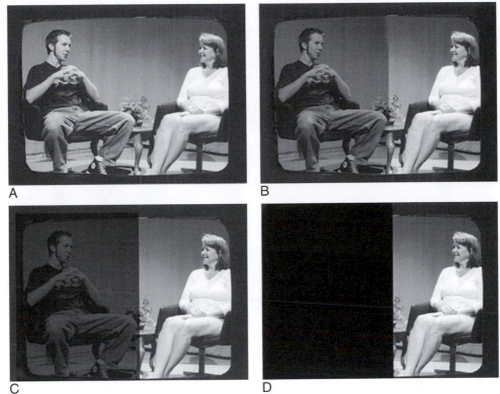

FIGURE 5.16 A fade to black shows the image slowly darkening until it disappears. A fade from black starts with a totally blank frame and then the first image slowly. Frame A shows an image on both halves in full view. Frame B shows the left side of the frame beginning to fade to black. Frame C shows the left side of the frame nearly faded all the way to black, and Frame D shows the left side of the frame completely faded to black. The right side of the frame has remained at full level in each frame.

Dissolve

A dissolve is actually a simultaneous fade-out and fade-in. One scene or shot fades out at the same time that another shot fades in to replace it. For a very short duration, the two shots are superimposed on one another. Dissolves are frequently used to conceal or smooth over gaps in time rather than emphasizing them as in a fade-out and fade-in. A very rapid dissolve is sometimes called a *soft cut* or *lap dissolve*.

Wipe

A wipe is a transition device created on a switcher, a special effects generator, or an optical film bench whereby one image or shot is gradually replaced on the screen by another. A wipe may begin on one side of the screen and move across to engulf the opposite side. It can also begin in the middle of the frame and move outward. Ending one shot by dollying or zooming in to a black object that fills the frame and beginning the next shot by dollying or zooming out from a black object is sometimes called a *natural wipe* (Figure 5.17).

Defocus

Placing one image out of focus and gradually bringing a replacement image into focus is called a *defocus* transition.

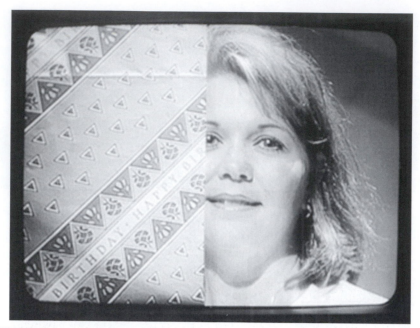

FIGURE 5.17 A wipe appears as one image is replaced by another with a straight line separating the two images. A wide number of different patterns separating the two images also may be used.

Swish Pan

A rapid movement of the camera on the tripod swivel or panning head causes a blurring of the image, which can be used as a swish pan transition from one scene to another. This transition is frequently accompanied by up-tempo music, which accelerates the sense of action and movement rather than creating a pause.

Special Effects

Split Screen or Shared Screen

Having one image occupy a portion of the same frame with another image is called a *shared screen*. When the frame is split into two equal parts by the two images, it is called a *split screen*. Sometimes these techniques make it possible to show two different but simultaneous actions on the same screen.

Superimposition

Having two different shots occupy the same complete frame simultaneously is called a *superimposition*. One shot is usually dominant over the other to avoid visual confusion. The superimposed images should not be excessively detailed or busy. In effect, a superimposition looks like a dissolve that has been stopped while in progress. Combining a long shot and close-up of the same person from different angles sometimes creates an effective superimposition (Figure 5.18).

Keying and Chroma Key

A specific portion of a video image can be completely replaced with a second image using keying or chroma key techniques. Titles and graphics can be inserted into a portion of another image. A scene from a still photograph or slide can be inserted into a blue- or green-colored area (e.g., a green or blue screen on the set) in a shot

FIGURE 5.18 A superimposition is a combination of two images created by stopping a dissolve at midpoint. Depending on the intensity of each image, part of one will bleed through the other.

using video chroma key. The monochrome blue or green portion of the latter shot is replaced with the inserted shot.

Matte and Blue Screen

A matte is used in film to black out an area in one image that will then be filled in with a second image. Matting is to film what keying is to video. Blue screening in film is equivalent to chroma key in video, because the blue screen area in one image is replaced by a second image.

Negative Image

A normal visual image is positive. A negative image reverses the brightness and darkness of the original image. Blacks become whites and whites become blacks. Colors turn into their complements. In television, simply reversing the polarity of the electrical picture signal can do this. In a film, a negative print can be made from a positive image.

Freeze Frame

A freeze frame is a continuing still image from one frame of a video or film shot created during postproduction. Usually the action stops by freezing the last frame of a shot, such as at the conclusion of a film or video program.

Digital Transitions

A wide variety of effects now can be created with a digital effects generator. Page turns, shots on each side of rotating blocks, a subject morphing into another subject, shots disintegrating into another shot, plus virtually any transition imaginable are all possible through the use of digital switchers and effects. The specific language and

FIGURE 5.19 A digital effect is any one of a number of transitions, such as page turns, unique patterns, or three-dimensional transitions.

naming of digital transitions remains in flux as the industry attempts to reach standards agreed upon among the many manufacturers of digital equipment. A caution for new directors: Use a special effect only when needed, not just because the equipment is capable of performing such effects. A special effect is not special if overused (Figure 5.19).

Scene Construction

A *scene* is a series of shots of action occurring in continuous time at one place. It is important to ensure that significant changes in camera angle or camera-to-subject distance occur between two successive shots within a scene. The camera angle should change at least 45 degrees with respect to the subject from one shot to the next, unless there is a significant change in camera-to-subject distance. A few aesthetic reasons for making a cut that involves a change of camera-to-subject distance are (1) to depict an action that was omitted in the previous shot; (2) to provide a closer look at an event or object; (3) to emphasize an object or action; and (4) to draw back and establish the setting. A cut from a medium shot to a close-up provides a closer look at an object or event, whereas a cut from a long shot to a close-up emphasizes an object or action. Cutting from a medium shot to a long shot helps to reestablish the setting and place the action in context or in broader spatial perspective.

A conventionally constructed scene might begin with a long shot or establishing shot to place the subjects within a specific setting. Then the camera gets progressively closer to the subject as the action intensifies, and finally the camera pulls back to reestablish the setting at the conclusion of the scene. An alternative approach is to begin a scene with a close-up and gradually pull back from shot to shot to reveal more and more of the setting as the action progresses. The latter approach is initially somewhat confusing and spatially disorienting, but it also arouses viewer curiosity.

Certain types of cuts involve severe changes in camera-to-subject distance, such as those from long shot to close-up or vice versa. In realist situations, these dramatic changes of scale should be used sparingly and primarily for emphasis, because they often have a distracting effect on the audience. More gradual changes of scale are less disruptive and provide a smoother transition. A new shot or image should serve a purpose different from that of the previous shot. It can anticipate the audience's next point of interest—that is, it can be psychologically motivated on the basis of viewer expectations. It can present additional or contrasting information by revealing actions that were hidden from a previous angle. In general, every shot should be cut as short as it can be without inhibiting its function. A good director separates essential from nonessential information to determine how long a specific shot will maintain viewer interest.

Continuity Editing

Continuity editing usually means creating a smooth flow from one shot to the next. Actions that begin in one shot are completed in the following shot with no apparent gaps in time. There is continuity in the spatial placement and the screen direction of moving and stationary objects from shot to shot. Conventional continuity can, of course, be disrupted in time and space. Gaps or jump cuts in the action can be consciously edited into a scene. Actions can be repeated over and over again, slowed down, and speeded up. But it is important to learn the basics of continuity editing before attempting to disrupt it. Beginning video and film directors need to first acquire some appreciation of the difficulty inherent in trying to maintain continuity and in meeting conventional viewer expectations.

Pace and Rhythm

The selection of long- and short-duration shots affects the pace or rhythm of a scene. A director must be sensitive to changes in pace and rhythm. To build a scene out of different shots, a director must match the tempo or rhythm of the editing to the subject matter and the audience's expectations. Rapidly cutting together many short-duration shots for a how-to film about woodworking, for example, distracts the audience's attention from the primary subject matter. Slow-paced editing for a soft drink commercial may be extremely boring and an ineffective persuasion technique. A fast-paced exposition and a slow-paced climax in a dramatic production usually fail to achieve the desired emotional effect and dramatic structure.

Compression and Expansion of Time

Directors can compress and expand time through editing, even while preserving the illusion of temporal continuity. For example, suppose that you wish to record the action of someone getting dressed and ready for work in the morning. A single shot of this activity that preserved exact temporal continuity might last 10 minutes or more in actual duration. But by recording different segments of action and editing them together, the essential elements of time activity can be preserved without creating any readily apparent gaps in time. How can this be done? Simply by cutting from a long shot of the action to a close-up of a hand or an object in the room, and then cutting back to a long shot in which the person is more completely dressed than could actually have occurred in the duration of the close-up.

A director can speed up an action by eliminating unimportant or repetitious actions between cuts. The action and time are condensed and compressed. The same technique can be used for someone crossing a street. For instance, we begin with a full shot or long shot of the person starting to step off one curb, then we cut to a medium shot and then a close-up of his or her feet or face. Finally, we present a long shot of the person reaching the other side of the street. This edited version of the street crossing might last just five seconds, although actually walking across the street takes more than 20 seconds. Condensing or compressing action can increase the pace and interest of actions. Actions can also be expanded through editing. An action can be shown, followed by the thoughts of one or more of the characters as the action occurs. In reality, the action and the thinking would have occurred simultaneously, but in a media production, each must be shown separately, lengthening the time it takes to depict the actual time of the incident.

Screen Directionality

Depicting a three-dimensional world in a two-dimensional medium presents the director with special problems of screen directionality. *Screen directionality* refers to the consistent direction of movements and object placement from one shot to the next. Inconsistent screen direction causes spatial confusion. What viewers actually see seems to contradict their expectations. This type of confusion can be effective in music videos and formative or modernist works of art. But, in general, maintaining directional consistency of looks and glances, object placements, and subject movements within the frame reduces viewer confusion by increasing spatial clarity in realist and functionalist works.

Directional Glances

It is important to record a consistent pattern of performers' spatial looks and glances within the frame to preserve an illusion of reality. The improper placement of a camera can result in confusing inconsistencies (which again can be useful in a modernist approach). A close-up of one character looking screen left at a second character is usually followed by a shot of the other character looking screen right to suggest that he is looking back at the first character. When one person looks down at another person, the other should look up within the frame of the second shot, and so on. The camera must be placed and the image framed so that there is directional consistency from one shot to the next.

The 180-Degree Axis of Action Rule

The 180-degree rule of camera placement ensures directional consistency from shot to shot. An imaginary line can be drawn to connect stationary subjects. Once the camera is placed on one side or the other of this axis of action, all subsequent camera placements must occur on the same side of the line to prevent a reversal in the placement of objects in the frame (Figure 5.20).

A moving subject establishes a vector line, and all camera placements are made on one side of this line or the other to maintain consistent screen direction of movement. If the camera crossed this line, a subject going from left to right in one shot would appear to be going in the opposite direction in the next shot. There are ways to break the 180-degree rule without creating spatial confusion or disrupting an illusion of reality. First, the camera can move across the line during a single shot, establishing a new rule on the opposite side of the line to which all subsequent shots must conform. A director can also cut directly to the line itself by placing the camera along the line and then cross over the line in the next shot to establish a new rule. Finally, the subject can change direction with respect to the camera during a shot and thus establish a new line.

180-DEGREE AXIS OF ACTION RULE

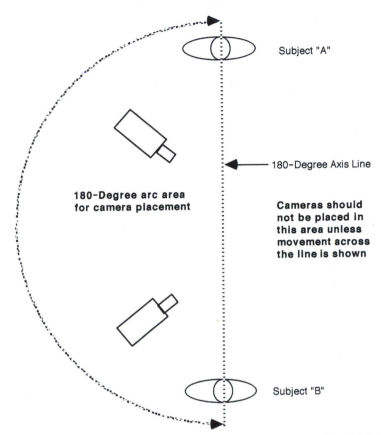

FIGURE 5.20 A line drawn through the two main subjects in a scene divides the studio plot into two areas, one on each side of that line. Once shooting in that scene has started on one side of the line, the rest of the scene must be shot from that same side, unless a shot moves from one side to the other while recording.

SOUND AND IMAGE INTERACTION

An overvaluation of visual images can lead directors to neglect accompanying sounds, but sound is an extremely important aspect of video and film production. Sound can complement and fill out the image. It can also conflict with corresponding images or produce an independent experience. Sound can shape the way in which images are interpreted. It can direct our attention to a specific part of the image or to things not included in the image. Some sounds and music have the ability to stimulate feelings directly. Sounds can create a realistic background or a unique, abstract, impressionistic world.

Sound and image relationships can be divided into four oppositional categories: (1) on-screen versus off-screen sounds, (2) commentative versus actual sounds, (3) synchronous versus asynchronous sounds, and (4) parallel versus contrapuntal sounds. Understanding each of these categories opens up a broad range of aesthetic possibilities. This section concludes with a separate consideration of combining music and visual images from two different standpoints: editing images to prerecorded music and composing original music for video and film.

Sound and Image Relationships	
On-screen	Source is visible
Off-screen	Source is not visible
Commentative	No obvious visible source (music)
Actual	Created from visible source
Synchronous	Matched visual movement
Asynchronous	Movement not matched to visual
Parallel	Blends with visual
Contrapuntal	Contradicts visual

On-Screen versus Off-Screen Sound

A sound coming from a source that is visible within the frame is called an *on-screen sound*. *Off-screen sounds* come from sources assumed to be just outside the frame. The use of off-screen sounds can enhance spatial depth. Noel Burch, a media theorist, has pointed out that an off-screen sound can seem to come from six possible positions outside the frame: from the left, from the right, from above, from below, from behind the wall at the back of the frame, and from behind the camera. The precise spatial placement of an off-screen sound is not always discernible. Stereophonic or multichannel sound obviously helps us to determine the position of an off-screen sound, but the effect is the same. Our attention is directed off-screen to the source of the sound, particularly if on-screen performers are looking in the appropriate direction. By arousing our curiosity, off-screen sound can set up an expectation of the visual presentation of its source. It can also break down some of the limitations of a visual frame, opening it up as a realistic window on the world, as opposed to a more abstract, self-contained, modernist aesthetic world.

Commentative versus Actual Sound

Sound and image relations also can be classified on the basis of the supposed actuality or artificiality of their sound sources. Commentative sound has no known source, whereas actual sound is presumed to come from some actual or real sound source either inside or just outside the frame. Spoken dialogue is usually actual sound. Narration is commentative sound, unless the narrator appears on-screen. Music can be either commentative or actual sound. Scoring is commentative sound, and source music is actual sound. Commentative sound effects, such as shrill metallic sounds that have no readily apparent source, can help to create an impressionistic, emotionally charged atmosphere. Commentative music, narration, and sound effects can be effectively used to reinforce specific feelings. Lush, romantic music, for example, might complement a romantic scene, such as the reunion of long-separated lovers, although such conventions easily become musical clichés.

Synchronous versus Asynchronous Sound

Synchronous sounds match their on-screen sources. Lip-sync sounds synchronize with the lip movements of the on-screen speaker. Sound effects match their on-screen sound sources. For example, the sounds of a runner's feet striking the pavement should be synchronized within the corresponding visual images. Music can also be said to be synchronous with visual actions or cuts that precisely follow the beat or rhythm. Asynchronous sound does not match its sound source. Poor quality lip-sync is asynchronous sound, such as a film dubbed into a foreign language that fails to match the lip movements of the speaker. But asynchronous sound is not always poor-quality sound. In fact, asynchronous sound offers many exciting aesthetic possibilities, such as providing a basis for contrapuntal sound. Commentative sound effects can be used asynchronously to contrast with their corresponding visuals. One example is the substitution of a train whistle for a woman's scream in Alfred Hitchcock's *The Thirty-Nine Steps* (1935). Commentative, asynchronous sound effects can produce emotional effects or meanings that counterpoint rather than parallel their accompanying visual images.

Parallel versus Contrapuntal Sound

The emotional effect or conceptual meaning of sounds and images can be virtually the same or completely different. Speech, sound effects, and music can parallel the meaning or emotions of the visuals, or they can counterpoint them. The term *counterpoint* in music refers to two separate and distinguishable melodies that are played simultaneously. The same term has been applied to image and sound interaction in video and film. Contrapuntal sound has an emotional effect or conceptual meaning that is different from its corresponding visuals. Sounds and images are aesthetically separate and often contrast with one another.

Parallel sound, like musical harmony, blends together with its corresponding visuals. Like musical notes played simultaneously and in harmony, sounds and images can have parallel meanings or emotions that are mutually supportive. Suppose that the visually depicted events are sad or tragic but the accompanying music is upbeat and in a major key, so that it communicates a bright, happy, strong feeling. In this case, the music counterpoints the corresponding visuals. The same thing happens when sad music accompanies a happy event. But when sad, minor key music accompanies a tragic scene, the sounds and images parallel one another in emotional tone.

Speech sounds and sound effects can parallel or counterpoint their corresponding images. For example, the film musical *Singin' in the Rain* (1952) begins with the main character, Don Lockwood, describing his path to Hollywood stardom. Lockwood gives a short autobiography to his fans in which he claims to have received his training and background at elite, high-class schools and cultural institutions. But what we see contradicts his voice-over narration. We see that he actually began his performance career in pool halls and bars and gradually worked his way into the movies as a stuntman. His elitist posturing provides a pseudo-sophisticated, tongue-in-cheek commentary on Hollywood. The meaning of what we see contradicts the meaning of what we hear, producing a powerfully humorous effect.

Composing Images for Prerecorded Music

The use of music in video and film is a rather complex art. It is important for directors to understand some of the basic aesthetic possibilities inherent in two approaches to combining images and music: (1) editing visual images to preselected, prerecorded music and (2) composing original music for video and film, even if the responsibility for the music is in the hands of a specialist, such as a music director, composer, or performer.

Visual images can be selected and ordered into a pattern that is prescribed by prerecorded music. For example, fast-paced music might be accompanied by rapid cutting of visual images and rapid action within the frame, and slow-paced music might call for less frequent cutting and slower movements. The visual action might reach its climax at the same time as a musical crescendo or swelling in the volume and intensity of the music. The timing of the visuals can be made to coincide with the timing of the music so that both begin and end at the same points and achieve a parallel structure throughout. Dancing and singing sequences require a high degree of synchronization and parallelism between the music and visuals. The music can be recorded in advance and used as a basis for the choreography. Prerecorded music establishes a basic structure and timing to which the performance and editing of visual images must conform, unless conscious asynchronization or contrapuntal relations between the sounds and images is desired.

Composing Music for Prerecorded Images

Music and Image Interaction
- Intensify the action
- Intensify the dramatic tension
- Establish the period or location
- Set atmosphere or mood
- Stimulate screen emotion
- Fill dead air

Another approach to music and image interaction is to compose original music for specific film or video sequences. Music composed for video or film usually serves one or more of the following functions: (1) intensifying the action or dramatic tension, (2) establishing the period or place, (3) setting the atmosphere or mood, (4) stimulating a specific emotion in conjunction with a character or theme, and (5) avoiding screen silence. Music rhythm can intensify action and create dramatic tension. The pace of music can increase with the speed of the action, such as a crescendo that accompanies a dramatic climax or crisis. Music can communicate time and place by virtue of its source, period, and style. Selecting a specific mode of music affects the overall mood or atmosphere. A specific melody can develop an emotion in conjunction with an important character or theme. Leitmotifs can intensify audience identification with specific people or characters and stimulate emotions. Finally, music can be used simply as a filler to cover silence or to attempt to create viewer interest during slow-paced visual action sequences.

Background music is all too frequently used to fill a void rather than to create a specific effect in conjunction with visual images. Careful selection and design of music is a much better approach to the problem. Original music for television and film can consist of sounds from a single instrument, such as a solo guitar or flute, or a fully orchestrated symphonic score. The number of musicians required and the complexity of the music can vary considerably depending on the specific needs and requirements of the project and the available budget. Sometimes a scarcity of materials and resources can be an advantage. Simple music and solo performers can be easier for beginning producers to obtain and control. New computer music programs and synthesizers make it easier to have original music composed, played, and recorded by one person. Apple's computer program Logic, which accompanies Final Cut Pro 6, facilitates the creation of film and video music, especially for directors and editors with limited composing experience and low budgets. Regardless of the sophistication of the music, video and film directors should make every attempt to collaborate with composers and musicians so that the music can be designed and performed for their specific needs. Original music can be tailored to a video or film production much better than prerecorded library music, but in some cases the latter is more cost-effective.

PREPARING THE SHOOTING SCRIPT

Directors begin to apply aesthetic principles to concrete production problems when they plan a production. Production planning is usually done on paper. Directors specify shots and sound effects for each scene in the script as they prepare a final shooting script (Figure 5.21).

After the shooting script is completed, shot lists are often written up for camera operators. Sometimes a storyboard consisting of still-frame drawings of every shot in the final shooting script is drawn up as a visual guide to production.

SHOOTING SCRIPT

1.   INT   WS   UNIVERSITY CLASSROOM   DAY   1.

    Classroom is full of students, some wide awake, gossiping, others sleeping or nodding off as they wait for the professor to arrive.

    2-Shot of Jane and Jack, Jane turns around in her seat to whisper to Jack.

JANE
(Quietly so only Jack can hear her.)
Are you sure there isn't going to be an exam
during tomorrow's class?

    CU Jack, he leans forward toward Jane.

JACK
(With a bravado, all-knowing tone)
Of course not, have I ever lied to you?

    The professor enters the room, downstage right, walks to the lectern and the room becomes quiet.

    MWS from back of classroom, students in foreground, Professor in background.

PROFESSOR
(Emphatically as a reminder)
If I am forced to repeat myself again, I WILL
be forced to give you your first examination in
tomorrow's class.

    MS Students as they react to Professor, groans, turning to each other in sympathy.

(DISSOLVE TO)

2.   EXT   WS   CAMPUS   DAY   2.

    The clouds suddenly darken the sky as rain, thunder and lightning start and the lights go out plunging the room into darkness.

FIGURE 5.21 A shooting script should provide the director with enough information to shoot the scene as closely as possible to the vision the writer had when writing the script. If the script is not clear, then the director must make decisions on specifically how to shoot the scene.

After carefully analyzing the script, a director begins to prepare a final shooting script by indicating specific types of shots, transition devices, and sound effects. Directorial terms for specific types of visual images and sounds must be thoroughly learned before a shooting script can be created. Shots are continuous recordings of actions within a scene made by a single camera. Abbreviations are used to specify camera placements and movements, such as ECU (extreme close-up) or MS (medium shot), which specify the desired distance of the camera from the subject. Where the camera is placed can have a considerable impact on what action is viewed or how a subject appears. Camera movements, such as CAMERA PANS RIGHT or CAMERA DOLLIES IN, are also specified in a shooting script, as are transitions between one shot and another, such as CUT TO, FADE OUT, FADE IN, and DISSOLVE. Camera movements add motion to the recording of a scene and can also change the perspective or point of view on a subject or action. Various transition devices are used to communicate changes of time or place to the audience. Sound effect designations, such as SFX (sound effect): PLANE LANDING, specify concrete sounds that should accompany specific images.

Preparing a final shooting script allows a director an opportunity to shoot and reshoot a video or film production on paper at minimal expense before actual recording begins. To compose a final shooting script, a director must understand a full range of aesthetic possibilities. There are many different ways to record a specific scene in any script. A director interprets the action and decides on the best shots, transition devices, and sound effects for each scene. Directors select specific recording techniques, such as different types of shots, for each scene on the basis of the aesthetic approach they have chosen. A director's overall aesthetic approach in large part determines the meaning of images and sounds by setting a context for interpretation. A realist approach often involves the use of techniques that help to preserve an illusion of reality through a transparent or unnoticed style. Modernist and postmodernist approaches call attention to techniques and highlight a director's manipulation and control over the recording medium and subject matter.

Some types and combinations of visual images and sounds can be realist in one context but modernist or postmodernist in another. For example, jump cuts are discontinuities in human actions or movements from one shot to the next. Because they disrupt the continuous flow of realist time and space, jump cuts are often considered a modernist technique, but they are also used in news and documentary interviews.

A jump cut indicates that something has been removed and is often considered more honest than using techniques that disguise the fact that editing has been done. From a modernist perspective, jump cuts, such as those in Jean-Luc Godard's *Breathless* (1959), call attention to directional control by breaking down the illusion of temporal continuity or the smooth, continuous flow of time from shot to shot. But from a realist perspective in news and documentary productions, jump cuts make it clear that the recording of an event has been edited.

PRODUCTION COORDINATION

Video and film directors are personnel managers as well as artists using the media of moving images and sounds. Directors coordinate production by working with their staff, crew, and performers. Frequent production meetings facilitate coordination.

A cooperative, collective effort has to be carefully orchestrated and managed by the director if a quality product is to be achieved. The director must be a good judge of character.

Production Meetings

Frequent production meetings provide the director and the production staff with an opportunity to work out important details and problems collectively. Before actual production, the director usually meets with key staff members, such as the producer, the art director or scenic designer, and the lighting director. The overall goals and objectives of the film or video project are clarified during these meetings. Everyone must understand the overall purpose and design of the production to prevent members of the production team from working at cross-purposes. Everything must be worked out and all problems solved before actual live video production, because live production means that there is no postproduction and therefore little or no room for mistakes during production.

The director must be able to communicate effectively with the staff if these problems are to be quickly and efficiently resolved. The more talented, independent, and opinionated the staff, crew, and performers are, the more likely it is that problems and disputes will arise, unless a common purpose has been collectively determined or hierarchically imposed at the beginning. The director's authority may be questioned, and his or her status with the staff, crew, and other performers jeopardized, if an unruly participant is allowed to dominate the proceedings. The director must be explicit and authoritative about commands. The director must also listen to the needs, desires, and problems of the staff, crew, and talent. Production meetings provide the director with an opportunity to exercise authority and give commands, but also to listen to the ideas, needs, and problems of others. Effective managers are often good listeners.

Casting

To cast a specific performance effectively, the director must have a firmly established interpretation of each character or role. Each role, however small, is important in terms of the quality of the final product, and a video or film program is often only as good as its worst performer. It is often said that almost any director can evoke an excellent performance from an experienced, talented performer but that good direction is most evident in the quality of smaller roles and bit parts. Good casting depends on a director's understanding of at least three factors: the audience, the character or role, and the physical appearance of specific performers. The natural look and feel of a performer is probably the most important factor in terms of his or her appropriateness for a specific role, although skilled actors can drastically change their appearance and still appear naturally suited to a role. Robin Williams did in *Mrs. Doubtfire* (1993) (Figure 5.22, A and B).

Casting sessions often consist of actors reading a short scene from the script so that the director and producer can evaluate their suitability for a role. Sometimes several actors will be auditioned before a part is cast. Directors often have to deal with performers who have different levels and types of acting experience. Inexperienced actors need to be explicitly told what is wanted. Most fail to understand or prepare themselves for the rigors of video and film acting. Inexperienced performers have difficulty relating to an awkward, unfeeling camera. Constant feedback and praise from a director can greatly improve the quality of a performance. Experienced professionals, on the other hand, may require more freedom in some situations and a firmer hand

FIGURE 5.22 The range actors can portray serves them well, especially if they are asked to take the part of someone as different from their own persona as Robin Williams was able to do in Twentieth Century Fox's production of *Mrs. Doubtfire* (A) and in Touchstone/Columbia Pictures' *Bicentennial Man* (B). (Courtesy of Twentieth Century Fox and Touchstone/Columbia Pictures.)

in others. Most directors work somewhere in between two extremes of management styles: Either a director allows the actor to find his or her role, or the director takes an authoritative approach in order to develop a consistent interpretation.

Rehearsals

Once the performers have been selected, a director can begin a preliminary run-through of the production by helping the actors to develop their specific characters. Preliminary practices of a performance are called *rehearsals*. Rehearsals sometimes begin with reading sessions, in which actors sit around a table and read their respective parts before actually performing them. Many rehearsals may be necessary before the actors are fully prepared to perform unerringly before the camera(s). All the bugs have to be worked out before a performance can proceed without problems or disruptions. The final rehearsal, which usually takes place with the sets fully dressed and the performers in costume, is called a *dress rehearsal*. It simulates the actual recording session in virtually every respect.

Multicamera and live productions usually demand more rehearsal time than single-camera productions, because entire scenes or programs are recorded at one time rather than broken up into segments for a single camera. The entire performance must be worked out to perfection so that even minor mistakes are avoided during actual recording. Actors in single-camera productions do not always know how one shot relates to another. Single shots are often recorded in isolation, and performers cannot build a performance in perfect continuity as they would on the stage or for a multiple-camera production. Close-ups are often recorded out of sequence, for example. The director must be able to provide the performer with a context that will help the actor achieve a proper performance level so that shots can be combined during postproduction editing. One of the director's primary responsibilities during rehearsal and production is to ensure that the actors maintain continuity in the dramatic levels of their performances from one shot to the next. Many directors prefer to have a complete rehearsal in advance.

Performer and Camera Blocking

The director usually stages and plots the action in two distinct stages: performer blocking and camera blocking. Before selecting final camera placements, angles, lenses, and so on, the director will frequently run through the basic actions to be performed by the talent. This is called *performer blocking*. A director must carefully preplan the entire performance in advance. Only rarely are the performer's movements precisely set during performer blocking alone. Instead, a general sense of the action is determined, which facilitates camera blocking and prepares the performers for actual recording.

Camera blocking refers to the placement of cameras so that they can follow the movements of the talent. Whether several cameras or a single camera will actually record the action, the director must be able to anticipate the types of shots that will provide adequate coverage, dramatic emphasis, and directional continuity from shot to shot. Shot lists can be drawn up and supplied to the camera operator(s). These lists are a helpful guide to camera operation during blocking sessions and actual production. Every consecutive shot in each scene for each camera is written on a piece of paper that the camera operator can tape to the back of the camera for easy reference. Shot lists indicate types of shots and camera movements called for in the final shooting script. In some recording situations, there is minimal time to block the cameras and the performers separately, and the two stages are combined. During camera blocking, the performers, director, and camera operator(s) exchange ideas and discuss problems as the action is blocked or charted on the floor or on location. The director refines his or her conception and interpretation of the script, making notations of any deviations from previous shot selections. Performers not only learn and remember their lines, they must also remember their marks, that is, the precise points where they must position themselves during actual recordings (Figure 5.23).

MULTIPLE-CAMERA DIRECTING

Directing several cameras simultaneously requires a different approach from that of single-camera recording. The preproduction planning stages are always extensive, because major changes are more difficult to make once recording has begun. Performers must learn the lines of dialogue for several scenes, because more script material will be recorded in a single session. Camera operators must anticipate what camera positions, lens types and positions, and framing they are to adopt for upcoming segments. Ample time and space must be provided for the cameras to be moved during recording. Every detail must be worked out in advance, and a detailed shooting script or camera shot sequence must be provided to each key member of the production team.

When the recording session has been properly planned and practiced, tremendous economies in time and expense can be accomplished by using multiple-camera recording. But a multiple-camera situation can also be extremely frustrating if a key individual is improperly prepared or the director has failed to anticipate all the problems that can arise. Murphy's law—**If anything can go wrong, it will**—is an

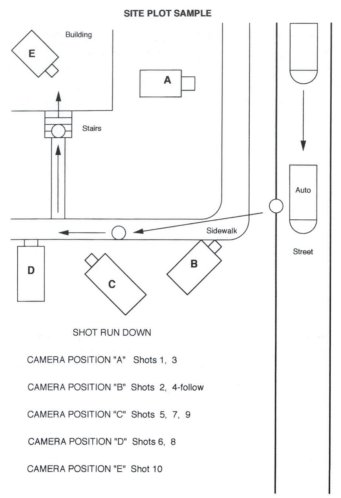

FIGURE 5.23 A director blocks performers and cameras before and during rehearsal in order to determine the best placement of each to provide the framing and movement intended for each shot. A plot drawn as if looking straight down on the scene helps the director to visualize where cameras and performers need to be blocked.

optimistic expectation in multiple-camera and live television recording situations where directors, crews, and talents are insufficiently prepared.

For multiple-camera recordings of uncontrolled events, such as sporting events, cameras are often placed in fixed positions. Each camera operator is responsible for covering a specific part of the action from one position. The director of a live production, such as coverage of a sporting event, may have to watch and control as many as 10 cameras, some of which are connected to slow-motion recorders. The director must be able to respond instantaneously to any action that occurs, rapidly cutting from one camera to another. The director selects from among the images displayed on a bank of television screens. Because only minimal scripting is possible, the action and atmosphere within the director's control room itself often become intense during a sporting event or similar production. Accurate decisions must be made quickly. To anticipate actions and cuts, directors must be intimately familiar with the particular sport.

Timing

An important function performed by the director is timing. The control of program pace in terms of the speed of dialogue, actions, and editing is one form of timing. As discussed in Chapter 4, Scriptwriting, dramatic pacing is a subjective impression of time in video, film, and sound productions. Through effective editing, a sequence of action can be made to seem longer or shorter in duration to the audience. Other types of timing are equally important in the production process.

Running Time

A director is responsible for ensuring that the program length or actual running time of a completed program conforms to the required length. In video production, *running time* should be distinguished from *clock time*. The latter refers to the actual time of day on the studio clock. Each video or film program or program segment has its own running time, which is the exact duration of the program, regardless of what time of day it is actually shown. During live productions, a timer is used to calculate the running time of each program segment so that the total running time will conform to the scheduled overall length of the program.

Timing in Production

Television commercials, public service announcements, and broadcast or cablecast programming must be accurately timed during production. When recording a commercial, for example, a director must obtain shots that will add up to exactly 10, 30, or 60 seconds. The screen time of the various shots and vignettes must add up to the exact screen time of the commercial format that has been chosen. Live video production demands precise screen timing with a timer as well as a studio clock, as the show cannot be reedited, lengthened, or shortened.

Backtiming is the process of figuring the amount of time remaining in a program or program segment by subtracting the present time from the predetermined end time. Music is sometimes backtimed so that it will end at the conclusion of a live production. This means that if the music should last three minutes, you backtime three minutes from its end and start playing it three minutes before the end of the program, gradually fading it up. In other words, if you want it to end at 6:59, you backtime it three minutes and start it at 6:56. In multiple-camera video production, the talent is often told how much time remains by means of hand signals. Five fingers, followed by four, three, two, and one, indicate how many minutes of running time remain for that segment. Rotating the index finger in a circle indicates that it is time to wind up a performance because the time is almost up. A cutoff signal (the hand cuts across the neck, as though the stage or floor manager's own head is coming off) indicates the actual end of a segment or show.

On-the-Air Timing

Prerecorded videotapes such as commercials, which will be inserted into a program as it is being broadcast or cablecast, must be accurately backtimed or cued and set up on a playback machine. A countdown leader displaying consecutive numbers from 10 down to 0 is placed just ahead of the prerecorded pictures and sound. The numbers indicate how many seconds are left before the start of the prerecorded material. The playback can then be *prerolled*, that is, begun at the appropriate number of seconds before the commercial is due to start.

Production Switching

In multiple-camera video production, the director supervises virtually all of the editing in the control room during actual production. Production editing is done by means of a switcher, a device that allows shots to be selected from among several different cameras instantaneously. The director usually commands the technical director (TD) to change the transmitted image from one camera to another. (In many local stations, the director actually operates the switcher.) The TD then pushes the correct buttons on the switcher. Each button on the switcher is connected to a different camera or image source. When the TD pushes a button, the switcher automatically substitutes one picture for another.

The TD and the director view these changes on television monitors as they are taking place. The images sent out of the switcher can either be directly transmitted and broadcast during live production or recorded on videotape. A videotape recording can be used for subsequent postproduction editing and delayed broadcast, cablecast, or closed-circuit showing. A switcher is both an electronic editing device and a special effects machine. The TD cannot only cut from one image or camera to another, but he or she can also fade in, fade out, dissolve, wipe, key, chroma key, and superimpose images. Various transition devices can be used in changing from one image or camera to another.

A switcher consists of a series of buttons organized into units called *buses* (Figure 5.24). There are three types of buses: preview, program, and special effects or mix. Individual buttons within each bus are linked to specific sources, such as Camera 1,

VIDEO SWITCHER

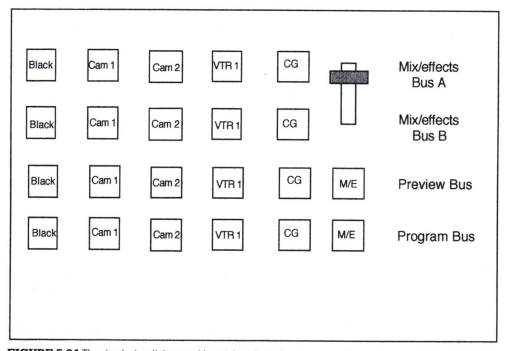

FIGURE 5.24 The simplest switcher would contain at least four buses: one for on-air (program), one to check shots ahead of time (preview), and two for mixing or wiping shots (mix/effect, or M/E). In addition to all other inputs to the switcher, the program bus must also contain a button for switching to the M/E bus.

Camera 2, Camera 3, a videotape player, a remote source, still store, character generator, digital generator, and a constant black image (Figure 5.24).

Each bus has one button assigned to each of these image sources. Thus, a bus allocated to previewing images before sending them out of the board, called a *preview bus*, would have at least nine individual buttons connected to the nine image sources cited earlier: Cameras 1, 2, 3, videotape player, remote source, still store, character and digital generators, and a constant black image. When one of these buttons is pressed, the image from that source appears on the preview monitor. A second bus having the same number of buttons is assigned to the actual program feed; on a simple switcher, this is the signal that will actually be transmitted or recorded.

A switcher having just two buses would only allow the TD to preview images and to cut directly from one image to another. If any special effects are to be created, the switcher must have special effects or mix buses. These two effects or mix buses are usually designated "A" and "B." To send any visual signal on the effects buses out of the switcher, a button designating the effects buses must be activated on a secondary program bus called the master program bus.

The master program bus acts as a final selection switch, determining what the switcher will transmit. The TD can select the program bus (which contains one of the nine visual sources) or the effects bus by depressing one of these two buttons on the master program bus. A master preview bus is also available on more sophisticated switchers, so that an effect, such as a split-screen or digital effect, can be previewed before recording or transmission via the master program bus.

Preset multilevel switches can handle complex digital changes of shots and sequences. Digital switchers are designed with switch sequence storage so that any number of shot changes can be set and stored in memory. As each switch is called for, the video operator simply calls up that specific change on the built-in computer without having to set each aspect of the switch such as multiple levels of keys and layers or complex transitions. Today's video switchers also must be able to change shots between standard definition (SD) and high definition (HD) video sources. Complex visual switches may also require matching audio sources changes to stay in sync with the production.

Director's Commands

A director must communicate accurately with the entire crew to coordinate a production effectively, but communication with the TD is critical because the TD's response and action determine what pictures will be seen on air or fed to the tape. Operating the switcher during production requires careful preparation and infallible communication between the director and the operator of the switcher. The TD must know in advance exactly what switcher operations the director will call for and the order in which he or she will call for them. It is easy to become confused and push the wrong button or misunderstand the director's commands. It is the director's responsibility to convey clear and distinct commands to the TD and to provide adequate time between the preparatory command and the command of execution.

Video and film directors have developed relatively precise terminology and methods with which to communicate with their cast and crew. The method is based on a two-step system of first warning of an impending command with a preparatory (prep) command, followed by a command of execution at the precise timing moment.

A preparatory command always begins with either the words "stand by" or "ready." This tells everyone that a new command is about to be announced, so pay attention. The prep command needs to be detailed and precise and clearly stated so that the crew and cast directly involved know what to prepare themselves for when the command of execution arrives a few seconds later. The command of execution needs to be as short and as precise as possible, because that command determines the precise moment when an action is to take place.

If the director wants Camera 3 to zoom in to a two-shot, for example, a typical command series would be as follows.

Simple Command Sequence	
PREPARATORY COMMAND:	Camera 3, stand by to zoom into a two-shot.
COMMAND OF EXECUTION:	Three-zoom.

More often a single command series is directed at more than one crew or cast member. The beginning command of a newscast might be directed at the TD (the switcher transition), the audio operator (to open a mic), the camera operator (who gets the opening shot), and the floor manager (to give the anchor a stand by and a cue to start talking).

Complex Command Sequence	
PREPARATORY COMMAND:	Stand by to anchor, ready mic, ready to fade in Camera 2 on the anchor.
COMMAND OF EXECUTION:	Mic, fade in 2, cue anchor.

The order of the commands and the precise nature of their execution are critical. Sloppy or inaccurate calls by a director will guarantee a sloppy production. Commands to the TD and camera operators are especially important because in both cases some preoperation activities may need to be carried out before the command can be followed. The switcher may need to have a complex set of buttons aligned or set up, or a camera or lens may need to be moved or adjusted before the shot is ready.

Live-on-Tape Recording

A live-on-tape (multiple-camera) director can use the techniques of live multiple-camera video to record events quickly and efficiently but also has the option to change the shot sequence during postproduction. This is accomplished by recording the images from several cameras simultaneously while at the same time making some editing decisions on the switcher that are recorded on a separate recorder. Editing decisions made during production can then be changed during postproduction by inserting different camera shots. This method gives the director maximum flexibility to produce a program economically in the shortest possible time without jeopardizing the quality of the final product, because changes can always be made later. In this way, multiple-camera recording techniques can be combined with the techniques discussed next, allowing the director to benefit from the advantages of both methods.

SINGLE-CAMERA DIRECTING

The number of cameras used and the order and time frame of recording or filming shots constitute the major differences between multiple- and single-camera directing. The types of shots are the same, but the physical arrangement and order of shooting those shots differ between the two production modes. Recording with a single camera usually takes longer than multiple-camera recording. The lighting, camera, and set are sometimes moved and readjusted for each shot. Better quality images are often obtained using this method, as fewer compromises have to be made in terms of recording logistics. Each shot is composed and the action repeated so that an optimal recording is made. But potential problems can arise in terms of discontinuity or mismatched action from one shot to the next. The director and the script continuity person must observe and duplicate every detail recorded or filmed in the master shot during the shooting of the inserts.

Both film and video use three different types of setups for one camera: (1) master shots, (2) inserts, and (3) cutaways. Single-camera recording normally begins with a shot of the entire action in a scene, or as much of the complete scene as it is possible to record in a single shot. This is often called a *master shot*. Master shots are usually, but not always, long shots. Specific actions occurring within the master shot are then repeated after the camera has been placed closer to the subject for shots known as *inserts*. Inserts are usually the medium shots and close-ups indicated in a script. Master shots and inserts may be rerecorded several times before an acceptable recording has been made. Specific recordings are called different *takes* of the same shot. A script continuity person then marks the shooting script (as shown in Figure 5.25) with the number of the exact shot specified in the script, and each take is circled at the beginning point of actual recording.

A line is drawn vertically through the script to the point where actual recording of that take ends. Inserts are normally extended before and after the exact edit points in the script to allow for overlapping action and a range of editing choices. A marked shooting script provides a complete record of actual recording in terms of master shots and inserts. *Cutaways* are additional close-ups and medium shots of objects or events that are not central parts of the action and are often not specified in the script. They can be inserted into a scene to bridge mismatched actions or to hide mistakes within or between a master shot and an insert. The master shot or long shot can act as a safety net in the event that matching medium shots or close-ups specified in the script do not prove satisfactory. A continuously running long shot or master shot can be quite boring in comparison with using several different long shots, medium shots, and close-ups for emphasis and variety. But the knowledge that the master shot covers the entire action and can be used at any point can be of some comfort to the editor.

Insert shots, which record some of the same actions as the master shot but from a closer camera position or a different angle of view, are called *inserts* or *cut-ins*, because they will be cut into the master shot. The director and the script continuity person must observe and duplicate every detail recorded in the master shot during the recording of the inserts. The actors must perform the same gestures, wear the same clothing, and repeat the same actions and lines of dialogue if actions are to overlap and match from one shot to the next. In extremely low-budget situations, where it is impossible to record several takes of each insert, a director is well advised to record a few cutaways for use in bridging mismatched actions between shots that

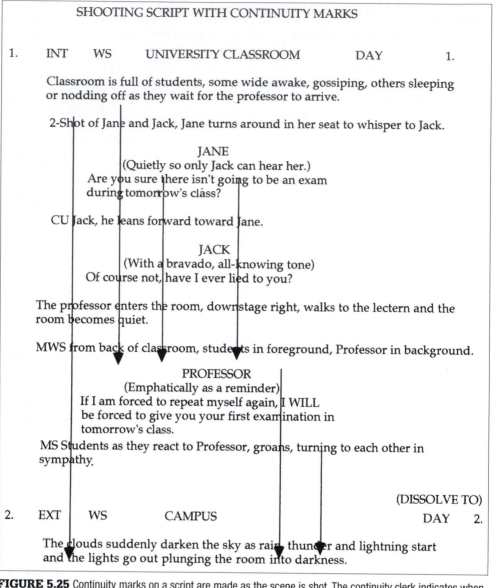

FIGURE 5.25 Continuity marks on a script are made as the scene is shot. The continuity clerk indicates when a shot starts and ends with codes agreed upon with the editor. Often the codes will indicate the framing of a shot as well as its length and the number of takes. These kinds of markings are invaluable to the editor during postproduction.

are discovered during postproduction editing. It is the director's responsibility to provide adequate coverage of events and actions so that a program can be edited with minimal difficulty. Good coverage provides insurance against costly reshooting.

Cutaways

Cutaways are shots of secondary objects and actions that can be used to hide mismatched action and to preserve continuity or simply to add depth and interest to the primary action of a film or television program. *Cut-ins* depict actions that appear within the frame of master shots, whereas *cutaways* depict actions and objects outside the master shot frame. In single-camera news recording, a reaction shot of the reporter or interviewer is sometimes used to bridge gaps or to avoid jump cuts in a condensed version of an interview or simply to provide facial expressions to comment on what is being said. Close-ups of hands gesturing and relevant props can also be used as cutaways. They can be inserted at almost any point to bridge mismatched action in master shots and inserts or simply to add more detail to the spatial environment. Cutaways provide an editor with something to cut away to when editing problems are discovered.

Shooting Ratios

All single-camera directors try to get an acceptable shot in as few takes as possible; nonetheless there can be considerable variation in shooting ratios from one production to another. *Shooting ratios*, which refer to the ratio of visual material shot to visual material actually used, can range from about 5:1 to 100:1 in different types of production situations. Obviously, more takes of each shot translate into higher shooting ratios. Network commercials often have the highest shooting ratios. At the other end of the spectrum, student productions often have shooting ratios as low as 5:1 or even 3:1, because of limited production funds. Low-budget situations call for highly efficient production methods.

Director's Terminology

Because a single-camera director is normally present on the set with the camera operator rather than isolated in a control room, as in multiple-camera production, he or she can communicate directly with the crew and talent. Directorial terminology for camera placements and movements is generally the same as that for multiple-camera recording, but a few commands are quite different. When the crew and the talent are ready to record a single shot, the director says, "Roll tape" to the videotape (in video) or audio (in film) recordist and "Roll film" to the film camera operator. When the tape or film is up to speed, the operator says, "Speed" or "Camera rolling." The director then calls, "Slate," and a grip or camera assistant slates the shot by calling out the scene, shot, and take numbers, which are also written on a board called a *slate*. In film, the slate has electronic or physical clap-sticks that are brought together so that separate sounds and pictures can be synchronized later. The scene, shot, and take numbers displayed on the slate are used as a reference during postproduction editing. They are usually written down on a camera report sheet, which is sent to the film laboratory or used by the videotape editor.

When the talent is ready and the slate has been removed from the shot, the director says, "Action" and the performance begins. When a shot is over or a problem develops in midshot, the director says, "Cut." If the director wants a scene printed for later viewing, the command "Print" will be given. The "Print" command is noted on the camera report. Because editing can be done during postproduction, there is no need for the director to communicate with a technical director (switcher operator) during actual production. Editing decisions will be made later (Figure 5.26).

Summary

Video and film directors are artists who can turn a completed script into a shooting script and produce works of art from recorded visual images and sounds. To prepare a shooting script, a director must know when to use different types of shots. Shots can be categorized by camera-to-subject distance, camera angle, camera (or lens) movement, and shot duration. Directors also know how to control various aspects of

FIGURE 5.26 The director on a single-camera shoot stands next to the camera to give directions to both the camera operator and the talent. Either the director or a production assistant keeps an accurate record of each shot on a camera log.

visual composition and image qualities, such as tone, scale and shape, depth, and speed of motion, and the use of various transition devices and special effects.

In scene construction, conventional continuity often begins with a long shot and gradually moves closer to the subject as the action intensifies. Continuity suggests an uninterrupted flow of time, with no apparent gaps or mismatched actions from shot to shot. Video and film are temporal and spatial arts. Classical continuity refers to the continuity of time and continuity of space maintained in many classical Hollywood films (e.g., most films made in Hollywood between 1920 and 1960).

The aesthetic use of sound is extremely important. Although sound can be used simply to accompany and complement the visuals, it can also be treated as an independent aesthetic element. There are four basic categories of sound: speech, music, sound effects, and ambient noise. A director must be familiar with the basic elements of music, such as rhythm, melody, harmony, counterpoint, and tonality or timbre, as well as different types of music. Sound effects are sometimes used to enhance an illusion or reality or to create imaginative sound impressions. Ambient noise, also called background sound, is present in any location and can be used to preserve temporal continuity and to create an illusion of spatial depth. A director can affect the perception of temporal continuity through the selection and ordering of sounds. Mismatched levels and gaps in the presentation of sounds can create discontinuity, thus disrupting the flow of time. It is possible to condense and expand time without disrupting the illusion of continuity, however.

Music composed for television or film often performs one of the following functions: intensifying the drama, establishing the period or place, setting the mood or atmosphere, stimulating a specific emotion in conjunction with a character or theme, or simply filling in and avoiding silence. The director and the composer should collaborate with one another, fully and creatively exploring the artistic potential of visual image and music interaction.

The director supervises the creative aspects of television and film production by coordinating the production team, initiating and chairing preproduction and production meetings, casting the film or television program with the producer and casting director, and organizing production rehearsals.

The director's function can vary considerably between multiple-camera and single-camera recording situations. The multiple-camera video director frequently sits in a control room isolated from the talent and crew during actual recording. In live and multiple-camera production, directors are usually directly involved in the selection of specific types of shots and in the creation of transition devices and special effects. The multiple-camera director supervises the movement of several cameras, using an intercom, and controls the editing by having the TD punch buttons on the switcher, changing the main signal from one camera or source to another. The single-camera director, on the other hand, is usually present on the set during the shooting and works directly with the talent and crew during the period of time between shots, when the camera is being moved and the lighting and sound recording devices reset. The editing of single-camera production is usually left to a specialist who cuts the film or electronically edits together videotape during postproduction.

EXERCISES

1. View a scene or sequence from a completed production repeatedly and write a postproduction shooting script or shot analysis for it based on actual shots in the finished product. Compare your shooting script or shot analysis for this segment to a published version to determine if you have made proper use of shooting script terms and concepts.

2. Take a segment from a completed and published script and attempt to transform it into a shooting script by adding specific shots, sound effects, and so on. Use techniques that are consistent with a realist, modernist, or postmodernist approach when creating your shooting script. Do this exercise for both a multiple-camera production and a single-camera production.

3. Record a television program without watching it. Then play it back without watching the screen. Determine if you are able to follow and understand the program without the visual side of the story line.

4. Record another program, only this time don't listen to it. Then play it back, and watch it with the sound turned down. Determine if you are able to follow and understand the program without the audio portion of the story line.

5. Using either of the tapes from Exercise 3 or 4, carefully listen to the sounds and create a chart by time in seconds. On the chart, indicate when there is music, sound effects, narration, wild sound, and dialogue. Keep each type of sound in a separate column to determine how much of the audio portion of the program is music, SFX, narration, wild sound, or dialogue.

6. Using either of the programs recorded in Exercise 3 or 4, create a chart showing each transition between shots. List cuts, dissolves, wipes, digital effects, and fades to or from black. Total the number of transitions and how many of each type were used in the production.

Additional Readings

Andrew, J Dudley. 1976. Major Film Theories, Oxford University Press, New York.

Benedetti, Robert. 2002. From Concept to Screen: An Overview of Film and Television Production, Allyn & Bacon, Boston.

Block, Bruce. 2008. The Visual Story: Creating the Visual Structure of Film, Video, TV and Digital Media, Focal Press, Boston.

Bordwell, David, Thompson, Kristin. 1986. Film Art: An Introduction, second ed. Knopf, New York.

Burch, Noel. 1973. Theory of Film Practice, Trans., Helen R. Lane. Praeger, New York.

Cury, Ivan. 2006. Directing and Producing for Television: A Format Approach, third ed. Focal Press, Boston.

Dancyger, Ken. 2006. The Director's Idea: The Path to Great Directing, Focal Press, Boston.

DeKoven, Lenore. 2006. Changing Direction: A Practical Approach to Directing Actors in Film and Theatre, Focal Press, Boston.

Douglass, John S, Harnden, Glenn. 1996. The Art of Technique: An Aesthetic Approach to Film and Video Production, Allyn & Bacon, Needham Heights, MA.

Gross, Lynne S, Ward, Larry W. 2007. Digital Moviemaking, sixth ed. Wadsworth, Belmont, CA.

Hanson, Matt. 2006. Reinventing Music Video: Next Generation Directors, Their Inspiration and Work, Focal Press, Boston.

Irving, David K, Rea, Peter W. 2006. Producing and Directing the Short Film and Video, third ed. Focal Press, Boston.

Kindem, Gorham. 1994. The Live Television Generation of Hollywood Film Directors, McFarland, Jefferson, NC.

Kingson, Walter K, Cowgill, Rome. 1965. Television Acting and Directing, Holt, Rinehart & Winston, New York.

Musburger, Robert B. 2005. Single-Camera Video Production, fourth ed. Focal Press, Boston.

Proferes, Nicholas. 2008. Film Directing Fundamentals: See Your Film Before Shooting, third ed. Focal Press, Boston.

Rabiger, Michael. 2007. Directing: Film Techniques and Aesthetics, fourth ed. Focal Press, Boston.

Rabiger, Michael. 2004. Directing the Documentary, fourth ed. Focal Press, Boston.

Shyles, Leonard C. 2007. The Art of Video Production, Sage.

Thomas, James. 2005. Script Analysis for Actors, Directors, and Designers, third ed. Focal Press, Boston.

Utterback, Samuel. 2007. Studio Television Production and Directing, Focal Press, Boston.

Ward, Peter. 2003. Picture Composition, third ed. Focal Press, Boston.

Watkinson, John. 2000. The Art of Digital Video, Focal Press, Boston.

Wilkinson, Charles. 2005. The Working Director: How to Arrive, Thrive, and Survive in the Director's Chair, Michael Wiese Productions, Studio City, CA.

Zettl, Herbert. 2008. Sight, Sound, and Motion: Applied Media Aesthetics, fifth ed. Wadsworth, Belmont, CA.

Zettl, Herbert. 2009. Television Production Handbook, tenth ed. Wadsworth, Belmont, CA.

Audio/Sound

- What are the aesthetics of sound?
- What types of mics are available?
- How are mics selected and placed?
- How is sound measured and controlled?
- What does sound perspective mean?
- How are sound signals connected?

Introduction

This chapter explores the audio production techniques and equipment used to record and control high-quality sound and sound perspectives. Quality audio is extremely important in media production. Poor-quality sounds can destroy the impact of high-quality visuals. High-quality sounds not only enhance accompanying visuals, but they can directly affect emotions and develop additional creative dimensions and responses.

Some directors feel that sounds and visual images should be almost completely independent of one another so that each component could stand entirely on its own, whereas others feel that sounds should reinforce accompanying visual images. The former approach is consistent with modernist aesthetics, whereas the latter reflects a realist approach to production. Some directors combine these approaches and suggest that high-quality sound should function well on its own as well as in combination with visual images.

Except for signal processing, editing, and distribution, no substantial difference exists between analog and digital audio production techniques. Greater care must be taken in all stages of digital audio production because of the increased frequency response and lower level of noise. Digital distribution systems are covered in Chapter 1, Producing: Exploiting New Opportunities and Markets in the Digital Arena, and editing technologies are covered in Chapter 10, Editing.

AESTHETICS OF AUDIO/SOUND

Audio/sound can be approached from the three aesthetic perspectives of realism, modernism, and postmodernism. A realist approach uses sound to stimulate an illusion of reality, reinforcing the temporal and spatial continuity of visual images. Modernist audio develops sound independently of accompanying visual images, breaking down realist conventions and stimulating more abstract impressions and visceral feelings. Postmodernist audio emphasizes listener participation within productions in order to emotionally involve the audience as much as possible.

TYPES OF MICROPHONES

The ability to duplicate quality audio in film, video, and audio-only situations depends on careful mic selection and placement. This means choosing a mic designed for the specific purpose at hand and positioning it properly. A microphone is a type of transducer. Transducers are devices that change one form of energy to another form of energy. Mics convert analog sound wave action into analog fluctuations in electrical voltage. A digital signal must be created by converting the analog signal through an analog-to-digital converter. Sound is created by the rapid vibration of objects and sound waves consist of rapidly contracting and expanding particles of air. A tuning fork, for example, causes air molecules to compress and expand as it vibrates, creating a sound pressure wave. As one arm moves forward, it pushes the air molecules, and as it moves backward, the air molecules, which are elastic or resistant to being pushed, expand again to fill the partial vacuum or void. Rapid vibration creates a pressure wave of alternately compressed and expanded air molecules. This pressure or sound wave moves in a relatively straight line and strikes other objects, such as the human ear or a microphone element. The eardrum vibrates in response to the sound wave and produces an auditory impression in the mind. A mic has an element that is sensitive to these airwaves and converts the wave action into corresponding fluctuations in electrical current. The electrical signal thus becomes an analog, or copy, of the sound wave. Once an electronic equivalent of the audio signal has been created, that signal may be converted into a digital signal for recording, processing, and maintenance of the highest quality during duplication.

Mics can be classified on the basis of the type of transducer element they use into three basic categories: dynamic, ribbon, and condenser. One type of mic element may be better suited to a specific audio situation than another.

Transducer Elements

A dynamic mic consists of a moving coil attached to a vibrating diaphragm or disc suspended between two magnetic poles. As the diaphragm vibrates with the sound wave, the coil moves up and down within a magnetic field and changes the voltage of the electrical current flowing through the coil. In general, dynamic mics are very durable, not extremely susceptible to wind noise, and relatively inexpensive (Figure 6.1).

A ribbon mic contains a narrow strip of corrugated foil suspended in a magnetic field. This ribbon vibrates in response to the difference in air pressure in front and

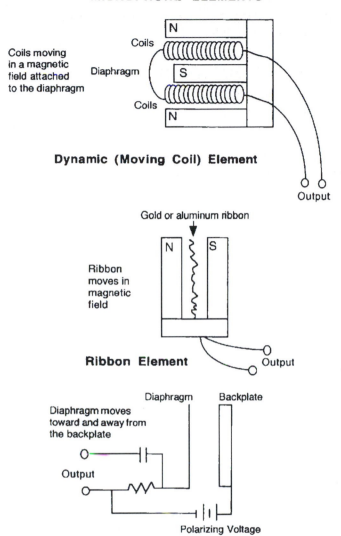

MICROPHONE ELEMENTS

Coils

Coils moving
in a magnetic
field attached
to the diaphragm

Diaphragm

Coils

Dynamic (Moving Coil) Element

Output

Gold or aluminum ribbon

Ribbon
moves in
magnetic
field

Ribbon Element

Output

Diaphragm moves
toward and away from
the backplate

Diaphragm

Backplate

Output

Polarizing Voltage

Condenser Element

FIGURE 6.1 The three transducer elements now used in microphones are dynamic, ribbon, and condenser. Dynamic transducer involves the movement of a thin diaphragm moving a coil of wires wrapped around a permanent magnetic. A ribbon transducer involves a thin corrugated strip of metal moving between the poles of a permanent magnet. A condenser transducer involves two thin plates of metal moving within a static-charged capacitance field.

in back of it and produces an alternating current along the length of a coil. The ribbon itself is quite fragile and can easily be damaged by simply blowing into the mic, although newer ribbon mics have been designed to be more durable but still are best confined to studio use. A ribbon mic usually produces a smooth, bass-accentuated sound, is preferred by many radio and television announcers for that reason, and it is ideal for digital recording because its warm sound accentuates high frequencies. Most ribbon mics are priced at the top of the range of professional microphones.

Condenser mics are relatively complex, compared to dynamic or ribbon mics. The element is a capacitor that requires two charged plates: a diaphragm and a fixed back plate. As the diaphragm vibrates, the space between it and the fixed plate changes in capacitance, that is, in its ability to pass an electrical current or signal. The strength of the electrical sound signal increases or decreases accordingly. The signal is very weak, however, and a preamplifier is required to boost the signal to a usable level. Additional current may be supplied to the preamplifier by a battery in the mic handle or by a power supply located in the mixer called a *phantom supply*. An electret condenser mic is constructed with permanently charged plates, reducing the power needed to operate the mic and the need for a built-in preamplifier. Condenser mics vary in price from relatively inexpensive to quite expensive, and some inexpensive cameras and cassette recorders have built-in condenser mics of lesser quality. A condenser mic generally reproduces high-quality sound, and with its built-in preamp can be considered quite sensitive.

Pickup Patterns

Mics can be classified according to their directional sensitivity or pickup patterns, as well as their transducer elements. Different recording situations require the use of mics that pick up sounds from a very narrow or a very wide area. Some mics pick up sounds coming from every direction, whereas others are sensitive to a very restricted area. The three basic categories of pickup patterns are as follows: omnidirectional, bidirectional, and unidirectional or cardioid.

An *omnidirectional mic* is equally sensitive to sounds from all directions, that is, from the entire 360-degree area surrounding it. A *bidirectional mic* is sensitive to sounds coming from two opposite directions. Its sensitivity drops off rapidly at 60 degrees on either side of these two opposite directional points. At 90 degrees (perpendicular to the two optimal sound source directions), it is almost totally insensitive to sound. Unidirectional mics are sensitive to sounds from one direction only (Figure 6.2).

A *cardioid mic* is a type of unidirectional mic so named because its pickup pattern is heart shaped. A cardioid mic is somewhat more sensitive to sound emanating from directly behind it, but it is very sensitive to sound coming from directly in front of it. A supercardioid mic is somewhat more sensitive to sound coming from the rear of the mic but has an even narrower optimal response area (about 60 degrees as opposed to 120 degrees for a cardioid mic). Shotgun mics are long, narrow tubes; they frequently have a supercardioid pickup pattern.

A multidirectional mic is constructed with more than one pickup head aligned to receive sound from different directions. Such a mic may contain as many as six heads placed for simultaneous recoding of 5.1 audio mounted in one fixture. The mic combination may be mounted directly on a camera or any other mic mounting system. The danger of using such a mic comes from any equipment noise near the mic being picked up by more than one head increasing noise levels (Figure 6.3).

Impedance

A third characteristic of microphones that determines their use and placement is impedance. Impedance is a complex measurement of the property of wires and equipment that determines the ability of a signal to pass through that piece of equipment. It is critical that all audio equipment be designed to match input and output impedances. For microphones, there are two basic impedance choices, high or low.

Microphone Pickup Patterns

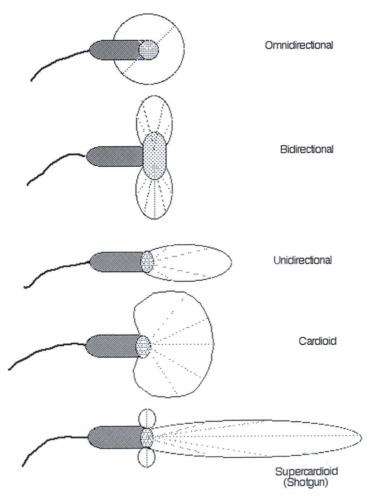

FIGURE 6.2 Three basic microphone pickup patterns of omnidirectional, bidirectional, and unidirectional may be modified or combined to create two additional patterns: cardioid or supercardioid or shotgun pattern.

High-impedance mics are low-cost amateur mics, whereas all professional mics are low impedance. High-impedance mics may be connected with wires that contain one conductor and a shield, which does not provide the maximum protection for the signal from outside interference. Low-impedance mics normally are connected with wires that contain two conductors and a shield, providing maximum protection for the signal.

MIC PLACEMENT AND SELECTION

Mic placement during recording can be either on-camera or off-camera. On-camera mics, such as a reporter's handheld mic, are visible to the viewer. Off-camera mics are not visible to the viewer. An off-camera mic can be hidden somewhere on the set or under a speaker's clothing, or it can be situated just outside the camera frame.

FIGURE 6.3 Recording raw six channel audio simultaneously may be accomplished using a multidirectional mic, which contains at least six different heads pointed in six different directions to provide the various sources needed for 5.1 channel programming. (Courtesy of Holophone Surround Sound Microphone Systems.)

On-Camera Mics

Hand mics are the most common on-camera mics. Mics that are to be handheld should be shock mounted; that is, they should be well insulated so that noise is not created as the performer moves the mic. Because the performer can move and control a hand mic, it does not always stay in a fixed position, and it generally has a relatively wide pickup pattern, such as omnidirectional or cardioid. It is wise to use a mic with a durable element, such as a dynamic or an electret condenser mic, in a handheld situation. An inexperienced performer should be instructed in how to keep the hand mic at a relatively constant distance from his or her mouth in order to keep the loudness relatively constant. A problem that frequently arises with the use of a hand mic is controlling the mic cable. Performers must learn to move the mic around without stretching the cable or tangling it (Figure 6.4).

Desk mics often have less durable elements than hand mics. If a desk mic is placed in a relatively permanent position, it does not have to be shock mounted. If a desk mic is to be removed from its mount and also function as a hand mic, as frequently occurs, it must have some of the same qualities as a hand mic. Most desk mics have cardioid pickup patterns and are placed one to two feet from the speaker. Sometimes a single bidirectional or omnidirectional desk mic can be used for two speakers to limit the number of mics needed (Figure 6.5).

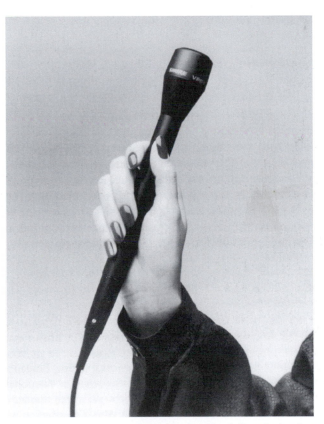

FIGURE 6.4 Hand microphones also may be mounted on a desk stand, floor stand, or boom, but they must be designed to fit comfortably in the hand with reasonable sensitivity. (Courtesy of Shure.)

FIGURE 6.5 A desk stand is designed to hold a microphone in position to pick up people seated at the desk. It usually works best for one person but can be placed between two people if their audio levels are nearly the same. (Courtesy of ElectroVoice USA.)

A *stand mic* is supported on an adjustable pole in front of the performer; thus, it offers a distinct advantage to a person who has his or her hands occupied with a musical instrument. The stand mic can usually be tilted and adjusted to a comfortable height for different performers. In general, more sensitive ribbon and condenser mics are used on a stand to record relatively soft sound sources such as stringed instruments, whereas dynamic mics with omnidirectional or cardioid reception patterns are often used for singers and amplified instruments. Sometimes more than one mic may be attached to a single stand: perhaps a condenser mic positioned from below to pick up the sounds of a guitar and a dynamic mic above to pick up the singer's voice (Figure 6.6).

A *lavaliere mic* also leaves a performer's hands free and does not require a stand that restricts his or her mobility. This type of mic, which is either hung around the performer's neck with a strap or clipped to a tie or outer garment, is relatively unobtrusive compared with a desk mic or a stand mic. Care should be taken in the placement of a lavaliere mic to ensure that it will not create noise by rubbing against rough clothing or jewelry. Lavaliere mics are often susceptible to cable problems because their cables are relatively thin and fragile. To guard against this on live broadcasts, performers such as newscasters often wear two lavalieres clipped together to create a dual-redundancy system, where one mic serves as a backup for the other. Only one mic at a time is live to prevent phasing problems, which are discussed later in this chapter. A lavaliere microphone can be hidden or concealed behind clothing, although this can lead to added rubbing noise (Figure 6.7).

FIGURE 6.6 A stand mic is designed to allow one or more people to stand on each side of the microphone, depending on whether the microphone is bidirectional, unidirectional, or omnidirectional. (Courtesy of Sony Corporation.)

Some handheld and lavaliere mics have battery-powered FM transmitters, which allow the speaker using the mic to move around quite freely without a restrictive mic cable. Wireless lavaliere mics can also be used as hidden mics by concealing the mic and its transmitter under clothing. An FM receiver at the audio input of the recording machine receives the transmitted signal. Although wireless mics can be extremely helpful in many difficult recording situations, they also have a number of pitfalls. Like any FM radio, the wireless receiver can pick up interfering signals, such as noise from CB radios. Batteries can expire in the middle of a recording, especially when performers forget to turn them off. Finally, wireless mics are more expensive to rent or purchase than wired mics (Figure 6.8).

Off-Camera Mics

Off-camera mics may be attached to a mic boom. A *mic boom* is a long pole that can be placed (usually above the heads of the talent) just outside the camera frame. It can also be hidden on the set. There are three different types of mic booms: fishpole, giraffe, and perambulator booms. A *fishpole boom* is an aluminum pole with a mic-mounting device at one end. Some fishpoles can be telescoped to allow for maximum extension during shooting and contracted for compact storage.

One disadvantage of the fishpole boom is that the length generally cannot be changed during recording. The boom operator must move as the talent moves. Also, the entire pole must be twisted to change the positioning of the microphone, making it somewhat difficult to alternate the placement of a directional mic between two different performers. The portability and flexibility of a fishpole gain may be increased by using an FM mic instead of a wired mic (Figure 6.9).

A *giraffe boom* is somewhat more bulky and less portable than the fishpole, but it allows for greater mobility and flexibility during recording. The giraffe is basically a fishpole gain attached to a three-wheeled dolly. It can be quickly and easily moved around the studio. It also has the advantage of allowing the operator to rotate the mic on a swivel to which the pole is attached. It requires only one operator and can be extended to different lengths during camera setups (Figure 6.10).

The *perambulator boom* is the heaviest type of boom. It has a large pole, which can be telescoped during a camera take; a swivel mechanism for rotating the mic; an operator platform, which can be raised and lowered; heavy-duty rubber tires; a guide pole, which requires the presence of a second operator to push or pull the boom around the studio; and a boom pan-and-tilt control. The perambulator boom is designed primarily for studio use. It is not very portable. It is counterweighted so that it can support a heavy microphone and a mounting device. Some perambulator booms allow an attached

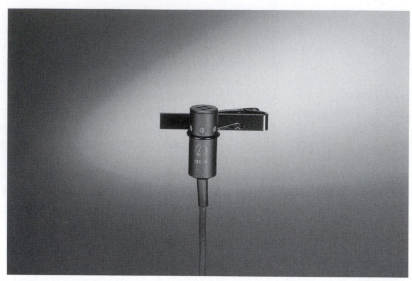

FIGURE 6.7 A lavaliere microphone is designed to be clipped to the clothing of the person speaking. The design of a lavaliere compensates for the microphone resting against the chest of the speaker, and the microphone is located below the speaker's mouth. A lavaliere should not be used as a handheld microphone away from the body. (Courtesy of Audio-Technica.)

FIGURE 6.8 A wireless microphone may be designed as either handheld, a lavaliere, or on a head mount. The transmitter may be built into the base of the handheld microphone, or the lavaliere and head mount may be connected to a small transmitter fastened to the body of the performer. (Courtesy of Audio-Technica.)

FIGURE 6.9 The fishpole's greatest asset is its portability. A fishpole and the attached mic are usually lightweight enough to be handheld for a relatively long period of time without excessively tiring the operator. (Courtesy of ElectroVoice USA.)

FIGURE 6.10 A giraffe microphone is a small boom generally used to pick up the voice of one or two persons in fixed locations.

microphone to be panned or moved a full 180 degrees, so that a highly directional mic can be used to pick up a moving performer or to switch from one speaker to another.

Boom Operation

Operating a boom demands great care and manual dexterity. Movements of the mic and the boom must be smooth, precise, and carefully planned. Excessively rapid movements of the boom or mic will create objectionable noise. The movement of the talent must be fully anticipated by the boom operator. If the boom operator has not preplanned the movements of the boom so that it can follow the talent, it will be difficult to maintain a constant sound level or to avoid crashing into other equipment on the set. The boom operator's job is to keep a moving sound source within the mic's primary pickup pattern. The operator listens to the sounds on headphones, which serve the same function as a viewfinder for a camera operator.

Omnidirectional mics are rarely used on a boom, even though using a boom might make it easier to follow the movements of the talent, because they simply pick up too much unwanted additional noise. Unidirectional mics seem to work best on a boom. They cut down on unwanted sounds by focusing on the sound source, and they provide good reception at a greater distance from the subject than mics with wider pickup patterns. This can be especially helpful when recording long camera shots with an off-camera mic.

Boom Placement

The optimum placement of a cardioid mic on a boom is one to four feet in front of and one to three feet above the speaking subject. In general, the boom operator should keep a uniform distance between the subject and the mic. Sometimes it may be necessary to vary this distance, however. To achieve proper sound perspective in single-camera recording, the mic may have to be slightly closer to the subject for close-ups and farther away for long shots (Figure 6.11).

An overhead boom can create harsh shadows that disrupt the image. The placement and movement of a boom must be carefully preplanned to prevent objectionable shadows on the set. Sometimes it is simply impossible to place the microphone directly overhead on a boom without noticeably affecting the lighting or camera and performer movements. In these situations, a fishpole boom may be placed at the bottom or side of the frame, or a hidden mic may be used.

Boom operators who are attempting to record the best-quality sound often place the mic as close to the subject as possible without the mic entering the camera frame. In multiple-camera production, the audio operator informs the boom operator when the mic has entered an underscanned TV monitor, which shows a portion of the picture not viewed at home. In single-camera productions, the camera operator carefully monitors the frame area. One strategy boom operators sometimes use to obtain good-quality sound is to place the mic within the camera frame during a rehearsal or blocking session. This forces the director, audio operator, or camera operator to ask for the mic to be raised out of the frame. This strategy ensures that the mic will always be as close as possible to the subject and forces the director to consider whether the camera placement is compromising the quality of the sound. Although directors usually are well aware of these limitations, a periodic reminder can go a long way toward preventing subsequent objections to the quality of the sound recording.

Hidden Mics

There are three different types of hidden or concealed mics: the hanging mic, the prop mic, and the concealed lavaliere mic. *Hanging* and *prop mics* are stationary, but the concealed *lavaliere* moves with the talent to whom it is attached. A stationary hanging mic can be attached to an overhead grid. It is usually an omnidirectional mic capable of covering a wide area of action. Its chief advantage is that it does not require a boom operator. Its obvious disadvantages are that it cannot be moved to vary or improve the audio during visual recording, and it often picks up ambient noises below it, such as footsteps and equipment being moved. Prop mics are microphones that are concealed on the set. A telephone at the center of a table around which several performers are seated can conceal a mic. Because a prop mic is stationary, it often has a relatively wide pickup pattern so that the talent does not have to stand immediately in front of the prop, calling attention to the presence of the mic or making it the focal point of a scene (Figures 6.12 and 6.13).

A *prop mic* can be extremely useful in situations in which it is difficult to use a boom, such as when the camera is shooting an extreme long shot or when the space is so confining that a boom necessarily affects the lighting. A concealed lavaliere mic is

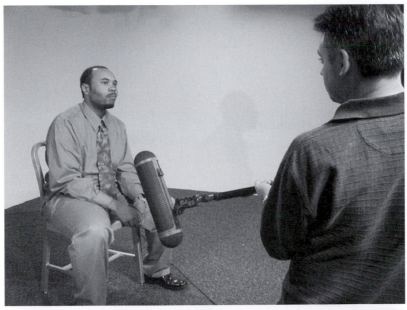

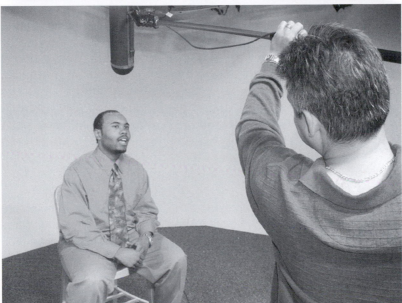

FIGURE 6.11 A handheld microphone boom may be placed above the speaker's head or below, depending on the noise at the location or the type of shot. The mic may be placed closer to the speaker's mouth if the shot is a close-up rather than a wide shot.

frequently used as a hidden mic for extreme long shots and complicated movements of the camera or talent. The concealed lavaliere mic may be wrapped in foam rubber and taped to the subject underneath his or her clothing. It should not be free to rub against garments or jewelry and create noise, and care must be taken to ensure that heavy clothing does not muffle the sound that the mic is intended to pick up.

Another solution to reaching sound without the mic in view of the camera is to use a *supercardioid* or *shotgun mic* (Figure 6.14).

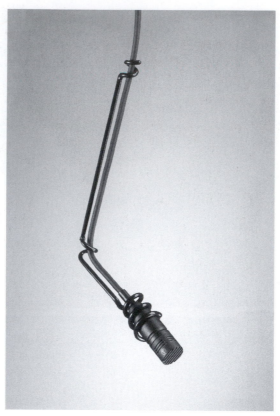

FIGURE 6.12 In an emergency, a microphone can be hung from a light batten over a sound source, but this works best if the person speaking stands in one position and the mic is a cardioid. (Courtesy of Audio-Technica.)

Wireless (RF) Mics

As media productions become more mobile, a need for a system of connecting audio sources with recorders and mixers without entangling wires brought about the development radio frequency (RF) wireless microphones. Each RF system consists of a microphone, a transmitter, and a receiver. Mics (usually electret) may be body mounted, head mounted, handheld, stand, or boom mounted. Each mic must be connected to a transmitter. A transmitter may be built into the base of the mic or plugged into the base of the mic, or a lavaliere mic may be connected with a short cable to a body-mounted transmitter. The receiver may be a small, battery-operated unit mounted on a camcorder or a larger A/C-powered unit feeding a mixer, public address system, or recorder (Figure 6.15).

The transmitters are designed to operate on one of three frequency bands: VHF, UHF, or ultra UHF. VHF equipment offers lower-priced equipment but may suffer a greater chance for interference from taxis, police officers, or other RF users. Units operating on UHF frequencies are designed specifically for radio and TV broadcasters for high-quality communication systems. Newer digital units operate above the UHF band offering the highest quality but are the most expensive. Antenna placement on both the transmitter and receiver is critical. Operation and positioning of all RF equipment should closely follow the manufacturer's recommendations.

FIGURE 6.13 If the production requires off-camera mics, a microphone also can be concealed in a set piece or hand prop on a set near where the actors will be talking.

FIGURE 6.14 The long reach of a shotgun provides sound pickup for documentaries, news gathering, and interviews in production situations that require quick and efficient operation. (Courtesy of Sennheiser USA.)

With smaller and quieter operating cameras, a mic mounted directly on the camera provides flexibility in movement, especially for news gathering and documentary productions.

Selecting the Best Mic

Selecting the best mic for a specific recording situation depends on an understanding of sound aesthetics and different mic characteristics. The more versatile and widely used mics are the *dynamic* and electret condenser cardioids. They have extremely durable elements and a pickup pattern about halfway between a full-range

FIGURE 6.15 High-quality, sensitive mics can be mounted directly on camera if the production requires that need, but this is not the best means of gathering sound except in unusual or emergency situations. (Courtesy of Sennheiser USA.)

omnidirectional and a narrow unidirectional mic. An on-camera mic can be hand-held (in this case they should be shock mounted) or mounted on a floor or desk stand. An off-camera mic can be suspended overhead on a mic boom just outside the frame.

A cardioid mic works best when it is relatively close to the speaker or sound source; thus, it is not always the best mic to use for long-distance pickup. If an off-camera mic must be used at some distance from the speaker during the recording of an extremely long shot, then a unidirectional condenser mic, such as a supercardioid shotgun mic, may be the best choice. The narrow pickup pattern isolates the primary signal from the surrounding space. The condenser element provides a stronger signal because of its built-in preamplifier. Care must be exercised when using a shotgun mic, however, so that noise coming from directly behind the speaker is not amplified along with the primary voice signal.

A second concern with the dynamic cardioid mic is that it is difficult to make inconspicuous on camera. A lavaliere condenser mic can be the size of a tie tack. It can be placed very close to the speaker without dominating the frame. It can also be completely hidden in a person's clothing. When connected to a tiny FM transmitter, it can even allow for freedom of movement without mic cables or for extremely long-range camera shots with extremely high-quality voice sounds. This can be an advantage when recording functional sound, but realistic sound perspective is better achieved by using a shotgun mic. The ribbon mic is best left to completely stationary performance situations, such as talk shows, interviews, or dramatic radio productions. The ribbon mic can be versatile in such a situation, because it is capable of producing a resonant sound. It can be set for an omnidirectional, bidirectional, or unidirectional pickup pattern so that several speakers, a single speaker, or two performers facing each other can use it. An omnidirectional dynamic or condenser mic is often used to record several speakers simultaneously. It can be suspended overhead in a fixed position or permanently positioned at a central location on the set.

Using Multiple Mics

Using a single omnidirectional mic is not necessarily the best way to record several different sound sources, such as several talk show performers. For one thing, even if the mic is centrally located, it will probably pick up a good deal of unwanted background sound along with the primary signals or voices. Using a different mic for each sound source provides better control and higher-quality sound recording, provided each mic can be placed close to its sound source. One advantage is that each mic can be selected for the particular characteristics of its sound source. For example, suppose that you are recording a singer on camera while a band is playing off camera. If the singer moves with a handheld mic, the loudness of the band music will vary with the mic direction, unless one or more stationary mics are set up specifically for the band.

These two sound sources should be separately controlled and combined (or mixed together), using two mic inputs on a recorder or a device called a mixer. The music now maintains a constant loudness. The singer can use a dynamic cardioid, while an omnidirectional dynamic or ribbon mic is set up for the band. Better yet, several different mics can be set up for different instruments in the band.

Separate mics can be set up for each individual speaker at a table. Each mic must be carefully placed, however, so that different mics do not pick up the same signals. This can lead to multiple-microphone interference, in which some of the sounds picked up simultaneously by two different mics cancel each other. Such cancellation is a phasing problem that occurs when similar sound waves passing through the same medium are 180 degrees out of phase with respect to each other. Phasing is sometimes used deliberately to create special audio effects, such as the noise of a robot or to disguise a speaker's identity.

The best way to find out if multiple-microphone interference exists is to set one mic at its proper level and then turn on the other mic. If the volume goes down rather than up when both mics are on, there is interference, which must be corrected by changing the distance between the two mics or their directional placement. Some sophisticated audio consoles allow the audio engineer to eliminate phasing problems electronically. Multiple-microphone interference can be prevented by keeping live mics well separated, using directional mics, and having them directed at different sound sources. If two subjects are seated close together, a single mic should be used for both, either by swiveling an overhead mic or a boom or by placing a stand mic or a desk mic with a relatively wide pickup pattern between them. When more than two people are involved, two or more mics should be set up so that they are at least three times as far apart as the subject-to-mic distances. This three-to-one rule ensures that there will be no phasing problems with multiple mics (Figure 6.16).

Another solution is multichannel recording, where each mic is fed to a separate recording channel on a computer sound application or digital audio workstation (DAW). Using multiple mics can also cause problems with excessive ambient noise. Each mic picks up the same ambient noise, and when more than one mic is used, the ambient noise adds up and can become disturbingly loud. Placing mics as close as possible to their sound sources so that loudness levels can be turned down reduces ambient noise in some instances. At other times, different speakers can simply share the same mic.

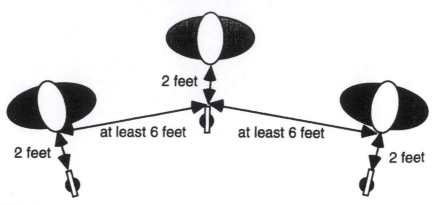

**MULTIPLE MICROPHONE PLACEMENT
THE 3-TIMES RULE**

2 feet

at least 6 feet   at least 6 feet

2 feet   2 feet

FIGURE 6.16 When using multiple microphones, the three-times rule should be followed. The rule indicates that each sound source (person) must be three times the distance from any other microphone as he or she is from his or her own microphone. Any closer and audio phasing may occur, causing the sound to distort.

Stereo Mic Placement

Stereo provides an additional spatial dimension by giving sound a directional placement from left to right. This is accomplished by recording sounds with at least two mics. Two cardioid mics can be arranged so that they crisscross one another, forming a 45- to 90-degree angle.

Each mic picks up sounds from a different direction. This setup works quite well for speech. Using two parallel cardioid mics separated by 10 to 15 feet and well in front of an orchestra or band works well for music. The sounds picked up by each mic are kept separate and recorded on different audio channels, which can then be played back through speakers that are spatially separated from one another. For proper balance, the mics must be adjusted so that a sound coming from a source directly between them creates a signal that is equally strong on both channels.

Cardioid mics are well adapted to stereophonic use because they are slightly more receptive to sounds directly in front of them than to sounds coming from the right or left. Stereophonic sound can be used to bring added realism or simply more spectacular audio effects to a film or television program. But stereo can also bring added production problems. In terms of production logistics, it is often difficult to record stereophonic sound on location. Handling additional mics and audio equipment inevitably leads to greater risks and problems. Stereophonic recording also complicates the postproduction process, because many additional sound elements must be smoothly combined and balanced during final mixing.

Mics with built-in dual pickup heads aligned for stereo recording allow for handheld recording of stereo programming as well as providing alternate means of placing mics for stereo sound pickup. Such mics appear to be the same as standard mono-mics but provide at least two channels of separate stereo audio.

Digital Mic Placement

Most equipment, including microphones, originally designed for analog sound systems emphasizes high frequencies to compensate for losses. Digital systems do not

FIGURE 6.17 Mics specifically designed for use with computers are equipped with an USB plug that carries the audio signal to the computer and power to the mic if needed. (Courtesy of Audio-Technica.)

suffer the same problem, so mics designed for analog systems used on digital systems tend to sound strident and shrill. Noises created in preamplifiers or other sources of noise that are not noticed in analog systems may become obvious in digital systems. Therefore, mics must be positioned to avoid emphasizing high frequencies by placing them off-center rather than straight out from a sound source (Figure 6.17). Some mics now are equipped to operate directly into the central processing unit (CPU) of a computer. The mic does not require an adapter of special cable because its impedance is matched to the computer audio board input.

Setting mics close also may cause distortions or noise that would not be obvious in analog systems but that would be heard in digital systems, because there is little or no masking of tape- or amplifier-created noise in a digital system. Some digital systems are also sensitive to overmodulation, creating another type of distortion to guard against.

SOUND-SIGNAL CONTROL

Controlling sound depends on understanding problems of level, signal to noise, and managing the signal as it passes through cables and operational equipment.

Audio Problems: Distortion and Noise

Distortion and noise are two different unwanted changes in an audio or video signal. *Distortion* is an unwanted change in a signal; *noise* is an unwanted addition to the signal. In both cases, audio may be distortion or noise in a specific production, or simply an additional audio element. Rock musicians often add distortion to their music for an effect. Someone trying to listen to a country-and-western recording would consider a classical music recording played simultaneously as noise. But, of course, to a classical music fan, classical music is not noise (Figure 6.18).

One of the most common problems encountered in audio recording is distortion. The most common type of distortion encountered by beginning media production students is loudness distortion, which occurs when a sound is recorded at a level that exceeds the limitations of the electronic system. The peaks or high points of the sound wave are flattened, and new, unwanted frequencies of sound are produced. The end result is a reproduction that sounds like there is some kind of variable interference or garble on the line. Loudness distortion is controlled by setting the volume so that it does not exceed the limits of the system. A volume unit (VU) meter, light emitting diode (LED) meter, or peak program meter (PPM) allows the recordist to set the volume controls as high as needed for a good-quality recording without distorting the sound. Digital audio systems are sensitive to loudness distortion. Levels must be monitored carefully while recording and editing.

There are basically two types of noise, ambient noise, discussed earlier, and system noise. *Ambient noise* comes from open mics fed into an audio console or tape recorder that pick up the sound of air ventilators, lights, cameras, or other devices. (Fluorescent lights frequently cause a hum or buzzing sound, for example.) A second type of noise is called *system noise*, which can come from the electrical recording system and equipment. Microphone lines placed too close to lights and electrical cables often create system noise, as do worn volume controls or bad circuit boards and cable connections. Tape hiss is inherent in any system using analog tape recordings. Most ambient noise and some system noise can be controlled, but most system noise is simply inherent in the recording equipment. A digital audio system cannot control ambient noise any differently than an analog system can, but a digital system does reduce system noise to a minimum level. Therefore, signal-to-noise ratios are less important in digital systems.

An important determinant of sound quality is a system's signal-to-noise ratio. This is the ratio of desired sounds to unwanted system noise. Many professional audio systems have signal-to-noise ratios of 55:1 or above; that is, the main signal is 55 times as loud as the system's noise level. Quality audio production requires the

NOISE   **ORIGINAL**   **DISTORTION**

FIGURE 6.18 There are two types of sound: noise or distortion. Noise is unwanted sound that's added the original sound, and distortion is an unwanted modification of the original sound.

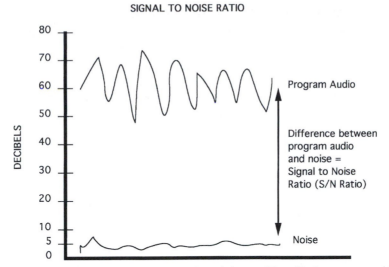

FIGURE 6.19 The ability to minimize the signal-to-noise ratio is one of the critical measures used to determine the quality of an electronic system. Noise inherent in magnetic-tape systems and noise picked up by cables are the leading creators of poor signal-to-noise ratios.

maintenance of high signal-to-noise ratios throughout all stages of the process. At each stage of duplication or reproduction, an analog system's signal-to-noise ratio will decrease, increasing the noise level. In digital systems, duplication or reproduction will not normally change the signal-to-noise ratio, thereby maintaining the same low level of noise (Figure 6.19).

Sound Intensity Measurement

Many different devices for indicating the volume intensity or loudness of a sound signal are used today. A less expensive tape recorder often has a red light that flickers with volume peaks. Overmodulation or loudness distortion is indicated when the light stays brightly lit for a continuous period rather than flickering intermittently. Other recorders employ a needle device that indicates loudness distortion when the needle enters a red zone. These less-expensive meters are quite small and do not have precise volume scales. More expensive meters are calibrated in specific units of sound intensity, such as volume units or percentages of modulation. There are basically three types of professional sound intensity meters: volume unit (VU) meters, peak program meters (PPMs), and light emitting diode (LED) meters. The VU meter has been the American standard. It is a special type of electrical voltmeter, which reads voltage shifts in electrical current as changes in sound intensity (Figure 6.20).

Needle readings are calibrated in both percentages of modulation and volume units or decibels (dBs). Approximately every 3 dB increase indicates a doubling of sound intensity. (A decibel is a logarithmic unit of sound intensity.) The modulation percentages are usually indicated on the lower scale of a VU meter. They range from 9 percent to 100 percent, the thresholds of signal detection and distortion, respectively. The upper scale indicates volume units or decibels. A reading of 0 dB usually corresponds to 100 percent modulation or peak loudness before distortion occurs, and the scale reads down on the left side and up on the right side (+1, +2, +3, and so on) of 0 dB.

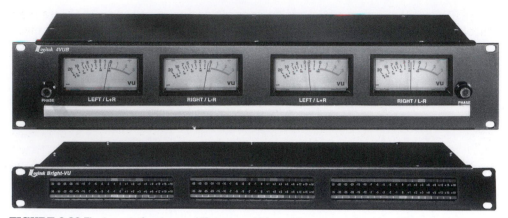

FIGURE 6.20 The top set of meters are VU meters, which read the average signal level. The set of meters on the bottom are LED meters, and they generally are set to read peak audio voltages. (Courtesy of Logitek USA.)

A VU meter provides an electrical analog to human hearing. It does not show instantaneous peaks and immediate distortion, but it does indicate the average sound intensity over a very short period of time. This average reading closely approximates the response of the human ear to peak sound intensities. In general, signals on a VU meter should register between 50 percent and 100 percent modulation, or between 6 dB and 0 dB. Below 50 percent modulation or 6 dB, the signal-to-noise ratio becomes relatively low. Above 100 percent modulation or 0 dB loudness, distortion occurs. Sounds that intermittently peak above 100 percent modulation, or 0 dB, for very short periods of time rarely cause noticeable distortion, but sounds that continuously pin the needle to its maximum above 100 percent modulation, or 0 dB, not only cause distortion but frequently cause meter damage as well. The audio operator continually watches the VU meter and makes minor adjustments in the sound level throughout a recording, using a volume-control mechanism such as a *potentiometer* (pot) or a sliding fader bar. Volume level adjustments should be made smoothly and slowly. Major shifts in volume level affect the noise levels and background sounds as well as the primary signal and change the sound perspective and dynamics of the recorded sounds.

The PPM (sometimes called a *modulometer*) is another type of loudness or voltmeter and is the European standard. Rather than averaging sound intensities, a PPM responds immediately to peak sounds. The human ear cannot perceive extremely rapid loudness distortion, but many PPM users believe that such distortion nonetheless affects a sound recording. Obviously an operator using a PPM or modulometer must respond to needle readings on the devices somewhat differently, probably more reservedly and slowly, than one would respond to a VU meter reading. Both types of meters facilitate sound signal control, however.

A third type of level monitoring is a series of light-emitting diodes (LED). The string of diodes lights as the level intensity changes, providing an accurate and easy-to-follow means of monitoring levels. The diodes usually are arranged in a row with at least two colors. A change in color indicates over modulation. LEDs measure instantaneous peak voltages and are considered the most accurate method of determining sound levels. The LED's small size, absence of moving parts, and minimal voltage requirements make it the ideal tool for measuring audio levels in digital equipment. The same criteria of setting proper levels determined years ago with VU meters also applies to using LED or PPI audio metering systems. Maximum levels of digital audio are more critical than analog, so proper monitoring while recording digital audio is imperative.

Some recorders have automatic gain controls (AGC) or automatic level controls (ALC) for mic input. An AGC prevents loudness distortion automatically. However, it also boosts the ambient noise level when primary sounds are at low levels, such as at pauses in dialogue. To avoid this problem, levels should be set manually using a VU meter with the AGC turned off, if possible. Peak limiters are sometimes more useful than AGCs, as these simply limit the upper level of loudness without automatically setting the basic recording level and running the risk of increasing ambient noise levels. But most professionals prefer to control recording levels manually. Volume levels on a digital recording must also be carefully set. Although digital signals are either off or on, they do vary in intensity. An overmodulated digital recording will suffer uncorrectable distortion or total loss of the recording (Figure 6.21).

Cables and Connectors

Professional mic cables have two conductor wire lines: a ground and a grounded shield. This type of balanced line is less susceptible to cable noise than an unbalanced line, which has a single conductor wire and a grounded shield. The two conductor lines are usually well insulated from each other, the ground wire, and the cable

FIGURE 6.21 Audio control boards vary from small portable boards (*top*) for field and postproduction facilities to large multi-input and multi-output boards (*bottom*) for motion picture mixing theaters and music recording studios. (Courtesy of Soundcraft Studer Group.)

exterior in balanced lines. Poorly insulated cables are much more susceptible to interference from other electrical cables and devices. Mic cables should never be placed near lighting instruments or electrical power cables, which can cause interference. Nor should they be wound tightly together or twisted in any manner that will reduce their life expectancy and damage the wire conductors. A less-expensive recorder sometimes has a mic attached by an unbalanced line cable with a single-prong miniplug at one end that is inserted into the front or side of the recorder. Balanced line cables are attached to three-prong XLR connectors, which can be plugged into mics, audio consoles, or tape recorders. These connectors have separate prongs for the two conductors and the ground. Male and female connector ends lock into each other so that they do not become disconnected easily (Figure 6.22).

It is probably a good idea to wrap two cables together in a very loose knot around the connectors, so that any pulling on the cables will pull the connectors together rather than apart. Even though this procedure may place considerable stress on the cables in the case of an accident, such as someone tripping over a cable, it would undoubtedly be more expensive to reshoot the entire sequence in the event of a complete disconnection. Care should be taken, of course, to minimize the amount of twisting and stress that occurs at the juncture of the cable and connector, because this part of the cable is extremely vulnerable to damage and wear. Also cables should be coiled carefully before storing. Two methods of coiling cables are the over-and-under method and the figure-eight method. Each system, when properly carried out, prevents internal twisting and damage to conductors inside the cable (Figure 6.23).

Mixing

An audio console or mixer is designed to combine sounds from several different sound sources, such as mics, tape recorders, and playback units. These devices can vary from an elaborate studio audio console to a simple multiple-input mixer, which allows for separate volume control over each input (Figure 6.24). Basically the audio console routes signals from sound sources or playback units to a control device or recording unit. It can send a signal from a particular mic or a playback unit to a recorder, so that

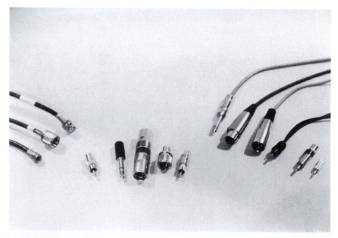

FIGURE 6.22 Audio and video signals are carried through different cable types and connected by a variety of connectors. On the left: three video cables, RF or F, UHF, and BNC. In the center: adapters, RCA to BNC, quarter-inch stereo to miniplug, an XLR male-to-male barrel, UHF to BNC, and RCA to miniplug. On the right: quarter-inch, XLR female, XLR male, RCA to quarter-inch adapter, and a microplug to miniplug adapter.

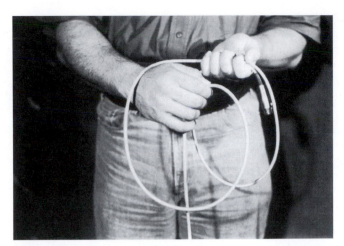

FIGURE 6.23 To properly coil cables, an over-and-under method may be used. This system protects the cable from twisting and provides a clean, straight unwinding when uncoiled for use.

a duplicate copy or dub can be made, for example. It can combine or mix together several sound sources into one (monophonic) or onto two or more (multitrack) sound-tracks or channels, which are recorded as a final or master audiotape.

In a digital board, the analog signals originating from mics, tape decks, or other non-digital sources are converted to a digital signal as it enters a digital mixer. Digital inputs are then combined with the converted analog inputs. From that point until the signal must be converted back to analog to feed speakers or headphones, the signal may remain in the digital format for processing and editing. Digital boards also provide for digital outputs to feed other digital signals including a digital transmitter. Some digital boards contain their own recording media. A computer hard drive, solid-state memory, or digital tape deck may be built into the board. Because a digital board is in essence a computer with multiple inputs and outputs, the processing of the signals, depending on the software, follows that of computer word processing: cutting, pasting, adding, deleting, and modifying with simple user-friendly controls. There will be more on this subject in Chapter 10, Editing. Some digital boards are labeled digital audio workstations (DAW) (Figure 6.25).

An audio console consists of a series of faders, each of which controls the volume level of a single input. The inputs can come from microphones, turntables, analog and digital audiotape recorders, compact disc (CD) players, or audio playbacks from videotape recorders. A single (or dual) master pot controls the output. Each pot or fader often has its own equalization controls for increasing or decreasing bass and treble (low frequencies and high frequencies) directly above or below it. In a digital board, signal control may be by faders or by computer controls or software operations (Figure 6.26).

Most audio consoles and mixers have two types of audio inputs: high impedance and low impedance. Impedance cuts down on the flow of alternating current; it is analogous with resistance in devices operated on direct current (batteries). Impedance and resistance are measured in ohms. High-impedance signals come from some nonprofessional mics, from playback machines, and from some signal-processing equipment. Low-impedance signals usually come from professional-quality microphones

FIGURE 6.24 Audio boards cover a wide range of styles and capabilities. Some are designed for specific production purposes. The top board is designed for radio control room operation, and the board on the bottom is used for television studio production. (Courtesy of Utah Public Radio, Logitek USA, and Wheatstone Corporation.)

FIGURE 6.25 A digital audio workstation (DAW) is designed for quick editing for talk radio, call-in clips, news actualities, promotional announcements, and commercials. It is designed to edit like a word processor with cut/copy/paste and precision scrubbing functions. (Courtesy of Fairlight, USA.)

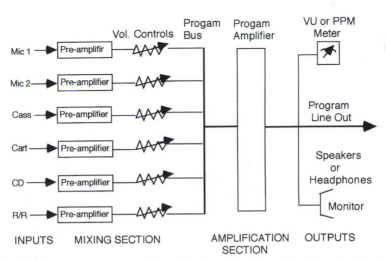

FIGURE 6.26 Audio mixing board circuits follow the basic pattern of preamplifying low-level inputs, mixing all inputs through a program bus, and monitoring the program output signals by viewing a metering system and listening on headphones or through loudspeakers. A parallel set of circuits carries signals for cueing or monitoring purposes without placing those signals on air.

and other equipment. Professional mics usually have an impedance of about 50 ohms, whereas playback units and other high-impedance sources are above 600 ohms.

An impedance imbalance or mismatch between the sound source and the mixer or console input will result in a signal that is either too loud and distorted or too soft and weak to be useful for recording purposes. Different sound sources can have different levels of sound intensity or signal strength (volts), as well as different impedances (ohms). These also require separate inputs or an audio console. Mic levels are usually lower than line levels from playback units. Preamplifiers in the audio console car boost a low-level signal to a higher level so that it equals that of other sound sources. When a high-level signal enters the console through a low-level input, distortion occurs. The level output of a mixer can be either high-level or mic-(low)-level, or, if amplified, the speaker level that is generally the highest level (Figure 6.27).

Any computer equipped with sufficient memory, a sound-processing board, and an audio-editing program can function as an audio postproduction board. The functions of mixing, equalizing, setting and varying levels, editing, and adding special effects are performed quickly with such a computer system. More detailed information on these topics may be found in Chapter 10, Editing.

Compression

The term "compression" in audio traditionally referred to a process of decreasing the dynamic range (loudest to quietest) of a signal. In the digital world, "compression" refers to a reduction in the amount of bandwidth required to record or transmit a digital signal. A compression system omits certain sounds unimportant or redundant in the overall signal so that the human ear does not recognize the loss. The amount of compression is stated as a ratio of 2:1, which means the bandwidth has been cut in half. The higher the compression ratio, the greater the possibility that the signal will lose enough of the signal that a discerning listener will detect a loss in quality. MP3 recordings are compressed to reproduce a signal lower in quality than a CD that is also compressed, but not as much.

The term codec (COmpressionDECompression) refers to a process or equipment that encodes or decodes data. To save storage space and time in moving files with high bytes of data, repetitious amounts of data are deleted. There are two basic systems

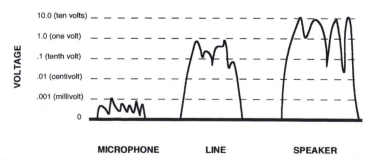

COMPARISON OF AUDIO LEVELS

FIGURE 6.27 The three primary audio levels vary in voltage from the very weak signal directly from a microphone, turntable pickup arm, and magnetic recorder playback head, to a middle level of a preamplified signal (called line level), and lastly to the high level of the output of an amplifier intended to power a speaker or speaker system.

in common use: lossy and lossless. In lossy systems, unneeded data are not transmitted or recorded. Tests indicate the deleted data generally are not missed. Lossless systems either do not compress the files or do so in such a manner that the deleted data are replaced or substituted for when decompressed. Lossy systems use far less space than lossless systems but offer a lower quality signal on reproduction.

A variety of mostly noncompatible audio codecs are used to record, store, and process audio files. The quality of the end product depends on the application required for the audio signal. High-quality soundtracks for motion pictures and network television program require the highest uncompressed audio. Mobile and handheld audio players monitored with headsets can operate with higher compression ratios to save on storage space and because the listener will not easily notice the lower quality.

Some Examples of Codecs Now in Use	
CD	Compact disc uncompressed audio files on optical disc
MP3	MPEG-1 Layer III Lossy compressed 11:1, lowest quality, bit rate can be chosen before recording
AAC	acc Advanced Audio Coding. Lossy compressed file system, higher quality than MP3
AC-3	Adaptive Transformer Code 3 Lossy compression file. Dolby 6 channel
AIFF	aiff Lossless interchange file format for storing audio files
FLAC	Open source lossless audio format. 2:1 compression
RealAudio	.ra Compression codec for Real/Video, uses variable bit rate depending on application: mobile, streaming, Internet
Shorten	.SHN Losslessy compressing file format. CD quality, replaced by FLAC, Wav
WaveForm	.wav Audio storing file format used on Windows PCs. Can store either compressed or uncompressed files

Console Operation

Once impedance and line levels of source and input match, the console operator can set the proper loudness levels for recording each sound source. To accomplish this on an audio console or mixer with a single VU meter or LED indicators, all of the faders should be closed, except for the one being set. If each input has its own VU meter, then it can be set independently from the others. The level for each input should be set between 80 percent and 100 percent modulation for an optimal signal-to-noise ratio. In some instances, such as background music and sounds, the level may be set somewhat lower for a proper overall balance between the sounds. Balance is an aesthetic concept that refers to the best proportion of sound intensities from the different elements, such as speech and music. Generally speaking, music must be toned or faded down to achieve a proper balance with accompanying dialogue or narration. In addition to balancing sounds, an audio operator should check for multiple-microphone interference by determining if the volume levels of specific sources increase as others are shut off. It is generally a good idea to label each fader with the number or name of the mic or sound source it carries for each sound source and fader in order to eliminate any confusion when adjustments have to be made during actual recording.

Recording and Mixing Commands

To perform well at the audio console or mixer, the audio recordist should be familiar with each of the following audio terms, cues, and commands:

> *Fade-in audio*. The sound intensity is gradually raised to an audible level, and its proper volume setting is increased from an inaudible or nonexistent level.
>
> *Fade-out audio*. The sound intensity is gradually lowered to an inaudible level.
>
> *Segue*. One sound source is faded out while another is immediately faded in without any overlap or dead air in between the two sounds.
>
> *Cross-fade*. One sound source is faded out while another is faded in over it. The sum of the two sounds should remain at a peak level.
>
> *Open mic*. The fader or pot for a specific mic is raised immediately to its proper level or is simply switched on.
>
> *Cut sound or kill sound*. The fader or pot is abruptly closed, or the channel switch is cut off.
>
> *Sound up and under* (or *bed sound*). The sound is faded up promptly to its proper level and then is faded down to a lower level, at which level it is still audible but less prominent, to allow for a voice to be balanced over the original background sound, usually music (Figure 6.28).
>
> *Backtime*. A prerecorded sound or music track is prepared so that it will end at a specified time. This requires a calculation that subtracts the length of the track from the end time of the production. The playback machine or audio file must begin at the exact backtime in order for the track to end correctly. The pot or fader assigned to it is not turned up until required, so that the sounds or music can be gradually faded in at the appropriate point. Many digital playback machines can be programmed to automatically backtime if data are properly entered.

SOUND PERSPECTIVES

The relationship of sound to space parallels that of a picture with three dimensions: left-right, up-down, and in front of or behind the listener. To duplicate audio realistically, the perception of these dimensions must be duplicated. The characteristics to be duplicated are distance and directionality. Sound that appears to be originating close by or far away may be recorded by placing the mic(s) close to or at a distance from the sound source. The sound indicating the size of the environment will be determined by the reflective or absorption values of the walls, furniture, or other objects in the space, and the size of the room. The direction of the sound can only be determined through the use of one of several multichannel systems to give the audience the sense that the sound is to the left, right, in front of, or behind.

Stereo Sound

Both stereo and surround-sound systems and modifications are attempts to duplicate the three-dimensional aspects of a sound environment. Stereo offers two or three channels of sound: left, right, and, depending on the size of the theater, a center channel. Reproduction of sound through the left or right channel to match the

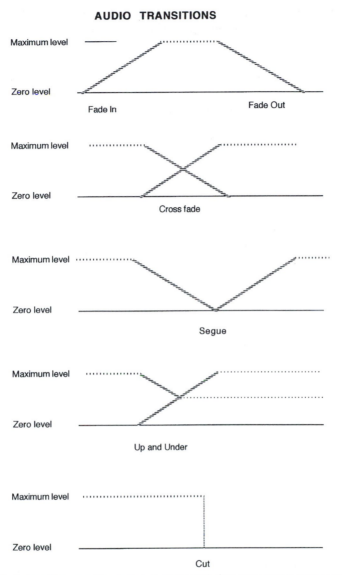

AUDIO TRANSITIONS

FIGURE 6.28 Audio transitions provide a means of mixing audio from two or more sources or a means of switching from one audio source to another.

objects originating the sound on the screen may add to the realistic effect but also may become confusing if overdone. Now that stereo television receivers are available, the impulse to split sound into left and right must be weighed against the realization that television is a close-up medium that requires audio to be concentrated in the center of the screen or balanced between the left and right channels.

Wide-screen films, on the other hand, offer much greater opportunities to utilize sound originating from the side of the screen matching the source of the sound. Care must be taken not to overbalance sound to one side or another, or else the audience seated on the opposite side of the theater may miss some critical sounds. In the recording industry, music is recorded either to duplicate the physical arrangement of the group (symphonic orchestras) or to enhance the vocals or a solo instrument (rock groups). Today music is recorded with the assumption that it will be reproduced on a stereo rather than monaural system.

Multichannel Sound

Surround sound was the next logical step from stereo in creating the realistic three-dimensional sound environment. Mixing the sound into at least four channels to be reproduced through speakers located in the four corners of the listening space enhances the sense of the original recording, but such a process increases the complexity of mic placement, mixing, and speaker location. Surround sound in the past has not proved practical for the average home or video production. Modification of the theory has opened new avenues for film sound. Most theaters today are capable of reproducing sound recorded on as many as 10 channels using three to four speakers lining the side walls of the theater to supplement the normal stereo and center speakers located behind the screen. Multichannel sound increases the illusion of both the width and depth of the picture.

Dolby Digital 5.1, 6.1, and 7.1 Sound and Beyond

Dolby Digital 5.1, 6.1, and 7.1 sound systems designed to complement advanced television systems requires six, seven, or eight channels of audio and six or seven separate speakers. The usual four-corner speakers (left front, right front, left rear, and right rear) are supplemented by two, three, or four additional speakers: one directly behind or under the screen for bass response, called a subwoofer, and the sixth directly behind or above the screen, called a front channel, and a seventh directly behind the audience (for 6.1) or a seventh and eighth (back left and back right for 7.1) behind the audience, which are called rear channels. The maximum effect of making the audience feel as if they are placed within the program occurs when each audio channel is properly programmed to carry the correct signal. Whether the complexity of Dolby Digital 5.1, 6.1, or 7.1 will discourage consumers from installing such a system to match their HDTV system will be determined in the next 5 or 10 years. As a production situation, a 5.1, 6.1, or 7.1 signal, consisting of six or seven channels, is complicated not only by the differences in apparent direction of the sources but also by the differences in equalization of the individual channels. Editing multichannel systems is complex and requires a deep understanding of the part each channel of audio plays in that particular production. Ultra-high-definition TV, still in development, plans on using 21 channels of audio for exhibition.

Summary

The aesthetic use of recorded sounds demands an understanding of realist, modernist, and postmodernist aesthetics as well as recording devices and their selection, placement, and control. A mic or microphone is a transducer that converts analog sound-wave energy into analog electrical energy. Mics can be classified into three different categories on the basis of their transducer elements: dynamic, ribbon, and condenser.

Mics can also be classified on the basis of pickup patterns: omnidirectional, bidirectional, and unidirectional mics, such as the cardioid and supercardioid or shotgun mic. Mics can be placed in on-camera and off-camera positions. Hand mics, desk mics, stand mics, and lavaliere mics are examples of on-camera mic positions. Mics on booms, such as fishpole, giraffe, and perambulator booms, as well as various hidden mics, such as the hanging mic, prop mic, and concealed lavaliere mic, are off-camera mics.

Selecting the best mic and mic position depends on an understanding of what mic characteristics and placements are best suited to a specific situation. Digital recording of audio requires greater care in mic selection and placement as well as noise reduction.

Sound signal control helps a sound recordist achieve the best-quality recorded sound by eliminating specific audio problems, such as loudness distortion and excessive ambient and system noise. A sound-measuring device, such as a volume unit (VU) meter or LED indicators, can be used to set the sound level as high as possible for optimal signal-to-noise ratio while avoiding loudness distortion. Balanced mic cables should be used to minimize noise and electrical interference.

Audio mixing is done on an audio console, mixer, or DAW. Mixing refers to combining several different inputs, such as different mics or playback machines, into a single (monophonic) or dual (stereophonic) output, which is directed to a tape recorder or some digital recording medium. Faders on the audio console, mixer, or DAW are used to adjust the volume gradually.

Audio operators using a console, mixer, or DAW must be familiar with basic audio terms, cues, and commands so that they can effectively communicate with the rest of the staff and crew. Sound perspectives should match the perspectives of the matching visual as well as the requirements of the drama or music. Perspectives include both distance and dimensionality.

EXERCISES

1. Practice following a person moving and speaking with a cardioid mic on a mic boom as he or she walks around a studio on a precise, preplanned route. Try to keep the mic one to four feet in front of and one to three feet above the speaker. Record the sounds on audiotape or videotape without changing the pot or fader setting on the recorder so that the initial volume setting is used constantly. Change the mic to a supercardioid or shotgun mic, and perform the same exercise. Did you keep a constant distance between the mic and the speaker? Was the mic always in the best position to pick up the speaker's voice? Listen to your recording critically for fluctuations in the loudness of the speaker's voice. Discuss what you could have done to improve recording consistency. Did the shotgun mic increase overall sound quality but make it more difficult to maintain a constant recording level?

2. Set up an on-camera narration videotape recording outdoors. Select a location that is relatively quiet. Bring along three mics: a cardioid hand mic, a small lavaliere mic, and a supercardioid or shotgun mic. Record the same on-camera narration with the speaker looking directly into the camera three times, once with each type of mic. Make sure that each mic has a windscreen, and position the speaker with his or her back to the wind, if possible. When using the shotgun mic, make sure that there are no loud sounds coming from directly behind the person speaking. Position the shotgun mic as close to the edge of the camera frame as you can without entering the frame. Have the speaker

hold the cardioid mic about six to nine inches from his or her mouth. Attach the lavaliere so that no clothing or jewelry rubs against it and the mic cable is well hidden. Compare the three.

3. Place two microphones of the same type side-by-side and an equal distance from a subject. Open both mics, and have the subject speak evenly and continually while closing one mic slowly and noting if there is a decrease or increase in the level of the audio output. Move the mics, so that they are more than three times the distance between the subject and the mics, and again close and open one mic, noting the change in level while someone speaks evenly and continually.

4. Place a microphone near the speaker of a CD player. Feed the mic through a preamp and an amplifier to a recorder. Monitor the recording as you play back the CD. Raise the level to the maximum capability of the amplifier, then back to a normal level as shown on a meter, then to a level that barely shows on the meter. Rewind the recorder, and play the recording back at a set level and listen for distortion when the level is too high and an increase in noise when the level is too low.

5. Feed three audio sources through a mixer. Start with one source, set a normal level, then open another source and bring it to the same level. Open a third source and bring it to a normal level. Note whether it was necessary to reduce the level on the first source as a second source was brought up to keep the sum of the two sources at the predetermined level. Note the change in overall level as the third source level is brought up.

6. Watch a DVD of a well-made motion picture. Note whether the audio always is at the same level or whether it changes with the positioning of the source of the audio. If you have access to a multiple-channel audio system, note which channel carries which sound, again depending on the location of the source in reference to the camera.

Additional Readings

Alburger, James. 2007. The Art of Voice Acting: The Craft and Business of Performing for Voice-Over, Focal Press, Boston.

Alten, Stanley. 2008. Audio in Media, eighth ed. Wadsworth, Belmont, CA.

Bartlett, Bruce, Bartlett, Jenny. 2005. Practical Recording Techniques: The Step-by-Step Approach to Professional Audio Recording, fourth ed. Focal Press, Boston.

Bartlett, Bruce, Bartlett, Jenny. 2007. Recording Music on Location, second ed. Focal Press, Boston.

Case, Alex. 2007. Sound FX: Unlocking the Creative Potential of Recording Studio Effects, Focal Press, Boston.

Eargle, John. 2004. The Microphone Book: From Mono to Stereo to Surround: A Guide to Microphone Design and Application, second ed. Focal Press, Boston.

Geoghegan, Michael, et al. 2008. Podcast Academy: The Business Podcasting Book: Launching, Marketing, and Measuring Your Podcast, Focal Press, Boston.

Grant, Tony. 2003. Audio for Single Camera Operation, Focal Press, Boston.

Gross, Lynne S, Reese, David E. 2001. Radio Production Worktext, fourth ed. Focal Press, Boston.

Hausmann, Carl, et al. 2007. Modern Radio Production, seventh ed. Wadsworth, Belmont, CA.

Holman, Tomlinson. 2005. Sound for Digital Recording, Focal Press, Boston.

Holman, Tomlinson. 2008. Surround Sound, second ed. Focal Press, Boston.

Howard, David, Angus, Jamie. 2006. Acoustics and Psychoacoustics, third ed. Focal Press, Boston.

Huber, David Miles, Runstein, Robert. 2005. Modern Recording Techniques, sixth ed. Focal Press, Boston.

Iuppa, Nicholas. 2001. The Complete Guide to Game Audio for Composers, Musicians, Sound Designers, and Game Developers, Focal Press, Boston.

Izhaki, Roey. 2008. Mixing Audio: Concepts, Practices, and Tools, Focal Press, Boston.

Katz, Bob. 2007. Mastering Audio: The Art and Science, second ed. Focal Press, Boston.

Keith, Michael C. 2007. The Radio Station: Broadcast, Satellite, and Internet, Focal Press, Boston.

McGuire, Sam, Pitts, Roy. 2008. Audio Sampling: A Practical Guide, Focal Press, Boston.

Newell, Philip. 2007. Recording Studio Design, Focal Press, Boston.

Newell, Philip, Holland, Keith. 2006. Loudspeakers for Music Recording and Reproduction, Focal Press, Boston.

Nisbett, Alec. 2004. Sound Studio: Audio Techniques for Radio, Television, Film, and Recording, Focal Press, Boston.

Rumsey, Francis. 2003. Desktop Audio Technology: Digital Audio and MIDI Principles, Focal Press, Boston.

Rumsey, Francis, McCormick, Tim. 2005. Sound Recording: An Introduction, Focal Press, Boston.

Watkinson, John. 2002. Introduction to Digital Audio, second ed. Focal Press, Boston.

Webber, Stephen. 2008. DJ Skills: Essential Guide to Mixing and Scratching, Focal Press, Boston.

Weis, Elisabeth. 1982. The Silent Scream: Alfred Hitchcock's Sound Track, Farleigh Dickinson University Press, Rutherford, NJ.

Weis, Elisabeth, Belton, John. 1985. Film Sound: Theory and Practice, Columbia University Press, New York.

Yale French Studies. 1980. Special issue on "Sound in Film," 60.

Yewdall, David Rush. 2007. The Practical Art of Motion Picture Sound, Focal Press, Boston.

Lighting and Design

- What are the aesthetics of light?

- How do light and color interact?

- What types of lighting instruments are available?

- How is light measured and controlled?

- How is scene design used in digital production?

Introduction

One of the most creative and visually exciting tasks in video and film production involves lighting and creating environments with sets, properties, costumes, and makeup. Visual artists refer to lighting as painting with light. A lighting director or director of photography can use lights just as effectively and expressively as any painter uses color pigments to evoke a specific mood or visual impression. An art director can create imaginary worlds or create actual times and locations and may place actors anywhere in the universe and at anytime in history by choices available to her. Lighting can be used to emphasize and dramatize a subject by bringing objects into sharp relief or contrast, or it can be used to soften and to harmonize. Lighting directly affects the overall impressions and feelings generated by recorded visual images. It is a complex art, but basic video and film lighting can be reduced to a limited number of concepts and techniques. This chapter introduces the basic aesthetic approaches, techniques, and equipment needed to design and control the lighting of moving images and the basic principles of designing sets, props, costumes, makeup, and their use in visual productions.

The expressive design and effect of a lighting setup and a scene can be described as realist, modernist, or postmodernist.

REALIST LIGHTING AND DESIGN

Realist lighting appears to come from actual light sources in a setting or location. Realist design simulates an existing setting or location with an emphasis on the illusion of reality, not necessarily reality itself. Because it enhances this illusion, realist lighting conforms to the audience's expectations of how a scene should normally or naturally appear in real life. In conventional popular dramas, the lighting is usually realistic. The major problem for the lighting director is to determine the actual light source in the scene. The brightest lights are positioned according to the direction and intensity of the central or main source of light. Directional lighting continuity is maintained from one shot to the next in the same scene. If the main source of light is a window, the direction of the lights basically preserves the spatial positioning of the window on the set. The same holds true for firelight or candlelight. The lighting director tries to match the natural scene under normal vision using artificial lights. Multiple shadows should be minimized, if not eliminated, so that the lighting rarely calls attention to itself. There is a logical consistency to the direction and intensity of the lighting, which has a presumed cause or real source. Maintaining basic principles of spatial perspective and proportional size are extremely important in realist design, because they help to sustain an illusion of reality. Sets are often constructed out of lightweight materials that give the impression of being real but are much easier to construct and move around than actual objects. Virtual sets and backgrounds are created or stored as computer files to be used on command and at the will of the director. Such virtual sets may take the form of interiors, exteriors, space, or any location within the imagination of the creative staff of the production. Few productions are completely realist. Some degree of modernist stylization is often needed to stimulate dramatic interest. Lighting and art directors use lighting and settings to bring out and emphasize specific aspects of a personality or setting. They highlight details that add depth to performers and actions. Strict authenticity often fails to stimulate emotions and viewer interest, and a purely realist lighting setup often seems flat and boring.

MODERNIST LIGHTING AND DESIGN

Modernist lighting has no real-life referent. The lighting and design directors are much freer to design a setup according to purely abstract or subjective emotional criteria—that is, to stylize the use of light or setting. The lighting director literally paints with light to create emphasis and spatial impressions. Modernist lighting tries to achieve a specific emotional effect or abstract design through non-naturalistic patterns of light. The actual sources of light are often of little interest.

Modernist lighting and settings stimulate emotions and create a dynamic visual impression. For example, the lighting setup for a musical variety program may light an empty stage with pools of colored light, creating abstract patterns. The mood or atmosphere can coincide with the central theme or emotion expressed by a song or dance. Even in a realist drama, a dream sequence might call for highly stylized lighting and location that mirrors the internal state of mind of the central character. These are often highly abstract and unrealistic visual sequences, but they effectively convey the character's feelings, emotions, and state of mind. Excessive or inappropriate stylization calls attention to the lighting and distracts viewer attention from the central message or information of a nonfiction program. It can also destroy the illusion of reality in a realistic drama, but the absence of any stylization at all leads to viewer disinterest. Innovative television programs and films by many experimental artists have shown how a formative or modernist approach to scenic design can break down conventional illusions of reality by ignoring spatial perspective and using highly artificial, stylized sets, backdrops, and lighting, such as those used on the *Entertainment Tonight* program.

POSTMODERNIST LIGHTING AND DESIGN

Postmodernist lighting and settings often mix a variety of styles drawn from different genres or modes, such as narrative fiction and documentary. For example, highly stylized Hollywood studio lighting and setting normally associated with fiction films is used to record documentary interviews in Errol Morris's *The Thin Blue Line* (1987) and a *Brief History of Time* (1992). The former film also mixes clips from old Hollywood B movies with contemporary interviews that features this highly stylized lighting. Postmodernist lighting offers a pastiche of styles, and it appeals to the emotions on a different level from most modernist or realist lighting and locations. By mixing concrete realism with abstract modernism as well as different styles, genres or modes of lighting and settings can evoke a complex emotional response in the viewer. Some music videos and rock concerts use postmodernist lighting effects and locations to bombard the viewer with powerful sensations unrelated to any realist action in the film or video or any specific thoughts or feelings inside the mind of a character. These lighting effects and locations reflect the complexity and diversity of contemporary life, art, and culture. For example, postmodernist lighting in *Batman Forever* (1995) relies on computerized lighting effects similar to those used at rock concerts to create a feeling of disorientation at a circus. By controlling the projection of Chinese and other ethnic symbols and motifs in exterior settings of Gotham City, the film creates a multicultural (drawn for different bodies of people) and multitemporal (drawn from different historical periods) pastiche of different cultures, times, and places through lighting in distinctly postmodernist ways. A blend of classical and modern, traditional and contemporary, elite and popular patterns and combinations of colors and textures can serve as the basis for postmodernist designs.

LIGHT AND COLOR

A variety of light sources can be used for television and film recording. Each of these can be distinguished in terms of the color temperature of the light it emits. Color temperature is usually defined in technical terms of degrees Kelvin (K). *Degrees Kelvin* is a unit of measurement that refers to the type of light that would theoretically be given off by a perfect light radiator (what physicists call a black-box radiator) when it is heated to a specific temperature. White light is actually composed of relatively equal amounts of all the colors in the visible spectrum; but light sources with different color temperatures emit slightly different amounts of the various color wavelengths (red, green, blue light), which together make up white light and the visible spectrum. Sunlight has a relatively high color temperature, about 5400 or 5600 degrees K, whereas tungsten or incandescent light, such as that given off by many living room lamps and some professional lighting equipment, has a much lower color temperature, about 3200 degrees K.

Sunlight has somewhat more blue light (short wavelengths) than does tungsten light, which has slightly more red light (long wavelengths.) As a result, a film stock or video camera designed or preset for tungsten light will record bluish images when it is exposed

COLOR TEMPERATURES OF LIGHT SOURCES

SOURCE	DEGREES KELVIN	MIREDS
Match flame	1700 K	588
Candle flame	1850 K	541
Sunrise or sunset	2000 K	500
Consumer lamps	2650 K–2990 K	317–345
Standard Tungsten/Halogen	3200 K	313
Photoflood	3400 K	294
Early morning, late afternoon	4300 K	233
Daylight photoflood	4800 K	208
HMI	5600 K	179
Typical noon	5400 K–5800 K	185
Carbon arc	5800 K	172
Overcast sky	6000 K	167
Summer shade	8000 K	125
Full summer sun	10,000 K–30,000 K	100

Comparable Degrees Kelvin for Fluorescent Sources

Warm white	3050
White	3500
Natural white	3700
Cool white	4300
Daylight	6500

FIGURE 7.1 The differences in the actual color of light sources range from full summer sun to a candle flame. Fluorescent light sources also vary over a range, but not as widely as incandescent and natural light sources.

under sunlight, and a film stock or video camera rated or adjusted for daylight (sunlight) will record reddish images under tungsten light. Because video and film recording devices are often more sensitive to these differences in color temperature than our eyes, specific light sources must be carefully selected and controlled (Figure 7.1).

Sunlight

Sunlight is a natural light source. Burning gases on the sun's surface emit light that has a relatively high color temperature when it reaches the earth's surface, or 5400 degrees K. Sunlight contains approximately equal proportions of all color wavelengths in the visible spectrum. Unless it is broken up and diffused by clouds, direct sunlight produces intense, harsh, contrasty light. This kind of light quality is called *hard* as opposed to *soft* light. It creates harsh shadows. Diffusion screens and reflectors can be used on location to reduce the intensity and contrast of direct sunlight and to create soft light. Indirect sunlight, often called *skylight*, has a higher color temperature than direct sunlight: from 6000 degrees K to 20,000 degrees K. Indirectly lit shadow areas also contain a higher proportion of ultraviolet (UV) light than areas lit by direct sunlight. To reduce the bluish cast that is often produced by this ultraviolet light, an ultraviolet or skylight filter can be placed over the camera lens.

Tungsten Light

One of the earliest sources of electrical lighting was Thomas Edison's incandescent bulb. An incandescent bulb consists of a tungsten filament in a glass-enclosed vacuum. A strong electrical current encounters considerable resistance at the filament, generating both heat and light. In general, a tungsten light source produces somewhat more light of longer wavelengths, such as red and orange, than of shorter wavelengths, such as blue and violet. Professional tungsten light has a color temperature of 3200 degrees K. Incandescent lamps in the home and office may emit a much lower color temperature.

The color temperature of all tungsten lamps decreases with age. Tungsten-halogen-quartz bulbs (usually called *quartz lights*) have become an important source of 3200 degree K indoor lighting. Caution needs to be exercised in the handling of quartz bulbs, however. They should never be touched, because the oil in your skin breaks down the quartz-like glass and reduces the life of a bulb. Quartz lights are usually rated in terms of the watts of electrical energy they consume. The most common sizes are 650 and 1,000 W.

Carbon Arc Light

Carbon arc lights produce intense light, which has very high color temperature. Light is produced by passing a spark between two carbon poles. Carbon arcs generally require vast amounts of DC electrical current and produce intense heat and noxious vapors and exhaust, which must be ventilated. The high intensity and high color temperature of arc lights make them useful for location production in combination with sunlight. However, they are extremely bulky and require special electrical generators on location.

Metal Halide Light

The latest development in location lighting is the metal halide light, three of which are in use today: halogen-metal-iodide (HMI), compact iodine daylight (CID), and compact source iodide (CSI). HMI and CID lamps provide light at approximately 5400 degrees K and now are replacing carbon arc lamps. HMI lamps, the most popular of the three, give almost four times the amount of light for the same electrical input as tungsten-quartz-halogen lamps. This light source produces high-intensity, high-color-temperature light (similar to daylight) with great efficiency. It generates little heat and operates on standard 120-volt, 60 Hz AC current (although a few use 220-volt current) ranging in power from 150 to 18 kW. Like fluorescents, HMIs are discharge type of light but designed with a specific spectrum of light. The pulse is set at 120 Hz and can cause flickering in film production and video productions unless film rates and scan rates are changed to avoid matching the rate of the ballast. HMI lights are frequently used to raise the lighting level at outdoor locations, which may be partially lit by indirect sunlight. HMI lights are fully glass-enclosed arc lamps that require separate start and ballast mechanisms to control electrical current. Smaller 10 W to 18 W units now are available for portable cameras and fast-moving production like documentaries and news coverage. They are also available in soft-lights and both open-faced and PARs. HMI lights can also be filtered so that they duplicate 3200 degree K tungsten light sources.

Fluorescent Light

Unlike all the other types of light sources discussed thus far, fluorescent light is discontinuous throughout the visible spectrum (Figure 7.2). Certain bands of colored light, such as bands of red, yellow, green, or blue light, are strong, whereas others are almost nonexistent in a fluorescent light source. Light is produced through phosphorescence rather than incandescence, and different phosphors produce different wavelengths of light. In film recording, color filters placed over the light source or camera lens can compensate for some of this spectral discontinuity, but there are so many differences between most fluorescent bulb types and brands that no simple filter or combination of filters will properly remedy every situation. Video recording devices can be at least partially adjusted for fluorescent light sources by white-balancing the camera under fluorescent lighting, but not for film. Professional fluorescent lighting instruments have been developed that produce highly intense but diffuse light of 3200 degree K color temperature using minimal electricity. Although these instruments are expensive, they are also highly efficient sources of fill light and now are available in small tubes and mountings for location and handheld shooting situations with the new small digital camcorders.

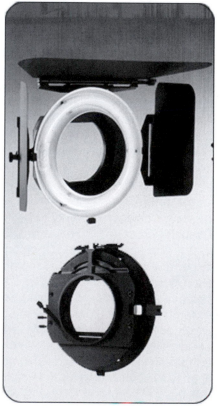

FIGURE 7.2 Fluorescent lamps are designed in various shapes and sizes depending on their uses—from circular to surround lens, to large banks for fill and even key light. (Courtesy of KimoFlo.)

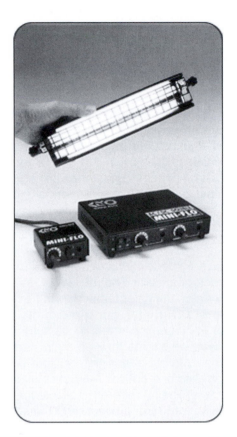

VistaBeam 600

FIGURE 7.2—CONT'D

Conventional fluorescent lighting often produces humming and flickering. The alternating current mechanisms used to create fluorescent light can cause flicker in a recorded image and produce an audio hum, which is easily picked up by even distant microphones and affects the recorded sound track, but professional fluorescent systems are designed to avoid hum and flicker. Because of negative audio and visual effects, it is often advisable to shut off conventional fluorescent lights, if possible, and to use professional fluorescent, tungsten or HMI lighting instead. Fluorescent fixtures designed for media production use may change color temperature by changing tubes with specific color temperature ratings. The intensity of each unit for any one scene may be altered by increasing or decreasing the number of tubes in each fixture. Fluorescents may act as either key or fill light, although generally they provide a soft flat light rather than a harsh controlled light. Fall-off from fluorescents is easily controlled by barn doors and the design of the fixture (Figure 7.2).

In some situations, such as certain industrial locations, it is virtually impossible to replace all the preexisting fluorescent lights in the room with other artificial lighting. In this case, one type of light source is selected as primary, and all other light sources are reduced as much as possible in intensity. Light sources having different color temperatures should not be used simultaneously unless filters can be placed in front of light sources, including windows, to change and equalize different color temperatures.

LED Lights

Light-emitting diodes (LED) lights are clusters of red, green, and blue LED chips controlled by a built-in microprocessor. The mixture of different chips and voltages applied to each chip determine the color temperature the fixture offers. The normal LED chip actually produces a blue light, but some of the light stimulates a yellow phosphor to compensate the blue to create a white light. The increased efficiency and luminosity of LEDs was developed through major breakthroughs in technologies of manufacturing chips, structural design, and light beam shaping, combining advances in solid-state physics and optics. The optics usually consist of two parts: a primary and secondary lens. The primary lens collects the light emitted by the LED close to the chip, combining it to form a beam, and the secondary lens blends the light beam colors together to form "white light." The result is a high-energy, efficient white light source that remains cooler to the touch. Typical LED luminous (energy) efficiency is near 90 percent compared to 20 percent or less with typical tungsten-halogen lights, resulting in high output light intensity with virtually no heat. Unlike traditional tungsten-halogen or HMI light fixtures with single lamps, multiple LEDs are packaged into panels with 50 or more LEDs, with each LED having its own reflector. Spot and flood illumination is accomplished by using different reflectors, usually varying from a 5-degree (spot) to a 50-degree (flood) beam angle.

Individual panels of LEDs are designed to produce a 5600 to 6000 degree K source. Panels may be dimmed without changing color temperature by changing the voltage applied to individual chips. Small panels may be mounted on a camera, easily running on 12 volts from a battery pack or from the camera's power source. Panels may be mounted on a stand or camera, taped to a wall, or handheld. The units are heat-free, flicker-free, and have a long life. As many as 140 small LEDs mounted in a 6.75 × 2.25 panel will provide 80 foot candles of light. A 5-inch diameter disk of chips will deliver 130 foot-candles of light. Groups of panels may be mounted in racks to provide a wide, even source of light suitable to act as fill light for an entire scene. Panels can be designed to be used as floods with a 50-degree spread of light or as a spot with a 20-degree spread. Panels can be fitted with barn doors, egg crates, filter frames, or intensifiers as needed (Figure 7.3).

White Balance

To adjust either video or film systems to various Kelvin temperatures, compensation must be provided. Video cameras can be adjusted to the degree Kelvin of the

FIGURE 7.3 LED fixtures come in different sizes and shapes, but primarily provide a flat even soft light. They may be used directly on a camera, as a fill light, as in small space powered by batteries. (Courtesy of LitePanels, Inc.)

light source through the process of white balancing. Once the lighting has been determined and set, the camera(s) are pointed at the subject area, focused on a white card. A switch is thrown on the camera or camera control unit and held until an indicator shows that the camera has adjusted its electronic circuits to that lighting temperature. A video camera must be white balanced again each time the location or light source has been modified. Some new digital cameras now contain automatic white balance circuits that "read" the color temperature of a scene and adjust internal circuits to maintain proper light color relationships. Video cameras are designed to operate under 3200 degree K tungsten lighting without filters. If operated under daylight or other 5,400-degree light sources, a filter must be inserted to compensate for the difference in light temperature. Normally an 85 (yellow-orange) filter is used (Figure 7.4).

FIGURE 7.4 With the proper filter placed between the video camera lens and pickup chips or tubes, the camera's internal circuits will automatically white balance when focused on a pure white card and when the white balance switch is thrown. Film camera white balance is dependent on the type of film stock and filter arrangement, not on the camera or the camera's internal operation.

Film systems, on the other hand, must match the film stock to the lighting temperature. If shooting under tungsten, a film balanced for 3200 degree K must be used, or daylight film with an 80 blue filter can be used. If shooting under daylight conditions, a film balanced for 5400 degree K or tungsten film with an 85 filter must be used to compensate for the difference in Kelvin temperature (Figure 7.5).

LIGHTING INSTRUMENTS

The housing within which a light source or lamp is encased is called a *lighting instrument* or *luminaire*. Lighting instruments can be generally classified according to the directness or indirectness and hardness or softness of the light they emit. Sharply focused and concentrated light produces harsh shadows and high contrast.

Diffused or softened light minimizes shadows and reduces contrast. Lighting instruments with lenses that sharply focus light are referred to as spotlights. Lighting instruments without lenses that have reflectors that spread and soften light are called floodlights.

Spotlights

Fresnel and ellipsoidal lighting instruments are two different types of spotlights. *Fresnel* refers to a specific type of lens, which bends the light so that it travels in a relatively narrow path. The term *ellipsoidal* refers to the shape of a mirror or reflector

MOTION PICTURE FILM EXPOSURE CHARACTERISTICS

NAME	LIGHT BALANCE	EI	FILTER
Color Negative			
Agfa XT 100	Tungsten	100/80	85
Agfa XT 320	Tungsten	320/200	85
Agfa XTS 400	Tungsten	400/250	85
Eastman EXR 50D	Daylight	12/50	80A
Eastman EXR 100T	Tungsten	100/64	85
Eastman EXR 200T	Tungsten	200/125	85
Eastman EXR 500T	Tungsten	500/320	85
Eastman HS Day	Daylight	80/250	80B
Fujicolor F-64	Tungsten	64/40	85
Fujicolor F-64D	Daylight	64	
Fujicolor F-125	Tungsten	125/80	85
Fujicolor F-250	Tungsten	250/160	85
Fujicolor F-500D	Daylight	64/250	80A
Fujicolor F-500	Tungsten	500/320	85
COLOR REVERSAL			
Eastman Ekta-day	Daylight	40/160	80A
Eastman Ekta-tung	Tungsten	125/80	85B
Eastman Ekta-HS-D	Daylight	100/400	80A
Eastman Ekta-HS-T	Tungsten	400/250	85B
Kodachrome 25	Daylight	6/25	80A
Kodachrome 40	Tungsten	40/25	85
BLACK & WHITE NEGATIVE			
Agfa Pan 250		200/250	
Eastman Plus-X		64/80	
Eastman Double-X		200/250	
Fuji FG		64/80	
Fuji RP		64/80	
BLACK & WHITE REVERSAL			
Eastman Plus-X Reversal		40/50	
Eastman Tri-X Reversal		100-125	

FIGURE 7.5 The design and manufacture of motion picture film stock determines whether the film is designed to be shot under daylight or tungsten light sources. The speed of film stock also is determined by the manufacturing process. Each of these characteristics can be adjusted with filters and processing modifications. (Courtesy of Eastman Kodak, Fuji Films, and Agfa Films.)

at the back of the instrument that concentrates the light rays focused by a lens. Both types of spotlights concentrate the light emitted by a lamp or bulb into a narrow, intense band of light (Figure 7.6).

Floodlights

The most commonly used types of floodlights are scoops, broads, soft lights, strip lights, and banks of Parabolic Aluminized Reflector (PAR) bulbs. These lights lack mirrors that focus light into a narrow beam. Instead, they diffuse or spread light, decreasing both its intensity and harshness. Scoops, broads, and soft lights usually consist of one, two, or three lamps and have somewhat larger and more diffuse reflectors than spotlights. Strip lights and PARs have several bulbs, each with its own built-in

FIGURE 7.6 The light pattern from a Fresnel lighting instrument is controlled by moving the lamp inside the fixture closer or farther away from the stepped lens in the front of the instrument and by adjusting the barn doors mounted on the outside front of the lamp (*top*). The light pattern from an ellipsoidal lamp is controlled by adjusting shutters mounted inside the case of the lamp between the lamp and the front lens. Barn doors also may be mounted on ellipsoidal lamps (*bottom*). (Courtesy of Arri and ETC Lighting.)

reflector, placed close to one another so that they diffuse and soften the light in combination. Strip lights may be equipped with colored lenses to throw a "colorized" wash onto a cyc, or cyclorama (a large plain background scenery, usually stretched cloth), or other neutral background. Floodlights are frequently used to light wide areas. They are also used to fill in the shadows created by spotlights and thereby reduce contrast within a scene (Figure 7.7).

FIGURE 7.7 Flood lamps are manufactured in a variety of shapes and sizes, but the purpose is to provide a soft, diffused light. Control of light from flood lamps is more difficult because of its diffused nature. (Courtesy of Lowell and Arri Lighting.)

Portable Lights

A wide variety of lighting kits are available for use on location. Portable lighting kits usu-ally have open, nonlensed lighting instruments, quartz lamps, and LEDs rated from 80 to 2,000 W. These instruments lack some of the controls of studio spotlights. Lighting kits contain several open-reflector quartz lights and collapsible light-mounting equipment, power cords, and other lighting accessories. Photofloods, such as Lowell Light units, are highly portable lamps with self-contained reflectors inside the bulb (Figure 7.8). Some lightweight lighting instruments have their own portable power supply or rechargeable battery pack. Battery-powered lights, such as the Sylvania Sun Gun, can be used in moving vehicles or on remote locations where a standard power supply is

FIGURE 7.8 Portable light kits are designed to provide the maximum amount of light output in small, easily moved and controlled lighting fixtures that also draw a minimum amount of amperage. The kits are designed to provide both spot light and flood light with a variety of designs or adjustments of the lamp fixtures. (Courtesy of Lowell Light.)

not available. The batteries should be fully charged, because the color temperature gradually decreases as the battery weakens and the voltage drops.

With the increase of available power in newer battery designs, more efficient luminaires, and cameras and films that are more sensitive, battery-powered lighting has become more practical. Standard alternating current power sources are still preferable to batteries for lights, whenever possible.

New Lamp Designs

Digital techniques in cameras as well as other electronic devices have led to new and inventive lighting fixture designs. Pursuing bright color and color constant light source has led to the development of a ceramic light source. Today's productions require smaller, easily portable, and flexible fixtures. Fixtures that allow the light source to be changed from incandescent, to fluorescent, to LED in one fixture that can be easily folded and moved in a light-weight container has led to several different designs fulfilling these characteristics (Figure 7.9).

Mounting Devices

Studio lighting is accomplished with overhead lighting instruments, which are attached to a grid. This makes it easier for cameras and performers to move about the studio floor without running into lights. The grid, which consists of a series of pipes suspended in parallel rows above the studio floor to which instruments are attached with C-clamps, is probably the most common type of grid. Safety chains or heavy-gauge wire loops ensure that no accident will occur if the C-clamp slips on the pipe. Another type of grid has a sliding track to which instruments can be attached and along which they can be moved (Figure 7.10).

A collapsible floor stand is one of the most frequently used light-mounting devices on location. The seven- or eight-foot stand telescopes for portability. Sandbags can be placed over the three legs of the stand for added stability. Lights can also be mounted on special clips and clamps, such as a spring-tension alligator clip, or simply taped to a wall with a strong adhesive gaffer's tape. The latter must be used with care as it sometimes damages paint or wallpaper on removal (Figure 7.11).

Shaping Devices

Light can be shaped, manipulated, and controlled by a variety of devices, such as barn doors, scrims, diffusers, flags, gels, cookies, and reflectors. These are often attached to a lighting instrument. *Barn doors* are black metal flaps that can be attached to the top, bottom, and sides of a lighting instrument. When properly positioned, they prevent light from spilling into areas of the set where it is not wanted. *Screens* are pieces of wire mesh that can be placed over the front of a lighting instrument to cut down the amount of light transmitted. *Scrims* and *diffusers* are pieces of translucent material, such as spun glass, that break up direct light and spread it out in all directions. *Flags* are opaque pieces of metal, plastic, or cardboard that prevent light from spilling into an undesired area.

Gels are flexible sheets of transparent colored plastic that can act as color filters when they are placed in front of light sources, such as windows or lamps. A gel can be used to convert 5400 degree K light coming through a window to 3200 degree K light, which is the same color temperature as interior room lighting. A *cookie* or *cukaloris* is a piece of

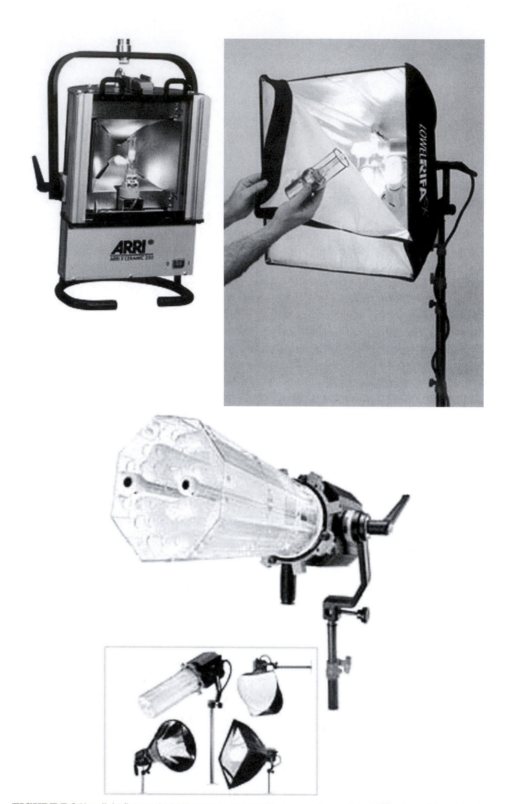

FIGURE 7.9 New light fixtures include ceramic replaceable sources in one fixture. (Courtesy of Lowell and Arri Lighting.)

FIGURE 7.10 The lighting grid in a studio is constructed to support both the batten, which carries the power to the pigtails, and the lighting instruments. The grid must be high enough to allow wide-angle shots, but it also must allow for space above the grid to dissipate the heat generated by the lighting instruments.

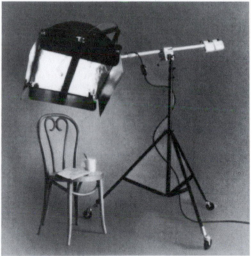

FIGURE 7.11 The design of portable light fixtures allows them to be mounted on floor stands, anchored by sand bags, hung from doorways, or clipped to other handy positions on the set. (Courtesy of Lowell Light and Colortran.)

opaque material with holes in it, which patterns the light into shadowed and brightly lit areas. Cookies are built to be slipped into a slot between the lamp and the lens of the body of an ellipsoidal spotlight. Reflectors provide indirect, reflected light, which is usually less harsh than the primary direct light. Sunlight, for example, can be reflected to function as fill light outdoors, whereas direct, unreflected sunlight functions as a key light (Figure 7.12).

LIGHT CONTROL

Electrical lighting in a studio can be controlled by means of patch panels and dimmer boards operated either electronically or digitally (Figure 7.13). A patch panel or electrical distribution center consists of a series of plugs for specific electrical circuits to which lighting instruments can be connected.

Lighting Control in the Studio

The voltage carried by each circuit can be controlled by a dimmer board. Each circuit has a limited electrical capacity, varying from about 20 to >50 amps. Using the formula watts = amps/volts (W = A/V), you can determine the maximum number of

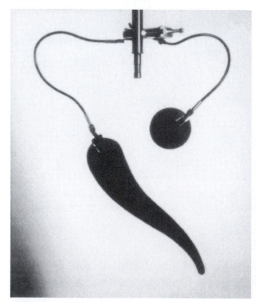

FIGURE 7.12 The control and shape of light as it falls on the set may be controlled by barn doors mounted on the front of the instrument, by reflecting light from a light surface such as an umbrella, or by placing scrims, flags, and diffusers between the lamp and the subjects. (Courtesy of Colortran and Lowell Light.)

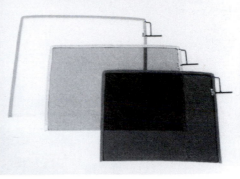

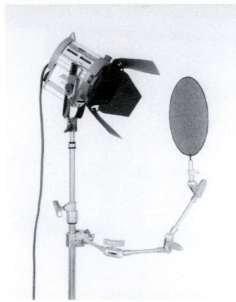

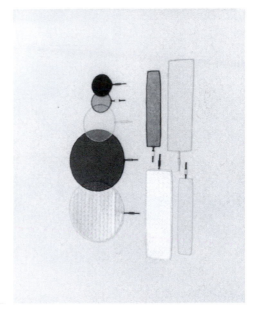

FIGURE 7.12—CONT'D

lamps that can be safely attached to each circuit without blowing a fuse or tripping a circuit breaker. For example, five 1,000 W, 110-volt lamps can be safely plugged into a 50-amp circuit, because each lamp will draw slightly more than 9 amps (watts/volts = amps; 1,000/110 = 9.1 amps per lamp; 5 × 9.1 = 45.5 total amps) (Figure 7.14).

For quick reference for calculating wattage and amperage in your head, use 100 volts instead of 110 or 120. This allows approximately a 10 percent safety factor. In the preceding examples, 1,000/100 = 10 amps; 10 × 5 = 50 amps.

The dimmer board is a useful means of reducing or adjusting light intensity for black-and-white production, but it is not very useful in this respect for color recording. A dimmer board reduces the light intensity by dropping the voltage, and dropping the voltage below 120 volts causes a consequent drop in color temperature, which is not

FIGURE 7.13 Light control patch bays may be designed to require physically placing patch cords into patch panels (*top*), or all connections can be performed through a computer program and computer-controlled distributor systems. (Courtesy of ETC Lighting.)

acceptable in color production. In color production, lighting intensity is reduced by moving a lighting instrument or using a scrim. To determine the result of moving a lighting instrument, the inverse square law may be used. This law of physics states that the amount of light change caused by increasing the distance between the light source and the subject will decrease by the square of the inverse of the change in distance.

Conversely, the amount of light change caused by decreasing the distance between the light source and the subject will increase by the square of the inverse of the change. For example, if the incident light from a lamp 8 feet from the subject measures 100 foot-candles and then the lamp is moved to 16 feet away (doubling the distance), the light will decrease by the square of the inverse of the change: ½ squared

OHMS LAW AS APPLIED TO LIGHTING SITUATIONS

The Wattage portion of Ohms Law is stated:

WATTAGE EQUALS VOLTAGE TIMES AMPERAGE
or
POWER = ELECTRICAL PRESSURE $\times$ ELECTRICAL FLOW

or stated as a formula:

W = V $\times$ A

a converse of the law is stated:

$$A = \frac{W}{V}$$

Either formula is simplified by using 100 V for Voltage although the normal Voltage in the U.S. is between 110 and 120 V, the difference provides a margin of protection.

The Wattage formula is used to determine how many Watts of lamps may be hooked to any one circuit once the Amperage of that circuit is known.

For example: typical electrical household or business building circuits provide 20 Amps of current, therefore:

W = V $\times$ A   W = 100 $\times$ 20   W = 2000 Watts

That means a total of 2000 watts of lamps and equipment could be connected to that one circuit.

If the total Wattage is known (total the wattage required to power all lamps & equipment) and then use the Amperage formula. If your location requires 2450 Watts of power then:

$$A = \frac{W}{V} \qquad A = \frac{2450}{100} \quad A = 24.5 \text{ Amps}$$

That means a circuit that provided at least 24.5 Amperage of current would be required. Neither a 15 Amp nor 20 Amp circuit would work, so either a 25 Amp circuit would need to be located, or the lamps would have to be split between a 15 Amp and a 10 Amp circuit or more likely two 15 amp circuits in order to provide enough current without blowing a fuse or breaker.

Using 100 for Voltage means that in most cases these calculations can be completed mentally, since it is easy to remember to multiply by 100 to obtain Wattage or divide by 100 to obtain Amperage.

FIGURE 7.14 As complicated as it may seem, calculating the amount of power required to power equipment and lighting instruments can be accomplished with simple formulas dividing or multiplying by 100.

is ¼, and ¼ of 100 foot-candles is 25 foot-candles. On the other hand, if the lamp's distance is cut in half to 4 feet, then the amount of light would increase by the square of the inverse of the change: $^2/_1$ squared is $^4/_1$ or 4; 100 × 4 is 400 foot-candles. It is obvious that it takes very small changes in the distance between the lamp and subject to make a major change in the amount of light reaching the subject (Figure 7.15).

Dimmer boards are useful for controlling entire banks of instruments simultaneously and for presetting a series of lamps for the next scene. Modern dimmer boards are computer controlled and allow an infinite number of individual instruments or series

INVERSE SQUARE LAW AS APPLIED TO LIGHTING SITUATIONS

The Inverse Square Law states that the light intensity falling on a subject will vary inversely by the square of the variation in the distance between the light source and the subject.

A simpler variation is that changing the distance between a source of light and the subject will result in a major change in the amount of light falling on the subject.

Stated as a formula:

$$I = \frac{1}{D^2} \, fc$$

When **I** is the change in light intensity and
D is the change in distance between the light source and subject.

An example:

If the measured light at the subject is 100 foot candles (fc) when D = 10 feet, and the D changes from 10 to 20 feet which is double the distance then:

$$I = \frac{1}{2^2} \, 100 \quad \text{(The distance doubled and the inverse of 2 is 1/2)}$$

$$I = \frac{1}{4} 100 \, fc$$

$$I = 25 \, fc$$

Or, if D changes from 10 to 5 feet, which is 1/2 the distance then:

$$I = 2^2 \text{ (The distance is 1/2 inverse of 1/2 is 2) } \times 100 \, fc$$

$$I = 4 \times 100 \quad \text{or } 400 \, fc.$$

Just remember moving a luminaire or the subject in relation to each other will modify the light measurement on the subject radically. A small movement will result in a great change in the light on the subject.

FIGURE 7.15 Calculating the amount of light falling on a subject as the lamp is moved back and forth is accomplished with a simple formula based on dividing by the square of the light source if the change in distance is increased, or multiplying by the square of the light source if the distance is decreased.

of instruments to be preset and changed at the press of a button. Computer control boards are designed to perform complex and rapidly changing light cues in variable combinations and number of cues (Figure 7.16).

Lighting Control on Location

Securing adequate electrical current for lighting on location presents more problems and hazards than does studio production. The most pressing problem is how and where to secure adequate power. If sufficient electricity is not available, portable gasoline generators are sometimes brought in. When using a private home or office, a lighting director and electrician may decide to tap the main power supply or to use the existing circuits. If the former course is taken, a qualified electrician must perform the operation of tapping into the 100 amp (or more) main supply, which can then be

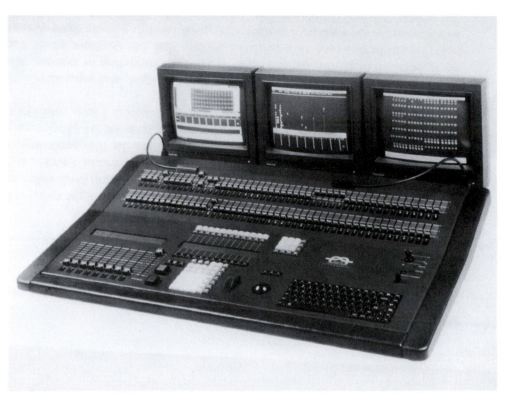

FIGURE 7.16 A modern computer-operated lighting-control dimmer board allows all of the adjustment functions of lighting instruments (except for moving the lamps) from the control board. (Courtesy of Colortran.)

channeled to a portable circuit board for distribution to individual instruments. If you decide to use existing circuits in the home or office, you can determine which outlets are on the same circuits and how many amps each circuit can carry by simply checking and closing a circuit at the main circuit box or fuse box and then testing outlets in the rooms where filming is to take place. Load demands should never exceed those specified at the circuit or fuse box, because excess power traveling along a line can melt the wires and start a fire. Any situation that requires an extensive amount of lighting and electrical energy demands the expertise of a qualified electrician.

LIGHT MEASUREMENT

The basic unit of light intensity measure is the foot-candle. One foot-candle is an agreed-upon standard that represents the approximate light intensity produced by a candle one foot away. The normal measurement range of a light meter is from 1 to about 250 foot-candles. A light meter is extremely useful in both video and film production for determining lighting levels and contrast within a scene, as well as for properly positioning and setting individual lights. In film recording, a light meter must be adjusted to the proper sensitivity scale or Exposure Index (EI) number (DIN in Europe) so that it provides the correct f-stop readings for the specific sensitivity of the film stock (Figure 7.17).

The three major light sources are key light, fill light, and separation light. The *key light* is the brightest, hardest light. It provides modeling or texture. *Modeling* refers to the appearance of a textured surface that has shadows where there are indentations in

FIGURE 7.17 Handheld light meters may be designed for different functions. The one on the left is designed primarily to read incident light, and the one on the right is designed to read reflected light, although both meters will read either incident or reflected light.

the surface. A surface with good modeling looks three-dimensional. *Fill light* is softened, lower-intensity light that helps to fill in some of the shadows created by the key light and to reduce the contrast between light and shadow areas. *Separation light* comes from behind the subject. It creates a halo effect, which outlines the subject and helps to separate it from the background.

Types of Light Meter Readings

There are two basic types of meter readings: incident and reflected. *Spot meters* are a specialized type of reflected meter. Another type of reflected reading may be gained through a meter built into the film camera or electronic circuits built into a video camera. This type of metering is called *through the lens* (TTL). Some light meters are capable of producing only one type of reading. Others can be used for several different types of readings. Each reading has a specific purpose in terms of lighting control. On some light meters, a white hemisphere or flat circle is placed over the photoelectric cell so that the meter can measure the intensity of the light falling on the subject, or the *incident light*. This white surface gathers and diffuses light falling on the meter from several directions. For a reading of direct light falling on the subject, the meter is pointed at the camera from the position of the subject (Figure 7.18).

A reading of incident or direct light is called an *incident reading*. Because such a reading measures the light falling on the subject, it is not affected by the reflectance of the objects to be recorded.

A measurement of indirect light—that is, light reflected by the subject—is called a *reflected reading*. The white covering is removed from the photocell for a reflected

FIGURE 7.18 To take an incident light reading, the meter should be held close to the subject pointing toward the light source(s). A wide-angle light meter with a diffusion cap provides the most accurate incident meter reading.

reading, and the meter is pointed at the subject from the camera. A reflected reading of the subject or whole scene averages the amount of light reflected by objects in the scene to determine the best overall exposure or base light level (Figure 7.19). A *spot meter reading* is the reflected light from a small isolated area within the frame. Spot meter readings are often used to take light readings of objects that are too far away to make an incident reading practical or from subjects that reflect far more or less light than the average subject in the area.

A *TTL* or *through-the-lens reading* provides a reflected reading of the exact image framed within the camera and can be used to adjust the lens automatically. Some TTL systems do not respond instantaneously to light changes, and the proper exposure lags slightly behind actual changes in light intensity. In essence, a video camera is a TTL meter. The operator can determine the proper exposure by reading an oscilloscope attached to the camera output or by gauging the contrast and exposure through the camera viewfinder, assuming the viewfinder is properly adjusted. The operator actually is viewing the reflected light in the viewfinder.

Determining Contrast Ratios

A light meter can be used in both video and film production to determine contrast within a scene. Apparent contrast within the image area can affect image clarity as well as the overall emotional mood. There are two important contrast ratios in any lighting setup: lighting ratio and contrast ratio. The mathematical relationship between light intensity in foot-candles or between f-stops on a light meter can be used to determine these specific ratios. (Foot-candles can be directly compared, whereas each higher f-stop number indicates a doubling and each lower f-stop a halving of the light intensity.)

FIGURE 7.19 To take a reflected light reading, the meter is held close to the camera and pointed at the major subject. A narrow-angle meter provides the most accurate reflected meter reading.

Lighting Ratios

Key-to-Fill Ratio

Key-to-fill ratio indicates the proportion of key light to fill light in any lighting setup. This is called the *lighting ratio* but should not be confused with the inherent contrast ratio of a video camera or film stock, as will be discussed in Chapter 8, The Camera. Lighting contrast is caused exclusively by lights. It is actually a comparison of key-plus-fill light to fill light alone.

Some fill light always spills over into the key light area and increases its intensity. An incident reading is taken of the key and fill lights together. Then the key light is shut off and a fill light reading is taken. A comparison of the two readings in terms of foot-candles or recommended f-stop readings indicates the key-to-fill light ratio. A key-plus-fill light reading of 250 foot-candles compared with a fill light reading of 125 foot-candles equals a 2:1 lighting ratio. One f-stop difference between the two indicates a 2:1 ratio, two f-stops a 4:1 ratio, three f-stops an 8:1 ratio, and so on. In most situations, video and film recording is done under a key-to-fill light ratio of 4:1 or less, unless a highly dramatic effect with high contrast is desired. Because video has less tolerance for contrast than film, it generally is advisable to use a 2:1 or lower key-to-fill light ratio in video recordings or film recordings that will be transferred to video. The key-to-fill ratio determines whether a high-key or low-key aesthetic of lighting is in effect. Low-key lighting has a high key-to-fill ratio, whereas high-key lighting has a low key-to-fill light ratio.

Key-to-Back Ratio

The relative proportion of key light to backlight is called the *key-to-back ratio*. In most instances, backlights and key lights should have approximately the same intensity. This ratio is usually kept at about 1:1 or 1:1.5. A weak backlight does little to separate the subject from the background or to create a halo effect. An extremely strong back-light, on the other hand, can cause an excessively bright halo to form around the subject's head and back.

Lighting Ratios (Incident Meter Readings)		
Key-to-fill ratio	=	Lighting ratio
250 fc:125 fc	=	2:1
Key-to-back ratio	=	Key to back ratio
375 fc:250 fc	=	1.5-1
Contrast ratio	:	(Reflected meter readings)
Brightest area	:	Darkest area
100 fc:5 fc	=	20:1

Contrast Ratios

Contrast ratios can be determined by taking reflected light meter readings of the brightest and darkest reflecting objects in the scene. A spot meter is a great help in isolating a specific object, although moving a standard reflected light meter closer to an object without interrupting the light falling on it accomplishes the same goal. Again, a comparison of light meter foot-candle or f-stop readings indicates the contrast ratio between the brightest and darkest reflecting areas in the scene. Video cameras cannot record a reflectance contrast ratio greater than 50:1 (approximately five f-stops). Some standard film stocks, such as color negative, can often record reflectance contrast ranges as high as 100:1 (six or seven f-stops).

Adjusting Contrast

There are several ways of altering a scene's contrast to make it more acceptable for visual recording. Specific lights that are too strong or too weak can be moved farther from or closer to the subject. Scrims and diffusion materials can be used to cut down on the light intensity. Additional instruments can be focused on the subject, although care must be taken to keep these multiple keys and fills close together so that objectionable multiple shadows are not created. Altering the lighting contrast ratio can affect the reflectance contrast ratio because the two are interdependent: objects reflect key and fill light. In some cases, a change in the color or brightness of props, sets, or costumes may be required to increase or decrease light reflectance.

SETTING LIGHTING INSTRUMENTS
Three- and Four-Point Lighting

Three-point and four-point lighting are realist techniques that help create an illusion of three-dimensionality and depth in two-dimensional media such as video and film (Figures 7.20 and 7.21). Three-point and four-point lighting setups use three specific types of light, which have different directional placements, degrees of softness and hardness, and intensities.

FIGURE 7.20 A subject lit with one harsh luminaire that represents the sun or major light source is called a key light. Such a lighting design is not flattering nor particularly revealing. Using both a key light and an additional softly diffused luminaire from the opposite side of the subject from the key light creates a more pleasant and useful subject.

FIGURE 7.21 To separate the subject from the background and to highlight the subject's hair, a luminaire is placed directly opposite the camera focused sharply down on the subject.

A fourth luminaire may be used to throw a pattern on the background, erase unwanted shadows, or light an area not covered by the other three luminaires.

Key Light

The key lights are the brightest and, in some ways, the most important lights on the set. The key light determines the overall recording or exposure level. The placement of a key light suggests the direction of the primary source of light within a scene, such as a window, an overhead light, the sun or moon, or even a candle or fireplace. When the key light strikes a subject directly from the front or camera side of the subject, few shadows or variations in surface texture are created and the result is a flat, uninteresting image. For optimal modeling and aesthetic effect, the key light should be 30 to 40 degrees away from the camera-subject axis, and it should light the short or narrow side of a face, that is, the side of the face that is least exposed to the camera. Moving the key light up and down, and from side to side, affects the direction and length of facial shadows and increases or decreases facial modeling.

Key light usually has a hard quality. The beam of light is narrowly focused and rarely if ever diffused or softened, except perhaps in a situation where softness is needed to create a romantic or light mood. The height of the key light affects the length of shadows falling on the set. Key lights should be placed high enough that long shadows do not spill onto the background from foreground subjects. The key light is usually placed much higher than the camera, unless a special effect is desired, such as the presentation of a flat, untextured image (in which case, the key light is at camera height) or a mysterious and horrifying face (in which case, the key light is placed lower than camera height). In multiple-subject setups, the same light that functions as a key light for one subject can also function as the fill light or backlight for another. The term *key light* simply refers to the brightest light source striking a subject from the camera's viewpoint. The specific instrument designated as the key light can change as the camera or subject moves.

Fill Light

Fill light is used to provide general illumination on the set and to fill in the shadows created by the key lights. Fill light is usually softer than key light. Reflectors or translucent materials placed in front of the lighting instrument are used frequently to diffuse the light. The fill light is often placed at approximately camera height or just slightly above so that shadows created by overhead key lights can be properly filled in. It is usually on the opposite side of the camera from the key light. The intensities and physical placement of the key and fill lights will determine to a significant extent the emotional mood and lighting atmosphere within the scene.

Separation Light (Backlight)

One or two separation lights complete the three-point lighting triangle or four-point rectangle. A backlight is usually placed above and behind the subject to create a halo effect that outlines the subject, separating it from the background. The backlight completes the three-point lighting setup, but it is not the only light that can be used to separate the subject from the background. In a four-point lighting setup, another separation light, called a *kicker*, may be placed exactly opposite the key light on the set. A kicker functions similarly to a backlight, but it is directed from the back and the side of the subject (usually opposite or facing the key light) rather than from directly behind and above the subject's back and head. Separation of subject and background through backlights and kickers is extremely important in black-and-white recording. The height of the backlight or kicker and its intensity in comparison with the key light affect the amount of separation that takes place.

Background Light

Background light illuminates the background or set. It affects every lighting setup and is extremely important in the overall aesthetic appearance of a scene. Although fill lights and key lights frequently spill over onto the background and partially illuminate it, it is important to light the background separately so that its appearance can be more carefully controlled. The amount of light cast on the background obviously affects subject/background separation. It can also affect visual emphasis within a scene. If the background is brighter than the subject, the viewer's attention will be distracted from the primary focus of interest. If the background is too dark, the set may look unnatural or the scene too high contrast. To add interest and texture to an otherwise flat, monochromatic background, patterns can be cast on the background to break it up and give it some modeling and texture. Although too much patterning can be distracting, a flat, monochrome, evenly lit background looks dull and unimaginative. The use of different colors for the subject and background can affect much the same separation in color production, but separation lights have not been entirely abandoned in color production because they add so much texture, dimension, and depth to the visual image. In an optimal three-point lighting setup, the keys, fills, and backlights form the points of a triangle or a Y. When a kicker and a backlight are used together, the four lighting points form a rectangle or an "X." Such ideal placements are rarely, if ever, consistently maintained. Only static, artificial, intensely boring still scenes with subjects and cameras that never move would allow for a permanent, perfectly triangular three-point or rectangular four-point lighting setup. A more typical situation is characterized by the constant movement of the subject(s) and cameras and a complex, constantly varying relationship between keys, fills, and backlights or kickers. The three-point and four-point lighting procedures outlined earlier simply provide a starting point and an idealized model that is necessarily and continually manipulated in complex recording situations.

Controlling Shadows

Background light should not be used to try to burn out shadows from foreground performers that fall on the background. The most effective means of eliminating bad shadows is proper placement of the key lights. Key lights should be placed high enough above the performers so that prominent shadows are not cast on background walls as they move around the set. Performers should also be kept at a safe distance from the back wall whenever possible. Another complicating factor in three- and four-point television and film lighting is the creation of objectionable shadows by microphone booms. Because the key light creates the most noticeable shadows, microphone-boom placement and movement must be arranged to minimize interference with the key lights. Sometimes this can be accomplished by adjusting the barn doors of the key lights so that light does not spill into the microphone boom area. In other cases, the key lights may have to be placed higher overhead than normal, so that boom shadows fall on the floor, rather than on more noticeable parts of the set. A microphone-boom shadow can often be hidden in a part of the set that is already riddled with a shadow pattern. Obviously, the planning of the lighting setup must include consideration of the placement and movement of the microphone boom, before the key and fill lights are firmly positioned.

Cross Key Lighting

Cross key lighting uses two key lights to light two subjects equally. A fill light is not needed because the spill light from the key lights acts as fill.

Lighting Moving Subjects

The discussion of lighting to this point has assumed that the subject to be recorded is relatively stationary. A moving subject significantly complicates a lighting setup. The major problem inherent in lighting a moving subject is how to maintain relatively consistent light levels as the subject moves about the set. Multiple key lights must be used to light a moving subject in the studio.

If a subject were to walk too close or too far away from a single key light, he or she would become too light or too dark, and realist continuity in lighting would be lost. Multiple key lights are hung at constant distances from the moving subject so that the subject can move from one key light to another without a noticeable change in lighting. Problems arise when key light beams overlap or when there are gaps of darkness between key lights. To prevent these problems, the barn doors or shutters on the key lights are adjusted so that key light beams are exactly adjacent to each other along the performer blocking line (where a subject will move on the set). As long as the talent follows this prearranged line of action and hits his or her marks, no gaps or overlaps of lighting will occur.

Low-Key versus High-Key Lighting

The terms *low-key* and *high-key lighting* originated in the studio eras of feature film production in Hollywood. They seem counterintuitive—that is, the terms mean the opposite of what we think they should mean. Low-key lighting refers to the minimal use of fill light—that is, a relatively high key-to-fill ratio. This kind of lighting creates pools of light and rather harsh shadows. Many Warner Bros. gangster films and detective films produced in the 1930s and 1940s used low-key lighting for aesthetic effect. However, a whole genre of Hollywood films called film noir (literally, "black film" in French) relied on low-key lighting in the 1940s. Low-key lighting evokes a rather heavy and serious mood or feeling that enhances the emotional atmosphere of certain types of films. Low-key lighting is similar to an effect in painting known as *chiaroscuro*.

This technique is evident in the paintings of Rembrandt, for example, where shafts of light illuminate central figures in the painting, while the remaining parts of the scene are dimly lit and heavily shadowed. Low-key lighting can have a similar effect in video and film, although contrast ratio differences between video and film call for different lighting techniques to create the same effect in the two media.

High-key lighting presents a brightly lit scene with few shadow areas. It has been suggested that during the 1930s and 1940s, Metro-Goldwyn-Mayer (MGM) studios used high-key lighting for its lavish musicals so that no detail in its elaborate and expensive sets would be hidden in the shadows.

In any case, the use of high-key lighting in musical comedies is another example of form following function. The term *notan* is often applied to high-key lighting. The word *notan* refers to the bright, low-contrast paintings of the Japanese master painters. The light, happy atmosphere stimulated by high-key lighting contrasts with the somber, mysterious, or threatening atmosphere of low-key lighting. Thus, an important consideration in selecting either high- or low-key lighting styles is attempting to match the form of the lighting to the specific function it is intended to serve.

Single-Camera versus Multiple-Camera Situations

In single-camera recording situations, the lighting is sometimes changed for each shot or each major change in camera position. Of course, changing the lighting slightly for each separate shot can be extremely laborious and time consuming. Subtle changes in lighting are made in realist productions, not drastic changes that call attention to the lighting. Lighting continuity from shot to shot and scene to scene will break down with too much shifting of lighting instruments. Feature films and network television commercials, which have big budgets, long shooting schedules, and large production crews, can better afford the luxury of lighting each separate shot perfectly than can lower-level productions.

The aesthetic expectations of audiences and the demands of clients make lighting a high priority in some single-camera productions. Still, the lighting for any single-camera production can benefit from the added time and care this production method affords. Because recording is continuous in multiple-camera production, the lights cannot be reset for different shots. Lighting decisions and compromises must be fully worked out before the actual recording. The same lighting setup is used for long shots, medium shots, and close-ups. The lighting director must be able to anticipate every camera angle and placement that will be needed before arranging and setting up the lights on the set.

Lighting for Digital Cameras

Digital cameras see light in the same way as analog cameras. The digital signal maintains an apparently higher level of resolution because no defects are added to the picture. For this reason, many fine details lost with an analog camera will stand out visibly in the digital mode. It is imperative, then, that light falls only on areas that need to be lit and that accurate lighting ratios are developed in the lighting plan. Sloppy work in all aspects of digital production, especially in high-definition production, such as set design and construction, costumes, and makeup, will become obvious in areas that would not show in an analog production. Lighting for digital signals simply requires greater care for the small details than lighting for analog signals. Although modern digital cameras are more sensitive than older analog cameras, requiring less base light, they still need well-balanced light sources. The difference between key and fill need not be as great on a digital set, but there is no such thing as a true realistic light situation. The lighting in a normal living room, office, or even an outdoor setting will not appear as a professionally lit scene; instead it will look like someone forgot you were shooting film or video and left the camera running. Some key or fill lights, with back or set lights are needed in a digital setting as well as any analog setting.

Lighting Plots

A specific lighting setup can be outlined or diagrammed on a piece of grid paper that represents an overhead scale diagram of the studio. This outline is called a *lighting plot*. The overhead lighting grid to which specific instruments can be attached is drawn onto the studio diagram. The basic elements of the set are added to this overhead view. The placements and movements of the talent and camera(s) can be added to the diagram after preliminary performer and camera blocking, so that the lights can be positioned accordingly. Lighting plots also may be created using specifically written computer programs that allow for manipulation of diagrams of sets, instruments, and performers. Such programs also allow for the printing of hard copies of the diagrams as well as storage of the files on discs for recall at a later time. The lighting director equipped with such computer programs uses the computer graphics to create these plots quickly and efficiently without tediously hand drawing each instrument and connection.

The program also will create lists of the instruments required and indicate patchboard connections. Several key lights may have to be arranged so that they maintain an even or balanced brightness on the moving performer throughout the set. Only when the exact blocking line of the talent is known can these lights be properly placed. The distance of the key lights from the talent can be determined by relying on the inverse square law (light intensity changes according to the square of the distance of the light source from the object) and the scale dimensions of the grid paper. One-quarter inch on paper may equal one foot of actual studio floor space for example (Figure 7.22).

Composing a lighting plot allows the lighting director to consider all relevant factors that can affect the selection and placement of lighting instruments before actual production. He or she must consider the placement and movement of the talent,

TYPICAL LIGHTING PLOT

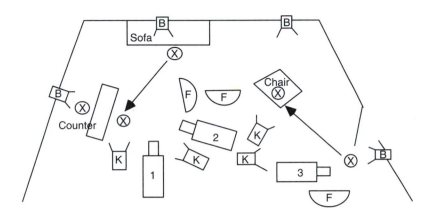

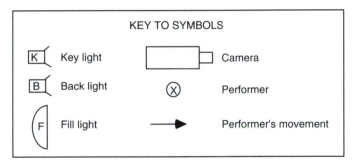

FIGURE 7.22 Lighting plots provide a means of carefully planning ahead of time for the placement of lighting instruments to avoid unnecessarily moving fixtures once the sets and blocking have been completed. The plot must be drawn to scale or it is of little value for accurate planning.

cameras, and microphone booms, as well as the electrical and spatial capabilities and limitations of the studio or location environment. The lighting plot must also incorporate many aesthetic or stylistic variables. It can be low key or high key; realist, modernist, or postmodernist. The lighting director must develop a lighting setup that is both aesthetically satisfying and practical from an engineering standpoint.

PRINCIPLES OF DESIGN

Design has three basic functions in a dramatic production: to establish the time, place, and mood; to reflect character; and to reinforce specific themes. A historical time period and setting must be easily identifiable. Costumes, sets, props, and titles denote a specific time and place at the same time that they reflect a specific style or mood. The mood or atmosphere results primarily from the abstract, emotional aspects of design elements and principles. Specific colors and shapes create an emotional mood that can reveal character and reinforce themes. The idea that you can tell a great deal about people from where they live and what they wear can be applied to scenic design. A cold, formal setting or costume reveals a great deal about a character, as does a warm, relaxed setting or costume.

An art director works with three basic principles of design: design elements, color, and composition in creating settings, properties, costumes, and makeup. The ways in which these elements are selected and combined determines the nature and success of each aspect of the design. The selection of design elements must support the themes, plots, and characterizations of a drama or the central message of a nonfiction production.

Design Elements

Design elements shares the same history, theory, and techniques as the same elements used in two-dimensional and computer graphic design.

Shape

A combination of lines creates a shape. An infinite number of different shapes reflect specific objects, but some common, recurring shapes with which all designers work are circles, squares, rectangles, triangles, ellipses, trapezoids, octagons, and hexagons. Shapes can carry symbolic meaning. A square-straight flat gives the viewer a different impression than a set constructed using circular and curved forms in the background.

Texture

Texture provides a tactile impression of form on the walls and on the surface of costumes. Texture can be real or represented. Real textures are revealed by directional light, which creates shadows and modeling on a nonsmooth surface. Represented textures, such as granite, marble, or wood grains, have smooth surfaces that create a tactile impression. The texture of a surface affects our perception of depth. A rough texture with heavy shadows provides a greater sensation of depth than a smooth, flat surface. A heavily textured material used in drapes or costumes can create a richness that relates to a theme of opulence, splendor, or decadence. Texture, like shapes, can create a sense of space that affects our emotions and relates symbolically to the major themes of a story.

Movement

Movement can be real or imaginary. The illusion of movement can be enhanced by the use of parallel diagonals in a set, for example. It can also be limited or reduced by the use of vertical and horizontal panels. Specific shapes and lines, such as spirals, concentric circles, and radial designs, can generate significant movement and space for actors to appear and work.

Color

The three aspects of color of primary importance to a designer consist of color harmony, color contrast, and the emotional or symbolic effect of color. Chapter 11, Graphics, Animation, and Special Effects, presents detailed descriptions and uses of color; they include contrast, harmony, gray scale, and emotional and cultural responses to color.

Composition

The arrangement and selection of sets, props, furniture, costumes, and actors within the frame make up the objects of composition combined in the following elements: balance, perspective, dimensionality, and image area.

Balance

Balance in a set can give the feeling of stability, or instability. If the design seems to be out-of-line unnaturally, then it has lost its stability. Balance also may be gained by using precisely matched objects on each side of the frame, such as two chairs set the same distance from the side of the frame. This would be a *symmetrically balanced* design. A set may still be balanced but not have precisely the same size and graphic weighed objects on each side of the frame. Instead, one or more objects of the same weight on each side of the frame may create an *asymmetrically balanced* design.

Perspective

Perspective refers to the arrangement of various elements to draw attention to the most important aspect of the image, which is called the *focal center*. A common focal center is the performer, but for the actor to be the focal center, the objects in the set must be arranged so that they do not overwhelm, hide, or distract from the actor. Placing the actor in or near the center of the set works, but it is boring. Arranging objects within the frame so that the viewer's eye follows the objects to the focal center accomplishes a greater purpose of the scene.

Dimensionality

The three-dimensionality of reality is created in either a video or film frame with a two-dimensional reproduction. To give the impression that the picture represents the 3-D world, an understanding of how the three dimensions relate to the frame is necessary. The movement or composition along a line running from left to right or vice versa is considered the *X-axis*. Any movement or composition running from the bottom to top, or vice versa, is considered the *Y-axis*. The *Z-axis* does not actually exist in a two-dimensional medium, but it can be depicted or created through the use of compositional arrangements within the frame. If objects are arranged at an angle, instead of straight across the frame, or if a series of objects diminish in size as they rise in the frame, a Z-axis is created. To avoid boring or static pictures, efforts should always be made to create a Z-axis in each sequence.

Image Area

An important determinant of composition in visual graphics is the aspect ratio or frame dimensions of the recorded and displayed image. As noted earlier, frame dimensions vary in television and film. The aspect ratio, or proportion of height to width, of standard television (SD) images is 4:3 or 1.33:1. The aspect ratio specifications for HDTV is 16:9 or 1.85:1; projected film images vary somewhat in terms of their aspect ratios, from 1.33:1 to 2:1 (Figure 7.23).

When HDTV images are viewed on a 4:3 standard television receiver or monitor or on a small screen on a mobile device, the viewer will either not see a portion of the image on both sides of the frame, or the signal will need to be broadcast in letterbox frame. *Letterbox framing* refers to a widescreen image shown in its full width, but a narrow band of black across the top and the bottom of the frame fills in the areas that are not included in a widescreen production. At one time, letterbox was considered an unacceptable method of showing wide-screen productions, but with the advent of HDTV it is not only acceptable but has become fashionable, with commercials being produced intentionally in letterbox format. Some mobile devices are designed with square or variable ratio screens so the designer can only guess as to what the viewer actually will see on those screens. It is therefore best to keep as much important information as possible well within the critical area of a standard 4:3 frame.

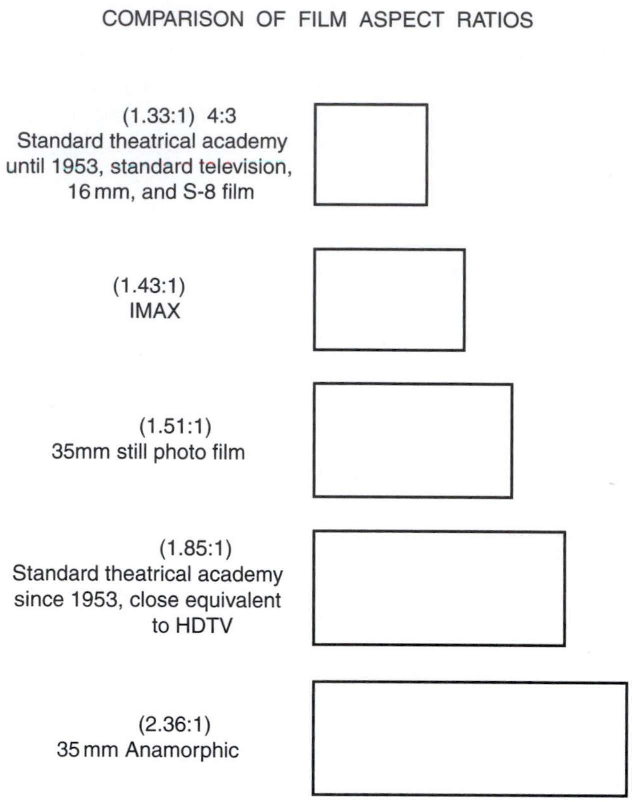

COMPARISON OF FILM ASPECT RATIOS

(1.33:1) 4:3
Standard theatrical academy
until 1953, standard television,
16 mm, and S-8 film

(1.43:1)
IMAX

(1.51:1)
35mm still photo film

(1.85:1)
Standard theatrical academy
since 1953, close equivalent
to HDTV

(2.36:1)
35 mm Anamorphic

FIGURE 7.23 If a 35 mm photographic slide is converted to SD, not all of the slide will be visible on the video screen. If converted to HD wide screen, all of the slide will be visible. The 35 mm slide is wider than 35 mm film but a smaller border at the top and bottom of the slide will be lost from scanning and reproduction. SD video and 35 mm film will have to be reproduced with either a black stripe across the sides or with a portion of the sides cut off to fill the frame top and bottom.

On-Set Design Elements

Set furnishings, props, costumes, and performer makeup are not completely independent elements in the production process. Elements of scenic design interact with each other and many other areas of production to create an overall visual impression. The most important interactions are those between scenic design and each of the following: lighting, performer movement, and camera and microphone placement. Important set elements, such as key props, can be emphasized by lighting them more brightly than other elements. The texture of a rough surface can be accentuated with side lighting, which creates textural shadows in the surface indentations. Colored lighting can drastically alter the color of set elements. A colored surface can only reflect wavelengths of light that are present in the light that illuminates it. Different lighting-contrast ratios and lighting styles can enhance a specific mood or atmosphere inherent in the setting.

The most commonly used types of on-set graphics are handheld cards, photographic blowups, and three-dimensional graphic set pieces. Handheld cards are images that a performer holds up to the camera during a scene. The talent controls the timing and placement of this type of graphic illustration.

Still photographs can be blown up or enlarged so that they provide a convenient background or backdrop on the set. Such photographs should have a matte rather than a shiny or glossy surface so that they do not reflect a great deal of light, and they should be positioned so that no glare or reflection is directed toward the camera lens. Three-dimensional structures placed on the set for illustration purposes are called *graphic set pieces*. A graphic set piece could be an item to be demonstrated, such as a piece of machinery, or an art object. Most on-set graphics can be scanned or shot and recorded ahead of time so that the framing can be precise and the camera is not tied up with a static shot unless it is necessary for the talent to handle the graphic or be part of the action involving the graphic.

Camera cards are usually placed on an easel, which is an adjustable display platform or graphics stand (Figure 7.24). The lights on the easel, which illuminate the card, are normally placed at a 45-degree angle from the card's surface to minimize light reflection in the camera lens.

Scenic Design

Scenic design is an important contributor to overall characterization and thematic meaning. The first stage of scenic design is analyzing the script to determine what kinds of sets, costumes, and makeup will be required. A script usually provides a clear indication of general time and place, even if it does not describe settings and costumes in detail. Judgments concerning time, place, mood, character, and theme can

GRAPHICS STAND

The stagehand stands behind the stand and drops each graphic on cue from the floor manager

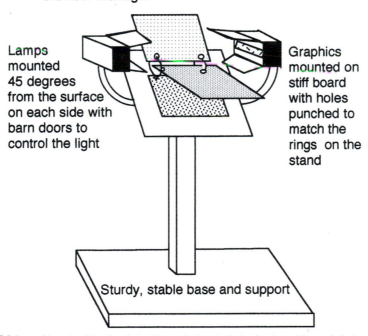

Lamps mounted 45 degrees from the surface on each side with barn doors to control the light

Graphics mounted on stiff board with holes punched to match the rings on the stand

Sturdy, stable base and support

FIGURE 7.24 A graphics stand is a handy tool to use in the studio to shoot graphics and photographs mounted on a stiff board. The lamps should be adjusted to prevent unwanted reflections and to light the stand from the studio fixtures. The graphics should be stacked with the first on the bottom and the last on top. All of the boards are held at the top and they are dropped to the stand one at a time on cue from the floor manager.

only be made after the script has been carefully and thoroughly analyzed. The script itself can be broken down into a list of specific times and places, in much the same way as a breakdown is done for production scheduling and budgeting. A designer can then note the specific psychological mood of the action and characters for each time and place. Finally, more abstract concepts, ideas, and themes that result from in-depth analysis can be integrated with and reinforced by the selection of specific settings, costumes, and makeup.

SET CONSTRUCTION

The design of specific physical sets can be conveniently divided into two stages: layouts or floor plans and actual set construction. Design research, layouts, floor plans, and costume sketches are considered *above-the-line expenses*. They are created before actual production and before a commitment is made to actual construction, so that changes can be made before more sizable *below-the-line construction* expenses have been incurred. Each stage of design from planning to execution results in a specific two-dimensional or three-dimensional product. By following these stages, a designer refines rough ideas into workable sets that can be efficiently and economically constructed, significantly contributing to overall program effectiveness. Before undertaking the work and expense of set design and construction, some designers may consider the use of a neutral background, called a *cyclorama* or *cyc*. A cyc is a heavy, monochrome curtain that provides a neutral set backdrop. It is convenient to set up in a studio and can be used for many production settings. A cyc will often suffice in many modernist and postmodernist situations (Figure 7.25). A cyc also may be used as a green chroma key screen background if washed with the proper balanced green lights.

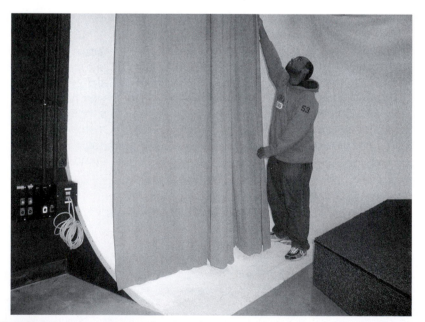

FIGURE 7.25 A sky cyclorama (skycyc) is a plain off-background that may be lit with a variety of different colors or patterns depending on the lighting instruments used. It also represents an infinite or nondescript background if that is called for in the set design. The cyc may be either a drape hung on a continuous rod to allow the drape to be moved and arranged as needed, or it may be hung as a hard cyc with both the corner and the section meeting the floor curved to add to the infinite background.

Virtual Sets

Design of computer-generated or virtual sets is done completely within one or more computer programs intended for that purpose. The same amount of research and planning must also precede the actual computer design as is accomplished for a set constructed of physical materials. Many Hollywood reporting and some news sets now are virtual sets.

During preproduction, a designer first draws a rough layout sketch for each set. These preliminary drawings are extremely important preproduction elements. They provide a focus for discussions at preproduction meetings, facilitate the estimation of set construction costs, and serve as a preliminary guide for the actual construction of sets.

A fully scaled floor plan translates actual set dimensions into a proportional ¼-inch or other convenient scale on a piece of grid paper. The designer creates a bird's-eye view of the proposed set in reduced dimensions that are proportional to the actual size of objects on the set. If a wall is to be 8 feet long, it will be 2 inches long on the scaled floor plan (eight ¼ inches = 2 inches). Using a fully scaled floor plan, a director can determine if there is sufficient room to move the cameras or talent from one position to another in the set. The lighting director uses a fully scaled floor plan to prepare the studio lighting. The final floor plan layout will include such things as scenery, set pieces such as furniture and props, and set dressings such as curtains. Skilled carpenters and painters translate the drawings into set materials that conform in every possible respect to the designer's original intentions.

Set Construction

Flats are relatively lightweight rectangular boards that are braced and supported by 2 × 3 inch or 2 × 4 inch boards on the back so that they are quite sturdy and durable. Various devices are used to connect flats together: rope tied over pegs, fastened with metal hinges, or secured with C-clamps. Angle braces usually support flats to keep them upright. *Risers* are hollow rectangular boxes that can be placed on the floor to raise a portion of a set. Risers might be used in a news set, for example, to raise the news desk and seated performers to camera height. Permanent sets are sometimes constructed out of more durable materials. A set that is going to be used day after day, such as for an evening news program, may be permanently secured to the studio floor for added stability. Because set materials are rarely viewed from behind, carpenters can cut costs by finishing only one side of a set piece and using inexpensive support materials.

Properties

The designer of a more realistic set must also select the necessary furniture and dressings, which fill in the set with objects and materials that add interest, realism, or atmosphere. *Props* or properties are functional furnishings that are integrated into the program. *Hand props* are actually handled by performers, whereas set pieces are simply interesting, perhaps symbolic, details on the set. Hand props are often used for bits of stage business or action, such as a gun kept hidden from the view of other characters (Figure 7.26). With virtual sets, blue-screen, or chroma key sets, the placement of props is critical because the actual set and environment cannot be seen by the actors or stage crew except by viewing a monitor.

FIGURE 7.26 Hand props are objects decorating the set that are small enough to be picked up and used by the performers.

COSTUME DESIGN

Most television and film productions require costumes and clothing that are selected and designed specifically for one show. For the majority of such productions, the wardrobe person procures costumes from rental houses that specialize in supplying costumes to theater, film, and video productions. In some cases, clothing manufacturers that want to advertise their products will supply the clothing. Higher-budget productions employ costume designers who create original costumes.

In terms of texture, designers know that shiny, highly reflective materials appear much brighter than thick or coarsely textured materials. Bold plaids and stripes call too much attention to themselves. The designer of video costumes and sets should consciously avoid certain fabric shapes and designs because they cause problems during recording. For example, parallel lines that are quite close together, as in herringbone cloth, can cause a moiré effect on a video screen. A moiré effect is a distracting vibration of visual images caused by the interaction of close-set lines in the materials being recorded and the video scanning lines. In television, the color blue or green, when used for chroma key, is usually avoided in costumes and sets (Figure 7.27).

MAKEUP

Video and film performers' makeup can be divided into two types: cosmetic and prosthetic. *Cosmetic makeup* enhances the appearance of performers by hiding imperfections, adding needed color, and accentuating their better features, and *prosthetic makeup* transforms the appearance of a performer's face through temporary plastic surgery and other corrective means. Prosthetic makeup can add years to a performer's appearance or entirely transform his or her physical appearance. Prosthetic makeup gives mobility to the expressive features of an actor and allows him or her some facial versatility in terms of playing many different roles. Prosthetic appliances can be used to make changes in the apparent age, race, nationality, and even sex of

FIGURE 7.27 Costumes and settings are crucial in the staging of historical films, such as the Miramax Films production of *Restoration* with Robert Downey, Jr., and fellow actors wearing the traditional clothing of the 18th century. (Courtesy of Miramax Films.)

an actor. Prosthetic appliances are usually made of foam latex, which can be applied to the performer's face and hands.

Cosmetic makeup enhances the beauty of a performer. It compensates for the heightened awareness of imperfections caused by film and video recording equipment and weak features in a performer's face. It also brings out the best features of a performer's face. Cosmetic makeup hides reddish cheeks and noses, beard lines, freckles, and blemishes. Eyes and lips are the most important aspects of a female performer's face. Makeup can hide or compensate for defects in these facial structures. If a female performer's eyes are too close together, for example, eyeliner can be placed on the outside edges of her lids to make them look farther apart.

Male performers often require makeup to cover beard lines, although many newscasters shave just before they appear on the evening news to avoid whisker stubble. Bright shades of cheek and lip color are generally avoided with males to prevent the appearance of a heavily made-up look. A weak chin can be made more prominent with a subtle accentuation of jaw lines and cheek color. Female performers are usually less concerned or embarrassed about applying makeup than are men, but properly explaining the technical need for makeup can help to assuage the timidity of inexperienced performers.

It is possible to hide blemishes and create a consistent overall facial color and texture by simply applying a base or foundation makeup to a performer's face. Gently rubbing with cold cream and numerous tissues will remove makeup. Remember that the purpose of cosmetic makeup is usually to enhance the appearance of a performer, not to call attention to itself unless, of course, a modernist approach is employed. The best way to check a performer's makeup is to test it with a live video camera or a digital camera. If it does not hide blemishes and improve the appearance of the talent, it should be removed and redone. The performer should look natural, except in postmodernist, avant-garde works. Makeup for digital cameras is more critical than with analog as the digital system's fine detail will show blemishes, wrinkles, or other skin faults more readily than with an analog camera.

Summary

Aesthetic lighting and design setups can be divided into three categories: realist, modernist, and postmodernist lighting. Realist lighting and settings attempt to recreate the presumed natural sources of lighting within a natural location. Key lights are used to maintain the consistent directional placement of the presumed central light source in a room, whereas fill lights reduce contrast to a normal or acceptable level. Lighting and settings can also be used in a modernist or stylized manner to achieve a particular atmospheric effect, psychological mood, or abstract design.

Light sources, such as the sun and incandescent, carbon arc, HMI, and fluorescent lamps, emit light of a specific color temperature. Daylight, carbon arc, and HMI light have higher color temperatures and a greater proportion of blue in comparison with red light than incandescent or tungsten light. Fluorescent light is discontinuous throughout the visible spectrum. Color film stocks must be selected and video cameras balanced for the color temperature of the primary light source if a normal color rendition is to be recorded.

Spotlights and floodlights are two different types of lighting instruments. Spotlights produce bright, narrow beams of light, and floodlights provide softer, more diffused lighting for wider areas. Lighting instruments can be secured to a variety of mounting devices, including overhead studio grids and lightweight portable light stands. Light-shaping devices, such as barn doors, scrims, flags, and cookies, help direct and control lighting and create shadow patterns.

Artificial lighting consumes significant amounts of electricity. Load limits for specific electrical circuits must be carefully observed to avoid dangerous overloading.

Light meters measure light intensity. An incident light meter reading measures the intensity of the light falling on a scene, whereas a reflected reading measures the intensity of the light reflected by objects in the scene. These readings help to determine image contrast, as well as the proper exposure level. Lighting ratios can be determined by using incident light meter readings to compare specific lights in terms of their intensity. Contrast ratios in a scene affect visual aesthetics and techniques such as low-key and high-key lighting.

Three-point and four-point lighting methods consist of a triangular or rectangular arrangement of three types of light: key light, fill light, and separation light. Basic three- or four-point lighting in television and film production is complicated by the movement of subjects and cameras, which gives a dynamic, constantly changing character to a lighting situation. Multiple key lights can be used to maintain consistent light levels as a subject moves through a scene.

A lighting setup should be carefully planned to avoid problems on the set, such as blocking difficulties, unbalanced light intensities, and microphone-boom shadows. A lighting plot, which presents an overhead view of the studio floor or actual location drawn to scale, can help a lighting director to organize and plan a lighting setup.

Low-key lighting refers to a relatively high key-to-fill light ratio that creates pools of bright light surrounded by dark shadow areas. It is frequently used to effect an atmosphere suitable for horror and gangster films and television programs, although it can be an effective dramatic device in many productions. High-key lighting, which has a low key-to-fill light ratio, presents few shadows and is frequently used in comedies and musicals.

Lighting for digital cameras requires greater care and control than lighting for analog cameras. The higher resolution of digital cameras (depending on their scan and line rate) reveals details in a picture that normally are not visible or obvious in an analog signal. For that reason greater care is needed to light well-balanced scenes with light falling only where it is necessary or important.

Scenic design involves three basic design principles: design elements, color, and composition. Design elements include lines, shapes, textures, and movement. Color and contrast are interrelated aspects of design, as are color and shape. Contrasting colors can be used to separate foregrounds and backgrounds and to create various shapes, and they can be used to define specific characters, settings, and themes.

Sets, set furnishings, props, costumes, and performer makeup are not completely independent elements in the production process. Elements of scenic design interact within each other and many other areas of production to create an overall visual impression. The most important interactions are those between scenic design and each of the following: lighting, performer movement, and camera and microphone placement. Sets are usually designed to facilitate the placement and movement of the cameras and microphones, as well as the talent.

Sets are designed to provide an environment for a production. The setting and properties must be practical and utilitarian for both the performers to be able to move and interact and for the director to be able to place cameras and microphones where they are needed. Makeup is used to hide blemishes and create imaginative characters.

EXERCISES

1. Design two sets of lighting plots for a specific dramatic scene: one for single-camera recording and another for multiple-camera recording. Make subtle changes of light placements for close-ups in the single-camera production that will enhance the view of the subject without disrupting the overall appearance of the lighting when the camera is moved to another perspective. Find

the best (compromise) position for lights used in multiple-camera production so that the subject looks reasonably good from many different camera perspectives at the same time.

2. Light a stationary, two-person interview, using cross-key lights and fill lights, creating a 2:1 key-to-fill ratio and a 1:1.5 key-to-backlight ratio.

3. Set up multiple key, fill, and separation lights, which will keep a moving subject lit by relatively constant light intensity, while maintaining a 2:1 key-to-fill ratio and a 1:1 key-to-backlight (or kicker) ratio.

4. If both film and video cameras are available, light a simple scene. Place the cameras side-by-side. Shoot several sequences after varying the light from high contrast to low contrast. Shoot some sequences with too much light and some with not enough by normal standards. After the film is processed, compare the reaction of the two media to changing light values.

5. Light a scene with tungsten fixtures near an open door. Follow the talent as they walk from the interior to the exterior. Note the change in white balance and the change in light level and its effect on the recording.

6. Find the breaker box in your home, office, or class building. Note the amperage rating of each circuit. If the breaker box is well marked, it will indicate where each circuit is located. Calculate how many light fixtures at what wattage you would be able to use in any one room of the building without blowing a breaker.

7. Design a realistic room interior on the basis of the description of a setting in a script, short story, or novel. Carefully select and coordinate furniture, props, sets, and costumes so that all of these elements create a realistic impression of time and place. Color and brightness levels of foreground and background elements, sets, and costumes should contrast but not clash with each other. Provide detailed layouts drawn to scale so that the set can be efficiently and accurately constructed. Incorporate elements into the set that are economical to obtain or already on hand, such as specific flats, props, set dressings, and pieces of furniture.

8. Use a cyclorama to create a setting that has no borders, where walls or ceilings meet so that space appears infinite. Use lighting to create abstract shapes, colors, and patterns that create a dramatic and unusual sense of space. Discover ways of manipulating the viewer's sense of spatial perspective by simply altering the lighting.

9. Using the description of a specific setting in a dramatic script, short story, or novel, find an existing building that meets the essential criteria needed to represent this place. Assess the difficulties inherent in using this facility from the standpoint of recording, and determine what elements will have to be removed or added to make this an ideal setting.

10. Preview a new film or television show, and analyze how the sets, costumes, and makeup establish or carry the mode, time of day, or time of history.

11. Complete a design package of scenery, lighting, costumes, makeup, and characters to fit a story you have written that takes place in a particular time and location.

Additional Readings

Alton, John, 1995. Painting with Light, University of California Press, Berkeley.

Baker, Georgia O'Daniel, 2000. A Handbook of Costume Drawing, second ed. Focal Press, Boston.

Barsacq, Leon, 1978. Caligari's Cabinet and Other Grand Illusions: A History of Film Design, The New American Library, New York.

Bellantoni, Patti, 2005. If It's Purple, Someone's Gonna Die: The Power of Color in Visual Storytelling, Focal Press, Boston.

Bermingham, Alan, 2003. Location Lighting for Television, second ed. Focal Press, Boston.

Box, Harry, 1999. Gaffers Handbook, Focal Press, Boston.

Box, Harry, 2003. Set Lighting Technicians Handbook, third ed. Focal Press, Boston.

Burum, Stephen, ed. 2007. American Cinematographer Manual, ninth ed. The ASC Press, Hollywood, CA.

Davis, Gretchen, Hall, Mindy, 2008. The Makeup Artist Handbook: Techniques for Film, Television, Photography, and Theatre, Focal Press, Boston.

Essig, Linda, 1997. Lighting and the Design Idea, Harcourt Brace, New York.

Fitt, Brian, Thornley, Joe, 2001. Lighting Technology: A Guide for the Entertainment Industry, second ed. Focal Press, Boston.

George-Pallilonis, Jennifer, 2006. A Practical Guide to Graphics Reporting: Information Graphics for Print, Web, and Broadcast, Focal Press, Boston.

Gloman, Chuck, LeTourneau, Tom, 2005. Placing Shadows: Lighting Techniques for Video Production, third ed. Focal Press, Boston.

Grotticelli, Michael, ed. 2001. American Cinematographer Video Manual, third ed. The ASC Press, Hollywood, CA.

Huaixiang, Tan, 2007. Costume Craftwork on a Budget: Clothing, 3-D Makeup, Wigs, Millinery & Accessories, Focal Press, Boston.

Jackman, John, 2002. Lighting for Digital Video and Television, CMP Books, San Francisco.

Lester, Paul Martin, 2000. Visual Communication: Images with Messages, Wadsworth, Belmont, CA.

Musgrove, Jan, 2002. Makeup, Hair, and Costume for Film and Television, Focal Press, Boston.

Rizzo, Michael, 2005. The Art Direction Handbook for Film, Focal Press, Boston.

Uva, Michael, 2006. The Grip Book, third ed. Focal Press, Boston.

Uva, Michael, Uva, Sabrina, 2000. Uva's Rigging Guide for Studio and Location, Focal Press, Boston.

Viera, Dave, Viera, Maria, 2005. Lighting for Film and Digital Cinematography, second ed. Wadsworth, Belmont, CA.

Williams, Robin, 2003. The Non-Designer's Design Book, second ed. Peachpit Press, Berkeley, CA.

The Camera

- How do digital and analog cameras differ?

- What determines how a camera is placed and operated?

- What part do lenses and optics play in camera operation?

- What types of digital cameras are used today?

- How do film and video cameras differ?

Introduction

Camera operators try to provide directors with the best possible pictures that will enhance a particular aesthetic approach. To accomplish this goal, they must know how to use basic image framing, composition, and camera movements and how to control numerous technical devices of the camera and lens. To record clear and distinct images, for example, camera operators must understand how lenses work and then place key information in sharp focus. Significant image depth—that is, placing a wide range of objects at various distances from the camera in sharp focus—can be an effective realist approach to camera operation. Image depth enhances the perception of spatial continuity, which, like temporal continuity, is one of the hallmarks of realist aesthetics. Limiting or restricting image depth can help to create a modernist perspective on everyday objects by isolating them from their surroundings and temporarily "making them strange" (a formalist and modernist characteristic), often providing an unusual perspective on them.

The differences between analog and digital cameras are subtle but important. These differences and comparisons will be explained later in this chapter. Film cameras also have benefited from the increased use of digital circuits. A professional film camera will have a video assist (video picture output) originated by one or more charge coupled device (CCD) or complementary metal-oxide semiconductor

(CMOS) chips. In addition, timecode signals may be recorded in a digital format for easier conversion in postproduction.

Some aesthetic aspects of camera use, such as composition and camera movement, were considered in terms of directing in Chapter 5, Directing: Aesthetic Principles and Production Coordination, but they bear repeating here from the standpoint of camera placement and control. After reading this chapter and before attempting to use any camera, you should read the instruction manual carefully for the specific camera you wish to operate. Continual practice with the camera is necessary to make it an extension of your eyes and body. Basic camera exercises, such as those recommended at the end of this chapter, can significantly improve your skills as a camera operator.

Potential camera operators should be aware of the capability of studio systems to include remote controls for all of the camera operations: panning, tilting, zooming, and even dollying and trucking across the studio floor. The cameras used on major network newscasts now are all remote controlled from the control room. One of the functions of a camera operator may be to operate several cameras simultaneously with remote controls while seated in the control room. The traditional setting of the electronic controls of cameras by a camera control operator before each production also has been replaced by a computer built into the camera control unit. With a single press of a button, the computer runs a complete check of all electronic circuits and sets the camera controls for that particular production.

CAMERA PLACEMENT

Placing a camera in the best position for recording realist or modernist images consists of three camera operations: framing, positioning, and movement. *Framing* refers to the arrangement of actions and objects within the camera frame. *Positioning* includes the selection of camera-to-subject distance and angle, whereas *movement* of the camera is accomplished by means of various camera-mounting devices.

Framing

Four key concepts help camera operators frame visual images: essential area, lookspace, walkspace, and headroom. *Essential area* refers to the safe recording area within the camera frame. All key information should be placed within the essential area of the frame so that it is not cut off by mistake. Objects and actions can be placed within the essential area by moving the camera closer to or farther away from the subject or by altering the focal length of a zoom lens. *Lookspace* is the frame area in front of an on-screen performer who is looking at an off-screen object or person. Leaving some space in the frame for the performer's look or glance creates the best spatial composition. Lookspace can be increased by panning the camera. *Walkspace* refers to the additional space left in the frame into which a performer can walk or run. When following a performer with a camera, as during a panning or trucking shot, walkspace should be placed in front of the subject within the frame. Otherwise, the edge of the frame acts as a restrictive border and the visual composition seems awkward (Figure 8.1).

Another important aspect of composition is providing an appropriate amount of *headroom*—that is, space above the performer's head within the frame. Too little headroom creates a sense of confinement, whereas too much gives an impression

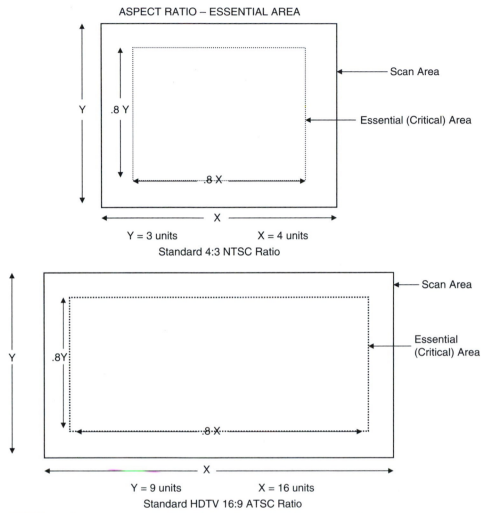

ASPECT RATIO – ESSENTIAL AREA

Scan Area

Essential (Critical) Area

Y

.8 Y

.8 X

X

Y = 3 units   X = 4 units

Standard 4:3 NTSC Ratio

Scan Area

Essential (Critical) Area

Y

.8Y

.8 X

X

Y = 9 units   X = 16 units

Standard HDTV 16:9 ATSC Ratio

FIGURE 8.1 Camera operators, whether of film or video, need to be aware that all viewers at home will not be able to see the subjects in their receivers in exactly the same way as operators see them in their viewfinders. There is a certain amount of picture loss around the edges because of the conversion and transmission process. This trims off a border around the picture that could amount to as much as 20 percent of the total picture. To be safe, a camera operator should include within the central 80 percent all subjects that are critical to the shot, while still keeping in mind that some people may see virtually everything the operator is viewing. Regardless of the aspect ratio, 4 × 3 or 16 × 9, the critical area still needs to be observed. Also a production may be shot and recorded on a 16:9 aspect ratio camera with the intention of using the video for both 16:9 and 4:3 production, requiring the camera operator to frame for both aspect ratios simultaneously.

of limitless space that sometimes dwarfs the performer. Of course, tight close-ups often have little or no headroom. Changes in headroom result from tilting the camera, moving the camera closer or farther away, or zooming the lens. The rules for framing in the 16:9 aspect ratio are the same as for framing at 4:3, except much more space is available on the sides of the frames that must be filled with some objects or filler. The frame still may be split into nine areas, and the rule of thirds still pertains. But the horizontal areas require greater planning and thought to maintain satisfactory composition, especially for objects that are predominately vertical in their individual framing.

Positioning

Camera operators also need to be familiar with the basic rules of camera placement and composition. For example, the 180-degree action-axis rule should be followed in camera placement, if the directional relationship of objects in the frame and subject movements is to remain spatially consistent from shot-to-shot. Crossing the line with the camera can reverse screen direction. In terms of composition, the rule of thirds, or dividing the frame into three parts both vertically and horizontally, allows the camera operator to place objects along the lines and at the intersection points to help achieve a satisfying frame composition. Additional compositional factors from the standpoint of aesthetics, such as symmetry or balance and closure, should also be considered (see Chapter 5, Directing: Aesthetic Principles and Production Coordination).

Camera operators and directors control the placement and movement of cameras and put aesthetic principles into actual practice. A specific terminology is often used to refer to common types of camera placements and movements. Terms such as *medium shot, dolly, pan, pedestal*, and *crane shot* have specific meanings when they appear in a final shooting script or shot lists supplied to the camera operators by the director.

A *close-up* is basically a head-and-shoulders shot of a person. An *extreme close-up* fills the frame of the camera with a character's face, a part of the face, or some specific object. Close-ups are used for emphasis, to achieve a degree of intimacy or involvement, or to focus the audience's attention on a particular detail. Used sparingly, close-ups can be an effective way of achieving dramatic emphasis. Close-ups are created by moving the camera closer to the subject or by zooming in.

A *medium shot* includes one-half to three-quarters of a character's body. The camera is placed farther away from the subject or the lens is zoomed out from a close-up. This type of shot is a compromise between the long shot and the close-up. Some details and facial gestures are readily apparent, but many broad actions of several characters can sometimes be included within the frame as well. A *two-shot* is generally a medium shot that presents two people or characters within the same frame. Television and film directors frequently frame an image as a two-shot so that the audience can see the actions and reactions of two characters simultaneously.

A *long shot* gives a full-body image of a character or characters. An *extreme long shot* might include a broad exterior vista. Long shots allow audiences to see broad action but do not provide emphasis or subtle details. The long shot is often called an *establishing shot* when it sets the character(s) in the context of the setting or location. Many standard scenes begin with an establishing shot to set the context or physical location and then cut to combinations of closer shots of specific actions and characters. A camera is normally placed at the subject's eye height in video and film production, but some shots call for a higher camera angle, whereas others call for a much lower camera position. These high- and low-camera angles can be used to simulate the spatial positioning and points of view of specific characters, or simply to provide perspectives that will exaggerate or reduce the apparent size of the object(s) in the frame.

Movement

Camera movements in midshot should be made only when they significantly improve our understanding of what is being presented. When overused, they can be visually distracting. Moving camera shots should begin and end with the camera stationary so that they can be intercut or combined with stationary camera shots.

When a camera is placed on a moving tripod or dolly, it can be moved toward or away from the subject. These camera movements are called *dolly shots*. They differ from *zoom shots*, which result from changing the focal length of a zoom lens. Dolly shots alter perspective—that is, they change the apparent spatial positioning of objects in a scene. They give the audience the feeling that they are actually moving through the scene, as well as shifting their perspective and focus of attention.

Physically moving the camera horizontally or laterally with respect to the subject is called a *trucking shot*. Trucking shots can be used to keep a moving subject in frame. A lateral movement of the camera in a semicircular path is called an *arc*. To perform a trucking shot or arc, the camera must be mounted on a wheeled dolly. Sometimes tracks are laid on the floor or ground so that the wheels of the dolly will follow a pre-arranged path. If the tracks are laid properly, minimal bounce of the camera will occur, even over rough terrain. During tracking, trucking, and dolly shots, it is often advisable to use a wide-angle lens to minimize the bouncing of the image. Telephoto lenses accentuate camera bounce.

A stationary tripod usually has a panning and a tilting device. A *pan action* slowly and smoothly rotates the camera from side-to-side on a tripod pivot, and a *tilt action* moves it up and down. These movements can be used to change the angle of view or to follow action. Panning too quickly can cause vertical lines or objects to strobe or flicker. Pans and tilts can also be used to follow performer movements. Tilts are often used to follow a performer sitting down or standing up. Like all camera movements, they usually begin and end with a well-composed stationary frame. A camera can also be physically moved up and down on a pedestal dolly. A hydraulic lift pushes the camera straight up or brings it straight down. This technique is called a *pedestal movement* and is used to adjust the camera for a high- or low-angle shot rather than to move the camera in midshot. A *crane shot* uses a long pivoting arm to move the camera up and down or from side to side in the studio or on location. It is usually reserved for wide establishing shots and is often used to move the camera in midshot.

Mounting Devices

Camera placements and movements usually require the use of specific camera-mounting devices in order to record steady images. Mounting devices for video cameras range from pistol grips to cranes. A *pistol grip* is used to handhold a lightweight, portable, small-format camera (Figure 8.2). This device is rarely used for professional recording. The *crane* is a relatively large mounting device, which consists of a long counterweighted arm on a four-wheeled dolly or truck. It allows a camera to be raised to extreme heights in a studio or field situation and usually requires several technicians to assist the camera operator in actually moving the camera. In between these two extremes we find the body mount, tripod dolly, and pedestal dolly.

Body Mount

A shoulder harness can be anything from a built-in camera mold or special body brace that fits perfectly over the operator's shoulder to a more elaborate servo stabilizer, such as a *Steadicam*, which minimizes vibration of the camera and allows the camera operator to move around freely. A body mount uses a complex system of

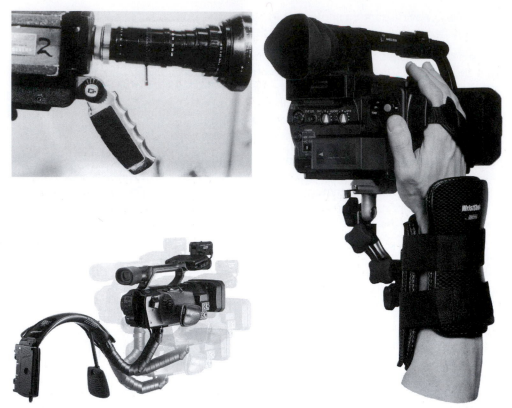

FIGURE 8.2 The smallest and most flexible camera mount is a pistol grip mounted on either the camera body or the lens. Using such a mount requires upper-body strength, because all of the weight of the camera and lens rests on the operator's shoulder and right hand. Much practice is necessary to learn to handhold a camera in order to provide a steady, unwavering shot. Other devices that help operators to steady a handheld camera include a support for the wrist and extended shoulder mounts. (Courtesy Sachtler and WristShot.)

springs and counterweights to smooth out the jerky movements of the operator and to simulate dolly or crane movements of the camera. A body mount can be used with a film camera as well as a video camera. (A Steadicam Jr. can be handheld with a lightweight video camera.) However, most body mounts position the camera in such a way that the normal film or video camera viewfinder cannot be used. The camera is usually at the operator's waist and is detached from his or her body. A video pickup is fitted into the camera viewfinder, and a video signal is fed to a small monitor on the top of the camera where the operator can view it. The video signal can also be fed to a recorder, so that immediately viewable television images are recorded at the same time as the film. Film, of course, cannot be screened until it is developed (Figure 8.3).

Tripods

A tripod is a three-legged device on which a stationary camera can be secured. The legs of the tripod can be extended to raise or lower the camera. Tripods are one of the most frequently used single-camera supports.

They usually consist of three extendible legs, with pointed spurs on the tripod shoes, a cradle and ball joint for leveling, a fluid head or other form of panning and tilting device, and a camera locking bolt. A *fluid head* allows the camera to be

FIGURE 8.3 Body mounts are manufactured to carry either film or video cameras of all sizes. They are designed with a built-in spring and gyro system to maintain positioning on a level and even keel as the operator moves about the set. (Courtesy of Cinema Products and Glidecam Industries.)

smoothly panned or tilted on the tripod. When used outdoors, the spurs of the tripod can frequently be secured in soft ground, but on hard surfaces and indoors, the spur must be secured in a *spider* (sometimes called a *triangle* or *spreader*), which provides a device for locking down the shoes of a tripod to prevent them from slipping. Tripods for small-format video cameras often have flat rubber shoes rather than pointed spurs and are intended for both indoor and outdoor use without a spider (Figure 8.4).

The head of a tripod frequently has a bubble device for proper leveling of the tripod. *Leveling* a tripod refers to making the camera horizontally level, so that the horizontal frames of the image are parallel with the horizon outdoors or the lines formed by the floor and the back wall, or the ceiling and back wall in an interior setting. The nut that secures the head to the tripod cradle can frequently be removed to allow the tripod head to be secured to another support device, such as a high hat. The *high hat* places a camera just a few feet above the ground, but well below the lowest tripod height. When it is equipped with suction cups, a high hat can be secured to almost any flat surface, such as the hood of an automobile or the top of a boat. A tripod can also be secured to a *hitchhiker*, which is a spider with wheels on it. The hitchhiker allows a tripod and attached camera to move around the studio and transforms a stationary tripod into a movable dolly.

Dollies

A *dolly* is a camera platform or support device on wheels, which allows the camera to move smoothly about a studio (Figure 8.5). A *pedestal dolly* can be vertically moved up and down to raise or lower the camera in midshot. A tripod can be attached to a hitchhiker to create a dolly. The wheels of a hitchhiker, like those of a pedestal dolly, can usually be locked to prevent movement of the camera. Three wheels give the

FIGURE 8.4 Tripods vary in size to match the size and weight of the cameras to be mounted on them. Specialized accessories include spiders to hold the tripod feet, quick release mounts to allow the camera to be quickly placed on or off the tripod as necessary to move to the next setup, and a high hat to allow the camera to be mounted close to the ground or on the side or top of a vehicle. Tripods may be designed to serve a variety of purposes using newer, stronger, and flexible materials. (Courtesy of Matthews Studio Equipment and Sachtler.)

hitchhiker or pedestal dolly ample stability and ease of movement, although care must be taken to plan the movement of a camera so that the bulky coaxial cables connecting the camera to the camera control unit do not get in the way. A dolly should never roll over audio or video cables on the studio floor.

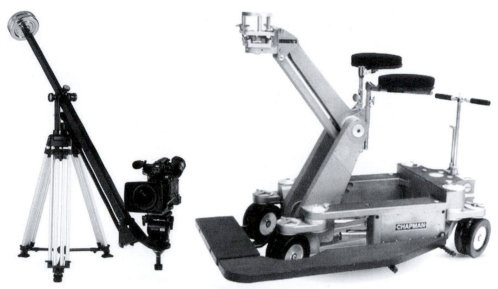

FIGURE 8.5 Dollies are constructed in a variety of shapes and sizes. These two are designed to be operated by hand rather than motorized. The dolly in the top photo is designed with the camera mounted in a yoke and with the operator and grip moving the camera and dolly as needed. The dolly in the bottom photo is designed for the camera operator to ride seated. (Courtesy of Miller Camera Support Equipment and Chapman/Leonard Studio Equipment.)

Various types of dollies and other mobile mounts can be used with film and video cameras. A *crab dolly* allows up-and-down pedestal movements. Some dollies, like the *Elemac spider dolly*, are collapsible yet extremely versatile and stable. Sometimes a wheelchair or moving vehicle, such as a car or van, can serve as an excellent dolly. A special mount, such as the *Tyler mount*, can be used to record vibrationless images from a helicopter or an airplane in combination with a special fluid-filled lens called a *dyna lens*. Finally, a *crane* can be used in studio or field productions to raise even the heaviest film camera to tremendous heights.

LENS CONTROL

Another way in which camera operators control the presentation of visual images is by using various camera lenses. A *camera lens* consists of one or more pieces of glass that focus and frame an image within the camera. Lens control begins with an understanding of basic optics.

Basic Optics

A *lens* is a curved piece of glass that causes light rays to bend. Because glass is denser than air, light slows down at the point where it enters the lens. Lenses bend light so that it can be controlled and projected in proper focus and size at a specific point behind the lens, where a light-sensitive material can record or transmit the image. The curvature of the lens, as well as the type of glass from which it is made, affects how much the light bends and, to a certain extent, determines the classification and function of a specific lens. Simple, single lenses fall into two basic categories: concave and convex (Figure 8.6).

Concave lenses, which are thinner at the center than at the edges, bend light rays away from the center of the lens, causing them to diverge from each other. *Convex*

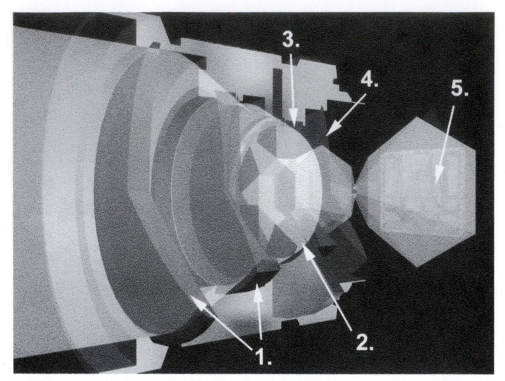

FIGURE 8.6 Typical parts of a lens are (1) a lens front surface, (2) an iris, (3) a concave element, (4) a convex element, and (5) a focal point.

lenses, on the other hand, are thickest at the center and bend light toward the center so that the light rays converge or intersect at a specific point behind the lens, known as the *focal point*. The distance from the optical center of a lens to its focal point is known as a lens's *focal length*. The curvature of a lens affects its focal length.

Lenses can be classified according to their focal lengths. For example, film and video lenses with short focal lengths are sometimes called *wide-angle lenses*. Beyond the focal point, the light rays diverge from each other, and at some area behind the lens, known as the *focal plane*, they form an inverted, reversed image of the objects that are reflecting light in front of the lens. Images at the focal plane are in acceptable focus; that is, the objects are clear and sharp. A piece of light-sensitive material, such as the front surface of a film or an electronic pickup chip, placed at the focal plane will record an inverted and reversed image of the original scene. Modern film and video lenses are composed of more than one piece of glass and are called *compound lenses* (Figure 8.7).

Aberrations

Compound lenses combine several concave and convex lenses in various configurations to cut down on disruptions of, or imperfections in, light transmission, which are called *aberrations*. A simple convex lens, such as a magnifying glass, creates several types of aberration, including field curvature, distortion, and chromatic aberration. *Field curvature* refers to the fact that the image projected by a simple convex

FIGURE 8.7 Lenses for video and film cameras come in a wide variety of sizes and purposes. Pictured are various variable focal length studio and field lenses. (Courtesy of Angenieux, Arri, and Canon USA Corporations.)

lens falls into best overall focus on a curved rather than a flat, plane, or image surface. Motion picture film and front surfaces of video pickup chips are flat, not curved.

Distortion is caused by changes in magnification that occur in different parts of the image projected by a simple, convex lens. *Chromatic aberration* refers to the fact that various color wavelengths bend at different angles when they enter a piece of glass, such as a prism or a simple lens.

A modern lens combines several concave and convex lenses to reduce these types of aberration. Modern lenses are also coated with substances such as magnesium fluoride that reduce the reflection of light entering the lens and therefore increase light transmission. The lens coating is usually placed on the outside element of a lens. Never touch the front surface of a lens with your finger. Body oils can etch the lens coating if they are not removed immediately with lens cleaning paper and proper cleaning solutions. Clean the lens with fluids infrequently, because repeated cleaning can wear down the lens coating. An air blower or camel hair brush usually does a good job of cleaning loose dirt off a lens. Lenses must be handled carefully, and cleanliness is essential.

Lens Perspective

Focal Length and Angle of Acceptance

Lens perspective, or the way in which a lens presents the spatial relations between the objects it records or transmits, varies with a lens' focal length and angle of light

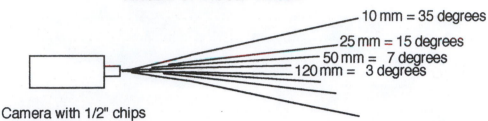

ANGLE OF ACCEPTANCE

10 mm = 35 degrees
25 mm = 15 degrees
50 mm = 7 degrees
120 mm = 3 degrees

Camera with 1/2" chips

FIGURE 8.8 The coverage that a lens allows the camera to cover is measured in the angle of acceptance. The shorter the focal length, the wider the angle of acceptance, and, conversely, the longer the focal length, the narrower the angle of acceptance.

acceptance. The *angle of acceptance*, or the angle at which a lens gathers light in front of a camera, is determined by the focal length of the lens and the format (size) of the recording medium. Shorter focal-length lenses generally have wider angles of acceptance than long focal-length lenses. Focal lengths usually range from 10 mm or less to 200 mm or more. Short focal-length lenses are usually called *wide-angle lenses*, whereas long focal-length lenses are frequently referred to as *telephoto lenses*. *Normal lenses* are so-called because they present an image perspective that seems to approximate that of normal monocular (single-eye) human vision (Figure 8.8).

Variable Focal Length Lens

A variable focal length lens (zoom) allows a camera operator to change the focal length of a lens from wide angle through normal to telephoto and vice versa by manually turning the zoom barrel (or by pushing the button for an electric zoom motor). Zoom-ins and zoom-outs in midshot are easily misused and overused by beginning students. A zoom-in should direct our attention to something within the frame, whereas a zoom-out presents new information, often clarifying the setting. A zoom-in or zoom-out during a shot should be made smoothly and precisely.

A zoom lens also makes it easier to change focal length between shots, because one lens does not have to be physically replaced by another on the camera. Changing the focal length magnifies and demagnifies the image. At a long focal length, the objects in the frame seem to be closer together, and at a short focal length, they seem to be farther apart. A zoom lens should first be focused at its maximum focal length (telephoto). This ensures proper focus at all other focal lengths, assuming the subject-to-camera distance does not vary, including the end point of a zoom-in. Zoom lenses are available in a variety of focal length ranges, with minimum focal lengths as short as 10 mm and maximum focal lengths as long as 200 mm.

Field of View

Field of view refers to the exact dimensions of the image framed by the camera. The field of view of an image captured by a specific film or video camera is largely determined by the focal length of the lens and the video or film format. Shorter focal-length lenses present a wider field of view than longer focal-length lenses when used in the same film or video format. But the field of view provided by any lens changes when the format of the recording medium changes. A 25 mm or one-inch lens provides a narrower field of view in 16 mm film or ⅔-inch video camera pickup chips than it does in 35 mm film, or the same lens provides a wider field of view for ½-inch or smaller

FIELD OF VIEW

FOCAL LENGTH	1/2" CCD/S-8 Film	16 mm Film	35 mm Film
10 mm	35 degrees	50 degrees	95 degrees
25 mm	**15 degrees**	**30 degrees**	**45 degrees**
50 mm	7 degrees	15 degrees	25 degrees
80 mm	4.5 degrees	7 degrees	15 degrees
120 mm	3 degrees	4.5 degrees	10 degrees
200 mm	1.75 degrees	3 degrees	6 degrees

Note: A 25 mm lens for a small format (1/2" CCD or S-8 film) is a telephoto lens, whereas the same focal length in a medium format (1" tube or 16 mm film) is a normal lens.
In a large format (35 mm film), the 25 mm lens is a wide-angle lens.

FIGURE 8.9 The field of view of a camera varies with the size of the sensor or the aperture opening of the film, and the focal length of the lens. A 50 mm lens would provide a narrow-angle shot on a small-format camera, a standard shot on a medium-format camera, and a wide-angle shot on a large-format camera.

chips. In short, lens classifications, such as wide-angle, normal, or telephoto, and fields of view for specific focal-length lenses vary from one format to another. Whether a specific lens is wide-angle, normal, or telephoto, and whether it has a wide or a narrow angle of acceptance and field of view, depends on both its focal length and the dimensions of the film or sensor format (Figure 8.9).

Image Depth

Image depth is a general term describing the overall range of distances and objects that appear to be in sharp focus within the frame. It can be affected by a variety of specific factors, including the type of lens used, various lens adjustments, the placement of the objects within the set (see Chapter 10, Editing), and the lighting (see Chapter 7, Lighting and Design). In this chapter, depth is considered from the standpoint of specific lens factors that affect one aspect of image depth, called *depth of field*. The primary factors creating depth of field are focus distance, lens aperture, and focal length. It is easier to understand the concept of depth of field by first explaining the primary factors that can be used to control it on a lens.

Focus Distance

Focus distance refers to the distance of the subject from the focal plane of a camera. On film cameras, the focal plane is indicated on the outside of the camera by a line drawn through the center of a circle. Focus distance can be accurately measured with a tape measure stretched from the focal plane to the subject. The focus ring on the lens barrel is adjusted according to the exact distance in feet or meters. On a reflex camera or video camera, focus distances can be set by simply turning the focus ring while viewing the subject through a properly adjusted viewfinder.

The *viewfinder diopter* on the reflex film camera is a device that adjusts the focus of a lens to the eyesight of a particular camera operator. This can be done by setting the lens focus ring on infinity and then looking through the viewfinder at an object that is at least 50 feet away. Turn the diopter focus ring until the object appears in proper focus and then lock down the diopter. Now the focus ring on the lens can be turned to set the focus on any subject regardless of its distance from the camera. A video camera does not have a viewfinder diopter or focus adjustment, because the viewfinder is usually a small black-and-white monitor; but for accurate focusing, the contrast and brightness of the monitor must be set properly.

Lens Aperture

An aperture is an opening through which light is allowed to pass. A camera has a fixed rectangular aperture or frame with a specific aspect ratio, where the film or pickup chip actually is exposed to light. A lens has a variable, circular-shaped aperture or iris, which allows the amount of light passing through the lens to be increased or decreased. The amount of light a lens transmits to a recording device can be controlled by varying the diameter of the lens aperture.

Lens aperture settings are calibrated in sequential f-stops or T-stops. The most commonly used measure of light transmission are *f-stops*, which have been mathematically calculated from a lens' physical characteristics. Some lenses have both T-stops and f-stops. *T-stops* provide an accurate index of actual light transmission by a specific lens. They are often used with zoom lenses, because the complex elements within the lens and the many air-to-glass surfaces can absorb a great deal of the light before it finally reaches the film or pickup tube. The most commonly labeled f- and T-stops on an aperture setting ring are 1, 1.4, 2, 2.8, 4, 5.6, 8, 11, 16, and 22. The higher the number, the narrower the opening in the lens, and thus the less light that is actually transmitted through the lens. It is sometimes helpful to conceive of the increasing numbers as reciprocals or fractions, that is, 1.4 = 1/1.4 and 16 = 1/16. Each higher f-stop represents a 50 percent decrease in light transmission from the f-stop immediately below it in numerical scale and two times the f-stop above it. Thus, an f-stop of 2 transmits half as much light through a given lens as an f-stop of 1.4 and twice as much as an f-stop of 2.8 (Figure 8.10).

Deciding exactly which f-stop to use is complicated by the many other variables that can affect exposure, such as the sensitivity of film stocks and pickup chips, as well as the amount of available light. In the 1930s, many Hollywood camera operators always tried to light a scene for an f-stop of 5.6. There were several reasons for this beyond mere habit. First, and most important in terms of image quality, every lens has an

LENS APERTURES - F/STOPS

FIGURE 8.10 The numbers designating f-stops seem to act in reverse to their actual function. A small number, such as f 1.4, actually is a relatively large opening in the aperture, but f 22 is a relatively small opening, allowing very little light to enter the camera.

optimum aperture, which is usually two to three full stops down from wide open. At an optimum aperture, such as a midrange f-stop of 5.6, the objects in focus are at their maximum sharpness. When the iris is closed down to a tiny hole, diffraction occurs around the blades of the iris, causing the sharpness of the image to be reduced. Such diffraction is more severe with wide-angle than with telephoto lenses. Studio camera operators selected 5.6 because even with poorer quality lenses, it consistently produced sharp images. Second, certain studios simply wanted to preserve a theoretical normal depth of field. A great deal of studio video recording today follows the same practice of using an f-stop of 5.6 for similar reasons.

Depth of Field

Depth of field refers to the range of distances in front of the lens that are in acceptable focus at the focal plane. Depth of field depends on the lens factors described earlier: (1) focus distance (which is usually the same as camera-to-subject distance), (2) lens focal length, and (3) the lens aperture or f-stop number. It also varies with the size of the recording format. Depth of field increases as the camera-to-subject distance increases, the focal length of the lens decreases, and the lens aperture narrows within a single format. Moving to a larger recording format increases the depth of field of a particular lens. For example, a 25 mm lens offers a greater depth of field when used with ⅔-inch diameter video camera pickup chips than when used with ½-inch pickup chips.

Depth-of-field charts for different focal-length lenses and film or video formats indicate the range of distances in front of a lens where objects will appear to be in focus at different lens settings. The range of distances is mathematically calculated from f-stop settings, focal lengths, and camera-to-subject distances. Obviously, focus does not immediately drop off beyond the nearest and farthest distances listed for each combination of focal length, camera-to-subject distance, and lens aperture setting. But the chart recommendations provide a relative standard for gauging depth of field and acceptable focus range (Figure 8.11).

Changing the focal length, either by changing lenses or by zooming out or in, obviously changes the depth of field. So does moving the camera closer to or farther away from the subject and changing the focus distance setting of the lens. The same holds true if the subject moves and the focus setting is changed. If a subject

DEPTH OF FIELD RANGES
16mm FILM - 25mm LENS

Hyper-focal distance	134.6'	96.1'	62.3'	48.0'	33.6'	24.0'	16.8'	12.2'	8.4'	6.1'
f-stop	1	1.4	2	2.8	4	5.6	8	11	16	22
Lens Focus	Near Far	Near Far	Near Far	Near Far	Near Far	Near Far	Near Far	Near Far	Near Far	Near Far
50'	36' 80'	33' 104'	29' 195'	25' Inf.	20' Inf.	16' Inf.	13' Inf.	10' Inf.	7' Inf.	5' Inf.
10'	9'3.5" 10'9.5"	9.5' 11'2"	8'9" 11'9"	8'3" 12'7"	7'9" 14'3"	7'1" 17'2"	6'3" 25'	5'6" 55'	4'7" Inf.	3'10" Inf.
3'	2'11.25" 3' 3/4"	2'11" 3'1.25"	2'10.5" 3'1.75"	2'9.75" 3'2.5"	2'9" 3'3.5	2'8" 3'5.25"	2'6.5 3'8"	2'5" 3.11.5"	2'2.5" 4'8"	2' 5'11"

FIGURE 8.11 The depth of field of a lens is determined by three factors: the f-stop, the focal length, and the hyperfocal distance, or the point of best focus. Each of these three can be manipulated to increase or decrease the depth of field, depending on the desires of the camera operator.

begins to exceed the depth-of-field range, the camera operator may have to adjust the focus distance setting, which is known as *pulling focus*. Sometimes a camera operator may intentionally try to limit the depth of field, either to isolate the subject from the background by putting the background out of focus or to shift the viewer's focus of attention by pulling focus from an object or face in the background to another in the foreground or vice versa. Depth-of-field limitations are extremely important in terms of the placement and movements of the talent, who must be accurately informed about the range of distances within which they can safely walk and still hit their marks during a shot. Controlling depth of field affects the perception and aesthetics of image depth within the frame, which was discussed more fully in Chapter 7, "Lighting and Design." A camera operator who learns the basic principles of depth of field can fully exploit the creative and aesthetic potential of film and television images.

VIDEO CAMERAS

Video and film cameras are sophisticated pieces of electronic and mechanical equipment. There are many different types of video and film cameras, which must be fully understood before they can be artistically controlled. This section considers basic camera design, function, operation, and artistic control.

Basic Video Camera

A basic video camera consists of pickup chip(s), a black-and-white or fold-out LCD viewfinder, a tally light, a lens, and all the electronic and mechanical controls needed to operate each of these devices.

Color cameras have one or more light-sensitive CCD or CMOS sensor chips. Even on color cameras, most studio viewfinders present black-and-white images, which show the camera operator what is being framed by the camera. The lens focuses light rays on the video camera pickup chips. Most modern cameras have a single zoom lens, which allows for power or manual control of the image size. Telephoto lenses magnify the image, whereas wide-angle lenses present a wide field of view and demagnify the image. The camera *tally light* is usually positioned on the top of the camera. It lights up to inform the talent and crew which of several cameras in multiple-camera production is actually being used for recording or transmission. Another tally light appears in the viewfinder to warn the operator when the signal from that camera is in use.

The Camera Chain

A basic video camera chain consists of five separate parts: (1) a camera; (2) a power supply; (3) a sync generator; (4) a camera control unit; and (5) an encoder, which combines the *luminance* (brightness or amount of light) and *chrominance* (saturation or amount of color and hue, or shade of color) channels of visual information into a single video signal. The power supply for American television systems consists of either 120-volt AC current for a studio camera or a 12-volt DC battery (usually) for a field camera (Figure 8.12).

A separate *sync generator* (which is housed inside a field camera) supplies the signal that ensures proper synchronization between the scanning of the camera pickup chip and the scanning of a video source or a monitor, such as a camera viewfinder.

BASIC COMPONENTS OF A VIDEO CAMERA CHAIN

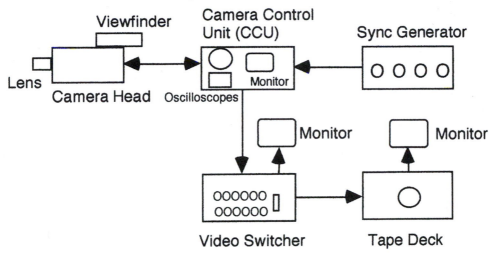

FIGURE 8.12 A basic camera chain consists of the following parts: the camera, its head, lens, and viewfinder. A camera control unit contains a vector scope, oscilloscope, digital signal monitor, and viewing monitor. A sync generator provides synchronizing signals. If the camera is used in a studio setting, then the signal is fed to a switcher with monitors and to a recording medium with its monitor. A portable camera has the camera control unit (CCU) and sync generator built into the camera body so that it can operate independently of any other equipment.

A *camera control unit* for a studio camera allows the video engineer to shade the camera, that is, to control the levels and color values in the video camera signal. This is done by adjusting the output levels and color of the pickup chips. Multiple cameras must be shaded and white-balanced so that all shots will be comparable in brightness and color. Field cameras have built-in controls, which also allow the color signal to be properly set for white balance and brightness. Many digital cameras contain circuits for presetting controls to maintain quality and consistency between cameras throughout a production.

Video Camera Filters

Two types of filter controls are used on video cameras: a filter wheel or a filter switch. A *filter wheel* consists of several different filters arranged around the perimeter of the wheel so that each filter can be positioned between the lens and the camera pickup tube(s). One of the wheel settings has no filter for normal studio operation. A *cap filter* on the wheel is opaque. It is used to protect the pickup tube when the camera is not actually recording. *Color correction filters* on the wheel alter the color temperature of daylight so that it corresponds with the preset color sensitivity of the video camera. *Neutral density filters* reduce the intensity of excessively bright light. The amount of light or brightness in a signal can also be controlled by adjusting the lens aperture or the brightness control on a field camera. A *filter switch* is commonly used on a portable video camera in place of a filter wheel. This switch allows a color-correction filter to be positioned between the lens and the pickup tube(s) when recording under sunlight.

Types of Video Cameras

The most basic distinction between video cameras many years ago used to be that of color versus black and white. But because of the standardization of color for most video situations, the most important distinctions today are those between standard-definition (SD) and high-definition (HD) cameras and whether the camera is capable of producing a picture in a 4:3 ratio or a 16:9 ratio or either of the scan systems: *interlace*—with two fields to a frame—or *progressive*—with a single frame made up of the total numbers of lines in the one frame, or scan rates of 480,720, or 1,080 lines of resolution. An additional consideration becomes important between those of field cameras, studio cameras, and convertible cameras, which can be converted for either field or studio use. Within each of these categories there is a variation in terms of image quality, and a distinction is often made between professional, prosumer, and consumer-quality cameras. *Prosumer* cameras are those designed for lower-level professional productions such as weddings and other social events, but they are of a higher quality than typical consumer equipment. Recorded images must be of high quality to be edited and duplicated for broadcast, and this usually requires more sophisticated and expensive equipment. The most sophisticated and highest quality cameras are those that maintain the video signal in the digital domain from the pickup chips to the built-in digital recorder or storage system. Most modern cameras are capable of creating both 4:3 and 16:9 pictures with a flip of a switch. Because most of the circuits within the camera and camera control units now are digital, varying between standard-definition and high-definition signals is easily accomplished. With the coming of high-definition television (HDTV), scan rates also vary from 480 lines to 1,080, and the method of scanning varies from interlaced to progressive. The recorder could be either a digital videocassette recorder, direct to disc, either DVD or CD-ROM, or a built-in computer with either a removable hard drive or RAM memory cards.

The image quality of a video camera should be matched with the format and quality of the videotape recorder being used. It is as pointless to use an expensive, three-chip, studio camera to make a miniDV original videotape recording as it is to use a digital recording system with an inexpensive single-chip consumer video camera. The characteristics and image quality of both the video camera and recorder must be compatible with the production expectations and standards of the specific task at hand (Figure 8.13).

DIGITAL CAMERAS

A digital camera contains three basic components: viewfinder, body, and optics. If the camera includes a recording medium, the recording unit makes a fourth component.

Viewfinder

The viewfinder may be a small 1.5-inch monochrome (black and white) monitor viewed through an eyepiece, as film cameras and consumer cameras have been constructed, or a larger 2.5-inch LCD color monitor that swings out from the side of the camera. This is also a common feature of consumer cameras. With an LCD monitor, the operator stands back from the camera and monitor rather than holding it on a shoulder close to the face. Each has advantages. The eyepiece monitor provides the opportunity for the operator to concentrate on what is visible in the viewfinder only and to not be distracted by other activities outside of the frame. For most shooting situations, the lack of a color monitor is not a handicap for the operator because framing, focus, and movement are prime concerns, not the color of the object in the frame. The monitor, either black and white or color, should be properly adjusted using the color bars signal to set contrast, brightness,

FIGURE 8.13 A professional video camera is a self-contained unit consisting of the camera head, lens, viewfinder, microphone, and built-in CCU and sync generator. The camera may be powered either by batteries or by an adapter pack from 100-volt power. (Courtesy of Ikegami Electronic Co.)

and chroma and not adjusted for the personal taste of the operator. All viewfinders show a certain number of functions or adjustments on the screen along with the subjects included in the frame. A tally light showing the camera is operating and recording, a zebra effect showing overmodulation, and battery and tape conditions generally are the minimum functions visible in the viewfinder. The viewfinder of a digital camera may show many more functions, often as a series of menus. Menus may indicate the adjustments for origin setup, display choices within the viewfinder, the recording medium setup, the camera setup, some possible shading or special effects available, and a series of switches required to operate the camera. Controls and choices of audio recording also are included in a menu. The operator must learn which menu contains the adjustments needed for a particular shot or setup and which adjustments are included in each menu. On the surface this makes operating a digital camera complicated, but at the same time it gives the operator of the camera/recorder a tremendous amount of flexibility in choosing how the recording will progress.

Body

The body of the camera contains the electronics starting with the charge coupled device (CCD) chips that convert light to a video signal. Newer professional cameras replace the CCD chips with complementary metal-oxide semiconductor (CMOS) chips. A synchronous generator keeps all of the signals in proper alignment, and an analog to digital converter must be included because the light entering the lens is an analog variation making the first electronic signal analog. Digital signal processing (DSP) circuits within the camera may vary from simple amplifiers to complex special effects amplifiers and circuits to create a variety of output signals, both analog and digital. All cameras have audio input circuits for both microphones and high-level audio. Once again, the analog signal from the mic must be converted to a digital signal for recording and distribution. A plug for a headset provides a means for monitoring the audio signal while recording and to check during playback. All professional and many consumer video cameras are multiformat output capable. That is, the output signal may be either analog or digital, a choice of line rate from 480 interlaced (i) or progressive (p), 720i or p, 1,080i or p, a frame rate of 24, 29.97, 30, 50, 59.97, or 60 fps, an aspect ratio of either 4:3 or 16:9. All of these variations are possible through the use of digital circuits within the camera body, yet the cost for such functions is minimal compared to analog cameras of 20 years ago.

Optics

The optic system for most digital cameras begins with a variable focal length (zoom) lens. Because the back focal distance is different in video cameras from film cameras, most video cameras are not able to use high-quality film lenses without an adapter. The lenses are designed to vary their focal length at least over a 10 to 1 range, and some professional lenses vary as much as 100 to 1. The major differences between optics for analog cameras and optics for digital cameras relate to quality. Because the resolution and reproduction capabilities of a digital system are much higher, the smallest aberration or fault in the lens becomes noticeable and objectionable. Automatic iris, focus, and zoom controls are common on all levels of lenses, but they are used sparingly in professional situations. Filters may be mounted between the lens and the prism blocks that split the light into the three primary colors, or a matte box may be mounted on the front of the lens to hold filters, scrims, and other light control devices. The prism block is considered part of the optic system, but it is not physically attached to the lens. The block, through the use of filters between the sections of the block, either stops certain colors from passing or reflects them in a different direction to separate the three colors to feed the three CCD or CMOS chips. The three colors are red, green, and blue. An equal combination of light of each of the three colors creates a white light. Any variation in the amount of each color creates any color of the spectrum.

Digital lenses differ from standard lenses primarily in quality of construction and the ability to reproduce light more accurately by reducing aberrations to a minimum and through modern coatings reduce reflections. Digital lenses are superior in their ability to reproduce wider contrast ranges and greater light transmission than standards lenses through very tight tolerances in design and manufacturing. SD lenses may equal HD lenses in resolution, but not in contrast transmission. Digital lenses must be designed for specific three-sensor cameras to match the camera's optical prism. Lenses for single-sensor cameras may be the same as high-quality lenses designed for use on modern film cameras. Because digital systems are designed to show much greater detail, HD lenses must be able to discern and reproduce fine detail in a wide range of lighting situations including low light settings.

Recording

The fourth segment of the camera is its recording section. This may be a tape deck, a CD or DVD laser burner, a solid-state chip, various types of memory cards, a variety of floppy discs, or a digital hard drive. Each of these drives may be either removable or permanently mounted within the body of the camera. The design of each camera is somewhat dependent on the recording medium, and this area of camera design is rapidly changing. The subject of recording media will be covered in greater detail in Chapter 9, Recording.

Types of Digital Cameras

The proliferation of different SD, HD, and digital cinema recording formats makes any neat, clear, and simple classification of digital video cameras into mutually exclusive categories difficult. Today, digital cameras are offered in a wide range of quality and price along a continuum from acceptable SD to the highest quality and expensive digital cinema cameras. Within this range or continuum, cameras may be separated into four basic types: (1) basic DV (including SD or DVSP, DVC PRO, and DVCAM) camcorders; (2) HDV camcorders; (3) HD cameras (including HDCAM SR, DVC PRO HD, and other full HD formats as well as broadcast HD; and (4) digital cinema cameras. Each category is vaguely separated by price, quality, and purpose. But there are no hard and fast divisions between camera types. The technology is changing so rapidly that a simple, inexpensive camera of today probably far surpasses the technical quality and at a much lower price than a camera of equal quality released two years ago, and that change will continue so that a camera of today will be outpaced in both price and quality within about two years of its manufacture and sale.

Basic DV Camcorder

Small, handheld single and multiple sensor cameras designed primarily for home and semiprofessional applications use ⅙-inch to ½-inch chips offering a 480 to 720 resolution highly compressed SD signal usually with interlaced rather than progressive scanning. Sensors rated at 6 megapixels or less recorded on miniDV tape, memory cards, of DVD-R disc. Prices range from several hundred dollars to near $1,000. The cameras are easy to operate in that they are basically point-and-shoot devices with almost all functions—focus, aperture, exposure rates—all automatically set. They are designed for quick, low-cost, fundamentally sound, but not highest quality signal output. Compared to professional SD formats, DVCAM and DVC PRO, are capable of recording at faster tape speeds, which reduces the possibility of drop out or lost picture information somewhat and produces slightly better quality images and sounds than standard DV or DVSP modes in consumer and prosumer cameras (Figure 8.14). As the size of digital cameras decreased, it became apparent that a camera could be designed that could be held in one hand, much as a

FIGURE 8.14 A basic DV camcorder may be as small as a consumer point-and-shoot or larger, with more professional controls and accessories. (Courtesy of Canon USA.)

still camera is held. A series of such cameras have been designed primarily for the consumer market, but the quality of the output, especially if the camera uses three chips, makes the miniature camcorder useful for news, television sales, streaming, and some professional productions. The handheld camcorders are designed with automatic focus, iris settings, white balance, and audio level controls. They come equipped with lenses that zoom in a range from 10:1 to 20:1. Most record on miniDV, discs, or memory cards. Some models are designed to output directly to the Internet for video streaming.

HDV Camcorder

The next most common type of digital camera now available to both the general pubic and professionals are HDV cameras. HDV is a compressed high-definition format that offers an inexpensive means of producing HD programs. The convenience and low cost of using standard miniDV tapes that are similar to or the same as those used in SD or DVSP recordings makes HDV very attractive to low budget producers. HDV cameras rely on greater flexibility in operation, higher quality of signal output, and a wider choice for the operator to determine how he wants the camera to operate in frame rate, aperture, focus, and either progressive or interlace scanning as well as choosing 720 or 1,080 resolution IN "I" (interlaces scan) or "P" (progressive scan) mode.

The camera may be operated at frame rates from 24, 25, 29.97 (for PAL and SECAM systems used in Europe and other countries), or 30 frames per second (fps), making it possible to create a production to be distributed as film, video, or via the Internet. Sensors range from ¼ inch to 1 inch and are either single with built-in color filters direct to lens or triple using a prism. The output may be either SD or HD at any of the rates required for that particular production. Prices range from $1,000 to $15,000 depending on the lens, accessories, and the recording media. Pixel rates vary between 5 and 10 megapixels. Built-in storage may be miniDV, digital Beta, built-in or removable hard drive, optical disc recorder, or any of several memory cards such as Secure Digital (SD), PCMIA (P2), SxS, GFCam, or Compact Memory flash card. These cameras are used in the field by documentary makers, independent feature producers, news videographers and freelancers working in industry or education. The major growth in digital cameras since the early 2000s has been in field cameras. As digital circuits assume responsibility for many previous manual functions, as the size decreased, as battery life increases, and as flexibility of operation increases, the field camera takes on a new, higher level of creativity for the operator and director. The increase in resolution and contrast range in field cameras moves them from handy production tools to truly high-quality creative tools. The smaller size and weight allows the camera to be held on a body mount, on the shoulder, or on any number of portable camera mounts. Increased battery life permits longer shooting sessions without changing batteries and also allows for the use of portable lighting fixtures powered by the camera battery. The flexible operation permits shooting under a wide variety of lighting conditions, instant changing of settings, and utilizing built-in effects and preediting functions (Figure 8.15).

HD and Broadcast Camera

HD field cameras are designed for HD sports, high-level documentaries, high- and low-budget television dramas, and live event coverage with pixel rates above 10 megapixels. Many of the technical specifications of HD cameras are similar but

FIGURE 8.15 HDV cameras usually use built-in miniDV tape decks or limited memory flash cards. The optics are superior to basic DV cameras but not as expensive or flexible as those used on HD or broadcast cameras. (Courtesy of Panasonic USA.)

slightly to considerably higher than HDV cameras. The main differences between HDV and full HD recorded images are that the latter treat each video frame individually rather than as aggregates. Full HD images are also less compressed than HDV images and they generally use 4:2:2 rather than HDV's 4:2:0 color sampling (standard DV or DVSP uses 4:1:1 color sampling). All of these differences add significantly to the data flow rates and storage requirements compared to HDV. Many of both categories are manufactured by the same corporations, who expand their line of offerings to meet the needs of their customers on many different levels of production requirements. The cameras, if used in the field, may feed the signal through Triax cables or fiber-optic cables to a central control room rather than to a built-in storage medium. Special zoom lenses with long ranges of up to 100:1 are needed for some sporting events and live coverage. As studio cameras, they have been designed for high-definition television (HD) digital signal origination, but many still are used to feed a standard definition (SD) analog or digital signal to take advantage of the superior quality of the originating HDTV signal. Such cameras are capable of delivering high-quality signals that are superior to the highly compressed HD signals of cameras, only they have greater flexibility to increase the quality level by taking advantage of higher-level technical specifications. Prices range from $10,000 to $150,000 depending on the technical specifications, lenses, accessories, and intended use (Figure 8.16). Studio cameras generally are equipped with zoom lenses capable of a focal length range of approximately 20:1. They are mounted on large, heavy, wheeled pedestal mounts. A pedestal mount with or without an operator is capable of dolling, trucking, panning, tilting, or zooming, and any combination of the movements. As they were originally designed, an operator would stand behind these cameras, but today many programs, such as news and game shows, have replaced the operator

FIGURE 8.16 Broadcast camcorders record directly onto a built-in hard drive, removable disk drive, or large memory flash cards and may be equipped with long-range zoom lenses for sporting events. Broadcast news cameras must be small, lightweight, and offer as many flexible characteristics as possible. (Courtesy of JVC, USA.)

in the studio with a single operator in a control room remotely operating several cameras simultaneously. The controls for the camera movements are preset in a specialized computer program, allowing each camera to have a series of shot positions preset to change with a touch of a button on the computer. Sports events cameras are seldom remote controlled, except for specific shots with cameras mounted in positions that are impossible or difficult for an operator to occupy, such as behind the backboard of a basketball court.

Digital Cinema Camera

DC cameras fall in the category of multipurpose because they are used both in the studio and in the field but are designed specifically to produce the highest quality signal for conversion to motion picture film or projection as a digital signal on a large theater screen. DC cameras use much larger CCD/CMOS chips, from ⅔ inch in 65 mm format to create a date stream instead of a video/audio signal, or they operate totally in an uncompressed or minimally compressed mode. DC cameras are not camcorders, because they are designed to feed either a large high-quality tape deck, a hard drive system, or a server rather than a portable media recording system (Figure 8.17). The most popular signal is a 4:4:4, 1,080 p at 24 fps, but a signal may be created with a resolution as high as 4,520 × 2,540 in the NHK Ultra HD system with 22.2 tracks of audio. The increasing possibility of projecting high-quality digital signals in theaters makes production of feature length stories more of a reality, and a greater number of cameras of different sizes, prices, and styles will be built to fill the need for these productions within this category of digital cinema cameras.

FIGURE 8.17 Video cameras are now equipped with all of the production accessories used in motion picture camera production. They are called digital cinematography cameras. (Courtesy of Ari, Dalsa, Sony, and Red Corporations.)

Specialized Digital Cameras

Micro cameras are subminiature cameras used for security, law enforcement, surveillance, and special shots used to cover sports, documentaries, and dramas where cameras shots are desired from hard-to-reach positions. Such cameras are small enough to be mounted on helmets, on race cars, on skiers, and on athletes who participate in other fast-moving sports (Figure 8.18). A micro camera has no viewfinder, all automatic operations, and a remote-controlled zoom lens or a single fixed focal length lens. Despite their small size (as small as 2 inches by 2 inches by 2 inches plus a lens not much larger), digital circuits create a reasonably acceptable output for professional productions. They use $\frac{1}{3}$-inch sensors and can operate in as little as 2,000 Lux light levels. The signal offers a full HDTV 1,920 × 1,080 resolution at 24 fps or other frames rates as needed. Few come equipped with attached recording media; instead, the camera is hard wired or connected wirelessly to a recorder at a safe, secure location or has a small transmitter attached that is similar to a wireless mic transmitter. Such cameras are labeled as pencil cams, doggie cams, and other names to fit their purpose.

A second type of specialized cameras developed primarily from military use require little light; they use light magnifiers and specialized lenses that respond to matching light sources not visible to the human eye but offering enough luminance to create a signal equivalent of a black-and-white picture.

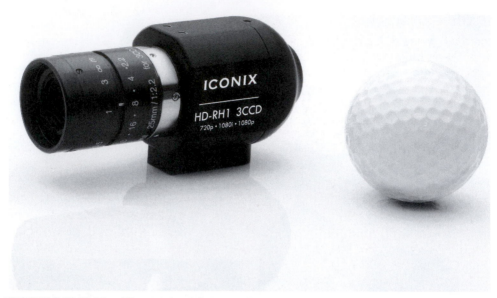

FIGURE 8.18 Miniature HD cameras may be as small as two inches by two inches, but they still create a full HD color picture. Their small size allows them to be used in places a regular-sized camera would not fit or would be too dangerous or inconvenient to place. (Courtesy of IconixVideo.)

FILM CAMERAS

Film cameras can also be differentiated on the basis of sound-recording capabilities. Mechanical or spring-wound cameras cannot run the film at a consistent speed and therefore cannot record synchronous or matching sounds. There are two basic systems by which electronic film cameras can record synchronous sounds: single system and double system. *Single-system* or *sound-on-film* (SOF) recording refers to the recording of synchronous sounds on the edge of the film as it runs through the camera. The camera records images and sounds at the same time. The sounds are recorded by a magnetic sound head, which is 18 (Super-8 mm) or 26 (16 mm) film frames ahead of the picture aperture, on magnetic tape striping on the edge of the film. During *double-system recording*, a separate high-quality audio-tape recorder records sounds, which can be played back in perfect synchronization with the recorded film images. The camera and sound-recording motors for double-system recording are usually crystal controlled for extremely accurate and precise recording and playback.

Types of Film Cameras

8 mm Cameras

Most Super-8 mm cameras have reflex viewfinders and are used for recording home movies; a few professionals prefer to work in this small format as well. Most Super-8 mm cameras are battery powered with automatic focus and iris settings. Synchronous sound on some Super-8 mm cameras can only be recorded at 24 fps. Some sophisticated Super-8 mm cameras can be used with separate synchronous sound tape recorders. Super-8 mm cameras use single and double Super-8 mm film cassettes which contain 50 to 100 feet of unexposed film.

16mm Cameras

There are many types of 16mm cameras. Some lack the ability to record synchronous sound, such as spring-wound mainspring-driven cameras that create considerable camera noise and run at imprecise speeds. Cameras that have quiet-running, battery-powered electric motors and film advance mechanisms are called *self-blimped* film cameras. Single-system sound-on-film cameras were once widely used for recording news footage; they have been replaced by electronic news gathering (ENG) video camcorders. A few film cameras are capable of both single-system and double-system film recording. Many self-blimped, double-system cameras are driven by crystal-sync electric motors that allow the camera to be used without any cable connection between it and a separate synchronous sound recorder. The absence of a cable connection allows for more freedom of movement and is particularly helpful in documentary situations. The camera operator can move about independently of the sound recordist (Figure 8.19). With the advent of the 9:16 aspect ratio, documentary and some commercial and dramatic cinematographers are using specially modified 16mm cameras, a format often referred to as Super-16mm, to shoot wide-screen productions by using a wider aperture. The film stock used for Super-16 productions is standard 16mm film, but the aperture in the camera exposes light in a path that is wider than a standard 16mm aperture. The extra space on the film stock is gained by using the soundtrack area used for standard 16mm films. Because the image size is larger than that of professional video camera chips, the quality is comparable for conversion to HDTV.

Unlike video cameras, whose viewing systems can be electronically controlled, the viewing system of a reflex film camera is often quite dim during actual recording. Film cameras are often focused with the aperture wide open (at the lowest f-stop) before the actual recording; when the aperture is closed down to the proper f-stop for recording, less light is transmitted to the viewfinder. Some viewing systems reflect only 18 percent of the light to the viewfinder, and a camera operator must become used to recording under difficult conditions. Sometimes a video tap (an electronic feed from the camera's viewfinder to a videotape deck) is attached to a film camera to monitor the image and to provide immediately viewable results.

35mm Cameras

It is important to note that 35mm motion picture cameras differ dramatically from 35mm still cameras. Still cameras run 35mm-width film horizontally through the camera, but 35mm motion picture cameras run the film vertically through the camera, recording film frames that are not as wide as still-frame slides. The aspect ratio and image size of a 35mm motion picture frame are thus quite different from a still-camera frame. A 35mm still-camera frame has a much higher aspect ratio (2.35:1) than video or 35mm motion picture film (1.33:1 or 3:4); thus, it is difficult to record complete slides on a motion picture or video camera (Figure 8.20).

Some smaller 35mm motion picture cameras, such as the Arriflex 35-3, are used exclusively for "mitt out" or without sound (MOS) nonsynchronous sound recording. Other, very bulky cameras, such as the Mitchell BNC and Panavision, are used almost exclusively for studio synchronous sound recording situations. A Panavision camera is frequently used for widescreen feature film recording in the studio. The latter has an extremely lightweight and portable stepchild, called the Panaflex camera, which is frequently used for feature film work on location. Only extremely high-budget feature

FIGURE 8.19 Today's 16 mm film cameras vary from lightweight, spring-wound, nonsync sound cameras to heavier cameras with built-in videotapes, crystal-sync systems, and sound-deadening blimp cases. They may be stripped down with few accessories or fully equipped with the accessories found on 35 mm feature film cameras. (Courtesy of Arri Corp.)

films use 65 mm cameras for original recording. Most 70 mm feature film prints are not made from 65 mm camera originals but rather from 35 mm original recordings that have been blown up to this larger format. Most 35 mm cameras are designed to shoot a variety of aspect ratios, from 4:3 to extreme wide-screen, depending on the design of the aperture or anamorphic lens. Professional motion picture camera recording in 16 mm, 35 mm, and 65 mm sets a very high standard in image quality, which is gradually being rivaled by EC-35 and HDTV cameras.

FIGURE 8.20 Today's 35 mm film cameras may vary in size from simple handheld to large multiformat cameras with a variety of accessories mounted to facilitate the best possible production. (Courtesy of Arri Corp.)

Camera Accessories

Many cameras have attachable matte boxes or lens hoods that shade the lens from direct sunlight and allow filters to be attached to the lens for color correction or special effects. A frequently used film camera accessory is the *cable release*, which minimizes the vibration to the camera when single-frame images are exposed individually. Another important film camera accessory is a *changing bag*, which is a black, light-tight bag that can serve as a portable darkroom for loading and unloading longer rolls of film wound on open cores.

Commercial productions, newscasts, dramatic programs on video or film, as well as documentaries required some means for talent to see and read a script while performing in front of the camera. A variety of prompter devices have been employed, from handheld cardboard "idiot cards" held next to the camera to computer-driven copy projected in front of the camera lens using two-way mirrors (Figure 8.21).

Quality audio can only be determined while working in the filed or for communication purposes using professional headsets that fit easily and carry signals accurately to the ears of the user.

CAMERA CARE

Cameras consist of extremely delicate instrument parts. They must be handled with great care because they can be damaged easily. Cameras should be kept clean and dry. Never leave a camera unprotected and exposed to elements such as rain, sleet, snow, or sand. Never leave a camera unattended or in a hazardous position where it is likely to fall or be stolen. Always make sure that you have sufficient battery power by charging batteries well before the actual recording begins. Nothing is more frustrating than having a group of people waiting around for the batteries to be recharged (Figure 8.22).

If the video camera has a built-in recorder, use the same operating procedures that you would use for a separate VCR (discussed in Chapter 9, Recording) to avoid having the tape jam within the recorder. Video cameras are even more sensitive to high heat and humidity than film cameras are, and therefore they require shading under intense sunlight, insulation from the cold, and careful use of videotape in high humidity. Digital cameras using solid-state recording media prove to be much more rugged than cameras equipped with tape decks or film cameras.

Operating a film camera requires extreme care and sensitivity to every possible malfunction of the equipment. Because film is expensive to record, minor mistakes can translate into significant financial losses, as well as reshooting time. Digital and solid-state equipment, on the other hand, can be viewed immediately and can be reused.

It is important to develop a checklist of camera operating procedures and to make sure that every item on the list is checked off before recording. First, make sure that the lens is clean and that no hairs or pieces of film are stuck in the film gate of the camera where the film is exposed to light. On professional film shoots for commercials, the operator usually removes the lens from the camera periodically to check the film gate for hair or debris, because the image must be perfectly clean. If a filter must be placed in the camera or on the lens, make sure that the filter is completely clean so that there will be no spots or marks on the film and no loss of light.

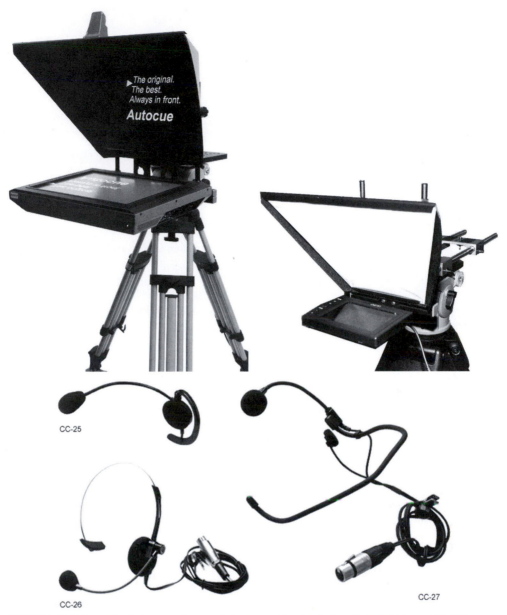

CC-25

CC-26

CC-27

FIGURE 8.21 Promoter devices may be mounted permanently on a studio camera, held to one side in the field, or mounted on a tripod in front of a field camera. Headsets may be held in place with an eye hook, around the back of the head, or a support over the top of the head. (Courtesy AutoCue/QTV and ClearCom.)

Carefully load the film into the camera and its magazine, and then run the film with the camera and magazine cover open to make sure that it is running properly and not tugging at the film gate, which will cause jittery images. Finally, close the camera and the magazine where the film is exposed and stored, and listen to a properly running and loaded camera. It has a characteristic sound. If this sound changes during actual recording, stop shooting immediately! Something is wrong. Open the camera and inspect the aperture area for problems. The film will probably need to be reloaded. Potential problems with a videotape deck also may be determined quickly by listening

CAMERA CARE

DOS

Keep clean and dry

Carefully clean film gate with each film load

Carefully check for dust/dirt with each lens change

Clean lenses properly and periodically

Clean filters before each use

Check for proper filter before each take

Protect from elements such as snow, ice, rain, dust, dirt

Check for properly charged batteries

Allow time for adjustments to changes in temperature and/or humidity

Insulate from extremes in temperature and humidity

Check for proper film and tape threading by listening and watching

DON'TS

LEAVE UNATTENDED ANY TIME

Bump, drop, or shake a camera violently

Leave exposed to public view in a vehicle

Leave tripod or pedestal head with pan or tilt control unlocked.

Expose to high heat, humidity, rain, salt water, or dust

Ignore changes in sounds when running

Assume anything

FIGURE 8.22 All cameras, whether video or film, must be treated as fine, sensitive pieces of expensive equipment. Careful handling requires knowledge of what can harm the camera and how to avoid damaging the camera either inadvertently or through ignorance.

carefully to the sound of the tape motor and drive movements. Follow the same care when loading tape, discs, or cards in digital cameras.

Summary

Camera operators must be thoroughly familiar with camera techniques and equipment to provide directors with the best possible visual images from the standpoint of a particular aesthetic approach. A camera operator controls image composition and camera placement by employing four key concepts: essential area, lookspace, walkspace, and headroom. Camera operators also employ the rule of thirds and realist conventions, such as the 180-degree action-axis rule.

Camera operators understand the best position and angle at which to place the camera in terms of camera-to-subject distance and high-angle versus low-angle camera positions. Camera movements alter spatial perspective and are often used to follow performer movements. Pans, tilts, and pedestal and crane movements can be made with a stationary tripod or camera-mounting device. Dollies, trucking shots, and arcs are accomplished using movable camera-mounting devices. Moving camera shots are used primarily to keep moving subjects within the camera frame or to reveal new information by altering spatial perspective.

Camera operators must understand how lenses function in order to control them. Lenses are curved pieces of glass that bend light in a predictable manner. Lenses help a camera operator control an image's field of view, brightness, focus, perspective, and depth of field. Lenses can be categorized by their focal lengths within a specific video or film format into wide-angle, normal, and telephoto lenses. Zoom lenses allow an operator to manipulate field of view by varying the focal length of the lens. A zoom lens should usually be focused at its longest focal length (telephoto). Varying the aperture, or iris, of a lens changes the amount of light transmitted through the lens. The depth of field of an image—that is, the range of distances in front of the lens that remain in focus—will vary with changes in focal length, aperture, and camera-to-subject distance or focus distance within a specific film or video format.

A video camera contains one or more light-sensitive pickup chips. The camera chain consists of a camera, power supply, sync generator, and a camera control unit. Video cameras can be divided into three basic categories on the basis of function: field cameras, convertible cameras, and studio cameras. Field cameras are lightweight and portable. They can range from consumer cameras to sophisticated and expensive digital video recording equipment that records the highest-quality images. Digital cameras are becoming smaller, use less power, and at the same time produce a higher-quality signal for a lower cost than previous video cameras. Digital cameras are usually divided into SD (standard definition), HDV, full HD (high definition), and DC (digital cinema) cameras, but there is a broad spectrum of digital cameras in terms of price and quality, ranging from inexpensive consumer-grade SD cameras to the highest-level digital cinema cameras. The use of videotape in camcorders is being replaced with disc, solid-state circuits, and flash and hard drive recording systems.

Film cameras can be divided into different levels of image quality on the basis of film formats, such as Super-8mm, 16mm, 35mm, and 65mm, which refer to the width of the film in millimeters. Professional film camera recording still sets a high standard of image quality, which is gradually being rivaled by digital video technology.

EXERCISES

1. Use a handheld or shoulder-mounted video camera to follow a person moving around in a random fashion outdoors. Maintain good framing and focus while following this unpredictable action. Move your body and the camera as slowly, smoothly, and deliberately as you can without missing any key action. View the recorded videotape to determine why problems occurred at certain points.

2. Use a dolly-mounted video camera to follow a person moving around in a random fashion within a studio. Maintain good framing and focus while following this unpredictable action. Move the dolly as slowly, smoothly, and deliberately as you can without missing any key action. View the recorded videotape to determine why problems occurred at certain points.

3. Select the best lens settings for each shot designated in a shooting script scene by determining the depth of field that will be necessary to keep the performers safely in focus throughout each shot. Remember that depth of field depends on the camera-to-subject distance, the focal length of the lens, and the aperture or f-stop opening of the lens.

4. Using a digital camera, open the menu and run through all of the possible settings, then set the camera for daylight shooting. Shoot a subject outdoors, then bring the camera under tungsten lights and shoot with the same daylight setting.

5. Record a short shot. Set the camera for a digital effect, and then add another shot. Build a sequence with a variety of digital in-camera effects.

6. Handhold a camera while seated in a car or van. Hold the camera away from your body, and try to anticipate bumps and changes in the motion of the moving vehicle while shooting subjects moving parallel to the vehicle.

Additional Readings

Brown, Blain, 2002. Cinematography: Theory and Practice, Image Making for Cinematographers, Directors, and Videographers, Focal Press, Boston.

Burrows, Thomas D., 2001. Video Production: Disciplines and Techniques, eighth ed. Focal Press, Boston, MA.

Burum, Stephen, ed. 2008. American Cinematographer Manual, ninth ed. The ASC Press, Hollywood, CA.

Compesi, Ronald, 2007. Video Production and Editing, seventh ed. Allyn & Bacon, Boston.

Elkins, David E., 2000. Camera Assistant's Manual, third ed. Focal Press, Boston.

Evans, Russell, 2006. Practical DV Filmmaking, second ed. Focal Press, Boston.

Fowle, Grant R., 1989. Introduction to Optics, second ed. Dove Publications, Mineola, NY.

Gross, Lynne S., Ward, Larry W., 2007. Digital Moviemaking, sixth ed. Wadsworth, Belmont, CA.

Grotticelli, Michael, ed. 2001. American Cinematographer Video Manual, third ed. The ASC Press, Hollywood, CA.

Hodges, Peter, 1995. The Video Camera Operator's Handbook, Focal Press, Boston.

Honthaner, Eve Light, 2001. The Complete Film Production Handbook, third ed. Focal Press, Boston, MA.

Lester, Paul Martin, 1995. Visual Communication: Images with Messages, Wadsworth, Belmont, CA.

Mamer, Bruce, 2009. Film Production Techniques, fifth ed. Wadsworth, Belmont, CA.

Medoff, Norman, Fink, Charles S., 2006. Portable Video: ENG and EFP, fifth ed. Focal Press, Boston.

Musburger, Robert, 2005. Single Camera Video Production, fourth ed. Focal Press, Boston.

Roberts-Breslin, Jan, 2008. Making Media: Foundations of Sound and Image Production, second ed. Focal Press, Boston.

Ray, Sydney F., 2002. Applied Photographic Optics, Elsevier Science and Technology Books, Boston.

Swartz, Charles S., 2005. Understanding Digital Cinema: A Professional Handbook, Focal Press, Boston.

Underwood, Rich, 2007. Roll: Shooting TV News: Views from Behind the Lens, Focal Press, Boston.

Uva, Michael, 2006. Video Shooter: Storytelling with DV, HD, and HDV Cameras, Focal Press, Boston.

Uva, Michael, Uva, Sabrina, 2001. Uva's Guide to Cranes, Dollies, and Remote Heads, Focal Press, Boston.

Ward, Peter, 2000. Digital Video Camerawork, Focal Press, Boston.

Whitaker, Jerry, 2002. Master Handbook of Video Production, McGraw-Hill, Boston.

Wheeler, Paul, 2007. High Definition Cinematography, second ed. Focal Press.

Zettl, Herbert, 2009. Television Production Handbook, tenth ed. Wadsworth, Belmont, CA.

Recording

- How do digital recording systems differ from analog systems?
- What makes up the video signal?
- How does digital video differ from analog video?
- What processes are used in recording film?

Introduction

Recording good-quality sound and images is extremely important, as poor-quality recordings can destroy the impact of what could otherwise be a high-quality production. Understanding how audio video and film recording devices work will help ensure that you consistently record good-quality sounds and images. Acquiring a basic understanding of media technology increases your ability to control aesthetic variables, whether they are realist, modernist, or postmodernist. If you understand the means by which images and sound are recorded, you can consistently obtain high-quality recordings of the intended production. Visual and aural media are based on digital and analog electronic, magnetic, and photochemical recording processes. This chapter introduces you to audio and video electronics, as well as film photochemistry.

ANALOG AUDIO

Analog recording produces a continuously varying magnetic optical copy of the electrical fluctuations stimulated by the original sound waves. The original sine wave variations of the audio signal are duplicated in sine wave variations, matching as closely as possible the original signal. Magnetic media passes over a magnetic sound-recording head, consisting of a magnet with a coil wrapped around it, which carries the electrical sound signal. As the voltage in the electric sound signal fluctuates, the magnetic field through which the medium is passed changes, recording the sound on the tape. A bias signal (30,000 Hz or above, which is outside the range of human hearing) produced by a bias head aligns the signal to record on the linear portion of the magnetization curve. In the playback mode, the medium is passed over a play-back head (in some decks the same head is used for both recording and playback), which picks up the prerecorded tape's magnetic variations and causes a weak electrical current passing through the magnetic head to fluctuate accordingly This signal is then amplified; that is, it is increased in strength and intensity so that it can be sent to a loudspeaker, headphones, or another recorder.

Audiotape Formats

Audiotape for either analog or digital recording is made up of particles of iron oxide or other metallic substances attached to a flexible support base. Tape formats can be categorized on the basis of two factors: the dimensions of the tape and the form in which it is packaged. Tape dimensions differ in terms of thickness and width. Audio quality generally increases with increasing tape thickness and head width and with the relative speed of the head to tape. The thickness of audiotape is measured in mils (thousandths of an inch). Tape thicknesses vary from 1½, to ¼ mil. Audiotape also comes in a variety of widths, from ⅛ inch, to two inch. Multitrack analog and digital tape recorders (each track is a separate tape path) require wider audiotape. As many as 64 separate tracks can be recorded on some multitrack machines using two-inch-wide audiotape (see Figure 9.2, presented later).

Audio signals in video recording are usually recorded directly on videotape in a variety of formats, which are discussed later in this chapter. Film audio may be recorded on a separate ¼-inch audiotape, onto full-coat film stock, on a portable digital recorder, or directly onto the film itself. In the latter case, the edge of Super-8mm or 16mm film is coated with magnetic material; this is called *magnetically striped film* (Figure 9.1).

Analog Audio Recorders

The enclosures in which tape is packaged and the type of machines on which the recordings are made provide another means of differentiating recording formats. Analog tape can be obtained in the form of cartridges and cassettes, as well as in open reels. Cartridges consist of continuous loops of 1½-mil, ¼-inch audiotape, ranging from a few feet to several hundred feet in length and from a few seconds to several minutes in duration. Cassettes are pairs of small reels encased in a plastic housing. The standard width of cassette tape is ⅛ inch, and the normal cassette tape recorder speed is relatively slow: 1⅞ inches per second. Open reel tape has the advantage that it can be edited (see Chapter 10, Editing), runs at higher speeds, and is available in a variety of tape sizes. Cartridges are quicker and easier to set up and recue—that is, to find the specified starting point (Figure 9.2).

Audiotape Speeds

The speed at which an audiotape is driven directly affects the amount of tape that is used and, more important, the quality of the tape recording. In general, faster recording speeds produce better-quality recordings. Analog tape recorders have a speed-control setting that can be adjusted to any of the following speeds: 15/16, 1⅞, 3¾, 7½, 15, or 30 *inches per second* (ips). Professional recordings of live music, if recorded on analog equipment, are usually made at tape speeds of 15 ips or above. Most multitrack sound analog recording is done at a speed of 30 ips. Simple voice recordings are frequently made at 7½ ips or even 3¾ ips.

LOCATION OF MAGNETIC STRIPE ON FILM

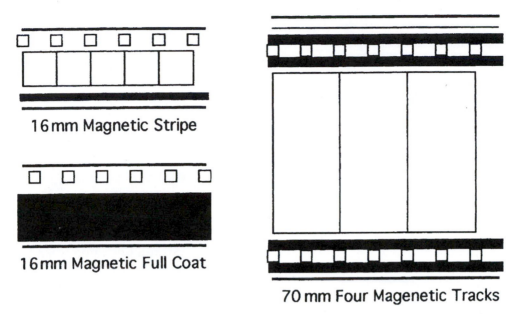

16 mm Magnetic Stripe

16 mm Magnetic Full Coat

70 mm Four Magenetic Tracks

FIGURE 9.1 Magnetic film tracks are laid down on the edge of the film if a picture also is recorded on the same stock. If the film is to be used for sound only, the track can be laid down in one or more paths down the middle of film as magnetic full-coat film.

FIGURE 9.2 The arrangement of audio tracks varies with the type of tape deck and the number of audio tracks, sync, pulse, or timecode tracks that need to be recorded.

AUDIOTAPE RECORDER TRACK LAYOUTS

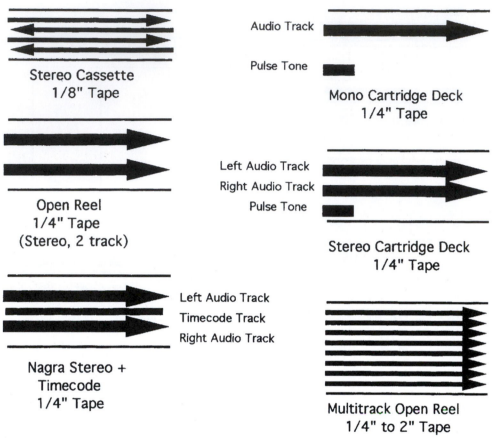

FIGURE 9.3 The common analog audiotape decks are ¼-inch reel-to-reel, broadcast cartridge, and a standard ¹/₈-inch cassette deck.

DIGITAL AUDIO

A digital audio recorder samples or evaluates the electrical sound wave thousands of times every second and gives an exact numerical value to the electrical sound signal for each specific instant of time. The numerical values are coded into a series of on-and-off electrical pulses, known as *binary code*. These are the same types of signals used by computer systems. These electrical pulses are not an electrical copy or analog of the sound wave. The only signal that is recorded is electricity that is either entirely on or entirely off, rather than different gradations of electrical current, as is the case in analog recording. Despite the increase in digital audio recording, the highest quality original sound recording is on an analog system that avoids the loss of conversion through compression and sampling and quantization (Figure 9.3).

The values of the recorded digital signal are determined by two factors: sampling and quantization. The analog signal is analyzed by periodically sampling its frequency. The more often the signal is sampled, the higher the quality of the digital signal. The rate must be at least twice the highest frequency to be reproduced. Today the standard sampling rates are 32 kHz, 44.1 kHz, and 48 kHz. To determine dynamic or loudness range, assigned binary bits determine how many different discrete audio levels can be

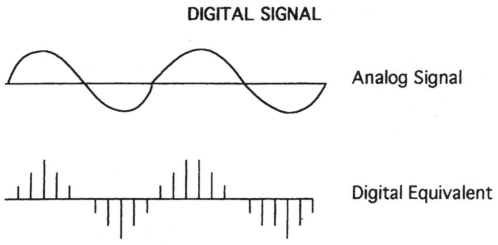

DIGITAL SIGNAL

Analog Signal

Digital Equivalent

FIGURE 9.4 An analog signal is a continuous signal equivalent to the frequency and level of the comparable audio signal. On the other hand, a digital signal is a series of pulses that "samples" the original sound at frequent intervals and then converts those samples to on-and-off digital signals that can be converted back to the original sound.

recorded. Standards vary from a low of 8 bits to a high of 128 bits. In both sampling and quantization, the higher the rates, the better the quality; but at the same time, the cost and amount of memory required increase (Figure 9.4).

Digital recording extends the recordable range of intensities and frequencies and virtually eliminates many other problems inherent in analog recording, such as tape noise, *cross-talk* (two recorded tracks on the same tape interfering with each other), and *print-through* (one layer of recorded tape bleeding through and interfering with another). *Flutter* (an unwanted fluctuation in pitch) is another common analog recording problem. Digital recordings can be duplicated without degradation of the signal and can produce a much more permanent record than analog recording. Fine gradations of analog signals can completely fade away and be lost forever, whereas a magnetic signal that is completely *on* or *off* can easily be restored to its original state as the *on*s begin to fade. For these reasons, digital recording has replaced analog recording as the professional audio standard.

Digital Recorders

Today there are four types of digital audio recording media: digital audiotape (DAT), audio-DVDs, CDs, and tapeless systems. DAT recorders operate in two different methods: stationary head (S-DAT), also called DASH, and revolving head (R-DAT) (Figures 9.5 and 9.6).

The design and operation of the stationary-head *DAT recorders* are much like analog decks in that a tape is drawn across a head or series of heads, depending on the number of tracks to be recorded at a set speed. A ¼-inch S-DAT recorder can record up to eight tracks plus sync tracks, and a one-inch deck can handle up to 32 tracks. DAT recorders used a type of preemphasis added to the recorded signal to recreate the "bass" values of analog recordings, but they do not need pre- and postbias adjustments to compensate for tape analog tape hiss. There are three different S-DAT compatible recording systems; all use metal-particle tape.

The R-DAT machines borrow from helical videotape technology by mounting the record heads in a revolving drum and wrapping the tape part way around the drum.

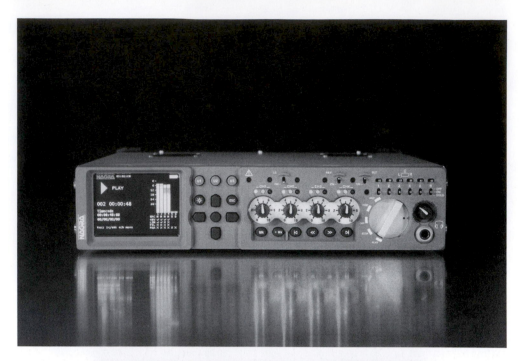

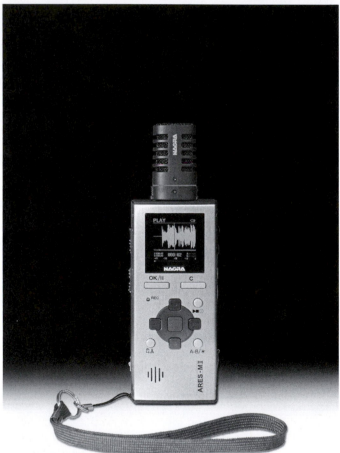

FIGURE 9.5 Digital tape decks operate in either R-DAT, or S-DAT, or DCC format. Digital decks, like analog, can record several tracks simultaneously in any of the formats. (Courtesy of Nagra.)

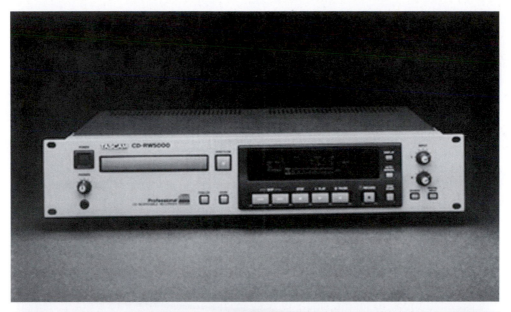

FIGURE 9.6 Audio may be recorded without using tape by recording directly onto computer floppy disks, a hard drive, or flash memory to be converted to another format. Audio can also be recorded directly or as a final format on CD discs. (Courtesy of Studer.)

The heads in the drum rotate in the opposite direction of the tape movement and, as in VCR technology, this movement increases the tape-to-head relative speed, thereby increasing the quality of the recording. There are several noncompatible S-DAT standards, but most R-DAT recorders are compatible, and because they can be manufactured in relatively small packages, they make ideal field recorders for video, film, and concert recording.

DAT was designed as a professional recording medium, and the two forms have found their niches in the recording industry. R-DAT also has become a backup tape format for nonlinear computer editors. If used for video recording, the signal is compressed, creating a recording that matches the quality of DV, now the most common low-cast video recording format.

With the rapid increase in computer memory and the lowering of costs, *tapeless audio recording* has developed and finds a place in the industry. Audio is simply fed into a computer and the digitized signal is recorded on one of several recording media: one or more computer hard drives, solid-state random access memory (RAM), flash drives, or some form of optical disc. The most common form of the latter is a write-once-read-many (WORM) drive, which has a high memory capacity, or a recordable compact disc (CD-R), or audio-DVD. With the advent of the Motion Picture Experts Group-Layer 3 (MP3) standard, audio may be downloaded from the Internet onto one of several digital music recorder/players. Each requires a digital signal input from either the Internet or any other digital source, such as a CD. Most of the small portable players play back from either disks or miniature memory chips for up to two hours at a time. It is clear that the question of copyright infringement using such technologies has become a major legal issue. Misuse of MP3 can bring heavy fines, prison penalties, and loss of the use of the Internet. The "free" use of downloading music from the Internet has been replaced with systems charging small fees for each download, a fair and equitable resolution of the problem.

It is possible today to feed a signal directly from a microphone into a computer, add any number of tracks, manipulate the signals in any manner desired, and output the finished signal to a digital format for distribution or playback without ever leaving the digital domain. Once the audio has been digitized, it may be edited as if the audio were a series of symbols in a word processor. The audio can be cut, rearranged, equalized, and mixed in any combination, depending on the complexity of the computer program. Once entered into the computer, the editing process is much more efficient than any other form of audio editing, but all of the audio must be entered into the computer in real time, which may be time consuming if there is much original material.

Digital audio processes have nearly replaced analog processes, but just as magnetic recording replaced electronic disc recording, and electronic disc recording replaced acoustical recording (although the majority of audio recording and processing are now through digital means), some analog audio recording will always be needed.

ANALOG VIDEO
Composite Video Signal

Video cameras transform and transmit visual images by converting light energy into electrical energy. The composite video signal of a visual image can be transmitted along an electrical conduit or wire in a closed-circuit system to a video monitor or a video recorder. The composite (or complete) video signal must be made up of three major components to be accurately recorded. The three components are the video signal, synchronization pulses (sync), and control track (CT) pulses.

Video Signal

The portion of the composite video signal that actually carries the voltages that are transformed into picture elements in a monitor and are recorded is called the *video signal*. That signal varies in voltage in direct proportion to the intensity of the light striking the camera sensor. In the component system, the video signal is a combination of all three basic pulses. In a composite color system, the video is more complex because there are three separate color signals combined out of phase, plus the basic component pulses. The advantage of the composite system is that it allows for better control of the color factors and avoids some of the color artifacts inherent in the component system, although composite requires more circuits. As in analog video systems, digital systems must maintain accurate and precise recording levels as well as specific digital and phase relationships between signals.

Synchronization Signal

For a video recorder or monitor to use the electronic signal transmitted from a camera, it must have some reference for the scan and the field rates of the picture. A synchronizing or sync signal, which functions like electronic sprocket holes, is fed either to the camera or generated internally in the camera during recording.

The sync signal is necessary for stable reproduction of the original signal. There are actually two sync signals: horizontal sync and vertical sync. The *horizontal sync signal* controls horizontal scanning and blanking, whereas the *vertical sync signal* controls the rate of the vertical scanning and blanking. These sync signals are passed along within the composite video signal so that all recipients of the whole signal will reproduce the picture at the same rate and direction as the camera originating the signal.

Control Track Pulse

A video recorder records a pulse signal, called a *control track (CT) signal*, that guides the playback video heads into position to accurately follow or track the signal laid down by the record head at the time of recording. A *servo capstan*—that is, a rotating tape drive cylinder with an accurate motor—varies the speed of the playback so that proper synchronization is maintained. It also moves the videotape through the recorder at the correct speed and ensures that it is aligned properly by the CT (Figure 9.7).

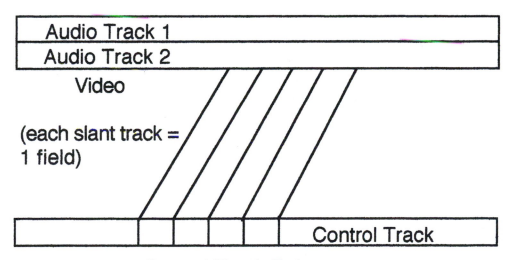

HELICAL TAPE TRACK POSITIONS

FIGURE 9.7 Helical videotape tracks follow a general pattern of several linear audio tracks, a linear control track, a linear timecode track, and video recorded at a steep angle in slashes across the tape by a video head rotating at a high speed in the opposite direction of tape travel. This method of recording video is necessary for the high head-to-tape speed required to record the high frequencies of video.

Monochrome and Color Video

A black-and-white system transmits only the brightness values of light, also called luminance, not hue or saturation. There are several different camera pickup systems for creating color video images. Some use only one sensor, and others use two or three. Light entering a video camera is divided into its red, green, and blue components by using color filters. The three-color information picked up by chips is then encoded as two chrominance or color signals, which are called the *I and Q signals*, and one luminance or brightness signal, which is called the *Y signal*. The signals are then digitized, as light striking each sensor creates an analog variation in voltages.

This chrominance and luminance information is then transmitted to the recording medium, where it is recorded. Light, as explained in Chapter 7, Lighting and Design, can be analyzed and manipulated on the basis of its three characteristics: hue, saturation, and brightness. Different wavelengths of light are perceived as different colors, or *color hues*, such as red, green, and blue. Color video and film systems are capable of recording and projecting a wide range of color hues. Like our eyes, these systems depend on three basic hues: red, green, and blue, called the *additive color system*. Light can be described in terms of its color saturation and brightness as well as its hue. The saturation of a specific hue indicates its *color purity*, that is, the amount of grayness the color contains. A vibrant but pure color of red, such as on a stop sign, is heavily saturated. In video, saturation is translated into a chroma or chrominance signal. *Brightness* refers to a light's intensity, its lightness or darkness. Bright lights have strong intensities.

In video, brightness is reproduced in the luminance signal. Black-and-white video and film recording devices are only sensitive to the brightness or luminance of a light, not its hue or saturation. Two distinctly different colors may contrast with each other to the naked eye, but if they are equal in brightness, a black-and-white recording depicts them as virtually identical. When recording in black and white, hue and saturation can generally be ignored, because brightness values are paramount. Hue, saturation, and brightness play key roles in video and film color recording processes. The basic principles of colored light, covered in Chapter 7, Lighting and Design, provide the basis for the recording processes of both video and film. Both the National Television Standards Committee (NTSC) and the Advanced Television Systems Committee (ATSC), the technical group formed to set the standards for digital and high-definition television, video signal reproduces color by keeping the three signals (I, Q, and Y) separate, either by combining them in one signal with each of the components out of phase with each other (the composite system) or by actually using three circuits to keep the signals separate (the component system).

Scanning Systems

Before discussing the method of recording a video signal, it is important to understand the scanning systems. There are two basic scanning systems: *interlace* and *progressive*. The United States and other countries that use NTSC standards for analog television use an *interlace system* of scanning to create and to reproduce the picture. Each picture is scanned twice: first the even lines are scanned, constituting one field, and then the odd lines are scanned, making up the second field. The two fields together make up a complete picture that is scanned every 1/30th of a second. Interlace is an efficient system, but it can introduce artifacts or distortions in the picture. Computer systems use a progressive system of scanning. Each frame is created by scanning every line in order to make a complete frame.

Improved modern technology has made *progressive scanning* a preferred system. Progressive systems can scan at the rate of 24, 25, or 30 frames a second. The recording process depends partly on the frame rate of the system in use, because the recording and editing systems must match the scan rate and the scan system used. As analog and standard definition (SD) systems are being replaced by high-definition (HD) systems, the number of lines and aspect ratios also are changing. The Federal Communications Commission (FCC) has ruled that 16:9 is the accepted wide-screen standard, and the number of lines may be either 525 or 625 for analog systems and 480, 720, or 1,080 active lines for digital systems. The end result is that there are 18 different combinations of aspect ratio, line rates, and progressive or interlace scan system standards set by the Advanced TV Systems Committee (ATSC) for advanced TV [ATV] — digital and high-definition — systems.

Helical Scan Recording

All videotape recorders, either analog or digital, now use the helical scan method of recording. Helical scan recorders use two or more video heads, which continuously record electrical video signals. As magnetic tape travels from left to right across the recording heads, the heads rotate in a clockwise direction, opposite to the movement of the tape. On a two-head recorder, each time a single head passes over the tape, it records a complete field of 262 half-lines of video in a 525-line system or 540 lines in a 1,080 system. At the exact instant that the first rotating head disengages from the tape, the second head engages it, so that a continuous recording of the television signal is made along the tape by consecutive heads. The passage from one head to the next corresponds to the *vertical blanking period* and is a crucial part of maintaining synchronization. The vertical blanking period is the time when the scan line is dropped to black and cannot be seen as it retraces to start a new scan line. The combined passage of the two heads records a complete frame of 525 or 740 lines (Figures 9.8 and 9.9). In a progressive scan system, two or four heads alternate, each creating a single frame as they pass over the tape. Instead of alternating scan lines, as in the interlace system, the progressive system scans lines continuously from the top of the frame to the bottom to create a single frame.

The videotape is wrapped around a semicircular drum, and the heads maintain continuous contact with a semicircular wrap of tape around the drum, moving in a downward diagonal direction as they rotate past the tape. Because the recording is made in a slanting movement of the head across the tape, a *helical scan recorder* is sometimes called a *slant-track recorder*. The linear speed of the tape passing the rotating heads in a digital recorder varies from 100 mm/second (approximately 250 ips) to 200 mm/second (approximately 500 ips). Although the speed of initial recording cannot be varied, a helical scan recorder can be slowed down or speeded up in playback to create slow- or fast-motion action. During slow motion, scan lines are repeated, but during fast motion, some lines are skipped. The image can also be stopped and the action frozen by repeating one recording line or complete field of the video image, called a *freeze frame*, which is often designated as the pause mode during playback. High-quality ½-inch helical scan recorders and digital recorders allow for special effects creation without sacrificing image quality.

FIGURE 9.8 The video head of a helical recorder contains from two to eight different recording or erasing heads depending on the complexity of the format.

Videotape Formats

Videotape contains iron oxide or other metallic particles that store electrical information in magnetic form. These microscopic particles are attached to a flexible support base, such as cellulose acetate or polyester (Mylar) (Figure 9.10). Videotape recorders (VTR) or videocassette recorders (VCR) are capable of both recording and playing back video information on reels or cassettes of videotape. The signals may be either analog or digitized video or audio signals.

The actual recording of video and audio signals is done by video and audio record heads, which also function as playback heads. The *audio* and *video heads* are usually separated from one another because the recording of a video signal requires a complex movement of the head with respect to the videotape, whereas an audio head remains stationary. Some tape decks record audio signals using rotating audio heads parallel to the video heads or record digital audio embedded within the digital video signal (called pulse-code modulation [PCM]). An erase head erases information previously stored on the videotape before recording new images.

D-9 (a component videotape format) uses separate heads for recording and playing back so instantaneous monitoring and even in-camera effects can be created using

TRACK LOCATIONS ON VIDEOTAPE FORMATS

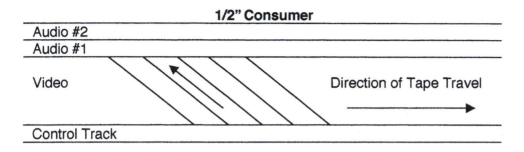

1/2" Consumer

Audio #2

Audio #1

Video   Direction of Tape Travel

Control Track

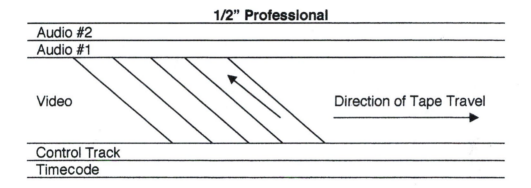

1/2" Professional

Audio #2

Audio #1

Video   Direction of Tape Travel

Control Track

Timecode

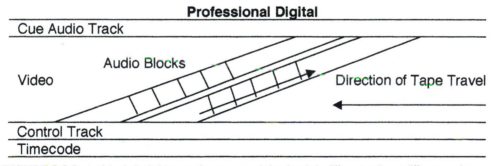

Professional Digital

Cue Audio Track

Audio Blocks

Video   Direction of Tape Travel

Control Track

Timecode

FIGURE 9.9 Each of the helical videotape formats records its signals in different paths, at different angles, and at different speeds. Each format historically was developed to provide a higher quality at lower cost. As time passes, the newer digital formats will replace the present analog formats.

both heads. The format, or width, of videotape ranges from 8 mm to 19 mm. Helical scan recorders use one of the following formats: 6.35 mm (¼-inch), 8 mm (⅓-inch), 12.5 mm (½-inch), or 19 mm (¾-inch) videotape. Small-format helical scan recorders use 6.35 mm (¼-inch) or 8 mm (½-inch) videotape. Digital recorders use tape from 6 mm to 19 mm wide. A variety of different helical scan systems have been developed for recording analog signals on ½-inch videocassettes: VHS, S-VHS, and Betacam SP; for digital recordings, digital Betacam, Betacam SX, D-3, D-5, and D-9. These systems all use ½-inch videotape in closed cassettes and helical- or slant-tracking techniques, but the actual scanning of the videotape is sufficiently different so that they are noncompatible systems. As an example, a D-9

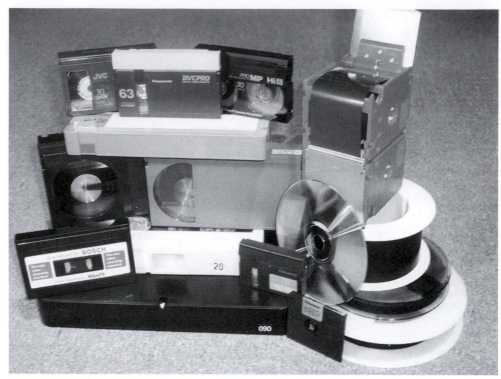

FIGURE 9.10 Audio and video recording stock is manufactured in a great variety of widths, thicknesses, and magnetic coatings depending on the purpose for which the tape is intended. The recording media today moves from magnetic tape to disc and on to solid-state media. From top down on the left: Mini-VHS, DVCPRo, Hi8, M-II, BetaMax, BetaSP, Quarter-cam, U-matic, DV. On the right: two-inch quad cart, two-inch quad open reel, EIAJ ½-inch, Type "C" one-inch. In front of the reels, a DVD and ½-inch floppy.

recording, which uses a slightly larger videocassette and a different loading mechanism, cannot be played on a Betacam SX machine and vice versa. As of this writing, four tape formats specifically designed for high-definition are available: D5-HD, based on D-5; D7-HD, based on DVCPro; D9-HD, based on Digital-S; and HDCAM and XDCAM-EX based on Betacam. Some other digital formats are available with upgrades or modifications that allow playing or recording an HD signal. Each season, new forms of digital and HD equipment are designed and produced, making it difficult to keep up with the latest available equipment. At the same time, many of the present formats may not find a market and may disappear within a year or two of their first appearance.

The digital systems are all high-quality recording systems, but they are also incompatible with each other (except for D-3 and D-5; and Beta, Betacam SP, and Digital Beta SX) or with any other ½-inch system. Some consumer ½-inch videocassette recorders are capable of running at a variety of speeds, so anywhere from one to six hours of recording can be made on the same videocassette. Some videocassette recorders are capable of recording and playing back several different types of television signals, such as NTSC, PAL, SECAM, and various ATSC using different types of electrical current. When large quantities of video or audio material needs to be recorded and accessed in a nonlinear manner, computers with maximum digital storage capacities are used. These systems are called servers (Figure 9.11).

FIGURE 9.11 A video server that is designed to record and play back digital video/audio cuts on a nonlinear basis. It emulates videotape recorders, cart machines, and video storage systems. (Courtesy of Philips Broadcast Television Systems Company.)

High-quality ½-inch analog and digital tapes used for professional recordings allow sufficient space for a control track, up to four soundtracks, a timecode track, and one video track. One-inch, once the professional broadcast standard, has been replaced by digital and ½-inch tape formats, solid-state, direct to disc, and hard drive media. Smaller analog consumer format videotapes can be broadcast when they have been channeled through an image stabilizer, known as a *digital time-base corrector*, or *TBC*. A TBC accurately synchronizes the scanning process by changing a conventional analog signal into a more easily controlled digital signal, thus providing high-quality video sync signals (see Chapter 10, Editing). Minor variations in synchronization that cause a picture to jitter are eliminated using a TBC, which makes it possible for smaller format recordings to be broadcast directly or dubbed up to better quality videotape formats.

Videotape Sound Synchronization

Synchronization between sounds and images is simple to maintain in videotape recording. A single videotape recording machine may be used to record picture and sound elements simultaneously on the same tape. In most videotape recording, on-set or synchronous sounds are recorded on the track located away from the edge of the tape. There is a slight distance separating the points at which the sounds and the picture are recorded on the videotape, because on most types of videotape recorders the video record and playback heads rotate but sound heads remain stationary. During electronic editing, then, the corresponding sound and images must be picked up from slightly different points on the tape. However, because videotape is always played back on a machine that has the same gap between images and sounds, this distance creates no real problem in terms of synchronizing sounds and images. Control track recording (discussed in Chapter 10, Editing) is an important reference for postproduction editing, although some machines provide another type of reference, called SMPTE timecode, which is discussed in Chapter 10, Editing.

DIGITAL VIDEO

Digital video technology is the same as digital audio, except that much higher frequencies and a greater quantity of recorded material must be handled. The original analog video signal is sampled and quantized, requiring up to 300 MB per second of recorded program, as compared with less than 100K per second for digital audio. Higher tape speeds or compression of the signal before recording allow sufficient video to be recorded without consuming an impractical amount of tape stock (Figure 9.12).

Signal Compression

The compression process removes redundant or repeated portions of the picture, such as the blue sky or white clouds. As long as there is no change in the hue, saturation, or luminance value, the digital program will "remember" the removed portions, then it will decompress and restore them when the tape is played back. This process saves space on the tape, disc, or chip, depending on the recording method. Compression allows a reasonable amount of programming material to be recorded, but the price is a slight degradation of picture quality.

The greater the compression, the greater the possible loss of quality. There are two basic systems now in use: JPEG, developed by the Joint Photographic Experts Group and originally intended for compression of still images, and MPEG, developed by the Motion Picture Experts Group and intended for compression of moving images. Each system offers advantages and disadvantages, and the possibility exists that

VIDEO RECORDING FORMATS

CAMERA	NTSC-DV	HDV JVC	HDV Sony	HDCAM	HDCAM SR	XDCAM SD	XDCAM HD	XDCAM EX	DVCPro 25	DVCPro 50	DVCPro HD
Quantization	8 bit	8 bit	8 bit	8 bit	10 bit	8 bit	8 bit	8 bit	8 bit	8 bit	8 bit
Compression	DCT IntraFr.	DCT IntraFr.	MPEG2 InterFr.	DCT IntraFr.	MPEG4SP IntraFr.	IMX IntrFr.	MPEG2 InterFr.	MPEG2 InterFr.	DCT IntraFr.	DCT IntraFr.	DCT IntraFr.
Compression Ratio	5:1	18:1	18:1	4:1	2,7:1 4,2:1				5:1	2,5:1	6,7:1
Color Sampling	4:1:1	4:2:0	4:2:0	3:1:1	4:2:2 4:4:4	4:1:1 4:2:2	4:2:0	4:2:2	4:1:1	4:2:2	4:2:2
Luma Resolution	720 × 576	1280 × 720	1440 × 1080	1440 × 1080	1920 × 1080	720 × 480 720 × 576	1440 × 1080	1920 × 1080	720 × 480 720 × 576	720 × 480 720 × 576	1440 × 1080
Chroma Resolution	180 × 480	640 × 360	720 × 540	480 × 1080	1920 × 1080	360 × 576	720 × 540	960 × 1080	180 × 576	360 × 576	720 × 1080
Picture Format	480i	720p	1080i	1080i/p	1080i/p	480i 576i	1080p	1080p	480i 576i	480i 576i	1080i/p
Frame Rates	30i	25/30p 50/60p	25/30i 25/30p	24/25/30p 25/30i	24/25/30p 25/30i	Variable	Variable	Variable	30i/25i	30i/25i	25p/25i
Audio Channels	2 or 4	2 or 4	12	4	12	4	4	4	4/2	4/2	8
Tape Size	¼"	¼"	¼"	½"	½"	Blu-ray	Blu-ray	SxS card	¼"	¼"	P2 Card
Play Time	80-270 mins.	80 mins.	80 mins.	49-155 mins.	124-155 mins.	25-50 GB	25-50 GB	16-32 GB	80 mins.	40 mins.	32-64 GB

FIGURE 9.12 As of the writing of this chapter, the formats listed in the text discussion are in use. Each year new formats are developed and perfected, in some cases replacing earlier formats. Compatibility between digital formats is rare.

new and better systems will be developed. Currently there are three MPEG systems: MPEG-1, MPEG-2, and MPEG-4. MPEG-2 was an improvement over MPEG-1, and MPEG-4 originally was written for interactive media intended for consumer use, but later developments have made the system applicable to HDTV and other high-quality and bandwidth-demanding formats (Figure 9.13). Additional MPEG standards have been developed by individual companies for their own equipment as technology continues to advance and develop.

Digital Videotape Formats

D-1 was the first industry-accepted digital format. The Society of Motion Picture and Television Engineers (SMPTE), the organization that sets standards in the visual fields, agreed upon the D-1 standard in 1986. It has become the universal, component digital standard. The signal is recorded on a 19 mm oxide tape, offering the highest-quality and most flexible recording system, but also the most expensive. It is capable of recording compressed HDTV signals, but it does not compress standard signals. It is especially useful for multilayering graphics, animation, and feature film special effects.

D-2 was the second SMPTE standardized digital system, but it is a composite system. It also records on 19 mm tape, but it requires special metal tape. D-2 is less expensive than D-1, can be modified to record in the component mode, and is commonly used by broadcasters. Neither D-1 nor D-2 is practical for use in a camcorder because of the physical size of the tape transport system. *D-3* and *D-5* are compatible systems, even though D-3 was designed as a composite system and D-5 as a

VIDEO COMPRESSION STANDARDS

LABEL	FUNCTION	ORIGINATING ORGANIZATION
H.261 or P64	Compressed video over telephone wires	Int'l Tele/Tele Consultative Commission
H.264	Compressed Internet video	Int'l Tele/Tele Consultative Commission
JPEG	Compressed still images	Joint Photo Experts Group & ISO
Motion-JPEG	Edited moving video	Joint Photo Experts Group & ISO
MPEG-1	Compressed moving images-CD video	Moving Pictures Experts Group & ISO
MPEG-2	Compressed moving images-DVD video	Moving Pictures Experts Group & ISO
MPEG-3	Compressed audio for MP3 files	Moving Pictures Experts Group & ISO
MPEG-4	Compressed Internet video	Moving Pictures Experts Group & ISO

FIGURE 9.13 To record and manipulate high-frequency video signals within a digital format, some method of compressing the signals needed to be developed to avoid requiring tremendous amounts of computer memory. Two basic systems and variations on those systems have been established, JPEG and MPEG. Researchers constantly work at developing newer systems that require less memory yet maintain the highest quality possible.

component system. Neither system compresses the video, and both use 12.5 mm (½-inch) metal tape. D-3 has a four-hour capacity on one reel, and D-5 offers two hours. D-5 is designed to record HDTV signals when the standards for that format are agreed upon.

Two systems created by competing videotape companies have not received standardization from SMPTE as of this writing. Both are being manufactured and are finding their individual markets. Sony developed *Digital Betacam* and *Betacam SX* to record on the same 12.5 mm metal tape stock as the Betacam SP recorder. They are also downward compatible with Betacam tapes. Digital Betacam is also a compressed component system compatible with the D-2 signal, but not with the D-2 tape.

Sony's newest format is the XDCAM that records directly onto specialized flash memory cards called SxS. Panasonic's highest level camera records onto its own flash memory cards, P2, a PCMCIA (Personal Computer Memory Card International Association) type card.

Since the late 1990s, nearly a dozen digital tape formats have been developed and marketed. *D-6* records on a 19 mm tape designed for HDTV. *D-7* (DVCPro) is one of the professional formats based on the consumer DV 6.35 mm format. Others are *DVCAM* and *DVCPro50*. In some cases, depending on the tape deck, the DV formats are compatible. *Digital 8* is the digital version of the Hi8 format and is downward compatible with the 8 mm formats. *D9*, or Digital-S, is based on the S-VHS format and in some cases is downward compatible with S-VHS. Tape formats will continue to disappear as solid-state recording media replace the mechanical tape systems. MiniDV cassette recorders are designed to record video in one or more of the following digital formats: Panasonic's DVC-Pro, DVC-Pro HD, DVSP (Canon and Sony DVSP formats are not completely compatible, however), Sony's proprietary DVCam, and HDV. Many of these formats can be recorded in 24, 25, or 30 frames per second (fps) in either I (interlaced) or P (progressive) scan mode.

Tapeless Video Recording

Video and audio signals may be recorded in digital form without using magnetic tape. Digital pulses may be recorded on random access memory (RAM) chips within a computer. RAM chips are capable of recording as much as 128 MB per chip. With compression, over an hour of video material can be recorded on one chip. The next level of tapeless recording is offered by flash memory or USB cards or sticks. The same memory system used in cell phones, digital still cameras, and other digital devices works well for recording digital audio and video. Secure (SD), MultiMedia (MMC), CompactFlash (CF), Memory Stick, xD-Picture Cards, and Smart Media (SM) are all physically slightly different, but the information recorded on each is compatible without additional circuits or equipment. Most do not need external power; only the most powerful and those designed for rapid recording and play back may need an additional power source.

The advantages of impressing production information on computer chips and flash memory are instant access, no moving parts, no maintenance, and no need to shuttle through other information. In addition, there are no physical aberrations, such as dropouts, tracking, or skewing, in digital pulses. There are no problems of compatibility, only possible differences in compression standards between computer programs. Relatively inexpensive personal computers can replace expensive digital tape decks.

Many of the same advantages exist if the digital pulses are recorded on computer hard drives or flash rives. Hard drives are now designed to hold multiple terabytes (1,000 GB) and can be disengaged from the computer, stored, and moved to another computer. The removable feature provides an advantage if more than one project is assigned to the same computer and for archiving the material. *Write-once-read-many* (WORM) CD and DVD optical discs also offer the same advantages, except that once they are recorded they are not erasable. Erasable and reusable optical discs, called *direct-read-after-write* (DRAW), exist. Prices for professional- and consumer-quality disc recorders have lowered to the point that CDs and DVDs are now an affordable and practical means of recording digital information on permanent or reusable discs.

FILM RECORDING
Basic Photochemistry

Photography uses light energy to transform the chemical properties of light-sensitive substances. Photographic film consists of light-sensitive materials, such as silver halide crystals or grains, attached to a flexible support base such as cellulose acetate. Silver halide forms an invisible latent image when it is exposed to light in a camera. Light stimulates a chemical change in silver halide crystals, which can only be made visible and permanent by developing the image in certain chemical solutions. The film image appears dark or opaque where it was struck by light and clear where the light energy was not strong enough to stimulate the silver halide crystals. The resulting image is called a *negative image*. It inverts the whites and the blacks of the original scene. A white wall appears black and a black curtain appears white (Figure 9.14).

To get a positive image, which reproduces the whites and blacks of the original scene, the negative film must be printed or copied onto another piece of film on a device called a *contact printer*. When the copy is chemically developed in the same manner as the negative film from which it was printed, it reproduces the correct whites and blacks. The bright areas in the original scene are now white and the black areas are black. This method, in which a negative is copied to produce a positive image, is called the *negative/positive process*.

An alternative approach to this two-stage, negative/positive process is known as the *reversal process*. The difference between negative/positive and reversal film is similar to the difference between snapshots and slides in still photography. Reversal recording is a single-stage process that produces a positive image after one development of the originally exposed film. The negative image resulting from initial exposure is converted to a positive image during several stages of development.

Reversal film produces a positive image immediately. It does not have to be printed to view the original scene, as does negative film. The size and composition of the silver halide crystals in large part determine the overall light sensitivity and graininess of the film stock.

BLACK-AND-WHITE FILM STOCK LAYERS

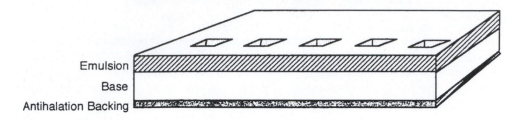

Emulsion

Base

Antihalation Backing

EMULSION RESPONSE TO LIGHT & PROCESSING

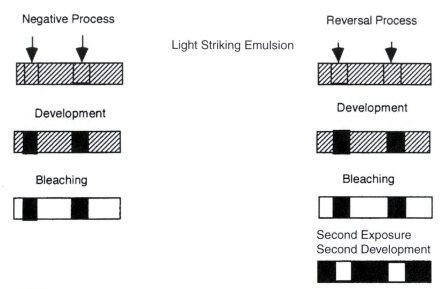

Negative Process

Light Striking Emulsion

Reversal Process

Development

Development

Bleaching

Bleaching

Second Exposure
Second Development

FIGURE 9.14 Black-and-white film consists of a layer of light-sensitive material, a flexible base, and an antihalation backing layer to prevent light from reflecting back through the base to the emulsion. Reversal film requires additional processing to create a positive image rather than a negative image.

Light sensitivity or film speed is rated in *EI*, which stands for exposure index. The American Standards Association rating, called *ASA* (or EI), or a German standard, called *DIN*, is often printed on the film package. These indices of a film's overall sensitivity to light provide a relative indication of how much light will be required to properly expose a specific container of film. Slower films, with lower numbers, require more light than those with higher numbers (Figure 9.15).

The term *graininess* refers to the size and visibility of particles in the film. A grainy image is one in which these particles are readily visible, and a fine-grain image is one in which they are not. Faster film stocks, which are more sensitive to light and therefore have higher EI numbers, generally have more visible grain structures than slower films, producing grainier images.

The size of the grain in the image can affect its *resolution* and *sharpness*, terms that refer to image clarity. Slower film tends to have higher resolution and sharpness

FIGURE 9.15 The label on a film canister provides all of the information the camera operator or director of cinematography needs to adjust the camera and make exposure decisions. The EI numbers indicate the film speeds for daylight or tungsten lighting, and the other numbers indicate the type of film (the left can is 7278, a high-speed, black-and-white reversal film sock), batch numbers, inventory, and order numbers.

than faster film. The size of the film grain also will determine the film's latitude, or the ability to reproduce a wide range of reflected light. Better films are able to reproduce an image in lighting with a 100:1 contrast range, but a standard video camera pickup tube has an effective contrast ratio of 30:1, and a video camera chip has a ratio of 50:1. If there is a wide range of dark-to-light reflecting objects in a scene, a video camera will not record as wide a range of grayscale as film. Many neutral tones will be recorded as completely black or completely white rather than as some shade in-between. In film, a full range of tones may be recorded. The effect of contrast ratio on lighting and scene design is discussed more fully in Chapter 7, Lighting and Design, because the difference between lighting for film and video is important (Figure 9.16).

Color Film

We have so far considered only the recording of different brightness levels of light on black-and-white film. Color film responds to different hues and saturations of light, as well as different levels of brightness. A color-film emulsion consists of a multilayered suspension of light-sensitive particles and color dyes attached to a flexible support base, such as cellulose acetate. When light enters a camera, it strikes three different layers of color dyes and light-sensitive particles. These layers are sensitive to blue, green, and red light, respectively. Light first strikes the blue-sensitive layer, where only the blue light affects the particles and dyes. The other colors of light then pass through this layer and a yellow filter, which removes excess blue light, before striking

LUMINANCE CONTRAST RATIOS

The difference between the brightest subject and the darkest subject for which detail can be seen is the contrast ratio. Different media are able to reproduce detail under different maximum contrast ratios.

Digital camera	30:1-50:1
Average film	250:1
Human eye	1000:1

Different lighting situations provide a variety of contrast ratios.

Foggy day	10:1
Average daylight	130:1
Bright day	800:1
White object next to black velvet lit by bright direct sun	2000:1

FIGURE 9.16 The contrast ratio of a medium determines how wide a variation in light reflectance values that medium can reproduce without losing either the brightest or the darkest values. Any attempt to reproduce a subject or frame containing a higher contrast range than the medium is capable of reproducing will result in either muddy dark areas or flared-out white areas.

the green- and red-sensitive layers. These layers are sensitive to blue light as well as their own wavelength bands. The blue-sensitive layer thus records the blue component, the green-sensitive layer records the green component, and the red-sensitive layer records the red component of white light (Figure 9.17).

Film Exposure

Film is exposed inside a lightproof mechanism called a *camera body*. A basic film camera consists of a *lens*, which focuses an image on the film; a *viewfinder*, which allows the camera operator to see the image that is being recorded; a *film feed and take-up mechanism*, which supplies film to the exposure area and rolls it up after it has been exposed; a *motor*, which drives the film through the camera; a *rotating opaque shutter*, which rapidly opens and closes to expose each frame of film; an *aperture*, which determines the dimensions of the frame that is exposed; a *pressure plate*, which holds the film flat against the aperture to ensure good focus; a *pulldown claw*, which intermittently grabs film sprocket holes or perforations to advance the film for each single frame or still photograph at the aperture; a *speed control*, which determines how many individual frames will be exposed each second; and a *run/stop button*, which turns the camera on and off.

Motion-picture film is perforated at regular intervals so that a camera and a projector can drive it intermittently. This intermittent movement allows a single frame of film to be held stationary while a rotating shutter opens up and allows light passing through the lens to expose the film. A projector uses the same mechanism to project recorded images through the lens onto a screen. The feed and take-up mechanisms push the film continually through the camera, whereas the claw pulls the film at the aperture. Film is constantly pushed and pulled through a 16mm camera at a rate of 36 feet

COLOR FILM EMULSION LAYERS

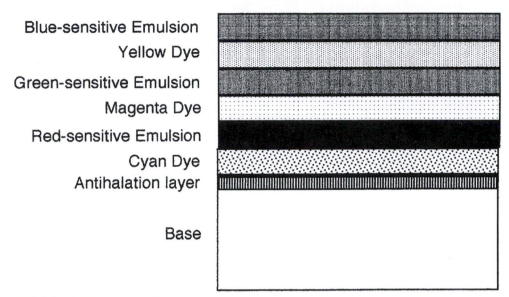

Blue-sensitive Emulsion	
Yellow Dye	
Green-sensitive Emulsion	
Magenta Dye	
Red-sensitive Emulsion	
Cyan Dye	
Antihalation layer	
Base	

FIGURE 9.17 Color emulsion film layers alternate specific color-sensitive layers with opposite color-dye layers. This produces a negative reproduction of the image exposed to the camera. Color reversal film, like black-and-white reversal film, requires additional layers and processing. Like black-and-white film, color film stocks come in negative or reversal processes and a variety of light sensitivities and contrast ranges.

per minute, or through a 35mm camera at 90 feet per minute. Normal sound speed exposes 24 frames per second (fps) in 35mm, 16mm, and Super-8mm.

The camera shutter and claw must be synchronized so that the shutter stays open when the claw disengages the film and retracts behind the aperture plate. At this point, the film is stationary in the aperture. Sometimes it is held stationary by a device known as a *registration pin*, which holds the film in firm registration—that is, it holds it very steady when it is not being pulled by the claw. The shutter must be closed when the registration pin retracts and the claw engages the film to advance it, or the film images will blur as they pass the light in the aperture.

The speed control allows the camera operator to alter the frames-per-second speed of the camera. Film recorded at speeds above 24fps will reproduce images in slow motion when it is projected or played back at normal sound speed (24fps). Camera images recorded at fewer than 24fps will produce fast motion. Thus, slow and fast motion are produced during actual recording in film, unlike video recording, which always occurs at 30fps. Increasing the film recording speed also changes the synchronized shutter speed and affects the amount of light exposing the film. Faster recording speeds produce more rapid shutter speeds and less light reaches each frame during exposure, because the duration of each exposure is reduced. To compensate for these changes in exposure, the lens must be adjusted so that more light passes through it and strikes the film when the camera speed is increased.

Motion Picture Formats

Motion picture film, which is exposed to light inside a camera, is available in a variety of formats or film widths, including 8mm, 16mm, 35mm, and 65mm formats. These distinctions between various formats refer to the width of the film in millimeters. The width of the film affects image size and quality, as well as the cost of supplies and equipment. There used to be two 8 mm formats: standard 8 mm and Super-8 mm. Super-8 mm cameras record images that are 50 percent larger than those of standard 8 mm cameras. Standard 8 mm is now virtually obsolete. All subsequent references in this book are to Super-8 mm, which is sometimes used for home movies, as well as for some independently produced, low-budget films.

The 16 mm format has been widely used for professional recording of industrial, educational, governmental, and documentary films, as well as some commercials and low-budget feature films, but now videotape productions are competing for the same markets. Some resurgence in the use of 16 mm film has come from new developments in Super-16. Such films are easily transferred to a video format for 16:9 widescreen broadcast on television and cable. Network-level commercials and television programs are recorded in 35 mm, as are most feature films. Some feature films are recorded on 65 mm film, which is then printed onto 70 mm film, with the added 5 mm being the width of the soundtrack area, for projection in large, specially outfitted theaters. Other 70 mm film prints for projection are enlargements or blowups from original 35 mm recordings (Figure 9.18).

Film stocks are available in different film lengths and loading arrangements or configurations. Super-8 mm film comes in a lightproof cartridge and is exactly 8 mm wide. It is normally packaged in 50-foot lengths, which lasts for two minutes and 46 seconds. Sixteen-millimeter film is available on daylight spools, which contain 100, 200, or 360 feet of film. It is also available on plastic cores, which simply provide a firm center on which the film is wound but do not protect the edges of the film from light. Film that comes on a core must be loaded in complete darkness. The standard length of 16 mm film cores is 400 or 1,200 feet. One hundred feet of 16 mm film, when exposed at 24 fps, runs for two minutes and 46 seconds. Thirty-five-millimeter film comes on cores in standard lengths of 100, 200, 400, and 1,100 feet. Ninety feet of 35 mm film runs for one minute at 24 fps.

Film stocks differ in terms of their perforation or sprocket-hole sizes and placements. Super-8 mm film has sprocket holes on only one side of the film, whereas 16 mm films are available with single-sided or double-sided perforations, which are called *single-perf* and *double-perf*, respectively. Magnetically striped 16 mm film has audio track in place of one row of sprocket holes. Thirty-five-millimeter film is always double-perf.

COMMON FILM FORMATS

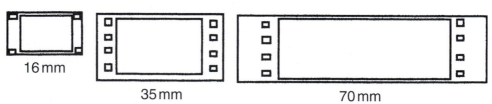

16 mm

35 mm

70 mm

FIGURE 9.18 Virtually all professional film now comes in one of three formats: 16 mm, 35 mm, or 70 mm film. Super-8 is still available for consumer use, and special large feature film formats also are in use such as IMAX, a wide-screen format.

Film Sound Synchronization

Synchronous sounds match their visual sound sources and are usually recorded at the same time as the corresponding visual images. Many different systems have been developed to synchronize recorded visual images with recorded sounds. Early in the 1950s, portable ¼-inch reel-to-reel tape recorders had the capacity to record a sync signal that allowed them to be used in conjunction with a motion picture camera. Today, separate digital recorders are used because they run to absolute speed and do not have to be connected to either the video or film camera to maintain sync, as long as the film camera receives a sync signal from a crystal control or the video camera is locked to its sync signal. This allows the separate recording of sounds that are synchronous with their corresponding pictures.

Single-System Film Recording

There are basically two different systems of synchronous sound film recording in common use today: single system and double system. Single-system recording, as shown in Figure 9.19, puts sounds and images on the same piece of film; usually, the sound is recorded on the edge of original motion picture film.

This technique is called *sound-on-film* (SOF). As a general rule, 35 mm film is not used for sound-on-film or single-system original recording. Sixteen-millimeter magnetic sound-on-film is recorded 28 frames ahead of the picture gate or film aperture. (Sixteen-millimeter optical sound-on-film is 26 frames ahead of the picture. Optical sound is created by exposing the edge of the film to light.) Super-8 mm sound-on-film is recorded 18 frames ahead of its corresponding pictures. These standard intervals allow the film driven through a camera to change from an intermittent movement at the film aperture, where a rapid series of still frames are recorded, to a continuous

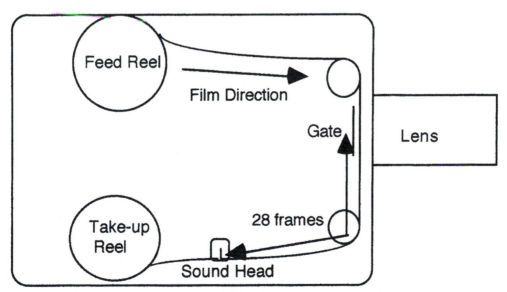

FIGURE 9.19 Cameras that record sound simultaneously with the exposing of the film are called single-system cameras. The sound-recording head must be located apart from the aperture, because the two cannot be physically located at the same place within the body of the camera. The sound head on a 16 mm single-system is located 28 frames ahead of the aperture. This separation must be taken into consideration when shooting original film to edit without transferring the sound to another medium.

movement over the sound-recording head. The same 28-, 26-, or 18-frame advance of sound ahead of the picture is standard in most 16mm or Super-8mm film sound projectors.

Single-system sound is commonly used for exhibition purposes. The final film prints marry an optical or magnetic soundtrack with their corresponding pictures on the same piece of film.

Single-system recording is used extensively in small formats, such as Super-8mm film recording. Editing problems arise from the fact that the sounds are always a specific number of frames ahead of the corresponding pictures. Sound-on-film yields an initial sound recording that is decidedly inferior in audio quality to a double-system film sound recording. If SOF is to be edited, either it must be shot with pauses in the voice track, so edits can be made without losing portions of the sound, or the soundtrack must be dubbed to a separate piece of film for double-system editing.

Double-System Film Recording

In double-system synchronous sound recording, the sounds and images are recorded on separate materials. (This approach is normally used for production and editing but not for final projection.) Rather than recording sounds directly on the edge of the film during production, an independent tape recorder is used, which can record and play back sound in exact synchronization with the corresponding images. There are two basic systems for synchronizing the recording of the separate sounds and pictures; the choice depends on both the camera and the recorder's speed as controlled by cable sync and crystal sync (Figure 9.20).

FIGURE 9.20 The camera and sound recorder stay in synchronization because they are both running with internal crystal sync or a synchronizing cable connects them.

Cable sync refers to the use of an electrical cable, which connects the camera to the tape recorder like an umbilical cord. The cable carries a 60-cycle-per-second sync signal, called *Pilotone*, which is generated by the camera. The Pilotone is recorded on the audiotape by a special sync head on the audiotape recorder. *Crystal sync* allows the camera and the tape recorder to be physically separated. This can be a distinct advantage because it increases the flexibility, mobility, and independence of sound and picture recording machines and operators, who are otherwise linked by an umbilical cable. For crystal sync, a crystal oscillator controls the speed of the camera so that the film is driven at a precise speed of 24 fps. The analog audiotape recorder uses a separate crystal oscillator to place a sync signal on the audiotape so that its original recording speed can be duplicated during playback and a digital recorder runs true to speed. Digital audiotape recorders also can be synchronized to film cameras using sync signals or the stable recording speed of a digital recorder to maintain sync.

Slating

Creating a common point where separately recorded elements of sound and picture match is called *slating*. In video recording, this generally is not necessary because the audio is recorded directly onto the tape as the picture, but it does provide a means of accurately logging scenes as they are shot. Normally a slate, sometimes called a *clapstick* or *clapboard*, is used for this purpose in motion picture production. The clapboard consists of a piece of wood with a hinged arm that makes a clapping sound when it strikes the bottom portion of the clapboard. This device produces a loud, recorded sound that can be matched to the corresponding visual image of the closing arm (Figure 9.21).

FIGURE 9.21 After both the camera and the recorder have reached speed, a production assistant holds the clapboard in front of the camera. The board contains information indicating the shot and take numbers, director and camera operator's names, and other information critical to the shot. Once speed has been reached, the assistant snaps the clapper shut smartly, creating a sharp, intense sound and a visual record that will be used to sync the film and soundtrack later during the editing process.

In the absence of a clapboard, a person can call out "Slate!" followed by a sharp handclap. If the separate sound and picture tracks are perfectly matched at the beginning of a shot, the editor can be reasonably sure that the entire cable or crystal-sync recorded shot will maintain synchronization. Slating is also used to identify the project title, director, and shot and take numbers during single-camera film or videotape recording. This information is written on the chalkboard surface of the slate or clapstick and is read aloud at the beginning of each camera shot. Thus, each take is fully identified on the film or videotape and the audiotape.

Some film cameras are designed for documentary shooting in situations where the use of a clapboard is impractical. They have an electronic means of providing a reference synchronization point for editing, called an *automatic slate*. At the beginning of each camera take, the first few frames (usually the first eight) of a picture are flashed or fogged with a small light inside the camera, and a signal that is separate from the Pilotone is sent to the tape recorder either by cable, if cable sync is being used, or by radio transmitter, if crystal sync is being used. This signal triggers a clap alarm, which creates an audible tone, known as the *bloop*. The proper flash frame of the picture can then be matched to the bloop at the beginning of the shot for editing synchronization.

Another development in slating is the *electronic clapboard*, which generates a tone that is fed to the camera and recorder and illuminates a continuously running SMPTE timecode visible to the camera and recorded on the edge of the film or on the videotape.

Summary

Understanding the technology that makes audio, video, and film recording possible helps us to obtain better-quality images. Recording media are based on digital, optical, electronic, and photochemical recording processes. Film uses a subtractive mixing process, with cyan, magenta, and yellow filters embedded in different layers of the film to subtract different color wavelengths from a white light source and to thereby produce a variety of colors on a screen. A video camera records and transmits visual images electronically using an additive color process of mixing red, green, and blue light to produce color video.

Videotape and film recording materials are available in a variety of formats. Among helical scan recorders, VHS videotape recorders use ½-inch (8mm) videotape, whereas others use 6.35mm (¼-inch), 8mm (¹⁄₃-inch), 12.5mm (½-inch), or 19mm (¾-inch) videotape. Digital recorders use tape from 6mm to 19mm wide. Super-8mm, 16mm (which includes Super-16mm), 35mm, and 65mm film require different cameras and recording equipment. Some ¼-inch videotape formats, such as DVPro, MiniDV, and DV CAM, reproduce high-quality images, but digital videotape recorders, from D-1 through D-9 and newer formats, provide even higher quality images. Four tape formats specifically designed for high definition are available: D5-HD, based on D-5; D7-HD, based on DVCPro; D9-HD, based on Digital-S; and HDCAM HD, which provides the highest-resolution videotape images. IMAX provides the highest-resolution film images.

The aesthetic use of recorded sounds demands an understanding of recording devices and their selection. Audiotape is available in a variety of formats in terms of tape sizes (widths and thicknesses) and tape enclosures, such as audiocassettes. An analog audiotape recorder converts the electrical audio signal to magnetic pulses stored on magnetic recording material. Digital recordings consist of a series of on-and-off pulses and are less susceptible to recording problems, such as cross-talk, print-through, and fading, than are analog signals which record the entire electrical signal. Tape speed directly affects the amount of tape consumed, and higher speeds generally produce higher-quality recordings. In general, the larger the tape size and the faster the speed, the better the quality of the recorded sound.

Film contains silver halide crystals, which form a latent image when they are exposed to light. These latent images become visible through chemical processing. There are two basic film development processes, negative and reversal, which are analogous to color prints and slides in still photography. Film generally has a wider contrast ratio than video. Some film stocks, such as color negative, can record and differentiate brightness levels that are more than 100 times as bright as the darkest object in a scene, yielding a contrast ratio of 100:1 or 200:1. The maximum contrast ratio in video is usually 30:1 or 50:1.

Film sound and images can be recorded on the same piece of film, which is called single-system sound-on-film (SOF) recording, or they can be recorded on separate sound and picture mechanisms, which is called double-system film sound recording. Double-system recording allows for more editing flexibility than single-system recording. Slating refers to the placement of a common starting point on the picture and sound recordings. It is also used to identify the project title, director, and shot and take numbers during single-camera recording.

EXERCISES

1. Find a CD recording and an audiocassette recording of the same music. Transfer both to a computer audio program, and compare the frequency response and dynamic range. Then compare the two to the original CD recording for the same characteristics.

2. Record the same scene on videotape and film. Then transfer the film to a videotape that has the same format as the originally recorded videotape. Compare the two videotape images in terms of image contrast, hardness and softness, and resolution.

3. Record and view several network television commercials. Try to determine which ones were originally recorded on videotape and which ones were recorded on film and then transferred to videotape. Do some commercials use the apparent contrast and hardness or softness of videotape and film to good effect? When might you prefer to use videotape or film for original recording?

4. Light a still life with subjects of various colors and reflectance values. Using both a film still camera and a digital still camera mounted side-by-side, shoot at least 10 exposures with various f-stop and shutter speeds. (The digital camera has equivalent shutter speeds.) Note the differences in the results.

5. Find at least two recorders that use different videotape formats, one analog, the other digital. Feed the same signal to both. Play back the signal on the same or equivalent monitors to compare the differences.

6. Using the tapes in Exercise 2, dub each tape onto an equivalent recorder, the analog to an analog recorder and the digital to a digital recorder. Then play back on equal monitors and compare the results.

Additional Readings

Alten, Stanley, 2008. Audio in Media, eighth ed. Wadsworth, Belmont, CA.

Ascher, Steven, Pincus, Edward, Keller, Carol, 1999. The Filmmaker's Handbook: A Comprehensive Guide for the Digital Age, Plume, New York.

Baxter, Dennis, 2007. A Practical Guide to Television Sound Engineering, Focal Press, Boston.

Cianci, Philip J., 2007. HDTV and the Transition to Digital Broadcasting: Understanding New Television Technologies, Focal Press, Boston.

Collins, Mike E., 2001. ProTools: Practical Recording, Editing, Mixing for Music Production, Focal Press, Boston.

Crich, Tim, 2005. Recording Tips for Engineers: For Cleaner, Brighter Tracks, Focal Press, Boston.

Hodges, Peter, 2005. An Introduction to Video and Audio Measurement, Focal Press, Boston.

Huber, David Niles, 2001. Modern Recording Techniques, fifth ed. Focal Press, Boston.

Maes, Jan, Vercammen, Marc, 2001. Digital Audio Technology: A Guide to CD, MiniDisc, SACD, DVD(A), MP3, and DAT, Focal Press, Boston.

McDaniel, Drew, et al, 2008. Fundamentals of Audio Production, Allyn & Bacon, Boston.

Moylan, William, 2006. Understanding and Crafting the Mix: The Art of Recording, second ed. Focal Press, Boston.

Rose, Jay, 2008. Producing Great Sound for Film and Video, third ed. Focal Press, Boston.

Rumsey, Francis, McCormick, Tim, 2002. Sound Recording: An Introduction, fourth ed. Focal Press, Boston.

Talbot-Smith, Michael, 2000. Sound Engineer's Pocket Book, Focal Press, Boston.

Watkinson, John, 2002. An Introduction to Digital Audio, second ed. Focal Press, Boston.

Watkinson, John, 2004. The MPEG Handbook, second ed. Focal Press, Boston.

Watkinson, John, 2008. The Art of Digital Audio, fourth ed. Focal Press, Boston.

Weis, Elizabeth, Belton, John, 1985. Film Sound: Theory and Practice, Columbia University Press, New York.

Wooten, Cliff, 2005. A Practical Guide to Video and Audio Compression: From Sprockets and Rasters to Macro Blocks, Focal Press, Boston.

Yewdall, David Rush, 2007. The Practical Art of Motion Picture Sound, third ed. Focal Press, Boston.

Editing 10

- What are the aesthetic approaches of editing?
- What are editing modes?
- How are editing te chniques used in digital productions?
- What techniques are used in mixing sound?
- How does film editing differ from digital editing?

Introduction

The craft of editing consists of selecting, combining, and trimming sounds and visual images after they have been recorded. In the digital age, editing can take place during both production and postproduction. While additional images and sounds are being recorded on location, even at great distances from the postproduction site, editing decisions can be shared between editing and production personnel via the Internet or satellite links. Editing can take place sequentially according to the production schedule or the script, or the editing of different sections or different components of a film or television program, such as sound effects, music, dialogue, and title sequences, can be done simultaneously and in parallel. Just as digital editing technologies are replacing analog technologies, parallel filmmaking and editing is replacing serial postproduction. Utilizing parallel editing techniques, directors and editors can continue to refine their editing decisions up until the last minute (Figure 10.1).

Whether they use parallel or serial techniques, editors need to understand basic terms and concepts that are important aspects of editing as a craft. For example, a film or video editor can trim a continuous recording of visual images, usually called a *shot*, by removing unwanted portions at the beginning or end of the shot. Trimmed shots can then be combined with other shots using various transition devices, such as cuts, fade-outs/fade-ins, or dissolves. A *cut* is a direct, instantaneous transition from one shot to the next. During a fade-out/fade-in, the first shot gradually disappears and is

EDITING PROCESSES

STAGE OF EDITING	MOTION PICTURES	VIDEO OR TELEVISION	AUDIO OR SOUND
PRELIMINARY	Rough cut and final cut of work print	Offline tape or in low-resolution nonlinear program in a computer	Record each source on separate tracks of multitrack recorder or enter each track into a multitrack computer program for nonlinear editing
FINAL	Conform original film to edited workprint or digitally edit in a computer	In high resolution nonlinear program in a computer following the EDL or online of original tape	From multitrack recorder of computer dub to stereo tracks in a computer to final mix for distribution

FIGURE 10.1 The two stages of editing media programs, whether audio, video, or film, follow the same basic pattern. During the preliminary stage, the material is assembled into a tentative order and pattern, and then during the final stage, the editing is completed as the production is trimmed and molded into its final form.

replaced by blackness. This is called a *fade-out*. It is followed by the gradual appearance of the second shot from blackness, which is called a *fade-in*. A *dissolve* consists of a simultaneous or overlapping fade-out of the first shot and a fade-in of the second shot. Unlike a fade-out/fade-in, the image never becomes entirely black during a dissolve. *Transitions* generally imply a change of time or place from one shot to the next. For example, a cut usually implies a very short, if any, temporal change from one shot to the next, whereas a dissolve suggests that some time has elapsed. However, a dissolve generally suggests a shorter passage of time than does a fade-out/fade-in.

Each different type of sound, such as speech, sound effects, and music, can be edited in conjunction with visual images. As noted in Chapter 6, Audio/Sound, sounds can be synchronous or asynchronous, on-screen or off-screen, and parallel or contrapuntal in meaning with respect to accompanying visual images. Separately edited speech, sound effects, and music tracks can be blended or mixed together to form one monaural soundtrack or several stereophonic tracks.

AESTHETIC APPROACHES

The director's aesthetic intentions regarding combinations of images and sounds are fully realized during editing. A good editor is both a practical problem solver, who comes to grips with the limitations of the visual and aural material that the director has provided, and a creative artist, who sometimes reshapes and improves this material through the use of imaginative editing techniques. Visual images and sounds can be combined using principles of editing derived from each of the three aesthetic orientations: realism, modernism, and postmodernism. Sound editing can be a complex process. Realist sound and visual recording, as discussed in Chapter 9, Recording, preserves a feeling of authenticity and accuracy of specific sounds and visual images, whereas realist sound and visual editing preserves a continuity of sounds and images in time and space. Generally speaking, time flows continuously and sequentially from one sound and visual image to the next. There are no apparent gaps or breaks in the audio action. Few editing situations are guided by one perspective alone. It is often effective to combine different approaches.

Realism

Many techniques used in classical fiction and nonfiction editing that preserve an illusion of reality are basically realist in aesthetic approach. Realist editing preserves spatial and temporal continuity from shot-to-shot. A smooth, unbroken flow of actions and events from one shot to the next maintains an illusion of continuity in time and space. A movement begun in one shot is completed in the next. A realist approach maintains the consistent directional placement of objects and movements in the scene by following the 180-degree axis rule, as discussed earlier. Directional glances must be consistent from one shot to the next. Sounds can follow the lead set by visual images, enhancing, filling out, and reinforcing the images they accompany. Realist sounds are usually synchronous, on-screen, and parallel in meaning with the accompanying images. If one person is looking up at another person in a close-up, then a close-up of the latter should show him or her looking down. Point-of-view shots can be an effective means of enhancing realism and intensifying viewer involvement and identification with specific participants in a scene. Even in a documentary, point-of-view shots can create a "You are there!" feeling that adds to the illusion of reality.

Realist editing also involves eliminating mistakes and clarifying and simplifying the message content. Flubbed lines of dialogue or narration are removed and replaced to achieve a proper balance between speech, music, and sound effects. Gaps and omissions in coverage are concealed whenever possible. Some mistakes simply cannot be corrected with the material provided. An editor may need to salvage an acceptable combination of images out of bad material, but sometimes bad material simply has to be reshot by the director or eliminated entirely from the final edited version. Realist editing often follows basic patterns of scene construction. A scene or sequence often begins with an establishing long shot and gradually moves closer to the subject as the action intensifies to reveal more intimate details of character and setting. The overall scene and setting can be reestablished with another long shot at the end of the sequence. A variation on this approach is to begin in close-up to arouse interest and attention, and then gradually use more distant shots to establish the setting and orient the viewer. Initial viewer disorientation is gradually overcome and message clarity is eventually reestablished, while interest is added to the scene. News stories and prerecorded interviews in documentaries are examples of situations that often call for a realist approach to editing. A reporter's or filmmaker's voice-over narration or the responses of an interviewee are often edited to maintain better message clarity and flow.

Modernism

A modernist approach to editing often deliberately disrupts spatial and temporal continuity between shots and sounds and calls attention to the editing process. Jump cuts, radical shifts in time and place, a rejection of conventional rules of scene construction, directionality, and continuity of voices, music, and sound effects all focus the viewer's attention on the manipulative powers of the artist and his or her control of the visual medium. A modernist artist is free to experiment with unusual combinations of shots and sounds without the constraints of logical clarity or realism. But an artist is not totally free of all constraints and structure. Both aesthetic unity and patterned disruptions of unity are achieved through a conscious and precise manipulation of aesthetic forms. Modernist sound editing often develops sound as an independent aesthetic element. Continuity of time and space are sometimes disrupted. Sounds may be asynchronous or contrapuntal with respect to accompanying visual images, and the audience frequently experiences the thoughts and feelings of the film or video artist, a fictional character in the story, or a social actor within a nonfiction work. In short, modernist techniques develop subjective impressions. Sound effects, for example, can create imaginative impressions of what a character is feeling, thinking, or experiencing rather than an illusion of objective reality or authenticity. The pace and meaning of music can contrast with or counterpoint the accompanying visuals, such as when slow-paced music accompanies rapidly paced visual action. The editor freely develops abstract audio relations and qualities. The sound in the films of Alfred Hitchcock is a good example of modernist sound editing within generally realist films.

Modernist approaches to editing often focus on abstract qualities and elements of design within and between shots, such as similarities and differences in shape, color, movement, and texture. Sharp diagonal lines can be juxtaposed with smooth curves and circular shapes. Visual rhythms can be established between shots that are related to audio rhythms in music and sound effects, for example. Modernist approaches to editing are often incorporated into specific sequences within more conventionally realist programming. Transition devices, such as a dissolve from one scene to the next, can rely on similarities in shape and color between the last shot of one scene and the first shot of the next. Deliberate breaks in temporal and spatial continuity can generate visual interest through temporary viewer disorientation in a more conventional work of fiction or nonfiction.

Postmodernism

A postmodernist approach to editing can take the form of a collage or pastiche that combines diverse images and sounds and modes of production. Postmodernist sound editing, for example, offers a pastiche of audio impressions, often mixing documentary, narrative fiction, and experimental modes. Documentary and fiction approaches to editing can be combined within a single scene. A dramatic enactment can be staged as a direct cinema interview, as in Mitch Block's *No Lies* (1974), or as a cinema vérité documentary about past or even future events, as in Peter Watkins' *Culloden* (1965) and *The War Game* (1966). A documentary, such as Errol Morris's *The Thin Blue Line* (1987), can edit together reenactments of events that occurred in the imaginations of different interviewees and witnesses. Hollywood feature films, such as *JFK* (1991) and *Forrest Gump* (1994), can edit historical documents, such as the Zapruder film of John F. Kennedy's actual assassination, together with an imaginatively staged fictional drama, or in the case of the latter film, can digitally manipulate the image to place a fictional character within the frame of documentary images.

In addition to mixing modes and editing techniques, a postmodernist approach to editing can actively engage the viewer/listener in the process of constructing the art-work. For example, an interactive multimedia production, such as *Explora 1: Peter Gabriel's Secret World* (1993), can allow the spectator to control the audio mixing or editing of various channels of his music within certain parameters determined by the project designer and computer programmers. A postmodernist approach to editing can highlight the performative and ephemeral aspects of a media production rather than the completion of a permanent, perfected text and work of art. It also encourages the participation of the spectator in the artistic process, rather than reinforcing the controlling presence of the individual artist (modernism) or the artist's transmission and preservation of the natural world or an illusion of a continuous reality (realism).

This chapter explores a variety of audio editing techniques, some of which reflect postmodernist, modernist, or realist aesthetics that are applicable to digital nonlinear, videotape, magnetic film, and audiotape editing technologies.

EDITING MODES
Fiction

Classical Hollywood conventions for shooting and editing fiction films and videos include master-scene shooting and continuity editing. A *master shot* consists of a rel-atively long duration shot that includes most of the action in a specific scene, usually recorded from a medium- to long-range camera distance with accompanying estab-lishing audio or mood music. Shooting a master shot allows the actors to achieve some degree of continuity in their performance before the action is broken up into shorter-duration shots with the camera closer to the actors. A master shot provides an editor with continuous coverage of the action. Closer shots can then be inserted into the master shot to intensify the action by revealing a character's facial expres-sions and gestures. For example, when two characters are talking to one another in a scene, alternating over-the-shoulder, shot/reverse shot close-ups of the two charac-ters (see Chapter 5, Directing: Aesthetic Principles and Production Coordination) are often inserted into the master shot so that their actions and reactions can be seen more clearly (Figure 10.2). The dialogue of each character generally matches the shot of the person speaking unless a reaction to the shot is expected.

Continuity editing refers to an editing system that developed in Hollywood and else-where beginning about 1910. It consists of a number of shooting and editing conven-tions that sustain an illusion of continuous time and place within a scene. For example, maintaining the 180-degree action axis or consistent screen direction from one shot to the next sustains the illusion of spatial and temporal continuity (see Chapter 5, Directing: Aesthetic Principles and Production Coordination). If a character moves from left to right in shot A but from right to left in shot B, he or she will appear to have dramatically changed direction without any passage of time. This may be perceived as a *jump cut*, that is, a mismatch in spatial continuity suggesting that a gap in time has occurred. When no mismatch in action or gap in time is apparent over a cut from one shot to the next, this is called a *match cut*. The sound also should match the shot to maintain continuity.

An editor must also be conscious of *eyeline matches*, that is, maintaining directional continuity in terms of characters' looks and glances within a scene. If one character looks screen left in shot A followed by another character looking screen right in shot B,

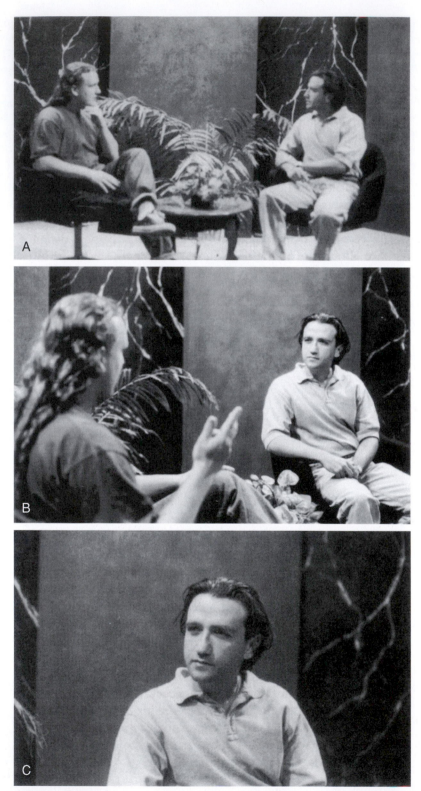

FIGURE 10.2 (A–C) The standard shot series in a scene starts with a long shot establishing relationships and positioning in the environment. A tighter medium shot brings the performers closer. A close-up will concentrate the audience's attention on a specific performer.

they will appear to be looking at (and perhaps talking to) one another. A common variation on the eyeline match is called a *point-of-view shot*. Here the editor cuts from one character looking in a particular direction to a shot of what the character is looking at from the character's approximate (usually over-the-shoulder) spatial position in the scene. Cutting back to a close-up of a character who has been looking at something in order to see his or her facial expression is sometimes called a *reaction shot*. Point-of-view and reaction shots not only maintain directional continuity; they can also enhance viewer identification with specific characters' points of view.

Sound levels and ambiance should match the shot—close mic for close-ups (CUs), some room noise for medium shot (MS) and medium long shot (MLS), and obvious reverberation for long shot (LS) and extreme long shots (XLS). The specific timbre of the sound should match the environment of the scene and individual shots.

Nonfiction

Partially or completely staged scenes in nonfiction productions sometimes rely on the master scene and continuity techniques used in fiction. Variations on these techniques have also been developed that take into account the difficulties of scripting and staging nonfiction events as well as the use of expository and rhetorical structures that can disrupt spatial and temporal continuity. A variation on master scene shooting and editing that is commonly used in news and documentary production, for example, is called *A and B roll editing*. "Talking head" interviews constitute the A roll (equivalent to the master shot), whereas additional recordings of various activities and events that illustrate what the interviewee is talking about constitute the B roll (equivalent to the inserts). The editor inserts B-roll material into the A roll, as the interviewee continues to be heard on one of the audio tracks. A- and B-roll editing adds viewer interest by interspersing rather static shots of a talking head with a wide variety of visual illustrations.

Master scene techniques can also be simulated during the editing of the interview itself. If the camera-to-subject distance or type of shot (long shot, close-up, and so on) varies through the manipulation of a dolly or zoom lens during the recording of the interview, an editor can sometimes change the order in which the interview statements were made by cutting directly from long shot to close-up, such as when a particularly revealing statement is about to be made, to intensify the impact. In this way, the basic effect of master scene shooting can be simulated during the editing process by cutting and reorganizing continuously recorded interviews. Viewer interest can be intensified further by then adding illustration materials. Similar techniques are often used with voiceover narration. Either the narration audio is edited first and then images illustrating the narrator's statements are added later, or the visuals are edited first and narration, which explains or complements the visuals, is edited and inserted later.

EDITING WORKFLOW

A change in the editing brought about by the move to digital processes has allowed different methods of taking advantage of those digital systems. Not only has the equipment used to edit visuals, audio, and graphics become much less expensive, but also, and more important, it is less complicated to use, allowing a wider range of people to learn to use the applications to edit their own and others' projects. The two major factors have been the tremendous increase in available memory at reasonable cost and the ability to move data rapidly and over multiaccess routes. Such a system also protects against loss of important data and frees creative staff to concentrate on production content instead of production processes. Multiple terabyte (TB) memory banks, internal memory systems in CPUs, and external servers have made the storage and handling of large quantities of data possible. In addition, Ethernet, wireless, and other data moving systems make local area networks (LAN) the basis for multi-user systems, allowing data to be moved among many workstations, monitors and storage media at will and at a reasonable cost. Instantaneous access to all aspects of a project while in process allows supervision on several levels without interference with the process and at the same time allows more than one editor to work on the same project simultaneously while viewing each other's individual work and the work as it is accumulated in its final form (Figure 10.3).

A method of utilizing these advantages developed over time, which is called workflow by the media industry. This title may be attached to several different methods of making media production more efficient; however, for this chapter the description applies to the entire production process but concentrates on postproduction steps. In this chapter, the process is described as a six-step process beginning with the most important step, planning, then moving through the acquiring of data, ingesting into the system, editing, finishing, and finally moving the final project to an output.

Planning

Despite the efficiency of the workflow system and of digital processes in general, much time and effort may be saved with clear planning on exactly how the process will move forward. Any plan must be made with the knowledge that the plan may be modified as alterations become obvious, but the more thoughtful the plan is to begin with, the fewer occasions you will need to make changes as the process moves forward. A thorough study of the script as well as carefully considered modifications made in the script while shooting, recording, or during preliminary storyboarding will lay the groundwork for a viable and practical plan.

Acquisition

Data may be accumulated as raw digital data, from either digital or analog videotape or audio tape, film, computer output, or from computer drive, solid-state, optical, or magnetic storage devices. Hand-drawn art, graphics, or photographs also may be acquired as analog inputs.

With the capabilities of converting any visual or audio source to a usable digital format, no restriction should be placed on the possible source of items to be used in a project. Of course, legal considerations also must be considered. The rights to any material not created by the producer must be cleared and paid for before even considering its use in a production.

Ingest

Again, the term *ingest* has several meanings and uses in different aspects of the media and the business world. In this consideration, the term includes analyzing and converting all media to a common format for further processing. The terms *ingest* and *capture* often are used interchangeably. Ingest usually means the clip has been processed within the camera via a specific code and then stored on a card such as P2 or SxS in a computer-readable form ready to be copied direct to a computer for editing. Capturing means the computer program must process video from a camera before

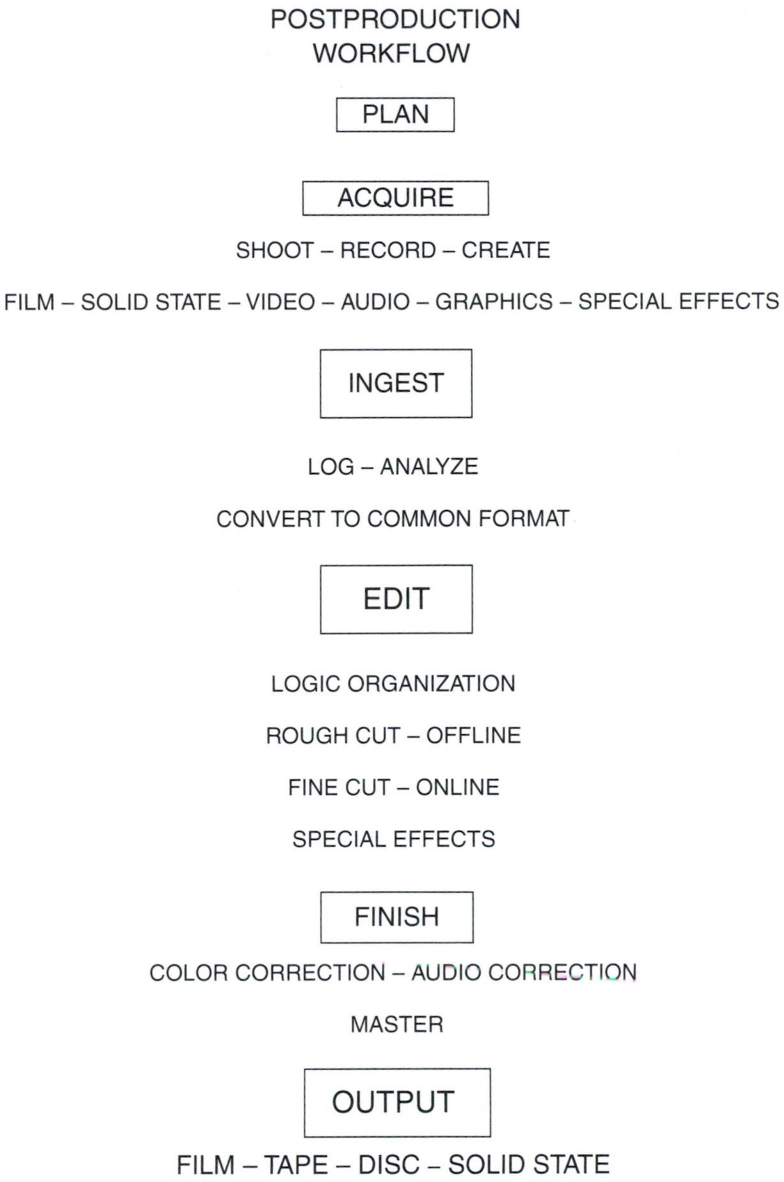

POSTPRODUCTION
WORKFLOW

PLAN

ACQUIRE

SHOOT – RECORD – CREATE

FILM – SOLID STATE – VIDEO – AUDIO – GRAPHICS – SPECIAL EFFECTS

INGEST

LOG – ANALYZE

CONVERT TO COMMON FORMAT

EDIT

LOGIC ORGANIZATION

ROUGH CUT – OFFLINE

FINE CUT – ONLINE

SPECIAL EFFECTS

FINISH

COLOR CORRECTION – AUDIO CORRECTION

MASTER

OUTPUT

FILM – TAPE – DISC – SOLID STATE

FIGURE 10.3 The workflow may be analyzed as a six-step process from planning to a final output. Each step contributes to the process without interfering in any other step while continuing the flow of data and creative effort from the beginning to the final product.

it can be imported to an editing program. Once all other material is gathered, then the next step in regard to the source, level of quality, or type of electronic or physical format is to preview and accurately log all material. It is important to determine the usability of each take, each frame, and each sequence, and precisely log the length, in and out cues, and location of the material on which the media are stored. Using timecode to accurately determine the location of such material is important. Make certain the timecode is consistent, either in real time or in drop-frame timecode. The individual shot and take numbers recorded from the slate at the beginning of each camera take are cataloged or "logged." Timecode or control-track numbers are often logged at this time as well. The editor makes notations to the log, indicating particularly useful or problematic shots and camera takes. These notations are often extremely useful.

> Workflow thus refers to the various technologies and processes used to acquire, ingest, and edit video and audio recordings. Workflows can be quite simple or extremely complicated. For example, acquiring video and audio information on a standard definition camera with a hard drive as Audio video interleaved files (AVI) files, which are then easily copied to a computer hard drive for editing and output as AVI files, is a relatively simple workflow. On the other hand, acquiring film or high-definition images recorded at 24 frames per second (24P or progressive scan in high definition [HD]) and then editing these images at 30 frames per second with 3:2 pull down (three frames of video for every two frames of originally recorded film or 24P video) before returning to 24 frames per second of 24P HD is a relatively complicated workflow for your project. Selecting the best workflow for your project ensures that you undertake the most efficient process that will also result in the highest quality edited project in the proper final format.

Editing Log

A production's editing log can be kept by either the director or production continuity clerk. The log indicates the precise location of takes, the description of the shot, and a judgment or notation of the take so that the editor will have some guidance as to which takes to consider using during the editing process, regardless of what technology and techniques are used to perform visual editing.

Timecode

A *timecode* is a series of digits that provides an exact reference for each frame. One of the most widely used timecodes has been standardized as the Society of Motion Pictures and Television Engineers (SMPTE) timecode. It is sometimes added to one of the tracks of the originally recorded videotape, or it is recorded during the vertical intervals between video fields. It consists of an eight-digit series of numbers beginning either with zero (called *zero start*) or with actual clock time in hours, minutes, seconds, and fields (60 per second). Thus, 01:00:00:01 indicates a point one hour and one field into the recording. Separate cassettes or reels of videotape can be differentiated by hours: 01, 02, and so on. The SMPTE timecode system requires a special generator and reader. The timecode can actually be viewed in the video image as a "burn-in" timecode, which can be helpful during offline editing to make editing notations, especially when using machines that cannot otherwise read the code, because the code is actually recorded in the picture area of the videotape.

Because the files are dubbed to a server, any editing is accomplished by using files withdrawn from the server. The files withdrawn are not the actual files in the server but copies called *virtual files*. Virtual files are used throughout the editing process without damaging or destroying the original files stored in the server. This means any number of experimental edits can be made with the virtual files without affecting the stored files in the server.

Once the material is well studied and a determination can be made of which files will be used, they are converted to a common format preferably at the highest level of the intended final project's distribution plan. Although most nonlinear editing applications can handle both standard definition (SD) and high-definition (HD) files simultaneously, it is best to use files that have been converted to the best common format to work with for the remainder of the project.

Compression

The conversion should be accomplished without using any (or an absolute minimum amount of) compression. Although these files will not be the final files used (the ones in the server will be used), to be able to make judgments on the quality of the material used, avoid compression wherever possible. This is especially true when moving the original files to the storage server; always avoid compression in any stage unless absolutely necessary especially if there are going to be several stages where compression may be required for distribution. Compression is necessary because of the large amount of bandwidth needed, especially for HD video files.

Computer storage units range from bits to gigabytes. A *bit* is the smallest amount of information a computer can handle. Eight bits make up a *byte*, 1,000 bytes equal a *kilobyte* (KB), 1,000 KB equal a *megabyte* (MB), and 1,000 MB equal a *gigabyte* (GB). It takes slightly less than 1 MB to store just one full frame of video information, depending on the compression ratio of the digitizing system. A full frame of standard definition digital video consists of 720 pixels horizontal by 480 pixels vertical, or a total of 345,600 pixels (720 × 480) multiplied by 24 bits of color (345,600 × 24 = 8,294,400 bits/8 bits per byte = 1,036,800 bytes or approximately 1 MB per frame) (Figure 10.4).

DIGITAL MEASUREMENTS

bit = 1/8 byte   8 bits = 1 byte

byte = 1/1,000 kilobyte (KB)   1,000 bytes = 1 KB

KB = 1/1,000 megabyte (MB)   1,000 KB = 1 MB

MB = 1/1,000 gigabyte (GB)   1,000 MB = 1 GB

GB = 1/1,000 terabyte   1,000 GB = 1 TB

Video frame requires nearly 1 MB

Pixel = smallest element of a picture

Video frame = 640 horizontal pixels × 480 vertical pixels = 307,200 pixels

Color video frame = 307,200 pixels × 24 bits of color = 7,372,800 bites or 921,600 bytes

1 second of video = 30 frames = 28 MB of memory

1 minute of video = 1,680 MB or 1.68 GB of memory

60 minutes of video = 100 GB of memory

Most consumer computer hard drives are limited to less than 1 GB of memory.

Professional computers require increased amounts of memory for nonlinear editing.

Both consumer and professional systems use some form of compression to reduce the amount of memory required for processing and editing.

FIGURE 10.4 The relationships between the measurements of the digital world are all based on the metric system. The amount of memory required for a specific amount of video or film depends on the compression system used. The amount of memory available in computers increases continually even as the prices continue to drop.

Digitizing audio, like digitizing video, requires considerable time and disk space. Audio can be digitized at the time of its original recording, using a separate digital audio-tape (DAT), disc recorder, or solid-state device, or an analog recording can be rapidly sampled and digitized during postproduction, either in conjunction with or separate from visual images. Unless the original recording has been digitized in a format that is computer readable, placing the audio information on a hard disk will generally take as long as the real-time duration of the original recording. The sampling rate and bandwidth of an audio signal can be varied during digitization to reduce the amount of storage space that is required. There are two steps to digitizing audio: setting the audio level controls and setting the audio resolution or quality. Setting the audio level controls avoids distortion and ensures a high signal-to-noise ratio in digital audio, just as it does in analog audio.

The quality of digitized audio and the size of the audio file also depend on the sampling rate and bit depth of the audio. The sampling rate for audio is similar to the frame rate for digitizing video. It measures the number of frequencies into which the sound is broken. The bit depth, which is similar to color depth in visuals, measures the number of tones per sample. A high sampling rate stores and reproduces very high quality sound. The higher the sampling rate and bit depth, the better the sound quality. Audio sampled at 22 kHz (kilohertz) (that is, at 22,000 cycles per second) and 8-bit resolution (8 bits equal 1 byte of computer information and storage) may be sufficient for monophonic speech and sound effects, but a sampling rate of 44 kHz and 16-bit resolution is probably the minimum required for stereo sound and music, which will require about twice the disk storage space.

During digitization, each NTSC standard definition analog video frame, which consists of two interlaced scanning fields that add up to 525 scan lines, is converted to a frame of 720 × 480 pixels that can be displayed in a noninterlaced mode on a computer monitor. As mentioned in Chapter 7, Lighting and Design, there are almost 30 (actually 29.97) video frames in each second of NTSC video, so it requires about 30 MB to store just one second of full-frame (720 × 480 pixels at 24-bit color), full-motion (30 frames per second) video. Consequently, just one minute of full-frame, full-motion video would require a storage capacity of 60 (seconds) × 30 MB, or about 1,800 MB (or 1.8 GB), which is a significant amount of storage space. Sixty minutes of full-frame, full-motion video would require a whopping 100 GB of storage space if the material is not compressed first. Most home computers have internal hard disk drives that provide 50 to 250 GB of storage space, and most professional editing systems use a 1+ TB hard disk drive. Obviously, even in the case of relatively large-capacity hard disk drives, some way to reduce the amount of storage space is usually required, especially for editing longer-duration projects.

The most common forms of storage space reduction used in digital nonlinear editing are compression, frame-size reduction, and frame-rate reduction. *Compression* refers to a reduction of the volume of information in order to force it into less storage space. Basically compression reduces the amount of information that must be stored in an individual frame, still image, or soundtrack by ignoring some pixel and color or redundant sound information during storage and then duplicating adjacent pixels and colors when the image is played back. Compression can also be achieved in motion video by storing only the pixels and colors and sound that change from one frame to the next and then duplicating stationary pixels and colors in subsequent frames during playback.

The volume of information can be reduced in still or motion images by using hardware and software compression, such as Joint Photographic Experts Group (JPEG) and Moving Picture Experts Group (MPEG). JPEG uses intraframe (within a single frame) compression to reduce the volume of information for each frame of video independently of every other frame and is frequently used for still photographs, but it can also be used for motion. MPEG is used exclusively for motion images because it involves both intraframe and interframe (between successive frames) compression. JPEG and MPEG compression are all applicable to digital nonlinear editing. As in videotape format changes, MPEG has been improved and there are now several new versions, including MPEG-2 and MPEG-4. MPEG-2 was created as an editing compression scheme, but it included some unwanted artifacts that have been corrected in MPEG-4.

Compression is usually indicated in terms of ratios, such as 2:1, 10:1, or 15:1. If it requires 1,800 MB of space to store a minute of full-frame, full-motion video, then a 2:1 compression ratio would require 900 MB of storage space, a 10:1 compression ratio would require 180 MB of storage space, and a 15:1 compression ratio would need only 120 MB of storage space. Why not use a 15:1 compression ratio all the time? The answer, of course, is that the quality of the images usually deteriorates as the compression ratio increases. The best compression—that is, the one that results in the least reduction in the quality of images—is usually achieved through a combination of hardware and software compression rather than through software compression alone.

Saving Space via Compression

One minute of full-motion video	=	1,800 MB
Compression	=	Space
None	=	1,800 MB
2:1	=	900 MB
10:1	=	180 MB
15:1	=	120 MB

Storage space can also be reduced by reducing the image quality, frame size, and frame rates of digitized images. For example, instead of editing full-frame video (720 × 480 pixels), an editor can work with quarter-frame images (160 × 120 pixels). At some point, reductions in frame size begin to affect image clarity and visibility. For example, it may be difficult for an editor to see clearly when the frame size of video images has been reduced from 720 × 480 to 180 × 120 pixels, or when images have been compressed by a 15:1 ratio. By the same token, a frame rate of 15 frames per second requires half the storage space as a frame rate of 30 frames per second, but again, the images may seem to flicker or strobe at reduced frame rates, such as when motion video is digitized at 10 or 15 frames per second. So an editor must decide what compression ratio, frame size, and frame rate she or he finds most comfortable and effective while working within the storage capacity limitation of a particular nonlinear editing system. An editor should also allow considerable time to digitize images, because images are frequently digitized in real time; in other words, it takes as much time to digitize images as the duration of the original recordings, and in some cases it takes more time.

Once compression factors have been determined, all files required for the project are downloaded onto the hard drive or external memory drive of the computer housing the nonlinear editing application. A check before downloading needs to be made to determine if enough memory is available to perform the editing process on the computer. Two types of memory need to be considered: random access memory (RAM) and storage memory; also important is the speed of the operating system. A 2-gigahertz (GHz) system is generally adequate, as is 800 MB+ of RAM memory and a 500 GB+ internal or external hard drive for storage. The RAM memory is used temporarily during the editing process and disappears when the computer is turned off (Figure 10.5).

Digital audio, unlike digital video, is not usually compressed when it is digitized, because digitized audio already requires considerably less storage space than digitized video, and audio compression could significantly reduce the quality of the audio signal. *Compression* in audio has two meanings: (1) compression refers to a reduction of the volume of information in order to force it into less storage space, and (2) compression prevents distortion during recording by, for example, reducing the loudness range of a singer who alternately sings very loudly and very softly. Compression in the second sense is rarely used while digitizing audio that was originally recorded as an analog signal, however.

Editing

As in organizing the entire workflow by reviewing scripts and written material before actually cutting and assembling clips in the editing project, a written equivalent of what the expected project will be will make the process more efficient and more creative in the long run.

One of the best uses of a cataloged list of the individual shots and camera takes that were recorded during production or during the logging process is for the editor to perform a paper edit. During a paper edit, an editor simulates the editing process on paper by cutting out each individual shot in a log and placing these shots

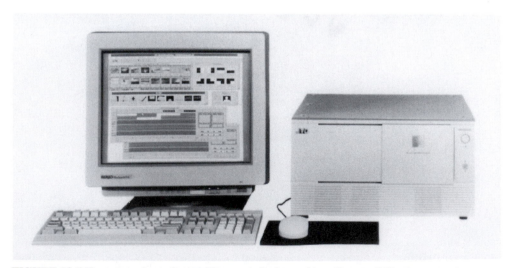

FIGURE 10.5 The screen of a nonlinear editor reveals the types of transitions available, the segments available to edit, the sound in visual form, timecode information, and running times of the production. Depending on the brand and model of editor, other characteristics of controls also may be visible on the screen. (Courtesy of Apple Computer.)

in the anticipated sequential order of the completed project. A paper edit can also be accomplished using written transcriptions of interviews with accompanying time-code numbers from the original videotapes in a documentary. Performing a paper edit is an effective method of determining whether or not there is sufficient coverage to complete the editing process. It is also an efficient and economical means of manipulating the overall structure of a media production on paper without incurring the expense and labor of actually editing the recorded images themselves. Documentary editors, who rarely have access to an extremely detailed script as a guide to postproduction, often rely on a paper edit to help them organize the editing process (Figure 10.6).

Digital nonlinear editing software offers several advantages over conventional means of editing film, audiotape, and videotape, including increased flexibility or creativity, as well as potential time and cost savings. A common cliché is that digital nonlinear editing is the equivalent of word processing and desktop publishing for audio, film, graphics, and video postproduction. The analogy holds for many aspects of editing that are shared by word processing and various digital nonlinear editing software programs. For example, most word processing software allows a writer to cut, copy, paste, and delete words, paragraphs, and pages of text. Digital nonlinear editing affords an editor similar flexibility in terms of instantaneously changing the order and duration of sounds and images. For example, clips of video or audio information can be cut, trimmed, copied, pasted, inserted, and deleted along a timeline (Figure 10.7).

A *clip* is usually the smallest unit of digital video (or audio) information that can be stored and manipulated during editing. It can range from just one frame to an entire movie in duration, but it often consists of a single shot, that is, a continuous camera recording or take. Digitized clips are usually imported (or copied) into a particular editing project file, where they are edited along a timeline with other images and sounds. Most editing software provides several windows or screens, including a project window, a timeline (or construction) window, a trimming window, a transition window, and a locking window. Different windows can usually be displayed simultaneously on one or more computer monitors. A *project window* usually contains the individual clips in alphabetical order based on the first letters of their written descriptions.

EDIT DECISION LIST (EDL)

EDIT#	REEL	DESCRIPTION	VIDEO IN/OUT	AUDIO IN/OUT	TRANSITION
001	3	WS-Ext	00:06:00:20 00:06:02:16	00:06:01:10 00:06:15:04	FI
002	3	MS-Ext	00:00:03:16 00:00:11:04		C
003	5	CU	00:10:02:15 00:11:29:05	00:10:02:15 00:11:29:05	D
004	2	CU	00:19:03:10 00:20:10:28	00:19:03:10 00:20:10:28	D

FIGURE 10.6 An edit decision list (EDL) is a precise listing (usually assembled on a computer) of each edit: its start point and end point, transition, and any special effects or differences in audio and video edit points. This becomes, in essence, a paper edit to be followed by the final edit, once the paper edit has organized the clips in a logical order (considering they may have been shot, recorded, or drawn out of order).

FIGURE 10.7 A nonlinear editing station consists of a computer for viewing and hearing the material being edited and for storing and manipulating the footage. The footage is not actually cut and spliced but is stored in the computer's memory in the order determined by the editor. Changes may be made quickly, easily, and many times over without damaging the original footage. Once the final edits are satisfactory, the final production can be fed out to either film or videotape for distribution. (Courtesy of Scitex Digital Video.)

The *timeline* or *construction window* displays a timeline that contains several video, audio, transition, and superimposition or special effects tracks and indicates the overall duration and order of the edited project. The *viewing window* allows you to view and set the in and out (beginning and ending) points for each clip. The *trimming window* is used for cutting directly (e.g., a straight cut) from one clip to the next. It usually displays the adjoining frames at the cut point between the two clips, allowing the editor to trim off video frames or add additional video frames from one or both clips on the timeline. A *transition window* displays dissolves and wipes that can be dragged or copied into the transition track of the timeline window wherever two separate video tracks overlap and a transition (other than a straight cut) from the first to the second clip is needed. Finally, a *locking window* allows the editor to lock together or unlock various visual and audio tracks in the timeline window, so that they can be cut and trimmed collectively or individually. Images from each motion video clip are often displayed as a series of representative still frames along the timeline, whereas audio is often displayed visually as a continuous, variable area soundtrack, where high peaks represent loud sounds and rapid fluctuations indicate high-frequency sounds. Clips can be copied and inserted at various points along the timeline, and they can also be deleted from the timeline and the remaining images and sounds attached to one another. Motion video and still-frame clips can also be placed in preliminary order using a storyboard display that presents one frame from each clip. A storyboard allows an editor to place the clips in rough sequential order before trimming precise cut points and adding various transition devices in the timeline window.

Every edit made using a digital nonlinear software program is a virtual edit. No digitized material is discarded when clips are trimmed, cut, or deleted along an editing timeline, because each clip is stored separately outside the timeline window. The timeline is in essence an edit decision list (EDL), which is, as noted earlier, a listing of all of the shots' in and out cues, durations, transitions, and audio cues. When the project is rendered to either a digital or analog output, the completed sequence will be created from the original digital source material. Every clip stored on a disk drive is instantaneously accessible in its entirety and can be grabbed in the project or clip window and reinserted at any point along the timeline. Many alternative versions of a scene or sequence can thus be quickly edited and examined without prematurely eliminating material that may be needed later. Transitions from one shot to another can be previewed, as can the superimposition of titles and various digital video effects without ever actually cutting, discarding, eliminating, or deleting any originally digitized video or audio. The ability to manipulate clips of video and sound along a timeline not only adds flexibility to the editing process, but it can also make editing more efficient and cost-effective. Clips can be rapidly trimmed, cut, inserted, and deleted. Digital nonlinear editing is extremely fast compared to physically cutting and splicing a conventional feature film; for example, and the time it takes to find and insert videotape images and sounds from a source onto a master videotape can be reduced dramatically by using instantaneously accessible digital clips along a timeline. The amount of time scheduled for postproduction editing can be diminished significantly, facilitating the editing of projects that require a short turnaround time, such as topical news magazine segments and minidocumentaries. Increased editing efficiency can also translate into cost savings that will affect the overall budget of longer-term projects, when an editor's time and salary can be reduced. Clearly, digital nonlinear editing offers a number of advantages in terms of flexibility and efficiency over conventional videotape, audiotape, and film editing.

Audio is often displayed visually as a continuous, variable area soundtrack, where high peaks represent loud sounds and rapid fluctuations indicate high-frequency sounds. Clips can be copied and inserted at various points along the timeline, and they can be cut, trimmed, and split into several clips as well as deleted from the timeline, leaving the remaining sounds attached to one another. The overall volume of a clip can usually be increased or decreased by adjusting an accompanying volume-control band. Fade-outs, fade-ins, and cross-fades can be created by adjusting the volume band,

and sounds can be increased or decreased at will throughout the clip, such as to bring a music track down and under a voice track. Rapid fade-ins and fade-outs of audio clips at cut points from one audio track to another often help to hide digital "popping" sounds, or digital noise, which is sometimes audible at cut points. (Some digital editing systems have programs that facilitate the elimination of digital popping sounds in this manner.) Clips can also be filtered, that is, the entire clip can have its frequency response altered. The high-frequency sounds can be reduced and the low-frequency sounds increased in intensity, for example. The reverberation or attack and decay of a sound clip can also be altered to enhance or diminish echo (Figure 10.8).

Digital nonlinear audio editing offers a number of advantages over analog editing. First, the quality of digital audio does not significantly diminish from one generation to the next, because the binary encoding of audio signals generally allows an editor to maintain a consistent signal-to-noise ratio throughout the editing process. Second, multiple audio tracks can be edited independently or in conjunction with one another. Third, most nonlinear editing programs provide a visual image of a soundtrack, which indicates fluctuations in loudness and pitch and allows the editor to quickly and easily find and mark precise edit points, such as the beginning or end of specific sounds.

FIGURE 10.8 The screen on a computer running a digital audio editing program shows what the sounds look like in various formats. When editing, an audio editor visually cuts, pastes, and modifies the virtual files as if they were a part of a word processing file.

Fourth, digital audio can be initially edited in conjunction with visual images, using a relatively simple editing program, and then the same audio can be fine-tuned independently using a separate, more sophisticated audio editing program before it is recombined with the visuals again. Because a digital nonlinear edited soundtrack can maintain exact synchronization with accompanying videotape or film images by using SMPTE timecode or film KeyKode as common reference points, it provides considerable editing flexibility. Digital film sound editing may require specialized software that maintains synchronization between the original film, which is usually recorded at 24 frames per second, and various soundtracks, including the originally recorded synchronous sound. This software or slave system resolves the audio playback to timecode, which can maintain synchronization with the original film. Achieving accurate lock to timecode allows a film sound editor to benefit from all the advantages of digital sound editing without losing synchronization between the originally recorded film and sound, when the final visual editing will be completed on film, such as for a Hollywood feature film.

The presence of the switcher, a video synthesizer, a special effects generator (SEG), or a digital video effect (DVE) in a computerized editing system allows many different special effects to be created. A variety of wipes, fades, dissolves, and key effects can be accomplished automatically on a postproduction switcher. A video synthesizer can manipulate an analog video in ways that are similar to digital effects generated by a DVE. That is, it can convert the component parts of a video signal, such as each color, into separate electrical signals that can be modified by a computer programmer. The height, width, depth, shape, clarity, or position of an image can be changed by turning a dial or flipping a switch. *Solarization* is a technique that relies on a separation between luminance and chrominance information in a video signal. The color can be drained out of the image to produce a high-contrast black-and-white image, which can then be synthetically colored by assigning different colors to different shades of gray.

It is possible to create a wide variety of special effects using digital devices, such as a DVE or a digital video manipulator (DVM). An image or full frame can be continuously compressed to a point of light. It can be expanded, stretched, freeze-framed, pushed off or on, made into an abstract painting-like image, and replicated as multiple images on a screen. The DVE or DVM can also be connected to the video switcher to create automatic chroma key tracking in which the size of the chroma key window can be automatically shaped and positioned. The inserted picture can be proportionately compressed and expanded to fill the window more efficiently and realistically than can conventional chroma key, especially when the main signal camera is tracking or moving, and thereby changing chroma key perspective. These kinds of digital effects can provide an editor with tremendous flexibility in terms of image manipulation during online editing (Figure 10.9).

A complete project that has been assembled from beginning to end is called a rough cut. Previously, a videotape edit was performed on a low-level videotape stock first, then called an offline cut. Later it was finished if the offline was found to be acceptable using the highest quality tape and was called an online cut. In digital editing, the offline-online method is no longer needed because changes can be made easily any point during the editing process until a finished project is approved. The final cut in digital editing is called the fine cut. To achieve the fine cut, additional shots such as cut-ways, cut-ins, and added transitions are made, along with adding the necessary music, sound effects, and special visual effects.

FIGURE 10.9 A digital effects generator creates a variety of effects not possible with an analog switcher or effects generator. A few of the possible effects are visible on the screen. (Courtesy of Sony Corporation.)

Finishing

In both video and film productions, the precise color balance within and between shots is completed after the fine cut has been made. The process is called color correction and is performed by a skilled technician on specialized digital equipment. Color correction may be done by the editor during the editing process while she or he is selecting and assembling shots, but it is better done after the program has reached a finished stage—the final audio equalization, level correction and preparation for synchronizing with the visual if that is part of the project.

During this stage, one of the advantages of the workflow process becomes apparent as all of the work is viewable at any time by producers or clients viewing the output of the computer(s) on a local area network (LAN) in their office located in the same building, across town, across the country, or even around the world. At the same time, the complexity of editing game programs, animation, and feature films using many special effects shots requires a staff of people, each an expert in his or her own field, working simultaneously on the same project. They all can view the work in progress, add their portion, and confirm the progress, as the workflow emphasizes the simultaneous collaborative creative process.

Output

The final stage of workflow is sending the signal to intended destination. That may be a live broadcast on television, cable, satellite, or as a streaming signal on the web. More commonly the signal will be stored on a medium for later use. It may be stored as a raw digital data, as a high-quality video and audio signal on a digital tape deck like D-1, on a lower-quality and higher-compression medium like a DAT, on disc, or on a hard drive solid-state storage medium. The project also may be converted to motion picture film for the longest archival life for storage because film will outlast any magnetic or optical medium now in production. Whatever the medium, care needs to be taken to make certain that the transfer is at the highest quality level as possible, even if immediate playback is scheduled to be on a low-level SD or mobile distribution system. Once lowered without compression, the quality lost cannot be regained. If the original production was shot on film, converted to a digital signal for postproduction, and then returned to a film format, the same rules hold true for maintaining the highest quality in each step of the transfer.

EDITING DIGITAL AUDIO
Synchronizing Sound Sources

One of the problems facing sound editors is to manage more than one audio track at a time and to keep them in sync if needed. There are two means of maintaining synchronization between one or more soundtracks originating at the same or different times. The technique used with either system is basically the same: one uses digital or analog audiotape and the other uses the ability of a sound application within a computer to record and process sound inputs individually or in groups. Multitrack audiotape recorders allow the sounds recorded on one track to be played at the precise speed at which the original recording was made while additional sounds are added on a parallel track. For example, music might be prerecorded on one track. This music could be played back while a singer's voice is recorded on a parallel track. Using this technique, several musicians and singers, for example, can each be recorded at different times and places. Narration can be recorded while the sound effects and music are played back, for example. When each of the different tracks has been properly recorded, they can all be mixed onto a single track. It is important to note that timecode-readable multitrack recorders can also be used to maintain synchronization between different tracks, as noted earlier. Multitrack recorders allow many soundtracks to be combined, such as those for narration, music, and sound effects. The same effect operates within a sound application in a computer. The first track is downloaded and saved in the file. Each additional source is added as a new track in the same file. Synchronization between the separate tracks is inherent in the tape because each track is recorded and played back on the tape parallel with the others.

The synchronization in computers is automatic, but depending on the application, a track can be "slipped" forward or backward to change or correct synchronization. This is impossible or extremely difficult to achieve using tape. To initially synchronize sounds with visual images, it is best to edit and mix in the same format as the accompanying visual images.

Sound Mixing Techniques

Sound mixing combines several sounds or soundtracks that are running simultaneously. Editing, on the other hand, pieces together sounds in sequence, usually on one soundtrack at a time. Mixing is a process by which various soundtracks are blended together or combined with each other. Individual soundtracks for speech, sound effects, and music, for example, are first edited into sequential order, often in conjunction with visual images, before they are mixed together to form one soundtrack. The volume and equalization, or EQ (the attenuation or amplification of specific frequencies), of each different audio channel or track is separately controlled using a fader and EQ controls on an audio console or mixer or within a digital editing program (Figure 10.10).

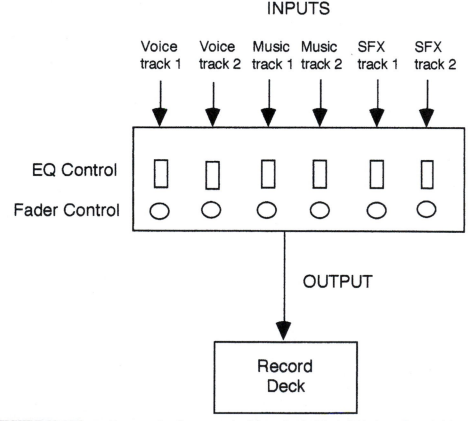

FIGURE 10.10 To combine several audio sources simultaneously, all of the individual sounds are fed through an audio mixer where the individual sounds can be equalized and levels can be properly set in relationship to each other before recording or downloading to a computer program.

It is extremely important to maintain a high signal-to-noise ratio in each separate soundtrack before the mix. During the mix, the audio level of one soundtrack can always be reduced. But speech, sound effects, or music that were initially recorded or dubbed at a low sound level cannot be increased in volume during the mix without simultaneously increasing the accompanying noise level and thereby reducing the quality of the audio. Whenever possible, sounds should be kept at their maximum level until the mix and then adjusted to accommodate other sounds. Properly recorded digital signals will not increase noise level when the levels are changed.

Automatic gain controls (AGCs) are sometimes used to maintain consistent audio levels during audio recording and dubbing. This method too often boosts background noise to unpleasant levels during nonspeaking passages. A *peak limiter* reduces excessively loud sounds without boosting background sounds. Both of these devices can affect the setting of maximum mixing levels.

During a mix, the sound editor adjusts the volume of one sound element with respect to another. Sounds can be superimposed on one another, and transitions between sounds, such as fades, cross-fades, and segues, can be created. During an audio *fade*, the *pot* (short for *potentiometer*, a type of volume control) or fader for a sound is gradually turned up or down. A *cross-fade* combines a fade-out on one track with a simultaneous fade-in on another track. A *segue* is an instantaneous change from one track to another. Sound mixes usually involve several playback units channeled through an audio console to a single (monophonic) or dual (stereophonic) track master tape. The editor or mixer operator must set the proper volume for each playback source and control all special effects and transitions. In digital editing, each track is adjusted individually before combining the tracks into a final monaural, stereo, or 5.1 output signal.

A mix is carefully preplanned on a mix log or audio cue sheet. A *mix log* or *audio cue sheet* indicates all the volume and EQ changes and transitions for every sound source the sound mixer must control. It is organized sequentially according to the overall time of the program. Changes in any sound source or the fader assigned to it are then listed under the column devoted to that source, indicating the precise time the change is to occur. The mixer operator consults the cue sheet as a guide to the adjustment of each individual sound source. For example, the opening music may have to be faded in at the beginning of the program, and a narrator's voice may then be faded in over the music a few seconds later. The music may have to be decreased in volume at this point so that it does not drown out the narration. Forty seconds later, the music may segue to another musical composition, which conveys a different mood or pace. Sound effects may have to be combined with this music, and at certain points, speech, sound effects, and music will probably occur simultaneously. Without a cue sheet, the editor or mixer could easily become confused during a sound mix (Figure 10.11).

Synchronous dialogue is generally recorded simultaneously with accompanying visual images. The sounds and images are then edited at the same time in the same format. When editing synchronous dialogue, an editor must be sensitive to the performance level, intonation, and accuracy of the speaker. Speech sounds that are radically different in intensity or intonation should not be edited together, even though their visual images match. Mistakes in the delivery of lines of dialogue should be removed. Compromises in editing synchronous speech sounds are inevitable, because editing together the best-quality images does not always result in the best-quality synchronous sounds.

AUDIO MIXING CUE SHEET

Production ——————————————————— Date ——————

Producer ———————— Director———————— Mixer ————————

Track A Dialogue 1		Track B Dialogue 2		Track C SFX		Track D Music	
Reel #1		Reel #2		Reel #3		Reel #4	
000	Dead Sync	000	Dead Sync	000	Dead Sync	000	Dead Sync
00:15	Sync pop	00:15	Sync pop	00:15	Sync pop	00:15	Sync pop
00:30		00:30		00:30	Crickets	00:30	FI Theme
				00:45	Slow fade		
					Hold under		
	Sam:						
01:10	(1st word)		Harold:				▼
	Hi, what's	01:20	Hi back to ya			01:20	FO
			▼				
02:00	(Last word)						
	Thanks, see ya						
					▼		
	FI = Fade In		FO = Fade Out				

FIGURE 10.11 The audio mixing log, or cue sheet, provides the mixing operator with a guide as to when to use sound from different tracks. The verbal and timing cues give precise locations for making transitions or adding effects.

The editor is sometimes forced to compromise between image quality and sound quality. An editor must be flexible and creative. For example, it may be necessary to use cutaways, such as a character's reaction to the speech of another character, to cover mistakes in synchronous dialogue. Two or more portions of the same on-camera speech can be combined to remove missed lines or poor inflection, but unless there are cutaways, visual jump cuts will result. An editor must constantly make decisions on the basis of what is least objectionable, poor-quality sounds or poor-quality images, when editing synchronous dialogue and visuals (Figure 10.12).

Looping (which gets its name from loops of film that repeat the same shots over and over) or *automatic dialogue replacement* (ADR) refers to the creation and replacement of lip-sync dialogue in the sound studio during postproduction. The visual images are repeatedly projected onto a sound studio screen while the talent attempts to repeat the lines of dialogue exactly in sync with the lip movements of the on-screen speaker.

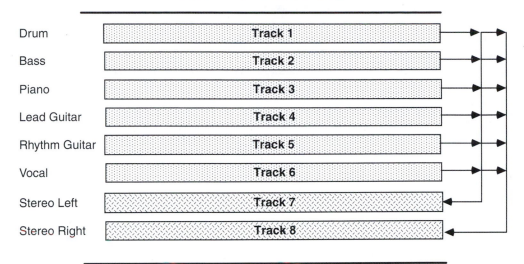

MULTITRACK AUDIO MIXING

Drum	Track 1
Bass	Track 2
Piano	Track 3
Lead Guitar	Track 4
Rhythm Guitar	Track 5
Vocal	Track 6
Stereo Left	Track 7
Stereo Right	Track 8

Tracks 1 through 6 are mixed in proper proportions for
a stereo mix and rerecorded in sync to tracks 7 and 8

FIGURE 10.12 Several individual audio tracks on a multitrack audiotape can be combined into a single or stereo set of tracks through the process of "ping-ponging." A multitrack recorder can be adjusted so that some heads are playback heads and others are set to record. Because they are aligned on one head stack, all of the tracks will be kept in sync. In a computer program, each track may be recorded individually in sync with previously recorded tracks.

These newly recorded speech sounds can be used to replace poor-quality original recordings. ADR is often done with the performer trying to speak in unison with the playback (via headphones) of the original, on-set speech, which is used as an audio reference. It is usually less expensive to replace defective dialogue than to reshoot the whole sequence. However, sound studio speech often seems dead and lifeless in comparison with the original recordings with which it must be intercut, unless the sound signal is properly processed. An editor must pay particular attention to the pace, intonation, and vocal quality of the specific lines of dialogue that are to be inserted within an originally recorded scene.

Nonsynchronous or voice-over narration is frequently used to provide a commentary on visual actions. Voice-over narration can be edited together from audio interviews conducted in the field, or it can be recorded after visual editing in real time with the narrator watching a preliminary edit of the film or videotape and pacing his or her speech to the changing shots and speed of the action. In the former case, the visuals are edited to the narration. In the latter case, the editor's job is to touch up various narration segments so that they coincide with specific visuals and any mistakes are removed. The pace of the narration may need to be speeded up or slowed down during recording or editing to accommodate specific visual sequences. Errors in delivery can sometimes be removed through judicious editing.

Sound Effects

There are basically three kinds of sound effects: prerecorded library effects, spot recorded effects, and actuality recorded effects. *Library effects* are cataloged and maintained on phonograph records, audiotapes, or CDs for storage convenience and accessibility (Figure 10.13). *Spot effects* are created in a sound studio to duplicate the supposed off-screen or on-screen source. *Actuality effects* are recorded outside the sound studio. They either accurately reproduce a particular sound or create a vivid sound impression. *Synchronous sound effects* are immediately dubbed to the videotape or film format of the visuals so that they can be edited in synchronization with corresponding visual images.

Library, spot, and actuality sound effects can all be placed in synchronization with visual images. Once the sound effect is dubbed to the proper format, it is edited into the videotape or film soundtrack accompanying the visual image. The sound of a door closing or a fist striking a face can be synchronized with the visual image of the action. In digital editing, the sound effect is usually dubbed to a separate file so that it can be inserted into the proper videotape frame. In film editing, the sound effect is dubbed to magnetic film, which will correspond frame-by-frame with the accompanying visual images. In both cases, the sound effect is precisely synchronized with its on-screen sound source.

In digital editing, a computer can be used to find and edit a collection of effects tracks on CD for either videotape or film. Computer storage, retrieval, and control allow a specific sound effect to be quickly accessed and its loudness, pitch, and duration to be altered and used in a variety of ways. For example, a single digitized sound of an airplane can be quickly found on a CD and then manipulated to create the complete illusion of an airplane circling an airport. Using this technique, a collection of basic sound effects can be used to provide an infinite variety of sounds. Each basic sound effect is cataloged and described as a computer file for easy selection and retrieval. It can also be stored digitally on a disk so that dubbing and signal processing does not result in any degradation of quality. Using the SMPTE timecode of an edited videotape for reference, a sound effects editor can select, order, and manipulate all the sound effects that will be needed. Once the computer program is created, the sound effects are automatically dubbed, ordered, and processed to the editor's precise specifications.

FIGURE 10.13 Sound effects libraries may be recorded on vinyl disks, audiotape, audiocassettes, CDs, or solid-state drives.

Editing Music

Music for a film or television program can come from a variety of sources. Library music, which has been prerecorded on a CD, audiotape, or phonograph record, is often used to accompany visual images and other sounds. For public exhibition, the rights to prerecorded music must be secured, as discussed in Chapter 3, Producing and Production Management. Original music can be recorded in a sound studio for a specific project. Either it can be recorded in advance of editing, so that visuals can be edited to the music, or it can be recorded after the visual editing has been completed, so that the performance of the music can be matched to the visuals.

After dubbing prerecorded music to the proper visual format, the editor carefully analyzes it by finding the precise frames where specific musical effects, such as rhythmic beats, crescendos, and changes in pace or tonality, occur. Visual images can then be added to the hard disk, videotape, or film and edited so that shot changes and changes in the intensity of the visual action and pace correspond with the music. Visual images can also be edited in counterpoint to the music, through the use of shot changes and visual tonalities and pacing that contradict rather than complement the music. Synchronizing music to preedited visuals can be quite complicated. Music is usually composed with specific visuals in mind. The tempo of the music may need to be adjusted so that specific effects coincide with the visuals they are intended to accompany. The edited visuals are normally played back while the music is being recorded and are used as visual cues to guide the pace and tempo at which the music is performed.

There are two basic approaches to the problem of mixing music and speech sounds. One approach is to lower the level of the music "down and under" immediately before the delivery of a line of dialogue or narration, and then return the music to a normal level after the speech has concluded. A second approach is to keep the music at a consistently low level. If music is mixed at its full value, the speech sounds that accompany it will be difficult to understand. Even when the music is kept at a consistently low level, it is important to have clear and distinct dialogue and narration. An underlying assumption of both of these approaches to mixing music and speech is that the speech must be clearly understood. But it is sometimes necessary to hear the music at its full value, particularly when its pace, intensity, and mood are essential to the establishment of a particular feeling.

Mixing music requires the smooth operation of faders on an audio console or sensitive adjustments within the computer program. The music must have a relatively consistent pace and original recording level at points where it is to be effectively faded in or out or cross-faded with other music, speech, and sound effects. Music that varies in intensity or seems erratic is difficult to fade in and fade out smoothly. Faders should normally be moved slowly so that one piece of music gradually blends into another piece of music or another type of sound. Sometimes popping on a sudden burst of music can be an effective transition device, a sort of musical punctuation. *Stingers* are short phrases of music, usually characterized by a rapidly descending scale or series of notes, which can also act as punctuation devices. In functionalist and realist situations, music is usually mixed smoothly and gradually with other types of sounds.

EDITING FILM

Film editing follows a series of stages similar to digital editing: from rough-cutting to conforming, the equivalent of online editing. The first stage includes viewing a copy of the originally recorded images called the *workprint*, *rushes*, or *dailies*; selecting and ordering specific shots and scenes; and continuing to the final stage, which involves conforming the original film to the edited workprint. Unlike digital editing, however, traditional film editing usually involves mechanical processes, such as physically cutting and splicing the film. Also like digital editing, conventional film editing is essentially a nonlinear process, because changes can be made in the overall length and order of the sounds and images at any time up to the completion of the rough cut. Today film images are normally transferred to video and digitized so that they can be edited more efficiently with a digital nonlinear editing system, but at some point, the original film must be cut if film prints are going to be made in a film laboratory and projected in a movie theater from a film print rather than a digital file. As a result of various postproduction efficiencies, digital nonlinear editing is rapidly becoming the preferred method of offline film editing or rough-cutting. Whether a film editor uses traditional mechanical techniques of rough-cutting or digital nonlinear editing techniques, a film editor has a great deal of freedom to experiment with a variety of takes and shot sequences and durations at all stages of the editing process until the conforming stage (Figure 10.14).

CAMERA REPORT

Roll No. _____

Page _____   Date _____

Client _____

Production _____

Director _____   Camera Operator _____

Camera _____   Magazine _____   Motor _____

Stock [   ]   Rated   [I.E.   ]

Print Circled [   ]   All [   ]   Takes _____

Scene	Take	T-Stop	Remarks

FIGURE 10.14 A camera report form lists all of the pertinent information that the laboratory needs to know in order to properly process the film that it describes. The form indicates which takes are to be printed and includes comments the editor may need to have while editing the workprint.

Synchronizing the Dailies

The recording and editing of film sound is usually kept physically separate from the recording of film images. Film sound is normally recorded on digital audiotape (DAT), which can be synchronized with the film recorded in a camera, as was described earlier in Chapter 9, Recording. One of the first tasks of film editing is to sync up the film visuals with their corresponding sounds. This is accomplished by finding a common starting point, such as the visual and audio marker at the beginning of each shot provided by a clapstick. Once the visual image of the closing clapstick or slate is linked up with the "clap" sound, the entire shot will be in proper synchronization. The editor combines all of the shots in this manner so that the director, producer, and cinematographer can screen them while production is still in progress. The editor screens and carefully catalogs this material while preparing for the rough cut. Today, film sounds and images are captured in digital form and synchronized on a digital film editing system.

Digital Film Editing

If the final distribution medium for a film project is videotape or a digital format, original film recordings are often immediately transferred to a digitized format for electronic editing. When film, videotape, and digital final copies are needed for different distribution and exhibition outlets, there are several options in terms of postproduction editing. One option is simply to make a film-to-digital file transfer of the completed film (Figure 10.15).

This option allows the editor to edit the film in digital nonlinear form and then use the timecode (videotape) and KeyKode (film) numbers generated by the EDL for final film editing or conforming. It is extremely important to use a digital nonlinear editing system that is designed specifically for film editing in order to solve two important problems that can arise: (1) a loss of synchronization between the separately recorded audio and video tracks and (2) a failure to accurately convert the frames-per-second speed back to 24 frames per second for film from the digital video, which has 30 frames per second. Audio synchronization can be maintained by using a video-to-film accurate editing program.

The frame-per-second differences between video and film mean that some video frames do not exist on the film, unless the video is recorded at 24 P, and then there is a direct correlation between video and film frames and conversion is simple. Computer programs were created in order to convert 24 frames per second of film to 30 frames per second of standard NTSC video. When using standard NTSC video, the computer program must be able to recognize which video frames actually have corresponding film frames (using both timecode and KeyKode) during editing in order to produce a conformed original film that is properly synchronized with the digitally edited soundtrack. A project can be shot as film, edited as digital images, and then conformed as film for both video and film distribution. This allows a producer to combine the image qualities and characteristics of film with the editing speed and convenience of digital nonlinear editing. Also, as high-definition television (HDTV) equipment and technology improves, shooting a documentary as well as a feature film on HDTV rather than film, editing it digitally, and then transferring it to film for distribution becomes a reality. Through "electronic cinema" such productions could be delivered directly to theaters without leaving the electronic format.

FIGURE 10.15 A CCD telecine film-to-digital conversion. Each film frame is scanned individually, allowing for color correction and filtering in real time as the film is converted to a digital signal. (Courtesy of Philips Broadcast Television Systems Company.)

Conforming

Once the film editing decisions have been finalized the original film is conformed to the edit decision list (EDL) conversion from timecode to key code numbers. Conforming is a professional skill that is often performed by a person called a *conformer*, particularly when a negative original must be cut together without error or getting the film dirty. All of the shots from the originally recorded film are permanently spliced into two or more rolls, called A and B (and C, and so on) rolls, using a cement splicer that physically welds two overlapping pieces of film together. During conforming, the individual shots must be divided into two rolls of alternating shots. One difference between 16 mm and 35 mm conforming is that there is sufficient space between frames in 35 mm to be able to make overlapping cement splices on a single roll, although a B roll is required for dissolves, fades, and superimpositions. Individual shots on an A or B roll of 16 mm film must alternate with black leader so that overlap splices always overlap into the black leader and are thus invisible when the film is printed. The completed A and B rolls are printed to a single piece of film, called an *answer print*, at a film laboratory, before a final viewable image is obtained. A film on which picture and soundtracks are "married" together is called a *composite print*.

A conformer prepares the original for splicing by pulling all the shots from the camera original and placing them on individual plastic cores, which are labeled and arranged in sequential order. An alternative approach is to simply pull each shot from its respective camera original roll as it is needed. The conformer makes a complete list of the edge number markings of the edited workprint, and the original camera shots are pulled on the basis of the edge numbers. The film is usually cut with a frame and a half extra at both the head and rail ends of an individual shot so that there is ample room for overlap.

Conformers usually adopt a standard set of procedures with no variations to avoid mistakes while cutting and splicing original film. Cleanliness is extremely important, because dirt and scratches will show up in the final prints. This problem is aggravated when using negative film, because the scratches and dirt then show up as white marks on the final prints. When all the shots have been prepared for splicing, the conformer places the A and B rolls in the gang synchronizer on the editing bench and proceeds to splice the shots alternately into one of the two rolls, leaving overlaps of specified lengths for dissolves and superimpositions.

The final conformed film must be spliced using a cement splicer, because a tape slice would show when the film runs through the printer. Like the tape splicer, the cement splice holds the film stock in precise position so that the sprockets are kept in alignment and the splice will fall on the frame line. The cement actually melts the base of the film stock so the two pieces adhere together to make a strong bond. Some splicers use a small heater to speed the setting process.

Combining the A and B Rolls

Once the A and B rolls are conformed to the workprint, they are sent to the laboratory so that they can each be printed in succession to a single roll of film, called an *answer print*. The answer print is a test printing of the A and B rolls, after they have been properly timed—that is, after the color and density of each shot has been adjusted by a laboratory professional, called a *color timer*. A composite print marries the A and B rolls together with a soundtrack so that the composite print can be run in a conventional projector. The composite print usually has an optical soundtrack, which is advanced ahead of the corresponding pictures by 26 frames in 16 mm or 20 frames in 35 mm.

Summary

Trimming and combining visual images and sounds define the craft or mechanics of editing, but any discussion of the overall process and art of editing must begin with a consideration of editing stages, systems, modes, and aesthetic approaches. In the digital age, editing occurs during production and postproduction stages, and parallel filmmaking and editing are replacing serial postproduction. The editing process consists of at least two stages: preliminary and final editing. During preliminary editing, images and sounds are repeatedly viewed before they are trimmed and combined, usually using a copy of the original recordings to create a rough cut or offline edited version. During final editing, the original recordings are online edited (video) or conformed (film) into a polished version that will actually be released to viewers and listeners.

Linear editing systems require an editor to add visual images and sounds in consecutive order from the beginning to the end of a piece. Most analog videotape and audiotape editing systems are basically linear editing systems. In nonlinear editing the overall duration of a production can be lengthened or shortened at any time, and images and sounds do not have to be edited in consecutive order from beginning to end.

Classical Hollywood conventions for shooting and editing fiction films and videos include master scene shooting and continuity editing. A master shot consists of a relatively long-duration shot that includes most of the action in a specific scene. Matching close-ups can be inserted into the master shot during editing. Continuity editing refers to an editing system that developed in Hollywood and elsewhere beginning about 1910. It consists of a number of shooting and editing conventions that sustain an illusion of continuous time and place within a scene.

Variations on master scene and continuity editing techniques have also been developed that take into account the difficulties of scripting and staging nonfiction events, as well as the use of expository and rhetorical structures that can disrupt spatial and temporal continuity. A variation on master scene shooting and editing commonly used in news and documentary production, for example, is called A and B roll editing. A and B roll editing adds viewer interest by interspersing rather static shots of a talking head with a wide variety of visual illustrations.

Sound mixing is a process of blending together simultaneous sounds or soundtracks. This includes transition devices such as fades, cross-fades, and segues. Blending together different types of sounds, such as speech, sound effects, and music, demands smooth and precise operation of the faders on an audio console or mixer. It also requires careful preparation of a mix log, which specifies different audio levels and transitions from one soundtrack to another. Specific principles of editing and mixing apply to different types of sound, such as speech, sound effects, and music.

Through a technique known as looping or automatic dialogue replacement (ADR), speech sounds can be added to and perfectly synchronized with preedited, prerecorded visual images. Voiceover interviews and narration are often edited before the selection of illustrative visuals.

There are three basic kinds of sound effects: library effects, spot effects, and actuality effects. Library effects are prerecorded on CDs, phonograph records, and audiotapes. Spot effects are specially recorded in the sound studio, and actuality effects are recorded in the field.

Visual images can be combined using principles of editing derived from each of the three aesthetic orientations: realism, modernism, and postmodernism. Realist editing preserves spatial and temporal continuity from shot to shot. A modernist approach to editing often deliberately disrupts spatial and temporal continuity between shots and calls attention to the editing process. A postmodernist approach to editing can take the form of a collage or pastiche that combines diverse images and sounds and actively engages the viewer/listener in the process of constructing the artwork.

One of the editor's first tasks is to organize and catalog all the recordings that the director has provided. In documentary productions that lack a detailed script, performing a paper edit from a catalog of shots and camera takes can help an editor efficiently and economically organize the editing process.

There are three types of editing technology and techniques: digital nonlinear editing, videotape linear editing, and film editing. Digital nonlinear editing software offers several advantages over conventional means of editing film, audiotape, and videotape, including increased flexibility or creativity, as well as potential time and cost savings.

A clip is usually the smallest unit of digital video (or audio) information that can be stored and manipulated during editing. It can range from just one frame to an entire movie in duration, but it often consists of a single shot, that is, a continuous camera recording or take. Digitized clips are usually imported (or copied) into a particular editing project file, where they are edited along a timeline with other images and sounds. Clips of video or audio information can be cut, trimmed, copied, pasted, inserted, and deleted along a timeline.

Videotape editing is usually divided into two stages: offline editing and online editing. Offline editing is often done in a smaller format or lower resolution images, and offline editing decisions are later performed on an originally recorded larger-format videotape or higher resolution images.

Film editing follows a series of stages similar to videotape editing from preliminary editing to final editing. Unlike videotape editing, however, traditional film editing usually involves mechanical processes, such as physically cutting and splicing the film.

Developments in digital editing have made it possible to edit film digitally in nonlinear form and then use the timecode (videotape) and KeyKode (film) numbers generated by the edit decision list (EDL) for final film editing or conforming. A project can be shot as film, edited as videotape or digital images, and then conformed as film for both videotape and film distribution. Once the film editing decisions have been finalized via the EDL, the original film is conformed to the edited timecode and KeyKode numbers.

EXERCISES

1. Edit together a short movie trailer or television promotion for a documentary or dramatic feature film, using an existing videotape that is in the public domain (that is, not copyright protected). View the videotape at least twice, writing down the control-track numbers for each shot or sequence that you think you might use in your trailer or promo. Then, using these notes, perform a paper edit of the sequence so that the edited promo, at least on paper, approximates a specific duration, such as one minute or three minutes. Then, using the paper edit, actually edit the sequence on videotape, or digitize the clips that you have selected and edit them using a digital nonlinear editing system. Remember that you are trying to promote the film. Therefore, you will want to select sequences that will attract viewers but not disappoint them by setting up false expectations that the film itself cannot fulfill. Basically you want to capture the essence of the film to promote it.

2. Edit your own version of a professionally recorded scene or sequence. Obtain a copy of the original, unedited recordings of a professional-quality production. The American Cinema Editor's (ACE's) annual student editing contest is a potential source of professional recordings or film rushes. After you have edited these shots in film, videotape, or digital form, compare your version with the version actually produced by a professional editor, and determine what you could do to improve your own editing.

3. Using a shooting script as your guide, prepare a mix log or audio cue sheet for combining all of the various sound elements that will be used in post-production editing. Although precise volume-control settings cannot be known until actual materials are prepared for a mix, virtually all other factors can be anticipated in advance. Try to compose separate and continuous soundtracks or channels on paper for each different type of sound, such as synchronous dialogue, narration, sound effects or background sound, and music. Indicate where one piece of music will cross-fade or segue to another, requiring separate tracks or channels, or where several different sound effects or background sounds must be combined. A mix log or audio cue sheet will graphically depict the depth and texture of sound by indicating when several types of sounds or soundtracks coexist, such as narration, sound effects, and music. Indicate which type of sound will be dominant if they will not all be of equal intensity. Determine the series of stages soundtrack preparation must go through if some types of sound must be premixed before the final master mix.

4. Replace some original sound (sound originally recorded with corresponding visuals) with library or spot effects. Grab an audio clip off a CD or digitize an analog audiotape recording of the sound effect. If you are using a digital nonlinear system, use the insert mode; if you are using electronic videotape editing, physically splice the new sounds into the existing magnetic film or audiotape soundtrack. Compare the edited soundtrack with the original for sound clarity and consistency.

5. After completing Exercise 1 or Exercise 2, shoot your own five-minute dramatic sequence and edit it on a nonlinear system. If a linear system is available, edit the same sequence using a linear system to compare the differences in ease of editing and the choice of edits.

6. Mix a voiceover narration track with music. Try to make the edits as smooth and indistinguishable as possible. Be careful to maintain consistency in terms of pace and timing in the delivery of narration. Find similar phrases of music on which to make an instantaneous transition from one piece of music to another. Pay careful attention to any discrepancy in terms of audio levels and background sounds when editing together speech, sound effects, or music recorded outside the studio. Fade the music down and under when the narrator is speaking, and fade the music up to its full volume when the narrator is silent for a reasonable period of time.

7. If film equipment is available, shoot and edit the same sequence as that discussed in Exercise 3 on film, and compare the two systems.

8. Dub an existing short dramatic video to a nonlinear system. Use actors to record new dialogue by watching the production. Record their audio on a separate system. Once the dialogue is recorded, synchronize that audio to the existing video.

9. Dub the film from Exercise 4 to a digital system, and edit the sequence on a computer.

10. Add music and sound effects to Exercise 4 as needed, including footsteps, doors opening, gunshots, or whatever sounds the drama calls for.

11. Produce an in-studio multicamera dramatic production by recording the output of all three cameras as well as the output of the switcher simultaneously. Produce the program as a "live" continuous production without any stopping or reshooting. Take the four tapes and edit them into a comprehensive program using a nonlinear system.

12. Dub a favorite music selection to a nonlinear system. Find another recording of the same selection. See if you can edit the two together to make a single selection by combining or alternating cuts.

Additional Readings

Amyes, Tim, 1999. Audio Post Production in Video and Film, second ed. Focal Press, Boston.

Benedetti, Robert, ed. 2004. Creative Post Production: Editing, Sound, Visual Effects, and Music for Film and Video, Allyn & Bacon, Boston.

Browne, Steven E., 2007. High Definition Postproduction: Editing and Delivering HD Video, Focal Press, Boston.

Case, Dominic, 2001. Film Technology in Post Production, Focal Press, Boston.

Clark, Barbara, Spohr, Susan, 2002. Guide to Post-Production for TV and Film: Managing the Process, second ed. Focal Press, Boston.

Compesi, Ronald J., 2003. Video Field Production and Editing, sixth ed. Allyn & Bacon, Boston.

Cousins, Mark, Hepworth-Sawyer, Russ, 2008. Logic Pro 8: Audio and Music Production, Focal Press, Boston.

Dancyger, Ken, 2007. The Technique of Film and Video Editing, fourth ed. Focal Press, Boston.

Derry, Roger, 2002. PC Audio Editing, Focal Press, Boston.

Fowler, Jaime, 2001. Editing Digital Film: Integrating Final Cut Pro, Avid, and Media 100, Focal Press, Boston.

Gloman, Chuck, Pescatore, Mark J., 2006. Working with HDV: Shoot, Edit, and Deliver Your High Definition Video, Focal Press, Boston.

Holman, Tomlinson, 2005. Sound for Digital Video, Focal Press, Boston.

Jacobsen, Jens, et al, 2005. Implementing a Digital Asset Management System: For Animation, Computer Games, and Web Development, Focal Press, Boston.

James, Jack, 2006. Digital Intermediates for Film and Video, Focal Press, Boston.

Kauffmann, Sam, 2006. Avid Editing: A Guide for Beginning and Intermediate Users, third ed. Focal Press, Boston.

Levin, C. Melinda, Watkins, Fred P., 2003. Post: The Theory and Technology of Digital Nonlinear Motion Picture Editing, Allyn & Bacon, Boston.

Maes, Jan, Vecammen, Marc, 2001. Digital Audio Techniques: CD-Minidisc, SACD, DVDA, MP3, fourth ed. Focal Press, Boston.

Mamer, Bruce, 2003. Film Production Techniques. Creating the Accomplished Image, third ed. Wadsworth, Belmont, CA.

Millar, Gavin, 1995. The Technique of Film Editing, rev. ed. Focal Press, Boston.

Osder, Jason, Carman, Robbie, 2007. Film Cut Pro Workflows: The Independent Studio Handbook, Focal Press, Boston.

Rose, Jay, 2009. Audio Post Production for Film & Video, second ed. Focal Press, Boston.

Rowlands, Avin, 2000. Continuity in Film and Video, fourth ed. Focal Press, Boston.

Sennenschein, David, 2001. Sound Design: The Expressive Power of Music, Voice, and Sound Effects in Cinema, Michael Weise Productions, Studio City, CA.

Staten, Greg, Bayes, Steve, 2008. The Avid Handbook, Advanced Techniques, Strategies, and Survival Information for Avid Editing Systems, Focal Press, Boston.

Watkinson, John, 2002. Introduction to Digital Audio, second ed. Focal Press, Boston.

Wright, Steve, 2006. Digital Compositing for Film and Video, second ed. Focal Press, Boston.

Graphics, Animation, and Special Effects

- What are the aesthetic choices of graphics?

- What are the principles of graphics?

- How is animation defined?

- What are the types of animation?

- What are graphic applications in digital productions?

- How do digital effects differ from optical or physical effects?

Introduction

Graphic functions can be divided into two categories: digitally created and physically created. In the studio, this includes the creation of scenery, props, and backgrounds. Graphics focus on the arrangement of letters, symbols, and visuals within the frame and the creation of complete backgrounds or virtual settings. All of the aspects of graphic design must be coordinated with one another to affect a consistent and unified approach to all elements that appear within the frame.

Graphic design should establish the time, place, and mood; reflect character; and reinforce specific themes. A historical time period and setting must be easily identifiable. Titles may denote a specific time and place at the same time that they reflect a specific style or mood. The mood or atmosphere results primarily from the abstract, emotional aspects of design elements and principles. Specific colors and shapes create an emotional mood that can reveal character and reinforce themes. The idea that you can tell a great deal about people from where they live and what they wear can be applied to scenic design. Cold, formal graphics reveal a great deal about a character, as does a warm, relaxed graphic. The opening titles warn the audience of the mood, genre, and often the time and location of the production.

Animation and special effects generate visual interest and can be used to create imaginative worlds that defy the physical laws of space and time. Animation simulates movement, allowing objects and characters to inhabit a unique world and to perform or record unbelievable actions that would be impossible in real life. Special effects generate interest and excitement, often allowing futuristic or historical worlds to come to life, dangerous actions and events to be simulated, and live-action characters to accomplish superhuman feats. Digital animation techniques now replace many physical special effects to create realistic-appearing scenes in film and video productions that could not be accomplished in any other manner. The same techniques allow corrections to be made in postproduction to save time and the extra expenses of having to reshoot mistakes made in original shots or to remove unneeded objects. Animation on the World Wide Web (WWW) has grown exponentially in the past decade.

AESTHETICS OF GRAPHICS AND ANIMATION
Realist Graphics

A realist graphic gives the appearance of an existing object, location, character, or background. Some three-dimensional animation used in commercials and settings cannot be distinguished from the real object by a casual viewing on whatever media it is recorded. The illusion of reality, not actual reality, is the critical point of a realist graphic. Virtual characters, known as avatars, duplicate as closely as possible the shape, color, movement of a human. If the avatar suddenly becomes something other than its original shape, that design might now move to become a modernist or postmodernist graphic because its depiction is far removed from any form of a realistic figure or object. Classifying graphics and any media art form within tight definitions of realism, modernism, or postmodernism may be difficult simply because an art form may easily transform or change its shape and depiction as part of its character or purpose within the plot. Both the original form and the final are classifiable before it changes shape and when it reaches its final shape. Realist graphics are rarely defined by their supposed fidelity to nature or reality alone. Almost every realist graphic has an emotional impact as some degree of subjective stylization. A realistic setting, title, or animation should convey a psychological impression that reinforces the central theme of a drama or the central message of an informational program. It can reflect warmth or coldness, tension or relaxation, simply by virtue of the colors, lines, and shapes it presents. It is even possible for a realistic setting to reveal a specific character's emotional state through the feelings that the design conveys.

Modernist Graphics

Modernist graphics are much more abstract than realist designs. The subjective feelings they arouse and the subjective impressions they convey are rarely tied to actual experience or production efficiency alone. Modernist artists usually have much freer rein to explore specific design elements or subjective impressions for their own sake. A designer may decide to call attention to textures, shapes, lines, and colors themselves. Visual innovations often stem from such formative experiments, which can be incorporated into more conventional narrative, documentary, or instructional programs. Experimental productions by many computer and animation artists have shown how a formative or modernist approach to graphics can destroy any sense of reality by ignoring spatial perspective and using highly artificial, stylized designs and formats.

Postmodernist Graphics

Postmodernist designs leave much of the visual perception to the imagination of the viewer. Graphics, color, and movement can be juxtaposed in a series of apparently unrelated images. Postmodernist designs often mix a variety of design styles drawn from different genres and historical periods. For example, the settings in the film *Who Framed Roger Rabbit* (1988) suggested 1940s Los Angeles in a semirealist way until the timeless, garish cartoon world of Toontown collided with the live-action world. The production design in *Chinatown* (1974) limited the color blue to appearances of the main theme, water, in 1930s Los Angeles, whereas pastel colors and art nouveau designs were reminiscent of the 1930s in the 1980s urban setting of the television series *Miami Vice*. Postmodernist designs sometimes appeal to the emotions and often are difficult to analyze or categorize, just as postmodernist paintings and writings are difficult to place in traditional categories. The distorted shapes, textures, and colors of the objects and characters in *Tim Burton's Corpse Bride* illustrates the combination of many different artistic styles, and forms mixing unusual colors, shapes, type styles, and distorting figures, which can serve as the basis for postmodernist designs.

PRINCIPLES OF GRAPHICS

A graphic artist or animator works with three basic principles of design: graphic elements, color, and composition. The ways in which these elements are selected and combined determines the nature and success of the design. The selection of design elements must support the themes, plots, and characterizations of a drama or the central message of a nonfiction production. These principles are the same as those of any designer using artistic tools such as set designers and lighting designers, as described in Chapter 7, Lighting and Design.

Design Elements

The elements a graphic artist uses are line, shape, texture, and perceived movement.

Line

Line defines the form of a graphic design. An independent line can be straight, curved, or spiral. Edges are lines formed by shapes or objects that overlap each other, such as a foreground door and background wall. Lines can be repeated to create parallel lines or concentric circles. They create a path or direction of movement for the eye. Converging parallel lines create an illusion of depth or spatial perspective, for example. Straight lines are more dynamic than curved lines and circles. They create a strong sense of directional movement. Smooth curves and circles communicate a smoother, softer feeling of more gradual movement. Norman McLaren's drawing directly on film in his *Hen Hop* as well as drawing on the soundtrack with straight lines for the soundtrack of *Blinkity Blank* illustrates an extreme use of lines only in a both graphic form and artistic use of line in a soundtrack.

Shape

A combination of lines creates a shape. An infinite number of different shapes reflect specific objects, but some common, recurring shapes with which all graphic artists and others use are circles, squares, rectangles, triangles, ellipses, trapezoids, octagons, and hexagons. Shapes can carry symbolic meaning. They can be repeatedly used in conjunction with specific people or settings to evoke specific themes. In the film industry, almost all classic animators used basic shapes to simplify their work. Three-dimensional computer animation also relies on basic shapes to create all of the charters and objects. Simple shapes as used in the award-winning Pixar films *Luxo Jr*. and *Tin Toy* are classic examples of using basic design elements to simplify and yet reinforce specific themes.

Texture

Texture provides a tactile impression of form. Texture can be real or represented. Real textures are revealed by directional light, which creates shadows and modeling on a nonsmooth surface. Artists can represent textures, such as granite, marble, or wood grains, on a flat two-dimensional surface by creating a tactile impression. Tactile is the sense of texture, how something feels by touch. The drawing texture of a surface can create a perception of depth. A rough texture with heavy shadows provides a greater sensation of depth than a smooth, flat surface. A graphic of heavily draped or folded material creates a richness that relates to a feeling of opulence, splendor, or decadence. Texture, like shapes, can create a sense of space that affects our emotions and relates symbolically to the major themes of a story. Weathercasters stand in front of a green flat, but the graphic artist with the help of computers creates the appearance of the countryside in depth with the textures of the mountains, water, and cities behind her to show the weather pattern and movement of rain and snow, even though the visual is two-dimensional.

Perceived Movement

Movement can be real or imaginary. The movement of performers on a set indicates real movement, whereas the illusion of movement stimulated by a series of still drawings or stationary backgrounds appears imaginary. In design, imaginary movement is just as important as real movement. The illusion of movement can be enhanced by the use of forced perspective lines drawn on the floor of the studio, for example. Transference can take place between real or imagined movement and otherwise stationary objects. A simple figure placed against a pulsating background will appear to dance or vibrate itself. A moving background can transfer the illusion of movement to a stationary figure placed in front of it. Movement throughout a stationary image is carefully controlled through changes in color, shape, space, and direction that guide the eye through a design. Movement also may be created by placing objects or character higher or lower, or closer or farther way from the camera in the frame which creates a perceived Z-axis in a two-dimensional frame. Hitchcock was exceptionally adept at framing subject in the frame to create movement without actual movement.

Color

The three aspects of color that are of primary importance to a designer are color harmony, color contrast, and the emotional or symbolic (cultural) effect of color.

Color Harmony

Various relationships between color pigments on a two-dimensional color wheel in large part determine the degree to which specific colors will harmonize with each other. A two-dimensional *color wheel* is a series of different colored chips or samples arranged in a circle from colors that are cool (short wavelengths of light), such as violet, blue, and green, to colors that are warm (long wavelengths of light), such as yellow, red, and orange. Traditional color judgments indicate that colors distant from each other on the wheel harmonize better than close colors, which tend to clash with each other. Several harmonious colors for sets and costumes can be selected by laying an equilateral triangle or square on top of a color wheel using the colors at the points. As the triangle or square is rotated, the group of harmonious colors changes.

Color Contrast

Different colors help separate objects in a scene through their mutual contrast. If two objects or shapes did not contrast with one another, they would appear as one object or shape. Contrast can help us perceive spatial depth. If specific colors of foreground and background are different, we will perceive their separation and hence spatial depth. Adjacent colors tend to interact. If you place a gray object against different colored backgrounds, it will appear darker or lighter depending on the color and brightness of the background. A particular hue takes on a completely different feeling depending on

COLOR RELATIONSHIPS

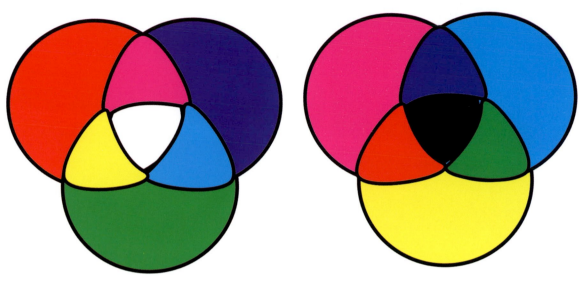

OVERLAPPING LIGHTS

SUPERIMPOSED FILTERS

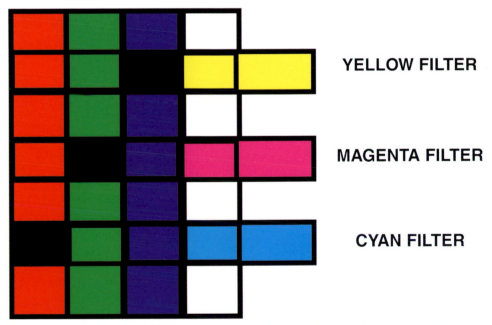

COLOR PLATE 1 The top left illustration shows what happens if pure primary colors (red, green, and blue) overlap, revealing the three secondary colors (cyan, magenta, and yellow); if all three primaries overlap, white light is reflected. The top right illustration shows what happens if white light is passed through filters of yellow, cyan, and magenta: the overlapping areas show red, green, and blue, and the center will have no light passed through since each of the three filters removes one of the three primary light rays. The bottom illustration shows the relationship of the three primary lights as they are passed through filters of the three secondary colors.

COLOR CHARACTERISTICS

Color is affected by surrounding colors. All of the center patches are the same color, but when surrounded by a lighter color or white it appears darker and if surrounded by a darker color or black, it appears lighter.

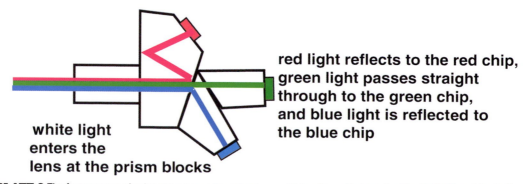

white light enters the lens at the prism blocks

red light reflects to the red chip, green light passes straight through to the green chip, and blue light is reflected to the blue chip

COLOR PLATE 2 The four squares of color show how adjacent colors and intensities affect a color. The illustration at the bottom shows light passing through the prisms in a typical three-chip video camera. White light (containing the three primary colors red, green, and blue) passes through the lens and enters the prism blocks. Red light is reflected toward the red chip, green light passes straight through to the green chip, and blue light is reflected toward the blue chip.

EXTERIOR LIGHT & FILTER COMBINATIONS

Exterior lighting-
For film - daylight stock
no filter in place.
For video - 85 filter in place
white balanced
under daylight.

Exterior lighting-
For film - daylight stock
with 85 filter in place.
For video - 85 filter in place
white balanced
under tungsten light.

Exterior lighting-
For film - tungsten stock
with no filter in place.
For video - no filter in place
white balanced
under tungsten light.

COLOR PLATE 3 Operating either a film or video camera under daylight conditions requires proper filters to be in place and proper white balancing in a video camera. The top photo shows a properly balanced video camera and daylight film in a film camera. The bottom photos show improper combinations of white-balancing in a video camera and mismatching filters and film stock in a film camera.

INTERIOR LIGHT & FILTER COMBINATIONS

Interior Lighting -
For film - tungsten stock
no filter in place.
For video - no filter in place
white balanced
under tungsten.

Interior Lighting -
For film - tungsten stock
with 85 filter in place.
For video - no filter in place
white balanced
under daylight.

Interior Lighting -
For film - tungsten stock
with 80 filter in place.
For video - white balanced
under tungsten light
with 85 filter removed.

COLOR PLATE 4 Operating either a film or video camera under tungsten lighting conditions requires proper filters to be in place and proper white-balancing in a video camera. The top photo shows a properly white-balanced video camera and tungsten film and lighting in a film camera. The bottom photos show mismatching filters and improper white-balancing in a video camera.

the hues that are adjacent to it. Complementary colors of the same intensity should not be placed next to each other, unless the intense contrast is intentional.

Maintaining brightness and contrast between different lines, shapes, and masses is extremely important when designing graphic images for television and film. A television graphic designer cannot rely exclusively on color contrast, because a television program may be received in either color or black and white. Adjacent colors should have a gray-value brightness contrast of at least 30 percent; that is, each object or shape should be 30 percent brighter or darker than the one next to it. Brightness contrast between different shapes and objects can be determined by using a gray scale (Figure 11.1). A *gray scale* consists of a sequential series of gray tones from white to mid-gray to black. Pure white has virtually 100 percent reflectance and video white approximately 90 percent, whereas pure black has 0 percent and video black approximately 3 percent. The midpoint on the gray scale is about 18 percent reflectance—that is, about 18 percent of the light falling on this shade of gray is actually reflected back to the eye. To maintain adequate brightness contrast, dark letters and shapes should be placed on light backgrounds, and vice versa (Figure 11.1).

Emotional Response to Color

Most designers believe that a general distinction can be made between warm colors and cool colors in terms of their emotional effect on an audience. Colors such as reds, oranges, and yellows create a sense of warmth in a scene. A romantic scene lit by firelight and surrounded by red, orange, and yellow objects on the set uses these warm colors to enhance a romantic mood. Caution should be used with reds and yellows in video recording, because video noise can occur in these colors on repeated generations of an analog videotape. Colors such as blue and green, on the other hand, are often considered to be cool colors. They are sometimes used to enhance a sense of loneliness or aloofness in a character, or a general mood that is related to a lack of human as well as physical warmth.

Cool colors tend to recede, whereas warm colors tend to advance. For example, pure hues of greenish yellow, yellow, yellowish orange, orange, and orangish red tend to advance and call attention to themselves, whereas pure hues of violet, red violet, blue, and blue-green tend to recede. Warm colors can convey a mood of passion or action, whereas cool colors tend to reinforce a sense of passivity and tranquility. The colors of sets, costumes, and graphic images must be selected with an eye toward their visual prominence, whether they recede or advance, as well as the degree to which they contrast with other colors. Colors that are repeatedly associated with specific objects, people, and settings can take on symbolic or thematic meaning. The red dress of a character in a drama can be used to signify sensuous passion. This color might contrast with the cool green or blue colors associated with a competitor for the affections of a male character.

Cultural Response to Color

Color symbolism also varies with different cultures. For example, the color white (or lack of color) to Japanese viewers may signify mourning, but for viewers from Western cultures, white often signifies purity and hope. The same color may have different connotations depending on its use in a specific film or television program. The color yellow may mean cowardice, sinfulness, or decay, yet it also can carry the meaning of spring, youthfulness, and happiness. Both blue and green also carry various meanings depending on people's cultural backgrounds. The use of color must be carefully considered based on the expected or targeted audience and their cultural background and traditions.

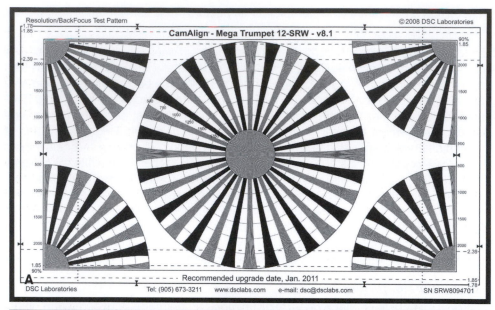

FIGURE 11.1 (A) Camera test charts contain a series of different lines, circles, and wedges of different thicknesses and positions in the frame. Such images enable the technician to both adjust the camera for maximum effectiveness and check the output of the camera. (Courtesy of DSL Labs.) (B) A color test pattern will show a variety of different colors as well as a gray scale chart containing a variety of specifically designed chips ranging from TV-white to TV-black on two strips. The center chip is pure black surrounded by pure white. This chart provides a standard against which a technician may adjust a video camera for maximum quality under the lighting conditions present and a means of comparing camera color output between cameras. (Courtesy of DSL Labs.)

Composition

A graphic artist organizes basic design elements by using principles of composition within the limitations of the visual frame. These principles can be applied to any visual design problem, including computer graphics and the arrangement and selection of on-set, off-set, or digitally designed graphics. They are concepts employed by designers in many other fields as well (see Chapter 7, Lighting and Design).

Balance

A design is balanced when there is an equal distribution of visual weight on each side of an imaginary centerline bisecting the image. Balance or equilibrium enhances unity and order. There are at least four different types of balance: symmetrical, asymmetrical, radial, and occult. *Symmetrical balance* consists of a mirror image of one half of a design in the other half. Identical but reversed elements are arranged on either side of the axis line, which seems to cut the design in two. *Asymmetrical balance* does not have completely identical elements or mirror reflections on either side of the axis line, but the weight or size of the elements on both sides is nonetheless equivalent. Asymmetrical balance permits a higher degree of variation and viewer interest than symmetrical balance. In *radial balance*, two or more similar elements are placed like the spokes of a wheel about a central point. This creates a strong sense of motion or movement around this point, while preserving balance. *Occult balance* is a sense of equilibrium achieved through the placement of unlike elements. Balance is intuited without reliance on conventions or rules. There is usually a strong sense of movement and a dynamic quality to the design (Figure 11.2).

Perspective

Perspective refers to the arrangement of various elements to draw attention to the most important aspect of the image, which is called the *focal center*. A common focal center is the main visual element, but more abstract aspects of a frame can also

EXAMPLES OF VARIOUS FORMS OF BALANCE

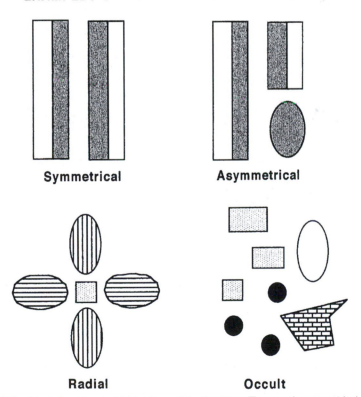

FIGURE 11.2 Graphic designs may be laid out in a variety of patterns. They may be symmetrical (exactly balanced on each side of the frame), asymmetrical (balanced visually on each side of the frame, but not exactly matched), radial (a pattern balanced around a central figure), or occult (without any obvious balance or symmetry).

function as focal centers. Designers rely on a number of basic principles of perspective, such as proximity, similarity, figure/ground, equilibrium, closure, and correspondence. All of these principles are based on the common ways in which our eyes and minds attempt to organize visual images (Figure 11.3).

Proximity

Objects placed near each other form common groupings. Conventional wisdom has it that graphic information should be grouped into common topics within the frame for greater intelligibility. It is unwise to try to pack too much information into a single graphic image. A second graphic frame is usually required when another topic is introduced or there is a great deal of information to convey about a single topic (Figure 11.4).

Similarity

The perception of similarity between shapes and objects in a frame provides another means by which graphic images can be organized. Objects with similar shapes, sizes, colors, and directions of movement are united into common groups. Any deviation from this similarity, such as a runner moving in the opposite direction from the pack or a red object in the midst of green objects, draws immediate attention on the basis of its lack of similarity (Figure 11.5).

PERSPECTIVE

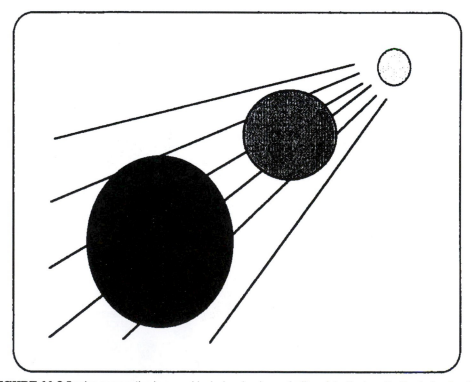

FIGURE 11.3 Forcing perspective in a graphic design develops a feeling of depth along the Z-axis (leading in and out of the frame—toward and away from the viewer), which does not actually exist in a two-dimensional medium. A design appears to have three dimensions by making some objects look larger while others appear smaller, or by appearing to converge toward the background.

PROXIMITY

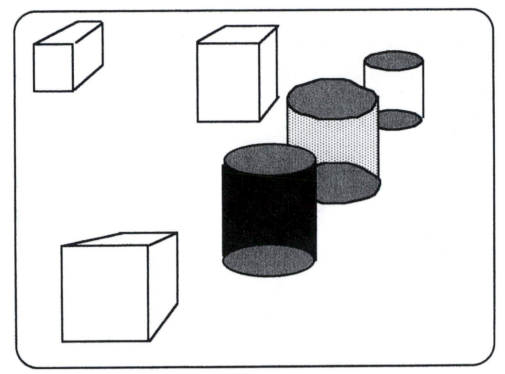

FIGURE 11.4 One way of graphically indicating that a group of objects belongs together is to group them close together in an obvious pattern. The cylinders appear to belong together, and the boxes do not.

SIMILARITY

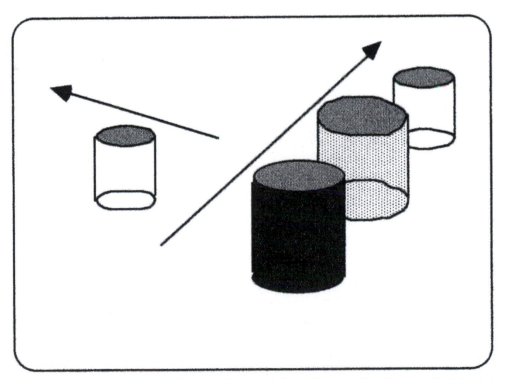

FIGURE 11.5 By grouping similar objects together in an obvious pattern, any other object, even if similar, that is not in the pattern will appear to move away from or at least not belong to the similar grouping.

Figure/Ground

Figure/ground refers to the relationship between backgrounds and foregrounds. Our eyes try to organize visual images into background fields and foreground objects. Some visual illusions are ambiguous, and we can alternate the foreground and background to create different shapes and objects from the same picture. A corporate logo or graphic marks that consist of letters and words, such as Eaton Corporation or PlayMakers Repertory Company, combine white and black letters that reverse figure and ground. The reversal in the PlayMakers logo suggests a rising curtain that is consistent with its theatrical subject matter. Symbols and signs that use figure/ground relationships can be effective means of gaining audience attention and communicating ideas (Figure 11.6).

FIGURE 11.6 A figure/ground illustration. The design conceals which part is the background and which is the foreground by alternating black and white within the type and the background. (Courtesy of the Repertory Company.)

Equilibrium

Another way in which our eyes try to organize graphic images is through a principle of equilibrium. An image in equilibrium is logically balanced and ordered. Equilibrium can be based on natural scientific laws, such as gravity or magnetic attraction, as well as a balancing of object weights and sizes on either side of a centerline in a frame. This organizing principle reflects a well-ordered, logical universe. When images defy a sense of balance or accepted physical or scientific laws, they are in disequilibrium, which can arouse interest but also cause distracting confusion (Figure 11.7).

Closure

Viewers have a natural tendency to try to complete an unfinished form, a principle that is called *closure*. An open form is ambiguous and leaves some questions unanswered. A partially hidden form can still be identified because we expect good continuation of a form off-screen or behind another object, but this is a projection of our need for closure onto the image. A designer can frustrate or fulfill our desire for closure by completing graphic forms or leaving them partially incomplete. The former seem stable and resolved, whereas the latter seem unstable, although they sometimes stimulate creative and imaginative impressions (Figure 11.8).

Emphasis

Brightness and contrast, size and placement, and directionality are devices that help create emphasis. Generally, a bright object attracts attention more readily than a dark object. Our eyes are drawn immediately to the brightest part of a design. However,

EQUILIBRIUM

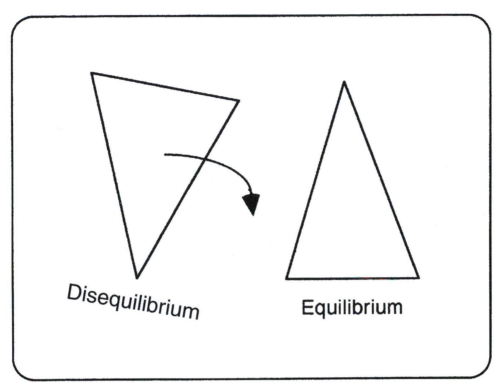

FIGURE 11.7 A triangle or other object with a broad base indicates a graphic arrangement of equilibrium, giving the arrangement a stable, firm graphic appearance. An arrangement with a smaller bottom or an object leaning without any visible support gives the audience a feeling of being off-balance or very unstable.

if the image is almost completely white, emphasis can be achieved by using contrasting darkness for an object. Objects in contrasting colors can create emphasis. Because warm colors advance and cool colors recede, emphasis can be created by using contrasting reds, oranges, or yellows for important objects.

The size or dimension of an object and its placement within the frame can also create emphasis. In general, large objects attract more attention than small objects. However, if most of the objects in an image are large, then a single small object is emphasized by virtue of its deviation from the norm. The placement of objects in a frame can also create emphasis. Closer objects are usually more prominent than distant objects. If several objects are grouped together, the one that is set apart acquires emphasis through variation and contrast. An isolated, individual object can be singled out from a group and thus be emphasized. If the single object outside the group is also different in size, brightness, or color from the members of the group, that emphasis is reinforced. One of the most common forms of directional emphasis is created by the use of converging parallel lines that direct the eye to a specific object. These lines enhance the illusion of perspective and depth at the same time that they add emphasis. The lines can be formed by natural objects, such as a row of trees or a road leading to a house, for example. Many different lines and shapes can direct the eye to various parts of the image, focusing attention in the desired direction.

CLOSURE

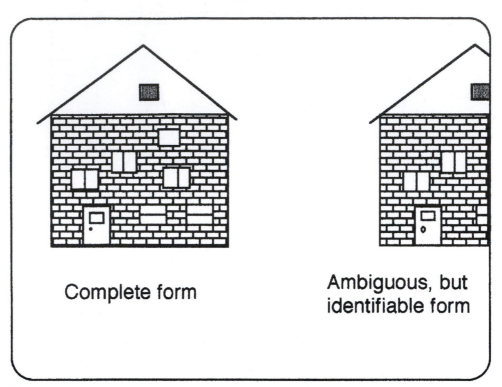

Complete form

Ambiguous, but identifiable form

FIGURE 11.8 The psychological condition of closure actually arises from an ambiguous or incomplete graphic that is designed to allow the viewer to fill in the rest of the picture through prior or common knowledge. A single house by itself will appear to be just that, a single house; but a row of houses may be depicted by only two houses, one on each side of the frame only partly visible. The viewer will fill in the rest of the houses and assume that there are more houses out-of-sight on each side of the frame.

X-Y-Z Axis

The three-dimensionality of reality is created in either a video or film frame with a two-dimensional reproduction. To give the impression that the picture represents the 3-D world, an understanding of how the three dimensions relate to the frame is necessary. The movement or composition along a line running from left to right or vice versa is considered the *X-axis*. Any movement or composition running from the bottom to top or vice versa is considered the *Y-axis*. The *Z-axis* does not actually exist in a two-dimensional medium, but it can be depicted or created through the use of compositional arrangements within the frame. If objects are arranged at an angle, instead of straight across the frame, or a series of objects diminish in size as they rise in the frame, a Z-axis is created. To avoid boring or static pictures, efforts should always be made to create a Z-axis in each sequence.

Readability

The size and amount of detail in an image affects *readability*, which refers to the ease of deciphering and comprehending graphic images. The size of a typeface or style of lettering, for example, is an important determinant of how easy it is to read a graphic image. Type of extremely small point size is usually avoided in video production

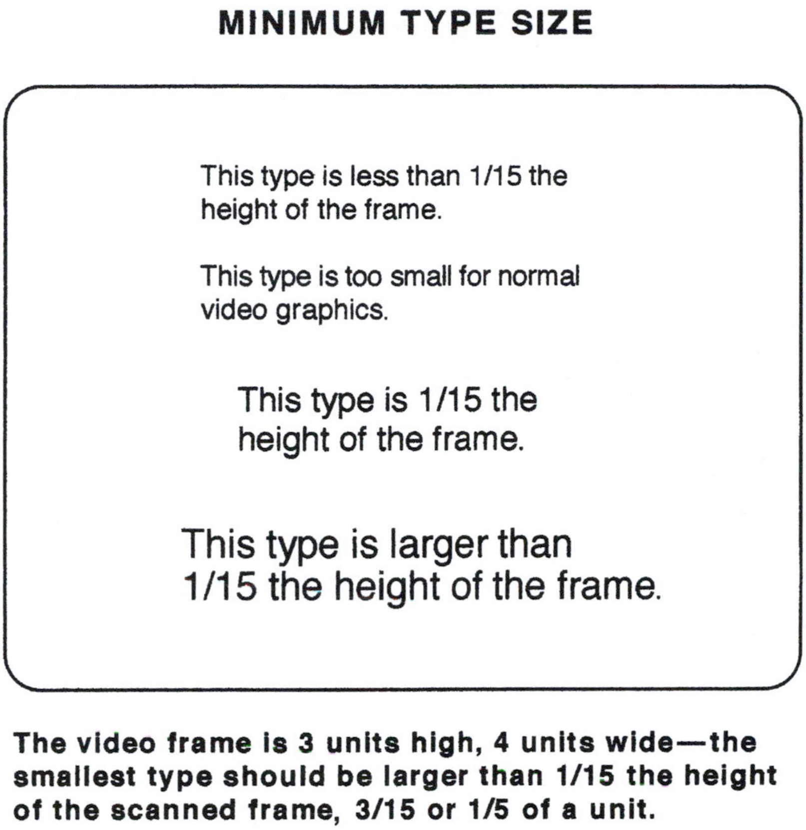

MINIMUM TYPE SIZE

This type is less than 1/15 the
height of the frame.

This type is too small for normal
video graphics.

This type is 1/15 the
height of the frame.

This type is larger than
1/15 the height of the frame.

**The video frame is 3 units high, 4 units wide—the
smallest type should be larger than 1/15 the height
of the scanned frame, 3/15 or 1/5 of a unit.**

FIGURE 11.9 In television production, partly because of the relatively low resolution of a home television receiver and partly because some of the audience may be watching on a small-screen receiver, graphic material in type form should not be smaller than 1/15th of the scanned height of the graphic.

because small titles are difficult to read on a film or television screen. *Point size* refers to the height of letters; the higher the point size, the larger the letter. (The text you are reading is in 10-point type.) Lettering sizes smaller than 1/15 of the full picture height should be avoided in television graphics (Figure 11.9).

Graphic artists also avoid finely drawn lettering and *serifs*, which are delicate decorative lines that are often difficult to reproduce. Because of the limited size, resolution, and sharpness of television images, boldface type is recommended for titles and subtitles. Plain backgrounds give prominence to foreground titles and lettering. A highly detailed or multitoned background is distracting. Good contrast between foreground and background tones and colors is essential for legibility. When titles are keyed over live-action images, bright lettering should be used, preferably with some kind of border, drop shadow, or edge outline, which gives greater legibility and three-dimensionality (Figure 11.10).

Image Area

An important determinant of composition in visual graphics is the aspect ratio or frame dimensions of the recorded and displayed image. As noted earlier, frame dimensions vary in television and film. The aspect ratio, or proportion of height to width, of standard television images is 4:3 or 1.33:1. The aspect ratio specifications for high-definition

UNCLUTTERED BACKGROUND

This background makes reading copy almost impossible.

Unreadable cluttered background.

This background makes reading copy possible by providing a cleared space.

"Boxing" important copy over a cluttered background works well.

This background is uncluttered making reading copy possible.

A satisfactory compromise is an uncluttered background.

If copy is the most important item, then a clear or no background is best.

The best solution for clarity is no background.

FIGURE 11.10 No font or important graphic should be framed in front of a busy background or a background with many small elements. If such a background must be used, the graphic can be framed within a plain box by defocusing the background or increasing the lighting contrast so that the important graphic will stand out and be clearly visible.

television (HDTV) is 16:9 or 1.85:1; projected film images vary somewhat in terms of their aspect ratios, from 1.33:1 to 2:1 (Figure 11.11).

When HDTV images are viewed on a 4:3 standard television receiver or monitor, the viewer will either not see a portion of the image on both sides of the frame or the signal will need to be broadcast in letterbox frame. *Letterbox framing* refers to a widescreen image shown in its full width, but a narrow band of black across the top and the bottom of the frame fills in the areas that are not included in a wide-screen production. At one time letterbox was considered an unacceptable method of showing wide-screen productions, but with the advent of HDTV it is not only acceptable but has become fashionable, with commercials being produced intentionally in letterbox format (Figure 11.11).

Scanning or Full-Aperture Area

The *scanning area* is the full field of view picked up by the camera sensor. The *full-aperture area* is the equivalent in film of this area. It refers to the entire field of view recorded on an individual frame of film.

If a graphic illustration or title card is shot live in the studio rather than created as a computer-generated graphic, then it must be framed in the camera so that it is slightly larger than the actual scanning or full-aperture area; this ensures that the edges of the

**COMPENSATING FOR DIFFERENCES
BETWEEN 4:3 & 16:9 FRAME RATIOS**

4:3 Broadcast, 16:9 Program

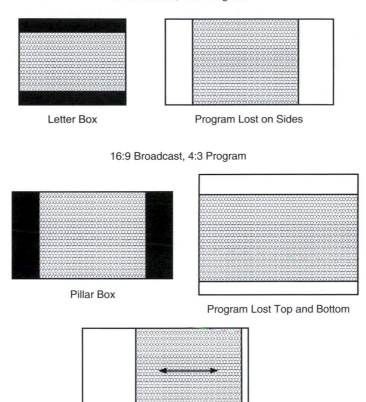

Letter Box   Program Lost on Sides

16:9 Broadcast, 4:3 Program

Pillar Box

Program Lost Top and Bottom

Pan and Scan

FIGURE 11.11 Motion pictures shot in the Academy Standard 4:3 ratio will be reproduced on standard television with full frame and no surrounding black bars. But 4:3 films or standard definition (SD) TV pictures on an HD wide screen will show black bars either on either side of the frame or the top and bottom of the frame will be trimmed to create a 16:9 aspect ratio. If a 16:9 or widescreen motion picture is broadcast on an SD monitor, the sides of the frame will be trimmed or the picture will be reduced and a black band will appear on the top and bottom of the monitor (known as the letterbox format). An HDTV 16:9 or widescreen movie will fit on a HDTV widescreen monitor without modifying the picture.

card do not appear in the frame. The scanning area should be about 1½ inches inside the outer edge of a 14-foot 11-inch or 11-foot 8-inch illustration or title card.

Essential Area

The *essential area* of the frame is the safe recording portion of the frame. Graphic information is placed within the essential area, so that it will not be cut off by somewhat overscanned TV receivers or film projector apertures. (Home TVs usually reproduce less than the full camera frame because the horizontal scanning is expanded.) The essential area of the video camera should allow at least a 10 percent border within the scanning area so that there is no possibility of eliminating essential information. If a graphic image falls within the essential area, an artist can be confident that all key information will be safely recorded and projected.

GRAPHIC DESIGN

Graphic design, like scenic design, is concerned with structuring pictorial content. Graphic images should be closely tied to overall scenic design, including sets and costumes. For example, the red titles and sepia-toned still photographs (black-and-white pictures with an overall reddish-brown color tone) at the beginning of *Bonnie and Clyde* (1967) foreshadow the violence and bloodshed to come and establish the 1930s' setting of the film through costuming and props in each photograph. A good graphic design organizes visual information so that it can be efficiently communicated to viewers. Graphic designs organize many different types of information, including lettering and illustrations. Titles are often the first images presented on a videotape or film, and they must set a context for what is to follow. Graphic titles and illustrations answer questions about who, what, when, where, why, and how or how much. Graphic images often convey information more directly than speech and live-action images. They can boil down complex ideas into simple concepts, which are represented by shapes, words, or numbers. Titles and illustrations can clarify the ideas inherent in more complex, live-action images and speech.

Principles of Graphic Design

The best titles often are very simple. Trying to convey too much information at one time produces ineffective or unintelligible messages. Each image should convey one general thought or idea. Everything presented within that image must contribute to a central theme. A complex array of statistics can often be boiled down to a simple graph or chart. Titles and subtitles that clarify visual information or give credit to contributors must be clear and concise. Good titles and subtitles do not crowd the image, yet title size is often used to convey their relative importance. Simple images are generally more intelligible images. They eliminate confusion and frequently have great aesthetic and emotional impact.

Types of Graphics

Graphics can be divided into two different categories on the basis of their placement and use during production: on-set and off-set graphics including computer-generated graphics.

Off-Set Graphics

Off-set graphics are generated somewhere other than with the live studio camera in the same studio as the production. They may come from a title card, computer-generated image, videotape, or a digital image fed directly into the switcher from a computer.

Computer Graphics

One of the most promising applications of computer technology to film and television production is computer graphics. The advantage of computer graphics systems, like that of the character generator, is that the images do not have to be recorded by a camera and individual frames can be digitally stored. Computer-generated images (CGIs) and graphics applications offer a wide range of fonts, font sizes, colors, and backgrounds. Movement, such as crawls, rolls, or digital transitions, is limited only by the particular model of computer. In addition, because the files are stored digitally, they can be called up and used immediately. A large number of files can be entered in advance of a production for insertion at the proper time and place (Figure 11.12).

FIGURE 11.12 A character generator (CG) is a relatively simple computer graphics machine designed to create lines of type, including numbers, and simple color graphics backgrounds or lines of type to be keyed over other video frames. (Courtesy of Scitex Digital Video.)

A variety of hardware and software systems are currently available for use in video and film production. Most systems allow the operator or artist to control all of the elements of graphic design, including line, shape, and color. Images can be created directly on the screen, using a light pencil, stylus, mouse, or keyboard. The artist can select and control various lines and shapes, as well as image size, color, and placement on the screen. It is also possible to use a stylus to trace a hand-drawn sketch or outline so that it can be computer manipulated and stored in disk form. Some computers have *frame-grabbers*, which allow the computer to manipulate a single video frame from a camera or VCR. Some computer software allows graphics programs to be integrated with animation programs to create apparent motion. Images can be placed in disk storage and accessed at any time. A graphics computer that has an SD or HD video signal output can be fed directly to a VCR or a switcher.

Partially because of convergence, a graphic designer must diversify to learn and use many skills and techniques handled in the past by individual operators. Now a designer must be familiar with all aspects of the field, including basic artistic principles (the same in either analog or digital), typography, photography, motion pictures, video, audio, animation and visual effects (VFX), and web technology. Basic concepts of design are unaffected by digital technology. The designer still must conceive and develop ideas and understand graphic principles and solutions, as well as composition, despite the wide scope of tools for exploring graphic concepts faster, cheaper, and over a wider range of solutions.

Graphic Applications

There are two basic types of graphic applications: bitmap and vector formats. Bitmap applications include Photoshop, Painter, and CorelDraw. Bitmap images are made up of a fine grid of individual pixels. Each pixel may be a different color. The combination of pixel color intensities in red, green, and blue will give the desired color, just as the screen on a video monitor provides many different colors from the combination of different intensities of the red, green, and blue guns in the cathode ray tube (CRT). To produce a graphic in bitmap, the application provides a series of tools to modify or edit the arrangement of pixels. Some of the tools are paintbrush, pencil, airbrush, cloning, color adjustment, masks, filters, and the ability to build layers with different objects in each unique layer. Bitmap graphics may be as simple as a single frame of type or as complex as the removal of wires and an unwanted building in a science fiction motion picture like the *Matrix* series (2002–2003).

Bitmap Formats

PICT (Apple Picture)	Used only for R-G-B files
BMP (Windows Bitmap)	Used only for R-G-B files
TIFF (Tagged Image File Format)	RGB and CMYK or indexed color
	Widely used for print; can be compressed without losing data
JPEG (Joint Photographic Experts Group)	Best for photos, especially Internet; compression can reduce file size but with some loss; should not be multicompressed
EPS (Encapsulated Postscript)	Reserved for vector files
GIF (Graphics Interchange Format)	Used only for web projects

Vector applications include Illustrator and Freehand. The vector graphic is determined by connecting strategically placed points on lines. Moving the lines at the point of contact creates a mathematical formula that determines the shape of the figure. The line may be connected, forming a shape that may be filled with color, textures, or gradients among other aspects. Each object is an individual item in the frame. The curves created by bending the lines into forms are called Bezier curves. Text can be converted to vector files and shapes and may be grouped and locked together. Layers and filters are available to build special forms and images. Vector files tend to be smaller than bitmap files.

Typography

The type fonts in computer graphics are based on historical terms spacing used in the print industry. The measurements are points (pt), pica, and inches: 12 points equal 1 pica; 6 picas equal 1 inch. So 12-pt type in the print world is $^1/_6$ of an inch; 72-pt type is 1 inch. But a computer screen is not necessarily the same size as a graphic printed from that file. Experience leads the designer to know the point size of their fonts, but the sizes are relative to everything in the frame. Computer graphic artists use points for type size, picas for column width, and inches for resolution (dpi) dots per inch. The space between lines is called leading, and the space between letters if adjusted is called kerning.

Type/Font Measurement

- Points (pt) = Type height
- Pica = Column width
- Leading = Space between lines
- Kerning = Space between letters
- Dots per inch (dpi) = Resolution
- 12 points = 1 pica
- 6 picas = 1 inch
- 12-pt type = $\frac{1}{6}$ of an inch high type
- 72-pt type = 1 inch high type

SEARCHING THE INTERNET

Browsers are applications that provide a means of searching or "surfing" the Internet. Browsers find a page by looking for that page's unique universal resource locator (URL). Once found, it displays that page on the screen using the hypertext markup language (HTML) instructions contained on that page. The page will appear instantaneously unless complex or moving graphics are included. Additional software like QuickTime or RealPlayer may be needed to translate video or flash for animations. The two major browsers are Safari and Internet Explorer.

Hypertext Markup Language (HTML)

HTML code is invisible to the viewer of a web page, but the code is buried within the page file, providing the instructions for the background color, font size, and object positioning in the frame. The code as written appears confusing but is very logical. Each line is preceded and followed by a "tag" that tells the browser how the line should be displayed. HTML may be written directly using text editors or by using a WYSIWYG ("what you see is what you get") program like Dreamweaver or GoLive. Graphics for the web are prepared in an image editor like Photoshop or a layout program like Quark Express or Freehand. Flash and ShockWave programs create animation and sound files to be embedded in a web page. The speed at which a viewer can download a web page depends on the size of the files and the method the viewer uses to download from the Internet. A 56 K modem will be very slow, but any of the broadband systems will download files much more quickly.

Interactivity

Interactivity is a relationship between the computer and the operator. Everything we do on a computer is a form of interactivity because the operator tells (asks) the computer to respond with some kind of an action visible on the screen. Web sites offer extensive interactivity with the operator given the opportunity to explore, modify searches, and gain access to files. The web designer needs to know how to create hyperlinks that connect one page, file, or source with another. The process of creating hyperlinks varies with the application used to create the link text. In essence, the application is told to "link" and given an URL as the next item in the link. Java and JavaScript are two leading languages designed to add interactivity to web pages. Special items such as rollover buttons, image maps, games, and animated texts may be programmed with a Java application. Other applications such as QuickTime, MP3, Windows Media Player, and RealAudio are used to compress sound and video files to be streamed for web distribution. Streaming allows a continuous flow of information on the web to be downloaded and stored on the receiver's computer drives.

Multimedia

Multimedia is the creation of audio and video and graphic programs distributed on a permanent medium rather than on the Internet. The technology used to create multimedia is similar to that of web pages. The major difference is between the restricted bandwidth of web pages and the much less restricted bandwidth of CD-ROMs and DVD systems. Multimedia programs produced for distribution on CDs are limited to the playback capabilities of individual computers. DVD multimedia programs deliver full color, motion, and 5.1 surround sound in uncompressed forms. Multimedia programs are produced using video and audio editing applications like Final Cut Pro and Director with animation and graphics added through After Effects and other graphic applications. The capabilities of editing programs for multimedia are constantly expanding, and at the same time the programs are becoming simpler to operate and cheaper to own.

The primary advantages of computer graphics systems are savings in time and convenience. In preproduction use, storyboards can be quickly and efficiently generated, and then modified immediately before actual production to mirror changes. Hard copies can then be printed for camera operators and other members of the production team. During production, illustrations such as charts, graphs, and drawings can be generated quickly and used immediately. Computer-generated graphics provide the background information for weather forecasts. Titles and lettering can be corrected immediately and then added to images to clarify the information they contain. All of this information can then be conveniently stored and accessed during production without using a camera. Images can also be modified efficiently and easily during production. Although sophisticated computer graphics systems are still very expensive, low-cost systems, such as those available with many home computer systems, can be inexpensively purchased and integrated into a television production facility.

On-Set Graphics

Set furnishings, props, costumes, and performer makeup are not completely independent elements in the production process. Elements of graphic design interact with each other and many other areas of production to create an overall visual impression. The most important interactions are those between graphic design and each of the following: lighting, performer movement, and important graphic elements. The most commonly used types of on-set graphics are handheld cards, photographic blowups, and three-dimensional graphic set pieces. Handheld cards are images that a performer holds up to the camera during a scene. The talent controls the timing and placement of this type of graphic illustration.

Still photographs can be blown up or enlarged so that they provide a convenient background or backdrop on the set. Such photographs should have a matte rather than a shiny or glossy surface so that they do not reflect a great deal of light, and they should be positioned so that no glare or reflection is directed toward the camera lens. Three-dimensional structures placed on the set for illustration purposes are called *graphic set pieces*. A graphic set piece could be an item to be demonstrated, such as a piece of machinery, or an art object. Most on-set graphics can be scanned and digitized ahead of time so that the framing can be precise and the camera is not tied up with a static shot unless it is necessary for the talent to handle the graphic or be part of the action involving the graphic.

Camera cards are usually placed on an easel, which is an adjustable display platform or graphics stand. The lights on the easel, which illuminate the card, are normally placed at a 45-degree angle from the card's surface to minimize light reflection in the camera lens. When the cards are attached to the easel by rings, they can easily be flipped, while maintaining perfect registration for the camera.

It is also possible to zoom in to different elements on a card or photograph. This adds dynamic movement to static images. Dissolving from one card illustration to another is another common technique. The camera should record a card or illustration directly head-on to avoid keystone distortion. *Keystone distortion* exaggerates the size of the top, bottom, left, or right side of a card when the camera positioning is slightly off dead center (Figure 11.13).

A section of the studio wall that is painted blue or green as the background for a weather report is commonly used as a graphic set piece in television news production. The weather board allows various weather maps and figures to be chroma-keyed behind the weather reporter. A whiteboard on which the talent can write or draw is also a graphic set piece. During elections, tally boards are entirely digital in operation.

Lettering and Titles

Graphic images can be divided into two additional categories, titles and illustrations, on the basis of the nature of the images themselves. *Titles* are various forms of lettering that either accompany illustrations and live-action images or are presented as

FIGURE 11.13 Keystoning is the effect created by shooting a graphic at an angle rather than straight on. The closer edge of the graphic will appear to be larger, and the farther edge will appear smaller when in reality they are the same size.

written text. They are created electronically on devices called a *character generator* or *graphics generator. Illustrations* are visual images, such as charts, graphs, and pictures. They can be hand-drawn, photographed, or produced with the aid of computer graphics equipment.

Lettering and titles are used to introduce the name of a film or television program and to list the credits or names of people who have contributed in some way to the production. The opening group of titles for a program is called a *title* or *credit sequence* (Figure 11.14).

Another common use of titles is to clarify live-action images. Subtitles or name keys are titles keyed in the bottom third of the video or film frame, indicating the person or place being shown. Finally, lettering and titles can be presented as pure text, that is, without any other visual accompaniment.

Textual materials are used to convey written information in the form of electronic newspapers, advertising, or financial statements.

Credit or Titles

Credit and title sequences present an opportunity for creative, abstract expression on the part of a graphic artist. They are carefully designed to communicate the central message and feelings of a film or television program. The opening credits or title sequence offer the audience an introduction to the basic subject matter of the program. It must arouse the audience's interest, excitement, and curiosity. Titles should integrate well with overall scenic design. Graphic design and lettering styles should be appropriate to the overall subject matter.

John Doe

FIGURE 11.14 To identify key performers, the name is typed on the character generator and then keyed over the medium close-up of the performer below his or her face but high enough in the frame to be visible to all viewers.

ANIMATION

Animation develops imaginative worlds by using single-frame recording techniques to make static images and objects appear to move; whether the medium is digital files, film, or video, the philosophy and basic techniques are the same. By breaking the motion of an object down into its component parts, an animator can control the movements of otherwise lifeless figures and images. Single-frame recordings of static images can create apparent motion when small changes in the positioning of objects occur between successive frames. Thus, animation creates apparent changes in position. Only 24/30 different images may be required for each second's duration of the final sequence, although single-frame versus double-frame animation is always a trade-off between smoothness and cost.

The animator's job is to create the desired illusion of movement. Animation is based on an animator's knowledge of time and motion. An animator must be able to break down motion into its component parts so that it can be artificially constructed out of static images. One of the best means of analyzing motion is to examine the individual frames of a live-action film. A live-action motion picture camera, for example, records 24 (25 in Europe) frames every second at standard speed. Each frame represents $1/24$th ($1/30$th in video) of the change in the subject's spatial positioning during one second. By looking at the amount of change that occurs between the successive frames of a live-action sequence, an animator can begin to determine how much change there should be in the position and movement of objects between successive animated frames.

It is not always necessary to record a different image for each film frame, however. A smooth illusion of continuous motion can often be obtained by recording two identical frames of each image or drawing position. Thus, only 12 different images will be required for each second's duration of the final sequence, rather than 24 images.

Storyboards and Animation Preproduction

An animated sequence often begins with the construction of a *storyboard*. A storyboard is a series of sequential sketches that depict the composition and content of each shot or key action in an animated sequence. A storyboard is similar to a newspaper comic strip. It helps a graphic artist or animator to visualize the entire sequence on paper before preparing the final images. The storyboard can be used to communicate the animator's basic idea and strategy to a producer. It can also serve as a blueprint or guide to the actual creation and recording of images.

Many animators design their storyboards in conjunction with prerecorded music, sound effects, or voice tracks. Because timing or synchronization between sound and images is often crucial to the success of an animated sequence, music and sound are initially recorded and analyzed. All of the detail is entered into a log sheet (often called an exposure sheet or *dope* sheet) (Figure 11.15).

Types of Animation

Many different types of images and objects can be animated, including hand-drawn illustrations, paper cutouts, puppets, clay figures, still photographs of live actions, and computer graphic images. All of these forms of animation are based on single-frame recording techniques. It is often helpful to distinguish between flat and plastic animation, as well as between film and digital animation. *Flat animation* is two-dimensional (2-D) and includes such techniques as cel animation, in which individual

EXPOSURE (Dope) SHEET

TITLE_____ SCENE_____ ANIMATOR_____ SHEET # _____

FRAME	ACTION	SETTING	LAYERS					CAMERA
			4	3	2	1	BG	

FIGURE 11.15 An animation exposure sheet, sometimes called a dope sheet, includes all of the information the camera operator needs to make the exposures and movements of the cels and to determie which cels to stack in the layer.

illustrations are drawn for almost every frame of a picture. *Plastic animation*, also called *stop-action* or *single frame* animation, encompasses the use of three-dimensional figures, such as puppets or clay figures. Single-frame recording of people and three-dimensional objects is sometimes called *pixillation*. In a sense, all of these techniques or types of animation elevate the animator to the status of director, editor, and scenic designer.

Flat animation refers to the recording of two-dimensional images using single-frame recording techniques. One of the most common forms of flat animation is *cel animation*. *Cels* are individual sheets of clear acetate on which images can be drawn or painted, usually with ink and opaque watercolors. Cels are preperforated with holes at one end so they can be inserted over the pegs of a movable table, called an *animation rostrum*, for precise registration and framing. An *animation stand* consists of a rostrum, lights, and a movable camera platform (Figure 11.16).

Cel animation gives the animator or graphic artist complete control over the design of the image. However, drawing each frame individually on a cel can be quite time-consuming and expensive, so many shortcuts are used to conserve time. Because cels are transparent, they can be sandwiched together to combine images drawn on different cels. A background cel can be used over and over again while changes are made in the placement of foreground objects, eliminating the need to redraw the background for each frame. Individual movements of characters' feet, hands, and mouths can be repeated or recycled with different bodies and backgrounds.

FIGURE 11.16 Layers of individual cels allow the animator to move some parts of the character or background, but not all at once. Layers of cels also may create a third dimension and sense of depth to the frame. The top illustration shows three individual cels from the left to right: the two space characters, then the moving pattern on the monitors behind the crew, and last the space ship interior as a background. The bottom illustration shows the three cels locked together for the complete frame ready to be recorded.

Another commonly used technique for cutting costs and increasing cel-animation effi-ciency is called *rotoscoping*. In rotoscoping, a sequence is first filmed in live action; the individual frames of the motion picture are then projected on a cel, and an outline of the objects in the frame is drawn and hand-colored. Subjects are normally photo-graphed against a contrasting background so that outlines are clearly visible. The drawn outlines are then colored like standard hand-drawn animation cels. Although rotoscoping makes the production of cels more efficient, it often produces images that are less aesthetically pleasing than hand-drawn animation. *Motion capture* (MoCap) takes rotoscoping one step further (see explanation under "Motion Capture" later in this chapter).

Hand-drawn illustrations are not the only flat images that can be animated. Paper or fabric cutouts and still photographs can also be set into motion. A paper cutout of a person or animal can be constructed so that it has moving body parts. It can then be placed over a variety of backgrounds so that it seems to come alive and move on the screen. A flicker effect can also be achieved by recording frames of colored paper in between frames of specific photographs or illustrations. The change in photographs can be timed to the beat of music. In this way what might otherwise be a boring pre-sentation of static images acquires kinetic energy. Still photographs and printed illus-trations, such as magazine images, can be animated through single-frame techniques, such as those used by Frank Mouris in his famous *Frank Film* (1978). Mouris's film is as much a feat of optical printing, discussed later in this chapter, as of animation (Figure 11.17).

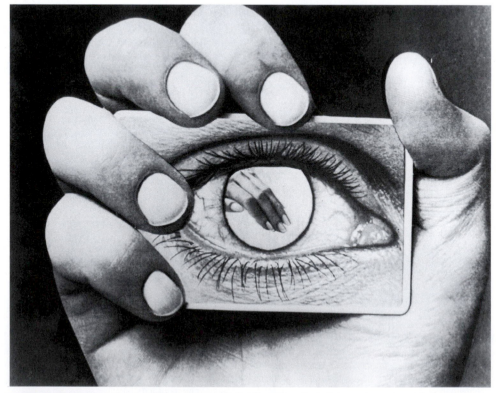

FIGURE 11.17 Frank Mouris specialized in producing films shot single-frame, often using collages of unrelated images shot in sequences as short as two to three frames for a rapid, eye-teasing format.

Plastic animation refers to the animation of many different types of 3-D figures and objects using single-frame recording techniques. Puppets, clay figures, miniature vehicles, and even still frames of live action can be animated.

Although hand puppets and marionettes are usually recorded in live action so that the mouth and body movements can be synchronized to speech or music, it is possible to animate more rigid puppets and clay figures by moving them slightly between frames.

Unlike the animator of flat, two-dimensional characters, however, the plastic animator must create a miniature three-dimensional world of sets and props within which puppets and figures will move. Careful attention must be paid to minute details. Backgrounds must be painted to scale, and everything must be proportional to the size of the figures. The camera is usually placed in a horizontal position with respect to the scene rather than above it, as with an animation stand. Miniature vehicles, such as cars and trucks, can also be animated through single-frame techniques. Sometimes these animated miniatures are used as a substitute for more costly and dangerous stunts and special effects in live-action films.

An animated three-dimensional figure sequence is shot much like a live-action scene, except that the pictures are recorded frame-by-frame. More than one camera is frequently used so that action does not have to be repeated for different shots, as in single-camera live-action recording.

Human figures can also be animated by a technique known as *pixillation*. Images of human beings can be pixillated by recording one frame, moving the image, and then recording another frame. Pixillation has been used in many films to animate images of human beings so that they seem to perform extraordinary feats. In Norman McLaren's famous film *Neighbors* (1955), two neighbors fight over their adjoining territory. This clever film offers a symbolic treatment of war by presenting a unique abstract image of human behavior and actions. In one scene, the human figures hover across the ground with no apparent movement of their limbs. McLaren achieved this image by photographing single frames of his subjects leaping into the air. Only the apex of each jump was recorded, making the people seem to hover over the ground.

Computer Animation

Computer animation programs are used for video and film productions. Virtually all commercials, all newscasts, and most television/cable and film programs use some form of computer animation or computer graphics. Some animation programs fully integrate graphics programs and animation programs so that still-frame graphic images can be used to create apparent motion. Graphic images can be originally designed on a computer monitor by using various computer commands and devices, such as a light pencil or stylus to draw on a television screen or an electronic tablet or a mouse to compose images on a computer screen. They can then be colored and manipulated by computer.

Live-action frames can also be grabbed or digitized by some computers for further graphic manipulation or combined with computer graphic images. Single-frame graphic images can be stored on disk. These images can be expanded in size for detailed work and then shrunk to a smaller size for actual presentation. The animator can manipulate the colors, lines, shapes, and size of the image. Motion is created by cycling different movements and using the computer to interpolate intermediate frames of motion between two static frames.

Computer animation programs allow for *interpolation*, another form of animation that uses paths and involves the drawing of lines through 3-D space. Using interpolation, the animator composes the first and last frames of a sequence, referred to as the *key-frames*, and the computer software then creates or interpolates the in-between frames Computer animation allows an almost infinite number of repetitions of the same image. Image cycling is facilitated by simply drawing the first and last frame of a sequence, interpolating the rest, and then recycling this sequence wherever it is needed.

Rendering is the final step in 2-D and 3-D animation. It is often the most time-consuming and memory-intensive stage of computer animation. The end product of rendering is the creation of a graphics file that can be combined with other graphics files to collectively produce the completed animation sequence. The time and memory required for rendering is often extensive, but it can be reduced by using shortcuts for color, procedure (mathematical approximations of "natural" patterns, such as marble or clouds), and texture (a graphic drawn on an object, such as a soft drink label drawn on a can) maps applied to images during the rendering process.

The greatest advantages of computer animation are speed and accuracy. Results are immediately viewable. An animator need not wait a day or a week for the film animation to be processed and printed at a laboratory. Images and frames can be quickly designed and accurately copied. They can be stored on disk for long periods of time and used again or redesigned for another animation sequence.

A completely computer-controlled illusion of three-dimensionality can also be obtained in films that combine live-action characters with computer-generated objects and backgrounds, such as *Tron* (1983) and *Who Framed Roger Rabbit* (1988).

The live-action subject is usually recorded against a blue screen or a monochromatic background so that it can be keyed or matted into a computer-generated scene. The availability of these combined animation and special effects techniques has allowed graphic artists to save time and experiment creatively with abstract visual images for film and video (Figure 11.18).

3-D Computer Animation

The differences between 2-D and 3-D computer animation involve the complexities of creating figures with a Z-axis dimension. The standard method is to follow the storyboard stage of 2-D drawing with the design and creation of a wireframe model of the figure. The wireframe is made up of a series of polygons that approximate the three-dimensional shape of the object. The wireframe model is then smoothed and rounded to a more realistic shape by creating the "skin" or outer surface of the object. Textures, shading, and lighting are added to enhance the 3-D effect. Once the figure is complete, the digital file that represents that figure must then be rendered, just as 2-D animation figures are rendered to a final form that may be output to film or video for combination with background, other figures, and added movement; the final form may also be distributed.

Motion Capture

Motion capture (MoCap) is a logical computerized extension of film rotoscoping philosophy. Subjects are wired with sensors located at critical points on the body. The sensors either emit a signal to a remote receiver or are wired directly to a computer with a special program that combines the position of each of the body parts with an animated character. As the subject moves arms, legs, head, or other body parts, the

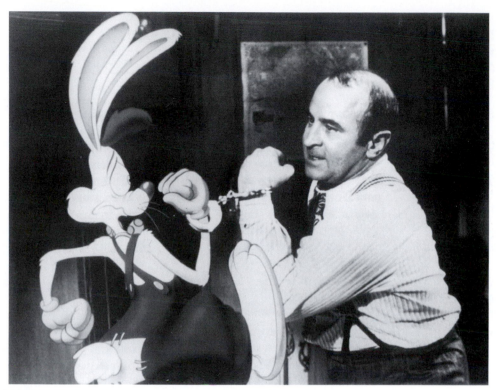

FIGURE 11.18 The Touchstone production of *Who Framed Roger Rabbit* (1988) combined live-action, cel-drawn animation and computer animation sequences in a startling yet realistic manner. (Courtesy of Touchstone Pictures and Amblin Entertainment, Inc.)

animated character moves the same amount and direction. The movements are accurately recorded in the computer program, allowing the animation to progress in real time as the actor(s) move. The process is not only a rapid means of animating movements, but also the body movements are accurate and realistic. The technology is still under development, and some animation purists do not totally accept MoCap as a legitimate form of animation.

Animation on the Web

Because of the limitations of the delivery systems on the web, web graphics and animation must be carefully designed so that they do not exceed the channels of delivery. Full-color, full-sized, moving images do not reproduce well on systems driven by the slower modem. As systems designed to move data at a higher rate are more widely used, the quality of animation on the web will improve. Today web art borrows from all forms and modes of animation and graphics. Two- and, in limited cases, three-dimensional graphics or animation can be downloaded with patience, plenty of memory, and a speedy delivery system. By comparison to other visual media, web art will remain somewhat primitive but full of opportunities for experimenting and plowing new artistic ground.

Flash

Flash is a multimedia, web-based graphics application using a frame-based timeline that allows *keyframing* and *tweening*. Keyframing is an animation technique used to simplify and speed up the animation process. A motion sequence consists of a starting framing in a selected position and an ending frame in another selected, usually different position. The two keyframes are drawn and noted in the program, a direction of movement and change in position or size if required is indicated, and then the program will "tween" the rest of the frames in-between to keyframes by doing the drawing and positioning. A file is created, saved, stored, and publish in a browser much like any web file application, but with few HTML codes. Flash requires minimum programming skills, some knowledge of HTM, some knowledge of basic computer animation, but is nearly WYSIWYG ("what you see is what you get"). The program is much faster than other animation programs and allows interactivity and buttons for insertion of other material. The application supports bidirectional streaming interactivity through the application ActionScript, which is similar to, but different than, JavaScript a commonly used web application.

Drawing images on flash uses vector graphics like Illustrator, which gives a clean image that can easily be manipulated including reducing or enlarging forms and shapes without losing clarity or quality of the image. Illustrator may be used with one of two levels of flash, either Lite or CS3 Pro for the more complex projects. Colors is easily accomplished, changing's shapes much like using Illustrator controls. Sound may be added and edited within the program or created externally and downloaded to the flash file as MP3 files.

Film Animation

Film animation requires the use of a camera that records single frames of motion-picture film. The camera is normally suspended above the artwork by mounting it on an animation stand. An animation stand consists of a camera platform attached to vertical poles or columns, so that it can be raised and lowered over the artwork. The camera platform is suspended above a large horizontal table, called a *rostrum*, which can be moved east, west, north, and south. The artwork is secured to this horizontal table by placing the hole perforations in proper registration over peg bars on the table.

A film animation camera is normally equipped with special controls for specific animation effects. A variable shutter, for example, can be used to fade out from or fade in to a specific piece of artwork. By rewinding the film to the beginning of a fade-out as indicated by the frame counter on the camera and then fading in on another piece of artwork, a dissolve can be created. Superimpositions are made by backwinding and double-exposing individual frames.

Images are electronically animated by placing a video camera on an animation stand and recording single video frames of the artwork on the table using the same techniques as used for film animation. An important difference between video and film animation is that the video camera records 30 frames per second (fps) instead of 24 fps. Single-frame video animation requires the use of a slo-mo (slow motion) recorder or a disk frame-storage unit, rather than a conventional VCR. A *slo-mo recorder* or *video animator* can be used to record individual frames for a 30-second animation sequence. The sequence can then be transferred to conventional videotape. A disk frame-storage or memory unit, such as that used to store pages of text and titles composed on a character generator, can also be used to record individual animation frames. Some memory units have a limited storage capacity, however, and others are capable of storing and immediately accessing hundreds of figures or pages.

One advantage of recording animation electronically is that the results can be viewed immediately. Film animators frequently have to wait several days or longer to see the results of their work. Video animation and film animation can be combined by recording a pencil test with a video camera using disk storage of single frames and instantly viewing the results on a monitor so that problems can immediately be uncovered and corrections made. The final cels are recorded with a film camera for optimum quality and maximum storage capacity.

SPECIAL EFFECTS

Special effects is in many ways a highly specialized area of media production. Producing most realistic effects was usually quite laborious and expensive in the past. Today, the widespread use of complex and convincing special effects in low-budget productions has been encouraged and simplified by the availability of relatively inexpensive digital image-processing programs that are built into many video cameras, as well as much digital nonlinear editing and special effects computer software. This section provides a broad survey of both traditional and contemporary special effects that are widely used in film, video, and multimedia production.

Special effects (visual effects [VFX] and sound effects [SFX]) can be divided into six basic categories: digital effects, camera effects, optical effects, models, miniatures, and physical effects. *Camera effects* include such features as fast and slow motion as well as single-frame (animation) recording. *Optical* and *digital effects* run the gamut of image-processing techniques, from *matting* and *keying* (where a portion of one image is replaced by another) to *morphing* (transforming one object into another, which is also called metamorphosis) and *compositing* (placing different layers of images on top of another). *Models* and *miniatures*, when combined with single-frame animation as well as matting and keying effects, can be used to put an object, such as a spacecraft, in motion or to create the illusion of a later century city by placing futuristic buildings into an existing location. Makeup can transform an actor into an android, a zombie, or a werewolf, whereas physical effects, such as fog, rain, and explosions, can contribute to the emotional mood of a sequence and generate viewer interest and excitement.

Digital Effects

Digital image processing has greatly reduced the amount of generational loss in image quality that has traditionally accompanied the creation of conventional film and video special effects. Digital effects can be divided into three areas: transitions, filters, and superimpositions, keys, or mattes; compositing; and morphing. *Transitions* are means of replacing one digital clip, which is usually a single image or shot, with another. *Filters* are means of altering a clip. *Superimpositions, keys*, and *mattes* are combinations of more than one clip that appear simultaneously within the same frame. *Compositing* involves combining different layers of visual information that can each be separately edited and animated using a digital nonlinear editing and an animation program, respectively. *Morphing* or *morphogenesis* refers to various techniques of transforming one shape or figure into another.

The types of transitions that can be created between one visual clip and another are virtually limitless. Most digital nonlinear editing and special effects programs offer a wide variety of transition devices as well as the capability of modifying the devices and creating custom transitions. Two of the most commonly used transitions are various dissolves and wipes.

During a *wipe*, one clip is entirely replaced by another clip, beginning in a specific area or several areas of the frame and gradually spreading throughout the frame. One clip can rise like a curtain, while the next is revealed behind it, or one clip can appear to push another off the screen. A wide variety of patterns, from pinwheels to clock hands, can be used to wipe from one clip to the next, and the movements of these wipe patterns or shapes throughout the frame can usually be adjusted.

A variety of *digital filters* allow a clip to be distorted, blurred, sharpened, smoothed, textured, and tinted or colored. Filters can also be used to pan, zoom, reverse motion, slow down, speed up, and flip a clip. The ability to alter the brightness, contrast, and color balance of individual clips allows an operator to function as a timer by smoothing out and eliminating subtle differences in color, brightness, and contrast between successive clips or shots or to function as a special effects artist by radically altering the original image and generating unusual and interesting effects. For example, all colors except the color red can be removed from a clip so that the entire frame is black and white except those portions of the image that are red in color. A clip can be blurred to simulate the point of view of a character whose vision has been altered. Various mosaic grids of squares or other shapes can be used to create interesting patterns, and an image can be *posterized* by limiting the color spectrum to just a few colors, or it can be *solarized* by blending negative and positive images to create a halo effect. By resizing clips, unwanted areas within the frame can often be eliminated, and zooms and pans can be created on stationary or moving images within a clip.

Compositing refers to combining different layers of visual images. One layer might be a model of a rocket ship moving against a neutral background as though it is taking off. Another might consist of an actual launch site recorded at Cape Canaveral. A third layer might consist of digitally animated images of ice particles falling through space. Each of these layers can be separated, edited, and combined into a composite image using a special effects program. This type of special effect was used to create composite images that simulated an Apollo spacecraft taking off in *Apollo 13* (1995).

Using these same techniques, motion clips, such as moving or talking lips, can be inserted in place of stationary images, such as the stationary lips of a character in the background scene, in order to animate a live-action image. Similar types of digital effects have been used in Hollywood feature films, such as *Forrest Gump* (1994), to allow prerecorded documentary images to be combined with studio recordings and to have historical figures appear to interact with and talk to fictional characters.

Morphing or *morphogenesis* refers to various techniques of transforming one shape or figure into another. Morphing can be accomplished in film animation by drawing individual cels that gradually change from one shape or form into another. Digital image processing and animation programs have facilitated the transformation process by allowing the computer to generate the gradual transformation from one figure, such as an automobile, into another, such as a tiger. Morphing is an effective technique for creating transitions from one image to another or for altering shapes, forms, and figures and creating imaginative worlds through the use of special digital effects.

Camera Effects

A significant number and range of special effects can be created within a film camera during initial recording. Some film cameras, for example, allow the frames-per-second speed to be altered from the normal sound speed of 24 fps. Recording rates in excess of 24 fps, such as 32, 48, and 64 fps, create slow motion when the processed film is projected at the standard projection speed of 24 fps. Recording rates less than 24 fps, such as 18 and 12 fps, create fast motion. Attaching an *intervalometer* to a film camera allows the frames per second to be significantly reduced to one frame every 1, 2, or 20 seconds, or even every few minutes or hours, to create *time-lapse recordings*, such as images of clouds rolling overhead or flower petals opening and closing throughout the day. Single-frame control of a live-action film camera allows for pixillation effects, which are described earlier in this chapter. Most digital cameras duplicate these same effects in camera also.

In-camera matte effects are created by blocking off a portion of the frame during the first exposure, rewinding the film, and then exposing the previously blocked portion of the frame. *Matte boxes* can have half of the frame filled with an opaque black filter, which is then reversed to cover the opposite half of the frame to create a split-screen image. First one side of the frame is exposed, and then the film is rewound and the opposite side of the film is exposed. In-camera mattes, which are finely cut out of metal, can also be inserted behind the lens closer to the focal plane. An actor can then play two different roles within the same camera frame. This is done by first filming the actor on one side of the screen, rewinding the film, and then filming the same actor on the opposite side of the screen. Painted skylines and other scenic additions can be made using the same in-camera matte process by dividing the frame horizontally rather than vertically. Filters can also be placed over a lens, such as a gauze or haze filter, to create a softer image. Cinematographers often carry a variety of transparent materials with them on location that can be used to diffuse the image during recording.

Video cameras can also provide built-in special effects controls. For example, fade-ins and fade-outs can often be created automatically at the beginning or end of a shot by depressing a fader control. Some cameras allow the speed of motion to be varied to create slow motion, fast motion, and time-lapse recordings. Other in-camera special effects include various forms of digital image processing, such as image patterning, blurring, solarization, and other visual image manipulations and distortions. Again, many of these in-camera effects can also be created during postproduction, such as digital nonlinear editing, although some experimental videographers prefer to create these effects during initial recording.

Optical Effects

One of the advantages of creating special effects during postproduction is that they can often be more carefully controlled at this stage than during the production stage. Mistakes made during production are often costly if a scene must be reconstructed and actors reengaged. Postproduction special effects are often "added on" to the initial recordings and rarely require the initial scene to be reshot.

A variety of optical film effects are still widely used today, including step printing, traveling mattes, and aerial-image printing. An *optical printer* is needed to create many special effects on film. A basic optical printer consists of a camera and a projector. The two machines face each other, and the lens of the camera is focused on the image from the projector. The camera and projector can be moved toward or away from each other to increase the size of the image. An optical blowup can be created by using a larger-format and a smaller-format projector. Using a smaller-format camera and a larger-format projector creates an optical reduction. The camera and the projector must be precisely positioned so that the full frame of picture in the projector fills the full frame of picture in the camera.

Optical flips can be achieved by simply rotating elements within special optical printer lenses. *Freeze frames* are made by exposing many frames in the camera while holding the same frame in the projector. *Stretch printing* slows down or retards the perceived action by printing each frame more than once. *Skip printing* is often used to speed up a slow-moving sequence by recording every other frame of the original film.

Wipes, split screens, and optical combinations of animation and live action involve the creation of special *traveling mattes*. *Mattes* consist of special high-contrast, black-and-white images that are made from normal film images or from artwork. For example, suppose a color title must be inserted into a background scene. The two images cannot simply be superimposed on one another, because the colors will bleed together rather than producing solid lettering. A black-and-white, high-contrast copy of the titles can be made, so that the black letters will block out the portion of the background image where the colored letters are to be inserted.

The optical printer must have three projectors to do this: one for the background scene, one for the matte (unless the matte and the background scene are *bi-packed*, or run physically in contact with each other in one projector), and one for the color titles. The combination of the three images is then recorded by the camera.

Wipes and split screens can be made from similar traveling mattes, which block out a portion of the screen into which a second image is then inserted. It is possible to combine live action and animation by using traveling mattes in this manner. One sequence can also be recorded against a blue or black screen so that another sequence can be inserted into the blue screen area. Many special effects in science fiction and horror films are achieved by using a blue screen process. Spaceships are often recorded as they move in front of a blue screen. This blue screen portion of the frame is then used to create a matte that blocks out the area of the frame where the spaceship should appear in a highly detailed background scene with stars in outer space. The spaceship is then inserted as a foreground object into this area.

Aerial image photography combines optical printing and animation by using a film projector with an animation stand. Live-action images can be projected from beneath predrawn cels, so that color titles or animated figures can be combined with live action. The opaque portions of the cel block out the background scene, which is projected underneath it so that the titles are superimposed over the background scene. The film camera suspended overhead records the combined image. Aerial image photography eliminates the need for special intermediate mattes, such as those that are used during film printing to block out or blacken areas of the frame into which titles and other images are to be inserted. However, aerial imaging requires bright projection illumination.

The choice between doing special effects on film, videotape, or through a digital medium is often a difficult one to make unless it has already been decided to use film or videotape for an entire production. The obvious advantage of digital video is the savings in overall production time. Effects can be set up and viewed immediately, without waiting for laboratory processing. Electronic effects facilities normally have sophisticated computerized editing and switching equipment, so that several images can be run simultaneously. Keys and mattes can be created instantaneously. Careful preplanning must go into the creation of a special electronic effect before entering the studio.

Optical film effects are time-consuming to produce, but a very high degree of control and precision can be achieved through multiple passes of the same artwork with film. It is also possible to make sophisticated special effects in films with very low cost equipment. A basic optical printer, consisting of a simple projector and camera on adjustable platforms, can be purchased for a modest sum, allowing freeze frames, step printing, superimpositions, dissolves, and many other optical effects to be created.

Models and Miniatures

Full-scale models and reduced-scale miniatures are used whenever a three-dimensional object or setting is needed that either does not exist or when it would be too expensive or dangerous to use an actual object. A miniature may be required for a historical setting that no longer exists, or a full-scale model may be needed for a spaceship that hasn't yet been constructed.

In some situations, such as when the camera must move within the shot, which requires a three-dimensional set to maintain realistic perspective, a painted two-dimensional background cannot be used to create the illusion of a specific location. In this case, a three-dimensional miniature of that location can be constructed to allow for camera moves. Usually when actions occur with a miniature, the camera records the action in slow motion to adjust for the difference in time-scale relations between full-scale and miniature environments. Motion must be reduced

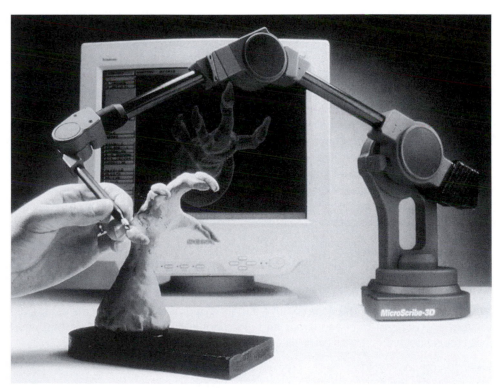

FIGURE 11.19 One of the methods of converting a solid object to a digital form is by tracing that form using a 3-D digitizer. The operator traces over all key surfaces of the object with a stylus until a full 3-D image has been transferred to a digital file. (Courtesy of Immersion Corporation.)

proportionately to the reduced scale of the miniature. When complicated miniatures and movements are required, it is often prudent to shoot test recordings at a variety of speeds before recording final takes or disposing of the miniature (Figure 11.19).

Effective use of miniatures and models requires careful preplanning, because these types of special effects are often extremely expensive. Similar types of coordination and planning are required, just the same as those that are demanded of an art director, director, producer, and cinematographer during full-scale, live-action production. Drawings are usually prepared and approved before miniatures and models are actually constructed.

Miniatures are difficult to record not only because of potential problems in perspective, scale, and speed of motion, but also because audience disbelief is often difficult to overcome. Larger-scale, highly detailed miniatures are usually required for longer shot durations where the audience will have an opportunity to carefully scrutinize them. When smaller, less-detailed miniatures are used, the editor often must keep the shot duration very short to reduce audience scrutiny and to maintain a willing suspension of disbelief.

Miniatures can take advantage of single-frame recording and matting or keying techniques to create apparent motion from stationary objects. A miniature spaceship or airplane, for example, can be recorded against a blue screen background while it is moved slightly along a suspended, invisible wire between each frame. Later a composite of the background scene and the moving aircraft can be made using photographic or electronic matting and keying techniques. Another advantage of miniatures and models is that they can be used to create inexpensive physical effects, such as various explosions, which would otherwise be too expensive to accomplish using actual objects and locations.

Physical Effects

Physical effects include wind, fog, smoke, rain, snow, fires, explosions, and gunshots. They require the guiding hand of a highly trained professional, especially when their use can endanger the safety of the cast and crew. Wind is usually generated by very large fans or aircraft engines and propellers whose speed and direction can be carefully controlled. Fog is often produced by combining smoke, such as from slow-burning naphtha or bitumen mixtures, and dry ice, which produces carbon dioxide. Most smoke-producing devices use either oil or water-based smoke fluid, which is heated above the boiling point to produce a gas that looks like smoke. Because all smoke is toxic to some degree, it should only be used in well-ventilated areas.

Rain, like wind and fog, is often used to accentuate a mood and atmosphere. Ground-level rain stands and overhead rain heads can be used to produce rain in limited areas, and the surrounding areas can be wetted down before shooting to sustain an illusion of a general rain shower. When rain effects are produced in a sound stage, it is extremely important to waterproof the floor, to have a means of drainage or water collection, and to avoid any contact between water and electrical equipment, such as lights, which could cause severe injury or even kill cast and crew members (Figure 11.20).

Snow can be created indoors or outdoors using a large, almost silent, wooden-bladed fan, which can also be used for rain effects, that is called a *Ritter fan*. Plastic snow can be dropped in front of the fan, usually from the top of the left side but never from behind (which would foul the blades and mechanism), by hand or a snow delivery

FIGURE 11.20 Most physical effects are the result of special effects crews using machines and chemicals to produce atmospheres and environments critical to the production, such as the Paramount crew on this Western set preparing to create wind. (Courtesy of Paramount Pictures.)

machine. Polystyrene granules can be added to create a blizzard effect. Outdoors, a variety of materials, in addition to plastic flakes, can and have been used to create snow, including shaved ice, foam machines, gypsum, salt (on windows and window-sills), and aerosol shaving cream on slippery surfaces.

Although fire effects can add excitement and visual interest to a scene, they are also extremely dangerous and should only be created by skilled professionals who know how to contain them. It is extremely important to have fire extinguishers on hand that can control all three classes of fire: Class A fires, which burn solid combustibles such as cloth, rubber, wood, paper, and many plastics; Class B fires, which burn flammable liquids and gases; and Class C fires, which involve electrical or electronic equipment.

Explosions and pyrotechnics are the most difficult special effects to perform safely. They need to be set up and supervised by experts who are thoroughly familiar with the setting, detonation, and control of explosions and fires, because they are potentially dangerous to cast and crew members. The U.S. Bureau of Alcohol, Tobacco, and Firearms controls explosives and pyrotechnics. A federal license is needed to use explosives, and information concerning their use can be obtained from the bureau upon request. Most explosions and pyrotechnics require remote detonation.

Bullet hits are created by remote detonation of small explosive devices, called *squibs*, which are positioned over body armor or a hit plate that protects the actor or stunt-man. Blood packs, consisting of plastic bags containing corn syrup and red food coloring to simulate blood, and squibs are glued onto the back of the actor's or stuntman's shirt. Wires running down the pant legs are attached to the squibs at one end and to the firing box for remote detonation at the other end. Sometimes the wires have break-away connectors at the ankles so that the actor or stuntman can break free of the wires just after the bullet hits have been detonated.

Summary

Graphic design can be approached from realist, modernist, and postmodernist perspectives. Realist sets and design formats depict an actual or general type of place or experience. However, a realist setting can provide an atmosphere that reflects the subjective state of mind or perceptions of a specific character. Modernist designs are relatively abstract and often reflect an abstract conception of space, a subjective feeling, or a state of mind. Postmodernist designs combine a variety of design styles and patterns and emphasize emotional responses and an intentional distortion of realistic visuals.

Graphic design involves three basic design principles: design elements, color, and composition. Design elements include lines, shapes, textures, and movement. Color and contrast are interrelated aspects of design, as are color and shape. Contrasting colors can be used to separate foregrounds and backgrounds and to create various shapes, and they can be used to define specific characters, settings, and themes.

Graphic artists design images that convey information. They use basic principles of design, such as simplicity, proximity, similarity, figure/ground, correspondence, equilibrium, and closure, to stimulate viewer interest. Graphic artists select lettering that is highly legible but also expressive. Titles and illustrations are designed and selected on the basis of their appropriateness for specific topics.

Animation and special effects generate visual interest and can be used to create imaginative worlds. Animation develops imaginative worlds by using single-frame recording techniques to make static images and objects appear to move. By breaking the motion of an object down into its component parts, an animator can control the movements of otherwise lifeless figures and images. Single-frame recordings of static images can create apparent motion when small changes in the positioning of objects occur between successive frames. Flat animation is accomplished with two-dimensional drawings and illustrations. One of the most common flat animation techniques is cel animation, in which an individual clear acetate cel is used for each frame. Plastic animation refers to the single-frame recording of three-dimensional figures and objects. Puppets, clay figures, miniature objects and vehicles, and even still frames of live action (a technique known as pixillation) can be animated. Three-dimensional figures are recorded using techniques that combine animation and live-action recording.

Computer animation generates images that can be recorded and stored as single frames on disk. Although 2-D computer animation continues to serve certain functions and even full-length features, 3-D computer animation has slowly become the creative leader in feature films and in television shorts. The greatest advantages of computer animation are speed and accuracy. Images can be immediately viewed as well as accurately recorded and rerecorded. Some computers interpolate the in-between frames if the animator simply composes the first and last frames of a sequence. A computer can also be used to interpolate the changes in two-dimensional or three-dimensional objects. Three-dimensional computer animation can be combined with live-action photography, opening up a whole new world of illusion and abstract art to film and television audiences.

Special effects allow futuristic or historical worlds to come to life and dangerous actions and events to be simulated. Special effects can be divided into five basic categories: camera effects, optical effects, digital effects, models and miniatures, and physical effects. Camera effects include such features as fast and slow motion as well as single-frame (animation) recording. Film recording rates in excess of 24 fps, such as 32, 48, and 64 fps, create slow motion when the processed film is projected at the standard projection speed of 24 fps, and film recording rates less than 24 fps, such as 18 and 12 fps, create fast motion. In addition to varying the speed of the images, some film cameras allow fade-outs, fade-ins, superimpositions, and reverse motion to be created during initial recording. Video cameras can also provide built-in special effects controls, some of which produce effects that are similar to in-camera film effects, such as fades and slow motion.

Optical film effects include step printing, traveling mattes, and aerial image printing. A basic optical printer consists of a camera and a projector. The two machines face each other, and the lens of the camera is focused on the image from the projector. Step printing is often used to speed up a slow-moving sequence by recording every other frame of the original film. Aerial image photography combines optical printing and animation, using a film projector with an animation stand. Live-action images are projected from beneath predrawn cels, so that color titles or animated figures can be combined with live action.

Physical effects include wind, fog, smoke, rain, snow, fires, explosions, and gunshots. They require the guiding hand of a highly trained professional when their use can endanger the safety of the cast and crew. Physical effects, like other kinds of special effects, can significantly contribute to the emotional mood of a sequence and generate viewer interest and excitement.

EXERCISES

1. Design a credit or title sequence for a specific production project. Determine how you can best use abstract graphic images and titles to introduce a production, or select live-action images on which titles can be keyed. Select a letter style or font that is consistent with the overall theme, message, and style of your project, and that creates an impression that reinforces the central theme of a drama or the central message of an informational program. It can reflect warmth or coldness, tension or relaxation, simply by virtue of the colors, lines, and shapes it presents. Your project will eventually be shown on a video screen, so be sure to use type sizes that are large enough for titles to be clearly legible.

2. Arrange six items of different sizes and shapes in a pattern within a single frame. Develop the maximum Z-depth effect, and follow the rules of composition. Record the arrangement from several different angles to see what creates the greatest depth and at the same time shows the objects to the best advantage.

3. Construct a storyboard for an animation project. Create frames for each shot that will appear in the completed sequence. Either draw each frame by hand, or use a computer graphics program to compose each one. Make sure that all camera and figure movements are relatively simple to reproduce using an animation stand or a computer animation program. Determine how many individual frames or changes of figure movement and motion from still-frame images

will be required. A series of single film or video frames in which recorded objects or materials gradually change their spatial position within the frame are recorded individually and sequentially. When they are played back at normal speed (24 fps in film or 30 fps in video), they produce apparent motion.

4. Animate cut out paper figures by placing them on an animation stand and moving them slightly between recordings of individual film or video frames. Vary the speed of movement and evaluate the results.

5. Shoot a series of in-camera special effects, such as slow motion, fast motion, reverse motion, pixillation, fade-outs, fade-ins, and split screens.

6. Digitize a short video sequence, divide it into separate clips, and then image process each clip using a variety of transitions, filters, and superimpositions, keys, or mattes using a digital nonlinear editing or special effects program.

Additional Readings

Arntson, Amy E., 2002. Graphic Design Basics, fourth ed. Wadsworth, Belmont, CA.

Bacher, Hans, 2008. Dream Worlds: Production Design for Animation, Focal Press, Boston.

Beauchamp, Robin, 2005. Designing Sound for Animation, Focal Press, Boston.

Beiman, Nancy, 2007. Prepare to Board: Creating Story and Characters for Animation Features and Shorts, Focal Press, Boston.

Birren, Faber, 2000. The Symbolism of Color, Citadel Press, Secaucus, NJ.

Bordwell, Dave, Thompson, Kristin, 2001. Film Art: An Introduction, sixth ed. McGraw-Hill, New York.

Corsaro, Sandro, 2002. The Flash Animator, New Riders, Indianapolis, IN.

Cotte, Olivier, 2007. Secrets of Oscar-Winning Animation: Behind he Scenes of 13 Classic Short Animations, Focal Press, Boston.

Fernandez, Ibis, 2002. Macromedia Flash Animation and Cartooning: A Creative Guide, McGraw-Hill, New York.

Fullerton, Tracy, 2008. Game Design Workshop: A Playcentric Approach to Creating Innovative Games, second ed. Focal Press, Boston.

Furniss, Maureen, 2008. The Animation Bible: A Practical Guide to the Art of Animating, from Flipbooks to Flash, Harry N. Abrams, New York.

Gahan, Andrew, 2008. 3ds Max Modeling for Games: Insider's Guide to Game Character, Vehicle, and Environmental Modeling, Focal Press, Boston.

Gauthier, Jean-Marc, 2005. Building Interactive Worlds in 3D: Virtual Sets and Pre-visualization for Games, Film and the Web, Focal Press, Boston.

Gordon, Bob, Gordon, Maggie, 2002. The Complete Guide to Digital Graphic Design, Watson-Guptill, New York.

Graham, Lisa, 2001. Basics of Design: Layout and Typography for the Beginners, Delmar, Albany, NY.

Griffin, Hedley, 2001. The Animator's Guide to 2-D Animation, Focal Press, Boston.

Hart, John, 2008. The Art of the Storyboard: A Filmmakers Introduction, second ed. Focal Press, Boston.

Hoffer, Thomas W., 1981. Animation: A Reference Guide, Greenwood Press, Westport, CT.

Horton, Steve, Yang, Jeung Mo, 2008. Professional Mange: Digital Storytelling with Manga Studio EX, Focal Press, Boston.

Kennel, Glenn, 2007. Color Mastering for Digital Cinema, Focal Press, Boston.

Kerlow, Isaac V., 2004. The Art of 3-D Computer Animation and Effects, John Wiley & Sons, Hoboken, NJ.

Kitagawa, Midori, Windsor, Brian, 2008. MoCap for Artists: Workflow and Techniques for Motion Capture, Focal Press, Boston.

Krasner, Jon, 2008. Motion Graphic Design: Applied History and Aesthetics, second ed. Focal Press, Boston.

Kuperberg, Marcia, 2002. A Guide to Computer Animation for TV, Games, Multimedia, and the Web, Focal Press, Boston.

Kuppers, Harald, 1990. Basic Law of Color Theory, second ed. Barrons, Hauppauge, NY.

Landa, Robin, 2000. Graphic Design Solutions, second ed. Onward Press, Albany, NY.

Lester, Paul Martin, 2000. Visual Communication: Images with Messages, Wadsworth, Belmont, CA.

Mack, Steve, Rayburn, Dan, 2005. Hands-On Guide to Webcasting: Internet Event and AV Production, Focal Press, Boston.

Mattesi, Mike, 2008. Force: Character Design from Life Drawing, third ed. Focal Press, Boston.

McCarthy, Robert E., 1992. Secrets of Hollywood Special Effects, Focal Press, Woburn, MA.

Meyer, Chris, Meyer, Trish, 2008. Creating Motion Graphics with After Effects: Essential and Advanced Techniques, Focal Press, Boston.

Michael, Alex, 2006. Animating in Flash 8: Creative Animation Techniques, Focal Press, Boston.

Miller, Dan, 1990. Cinema Secrets, Special Effects, Apple Press, London.

Mitchell, Mitch, 2004. Visual Effects for Film and Television, Focal Press, Boston.

NFGMan. 2006. Character Design for Mobile Devices, Focal Press, Boston.

Olson, Robert, 1998. Art Director: Film and Video, second ed. Focal Press, Boston.

Patnode, Jason, 2008. Character Modeling with Maya and ZBrush: Professional Modeling Techniques, Focal Press, Boston.

Pender, Ken, 1998. Digital Colour in Graphic Design, Focal Press, Boston.

Purves, Barry J.C., 2007. Stop Motion: Passion, Process and Performance, Focal Press, Boston.

Richter, Stefan, Ozer, Jan, 2008. Hands-on Guide to Flash Video: Web Video and Flash Media Server, Focal Press, Boston.

Rickitt, Richard, 2006. Designing Movie Creatures and Characters: Behind the Scenes with the Movie Masters, Focal Press, Boston.

Roberts, Steve, 2007. Character Animation: 2D Skills for Better 3D, Focal Press, Boston.

Sawicki, Mark, 2007. Filming the Fantastic: A Guide to Visual Effects Cinematography, Focal Press, Boston.

Shaw, Susannah, 2008. Stop Motion: Craft Skills for Model Animation, second ed. Focal Press, Boston.

Simons, Mark, 2000. Storyboards: Motion in Art, second ed. Focal Press, Boston.

Subotnick, Steven, 2003. Animation for the Home Digital Studio: Creation to Distribution, Focal Press, Boston.

Sullivan, Karen, et al., 2007. Ideas for Animated Shorts with DVD: Finding and Building Stories, Focal Press, Boston.

Whitaker, Harold, 2002. Timing for Animation, Focal Press, Boston.

White, Tony, 2006. Animation from Pencils to Pixels: Classical Techniques for the Digital Animator, Focal Press, Boston.

Wilkie, Bernard, 1996. Creating Special Effects for TV and Video, third ed. Focal Press, Boston.

Williams, Robin, 2003. The Non-Designer's Design Book, second ed. Peachpit Press, Berkeley, CA.

Winder, Catherine, Dowlatabadi, Zara, 2001. Producing Animation, Focal Press, Boston.

Wright, Jean, 2005. Animation Writing and Development: From Script to Pitch, Focal Press, Boston.

Wright, Steve, 2008. Compositing Visual Effects: Essentials for the Aspiring Artist, Focal Press, Boston.

CHAPTER

The Future and Your Career 12

Introduction

From its inception in the twentieth century, electronic communication has been a rapidly developing, expanding, and changing field. In the twenty-first century, changes occur faster, reach farther, and show few signs of a predictably clear and predetermined path. Despite the sometimes unsettling nature of the changes in electronic communication, there are some constant or persistent tendencies, such as economic and technological convergence, which continue to offer outstanding opportunities for students who plan to enter the media production job market now and in the near future. Convergence on two levels will continue to have a significant impact on employment in the field.

ECONOMIC CONVERGENCE

First, corporations will continue to merge and combine, not only within the same industry, but across all communication industries: radio-TV stations, networks, publishers, cable companies, production units, billboard companies, and theme parks all will be owned and controlled by the same corporation. Because of the higher costs of newer digital formats and equipment, companies must learn to use and market the equipment, facilities, and communication technologies in new and different ways. For example, the health industry experiments with using a game toy such as Wii as an efficient tool for motivating physical therapy in patients.

Communicators must face the realization that their traditional competitors will not be their greatest competition of the future. New concepts of using communication tools will be developed by people who are completely divorced from traditional communication activities but will find ways to skim off customers and users of media. To continue to survive in any field of communication, thinking must go beyond where communication has been or is right now. The economy of the entire world will have a much more dramatic effect on the economy of the United States and industries once considered centered in the United States such as the motion picture industry and broadcasting. The emerging industrial powers of China, India, and Russia must be taken into account for any future communication plans.

TECHNOLOGICAL CONVERGENCE

Traditionally distinct media technologies, such as video, film, digital discs, mobile phones, other telecommunication devices, computer games, and the Internet, will continue to merge, combine, and come closer together throughout the twenty-first century. Digital systems and communication will continue to change rapidly in ways that cannot be fully anticipated. Decreases in size, lowering of costs, increases in efficiency, memory, and the ability to pass information rapidly all will occur. Changes in methods of storage from moving parts, to solid state, from magnetic to optical or the next medium will surprise even the scientists of today. Television as we now know it will develop or accept both new and different means of delivery or it will disappear as the chief entertainment mass medium. Expanding uses of both broadband services and mobile services will become more popular. The public anticipates and apparently desires better and higher-quality video in HDTV, HD radio, and 3-D motion pictures. At the same time, widespread interest expands in distributing media in low-quality systems on mobile and miniature receivers, highly compressed audio on transportable listening devices, and viewing movies on compressed files on the Internet.

IMPACT OF CONVERGENCE ON EMPLOYMENT

Employees will be expected to meet the demands of converging industries and technologies by offering flexibility in skills and abilities to perform whatever functions are required, regardless of the medium or location of operation. The day of the specialist camera operator, editor, producer, or even writer may well be gone from the broadcast and media industries. This convergence of skills has come from two directions. On one hand, the new smaller, higher-quality equipment allows a single skilled person to research, write, shoot, edit, and distribute his or her own work. Media festivals, independent cable channels, and participating web sites provide a variety of distribution outlets without having to deal with major studios or television stations. At the same time, small, highly efficient equipment allows major production units to reduce the number of employees required for any one project, especially if the key personnel are highly skilled and capable of assuming multiple positions and responsibilities.

Finally, the world, and therefore the industry, will have to become more green, that is, more ecologically minded. Increasingly efficient uses of power supplied by nonpolluting sources are a growing necessity for ecological survival. Learning to cut power use with the help of better-designed equipment and more efficient use of space, facilities, and materials will be demanded in the future. Competition will grow, not only among traditional communicators such as broadcasters, cable companies, and film producers but also among new groups of creative people who are not bound by old, traditional methods of operating and who are willing to try more new efficient methods of creating competitive work in this changing world.

PREPARATION FOR A MEDIA PRODUCTION CAREER

Your knowledge and inventive use of communication is the key—software and brain ware, not just hardware, will determine the future of electronic media, especially for you as a media producer, operator, or writer. Each step in the move of communication to the digital world has done so only with the combined cooperation of corporations, manufacturers, and finally you as the person who determines the final outcome of each step of the process. As a media professional, you will need to study a variety of subjects, some not *so* obviously related to your chosen career. Knowledge of the arts and culture is essential as whatever you will create is a form of art and a contribution to culture. A serious study of the arts at a minimum—consisting of a semester or a quarter of music appreciation, art history, and the history of theater—is a necessary foundation for an understanding of our culturally based art world. Greater study in depth of each field will pay dividends in your future as you progress in your media production career. Additional courses in creative writing, economics, and psychology beyond required general studies will help answer questions and solve problems that you cannot anticipate in your career at its beginning. Spend as much time as you can in your communication classrooms gaining a deep knowledge of the communication process, how and why it works, and the basics of communication theory along with a knowledge of the value of rhetoric and how mass media affects the audience, both in positive and negative means (Figure 12.1).

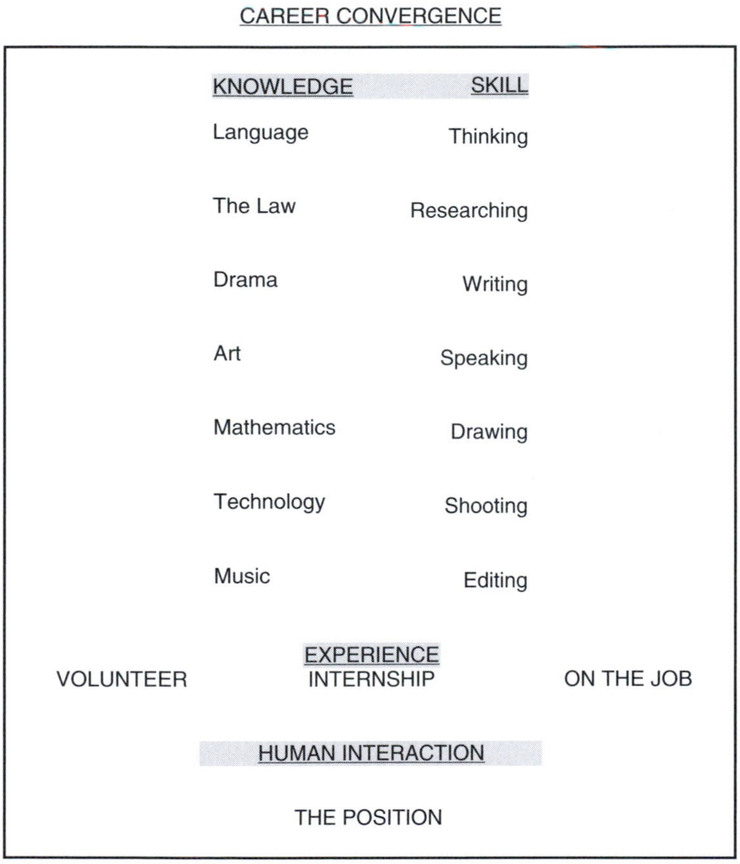

CAREER CONVERGENCE

KNOWLEDGE	SKILL
Language	Thinking
The Law	Researching
Drama	Writing
Art	Speaking
Mathematics	Drawing
Technology	Shooting
Music	Editing

EXPERIENCE

VOLUNTEER   INTERNSHIP   ON THE JOB

HUMAN INTERACTION

THE POSITION

FIGURE 12.1 While preparing for a career in media production, a potential employee needs to converge all of her or his accumulated knowledge and skills to face the uncertainty of the position available at the time of application. All of the general and specific knowledge available in a well-rounded academic program provides the basis for the career to move forward. Gain experience on as wide a platform as possible while developing one of the most important characteristics an employer looks for—the ability to interact on a professional level with supervisors, peers, and subordinates.

Today, new technology and audience demands provide you with two extremes: high-definition wide screen or low-definition on a miniature screen. HDTV or mobiles, each demand a different type of technical production knowledge and skills and as of now, there is no certainty as what type of creative production will serve each better than the other. Technology will continue to require workers with a broad range of skills who are dedicated to their careers above all else. The premium skill you will depend on is your ability to apply your best skills, knowledge, and interests to whatever market or audience exists.

Despite the industry's continuous cries for new talent, the competition always will be tough; getting the first job without experience, when experience is the first requirement, will not change. Follow the suggestions in this chapter, and through hard work, persistence, and dedication that break will come your way. In your lab courses, spend as much time as possible practicing and learning new techniques beyond your own individual interests. Spend time on operating and learning aspects of the media process that you may not care for now; keep in mind that you must be prepared for whatever opportunity may present itself during your career. Volunteer to offer your media skills wherever you can and gain as much experience in as many different settings as possible whether you are paid or not; the best pay you can gain early in your career is practical hands-on experience. The best way to obtain such experience is to earn and work in an internship.

Internship

An internship must be earned. Depending on the policy of your school and the companies that offer internships, there are minimum qualifications placed as an intern. An internship does not replace coursework. Don't expect an intern host to teach you everything you need to know to work in the field of your choice. The knowledge and skills you acquired in school should prepare you to qualify for an internship that may lead to an entry-level position. The best internships are competitive internships that are designed to be true beginning work experience—that is, they provide actual work experience in a variety of areas where experienced employees supervise and evaluate your work on a continuing basis. Companies, organizations, and associations that clearly understand the virtues and values of internships to themselves and the industry as a whole set up competitive internships. Examples of such organizations are the Academy of Television Arts and Sciences and the Belo Corporation.

Noncompetitive internships, unless closely supervised by the school, can vary considerably in quality and value, but one means of ensuring greater value is to rely on former students, alumni, family, friends, and faculty to help find a good internship. Someone directly connected to your school or to you personally, someone who knows you or has been in your place and knows what you've been through, can provide good guidance and sage advice concerning internships, leading to a worthwhile experience. Once you obtain an internship, you must demonstrate your willingness and ability to work and perform every reasonable task, however menial the task may seem at the beginning of your internship. If you have chosen your internship well and continue to display enthusiasm for your work, you may be given a bit more responsibility and an opportunity to experience a greater variety of work areas, tasks, and duties as your internship progresses.

You should wait until near the end of your academic career before enrolling in an internship program. There are two reasons for this decision. First, you need the education and background to prepare you for the internship. Second, if the internship works well and you are offered a full-time job, you don't want to have to choose between accepting the offer and quitting school before you graduate or turning the offer down because you must obtain your degree. Any company that offers you a full-time position while you are completing an internship will be willing to wait if you are in your last semester of school. Also, if you accept an internship during the fall or spring semester, make certain you carry as light an academic load as possible. To take full advantage of an internship, free yourself of as many obligations as possible to concentrate your energies and time on the internship.

If you apply for an internship during the summer, expect very heavy competition, because many schools allow students to intern only during the summer. During the internship, work to prove you will make a good employee. Perform any job assigned to you and be positive about all of the activities that your host asks you to do, even if some of them are boring, repetitious, and not at all what you thought the industry was all about. Ask questions; don't hesitate to ask if you can perform work not assigned to you, but ask first and make certain you know what to do and then do the job well.

Internship Keys

Types of Internships
- Competitive internship
- Paid internship (with or without academic credit)
- Unpaid for academic credit internship
- Volunteer internship at nonprofit organizations (with or without academic credit)

Cautions
- Remain under the close supervision of your faculty advisor.
- Remain in close contact and supervision with the human resources office of the company.
- Avoid unfulfilling nonvalue busywork, but accept intern-level work that fits your experience.
- Treat each requested assignment as an opportunity to learn new and valuable experience.
- Always present a professional appearance, in action, dress, relationships and speech.
- Understand the intern level in the hierarchy of the company and respect all other employees.
- Use the experience to develop contacts for future employment.
- Immediately report any physical or sexual harassment to your faculty advisor and to the human resources office.

Be aware of two negative incidents that may occur during an internship. First, if your assignments consist of only clerical work—answering telephones, getting coffee, running errands, or sitting around just watching people work—you have the right to report this to your school's intern supervisor, your supervisor on the job, or the company's human resources (HR) office. Expect to be assigned to low-level jobs during an internship, but an internship is also an educational activity, so if there is no potential for learning it is of limited value to you. Your school needs to be aware of your insufficient work assignment. The second is the more serious matter of sexual harassment. If you feel threatened at any time or are approached by an employee in an offensive manner, report the incident immediately to the HR department and your school's intern supervisor. At the same time, make certain you dress appropriately and act professionally toward all employees at all times.

An intern should not be expected to replace a full-time employee. This may be a difficult judgment to make, depending on the type of company and the manner in which the company assigns work to its employees. Too often a company will attempt to avoid hiring the full-time staff they need by taking on as many interns as possible and assigning each of them part of the job of an employee. The school's intern supervisor is responsible for making this determination, but the problem may not be obvious unless students notify her or him of the situation when they fill out their weekly reports. An internship at a for-profit company must be performed for academic credit or some level of pay. Labor laws and legal responsibilities can only be fulfilled with credit or pay. The rule does not apply to nonprofit corporations such as public broadcasters, such as PBS and NPR stations. You may volunteer as an intern with those organizations, but the job responsibilities are the same at a for-profit company and in some cases the opportunities for excellent work experience are better at nonprofit operations. Other nonprofit organizations that use media production, such as churches and charitable organizations like the Red Cross or the Cancer Society, also may offer internships with or without credit or with or without a small stipend. Don't expect a for-profit organization such as broadcast outlet to pay you, but the organization may offer a small amount to cover your travel expenses to the facility. Pay should not be an issue, except when it is required by law; for an internship, the work experience, the opportunity to prove you are a responsible, hard-working employee, and, almost as important, the opportunity to start to build a file for networking are your forms of payment. A critical value of an internship is networking, and its value and use are described later in this chapter.

As part of your preparation to serve an internship, you should begin assembling your job application file consisting of four documents: your résumé, cover letter, portfolio of your work, and a package of personal information for interviewing and for filling out application forms. Specific instruction on how to handle these documents is explained later in this chapter.

Job Search

Although some businesses (broadcasting and companies funded by the federal government) must by law advertise publicly for any open position, other companies do not have to advertise openly. Even advertised positions may be filled immediately, often from within the same company. Relying on advertising is a poor method of finding potential job openings. Some of the best methods of learning about job openings come through networking, knowing people in the industry, being related to someone in the field, or serving a semester as an intern. Joining a professional organization such as the student branches of the Radio TV News Directors Association (RTNDA), the Broadcast Education Association (BEA), the University Film and Video Association (UFVA), or the Gamer's Association will teach you from the inside about that business and will give you access to people working in the industry and in position to know of openings. Belonging to a newsgroup, monitoring blogs, and keeping in close contact with your professors who have contacts in the business provide potential career contacts that will widen the opportunity for you to find possible job openings.

The Job Search

- Develop Search Method
- Research
- Potential employers
  - Potential positions
  - Yourself—gather all personal information
- Application Process
  - Create a résumé
    - Narrative format
    - Outline format
  - Write a cover letter
    - For specific company
    - For specific position
    - Professional format
    - Critical closing paragraph
  - Create a portfolio
    - Only best work
    - Professionally mounted

The search for that first job, or, for that matter, each job as you move through your career, consist of three basic steps: finding the opportunity, preparing the paperwork, and surviving the interview.

The technique known as networking serves as the most efficient way to locate most media-oriented jobs. The paperwork consists of four parts: a package of your personal information, a cover letter, your résumé, and your portfolio. The heart of interviewing involves preparing for the interview. More about interviewing and paperwork details are described later in this chapter.

Networking

The first step in building a network consists of sitting down and creating a list of everyone you know, everyone your family knows, and everyone your friends know in the media business. Let them know you want to find a position in the industry. The list needs to include the complete name (proper spelling), title, company, address, phone number, and e-mail address of the possible contact. This list also should include all of the contacts you have developed at your internship (see the Internship section presented earlier), those you have met while volunteering at nonprofits, and even the names of people you read about in the newspaper or professional publications. This is the first of several research phases you will go through in your job search, so approach this phase as a very important one. Take accurate notes and think in the broadest terms of finding contacts that might lead you to potential positions, but also consider people who might assist you in your search.

Each of the media fields publishes some type of listing of all of the companies in that field. In broadcasting, it is an annual publication titled *Broadcasting Cablecasting Yearbook*. It is an expensive volume, but most large libraries carry the latest copy. It lists all broadcast stations, cable channels, many production companies and companies associated in some manner with broadcasting. The list includes addresses, phone numbers, and the names and titles of management-level employees. Motion Picture Enterprises Publications, Inc. publishes quarterly guides listing everyone in the film/video industry: suppliers, companies, equipment manufacturers, and freelancers. Copies often are distributed to media production faculty or may be gained by visiting www.mpe.net. Before you call or write to an individual, call the company first and make certain that person still holds that position. Managers come and go at a high rate in media production, and you don't want to ask to speak to or mail a résumé to the incorrect person. Don't ignore personal contacts. Check with all of your relatives and friends, and ask if they know someone in the business or at the company you are interested in. Don't hesitate to use the names of your family members or friends when you request an interview, after you have gained their permission. As an absolute rule, never use another person's name without specifically asking permission to do so, and that includes using the person as a reference. More about references later.

As part of your job search research, explore market sizes and know the differences between a major market, a middle market, and a smaller market. Larger markets seldom hire inexperienced people unless it is at a small operation within that market. Middle markets will consider some inexperienced people for their lowest-level entry positions. Small markets often welcome people who are willing to start in a small operation to learn the business and get the experience needed for a major market or company. It is much less costly to make mistakes while learning about a business when the financial stakes are not high; forgiveness comes easier in a small operation because your pay is low enough to make up the difference. Explore industries that are just beginning the move to the digital or interactive world. They will be expanding and needing people with digital training, especially multiskilled employees. This includes newspapers, magazines, radio stations, television stations, cable channels, film studios, and small independent production houses. If they have not yet started to use digital media including web sites, news groups, and other interactive forms, they will need qualified help.

If you are working already but want to move on to another job, be aware that the person who may hire will want to talk to your present boss. You can ask for confidential respect, up to a point. At some time you are going to have to be honest and upfront with your present employer about your search for another job. Also make certain you give proper notice—two weeks minimum. Show your present boss the same consideration that you would expect him or her to show you.

APPLICATION PROCESS
Résumé

Although a cover letter precedes a résumé, writing your résumé first will organize the information you will need when the time comes for you to write cover letters as you prepare for each job application. Your cover letter describes who you are, how you got to where you are, and where you want to go. It needs to be succinct, comprehensive, accurate, and absent any typos, grammatical errors, or superfluous fillers. Your résumé may be organized as either a list of all of your information, aesthetically arranged on the page, or a narrative written as a short monologue of who you are. If you feel you have narrative writing skills, the latter form may seem to offer an opportunity to show your creative writing ability, but be very careful of this format (Figure 12.2). A résumé's basic purpose is to succinctly tell someone who you are in a form that quickly reveals the critical information the reader wants to know. The narrative

	Megan O'Brien	
816-532-3625	2835 Granite Kansas City, MO 64131	sjones@comcast.net

EDUCATION
The University of Missouri-Kansas City   June 2009
Bachelor of Arts
Major: Communication
Minor: Computer Graphics
GPA 3.6

EXPERIENCE
May 2008–present   Brandon, Fife and Lewis, Advertising   Kansas City, MO
Receptionist
Handled telephone and guest duties
Entered data and typed letters, proposals, and scripts

May 2007–May 2008   Outback Steakhouse   Overland Park, KS
Waiter/bartender
Accurately handled cash register, tended bar, and waited tables
Trained income employees

HONORS and ACTIVITIES
Communication school scholarship, two years
Member Omicron Delta Kappa Honorary
Writer, producer, director UH TV
Volunteered for various community fund raisers
Internship, WDAF-TV

ADDITIONAL INFORMATION
Proficient with both PC and Mac operating systems, MS Word, Excel,
PowerPoint, FileMaker Pro, Photoshop, Illustrator,
Final Cut Pro, and other editing systems
Attended NAB conference, completed media production workshops,
and attended broadcast lectures and panels

REFERENCES

Michael J. Brandon
Partner
Brandon, Fife, and Lewis, Advertising
1235 North Loop West
Kansas City, MO 64105
816-862-1860
mjbrandon@att.net

Wendy Adair
Manager
Outback Steakhouse
2100 195th St.
Overland Park, KS 66207
913-3650-4122
wadair@outback.com

Jennifer Ayles, Ph.D.
Director, School of Communication
UMKC
Kansas City, MO 68108
713-743-2108
jayles@umkc.edu

FIGURE 12.2 An outline résumé lists important information in a manner that is easy for the interviewer to read and pick out the critical information she or he needs to know.

form requires a thorough reading and therefore requires more time and effort on the part of the reader. Whichever format you choose, keep in mind the KISS rule—Keep It Simple and Succinct. Contain it to one page if possible and no more than two pages if an additional page of references is called for. Don't try to be humorous, especially in the narrative form; save showing your writing skills for your portfolio. Avoid overly unique design, layout, paper, and font styles. Make it readable but enjoyable at the same time. Keep in mind that the reader may glance only at the first part of the front page; make it stand out and stick in the reader's mind so that he or she will continue reading the entire document. Begin with your full name, the one you want the potential employer to call you by; do not use nicknames unless you are stuck with one. Include accurate contact information: your address, phone numbers indicating whether each is a cell or land line, and your e-mail address and web site if you have one and you want the potential employer to see it. This is a good time to clean up your web site and any other site with your name on it. Keep in mind that your potential employer may have the company's research staff do an online search for your name. Your contact information must be accurate and current. If you are about to return home or move to a new city, make certain you can be found easily. No one will want to hunt you down. If the first try to reach you fails, the potential employer will go to the next candidate and dump your résumé.

The order of the next list of items depends on the job you are applying for and the strength of several of your past characteristics. For someone just graduating, list your schooling first. List each school's full name and location if the name does not clarify its location (do not list high schools, unless you attended a specialized school that taught media production), the date of graduation, and your GPA if it is over 3.0. Indicate your major and minor if it adds to your value (for example, do not list animal husbandry unless you are applying to a veterinarian publication). If you attended more than one college, list only the last one unless the others included specialized media training. List honors awarded and extracurricular activities, especially if they represent any form of media connection. Any media production work, publications, or research needs to be listed (Figure 12.3).

Fraternity or sorority activities may be listed only if they involved responsible or elected positions. Other elected campus responsibilities also may be listed, but only if there is space and the activity indicates some value to your future career. If your employment record includes items that specifically prepared you for a production career, then list important employment next. Employment could be listed ahead of education if your job record contains media experience. List jobs by the title of your job followed by a very brief description of your duties as they either apply to your career choice or indicate specialized responsibility or management experience. List only those positions that would impress a prospective employer, but be prepared to fill any gaps with a package of personal information to be presented later during your interview. If as part of your job experience you were involved in research, in media production, or worked on publications, list those items under the employment record, but indicate where and how you participated. Specialized computer and media production skills, language proficiency, and international travel experience round out your life's history.

You must make a judgment about what is most important and fit the information neatly on the page so that it reads easily and quickly. Often your references may be on a separate last page. You may change the references depending on the company and job requirements. List at least three people who know your work habits and your writing skills. Do not list your religious contacts—they never say bad things about anyone, and your prospective employer wants to know the truth about you. Make the reference choices based on your perceived knowledge of the individual's personal attitude toward you and her or his willingness to respond to specific questions about

RESUME

Greg McCamasters   November 20, 2008
9160 South Breaswood
Houston, TX 77035
713-574-2323
gmcc@aol.com

OBJECTIVE: To become as versatile as possible in writing for electronic media. I have
educated myself with everything from designing my own web page to writing series of scripts
for various media productions.

EDUCATION: Attending University of Houston's School of Communication with a degree
to be awarded December 2008 with an overall GPA of 3.63.

EXPERIENCE: I wrote two scripts on drug abuse and AIDS prevention, which were
selected to be produced and distributed to the student body. While at the University of Houston
each of the scripts I wrote in class were produced. A video copy is attached to this resume. I
also directed and edited each of the accepted scripts.

SKILLS: I have been trained to operate both linear and nonlinear editing programs
including Final Cut Pro. I am conversant with MS Word, Photoshop, and Excel programs.

AWARDS: Was the recipient of the Outstanding Academic Achievement-
Extraordinary Student award for four consistent years of high school participation.
I was awarded one of the University of Houston's outstanding Academic Achievement
Scholarships.

WORK EXPERIENCE: One year as a YMCA lifeguard, three years as assistant manager of
an antique store, and for the past three years as the manager of the dairy department at
Safeway.

REFERENCES ATTACHED.
PRODUCTIONS ATTACHED.

FIGURE 12.3 A narrative résumé appears to be a short story of who you are, but it is more difficult for the reader to recover the critical information needed in an application.

you and your production ability. Do not list anyone unless you have contacted the person first and made certain he or she is willing to act as a reference *and* remembers who you are. It may be helpful to send your contact a copy of your résumé by letter or e-mail to help the person remember you. If your contact is a teacher, specify the classes you took from that person, the grades you received, and the dates of the classes. Don't lie about the grade; some professors keep grade records until they die. While asking for permission to use the professor as references, make certain you have the correct spelling of his or her name, the professor's present title, and an accurate address, phone number, and e-mail address. Most prospective employers want to talk directly to references but do not want to spend much time trying to track them down. If an employer can't find the references, she or he will go to the next applicant.

Cover Letter

Your cover letter will offer the first impression to a potential boss. Research and write it as the best prose you have ever created. If you have completed the research suggested for your résumé, then you have completed much of the background work necessary for your cover letter. Each job you apply for requires a separate cover letter written specifically for that job and company. The well-written cover letter accomplishes three goals. First, it is your introduction to a complete stranger. Show your best side, personally as well as professionally. Second, it shows that you know what the company produces and what you offer that will benefit the company. Third, it gives enough of your background and experience to make the prospective employer want to meet and interview you to find what else you can give to the company (Figure 12.4).

Remember, this is a business letter. Use a standard business letter format; this is not the place to show your creativity, rather your ability to be responsible and organized. Start with a business heading—the name, title, company, and address of the person you are approaching or answering—nicely spaced on the upper left side of the page. Don't forget to date the letter just above or at the top line of the heading. Make certain you spell the person's name correctly and use her or his correct title. The greeting should be to the specific person, never "To Whom It May Concern." The best addresses are Mr., Dr., or Ms. followed by his or her full name. Your first line may explain why you are writing, but only if there is a specific reason such as answering an advertisement or responding to a letter. Don't waste your time with a lengthy explanation, get to the point. Briefly outline your qualifications (leave the details to the résumé) and explain why you would be a good fit for the job. Indicate if you have enclosed your résumé and if you also enclosed any production samples in a portfolio, on a DVD, or on a web site for which you have provided a link. Be sure to specify which job you are applying for. Never say "any job available." If the compavny is not hiring for the job you ask about, something else may be available, but give the interviewer the opportunity to indicate that fact. Never try to rationalize why you want a job at that location. The prospective employer does not care if you want to be near a beach, if you have relatives nearby, or you like mountains. Your last paragraph must include a statement that you will follow the letter with a phone call within a week or 10 days (specify which) and then be sure to call within that time block. Within that statement, indicate the reason you will call is to give the person a chance to discuss your résumé, and to give you a chance to answer any questions and if possible arrange for an interview. This last paragraph is as important as the first line of the letter. It indicates you are willing to take the initiative by following the letter with the call, not just sitting back waiting for a response. This is a little pushy, but remember, you have to find some way to stand out among the hundreds of other people applying for the same job. Sign off the letter with a closing such as "Sincerely," a handwritten signature, your full name, and a block listing of all of your contact information. Lay out the material in an open but compact design. Use white space to separate sections; don't cram the entire body in a clump at the top of the page, but spread it out for a pleasing visual appearance.

Megan O'Brien
2835 Walnut
Kansas City, MO
64131
816-532-3625
mobrien@comcast.net

May 20, 2009

Mr. Charles Profiot
Operations Manager
KGFO-TV
P.O. Box 7777
Kansas City, MO
64555

RE: Production Associate Position

Dear Mr. Profiot:

My media production experience and academic training provides the basis for consideration as a production associate at KGFO-TV. I will graduate this month with honors in communication and a minor in computer graphics. While at the university, I worked all positions at the student-operated television station including writing, producing, and directing a weekly public affairs program.

I spent last semester as an intern at WDAF-TV as a production assistant operating studio equipment and assisting the directors and producers. I suggested ideas for programs at Channel 4, where they were accepted and aired successfully. During that time, I watched your operation and believe I could be of benefit to you and KGFO-TV.

I feel my broad liberal arts education, including study of theater, art, and music as well as the study of media history, communication law, and audio, video, and computer graphics production courses with a GPA of 3.6, prepares me for a career in media production.

I worked part time while attending school, paying for part of my education and gaining valuable work experience. My former employers and references will honestly evaluate my work habits and potential for a career in electronic media.

I look forward to meeting you and will call on Monday, May 25, to discuss my application and for an interview. Thank you for your consideration.

Sincerely,

Ms. Megan O'Brien
816-532-3625
mobrien@comcast.net

Enc: Resume, references

FIGURE 12.4 The cover letter is the first impression an interviewer will have of you. Make it speak well of you. Make it professional and to the point, and summarize, but do not duplicate, your résumé.

Portfolio

A portfolio is not an afterthought. It is not something that you throw together immediately before you begin your job search. It is a succinct and engaging summary of your best work, and it is the culmination of several years of accomplishments. Throughout your academic career, you should be designing, planning, and completing short works of high quality that help build your portfolio. You should submit these works to student film, video, audio, and Internet contests, screenings, festivals, and exhibitions where your work might receive some kind of recognition or awards. Your portfolio provides a means for you to show what you are capable of doing and have accomplished in the past. As an artist, you are proud of your work, and you want to show it in the best light possible. Your portfolio is the setting to do just that. The approach you use may follow two different paths: (1) show at least one example of each type of production that you are capable of, or (2) create a portfolio containing only one type of work. The latter selection is best used if you are applying for a specific job such as an editor or as a news videographer for a television station. Some jobs require a range of work, from short spots or news clips to lengthy documentary or longer dramatic shooting. A portfolio for that type of job should include as wide a range of samples as possible. If you are talented in several different genres, use the best sample of each, but be sure to include only excellent samples to show your abilities. An important consideration requires that you include only your best work. The impulse to include every piece that you like or have an emotional attachment to creates a mediocre portfolio. It is better to have one excellent example of your work rather than one good one and several mediocre ones. The viewer will remember the mediocre samples. Choose wisely and critically as if you are looking at someone else's work, not your own. If there were production restrictions beyond your control, you may explain, but do not rationalize or excuse poor or mediocre work—just don't include it in the portfolio (Figure 12.5).

Once you have chosen your work, use only clean copies, preferably a DVD or some other ubiquitous digital disc format. Media formats change, but most operations today can review a standard burned DVD or CD. Check every clip for production errors or bad edits. Make certain each video clip is carefully dubbed with color bars, slate, and professionally formatted. Each clip slate should have your name on it. Few examiners will look at the entire portfolio, so make certain the first few clips are the very best and will entice the viewer to look further into the samples. A separate slate with a brief explanation preceding each sample will give a context for the work. A written table of contents with tabbed pages describing different examples will facilitate scanning through the portfolio. All written material should be mounted in some type of loose-leaf binder if more than one page. The DVD or CD case should have a clean, professional appearance; again save your creativity showcase for what's inside the DVD or CD, not the case itself. But it needs to be carefully labeled on both the front surface and on the disc. The labels need to be visible and contain your name and contact information. Selling production is a brutal business. Production managers; news directors; film, TV, game, and web producers; and agency managers all are busy people often faced with a deluge of portfolios and submissions. If your presentation does not grab them within the first 30 seconds, your work may never receive full consideration. Every portfolio won't appeal to every interviewer; you may need to redesign the portfolio for each different type of job that you apply for. Often your portfolio will not be viewed until you have been given an interview and as a part of that interview you will be given the opportunity to show your portfolio. If you have prepared it well, it should speak for itself, relying only on you for explanations or more detail about your experience.

If you mail your portfolio, make certain you have copies of all of the work contained in the package. Carefully package the DVD or CD and accompanying material to make certain it will not be damaged in shipment and will arrive at its destination on time. A little money spent at this point will pay dividends in the long run. Also include a prepaid, self-addressed return-shipping label if you expect to have the portfolio returned.

PORTFOLIO PREPARATION

1. Research Company

    Know who will view portfolio

    Learn what they will look for

    Choose works that fit the job

2. Choose Selections

    Review all of your work

    Select ONLY the best

    Select ONLY Professional quality examples

3. Create Portfolio

    At this time DVD is the best format

    Clean each selection: no bad edits, clean audio, black in and out

    Begin recording with slate:

    >   Name, email address, phone numbers, mailing address

    >   Table of Contents: title, length, medium each selection

    End recording with repeat of slate

    Restrict recording to ten minutes maximum, better a tight five minutes

4. Mounting

    Clearly label disc

    Clearly label disc sleeve

    Place in foam shipping pack with slate label on outside

    Include a self-addressed return label inside pack

Expect to leave cover letter, resume with disc

Do not expect the disc to be returned.

FIGURE 12.5 Your portfolio provides a way of showing your best work and what you are capable of accomplishing. Make it professional, show only the best work, and keep it simple and accurate.

Interviewing

For most people, including those who have gone through the process more than once, interviewing for a job can be an uncomfortable situation. It doesn't have to be, if you prepare yourself and your materials well. Remember, both you and the interviewer have a common goal, so find out if you fit the requirements the interviewer has for a position. The session need not be a confrontational battle, but a give and take during which you explain who you are, what you are capable of doing, and how it fits with the needs of the company. If there is no fit, then don't take the rejection personally. It is better you don't accept a position that doesn't match your interests or capabilities than take on a job that will make you unhappy and not allow your creativity to blossom.

Interview Process

- Arrange an interview.
- Arrive on time.
- Maintain a professional appearance.
- Prepare for questioning.
- Know yourself well enough to sell yourself.
- Negotiate pay, conditions, and benefits.
- Follow up with e-mail or a phone call.
- Don't give up—persistence will be rewarded.

To begin with, it is crucial for you to be yourself—your adult self, not your campus comedian and style leader. If you are interviewing with a middle-of-the-road or more conservative media organization or company, avoid extremes of clothing, hairstyle, metal accessories, and tattoos. Although many companies that specialize in artistic and creative works may be more concerned about your abilities and talents than your appearance, it might be better to appear somewhat more conservative at the first meeting and show your creativity in appearance later, once you are on the payroll. This caution is especially important if your interview is with the HR department representative, not the head of the department you expect to work for. At the same time, the interviewer does want to know who you really are and if you will fit in with the rest of the employees, but she or he is interested in your most responsible adult you, not your most immature undergraduate you. Concentrate on the job by giving the impression of a dedicated and task-driven potential employee. Be willing to start at or near the bottom of the rank and file. Of course, no one wants to stay in that position very long—more than two years in an entry-level position may mean that there is no possibility of moving up and it's time to look for a position at another company. The amount of money you make should not be the major motivating factor in the choice of your first position. Find work that gives you the opportunity to prove yourself, get experience, and develop those all-important networking contacts. Once you are working, then you will have the opportunity to submit proposals, games, web designs, and story ideas with some chance they will be viewed as coming from a professional. Don't expect to follow a linear path from your first job until you reach your final goal. Often, that path will not appear because as you work toward your goal, it will change and you will discover more satisfying opportunities that you didn't even know existed when you left school. Thoroughly research the company, the job you want, and the work you may be expected to perform. Be prepared to answer questions that reveal your knowledge of all of those subjects. You may not be asked detailed questions at the first interview, but knowing what you have learned from your research will give you confidence in talking intelligently about the company, and confidence is one of the best characteristics to show during an interview. Arrive on time fully prepared for both the face-to-face part of the interview and, depending on the size of the company, a stack of forms to fill out.

To prepare for the forms as part of your research—research yourself. Arrive with every possible bit of information about your past that the potential employer might be interested in. The list needs to include your past three to five residences, the addresses and whom you paid your rent to, your past three to five employers, supervisors, pay rates, addresses, and telephone numbers. You may be asked to name someone to contact in case of an emergency and that person's contact information, what medical insurance you have, and your primary doctors. After you have been hired, you may need to list family members: spouse, children, or anyone else for whom you may be responsible. You may be asked to make decisions on what type of medical coverage and retirement programs you want to enroll in. Some of these decisions arrive fast and furious and may have important bearings on your future. Think about them in advance to be able to make accurate and beneficial choices for you and your family.

Depending on the company and what position you are applying for, you may be asked to submit to an examination or test. If you are applying for a job as an editor, you may be asked to quickly cut a story, commercial, or treatment with basic information provided. The interviewer may intentionally ask you to complete another test or application in your handwriting, or he or she may give you access to a computer. Your portfolio should provide this type of information, but some companies will want to see if you can work with basic information against a deadline. If your primary interview is by telephone, it may be a conference call with several other people listening and possibly asking questions. At the beginning, ask for each person's name and title and try to remember what their voices sound like. Don't hesitate to pause after each question is presented and think carefully before you answer, but don't wait so long that they wonder what you are doing on the other end of the line. Have a copy of your résumé, cover letter, and portfolio in front of you as references. Also keep close at hand a copy of all of your personal information so that you can provide quick answers if asked.

Negotiating pay and benefits is a difficult challenge for all new employees, but even more so for creative applicants. We all know what we think we are worth, but it is difficult to face someone across a desk in a suit and demand that figure. Again, begin this part of the process with research. Find out what that company or similar companies in the same market size pay beginning employees in the position for which you are applying. Don't be afraid to ask for that figure if you are offered less. Knowing your own value again shows confidence, but don't argue. If you are told the figure is the maximum the company is willing to pay, don't walk out the door. Explore other perquisites (perks) such as car or clothing allowances, provided equipment, overtime pay, moving expenses, or a signing bonus. Don't take rejection personally; try to assume a pleasant negotiating stance, not an argumentative position. If you cannot come to terms satisfactory to you, don't hesitate to thank the interviewer for her or his time and for considering you for the position. Leave your résumé and cover letter in case possible future positions or budget changes allow you to accept a position with that company later. If the rejection comes from a complete lack of your fitting with this company, always ask if the interviewer knows of any other open positions with that company or any other company. Always leave on a positive note, even you though may be disappointed and hurt.

If the interview ends with a "We'll call you," be sure to ask how soon you might expect a call. If you are told or the ad you answered says, "don't call," then don't call. Wait a reasonable amount of time, two to three weeks maximum, and then send an e-mail inquiring about your interview. Persistence pays. Always follow up and maintain contacts. Once a month stop by or contact any person you have met at the company who is in a position to hire you. This person may eventually come looking for you. Even the busiest of HR people will reply to an e-mail. This may give you a quick rejection, but that is better than not knowing whether to pursue other possibilities and get on with your search. Most companies will have the courtesy to respond within a reasonable amount of time, but there may be extenuating circumstances beyond their immediate control. They may be waiting for budget clearance, depending on the job, or they may be waiting on security or personal clearance information. At this point, patience is a virtue, but don't ignore other possibilities while you wait.

Sending blind inquiries may yield a result, but be prepared to send hundreds if not more to get one or two responses. Never send unsolicited portfolios. They will be returned unopened or destroyed. Unsolicited résumés and cover letters may receive some limited attention.

Freelancing

Freelancing allows you the opportunity to work for yourself or your own company by finding an individual project and selling your services to the client. It would be best to avoid freelancing until you have had several years experience working on staff at other companies, saved money, and built a list of clients and potential clients. You will need to sell yourself or work with a partner who enjoys the selling end of the game. When you first start, you may have to accept projects that don't offer the creativity or even the pay you would prefer, but early on you can't be too choosy because you need to build a sample reel of your work. Do follow a set of ethics, and never take a job that you can't philosophically accept. As a freelancer, the second major problem after getting work is getting paid for it. The standard in the industry is to be paid on the one-third system. You bill and receive one-third of the budgeted figure on acceptance of the idea and on a signed contract. Then you bill one-third and collect on acceptance of the rough edit, and you bill the final one-third on completion and final acceptance. Finding quality clients and collecting your legitimate fees for creative personnel are onerous and annoying parts of the field.

Representation

The problems of finding jobs and clients, negotiating salary and fees, and collecting the money owed created the field of artist representation. At a certain level in your career, you may feel you would prefer to leave those awkward and unpleasant activities to an agent or representative. The agent's responsibility permits him or her to sell you and your work for a 10 percent cut of whatever your fee is. That means unless an agent gets you work, he or she doesn't make any money. At the same time, the agent becomes a liaison between producers, station managers, and company HR departments to bring to them only the best possible person to fill the job the company needs. That means an agent won't represent you unless you have had experience, can produce what is needed, and make a good appearance for an interview or a pitch. You must give the agent work to sell—an agent can't wait until he finds a job then have to wait for you to turn out a recording. Give the agent good work and the agent's job is to find a producer who needs that type of work. There must be a good deal of mutual trust between you and your agent, so don't sign with an agent until you are ready, have the work to sell, and you have carefully researched to make certain you have found the correct match for you in an agent.

For freelancers, an agent is almost a necessity. Producers and publishers normally will not speak directly to you as a producer. They are afraid that if they look at your work, they may be sued for stealing your work. If they go through an agent, a record exists of the transaction. An agent is not a union steward; although your agent can negotiate for you, you must handle grievances yourself, through a manager (another 10 percent off the top), a lawyer, or one of the professional guilds or unions. Their major responsibility is to write contracts for staff and freelance writers as a group who work for signers of contracts.

The two levels of professional organizations that represent media workers are guilds and unions. Guilds represent above-the-line employees; they include the Producers Guild (PGA), the Directors Guild (DGA), and two branches for writers, the Writers Guild of America East represents TV writers, and WGA-West represents film and network writers (WGA). Below-the-line employees are represented by unions; they include the American Federation of TV-Radio Artistes (AFTRA), the International Brotherhood of Electrical Workers (IBEW), the National Association of Broadcast Employees (NABET), the International Association of Theatrical and Stage Employees (IATSE), and other smaller unions. Each union represents various areas of the industry depending on contracts signed with producers or corporations. The basic concept for both guilds and unions is to set minimum pay and benefits for members and to provide maximum work hours and working conditions to protect the members. Negotiating for individuals is not part of their responsibility. If a disagreement goes beyond the conditions written into the contracts between the union/guild and the employer, the individual or an attorney representing the individual must handle those factors.

Summary

Finding work as a media production worker for both staff and freelancers follows the same pattern. The best search philosophy requires a three-step plan. First, conduct a detailed search based on research you have gathered on the companies who might be hiring, and develop contacts from friends, family, and your internship. An internship is one of the most beneficial activities you as a soon-to-graduate student can engage in to prepare yourself for building contacts and learning on a practical level what a job in the field of your choice actually is like.

Once you have established a reasonable goal, your next job is to prepare the paperwork you will need in order to apply for and gain worthwhile employment. You must write a cover letter tailored for each individual company and position, create a résumé that describes you completely but succinctly (who you are and what you are capable of giving to an employer), and put together your portfolio. Each must be carefully and professionally prepared, because they each represent who you are and what you are capable of doing. Ideally, an interview will follow, and again you need to do background research into the company, what the company produces, what its pay scales are, and how your skills may be attractive to the person doing the hiring.

Be Sure To

Once you are working, staff or freelance, here are some helpful hints:

1. Avoid legal complications from copyright, patents, and trademarks under intellectual property laws.
2. Aggressiveness and competitiveness are positive values, but they require restraint.
3. Small business anti-golden rule: What goes around comes around. Whatever dirty deed you do to someone else in the business, the chances are very good that the person will have the opportunity to pay you back plus more.
4. Get organized fast, and stay organized.
5. Your first job probably won't last long; prepare for numbers 2 and 3 right away.
6. Accept constructive criticism and reviews as a positive means of improving.
7. Be flexible, multiskilled, and constantly learn new techniques.

EXERCISES

1. Assemble all of the personal data that you will need to fill out employment forms.

2. Using the *Broadcasting Cablecasting Yearbook*, compile a list of all of the companies (TV stations, radio stations, cable companies) that you are interested in working for, and call to make certain the person you need to send an application to still works there and that the company is still accepting applications.

3. Using the Gamer's annual guide, find a game company near your location, and call for an interview.

4. Google NABET, IATSE, and IBEW; check their web sites for instruction on applying for jobs in those industries.

5. Do the same for RTNDA and the National Association of Broadcasters (NAB).

6. Create your résumé, then have someone in the industry look at it and critique it.

7. Write a cover letter for a specific company after you have researched the company and the job opportunities and have determined what you can offer the company and how you would fit in with its operation.

8. Study all of your creative work, list the few that are of professional quality, and describe how you would assemble a portfolio package.

Additional Readings

Print

Bermont, Todd, 2004. 10 Insider Secrets to a Winning Job Search, Career Press, Franklin Lakes, NJ.

Bucy, Erik P., 2002. Living in the Information Age: A New Media Reader, Wadsworth, Belmont, CA.

Edwards, Christina, 2003. The Gardner's Guide to Finding New Media Jobs Online, GGC, Herndon Lane, VA.

Fedorko, Jamie, 2006. Intern Files: How to Get, Keep, and Make the Most of Your Internship, Simon & Schuster, New York.

Kent, Simon, 2005. Careers and Jobs in Media, Kogan Page, London, UK.

Levy, David B., 2006. Your Career in Animation: How to Survive and Thrive, Allworth Press, New York.

Miller, Carolyn Handler, 2004. Digital Storytelling: A Creator's Guide to Interactive Entertainment, Focal Press, Boston.

Oldman, Mark, ed. 2007. Vault Guide to Top Internships, 2008 Edition, Vault, New York.

Reddick, Randy, King, Elliot, 1996. The Online Student: Making the Grade on the Internet, Harcourt Brace College Publishers, Fort Worth, TX.

Taylor, Jeffrey, Hardy, Douglas, 2004. Monster Careers: How to Land the Job of Your Life, Penguin Books, New York.

Web

www.cpb.org/jobline
www.nab.org/bcc/JobBank
www.gamejobs.com
www.rileyguide.com/comp.html
www.iwantmedia.com/job

GLOSSARY

1394 See IEEE 1394, Firewire.

AAC (Advanced Audio Codec) An advanced version of MP3 also known as MPEG-2AAC.

AAF (Advanced Authoring Format) A file format standard developed by a group of manufacturers and users of editing systems.

"A" ROLL The primary roll of film or tape in editing; generally includes the master shots.

A/B ROLL An editing process that uses two separate rolls (cassettes or reels) of tape or film. Each roll contains alternate shots of the sequence, thus enabling the editor to use transitions other than straight cuts between shots.

A/D Analog-to-digital conversion. Also called digitization.

ABERRATIONS Disruptions of or imperfections in the light transmission of a lens.

ABOVE-THE-LINE COSTS Production costs relating to producer, director, writers, and stars. See Below-the-Line Costs.

AC-3 (Audio Coded #3) Also known as Dolby Digital; developed as one of several required audio formats for DVD-video and ATSC digital TV.

ACADEMY APERTURE The size of the frame mask in 35 mm cameras and projectors (1.85:1) as standardized by the Academy of Motion Picture Arts and Sciences.

ACADEMY LEADER A strip of film containing a sequence of numbers indicating the exact number of seconds remaining before the beginning of a film or videotape.

ACCEPTABLE FOCUS The adjustment of the lens so that the important objects are clear and sharp.

A. C. NIELSEN A marketing and research company that measures and compiles statistics (ratings) on television audiences.

ACQUISITION Gathering of material from the original source.

ACTUALITY Reporting of a news story on the actual location.

ADAPTATION A relatively faithful translation of a play or piece of literature into a film or television program.

ADDITIVE COLORS The colors used in mixing light and upon which both film and video signals are based: red, blue, and green.

ADI (Area of Dominant Influence) The region covered by ratings of the Arbitron ratings company of one major metropolitan area or area covered by stations covering the same market. Similar to DMA.

ADR (Automatic Dialogue Replacement) A process allowing actors to rerecord their lines as they view a playback of their performance.

ADSL (Asymmetrical Digital Subscriber Loop) A digital transmission technology that allows local telephone companies to deliver video services to homes and businesses over copper wires.

AERIAL IMAGE Refilming a projected film image. Other images may be combined using mirrors or single-frame film techniques.

AES/EBU (Audio Engineering Society/European Broadcasting Union) A digital audio standard adopted worldwide.

AESTHETICS The study and analysis of creative works.

AFFILIATE A broadcast station carrying a network's programs, but not owned by that network. See Owned and Operated.

AFM (American Federation of Musicians) A union that represents professional musicians.

AFTRA (American Federation of Television and Radio Artists) The union that represents radio and television performers and, in some markets, directors and associate directors.

AGENT A person who represents a creative person in finding work, negotiating benefits, and guiding the client's career.

AIFF (Audio Interchange File Format) A standard file format for storing audio files.

AL JAZEERA An Arabic based news network, broadcasting in many mideastern languages and in English.

ALIASING A noticeable "jagging" of a computer-created image caused by a sampling rate that is too low.

ALLIGATOR CLIP A light-mounting device consisting of a spring-held clamp that somewhat resembles the jaws of an alligator.

AMBIENT The prevailing location environment; in audio, the background noise present at a location.

AMORTIZATION The depreciation of the value of equipment and facilities over time for tax purposes.

AMPLIFY To increase levels electronically.

AMPLITUDE The instantaneous value of a signal; the electronic equivalent of level or loudness in audio.

ANALOG An electronic signal that is constantly varying in some proportion to either sound, light, or a radio frequency.

ANAMORPHIC Optically squeezed wide-screen film images, which require special lenses for recording and projecting.

ANCHOR, NEWS A newscaster who reads the news in the studio; may or may not have written, covered, or reported the story.

ANCILLARY MARKETS Secondary sales possibilities for a program after it has completed its first run on a network and in the theaters. Also called back-end.

ANGLE OF ACCEPTANCE The angle at which a lens gathers light in front of the camera.

ANIMATION A process of creating the illusion that inanimate objects are moving.

ANIMATION STAND The mounting for the animation camera, lights, and table for shooting animation cels. Sometimes called a rostrum. See Cel Animation.

ANSWER PRINT The first color-corrected film print returned to the editor from the laboratory to make certain it was printed according to the directions provided.

ANTAGONIST The character in a drama that opposes the heroes.

APERTURE (Iris) The size of the camera lens opening, measured in f-stops.

APPLICATION A computer program designed to permit certain types of work to be accomplished.

ARBITRON A research and study company specializing in radio station ratings.

ARC Movement of the camera in a semicircular pattern.

ART DIRECTOR In film and video productions, the person who supervises the overall production design, including sets, props, costumes, settings, and even locations.

ARTIFICIAL INTELLIGENCE (AI) (1) A computer program that mimics the human mind. (2) In computer games, a method of inserting text-based dialogue.

ASA (American Standards Association) The rating of a film's ability to reproduce images based on the amount of light required. See Exposure Index (EI) and DIN (European Standard).

ASCAP (American Society of Composers, Authors, and Publishers) One of three major music licensing organizations charged with collecting residual fees due composers and musicians.

ASCII (American Standard Code for Information Interchange) A universal digital standard for reading binary digits that can be read by almost all computer operating systems.

ASF (Active Streaming Format) Microsoft's streaming format for Windows Media system.

ASPECT RATIO The mathematical ratio between the vertical and the horizontal measurements of a frame of video or film.

ASSEMBLE EDIT The sequential arranging of shots in a linear manner. May be accomplished on raw tape without previously recording a control track.

ASSISTANT DIRECTOR (AD) In film production, the person who helps the production manager break down the script during preproduction and helps the director keep the talent and crew happy during production.

ASSOCIATE DIRECTOR (AD) In video production, the person who relays the director's commands from the control room to the studio floor, keeps accurate time, and assists the director as needed.

ASYMMETRICAL (1) In computers, a system that provides unequal send-and-receive signal speeds. (2) In graphics, a layout with different shapes and sizes on the center dividing line.

ASYNCHRONOUS (1) A sound that does not match its actual or presumed on-screen source. (2) In computers, signals running at different speeds.

ATM (Asynchronous Transfer Mode) A high-speed, fixed-packet data standard that works with telephone systems, but not necessarily with LANs or WANs.

ATMOSPHERIC EFFECTS Environmental special effects such as fog, rain, snow.

ATR (audiotape recorder) A tape deck based on an analog linear system of recording audio on a plastic-based tape coated with a material that can be magnetized. Generally the tape transport is based on an open-reel system.

ATSC (Advanced Television Systems Committee) An industry group that sets standards for digital television in the United States.

ATTENUATE To decrease or lower the levels of a signal or parts of a signal.

ATTRIBUTE, ATTRIBUTION To define, identify, or describe a characteristic or quality.

ATV (Advanced Television) In the United States, includes digital television and high-definition television.

AUDIENCE-SURVEY RESEARCH To collect information on audience preferences and analyze tends or possible audience reactions.

AUDIO (1) The sound portion of the videotape. (2) Frequencies within the normal hearing range of humans.

AUDIO CONSOLE An audio board through which sounds are channeled, amplified, and mixed during production or postproduction. See Mixer.

AUDIO CUE SHEET (Mixing Log) A listing of audio tracks and their relationship as a guide to the editor for making precise transitions and equalization.

AUDITION (1) An audio circuit designed to allow the operator to hear selected sounds without those sounds being recorded or going on the air. (2) A talent tryout session for directors and producers to watch and listen to prospective performers before casting them in a production.

AURAL Having to do with sound or audio.

AUTHORING In interactive writing, the creation of flowcharts or copy for the computer screen.

AUTOMATIC GAIN CONTROL (AGC) A circuit that maintains the audio or video level within a certain range. Prevents overdriving circuits, which causes distortion, but can increase signal-to-noise ratio.

AUTOMATIC LEVEL CONTROL (ALC) See Automatic Gain Control (AGC).

AVAILABLE LIGHT Illumination existing at a location; sometimes called ambient light.

AVI (Audio Video Interleaved) A file format similar to MPEG and Quicktime for Windows.

AXIS OF ACTION (also called 180-Degree Line) An imaginary line formed by the performer's direction of movement or by drawing a line through major stationary objects. Screen directionality will be maintained as long as the cameras do not cross this line.

"B" ROLL A second roll of film or tape used in editing; usually includes cutaways and cut-ins.

BACKGROUND LIGHT Light used to illuminate the set or background without lighting subjects in front of the set.

BACKLIGHT Light placed behind the subject, opposite the camera; usually mounted fairly high and controlled with barn doors to prevent light from shining directly into the camera lens.

BACKTIME To calculate the start time of a prerecorded soundtrack so that it will end at a specified time.

BAFFLE A panel designed to absorb or reflect sound.

BALANCED MICROPHONE LINE A mic line that consists of two internal conductors surrounded by isolation and a wraparound ground mesh.

BALL JOINT The part of a tripod head that can be rotated to level the camera.

BANDWIDTH The amount or volume of information that can be transmitted though a communications link.

BARNDOOR Movable metal flaps attached to lighting fixtures to allow control over the area covered by the light from that lamp.

BARNEY A soft sound insulator placed over a film camera to kill camera noise during synchronous recording.

BARREL A cable adapter designed to connect two cables ending in similar plugs.

BARTER SYNDICATION A system of distributing programs in which the syndicator retains a certain number of commercial slots and markets them, keeping the income.

BASE The shiny side of a piece of film and some tapes. The physical support for either film emulsion or tape oxides.

BASE LIGHT LEVEL The maximum amount of light required to achieve a recording.

BASE MAKEUP Makeup that hides blemishes and creates a consistent overall facial color.

BASS The low-frequency end of the audio spectrum.

BAUD Number of symbols per second. A measure of data-transmission speed.

BED SOUND Lowering a background sound for simultaneous narration. Also called down and under.

BELOW-THE-LINE COSTS Those production costs of a cast and crew and their work, with the exception of the producers, director, writers, and stars. See Above-the-Line Costs.

BETACAM Half-inch professional videotape format developed by Sony specifically for use in camcorders; has replaced the ¾ U-matic as the predominant news-gathering video format.

BETACAM SP An improved Sony Betacam format. Uses metal tape but is downward-compatible with Betacam.

BETACAM SX Digital Betacam format.

BIAS A high-frequency current mixed into a recording circuit that acts as a carrier of the audio to ensure a linear response.

BI-DIRECTIONAL A microphone that picks up sound from the front and back but rejects most sound from the sides. The pickup pattern appears in the shape of a figure eight.

BINARY A number in base 2; an either/or comparison. Computer systems are binary systems.

BIT (Binary Digit) The smallest piece of information usable by a computer, either on or off.

BIT DEPTH A measurement of the number of tones per sample in an audio digitization process.

BLACK BURST A composite video signal including sync and color signals, but the video level is at black, or minimum.

BLACK LEVEL The normal level for pedestal or video black in a video signal. See Setup.

BLEED Space beyond the critical or essential area that may be seen on some television receivers but not on others.

BLIMP A hard-shell sound insulator placed over a film camera to deaden camera noise during synchronous sound recording.

BLOCKING Working out talent and camera positions during a rehearsal.

BLOG, BLOGGING Contraction of "web log," a web site operated by an individual with regular entries of information, opinion, and philosophy. The act of making entries in a blog.

BLOOM The effect seen when a video signal exceeds the capabilities of the system; white areas bleed into darker areas.

BLOOP (1) An audible tone recorded simultaneously with a flash of light for the purpose of synchronizing images and sound during editing. (2) To remove specific sounds from a soundtrack.

BLOW UP Print a film on a larger format in an optical printer.

BLUE-RAY (Blue Laser Disc, BD) The next-generation of optical disc after DVD; offers at least five times greater capacity for HD recording.

BMI (Broadcast Music, Inc.) One of three major music-licensing organizations charged with collecting residual fees due composers and musicians.

BMP (Windows Bitmap) A visual red, green, blue (RGB) computer format developed by Microsoft.

BNC (Bayonet Neill-Concelman) A type of twist-lock video connector, now the most common for professional equipment.

BODY MIC A microphone concealed or hung directly on the body of the performer, sometimes called a lapel or lavaliere mic.

BOOM The movable arm from which a microphone or camera may be suspended to allow for movement to follow the action.

BOOMERS The generation of American born following World War II (1945) and early 1960s.

BOOST To raise or increase the level of a signal or portion of the signal.

BOX OFFICE RETURNS The amount of money paid to theaters for tickets purchased by moviegoers for specific films.

BRANCHING (1) In a drama, various paths a character may take in action. (2) In multimedia, various paths that a viewer may take by following links on a web page.

BREAKDOWN SHEETS A listing of facilities, material, equipment, and personnel needs for production at a specific setting called for in the script, which is filled out during script breakdown.

BRIGHTNESS The intensity of light.

BROAD A type of open-faced fill light, usually rectangular in shape.

BROADBAND CARRIER A high-capacity transmission system used to carry large blocks of information on one cable or carrier: coaxial cable, microwave, optical fiber.

BROADCASTING The sending of video and audio signals by attaching them to a carrier wave of electromagnetic energy that radiates in all directions.

BSS (Broadcast Satellite Services) International video satellites on "C" and "Ku" bands.

BUBBLE Leveling device mounted on a tripod pan head consisting of a tube containing a liquid with a bubble of air trapped inside. Centering the bubble on a circle or crosshair indicates that the pan head is level.

BUDGET An itemized list of actual or estimated production costs.

BUFFER A block of computer memory set aside for temporarily holding data.

BURN A condition caused by exposing camera tubes to excessive light levels. An image is retained on the face of the tube that is the negative of the original subject.

BURNER A device to convert digital signals to an optical laser disc, either DVD or CD.

BUS (1) A group of buttons on a video switcher devoted to different sources but sending the chosen signal to a predetermined output: preview, program, or special effects. (2) A wire that carries a series of signals to a common output.

BUZZWORDS In advertising, phrases or words that have strong appeal and that the audience recognizes.

BYTE Eight bits; the standard amount of information used to define a single character.

"C" FORMAT One of three one-inch helical videotape formats specified by the SMPTE. "C" had become the analog production standard for studios in the United States until the development of digital formats.

CABLE RELEASE A device that allows a film camera to be operated from a distance, often used for exposing single frames.

CAMCORDER A camera-recorder combination. Designed originally for news coverage, but now becoming popular for electronic field production (EFP) and other field productions.

CAMEO A lighting technique in which foreground subjects are lit in front of a completely black background.

CAMERA CHAIN A complete video camera unit consisting of a camera, a power supply, a sync generator, a camera control unit, and an encoder.

CAMERA CONTROL UNIT A series of circuits that provide the signals and controls for operating a video camera.

CAMERA REPORT A listing of individual camera shots either as they are made in the camera on location, or a listing of shots to be processed by the film laboratory.

CAPACITOR An electrical device that can store an electrical charge and alter the flow of electronic signals by changing the electrical current passing through it.

CAPSTAN The rotating shaft that presses against the videotape to keep the tape running at a constant speed.

CARBON ARC LIGHT An intense light of approximately daylight Kelvin temperature that is emitted by electrically burning carbon rods.

CARDIOID MIC A specialized unidirectional microphone with a heart-shaped pickup pattern.

CARTRIDGE A self-contained continuous loop of audiotape or film.

CASE The upper or lower style of letters. Uppercase letters are capital letters; lowercase letters are small letters.

CASSETTE A prepackaged container of either audio, videotape, or film containing a specific length of tape or film stock, a feed reel, and a take-up reel. U-matic, Betacam, VHS, DVC tape systems, and Super-8 film all use cassettes.

CASTING The process of auditioning and selecting performers for a production.

CATHARSIS An element in drama that functions as an emotional release for the audience.

CATHODE RAY TUBE (CRT) A television picture tube.

C-BAND The range of frequencies from 4 to 8 GHz used by many satellite companies.

CCD See Charge-Coupled Device.

C-CLAMP An attachment device shaped like a "C" that can be used to secure lighting instruments to the grid or to connect flats and other set pieces.

CD (Compact Disc) A five-inch digital laser disc, generally used for music recordings but also used for computer and video recording.

CD-I (Compact Disc-Interactive) A large-memory CD that can deliver 2 to 16 channels of video and/or audio and up to 16 hours of audio; designed to provide the programming for interactive systems.

CD-ROM (Compact Disk-Read-Only Memory) A permanently recorded CD disc.

CED (Capacitive Electronic Disc) One type of video disc.

CEL Short for celluloid. The base material used to draw individual animation frames.

CEL ANIMATION The process of drawing and shooting as many as 24 cels per second. Each cel is a drawing on a clear acetate sheet. Cels showing foreground, midground, and background may be layered to give the impression of three dimensions.

CEMENT SPLICE A device with cutting blades and clamps for welding two pieces of film together with cement (often with a warming element).

CERAMIC LIGHT SOURCE A light source using a high-temperature ceramic composite and gas phase for selective emission. Provides 3200 K output at one-fourth the power consumption of a Halogen source.

CHANGING BAG A light-tight black cloth or plastic bag used to load or unload camera magazines with film wound on cores.

CHANNEL (1) A separate audio signal. (2) A separate broadcast signal.

CHARACTER A single letter, number, or symbol used as a means of describing information in a graphic form.

CHARACTER GENERATOR (CG) A computerized electronic typewriter designed to create titles or any other of numeric or alphanumeric graphics for use in video.

CHARGE-COUPLED DEVICE (CCD) (1) Light-sensitive silicon chips. Replaced camera tubes. (2) A solid-state element designed to convert light to electronics; replaced the pickup tubes in video cameras.

CHIAROSCURO LIGHTING Lighting accomplished with high-contrast areas and heavy shadows.

CHIP A semiconductor integrated circuit. Depending on design, can replace tubes, resistors, and other electronic components. This light-sensitive chip, which replaced the camera tube, was the most important development for electronic field production (EFP).

CHROMA The color portion of the video signal that includes both hue and saturation.

CHROMA KEY A method of combining two or more levels of pictures from more than one source. The process depends on the background behind the foreground subjects being a solid single color, usually green or blue. A specific type of effects generator ignores the blue or green background so that the foreground subject appears in front of the other signals.

CHROMATIC ABERRATION Visual distortion occurring when different color wavelength bands bend at different angles and intersect at different points behind the lens.

CHROMINANCE (Chroma) The color portion of the video signal.

CHRONOLOGY The timing sequence of events in a story.

CID (Compact Iodine Daylight) Lighting lamp using less wattage than Tungsten and providing near daylight color temperature light.

CINEMA VÉRITÉ Literally "cinema truth," a style of documentary filmmaking in which the camera runs continuously while recording unstaged events.

CINEMATOGRAPHER The operator or supervisor of a motion picture camera; over the years, this term has also been used to refer to those who operate a video camera.

CINERAMA A widescreen film process (1939–1963) that used three cameras and three projectors placed side-by-side.

CLAMPS Locks placed on the end of a rewind spindle on a film-editing bench to hold the film reels tight on the spindle.

CLAPSTICK A hinged arm on a board used to make a highly visible and audible reference point at the beginning of a synchronous sound film that is to be shot and recorded.

CLEAR LEADER Film or tape that has no magnetic or emulsion coating and is thus completely transparent base material.

CLEARANCE The process of applying for and receiving permission to use a person's talent, appearance, or property.

CLIMAX The decisive point in a drama, where the central conflict becomes so intense that it must be resolved; the central crisis in a drama.

CLIP (1) A single sequence of frames. (2) To cut or restrict.

CLOCK TIME (1) The actual time of day. (2) The reference code often used for SMPTE timecode recordings.

CLOSED SHOP Businesses or industries that require all employees to be members of a guild or a union.

CLOSED-CAPTION A form of teletext designed to permit the hearing impaired to read the dialogue and a description of the action of a program. The copy is keyed into a window at the bottom of the frame. A special decoder attached to or built into the receiver is necessary to be able to view the copy.

CLOSED-CIRCUIT A self-contained wired system, as opposed to a broadcast system.

CLOSE-UP (CU) Camera framing showing intimate detail; often a tight head shot.

CLOSURE Psychological perceptual activity that fills in gaps in the visual field.

CMOS (Complementary Metal-Oxide Semiconductor) A solid-state chip that is light sensitive, used as a camera pickup chip.

COAXIAL CABLE A metal cable consisting of a single conductor surrounded by another conductor in the form of a tube designed to carry high frequencies without loss or distortion.

CODEC A combination encoder and decoder of electronic signals in one piece of equipment.

COERCION To cause someone to think or act in a certain manner.

COFDM (Coded Orthogonal Frequency Division Multiplexing) A modulation system used in both digital television and DAB systems.

COLLABORATION To work together in a create endeavor.

COLLAGE To combine a variety of different individual items to create a single creative image: in graphics, film, audio.

COLOR BARS Electronically generated pattern of precisely specified colors for use in standardizing the operation of video equipment.

COLOR CONTRAST Visible differences between adjacent colors, in terms of hue and saturation.

COLOR CORRECTION During the postproduction phase of a visual project, adjusting the shades and tints of colors to compensate for an incorrect exposure or to create an effect.

COLOR HARMONY Colors that create a pleasing impression when used or presented together.

COLOR-REVERSAL INTERNEGATIVE (CRI) A color-reversal print of an original negative that produces another negative to be used to make many prints by saving the original negative from the wear and tear of multiple printing passes.

COLOR TEMPERATURE See Kelvin Temperature.

COLOR TIMING The art of setting the best color and density for the printing of each shot in a film.

COLOR WHEEL Color chips arranged in a dimensional circle to show the relationships between hue (chrominance), saturation, and luminance (brightness).

COMEDY A type of drama characterized by a less serious attitude toward life and an acceptance of its absurdities and incongruities.

COMET-TAILING A lingering afterimage of a bright light or reflecting object passing by the camera.

COMMENTATIVE SOUND Sound that has no visible source and that seems to comment on the visual action.

COMMERCIAL TIE-INS Using a retail product within a media production to promote and sell the product without appearing as a formal commercial. Also using a retail product to promote and sell and media production.

COMMERCIALS Paid brief messages that advertise products, companies, names, and services.

COMMON CARRIER The FCC's classification of transmission systems open to public use for fees. The operators are not allowed to control the content of the messages. Telephone, telegraph, and some satellite systems are regulated as common carriers.

COMPATIBILITY (1) That two systems can operate together. (2) That a tape recorded in one format can be played back in another. (3) That two different types of signals, such as NTSC and ATV, can be viewed on the same system.

COMPLEMENTARY COLORS Colors that are opposite each other on a color wheel or that, when mixed together, result in gray.

COMPONENT A signal (often video) in which unique parts are divided and transported or recorded separately. A component video signal may have the luminance and synchronous signals separated.

COMPOSITE A signal (often video) that contains all of the necessary signals in one combined signal. A composite video signal contains both picture and synchronous signals.

COMPOSITE PRINT A single film containing both the picture and soundtrack.

COMPOSITE SIGNAL A complete video signal, including sync pulse.

COMPOSITING Combining different payers of visual images in a computer graphics or animation program.

COMPOSITION The arrangement of visual elements with the frame.

COMPOUND LENS A lens made of more than one piece of glass or plastic.

COMPRESSED VIDEO A video signal that has repetitive and redundant portions removed, leaving only changes that occur between frames. Allows high-frequency video signals to use less memory and bandwidth.

COMPUTER CHARACTER (CC) (P.4.32) A symbol of a computer individual or object created by an artificial intelligence scriptwriter.

COMPUTER GRAPHICS Pictorial images and illustrations created on a computer to be used in video and/or film productions.

COMPUTER-GENERATED IMAGERY (CGI) Images created entirely within a computer system.

CONCAVE The shape of a lens that bends light away from the center of the lens, causing the light rays to diverge from each other.

CONDENSER MIC A transducer that converts sound waves by a conductive principle. Requires a built-in amplifier and a power source. Also called electrostatic or capacitor.

CONFLICT A point of contention, disagreement, or competition in a story.

CONFORMING The final film-editing process of actually cutting the original negative into separate rolls and syncing it with the sound for delivery to the laboratory for printing.

CONTACT PRINTER A film-printing device in which original film is placed in direct emulsion-to-emulsion contact with the copy or print being made from the original.

CONTENT The substance of a work of art.

CONTIGUOUS Next to, adjacent to.

CONTINGENCY FUND Percentage (usually 10 to 20 percent) of a budget added to cover any costly delays or unforeseen production problems.

CONTINUITY (1) A depiction of continuous action. (2) Scripts, especially of commercials. (3) See Script Supervisor.

CONTRAPUNTAL SOUND Sound that is presented simultaneously with visual images but is unrelated or contradictory in terms of meaning or emotional effect.

CONTRAST RANGE The ability of a camera to distinguish between shades of reflected black-and-white light: TV, 30:1; film, 100:1; human eye, 1000:1.

CONTRAST RATIO The ratio of light measurement between the difference of maximum reflectance, as measured with a light meter, and minimum reflectance on a set.

CONTROL TRACK Synchronizing signal recorded onto a videotape to align the heads for proper playback.

CONTROL TRACK EDITING Choice of edit points determined by counting pulses recorded on the tape.

CONTROLLER A specialized computer designed to accurately maintain control over a series of videotape decks during the editing process.

CONVERGENCE Separate technologies combined or cooperate together to create new technologies or means of performing similar tasks; newspaper, radio, TV, Internet news operations.

CONVERTIBLE CAMERA A video camera that can be either used in portable field productions or mounted with studio accessories for in-studio productions.

CONVEX The shape of a lens that bends light toward the center of the lens so that light rays converge or intersect at a specific point, beyond which the image is inverted.

COOKIE See Cukaloris.

COPY The words on a script.

COPY STAND A flat table with lights that illuminate artwork for an overhead camera.

CORE A plastic wheel upon which film can be rolled; unprocessed film placed on cores must be protected from light and loaded in a camera or magazine in complete darkness.

COSMETIC MAKEUP Facial and body makeup designed to hide imperfections and accentuate a performer's better features.

COSTUME DESIGNER The person who designs and supervises the making of clothing for talent.

COUNTDOWN LEADER A section of film or tape with a decreasing sequence of numbers indicating the amount of time remaining before the start of a film or tape.

COUNTER A meter designed to indicate either a position on a reel of tape or film or the amount of tape or film already used. May be calibrated in revolutions, frames, feet, meters, or time.

COUNTERPOINT The simultaneous presentation of two contradictory visual or sound sequences.

COVER LETTER Describes an applicant for a job. It precedes or accompanies a résumé or interview.

CPB (Corporation for Public Broadcasting). A private, nonprofit organization created by Congress in 1967 to invest federal funds in public broadcasting; to help fund National Public Radio (NPR) and PBS.

CPM (Cost per Thousand) The cost of exposing viewers to a commercial. Based on ratings of the program in which the commercial is scheduled to run.

CPU (Central Processing Unit) The main circuits that process digital information in a computer.

CRAB DOLLY A four-wheeled camera support on which an operator can sit and operate the camera while it is being moved.

CRADLE The dish on the top of a tripod into which the ball joint of a tripod head or camera mount is placed.

CRANE A relatively large camera mount consisting of a long counterweighted arm on a four-wheeled dolly.

CRAWL Credits or other graphic material moving from the bottom of the frame to the top.

CREDITS Lists of the names and functions of the people who have contributed in some way to a production.

CRISIS An intensification of the central conflict in a drama, usually involving a threat to someone or something.

CRITICAL AREA (Essential Area) Space occupying approximately 80 percent of the center of the video frame. This area will be seen with relative surety by the majority of the television receivers viewing that particular program. The 10 percent border outside of the critical area may not be visible on many receivers.

CROSS-FADE A transition in which one sound source fades out at the same rate as another is faded in.

CROSS-TALK Signal leakage between two channels.

CRYSTAL OSCILLATORS Small bits of quartz that oscillate at an unchanging rate and that can be used to regulate the speed of cameras and recorders.

CRYSTAL SYNC Separate crystal oscillators in the camera and recorder stay in sync without interconnecting cables.

CSI (Compact Source Iodide) A lighting lamp that uses less wattage than Tungsten and provides near-daylight color temperature light.

CUE (1) Signal to start talking, moving, or whatever the script calls for. (2) To ready material to be played back or edited by running and stopping a tape, film, record, and so on, at a specified spot.

CUKALORIS (Cucaloris) A metal filter with cutout patterns designed to be placed in front of or inside of lamps to throw a pattern or mottled shadows. Sometimes called a cookie.

CUT (Take) (1) Cue to stop an action and so on. (2) An instantaneous change in picture or sound. *Cut* is considered a film term and *take* a video term, but they have become interchangeable.

CUTAWAY Close-up shot of an image related to, but not visible in, the wider shot immediately preceding or following it.

CUT-IN Close-up shot of an image visible in the wider shot immediately preceding or following it.

CUTOFF POINT The frame that begins or ends a sequence.

CYCLE Time or distance between peaks of an alternating voltage; measured in Hertz.

CYCLES-PER-SECOND (CPS) The number of vibrations or successive waves of sound passing a specific point in one second.

CYCLING An animation technique for repeatedly using the same movements of hands and feet or other body parts.

CYCLORAMA, SKYCYC, CYC A plain gray or off-white screen that hangs in a studio to provide an "infinite" background.

D1, D2, D3, D5, D6, D7 (DVCPro), D9 (D-S), D16, SX Beta Digital videotape formats.

D/A Digital-to-analog conversion.

DAB (Digital Audio Broadcast) A wireless digital terrestrial broadcast service. Also known as IBOC/DAB. A digital signal carried on a standard AM or FM radio broadcast.

DAILIES A one-light print of the previous day's film shooting for checking the quality of that day's shooting. See also One-Light Print.

DAM (Digital Asset Management) A movement toward operating digital systems with one central control to allow exchange of files seamlessly between units.

DARS (Digital Audio Radio Services) Proposed satellite digital radio broadcasting.

DASH A stationary head digital recording device, also called S-DAT.

DAT (Digital Audiotape) A series of formats designed to record audio in the digital domain, rather than analog. Formats include R-DAT (rotating-head), S-DAT (stationary head), and others being developed at the time of this writing.

DATA Any information used in any project or process, analog or digital.

DAW (Digital Audio Workstation) A combination of software and hardware designed to facilitate the recording and editing of audio signals.

DAYLIGHT SPOOL A metal or plastic reel covering the edges of unprocessed film so that it can be loaded into a camera in daylight.

DBS (Direct Broadcast Satellite) (1) A system of relaying television programs from a satellite directly into the home without being retransmitted by either a cable or TV broadcast station. (2) A high-powered, high-band satellite television transmission system.

DECIBEL (dB) Logarithmic unit of loudness. A dB is one-tenth of the original unit, the Bel.

DECK In media, refers to a machine that plays or records audio or video signals.

DEFICIT FINANCING Producing a program at a loss on its first broadcast, depending on making a profit when the program goes into syndication.

DEFOCUS To roll the focus ring of a lens so that the image is out-of-focus.

DEGREES KELVIN See Kelvin Temperature.

DEMODULATION The separation of a program signal from the carrier wave.

DEMOGRAPHICS Characteristics of an audience or group of people in terms of age, gender, income, or other social factors.

DEPTH The illusion of three-dimensionality in visual composition; the "Z" axis.

DEPTH OF FIELD (DOF) The range of distances from the camera within which subjects remain in acceptable focus.

DEVELOPER The chemical solution that brings out the latent image on photographic film.

DGA (Directors Guild of America) Represents directors, in both film and television, in issues related to working conditions and rights.

DIALOGUE Speech between performers, usually seen on camera.

DIAPHRAGM (1) The adjustable opening that varies the aperture size of the lens. (2) The element in a microphone that vibrates according to the pressure waves in the air created by the sound source.

DICHROIC Filters designed to reflect certain colors of light and pass others.

DIFFRACTION Spreading or scattering of light that often occurs around the ball of the iris in the lens.

DIFFUSER Translucent material that breaks up and scatters light from a lighting fixture to soften it.

DIGITAL Binary-based, constant-amplitude signals varying in time. Provides signal recording without noise or distortion.

DIGITAL CINEMA (DC) (formerly called Electronic Cinema) The distribution and projection of feature film through a high-definition digital video system.

DIGITAL FILTER The application features that allow an artist to distort, blur, smooth, or texture an object.

DIGITAL LIGHT PROCESSING (DLP) A rear-screen video display system based on rotating mirrors.

DIGITAL SIGNAL PROCESSOR (DSP) A circuit designed to change the analog output of a CMSO or CCD chip to a digital signal.

DIGITAL VIDEO MANIPULATOR (DVM) (also called a Digital Effects Switcher) A special effects device that uses digital circuits to create unusual images.

DIGITAL-S A digital video-based tape-recording format.

DIGITIZE To create a digital equivalent of an analog image by sampling and converting it to the binary system.

DIMMER BOARD An electrical control center for lighting that alters the voltage to different circuits in a patch board and thus changes the light intensity of the instruments in those circuits, which also affects the color temperature of the light.

DIN (1) Deutsche Industrie Normen: The German standards organization. (2) DIN usually refers to a type of plug-jack.

DIOPTER An adjustable lens allowing the operator to match his or her eyesight with the viewfinder.

DIRECTOR Commands the creative aspects of a production. In the field, makes creative decisions; in the studio, calls the shots on live productions; and in the editing room, provides opinions.

DISC/DISK Hard recording drives: disc drives are recorded optically, disk recorded magnetically.

DISCRETE 5.1 AUDIO A six-channel audio-delivery system with speakers placed on the left, right, center, left-rear, right-rear, and including a subwoofer.

DISH A parabola-shaped antenna designed to receive satellite or microwave signals.

DISSOLVE Transition of one image fading into and replacing another. If stopped at the midpoint, it is a superimposition. Also called a lap.

DISTORTION An undesirable change in a signal or either light, sound, or video.

DISTRIBUTION The supply of media programming to exhibitors from the producers. The equivalent to wholesellers in the retail business.

DISTRIBUTION AMPLIFIER (DA) Electronic amplifier designed to feed one signal (audio, video, or pulses) to several different destinations.

DISTRIBUTORS Companies and organizations that rent films to exhibitors and theater owners.

DMA (Designated Market Area) The local ratings area used by the Nielsen Media Research Company.

DOCUDRAMAS A type of historical or biographical drama based on actual events but modified for dramatic and aesthetic purposes.

DOCUMENTARY A nonfiction film or videotape that explores a topic in depth with the purpose of making a specific point.

DOLLY (1) Three- or four-wheeled device that serves as a movable camera mount. (2) Movement in toward a subject (dolly in) or back away from a subject (dolly out).

DOUBLE PERF Film with sprocket holes on both sides or edges.

DOUBLE-SYSTEM RECORDING Recording synchronized sound on a recorder that is separated from the camera that is recording the matching images.

DOWNLINK Transmission path from a satellite to a ground station. Sometimes used to describe the ground station capable of receiving a satellite signal link. See Uplink.

DOWNLOAD The process of transferring electronic information from one source, circuit, or storage medium to another. A combination of various elements that affect the pace at which actions unfold and the emotional response of the audience.

DRAW (Direct-Read-After-Write) Erasable and reusable optical disc.

DRESS REHEARSAL The final rehearsal or dry run of a production with all costumes, props, and other production units before the actual recording.

DSL (Digital Subscriber Line) A system designed to allow a standard telephone line to carry digital information at a rate much faster than using a standard digital modem.

DUAL-REDUNDANCY Using two of a single element, such as microphones, in case one of them fails during a critical production.

DUB (1) Copying a recorded signal from one medium to another. (2) Replacing or adding voice to a preexisting recording.

DUBBERS Mechanical/electronic equipment to copy videotape, audiotape, or film soundtracks.

DUPE To duplicate; to make a copy of a tape, film, or disk.

DUPE NEGATIVE A negative copy of an interpositive that is used to make multiple prints of a negative original film.

DV (Digital Video) Any of several videotape formats for recording a digitized signal.

DVC (Digital Videocassette) Any of several digital videotape formats.

DVCPro, DVCPro50, DVCPro100 Digital video-based compatible recording formats.

DVD (Digital Versatile Disc or Digital Video Disc) A laser disc capable of storing from 8 to 18 GB of digital information, such as a two-hour movie with eight separate soundtracks and 32 subtitle tracks for international distribution.

DVD-R, DVD+R DVD discs for one-time-only recording.

DVD-RW, DVD-RAM, DVD+RW DVD discs that may be recorded multiple times.

DVE (Digital Video Effects) A video switcher used to create digital effects.

DVM (Digital Video Manipulator) See DVE.

DVSP, DVCAM Comparable medium-level digital recording formats.

DYNAMIC MIC A transducer designed to convert sound to electronics by using an electromagnetic coil attached to a lightweight diaphragm.

DYNAMIC RANGE The loudness range from the softest to the loudest that can be reproduced by any system without creating distortion.

EBU (European Broadcast Union) The world's largest professional broadcast and standards-setting association.

EC (Electronic Cinema) A digital video camera with a high-quality output nearly equaling that of 35 mm film.

EDGE NUMBERS Consecutive reference numbers printed on the edge of a piece of film.

EDIT CONTROL UNIT An electronic device that controls the editing manipulations of videotape recordings.

EDIT CUE A cue that activates an edit at a specific point on the tape.

EDIT DECISION LIST (EDL) A list of precise locations of edit points. May be generated manually or by computer.

EDITED MASTER The final product of online editing.

EDITING TEMPO The pace of editing. The subjective apparent speed of objects, as different than the speed of editing, the actual number of edits and their length.

EDITOR A tape or film specialist charged with assembling stories from footage and recordings to create the final production.

EFP (Electronic Field Production) A single-camera video production taking place at remote locations from the studio.

EFP UNIT A van containing equipment for a single-camera video-recording session at a remote location.

EIAJ (Electronic Industries Association of Japan) Standards-setting organization of Japan. At one time referred to a specific ½-inch open-reel videotape system.

ELECTRET A permanently charged element or capacitor in a condenser mic.

ELECTRONIC CINEMATOGRAPHY (EC) (now called Digital Cinema) Shooting a feature "film" with HDTV cameras and recording on videotape, not film.

ELECTRONIC NEWS GATHERING (ENG) Process of researching, shooting, and editing materials to visually report on occurrences of interest using video cameras and electronic editing specifically for newscasts.

ELECTRONIC PROJECTION Large-screen video-image projection systems, often using multiple monitors or split frames with different images in each frame.

ELLIPSOIDAL A lighting instrument with a mirror reflector in the shape of an ellipse, which produces intense, harsh spot lighting.

EMULSION A chemical layer containing the light-sensitive materials on photography and motion-picture film. The makeup of the emulsion determines how sensitive to light the film is and is rated accordingly.

ENCODING Adding additional signals or data, such as timecode and cues of close-caption information, to an existing signal or recording.

ENHANCEMENT A multimedia element such as a link to the World Wide Web.

ENT Abbreviation for interior, a location artificially lit.

EPS (Encapsulated PostScript) A visual computer format used for vector files.

EQUAL TIME The FCC's rule requiring stations to sell airtime to all candidates for a political office if they sell to any one candidate.

EQUALIZATION (EQ) The manipulation of frequencies to correct or compensate for deficiencies in an electronic signal by boosting or attenuating certain frequencies.

ERASE HEAD A device on a recording machine that is used to align all metal particles on magnetic tape before recording and in doing so remove any previously recorded signals.

ERROR RATIO (RATE) A measurement of the number of digital errors in a single signal.

ESSENTIAL AREA The area of the full frame within which critical information should fall so that it will not be cut off by a television receiver. See also Critical Area and Safe Action Area.

ESTABLISHING SHOT (ES) A shot in which the camera is generally located at a sufficient distance from the subjects to record their actions in the context of their surroundings, thus firmly establishing place, time, and relationships.

EVENT A single activity during an editing session.

EXHIBITION The public showing of a work of art, including film, video, graphics, or sound.

EXHIBITORS Film theaters and theater owners.

EXPOSITION A structural element in a drama whereby characters are introduced or settings presented, providing background information and setting a specific mood.

EXPOSURE The presentation of film to light.

EXPOSURE INDEX (EI) A rating of the sensitivity of a specific film stock to light. See DIN and ASA.

EXPOSURE LATITUDE See Contrast Range.

EXTERIOR (EXT) A setting or location outdoors.

EXTREME CLOSE UP (ECU or XCU) The tightest framing of a shot in a sequence—for example, just the eyes or hands of a subject.

EXTREME WIDE SHOT (EWS or XWS) The widest shot of a sequence—for example, an entire city block or football stadium.

EYELINE MATCHES Editing between shots so that the direction an actor is facing matches.

"F" A type of cable connector for a cable intended to carry a modulated signal or signals. See RF.

FACILITIES (FAX) Technical equipment, lights, cameras, microphones, studios, editing rooms.

FACSIMILE (FAX) Transmission of information by optical/electronic system through telephone lines.

FADE-IN OR FADE-OUT A gradual change in signal either from zero to maximum or maximum to zero, in audio, film, or video.

FADER A sliding knob that can be pushed up or down the scale to increase or decrease the audio level.

FADER BAR A movable control for increasing or decreasing the intensity of a video signal on a switcher.

FAST FORWARD A machine operational setting for rapidly advancing tape or film.

FAST MOTION Recording images at a slower speed than normal playback speed so that when played at normal speed, the images move faster than normal.

FEDERAL COMMUNICATION COMMISSION (FCC) The U.S. federal government agency charged with the supervision and regulation of all electronic communication media in the United States.

FEDERAL TRADE COMMISSION (FTC) The U.S. federal agency that monitors and oversees trade practices in many industries, including radio and television advertising and industrial market structure and competition.

FEED (1) The part of a recording device that supplies tape or film. (2) A source of video or audio information supplied to a station or studio.

FEEDBACK A continuous sound loop from a microphone through an audio amplifier to a speaker that is picked up by the microphone, creating a loud squeal. Feedback also can occur with recording/playback units that form a continuous loop, imitating reverberation.

FIBER OPTICS Glass strands designed to carry communication signals modulated on light waves rather than radio waves.

FIELD One-half of a complete television picture; 265.5 lines of the 525 NTSC system occurring once every 60th of a second. Two fields make a complete frame.

FIELD CURVATURE An aberration of an image that shows softer focus on the edges than in the center of the image or vice versa.

FIELD GUIDE A transparent sheet that indicates the proper field and spacing for character movement and artwork on an animation stand.

FIELD OF VIEW The exact spatial dimensions of the framed image in front of the camera.

FILL LIGHT Soft, shadowless light used to reduce contrast and lighten shadow areas. Usually placed on the opposite side of the camera from the key light and low enough to remove harsh shadows.

FILM (1) Light-sensitive material that is exposed to light in a camera to record images. (2) Refers to the whole process of recording, distributing, and viewing images produced by photochemical and mechanical means (excluding video).

FILM PROJECTION The presentation of a film image on a screen by passing light through exposed and processed film in a film projector that is focused by a lens on the screen so that it can be viewed.

FILM PROJECTOR A device that can play back a completed film and project it on screen while amplifying the accompanying soundtrack.

FILM STOCK The unexposed film described in terms of format, sensitivity, process, and graininess.

FILM VIEWER A device that projects a film image during the editing process.

FILM-TO-VIDEO TRANSFER Duplicating a film to video through a telecine or flying spot scanner.

FILTER (1) A colored or textured semiopaque element placed between the subject or lens and the focal plane of the camera. (2) A series of electronic elements used to equalize signals.

FILTER WHEEL A collection of filters arranged on a circular device mounted between the lens and pickup system that allows the camera operator to chose which filter to use as needed.

FINE GRAIN A film stock with small particles that reproduce at a high level of resolution.

FIREWIRE See IEEE 1394.

FISHPOLE A handheld, expandable mic boom.

FIXING Placing film in a chemical solution that permanently "sets" the developed image as part of the process.

FLAC An open-source lossless audio format that uses 2:1 compression ratio.

FLAG An opaque piece of material hung between a light and a subject or set to control light or throw a shadow.

FLASH DRIVE (USB, memory drive, thumb drive, jump drive, sneaker drive, compact flash drive). A portable solid-state magnetic memory recording device.

FLASH FRAME An unwanted frame between two edited shots.

FLAT ANIMATION Two-dimensional items used to create animation, usually individual cels or collages of flat objects.

FLATBED A horizontal film-editing machine.

FLATS Relatively lightweight background sections that can be lashed together to create a continuous wall in a studio.

FLOODLIGHTS Lighting instruments without lenses that have reflectors and diffusers to spread and soften the light that the lights emit.

FLOOR MANAGER (FM) The director's representative on the studio floor who relays commands to the talent and crew during live or multiple-camera video production.

FLOOR PLAN A scale drawing of the studio used in planning scenery design and construction, lighting, and camera and performer blocking.

FLOOR STANDS Three-legged poles that can be raised and lowered, to which lighting instruments and flags can be mounted.

FLOPPY DISK A flat, flexible magnetic medium designed to store and physically transfer computer data.

FLUIDHEAD A camera mount filled with a fluid that helps the operator create smooth camera pans and tilts.

FLUORESCENT LIGHT Light produced by a fluorescent lamp that creates a soft light that does not produce a specific Kelvin temperature.

FLUTTER An audio distortion caused by short and rapid variations in the speed of the reproducer.

FM (Frequency Modulation) Audio broadcasting with a wide frequency range and much freedom from noise.

FOCAL DISTANCE The distance of the subject from the focal plane of the camera.

FOCAL LENGTH The distance from the optical center of a lens to its focal point.

FOCAL PLANE The area behind a convex lens at which the light rays form an inverted image.

FOCUS RING The ring on the barrel of a lens that allows the focus to be changed.

FOOTAGE AND FRAME COUNTER A device that indicates the elapsed tape or film length and duration in feet, frames, or minutes, seconds, and frames.

FOOT-CANDLE (FC) A basic unit of light intensity, theoretically the amount of light from one candle that falls on a one-square-foot board one foot away from the candle.

FORM The method of creating a work of art.

FORMAT (1) A rough outline of a script, often used for newscasts and documentaries. The format is the blueprint for the program, not the word-for-word script. (2) A specific type or size of film, audiotape, videotape, or digital medium. Typical film formats are 70 mm, 35 mm, 16 mm, or S-8. Analog audiotapes are usually described by the width of the tape: ½ inch, one inch, or two inches. Digital formats may be set by the electronics, not the size of the tape. There are more than 20 different analog and digital videotape formats.

FOUR-PLATE FLATBED EDITOR A film editing table with one set of plates for sound, another for picture.

FOUR-WALLING A means by which an independent film producer can distribute and exhibit his or her own film by renting out a theater for a fixed fee.

FRAME (1) Complete video picture, made up of two 262.5 line interlaced scanned fields. There are 30 frames a second in the NTSC system. (2) The outline of the available area in which to compose a video picture. Today's NTSC standard is a frame three units high by four units wide.

FRAME GRABBER An operation within a computer application that allows a computer to convert a single video or film frame to a computer frame for modification and manipulation.

FRAME STORE A digital memory device that scans and stores a complete video frame in order to produce some special effects.

FRANCHISE A license granted to a cable TV, DBS, or telephone company by a civic unit (city, county) to provide electronic communication services to that unit's citizens.

FREELANCE Working on contract, not as a full-time employee.

FREEZE-FRAME Holding the same frame of video or film so that motion is completely stopped.

FREQUENCY The number of complete cycles an electrical signal makes in one second. Measured in hertz, Hz.

FREQUENCY DISTORTION An unequal reproduction or elimination of some frequencies.

FREQUENCY RESPONSE A measurement of a piece of equipment's ability to reproduce a signal of varying frequencies.

FRESNEL A spotlight equipped with a stepped lens that easily controls and concentrates light.

F-STOP A measurement of the size of opening that allows light to pass through an iris or aperture.

FTP (File Transfer Protocol) A system for transferring digital signals.

FTTH (Fiber to the Home) Wiring fiber-optic cable directly to an outlet on a residence instead to a district terminal box on the street.

FULLCOAT A film stock completely coated with magnetic recording medium designed to record one or more individual tracks of sound. The recording is kept in sync with the picture by the match of the sprockets and recording speed with that of the picture.

FULL-PAGE SCRIPT A script format organized around scenes, in which both the visual and audio information appear in the same paragraphs.

FULL SHOT (FS) An extremely wide shot that takes in the entire setting of a scene or sequence. See also Establishing Shot.

FUNCTION To the consumer of art, the reason why it is art.

FUNCTIONAL Referring to sets or lighting. Designed for a specific purpose to serve the needs of the production.

GAFFER The senior electrician on a crew.

GAFFER'S TAPE A strong, gray-colored tape used for securing lights and light-mounting devices, among many other objects.

GAIN The amount of amplitude of an electronic signal. Usually measured in dB.

GANG SYNCHRONIZER Several wheels or hubs with sprocketed teeth that hold different reels of film in exact registration frame-for-frame as they are moved back and forth.

GAP The small distance between the poles of tape heads, usually measured in microns.

GATE The area of the film camera or projector where the film is exposed to light.

GBIT/S Gigabits per second, billions of bits per second.

GELS Flexible sheets of transparent-colored plastic used to create colored light or alter the color temperature of a light source.

GENERAL PURPOSE INTERFACE (GPI) An electronic device controlled by remotely activated electronic switches. With GPI, a computer can control a large number of different components from one location.

GENERATION Each level of copies of a medium. The original is the first generation, the next copy is the second generation, and so on. In analog systems each generation adds additional degeneration of the signal.

GENLOCK The process of tying two different synchronous systems together so that a smooth transition may be made between the two. Also necessary when converting computer signals to video and vice versa.

GENRE A type of programming, such as western, comedy, and so on.

GIF (Graphics Interchange Format) A computer web page format.

GIGABYTE A unit of measurement of information or computer storage of exactly 1 million bytes or approximately 1.09 billion bytes.

GIGAHERTZ A measurement of frequency; 1 billion Hertz.

GIRAFFE Small mic boom mounted on a tripod on wheels usually designed for limited mic movement.

GOBO (1) In video, a set piece that allows a camera to shoot through it, such as a window. (2) In audio, a movable sound reflector board. (3) In film, a movable freestanding pattern cutout similar to a cookie. (4) On stage, the equivalent of a cookie.

GRAININESS The degree to which grains or crystals of silver halide are visible in a film stock after development and projection.

GRAPHICS A design consisting of shapes and colors to produce an object of some significance.

GRAPHICS GENERATOR A digital unit designed to create and combine pictures with type. Sometimes called a paint box.

GRAYSCALE A multiple-step reflectance intensity scale for the evaluation of a picture. Generally a 10-step scale is used for television, between video white and video black.

GRID A system of pipes hanging from the ceiling of a studio design, used to mount lighting instruments.

GRIP A stagehand; a crew person who moves sets, props, dollies. The head stagehand is the key grip.

GROSS DISTRIBUTOR RENTAL RECEIPTS The total amount of money paid to motion picture distributors by theater owners for the rental of a particular film.

GROUND STATION The terrestrial end of the satellite communication link.

GUILLOTINE SPLICER A film tape splicer that uses unperforated tape that it cuts off and perforates in a downward movement of the handle.

GUN A part of a picture and a camera tube that shoots a stream of electronics at the faceplate of the tube.

HANDHELD CARDS Illustrations that a performer holds up to a camera during a production.

HANGING MICROPHONE A microphone suspended from the ceiling or grid.

HARD COPY Generally refers to a printed copy on paper of a computer output, rather than a floppy disk.

HARD DISC DRIVE A rigid magnetic disc that is removable or is installed internally in a computer and that stores large quantities of data.

HARD LIGHT Direct light that creates harsh shadows.

HARDWARE Mechanical, electronic, or magnetic equipment rather than software, the material recorded, or computer programs.

HARMONIC DISTORTION Distortion of the primary signal by harmonics of the primary signal, usually caused by overmodulation.

HARMONICS Sounds that are exactly one or more octaves above or below a specific sound frequency.

HARMONY The combined effect of playing several consonant tones simultaneously.

HD DIGITAL RADIO (IBOC) IN BAND ON-CHANNEL A method of transmitting digital radio and analog radio broadcast signals on the same frequency.

HDDV, VDVD, HD-VMD A series of new advanced high-definition disc formats.

HDV (Cameras) An inexpensive high-definition digital recording format uses MPEG2 compression to allow recording on DV or MiniDv tapes designed originally for SD recording.

HEAD A pan head supports the camera and is designed to allow both horizontal and vertical movement of the camera.

HEADEND The cable companies' central control center where incoming signals from off the air, satellites, and other sources are distributed to output lines to the subscribers.

HEAD LEADERS The beginning leaders placed on film for editing and projection purposes.

HEADPHONES Small audio transducers mounted on a frame and worn over the head to feed sound to the wearer's ears.

HEADROOM (1) The space above the head of a person in the frame. (2) The amount of audio or video level that a piece of equipment can handle above the normal 100 percent modulation without causing distortion.

HELICAL SCAN Videotape with multiple recording heads that records information in long slanting tracks; each track records one field of information.

HERTZ (Hz) Measurement of frequency. Number of complete cycles completed in 1 second.

Hi8 A semiprofessional 8 mm videotape format developed by Sony for the prosumer (professional/consumer) market.

HIERARCHICAL A system of management that flows the channels of lines of authority on level at a time from top to bottom.

HIGH-ANGLE SHOT A shot in which the camera is placed high above the subject, tending to reduce its size and importance.

HIGH-DEFINITION TELEVISION (HDTV) One of several subcategories of Advanced TV (ATV). Attempt at creating a video system nearly equal to 35 mm film in resolution and aspect ratio.

HIGH HAT A minimal platform designed to mount a pan head allowing for shots close to the ground or to mount the camera on a car, boat, or airplane.

HIGH-KEY LIGHTING A brightly lit, low-contrast scene created by equal intensities of key and fill light and a low key-to-fill ratio. Also called Notan.

HITCHHIKER A spider on wheels.

HMI (Halide Metal Iodine) A high-intensity, high-color temperature light produced by an energy-efficient HMI lamp.

HOLOGRAPHIC A method of creating a 3-D image by using light scattering reconstruction techniques.

HOOK A dramatic device that grabs the audience's attention and secures involvement in the story.

HORIZONTAL BLANKING The period of time in a video signal when the electron beam is shut off while the scan returns to start the next line.

HORIZONTAL SYNC The part of the video signal that keeps all of the equipment synchronized.

HOT SPLICER A cement splicer with a built-in heating element.

HTML (Hypertext Markup Language) A computer language used for formatting documents to be transferred through the World Wide Web.

HUE A specific wavelength band of light, such as red, green, or blue.

HUM Low-frequency noise in audio or video equipment, usually induced by alternating power lines or stray magnetic fields.

HUT (Homes Using Television) A means that ratings companies use to compare audiences for programs by listing the number of TV sets in use at any one time.

HYPERCARDIOID An extremely directional microphone pickup pattern.

HYPHENATE A performer, crew, or staff member that performs more than one function; for example, producer-director.

IATSE (International Alliance of Theatrical Stage Employees) A union that represents stagehands, projectionists, and many other crafts of the television and film industry.

IBEW (International Brotherhood of Electrical Workers) A union that represents crew members in major U.S. markets.

IBOC (In-Band On-Channel) See DAB.

ICON A graphic symbol.

IEEE 1394 (FIREWIRE) A low-cost interface to connect digital equipment developed by Apple Computer.

IFB (Interruptable Foldback) A communication circuit that allows the director or associate director to talk to television performers while they are on the air.

ILLUSTRATIONS Stationary visual images such as charts and still photographs.

IMAGE DEPTH The range of images that appear to be in focus within any one frame.

IMAGE ORTHICON (IO) An early video-camera tube. The development of the IO opened the way for reasonably mobile studio and remote cameras.

IMAGE PERSPECTIVE The apparent depth of the image and the spatial relationships of objects.

IMAGE TONALITY The overall appearance of the image in terms of its apparent contrast and color.

IMAX A wide-screen film format shot on 65 mm film running horizontally past the lens. The image is 10 times larger than a standard 35 mm film frame and is projected on a curved screen.

IMPEDANCE Apparent AC resistance to current flowing in a circuit. Measured in ohms.

IN-CAMERA EDITING Shooting a sequence of shots on film or videotape so that they do not have to be edited in postproduction.

INCANDESCENT LIGHT Inert-gas-filled electric lamp emitting light and heat from a glowing filament. A typical lamp is the Tungsten-halogen lamp used in most production instruments, as well as the standard household lightbulb.

INCIDENT LIGHT Illumination from a light source. Measured in foot-candles or Lux by pointing the light meter at the light source.

INCIDENT METER READING A light meter reading of the intensity of light falling on the subject.

INCIDENTAL CHARACTERS Minor background figures in a story who often add texture, interest, and depth.

INDEPENDENT A producer, distributor, director, writer, or station that is not affiliated with a network or national company.

INFORMATIONAL A type of media production specifically designed to instruct or pass data or facts to the audience.

INGESTING Analyzing and converting media to a common format for further processing. Also called capturing.

IN-HOUSE A production unit that creates programming for the organization or institution of which it is a part.

IN-POINT The starting point of an edit.

INPUT The signal entering a system or an electrical unit.

INSERT A recording of specific actions in a scene to be inserted into a master shot, usually close-ups.

INSERT EDIT Assembling a videotape production by adding video and audio signals to tape stock that has already had control track recorded on it. Insert edits also can be made over existing edited tape.

INSTRUCTIONAL PROGRAMS Educational films or videotapes designed as teaching aids for the public, students, or employees.

INTERACTIVE MEDIA Communication systems that permit two-way interaction between electronic stations (video monitors, computers). May depend on stored programs such as games or shopping networks.

INTERCUTTING A relatively rapid alternation between two or more different shots.

INTERIOR (ENT) Setting or location inside of a building or structure.

INTERLACE SCANNING The method of combining two fields of scan lines into one frame.

INTERNEGATIVE A copy of the A and B film rolls onto a single negative film that can be used for printing multiple positive release prints.

INTERNET A public computer network, originally developed by the military, now linking home, education, science, and business computers.

INTERNET PROTOCOL TV (IPTV) A system designed to deliver television signals over the Internet using a broadband connection.

INTERNET SERVICE PROVIDER (IPS) A company that provides access to the Internet to individual subscribers using dial-up or DSL connections.

INTERPOLATION An animation technique in computer graphics that allows the animator to compose the first and last frames of an action sequence from which the computer then generates the images in-between.

INTERPOSITIVE A print using negative stock of the original negative that then creates a positive image.

INTERVALOMETER A device that allows a video or film camera to take a single frame at preset times, creating a time-lapse series.

INTRO The abbreviation for introduction.

INVERSE SQUARE LAW A mathematical analysis of changes in alternating energy. The amount of energy is inversely proportionate to the change in distance. The formula is easily applied to calculating lighting and audio levels.

IPOD A portable media player designed and sold by Apple, Inc. Available since 2001. May also be used to store and transport data.

IPS (Inches per Second) The method of measuring the speed of tape, film, or other longitudinal media.

IRIS See Aperture.

ISDN (Integrated Services Digital Network) A type of dial-up telephone system offering speeds of up to 128 kilobytes per second.

ISO See Exposure Index.

ISOLATED CAMERA A camera that feeds its own videotape recorder and is available for live shots in a multiple camera production, such as an athletic event.

ITFS (Instructional Television Fixed Service) A microwave video-delivery system licensed to educational institutions.

JACK A receptacle for plugs usually mounted on equipment or walls of a studio or control room.

JARGON The terminology and slang used in a particular field.

JINGLES Music and lyrics used in commercials that are quickly associated with the product advertised.

JOG CONTROL A circular dial used to either move slowly or rapidly, forward or backward, from one frame or section of an edit to another.

JOYSTICK A level on a video switcher or computer that allows the operator to select specific placement of a wipe, key, cursor, or other special effect or operation.

JPEG (Joint Photographic Experts Group) A compression standard for single frames.

JUMP CUT Any one of several types of poor edits that either break continuity or may be disturbing to the audience.

KELVIN TEMPERATURE A measurement of the relative color of light. Indicated as degrees Kelvin (K). The higher the temperature, the bluer the light; the lower the temperature, the redder the light.

KERNING A measurement of space between letters.

KEY The process of combining two or more images without the background image bleeding through the foreground image. See also Chroma Key.

KEYING or TO KEY Inserting or embedding one video signal into another.

KEYKODE A Kodak film method of labeling individual frames on the film stock. Can be digitized for conforming.

KEY LIGHT The apparent main source of light. Usually from one bright light above and to one side of the camera.

KEYSTONE DISTORTION The effect of an object shot at an angle rather than square on.

KEY-TO-BACK RATIO A comparison between the amount of light on the subject from the backlight and the amount of light on the subject from the key light.

KEY-TO-FILL RATIO A comparison between the amount of light on the subject from the key light and the amount of light from a combination of key and fill lights.

KICKER A light focused from the side on the subject or on a particular section of the set.

KILL To turn off a light, camera, or audio feed.

KILOHERTZ (kHz) A measurement of alternating energy; 1,000 hertz.

KINESCOPE A film recording of a live or taped video production, now replaced by tape-to-film transfers.

KU-BAND The range of frequencies between 11 and 14 gigahertz increasingly used by communication satellite companies.

LAB REPORT See Camera Report.

LAG Characteristic of a camera tube in which a picture trails its own images as the camera moves. Lag increases with the age of the tube.

LASER (Light Amplification by Stimulation of Emission of Radiation) A single-frequency beam of high-powered light.

LASER DISC A type of video or audio recording made by a laser disc scanning minute holes in a metal disc encased in a plastic covering.

LAVALIERE (Lav) A microphone worn around the neck. Also sometimes called a lapel mic when clipped to a tie or the front of clothing.

LAYBACK The process of rerecording a track in sync after it has been modified. Usually refers to audio tracks after sweetening.

LAYOVER Transferring the edited soundtrack to a multitrack recorder for final sweetening.

LEADING A measurement of space between lines.

LEAD STORY The most important story of a newscast, usually the first story in the newscast.

LEGAL RELEASE A statement releasing a producer from future legal action, signed by nonprofessional people appearing in or providing materials for a production.

LEITMOTIFS Musical themes associated with specific characters in a production.

LENS Glass or plastic designed to focus and concentrate light on a surface to form an image.

LENS CAP An opaque covering used to slip over the end of a lens to protect the surface from damage and to protect the image device from excessive light.

LENS COATING A substance placed on the surface of a lens to reduce the scattered reflection of light entering the lens, which increases the light transmission of that lens. Also used to protect the lens from moisture, scratches, and dirt.

LENS HOOD A device for shading the camera lens from direct sunlight or from artificial light emitted opposite the camera.

LENS PERSPECTIVE The spatial relationships of objects revealed in an image after the image has passed through a lens.

LETTERBOX A term describing the presentation of 16:9 format programming on a 4:3 medium that leaves black bands at the top and bottom of the frame.

LEVEL (1) Relative amplitude or intensity. Used to indicate light, audio, video, and other electronic signals. (2) Aligned with the horizon.

LEVELING Adjusting a camera or light fixture to be parallel to the horizon.

LEXISNEXIS (sometimes called either Lexis or Nexis) Searchable legal databases designed for lawyers and law students to access as many law cases, corporate, civic, and accounting files as have been digitized.

LIBRARY EFFECTS Sound effects cataloged and accessible in a prerecorded form on computer discs, CDs, audiotape, or vinyl discs.

LIBRARY SERVER A storage computer that keeps track of all broadcast elements in a studio or station.

LIGHT Electromagnetic energy that stimulates receptors in the eyes.

LIGHT-EMITTING DIODE (LED) A solid-state component that emits light when a small voltage is applied. Useful as a level or operating condition indicator.

LIGHTING DIRECTOR In video production, the person who designs and supervises the lighting setup. In film, the title is director of photography (DP).

LIGHTING INSTRUMENT The housing within which a light source or lamp is enclosed.

LIGHTING PLOT A scale outline of a lighting setup on grid paper that represents the studio floor, providing an overhead view of the relationship of lighting instruments to sets and actors.

LIGHTING RATIO The numerical ratio of the amount of light falling on a subject from the key light against the amount of light falling on a subject from the fill light.

LIGHT METER (Exposure Meter) An instrument used to measure the intensity of light. May be calculated in foot-candles, Lux, or f-stops.

LINE LEVEL A signal amplified enough to feed down a line without fear of degradation. A microphone level is lower than line level; a speaker level is higher.

LIP-SYNC The process of matching the movement of performers' mouths with the words they are speaking.

LIQUID CRYSTAL DISPLAY (LCD) A flat-screen monitor based on modulated liquid crystals.

LIST MANAGEMENT The process of making alterations, trims, or shifting of segments in editing decisions in a computerized editing system.

LIVE ON TAPE A multiple-camera video production recording as if it were live, but allowing for some postproduction.

LOAD To transfer date or information to an analog or digital storage device.

LOCATION The area or site of a production. Usually refers to sites away from studios.

LOCATION SCOUT A person who locates sites for media production shooting.

LOCKING WINDOW A monitor window that allows audio and video to be edited simultaneously.

LOG A listing of shots as they are recorded on tape.

LONGITUDINAL Lengthwise; in media, refers to the method of recording audio and control track signals.

LOOKSPACE The space in front of a figure in a frame to give the figure "room" to move or exist within that frame.

LOOPING The process of rerecording audio during postproduction. Also now called automatic dialogue replacement (ADR).

LOSSLESS A codec that either does not compress the files or does so that circuits replace the data on decompression.

LOSSY A codec that compresses data but maintains reasonable quality by deleting only information not required or missed.

LOUDNESS The perceived intensity of audio. Depends on the intensity and saturation of the sound, as well as the sensitivity of the listener to a range of frequencies.

LOUDNESS DISTORTION Disruption in a sound signal caused by overmodulation.

LOW-ANGLE SHOT A shot in which the camera is placed closer to the floor than a normal camera height. This angle tends to exaggerate the size and importance of the subject.

LOW IMPEDANCE A type of electrical signal created by most professional microphones and some playback equipment.

LOW-KEY LIGHTING A lighting aesthetic characterized by pools of light and harsh shadow areas created by minimal fill and a high key-to-fill ratio. Also called chiaroscuro.

LPTV (Low-Power TV) Television stations licensed by the FCC to broadcast using limited power to cover areas or markets not served by major market TV stations.

LUMINAIRE See Lighting Instrument.

LUMINANCE The brightness component of a video signal.

LUX European measurement of light intensity. There are approximately 10 Lux to 1 foot-candle.

MAG TRACK Short for magnetic sound film track.

MAJOR DISTRIBUTORS (Studios) The largest film distributors who receive the bulk of the distribution receipts from their films: Disney, Warner Bros., Twentieth Century-Fox, Universal, and Paramount.

MAJOR MARKET One of the top 100 metro areas in number of TV households.

MASTER The final product of an audio or video editing session.

MASTER CONTROL The room to which all video and audio signals of various production studios are fed for distribution, broadcasting, or recording.

MASTER SHOT An extended wide shot establishing the scene and often shot during the entire length of the sequence. Intended to be broken down in the editing process.

MASTER TAPE The final result of an editing session.

MATCH CUT An edit between two shots that maintain continuity to make the edit almost invisible.

MATTE (Traveling or Stationary) An opaque covering over the lens of a camera that allows for reexposure of the covered area later in film or in video to create an irregular shape for a special effect.

MATTE SHOTS Combinations of different images in the same frame.

MECHANICAL INTERLOCK A physical connection between different machines or portions of machines that causes them to run at the same speed when driven by the same motor.

MEDIUM CLOSE-UP (MCU) Relative average framing for a shot. Often framed from the waist up.

MEDIUM SHOT (MS) Wider than an MCU, often framed head to toe.

MEGAPIXELS One million pixels, a convenient unit of measurement of pixel count in light sensors.

MELODY A series of musical notes or tones that create a structured unit or order.

MEMORY The measurement of the amount of digital storage of data.

METAMORPHOSIS An animation technique in which one figure is gradually transformed into another figure of an entirely different shape.

METRONOME A device used by musicians to provide a regular beat or rhythm.

M FORMAT (M-II, Recam) Panasonic's professional ½-inch format. Originally sold by RCA as Recam, then upgraded to M-1. No longer manufactured.

MIC LEVELS The lower electrical signal strength of a microphone output as compared to line levels of amplified signals.

MICROPHONE A transducer that converts sound waves into comparable fluctuations of electrical current.

MICROPHONE BOOM A long pole to which a microphone is attached so that it can be held just outside of the camera frame.

MICROWAVE (1) A high-frequency carrier for both audio and video signals. Operates only a line-of-sight path. (2) An oven used for heating the crew's lunch.

MIDI (Musical Instrument Digital Interface) A system designed to allow musicians to connect musical instruments in a digital format.

MIL A unit of measurement (.001) used to designate tape thickness.

MIMETIC An adjective indicating an object or characteristic of imitation or mimicry.

MINIATURE A three-dimensional replica of a set or prop to be used as a substitute for a full-sized construction. Also called a model.

MINIDISC (MD) A small optical disc developed by Sony as an alternative to audio CDs. Now used as a general recording medium.

MINIDV A small audio or video digital recording tape most commonly used as the medium for small camcorders.

MINIPLUG (⅛-inch) An audio connector designed for small equipment. A scaled-down version of the ¼-inch phone plug.

MIRROR SHOTS (1) The use of two mirrors to make a large periscope that can be used for overhead video camera shots. (2) A partial mirror can be used to combine two film scenes in one take.

MIRROR SHUTTER A reflective coating on the front of a shutter that intermittently deflects all the light to a reflex viewfinder as the film is advanced in the camera.

MIXER A piece of electronic equipment designed to combine several signals. Usually refers to an audio board or console.

MIX LOG SHEET (Audio Cue Sheet) A list of all volume changes, transitions, and equalization changes for a sound mix.

MMDS (Multichannel Multipoint Distribution Service) A video delivery system using line-of-sight microwave with four or more channels operated by a single company. Often called "wireless cable"; similar to ITFS.

MODEL See Miniature.

MODELING Highlighting the appearance of a textured surface through the use of shadows.

MODERNISM A work of art using factors other than realism to express its concept.

MODULATOR An electronic component designed to impress one signal on another, usually of a higher frequency.

MODULE A small device designed to provide a single specialized function.

MODULOMETER (PPM) A peak reading voltmeter designed to monitor levels of audio signals.

MOIRÉ EFFECT A distracting vibration of visual images caused by the interaction of narrow stripes in the design of the material being recorded.

MONAURAL (Mono) A single track of audio.

MONITOR (1) To listen to or watch audio or videotapes or off-air programs. (2) A device used to view video signals. Much like a TV receiver, but it is usually much higher quality and generally does not have an RF section for off-the-air monitoring.

MONOCHROME Black-and-white film or video.

MORGUE Library, reference files, or storage for used scripts, tapes, maps, and other reference material.

MORPHING or MORPHOGENESIS An editing technique that uses matching shots to slowly transform from one image to another.

MOS (1) Metal oxide semiconductor. A type of camera chip that replaces the camera tube. (2) A film term indicating that a shot was recorded silent, or as the early German film directors said, "Mit out sound."

MOTIF Imagery that is repeatedly used in an artistic work to add depth and symbolism.

MOTION CAPTURE (MoCap) An animation technique used to duplicate movement by fastening electronic or magnetic sensors throughout a body and following them to a computer for recording and manipulation.

MOTION CONTROL A computer-controlled system for camera or object movements to match other exposures of background scenes for keying in video or double exposure in film.

MOVIEOLA The traditional mechanical film editor.

MP3 A highly compressed audio system based on the third level of MPEG. Used to download music from the World Wide Web.

MPEG (Motion Picture Experts Group) A series of video compression standards.

MSO (Multiple System Operator) A cable company that owns and operates more than one cable system.

MULTICAMERA PRODUCTION (Multiple-Camera Production) The use of several film or video cameras to record the same action simultaneously from different viewpoints.

MULTIMEDIA A program combining text, graphics, sound, animation, video, or a combination of any three media.

MULTIPLANE ANIMATION Animation shot on an animation stand that holds several levels of cels separated so they may be lit and moved individually. Invented by Ub Iwerks for Walt Disney.

MULTITRACK An audiotape recording with from 2 to 64 separate tracks recorded on the same audiotape.

MUNSELL COLOR WHEEL A three-dimensional model of colors that shows different color samples by hue, brightness, and saturation.

MUSIC LIBRARIES Collections of musical recordings that require a minimum royalty payment for use on media productions.

NABET (National Association of Broadcast Employees and Technicians) A union that represents crew members and in major markets everyone at an operation.

NANOSECOND A measurement of time, one-billionth of a second; .000000001 second.

NARRATE To tell a story or provide a commentary on events.

NARRATION A verbal commentary on the events taking place within a fiction or non-fiction media production.

NARRATIVE A story that is told or narrated by someone.

NARROWCASTING Aiming programs at a specific nonmass market.

NAT SOUND (Natural Sound) Ambient sound that exists on location and is recorded as a story happens. Often used as background for a voice-over. Sometimes called wild sound.

NATIONAL ASSOCIATION OF BROADCASTERS (NAB) Professional organization of radio and television broadcasters.

NATURALISTIC LIGHTING Lighting that appears to come from known or presumed actual sources in the setting or location.

NATURAL WIPE A transition that leaves the viewer feeling there was no transition because the edit appeared to flow realistically.

NEEDLE-DROP FEES The payment of music or sound effects fees according to the number of times the cut is used rather than a yearly fee.

NEGATIVE A type of film that produces a reversed brightness image when developed.

NEGATIVE/POSITIVE PROCESS A means of producing projectable film images in two steps by first exposing and developing negative film and then printing that negative film on negative stock to produce a positive print.

NET DISTRIBUTOR RENTALS The amount of money a distributor receives from theater rentals of films minus the distributor's own costs.

NET NEUTRALITY A policy to guarantee free access to the Internet and the web without constraint by government or corporations.

NETWORK A company distributing programs to stations interconnected but not owned by the network. The FCC defines a network if it distributes at least 15 hours of programming a week to at least 25 affiliates in at least 10 states. Today there are six television networks: ABC, CBS, Fox, NBC, Universal/Paramount, and Warner Bros.

NEUTRAL DENSITY A type of filter that decreases light passage without changing the color value of the light.

NEWSFILM Before small camcorders became practical in the late 1970s, all news stories were shot on 16 mm film, edited, and then projected on a film chain or telecine, a projector-camera video combination used to convert film to video.

NEXIS See LexisNexis.

NICHE A small specialized area of programming or genre.

NIELSEN RATINGS Television audience information researched by the A.C. Nielsen Company, consisting of shares, ratings, and demographics.

NOISE Any undesirable additions to a signal.

NOISE REDUCTION The elimination or diminishing of audio noise by means of signal-processing devices.

NONFICTION The depiction, description, or presentation of actual, unstaged events.

NONLINEAR EDITING (NLE) Editing out of sequence.

NONREFLEX A camera that has a separate viewfinder as opposed to one that allows the operator to look directly through the objective lens.

NONTHEATRICAL FILMS Films that are not produced for or shown in commercial theaters. Today, a direct-to-video film can gross more than a major motion picture.

NORMAL LENS A lens that presents an image perspective that approximates the vision of a monocular (single-eye) human. A midrange focal length.

NOTAN A lighting style similar to Japanese watercolors: high key, few shadows, evenly lit.

NTSC (National Television Standards Committee) (1) The organization charged with setting the television standard in the United States in the early days of television. (2) The television standard now in use in North America, much of South America, and Japan.

NTSC COLOR STANDARD The television standard first used in the United States for color TV transmission. This standard uses 525 interlaced lines scanned at the rate of 60 fields and 30 frames per second.

NVOD (Near Video-on-Demand) A pay television system providing programming when requested.

OBJECTIVE LENS The lens on a camera that is used to record the images.

OCCULT BALANCE Choosing colors by intentionally pairing unlike elements.

OFF-CAMERA MICROPHONE A microphone that is invisible to the audience.

OFFLINE Using the lowest-quality and lowest-cost editing system suitable for a particular project.

OFF-SCREEN SOUND A sound coming from a location not viewed by the audience.

OMNIDIRECTIONAL Microphone pickup pattern that covers 360 degrees around the mic.

OMNISCIENT POINT OF VIEW In literature, a narrative written in the third as opposed to the first person. In media productions, a story told from a relatively objective perspective or camera viewpoint.

OMNIVISION (also called OMNIMAX) A large film format shot on 65 mm film but projected through a fish-eye lens on a dome above and around the audience.

ON-CAMERA MICROPHONES Microphones visible to the audience.

ONE-LIGHT PRINT A quickly made film copy of the original film processed without adjustments to give the director and director of photography an accurate picture of what was shot and recorded on the film, shot-by-shot.

ONLINE Using the highest-quality and highest-cost editing system suitable for a particular project.

ON-SCREEN SOUND Sound emanating from a source clearly seen by the audience.

OPAQUE BLACK LEADER Film leader that is coated with an opaque layer so that light cannot pass through it. Used in conforming process to separate shots on the "A" and "B" rolls and as leader before and after the beginning and ending of the film.

OPEN MIC The instruction from the director to the audio operator to bring the pot or sounds faded up on a particular mic.

OPERATING SYSTEM Software responsible for controlling the hardware in use.

OPERATOR The person whose main responsibility is to operate equipment, as contrasted with technicians whose main responsibility it is to install, repair, and maintain equipment, and engineers whose main responsibility it is to research, design, and construct equipment.

OPTICAL DISK A laser recording medium for digital, video, or audio information. A vast amount of data may be stored in a relatively small space and can be designed to record once or record many times. CDs and videodiscs are examples of optical discs.

OPTICAL PRINTER A device consisting of a projector aimed at a camera that can be used to create special effects.

OPTICAL SOUND Sound recorded optically on the edge of film where variations in intensity are recorded as variations in density or the width of the film exposure.

OPTICS/OPTICAL Having to do with lenses or other light-carrying components of a video or film system.

OSCILLOSCOPE Test equipment used to visualize a time factor system, such as a video signal. Shows a technician what the picture looks like electronically. Also may be used to analyze audio or other signals. See also Waveform Monitor.

OUTLINE A topic-by-topic listing of sequences/scenes of a production.

OUT-POINT The end point of an edit.

OUTPUT Signal leaving a system or electrical unit.

OUTTAKES Recorded shots that are discarded entirely and do not appear in the final edited version of a media production.

OVEREXPOSURE Excessive exposure of film or video camera to light so that the quality of the image suffers and appears as washed out or overly bright.

OVERHEAD SHOT A shot from a camera that is placed directly overhead. This shot can be duplicated with the use of two mirrors. See Mirror Shots.

OVERMODULATION Adjusting the sound intensity so high that it exceeds the limits of the equipment and causes distortion.

OVERSCHEDULE A production that has exceeded the time limitations specified in the production schedule.

OVER-THE-SHOULDER SHOT (OS) A shot in which the camera is placed behind and to one side of a subject so that the shoulder of that subject is visible in the foreground and the face or body of another subject is in the background.

OWNED AND OPERATED A station actually owned by one of the networks. See Affiliate.

OXIDE One type of metal coating used on magnetic tape and discs.

P2 (PCMIA—Personal Computer Manufacturer Interface Adapter) A specialized memory card design by Panasonic for their broadcast digital cameras, can record either 16 or 32 GB.

PACE A subjective impression of the speed of sounds or visuals.

PACKAGE A marketable combination of production elements such as well-known stars, director, writers, and creative staff.

PACKET A unit of information transmitted as a whole unit between devices.

PAL (Phase Alternating Line) A color television standard used in England and many other countries around the world. It is based on a 625 interlaced line, 25 frames per second system. It is not compatible with the United States NTSC standard.

PALETTE A variety of colors.

PAN Horizontal movement of the camera, short for panorama.

PANHEAD A mechanism designed to firmly hold a camera on top of a tripod, pedestal, or boom while allowing for smooth, easily controlled movement of the camera horizontally (pan) and vertically (tilt). May be mechanical, fluid, geared, or counterbalanced.

PANSCAN A system of converting widescreen motion pictures to the 3 × 4 television scan area. A print is made by panning across the film, centering on the most important areas of characters.

PAR (Parabolic Aluminized Reflector) A fixed focus luminaire that resembles a household flood lamp. PARs are mounted from 4 to 12 in a rack to give even controllable floodlight.

PARABOLIC MIC A focused, concave, reflective, bowl-shaped surface with a mic mounted at the point of focus. Used to pick up specific sounds at a distance. Commonly used during sporting events.

PARALLAX The discrepancy between the framed image in an objective lens and the image in a separate viewfinder in a nonreflex camera.

PARALLEL SOUND Sounds that complement or have a supporting effect on the visual.

PATCH BAY A panel with wires connected to equipment in a control room to allow for flexibility in distributing signals to and from amplifiers and mixers. Also called patch board or patch panel.

PATCH CORD A short cable with plugs on each end designed to interconnect equipment wired to a patch bay.

PAUSE A mode or function on a recorder or player that holds the medium in position without stopping, but preventing an advance.

PAY CABLE Cable programming channels that must be paid above the amount for the basic service.

PBS (Public Broadcast System) A partial federally funded television network. Stations are not necessarily interconnected directly, but stations bicycle tapes and satellite program feeds between them to air on their own schedule.

PCM (Pulse Code Modulation) A digital conversion system.

PDA (PERSONAL DIGITAL ASSISTANT) A handheld computer design as a record keeping and communication tool.

PEAK PROGRAM METER (PPM) A standard device for measuring sound intensity of loudness. It measures the peaks rather than the average as is measured in a VU meter.

PEDESTAL (1) Electronic calibration between blanking and black level. (2) Hydraulic, compressed air, or counterbalanced studio camera mount. Designed to permit the camera to be raised straight up or down effortlessly and smoothly.

PENCIL TEST A film shot of simple sketches of an animation production to check timing and other aspects of the production.

PERAMBULATOR A large, wheeled, platform-mounted boom that a mic boom operator rides. Capable of swinging a mic over a large area.

PERFORATIONS (Perfs) The sprocket holes at the sides of film or fullcoat. Single-perf means sprockets on one side only; double-perf means sprockets on both sides.

PERQUISITES (Perks) Extra benefits offered beyond regular pay.

PERSISTENCE OF VISION A physical and psychological phenomenon of sight that allows a series of still images to create the illusion of motion. One of the phenomena based on which the images in animation, motion pictures, and television appear to move.

PERSPECTIVE The illusion of spatial distance in a two-dimensional medium.

PHANTOM POWER 48 volts required by condenser mic preamplifiers located in the mic. If the mic does not carry its own battery power, it may be supplied through the mic line by the mixer or recorder.

PHASE The relationship of two signals differing in time, but on a common path.

PHASING PROBLEMS The cancellation of certain frequencies caused by placing microphones too close together when they are picking up the same source.

PHI PHENOMENON The illusion of apparent motion from rapidly flashing stationary lights and objects used in the animation process.

PHOSPHORS Light-emitting optoelectronic semiconductors inside a video picture tube.

PHOTOELECTRIC CELL The transducer in a light meter of a film projector that converts light energy into an electronic signal.

PHOTOFLOOD Lamp with self-contained reflectors that do not require a lighting instrument.

PHOTOGRAPHER Originally, a person taking still photographs. In some markets, the term was applied to news cinematographers, and even today it sometimes is applied to videographers.

PHOTOGRAPHIC FILM A light-sensitive material, consisting of silver halide particles attached to a flexible support base that yields visual images after proper exposure to light and chemical development.

PICA A measurement of the horizontal size of type; 1 pica = $\frac{1}{6}$ inch.

PICKUP PATTERN The area or space surrounding a microphone within which the sensitivity to sound is the greatest.

PICKUP TUBE A device that converts light entering a video camera through the lens into electrical signals. Now replaced by solid-state chips.

PICT A visual red, green, blue (RGB) format designed by Apple.

PILOTONE A particular type of sync signal used in synchronous film recording.

PISTOL GRIP A handheld camera mount.

PITCH The perception of or human response to different sound frequencies.

PIXEL A single element of a computer or television picture. Picture resolution may be measured by the number of pixels in a set space.

PIXILLATION A system of single-frame animation that records only a portion of a live action, creating a floating or jerky movement of subjects.

PLASMA DISPLAY PANEL (PDP) A flat-screen monitor based on a gas-filled panel.

PLASTIC ANIMATION Animating three-dimensional objects.

PLATES The platters on a flatbed film-editing machine that feed and take up film and tracks.

PLAYBACK The mode or machine operational setting for viewing or listening to a prerecorded signal.

PLAYBACK HEAD A magnetic device capable of transforming magnetic changes on a prerecorded tape into electronic signals.

PLAYER CHARACTER (PC) The actor in a computer artificial intelligent production.

PLOSIVE SOUNDS Sounds made by the human voice that tend to "pop" a microphone. Sounds beginning with the letters "p" and "b," among others.

PLOT A scale drawing of the location of a shoot.

PLUG A mechanical connector fastened to the end of a cable. Designed to mate with a matching jack mounted on equipment or on the wall.

PLUMBICON A type of video pickup tube; one of the last developed before being replaced by chips.

PODCAST A miniature video or audio production designed to be distributed over the Internet using a syndication method for playback on media players and computers.

POINT OF ATTACK The beginning of a drama that usually generates interest and excitement.

POINT OF VIEW (POV) A camera angle giving the impression of the view of someone in the scene.

POINT SIZE A measurement of the height of type fonts.

POLARIZER FILTER A glass or plastic filter that reduces glare when properly adjusted over a camera lens and/or lights on an animation or copy stand.

POOL FEED A common video or audio feed to supply more than one operation. Often set up for such restricted coverage as presidential appearances or in times of extreme emergencies or tragedies.

PORTABLE LIGHTING KIT A self-contained lighting unit for field production consisting of several lighting fixtures, stands, filters, accessories, and cables.

PORTFOLIO A collection of a creative person's work; may be in written, visual, graphic, or aural form organized in a compact professional appearing manner to impress a prospective employer.

POSITIVE A type of visual image that reproduces the brightness of the original scene when it is processed or played back.

POSTERIZED Changing a graphic by using a few colors to give the appearance of a printed poster.

POSTMODERNISM Art that depends on the participation of the audience, if not physically, at least in a close mental form.

POSTPRODUCTION The final stage of the production process, during which recorded images and sounds are edited and the production is completed for distribution.

POT Short for potentiometer, a variable resistor used to change the voltage of an audio or video signal.

POWER AMPLIFIER An electronic circuit designed to amplify signals to a high enough level to power speakers or transmit signals over long lines.

POWER PACK Batteries used to power a piece of portable equipment.

PPM See Modulometer.

PPV (Pay per View) A cable service paid for on an individual program basis rather than on a monthly basis.

PREAMPLIFIER (Preamp) An electronic circuit designed to amplify weak signal to a usable level without introducing noise or distortion.

PREBLACK The process of recording either a black video signal or color bars with a control track on videotape stock in preparation for insert editing that requires a control track prerecorded on the tape.

PREMISE A concise statement that sums up the story or subject matter.

PREPRODUCTION The preparatory stage of production planning that takes place before actually recording sounds and visual images.

PREROLL The amount of time needed in advance of making an edit or starting a film, audio, or videotape for playback or editing.

PRESSURE PLATE The surface inside a film camera that keeps the film flat in the gate at the aperture.

PRETESTING OF AUDIENCES A system of exposing a group that represents the potential audience to determine the positive or negative reaction to the program.

PREVIEW To view an image source without sending it to its assigned destination.

PREVISUALIZATION (PRE-VIZ) The computerized method of creating an animated storyboard of a production to study and test ideas before sets are constructed or expensive crews and casts are assembled. A method of rehearsing without crew or cast.

PRIMARY COLORS The basic colors used in lighting and filters: red, green, and blue.

PRIME LENS A fixed focal-length lens.

PRIME TIME In general practice, the television broadcast evening hours programmed by the networks between 8 p.m. and 11 p.m. for the east and west coasts, and 6 p.m. and 10 p.m. for the Midwest and mountain states.

PRINCIPAL CHARACTERS Friends and foils of the central character(s).

PRINTING The process of making a copy of a film.

PRINT-THROUGH A signal that has bled through from one layer of recording tape to the next.

PRINT-THROUGH EDGE NUMBERS Numbers from the original film that are printed through to the workprint by using an edge light during the printing process.

PRISM A glass or plastic block shaped to transmit or reflect light into different paths.

PRODUCER The person in charge of a specific program.

PRODUCTION The stage of the production process during which production materials and equipment are set up and sounds and images are actually recorded.

PRODUCTION DESIGN The coordination of scenic design and other artistic aspects of production, such as lighting.

PRODUCTION DESIGNER The crew person who heads the production design team.

PRODUCTION MANAGER In feature-film production, the person who breaks down the script into its component parts for budgeting and scheduling and who supervises the allocation and use of studio and location facilities.

PROGRAM (1) To set a function of a pot, fader, or other control. (2) A complete production package ready to be broadcast or distributed.

PROGRESSIVE SCAN A monitor or camera scan system that creates a complete frame with one continuous sweep top-to-bottom and left-to-right. Used in PAL, SECAM, and computer systems. Proposed as one of HDTV's systems.

PROJECT WINDOW In an NLE monitor, shows individual clips in a predetermined order.

PROMPTER A device or person that provides the talent with the copy as they work on camera. Copy can be handheld beside the camera or a signal can be fed to a monitor mounted with a mirror to project the copy in front of the camera lens so the anchor, for example, can look directly into the camera. This signal may be coming from a black-and-white camera shooting pages of the script or from a signal fed directly from a computer.

PROPERTIES (Props) Functional set furnishings that play a part in a video or film program.

PROPOSAL A concise summary of a project intended as a sales tool to accurately describe a production and to sell a sponsor on funding.

PROSTHETIC MAKEUP Makeup and devices designed to transform the appearance of a performer's face or body through temporary "plastic surgery."

PROSUMER A category of producer and equipment that falls below that of a professional but at a higher level than a consumer.

PROTAGONIST The hero or main positive character of a drama.

PROXIMITY EFFECT A change in the audio pickup by moving the source too close to the microphone; can be used to give the appearance of lowering the human voice.

PSA (Public Service Announcement) A noncommercial radio or TV spot.

PUBLIC ADDRESS (PA) A sound-reinforcing system designed to feed sound to an audience assembled in a large room or other space.

PULLDOWN CLAW The square pin that grabs each sprocket hole of a film in the gate to advance a single frame in the aperture for exposure.

PULLING FOCUS Adjusting camera focus while shooting.

PURE TONE A single sound frequency.

QUADRAPLEX (Quad) The first practical professional videotape format. Used two-inch tape pulled across four heads to achieve a high-quality signal. No longer manufactured.

QUARTER-INCH PLUG (Phone) Audio connector used for many years for high-impedance signals. Still used in some consumer equipment and patch panels.

QUARTZ LIGHT A Tungsten light source consisting of a Tungsten filament, a quartz housing, and halogen gas.

RADIAL BALANCE A method of choosing colors by examining their relationship on a color wheel.

RADIO MICROPHONE (wireless mic) A microphone connected to a small FM transmitter worn by the performer broadcasting a short distance to a receiver connected to the audio mixer. This allows the performer to operate with trailing wires.

RAID (Redundant Array of Independent Disks) A server made up of a series of interconnected memory storage disks.

RAM (Random Access Memory) Semiconductor-based memory within a computer or other digital device. Usually deleted when power is removed.

RASTER The complete sequence of lines that make up the field of lines creating a video picture.

RATING Estimated percentage of TV households tuned to the same program at any one time.

RAW STOCK Unexposed film, video, or audiotape that has not been recorded.

RCA The American corporation that promoted the NTSC video system, the developer of many early television inventions, and the original owner of NBC radio and television.

RCA PLUG (phono) Audio and video connector designed originally for use only with the RCA 45-rpm record player. Now used as a consumer audio and video connector. Some professional equipment uses this plug for line-level audio. Not to be confused with the phone plug (¼ inch).

R-DAT Revolving head digital recording system, generally listed as DAT.

REACTION SHOT Close-up of a character's reaction to events.

READABILITY The ease of comprehending visual material accurately.

REALAUDIO (.ra) Compression codec for Real/Video uses variable bit rate depending on application; mobile, streaming, Internet.

REALISTIC LIGHTING Lighting that conforms to the audience's conventional expectations of how a scene should appear in "real" life.

REALISTIC SETS Sets designed to represent a specific or general type of place with which an audience is presumed to have some familiarity, usually filled with "naturalistic" details.

REAR PROJECTION A projection of a slide or film on a screen behind the performers on a set.

RECEIVER A television or radio set capable of decoding a broadcast signal.

RECORD MODE A machine operational setting for recording pictures and/or sound.

RECORDING HEAD A magnetic device that transforms electronic signals into changes in a magnetic field so that sounds and pictures can be recorded on tape.

RECORDING INDUSTRY ASSOCIATION OF AMERICA (RIAA) A trade group that represents the recording industry in the United States.

REDUCTION A transfer of film to a smaller format on an optical printer.

REEL-TO-REEL RECORDER A device that can record and/or play back sounds on an open reel of tape.

REFERENCE WHITE A white card or large white object in the flame that can be used for white balancing or the proper color adjustment of a video camera.

REFLECTED LIGHT Illumination entering a lens reflected from an object. Measured with a reflected light meter pointing at the object from the camera.

REFLECTED READING A light-meter reading of the intensity of light reflected from the subject and/or background.

REFLECTION A bouncing back of light from an object.

REFLECTOR A flat or curved surface that light can be bounced off to create indirect light on a set or location.

REFLEX A type of camera that allows the operator to look directly through the objective lens.

REFRACTION Light changing direction as it passes through transparent surfaces.

REGISTRATION The alignment of either electronic or physical components of a system; especially important in tube cameras.

REGISTRATION PIN A device on some film cameras that holds the film steady while a frame is being exposed to light at the aperture.

RELEASE (1) Legal document allowing the videographer to use the image and/or voice of a subject. (2) Public relations copy.

RELEASE PRINT A final copy of a film with soundtrack that is distributed and exhibited.

REMOTE NONLINEAR EDITOR (RNLE) An editing station set up in a remote vehicle or suitcase to be used in the field.

REMOTE PRODUCTION A video production performed outside of the studio.

REMOTE VAN A large video production semitrailer containing a virtual studio control room and all of the equipment normally in a video studio for high-level coverage of sports and entertainment events.

RENDER To convert a data file to an actual audio or video recording.

REPORTER A newsperson who is responsible for researching, gathering, and writing news stories. May or may not appear on camera or in the studio.

RESEARCH The process of investigating and uncovering sources of information about prospective video or film audiences and/or the facts necessary to write a script.

RESIDUALS Payment made to performers for repeat uses of programs and commercials in which they appear.

RESOLUTION (1) Ability of a system to reproduce fine detail. In video there are limits imposed by the NTSC video system. (2) Overcoming the central conflict in a drama and fulfilling the goals and motivations that have stimulated the dramatic action.

RESPONSE CURVE A graph of the sensitivity of a piece of audio equipment to different frequencies.

RÉSUMÉ A comprehensive listing of an individual and their work and academic history.

REUTERS An international news network based in Europe but with newsgathers working around the world.

REVERBERATION The delay between direct and indirect sounds.

REVERBERATION UNIT A signal-processing device that can create sound reverberation or echo.

REVERSAL PROCESS A means of producing projectable film images in a single step by using a type of film stock and development process that produces positive images from a single exposure and development.

REVERSE-ANGLE SHOT A shot in which the camera faces in exactly the opposite direction from that in which it faced in the previous shot.

REWINDS Rotating spindles on a film-editing bench used to advance and rewind the film.

RF (Radio Frequency) (1) Those frequencies above the aural frequencies. (2) A type of plug attached to a cable designed to carry a modulated signal.

RHETORICAL PERSUASION A method of convincing an audience of your point of view through reason, emotion, and personal appeal.

RHYTHM The beat or tempo of music or editing that affects the perception of speed or pace.

RIBBON MIC A transducer using a thin gold or silver corrugated ribbon suspended between the poles of a magnet to create an electrical output.

RIGHT-TO-WORK LAWS State statutes prohibiting unions from enforcing closed shops or requiring union membership of all employees covered in a contract.

RISERS Hollow rectangular boxes or platforms to be placed on the studio floor to raise a portion of the set.

RISK CAPITAL The money a person or company invests in a high-risk project such as motion picture or a television series.

RITTER FAN A mechanical device used to create snow or rain scenes.

ROSTRUM A movable table with an animation stand on which artwork is placed for precise framing and movement from one cel to another.

ROTOSCOPE A means of producing lifelike animation by filming a subject moving and then projecting each frame under a transparent drawing board and tracing the subject's position.

ROUGH-CUT The initial selection and ordering of shots and scenes in a production.

ROYALTY FEES Money paid to composers, authors, and performers for the use of copyrighted materials.

RUB-ON LETTERS Individual letters that can be transferred to any flat surface to make titles by rubbing on the plastic sheet holding the letters.

RUNDOWN SHEET A basic outline of a program that simply indicates the time and order of specific segments. See Format.

RUNNING TIME Actual program length or duration of a program.

SAFE ACTION AREA The approximate 90 percent of the television scanned area that can be reproduced on most home television receivers. Compare this to critical and essential areas.

SAG (Screen Actors Guild) The union that represents most film performers.

SAMPLING The process of taking periodic measurements of a signal.

SANDBAG A bag filled with sand used to steady lamp stands or other set pieces.

SATELLITE Geostationary orbiting space platform with transponders to pick up signals from the earth and retransmit the signals back down to earth in a pattern, called a footprint, that covers a large area of the earth.

SATURATION The intensity of a signal, either audio or video, but especially used as the third of three characteristics of a color video signal. See Hue and Brightness.

SCA (Subsidiary Communication Authorization) FCC permission for a company to use subcarriers on existing channels for audio or data transmission.

SCALE The apparent size of objects within the frame.

SCAN LINE A horizontal line of phosphors in a television receiver or video monitor, or optoelectronic semiconductors in a pickup tube.

SCANNING AREA The full field of view picked up by the video camera pickup tube.

SCENE A series of related shots, usually in the same time and location.

SCENE SCRIPT A full script without individual shots indicated.

SCENIC ARTISTS Craftspeople who compose detailed sketches, drawings, and set layouts.

SCENIC DESIGN The overall artistic control and coordination of sets, props, costumes, and makeup.

SCENIC DESIGNER In video and film productions, the person who supervises the overall production design, including props and costumes.

SCOOP A lighting instrument with an open bowl reflector that produces soft floodlight.

SCORE Music composed for a specific film or videotape.

SCOUTING REPORT A complete report of the facilities available and the equipment needed for a location production at a specific site. See Site Survey.

SCRAMBLING Modifying a video signal so it cannot be received without the proper decoder. Pay cable channels are scrambled.

SCREEN A nondiffusion scrim or what films are projected on.

SCREEN DIRECTIONALITY The left-to-right or right-to-left movement and placement of objects in successive two-dimensional images or shots.

SCRIM A metallic or fabric filter placed over a lighting instrument to diffuse and soften the light.

SCRIPT The complete manuscript of all audio copy and visual instructions of a program, whether it is a film, audio, video, or multimedia production.

SCRIPT BREAKDOWN Reorganizing the script in terms of specific settings so that production can be scheduled and an accurate estimate of the budget can be made, in terms of equipment and personnel needs at each setting and on each scheduled day of shooting.

SCRIPT CONTINUITY The dictates of the script, in terms of temporal and spatial details, that must be maintained during production.

SCRIPT OUTLINE A semiscripted format in which only a portion of videotape or live television program, such as the opening and closing segments, is fully scripted, if other elements are to be ad-libbed. See Format and Rundown Sheet.

SCRIPT SUPERVISOR The person who maintains continuity in performer actions and prop placements from shot to shot and ensures that every scene in the script has been recorded.

SCRIPTWRITING The process of creating a written outline for a videotape, live television program, audio production, or film.

S-DAT See DASH.

SDTV (Standard-Definition Television) 525- or 625-line digital television.

SEARCH-AND-CUE FUNCTION A machine operational setting that allows a playback machine to search for specific cues on a prerecorded tape.

SEARCH FUNCTION A function on a videotape recorder that allows a specific point on the videotape to be found by moving the tape very slowly.

SECAM (Sequential Couleur Avec Memoire) The color television system developed by the French and in use around the world in many countries.

SEG (Screen Extras Guild) The union that represents extras, or performers who do not speak on camera or have specific actions to perform.

SEG (Special Effects Generator) A video switcher capable of creating effects as transitions.

SEGMENT A portion of a program or spot.

SEGUE The immediate replacement of one sound source with another.

SEL SYNC An internal means of synchronization within an audiotape, which can be used to record consecutive soundtracks in synchronization with each other.

SELECTIVE FOCUS Using depth of field to direct the viewer's attention to certain areas of the scene by varying those elements in and out of focus.

SELF-BLIMPED A film camera that is completely sound insulated for synchronous sound recording. See Blimp.

SEMISCRIPTED A partial description or outline of a videotape, live television program, audio production, or film.

SEPARATION LIGHT A general lighting term that includes backlights and kickers, which both help to separate foreground subjects and backgrounds.

SEPIA TONE An antique brown tone to a graphic or photograph.

SEQUENCE, SEQUENTIAL Individual shots edited into scenes and individual scenes edited together to make a story.

SERIF Fine lines on the bottom and top of letters of some fonts. Serifs do not show well on scanned media.

SERVER A solid-state digital recording device designed to record and play back digital vide/audio files as nonlinear signals.

SERVO CAPSTAN A capstan with an accurate motor that varies the speed of the playback to maintain proper synchronization between a video recorder and playback machine.

SET DESIGNER In large-scale productions, the person who does the actual drawing of set floor plans, elevations, and layouts and supervises the construction of sets.

SET FURNISHINGS Furniture and props that fill out a set.

SETTINGS Specific exterior and interior places and locations specified in a script.

SET UP Assemble equipment and people in preparation for rehearsing a production.

SETUP Same as pedestal and black level; electronic calibration between blanking and black level.

SHADING Adjusting the brightness level, light sensitivity, and color of a video camera.

SHADOW MASK A series of windows or aperture deflectors inside a television picture tube that prevents electrons from each gun from striking the wrong color light-emitting phosphors.

SHARE The estimated percentage of HUTs watching a specific program at one time.

SHARPNESS A rating of the edge clarity and focus of images reproduced in video or film production.

SHOCK-MOUNTED MICROPHONE A microphone designed to minimize all vibrations and noise except those inherent in sound waves.

SHOOTING RATIO The ratio of material recorded during production to that which is actually used in the final edited version.

SHOOTING SCRIPT A script complete in all details, including specific shot descriptions.

SHORTEN (.shn) Lossless compression file format. CD quality, replaced by FLAC, Wav.

SHOT (1) One continuous roll of the recorder or camera. (2) The smallest unit of a script.

SHOTGUN Ultra-unidirectional microphone designed to pick up sound at a distance by excluding unwanted sound from the sides of the mic.

SHOT SHEET A listing of all shots in the order they are to be made, regardless of their order in the script.

SHOULDER HARNESS A body brace used as a camera mount.

SHUTTER An opaque device in a film camera that rapidly opens and closes to expose the film to light.

SHUTTLE Movement of videotape back and forth while searching for edit points. Usually done at speeds faster or slower than real time.

SIGNAL LEVEL The signal strength of the electrical current from recording and playback equipment.

SIGNAL PROCESSING Manipulation of the electrical sound signal.

SIGNAL-TO-NOISE RATIO (S/N Ratio) The mathematical ratio between the noise level in a signal and the program level. The higher the ratio, the better the signal.

SINE WAVE A graphic of voltage variations from zero to a maximum, back to zero, to a minimum and back to zero.

SINGLE-CAMERA PRODUCTION The use of a single video or film camera to record a videotape or film in segments.

SINGLE-PERF Film with sprocket holes on only one side or edge.

SINGLE-SYSTEM RECORDING Recording a synchronous soundtrack within the camera on the same roll of film as the pictures.

SITE SURVEY A detailed listing of all the information needed to shoot on location at a certain site.

SKEW Tension adjustment during videotape playback. Visible as a "bending" at the extreme top or bottom of the picture.

SKYLIGHT Indirect sunlight that has a higher color temperature than direct sunlight.

SLANT TRACK See Helical Scan. Videotape with multiple recording heads that records information in long slanting tracks; each track records one field of information.

SLATE Several frames identifying the shot, tape, or film reel number, or other logging information. Usually recorded at the beginning of the tape.

SLIDES Still photographic transparencies that can be projected.

SLIDING TRACK An overhead light grid to which lighting instruments are attached so that they slide into position along the track.

SLIPPING Moving a track (usually audio) forward or backward in relationship to the picture or visual.

SLO-MO DISC RECORDER A video recorder that records live-action images on a rotating disc so that they can be played back in slow motion, such as for game analysis in a sports broadcast.

SLOW MOTION Recording images at a faster speed than the normal playback speed.

SLUG An identifying name for a news story; usually only one or two words.

SMATV (Satellite Master Antenna Television) A "private" cable system. Often used by apartment or hotel complexes to serve all of their units.

SMEARING See Comet-Tailing.

SMPTE (Society of Motion Picture and Television Engineers) A professional society of members who are predominantly interested in the technical side of motion pictures, radio, and television. The official organization for setting technical standards for film and video in the United States.

SMPTE TIMECODE A binary code accurately setting hours, minutes, seconds, and frames used to synchronize audio, video, and film media.

SOFT CUT A very rapid dissolve.

SOFT LIGHT Indirect, diffused light that minimizes shadows.

SOFTLIGHTS Large light fixtures that emit a well-diffused light over a broad area.

SOFTWARE Material recorded on audio, video, or computer media. Contrast with hardware.

SOFT WIPE A slight superimposition at the point where two images intersect during a wipe from one to the other.

SOLARIZATION A technique that drains the normal color from a visual image and replaces it with artificially controlled colors.

SOLID-STATE MEMORY (Flash Memory, Minicard, MicroSD card, Smart Media, Multimedia [MMC] cards)

SOP (Standard Operating Procedure) Predetermined methods of completing a task. Often set by corporate or upper-management policy.

SOUND AMPLITUDE The intensity and height of a sound pressure wave.

SOUND EFFECTS Sounds that are matched to their supposed visual sources during postproduction editing.

SOUND FIDELITY The accuracy or illusion of reality inherent in a sound recording.

SOUND FREQUENCY The rapidity with which air molecules move back and forth in direct relation to the vibrations of the sound source.

SOUND INTENSITY The amplitude of a sound wave, which is perceived as a specific loudness level.

SOUND-ON-FILM (SOF) See Single-System Recording.

SOUND PERSPECTIVE An enhanced perception of distance achieved through the use of different volume levels for near and far sounds.

SOUND PRESSURE WAVE The compression and expansion of air molecules in response to the vibrations of a sound source.

SOUND TEST A test setting of the sound level before the actual recording takes place.

SOUND UP AND UNDER Instruction to cut the sound in at its proper level and then fade it down to a lower level where it is still audible but less prominent.

SOUND VELOCITY The speed of a sound pressure wave.

SOURCE MUSIC Music that comes from a source within the actual scene portrayed on screen.

SPACERS Small wheels used to fill the gaps between take-up reels on a film-editing bench so that their spacing matches the spacing of the individual hubs or wheels in a gang synchronizer.

SPATIAL DISTORTION An aural imbalance during stereophonic playback or recording that results from a faulty positioning of the sound source.

SPECIAL EFFECTS GENERATOR An electronic device usually installed in the video switcher, which is used to produce wipes, split screens, and inserts.

SPEED OF ACTION The speed of the movement of objects within the frame.

SPIDER An adjustable device into which the spurs of a tripod are placed on a flat, hard surface.

SPLICING Physically cutting and cementing magnetic tape or film while editing.

SPLIT An agreed-upon division of box office receipts between exhibitors and film distributors.

SPLIT-BEAM A reflex viewing system in which mirrors between the lens and the viewfinder eyepiece continuously deflect about 18 percent to 20 percent of the light.

SPLIT EDIT An edit made in which the audio and video are assigned separate in- or out-points so that the signals do not start or stop at the same point in time.

SPLIT-PAGE SCRIPT A script that has the visual specification on the left side of the page and the corresponding audio specifications on the right side.

SPLIT SCREEN A special video effect in which one image occupies a portion of the frame and another image occupies the remaining portion.

SPLITTER BOX A device used to feed an input signal to more than one output. Commonly used at news conferences to avoid a jumble of microphones by splitting the feed from one mic to all those covering the event.

SPOT EFFECTS Specific sound effects created expressly for a videotape, live television program, or film in a sound studio.

SPOTLIGHTS Lighting instruments with lenses that sharply focus the light they emit, producing intense, harsh lighting.

SPOT METER A light meter designed to read a very small area of reflected light.

SPOT READING A light-meter reading of the intensity of the light reflected by the subject in a very narrow area as determined by the angle of acceptance of the spot meter.

SPREADER See Spider.

SPROCKET HOLES The perforations in a piece of film that allow it to be advanced or driven through a camera or projector.

SPROCKET TEETH Metal teeth that drive a piece of film through a camera, projector, or editing device by engaging the sprocket holes.

SPUN GLASS A flexible light diffuser made out of fiberglass.

SPURS Points on the end of a tripod, which can be stuck into soft ground.

SQUASHING AND STRETCHING Animation techniques that exaggerate and caricature motions by accentuating the initial and ending movements of an action, such as running or jumping, to make them seem more active.

STAGE MANAGER The person who supervises the use of studio space, such as the setup and breaking down of sets and props on the studio floor. See Floor Manager.

STAND MICROPHONE A microphone designed to be secured to a mic stand, which can be raised or lowered to conform to the height of the speaker.

STEADICAM A servostabilizer camera mount attached to the operator's body to minimize camera vibrations when the operator moves with the camera.

STEREOPHONIC SOUND The separation of sounds coming from the right and the left during recording and playback, which preserves the directionality of sound sources.

STINGERS Short phrases of music, usually characterized by a rapidly descending scale or series of notes, used as punctuation devices.

STOCK FOOTAGE Film, video files, or audio files gathered and kept in storage until need for a future project.

STOP MOTION Filming or taping subjects one or two frames at a time.

STORYBOARD A series of drawings indicating each shot and accompanying audio in a production.

STORY LINE A one-two sentence description of a production that completely describes the production.

STORY TIME The supposed historical time of events presented in a television program or film.

STREAMING A collection of data sent in a sequential fashion through a system used to send audio, video, and other digital signals through the Internet.

STRIKE (1) A command and action to tear down sets, pack up equipment, and clear an area following a production. (2) A work stoppage action in a labor dispute.

STRINGERS Freelance reporters or video cinematographers who are paid by the story or are retained by a news operation but who are not on full-time staff.

STRIP LIGHTS A series of lights connected in a straight line.

STRIPPING Broadcasting a TV program at the same time of day, five days a week, usually a syndicated program.

STROBE A visual fluctuation or vibration as if lights were flashing on and off.

STUDIO A controlled, indoor production environment designed expressly for video, audio, or film recording.

STUDIO PRODUCTION The recording of audio, video, or film images inside a controlled production environment.

STYLIZED LIGHTING Lighting that is intended to achieve a special kind of emotional effect or abstract design through nonnaturalistic patterns of light.

STYLIZED SETS Abstract, imaginative settings that reflect an artistic style or give external form to an interior state of mind, such as a specific character's subjective state of mind.

STYLUS A handheld drawing tool used in place of a pen or pencil to create graphics on a computer screen.

SUBJECTIVE POINT OF VIEW A story told from the perspective of a specific character or participant in the action.

SUBJECTIVE SHOT A presentation of images supposedly dreamed, imagined, recollected, or perceived in an abnormal state of mind by a character or participant in a videotape or film.

SUBPOENA An order of the court to appear as a witness. May include an order to release sources, notes, or original and edited recordings.

SUBTEXT Within any media production there are stories and messages that are not openly or obviously spoken or acted that still carry an emotional impact to the production.

SUBTITLES Titles placed in the bottom third of the video or film frame that clarify the image or present the spoken dialogue in written form.

SUBTRACTIVE COLOR The process of using color-absorbing filters to subtract specific wavelengths of light from a white light source and produce the various colors of the visible spectrum.

SUBWOOFER A bass speaker designed to respond to extreme low frequencies.

SUPERCARDIOID A highly directional microphone pickup pattern.

SUPERIMPOSITIONS (supers) Two or more simultaneously fed video signals, stopping a dissolve at the halfway point.

SUPERSTATION A local television station whose signal is satellite delivered to cable systems across the company. WTBS of Atlanta and WGN of Chicago are such stations.

SWEETENING The process of equalizing, setting levels, and mixing voices, music, and sound effects into a master audio recording.

SWISH PAN A rapid horizontal movement of the camera while recording. May be used as a transition device.

SWITCHER (1) In multicamera or postproduction, a device used to change video sources feeding the recording tape deck. (2) The person operating the video switcher.

SYMMETRY The degree to which composition within a camera frame is balanced.

SYNC GENERATOR An electronic device that produces various synchronizing signals necessary for the operation of the video recording system.

SYNC HEAD An additional recording head on a synchronous sound recorder, used for recording the sync signal.

SYNC SIGNAL A regular wave of electrical current, which can be used as a speed reference for sound and picture synchronization.

SYNCHRONOUS (sync) Signals locked in proper alignment with each other; sound and picture locked together; all the various video signals in their proper relationship to each other.

SYNCHRONOUS SOUND RECORDER A device capable of recording sounds in synchronization with the images recorded by a film camera.

SYNDICATED PROGRAMMING Commercial television programs and films that are distributed directly to local television stations, bypassing the major television networks.

SYNOPSIS A short paragraph that describes the basic story line of a script.

TAKES Individual shots of a single action. There may be several takes of the same shot in single-camera productions, from which one will be selected for use in the final edited version.

TAKE-UP The part of a recording device that collects the tape or film.

TALENT Anyone who appears on camera or before the microphone.

TALK-BACK SYSTEM An intercom system in a television studio, used for communication between the creative staff in the control room and the crew on the studio floor.

TALLY LIGHT A light on the top of a video camera that informs the talent and crew which of several cameras has been selected for recording or transmission at a particular time.

TAPE SPLICER A device with a cutting blade and guide for combining different pieces of film or audiotape with transparent tape.

TAPELESS RECORDING Recording electronic signals on either optical discs or solid-state media.

TECHNICAL DIRECTOR (TD) In video production, the person who operates the switcher at the commands of the director.

TELCO A common name for a telephone company.

TELECINE An optical/electronic system of transferring film to videotape. Once called film chain.

TELECONFERENCE A live exchange of video and audio information over a long distance via satellite, microwave, or web links.

TELEPHOTO Long focal-length lens.

TELETEXT Text and graphics broadcast along with a TV signal for especially equipped TV receivers.

TELEVISION The electronic transmission and reception of visual images of moving and stationary objects, usually with accompanying sound.

TELEVISION QUOTIENT (TV-Q) A popularity index of television performers, which is sometimes used to ensure program success and aid casting decisions.

TEMPORAL CONTINUITY A continuous flow of events without any apparent gaps in time.

TENT An opaque sheet of material suspended over a subject to diffuse and soften the light.

TERABYTE (TB) A measurement of bandwidth and data storage; 1,000 gigabytes or 1 trillion bytes.

TERRESTRIAL A signal tied to the land such as broadcast radio and television that must be broadcast from a tower on land, as opposed to satellite or cable media not tied specifically to a land-carried signal.

TEXTURE The roughness or smoothness of a surface.

THEATRICAL FILMS Films produced for commercial theaters.

THEME (1) A central concept, idea, or symbolic meaning in a story. (2) A repeated melody in a symphony or other long musical composition.

THREE-OR-FOUR POINT LIGHTING A basic lighting technique that helps create an illusion of three-dimensionality by separating the subject from the background, using key, fill, and separation light.

THREE-SHOT A camera setup in which three subjects appear in the same frame.

THREE-TO-ONE RULE To avoid phasing problems, two or more microphones that are used simultaneously should be placed at least three times as far apart as their subject-to-mic distances.

THROUGH THE LENS (TTL) A type of light meter that measures the amount of light actually coming through the lens of a camera.

TIFF (Tagged Image File Format) A visual computer format used in print media.

TILT A vertical pivoting of a camera.

TILT SHOT A camera shot accomplished by moving the camera up and down on a swivel or tilting device.

TIMBRE See Tonality.

TIME-BASE CORRECTOR (TBC) An electronic device used to lock together signals with dissimilar sync. Also may be used to correct for phase, level, and pedestal errors in original recordings.

TIMECODE A time-based address recorded on videotape to allow for precise editing. SMPTE timecode is the one most universally used at present.

TIMECODE EDITING A choice of edit points selected by using sequential code recorded on the tape.

TIME-LAPSE SEQUENCE A visual segment that has been pixilated or compressed in time.

TIMELINE (Construction Window) The monitor window in a NLE showing the chronological arrangement of shots and transitions.

TITLE SEQUENCE See Credits.

TITLES Lettering recorded within the visual frame that identifies the visual images or adds text to the videotape, live television program, or film.

TONALITY The particular quality or unique characteristics of a musical instrument or voice.

TOPIC RESEARCH The process of gathering accurate information about a prospective program's subject matter.

TOTAL AUDIENCE MEASUREMENT INDEX (TAMI) An NBC-TV viewership analysis method that involves contracting with a variety of different audience measurement systems including the Internet, mobile viewers, and social networks to arrive at the most accurate ratings. First tried with the 2008 Olympics.

TRACK A separate tape path.

TRACKING (1) Aligning playback heads on a VCR with the original pattern of video recorded on tape. (2) Movement of a camera to the left or right, usually while mounted on a set of tracks for maximum smoothness and control.

TRAGEDY A type of drama that has a serious tone and often focuses on the misfortunes and problems of life.

TRANSDUCER Any electronic device used to convert any form of energy to another form; a video camera transduces light to video; a microphone transduces sound to electronics; a speaker transduces electronics to sound.

TRANSFER A copy of a recording in which the format is changed.

TRANSFERENCE Changes in perception, as between real and imaged movement.

TRANSFORMER A magnetic voltage or impedance-changing device.

TRANSISTOR The original semiconductor that replaced the vacuum tube.

TRANSITION DEVICES Various means of changing from one shot to another to suggest changes of time or place.

TRANSITION WINDOW An NLE monitor that shows transitions available for editing.

TRANSMISSION Moving signals from one to one or more points.

TRANSPONDER A satellite section that receives and retransmits a signal or series of signals on a single frequency.

TRANSVERSE TRACK See Quadraplex.

TRAVELING MATTE A film matte that moves across the image to create special effects.

TREATMENT A narrative description of a production. It should read more like a novel than a script because it is intended for a nonmedia person.

TREBLE High frequencies of the audio band.

TRIANGLE See Spider.

TRIAX A type of camera cable designed to carry many signals imbedded on a single carrier.

TRIM IN/OUT The process of making small adjustments in the in- and out-points of edits.

TRIMMING WINDOW The monitor in NEL that shows two shots for creating a straight cut.

TRIPOD Three-legged portable camera support.

TRUCKING SHOT A shot in which the camera moves from side-to-side on a wheeled dolly.

T-STOP A unit of light transmission for a lens based on actual tests of light transmission.

TUNGSTEN LIGHT Relatively efficient gas-filled light source of approximately 32,000 degree K temperature.

TWO-SHOT A camera shot including two subjects.

TV-Q (Television Quotient) A method used to determine the popularity of performers and programs on television.

TYLER MOUNT A helicopter or airplane camera mount that reduces vibration.

TYPO Short for typographical error, to be avoided at all cost in any written material presented digitally or on hard copy. Usually misspelling, incorrect grammar, or misplaced punctuation.

TVRO (Television Receive Only) A satellite downlink system that cannot uplink a signal. Home satellite receivers are TVROs.

UHDTV (Ultra-High-Definition TV) An experimental high-definition video system designed by the Japanese broadcasters, NHK. The system features resolution of 7,680 × 4,320 pixels and is four times wider and higher than ATSC HDTV. Scheduled to start broadcasting in 2015.

UHF (Ultra-High Frequency) (1) Frequency band for television broadcasting channels 14 through 69. (2) An older, large, threaded type of video connector.

ULTRACARDIOID The most directional (narrowest) microphone pickup pattern available; sometimes called a shotgun microphone.

ULTRA VIOLET LIGHT Invisible light that has a shorter wavelength than visible light but can nonetheless affect film and is present in outdoor shadow areas.

U-MATIC Three-quarter-inch videotape format created by Sony in the early 1970s that revolutionized video newsgathering. Has been upgraded by a compatible U-matic SP format.

UNBALANCED MICROPHONE LINE A mic cable consisting of a single conductor that is less well insulated than a balanced line and thus more susceptible to cable noise.

UNIDIRECTIONAL A microphone pickup pattern from a single direction. Comes in a variety of degrees of pickup angle, from cardioid to super unidirectional (shotgun).

UNION AND GUILD CONTRACTS Agreements regarding salaries, working conditions, and so on, made between various craft, trade, and talent unions or guilds and television, audio, and film producers.

UNIVERSAL SERIAL BUS (USB) A computer connectivity standard designed to allow digital data to be passed among many different formats, applications, and operating systems without modification.

UNSCALED LAYOUT A bird's-eye view of the studio and set giving a rough approximation of the material that must be constructed.

UPLINK A transmission path from an Earth-based station up to a satellite. Sometimes used to describe the ground station capable of sending a satellite signal. See Downlink.

UPRIGHT A vertically arranged film-editing machine.

URL (Uniform Resource Locator) The address system used to access sites on the World Wide Web.

VARIABLE FOCAL-LENGTH LENS (Zoom) A lens that can have its focal length changed while in use.

VARIABLE SPEED MOTOR An electric drive motor whose speed can be varied and controlled.

VECTORSCOPE Electronic test equipment designed to show the color aspects of the video signal.

VÉRITÉ The art of filming/recording to create realism without modifying the action.

VERTICAL BLANKING The period of time that the television electron beam is shut off, while the beam jumps from the bottom of one field or frame to the top of another.

VERTICAL INTERVAL TIMECODE (VITC) Time address recorded within the vertical interval blanking instead of on a separate linear track.

VERTICAL SYNC A portion of a television signal that controls the rate of vertical scanning and blanking.

VFX (Visual Effects) Also called special effects (SFX).

VHF (Very-High Frequency) The frequency spectrum includes television channels 2 through 13.

VHS, S-VHS JVC-developed consumer VCR system; VHS stands for Video Home System. "S" in S-VHS stands for "separate," because it is a semicompatible component recording system rather than a composite system.

VIDEO (1) The picture portion of an electronic visual system. (2) All-inclusive term for electronic visual reproduction systems; includes television, cablevision, corporate media, and video recording.

VIDEOCASSETTE A self-contained set of reels with videotape.

VIDEOCASSETTE RECORDER (VCR) A machine that can record video and audio signals on cassettes of videotape.

VIDEODISC An optical disc loaded with video and audio material, most often motion pictures or training tapes or films.

VIDEO ENGINEER In video production, the person who adjusts or shades the cameras for optimal recording and monitors the videotape recording equipment.

VIDEOGRAPHER The proper term for the operator of a video camera.

VIDEO METERS Meters on a videotape recorder that indicate the strength of the video portion of the television signal.

VIDEO NOISE Static or unwanted light in a video image.

VIDEO SYNTHESIZER A device that allows an artist to manipulate the analog or digital signal of a video image so that colors and shapes can be creatively altered for special effects.

VIDEOTAPE Magnetic substance-coated, plastic-based tape used for recording video and audio signals.

VIDEOTAPE EDITING UNIT An electronic editing system consisting of a playback videotape recorder (VTR) or VCR, a recorder, and an editing control unit.

VIDEOTAPE RECORDER (VTR) A device that records audio and video signals on open reels of tape rather than closed cassettes.

VIDEOTEX An interactive computer graphics database that may be accessed through a modem, cable television, or other lines of electronic communication.

VIDEO-TO-FILM TRANSFER Copying a videotape on film; was once called kinescoping.

VIDICON A type of video camera tube that replaced the Image Orthicon. It was lighter, smaller, and more durable and provided higher resolution.

VIEWFINDER The miniature video monitor mounted on the camera so that the operator can see what is framed by the camera.

VIEWFINDER DIOPTER An adjustment on a viewfinder that allows an adjustment to match the vision of the operator's eyesight.

VISUAL The video and picture portion of the program.

VIRTUAL EDIT An edit location existing only in the software addresses of the edit rather than in a tangible or physical location.

VIRTUAL FILE A copy of a file that is used for editing without destroying the original file.

VIRTUAL REALITY (VR) Video, audio, sensory computer-controlled effects designed to create an artificial environment or movement.

VIRTUAL SET A computer file that duplicates the appearance of a television or film studio that can be inserted behind any foreground object. Such sets do not require any construction or lighting of the set because all characteristics are created in a computer file.

VISUALIZATION The creative process of transforming a script into a sequence of visual images and sounds.

VISUAL STYLE The particular approach taken by a director to the visual presentation of events in a videotape, live television program, or film, including the selection of specific camera placements, movements, and types of shots.

VOICEOVER (VO) A story that uses continuous visuals, accompanied by the voice of an unseen narrator.

VOLTS An electronic measurement of the pressure available at a power source. In North America the standard is 110–120 V.

VOLUME The measurable loudness of a sound signal.

VOLUME UNIT (VU) The measurement of audio level. Indicates the average of the sound level, not the peak.

VU METER The volume unit meter, which indicates the relative levels of sounds passing through a sound system.

WALKSPACE The space in a frame in front of a moving subject to avoid the appearance of the subject running into the side of the frame.

WATTS The measurement of power used in a piece of electrical or electronic equipment.

WAVEFORM (.wav) An audio storing file format used on Windows PCs; can store either compressed or uncompressed files.

WAVEFORM MONITOR An electronic measuring tool; both oscilloscopes and vector-scopes are waveform monitors.

WAVELENGTH The distance between the crest or valleys of each successive wave of energy in light or sound.

WEDGE A plate fastened to the bottom of a camera that allows it to be quickly mounted to a tripod equipped with a matched slot.

WGA (Writers Guild of America) Represents writers in film and television for basic pay, working conditions, and rights.

WHITE BALANCE The electronic matching of the camera circuits to the color temperature of the light source.

WHITE LEVEL (Gain) The level of maximum voltage in a video signal.

WIDE ANGLE A lens with a relatively short focal length and wide field of view.

WIFI The trade name for wireless technology IEEE 802.11 used on home networks, mobile phones, and video games.

WII A Nintendo digital game that uses a handheld wireless control to duplicate hand and arm movements of actual games.

WILD SOUND Ambient background sound. See Nat Sound.

WIND NOISE Unwanted sound caused by air blowing over the pickup elements of a microphone.

WINDOW DUPE A copy of a videotape that has the SMPTE timecode recorded so that it is visible in a "window" for viewing, for logging, or locating specific points on the tape during the editing process.

WIND SCREEN A plastic foam covering placed over a microphone to inhibit wind noise.

WIPE An electronic special effects transition that allows one image to be replaced by another with a moving line separating the two pictures. Stopping a wipe in mid-movement creates a split screen.

WIMax A wireless technology designed to deliver broadband files as an alternate to wired broadband systems. Technology IEEE 802.16.

WORKFLOW An organized system of planning and carrying out a process in a logical step-by-step manner from the beginning until the end of the process.

WORKPRINT An edited master recording video or film used in offline or preliminary editing stages.

WORLD WIDE WEB (WWW) A distribution information network consisting of web sites accessed through individual URL addresses offering text, graphics, and sound.

WOW An audio distortion caused by a change in speed of either the record or playback equipment.

WRATTEN A series of filters originally designed for photography but adapted for use in cinematography and videography.

WWW (World Wide Web) An international computer communication network created in Switzerland.

WYSIWYG (What You See Is What You Get) A description of the comparison of what is shown on the screen and what actually is printed or recorded.

X-AXIS The plane running horizontally to the camera.

XLR PLUG A professional audio connector that allows for three conductors plus a shielded ground. Special types of multipin XLRs are used for headsets and battery-power connectors.

Y-AXIS The plane running vertically to the camera.

YELLOW-INK EDGE NUMBERS Edge numbers printed by a laboratory on the film, as opposed to edge numbers placed there by the film manufacturer.

Y SIGNAL See Luminance.

Z-AXIS The plane running away or toward the camera.

ZERO START The beginning point of SMPTE timecode on a videotape recording.

ZOOM See Variable Focal-Length Lens.

Index

Page numbers followed by "f" denote figures; those followed by "t" denote tables